THIRD EDITION

Archaeology

The Science of the Human Past

Mark Q. Sutton
California State University–Bakersfield

Robert M. Yohe II
California State University–Bakersfield

PEARSON

Boston   New York   San Francisco
Mexico City   Montreal   Toronto   London   Madrid   Munich   Paris
Hong Kong   Singapore   Tokyo   Cape Town   Sydney

To our wives,
Melinda and Belinda

Series Editor: Dave Repetto
Series Editorial Assistant: Jack Cashman
Editorial Production Service: Omegatype Typography, Inc.
Composition Buyer: Linda Cox
Manufacturing Buyer: Debbie Rossi
Electronic Composition: Omegatype Typography, Inc.
Cover Administrator: Joel Gendron

For related titles and support materials, visit our online catalog at www.ablongman.com.

Between the time Web site information is gathered and then published, it is not unusual for
some sites to have closed. Also, the transcription of URLs can result in typographical errors. The
publisher would appreciate notification where these errors occur so that they may be corrected
in subsequent editions.

ISBN-13: 978-0-205-57237-3
ISBN-10:   0-205-57237-5

Printed in the United States of America

10 9 8 7 6 5 4 3 2 1   RRD-VA   11 10 09 08 07

Photo credits appear on page 440, which constitutes an extension of the copyright page.

ABOUT THE AUTHORS

Mark Q. Sutton decided to become an archaeologist when he was 10 years old after reading a book on archaeology. In 1968, while still in high school, he took advantage of the opportunity to participate in archaeological excavations conducted by the local community college. He went on to earn a B.A. (1972), an M.A. (1977), and a Ph.D. (1987) in anthropology. He worked as an archaeologist for the U.S. Air Force, the U.S. Bureau of Land Management, and various private consulting firms and taught at a number of community colleges and universities. He has been at California State University, Bakersfield, since 1987 and is a professor of anthropology. Dr. Sutton has conducted hundreds of surveys and has excavated at more than 100 sites in western North America. He has published over 150 books, monographs, and articles on archaeology.

Robert M. Yohe II received his B.A. in anthropology at California State University, San Bernardino, in 1983 and his M.A. and Ph.D. in anthropology from the University of California, Riverside, in 1990 and 1992, respectively. From 1990 to 1993, he served as assistant director and then director of the Cultural Resources Facility at California State University, Bakersfield, and was an adjunct lecturer in the Department of Sociology and Anthropology. In 1993, Dr. Yohe was appointed State Archaeologist and administrator of the Idaho State Historic Preservation Office. He also served as director of the Archaeological Survey of Idaho and Deputy State Historic Preservation Officer. During this same period, he taught anthropology courses at Boise State University. In 1996 he was appointed interim State Historic Preservation Officer, a position he held until his departure in late 1999 to join the faculty at California State University, Bakersfield, as an assistant professor of anthropology. He is now an associate professor of anthropology and also serves as director of the Museum of Anthropology at CSUB, the Center for Archaeological Research, and the Laboratory of Archaeological Sciences at CSUB. Dr. Yohe has conducted research in the deserts of western North America for the past 26 years. More recently, he has conducted excavations in Middle Egypt to recover mummies dating to the Roman period.

BRIEF CONTENTS

CONTENTS

part 1   WHAT IS ARCHAEOLOGY?

Archaeology is the study of past peoples and societies and is often considered a subfield of anthropology. The goals of archaeology are to discover, describe, interpret, explain, and understand the past through the analysis of the materials left by past peoples. Professional archaeology grew out of the European interest in the remains of prehistoric peoples and classical civilizations. Contemporary archaeology employs a variety of theoretical approaches and emphases that provide a fascinating picture of the past.

chapter 1

The Science of Archaeology   1

c h a p t e r **2**

Backgrounds of Archaeology   31

c h a p t e r **3**

The Development of Contemporary Archaeology 55

part II   OBTAINING INFORMATION ABOUT THE PAST

To discover the record of the past, archaeologists obtain information by investigating archaeological sites, which contain artifacts, ecofacts, cultural features, evidence of architecture, and human remains. Key concerns are how sites were formed and transformed and how remains were preserved. To obtain information, archaeologists conduct fieldwork: they seek, find, record, and excavate sites and classify and analyze finds. Determining how old recovered materials are is an important task accomplished using a number of methods. The analysis of the remains of past people themselves, with the goals of determining their anatomy, genetics, and health, is also important. Computer and space-age technologies are vital to this process both in the field and in the lab.

chapter 4

The Archaeological Record 79

c h a p t e r **5**

Conducting Fieldwork   111

chapter 6

Classification and Analysis of Artifacts 141

chapter 7

Determining Time 164

chapter **8**

Bioarchaeology: Human Remains   192

p a r t III INTERPRETING THE PAST

Archaeologists use the information they obtain to interpret the record of the past. They can determine
how people made their living, how they adapted biologically and culturally to their environment, and how
they attempted to control or modify their environment. The domestication of plants and animals and the
rise of agricultural societies are key areas of inquiry. Archaeologists can infer people's settlement patterns,
population characteristics and movements, political organization, social stratification, gender roles, religious
practices, cultural symbols and art, and beliefs and values. It is also possible to reconstruct specific cultural
events as well as patterns and trends in people's cultural history, including changes brought about by new
technologies and cultural contacts through migration, trade, warfare, and conquest.

c h a p t e r 9

Environment and Adaptation 222

c h a p t e r 10

Understanding Past Settlement and Subsistence 250

c h a p t e r 11

Interpreting Past Cultural Systems 287

chapter **12**

Understanding Culture Change   322

part IV PUBLIC ARCHAEOLOGY

Archaeology and the science and politics of archaeology have special relevance today. Cultural resources and historic and prehistoric sites need to be preserved and managed, not only for their own sake but also for the education of future generations, the solving of mysteries, and the application of past knowledge and skills to present challenges. Archaeological findings and interpretations can and should be applied to the realities of the present day and the possibilities of the human future. With enhanced computer-based technologies, for example, archaeology more than ever before can model explanations of the past and propose solutions to contemporary problems of environmental and cultural adaptation.

chapter 13

Cultural Resource Management 351

chapter **14**

Archaeology in the Real World   382

TO THE INSTRUCTOR

Our main objective in writing this text was to provide an introduction to the broad and fascinating world of archaeology from the scientific perspective. Like all researchers, we have a bias in our approach to the study of the past. We view and interpret the past from the perspective of empirical science. Although some archaeologists believe that there are many pasts, we believe that there is only one empirical past. We agree that different people in the past had varying beliefs, views, and agendas, and we believe that each of these perspectives was real. This makes the past very complex but still empirical. We acknowledge and value the perspectives of other approaches and believe that they, too, can be incorporated into the empirical science of archaeology. We include their important contributions to archaeology in our book.

In our text, we wanted to discuss not only the theoretical aspects of archaeology but also practical applications of what is learned about the past, as well as ways in which that information can be used to improve the present. Archaeology is in a unique position to illuminate how past people faced the challenges of their times and environments and how they adapted—or why they did not. The archaeological record contains a vast storehouse of valuable knowledge and skills, and we should discover and learn from it.

In writing this textbook and providing examples, we drew on our own broad experiences as archaeologists who have worked in government, private industry, and academia. Although our topical experience is broad, our geographic experience is focused on western North America. To expand the geographic coverage, we included examples of the work of a number of our colleagues. Thus, readers have the benefit of the experiences of researchers from around the world and a wide range of archaeological sites across the globe.

Any textbook is a work in progress, and with the dynamic discipline of archaeology this is especially true. We have used a combination of new information and input from students, colleagues, and other reviewers asked specifically to evaluate the previous editions of this text to make changes to this edition that we feel make it more user-friendly and an overall better resource for students.

This third edition incorporates a number of changes. We expanded several sections, added a new sidelight, updated many items, and corrected a number of errors. We received input from several reviewers and from a number of students in our classes and did our best to address those suggestions (some, however, asked for things we thought went beyond an introductory book).

The text is organized into four major sections. In Part I, "What Is Archaeology?" we define the field, discuss the nature of scientific inquiry, and provide a history of the discipline.

Our goal is to provide students with a basic understanding of what archaeology is and how it operates. In Part II, "Obtaining Information about the Past," we define the fundamental concepts and methods in archaeology: sites, artifacts, ecofacts, remote sensing, excavation, and so on. We discuss how archaeologists obtain and classify information, and how they control for time through the available dating methods. Part III, "Interpreting the Past," covers how archaeologists analyze information to formulate and test models of what happened in the past. This is probably the most difficult aspect of archaeology, for both students and professionals. It is one thing to find and describe a broken pot, but it is another to really understand the cultural system in which that pot and its maker operated. This remains the challenge.

In Part IV, "Public Archaeology," we outline the field of cultural resource management and the laws and regulations that deal with archaeology, both in the United States and around the world. This is an important aspect of the field because much of the actual work done in archaeology is in response to development and preservation. Archaeology is not immune to politics, and we discuss some of the issues that face the field today, including the role of native peoples in the interpretation of their own heritage. Finally, we argue that archaeology can contribute to many contemporary issues, from environmental problems to law enforcement. Archaeology is truly a holistic science.

Special Features

CHAPTER OPENING OUTLINE Each chapter begins with an outline of the material covered in the chapter.

CHAPTER OPENING STORIES A compelling story of a real archaeological adventure that expresses the main theme of the chapter follows the opening outline.

HIGHLIGHTS Each chapter contains three or four Highlights—accounts of fascinating topics or sites related to specific sections of text. The Highlights focus on historical, classical, and

prehistoric archaeology from diverse archaeological regions around the world. At the end of each Highlight are questions to stimulate students' independent thinking.

LOCATION MAPS   Within each chapter is a map showing the location of regions and sites discussed in that chapter.

CHAPTER-ENDING PEDAGOGY   Each chapter ends with a summary, a list of key concepts, and an annotated list of suggested readings. There is also a ContentSelect feature with carefully selected search terms to encourage students to research articles from the ContentSelect online database, access to which is provided in the *Research Navigator: Anthropology* booklet that can be packaged free with *Archaeology: The Science of the Human Past,* third edition.

GLOSSARY AND INDEX   The glossary at the back of the book provides definitions of the key terms. The comprehensive index allows readers to locate concepts and archaeological localities throughout the text.

Supplements

Along with this textbook come many supplements to assist instructors in using the book and to enrich the students' learning experience. Most of the student supplementary resources are available free when packaged with *Archaeology: The Science of the Human Past,* third edition. Contact your publisher's representative for ordering information.

ANTHROPOLOGY EXPERIENCE WEB SITE   The Anthropology Experience site provides online resources for the four fields of anthropology. Illustrated text is provided with introductory content that incorporates photographs and downloadable figures and tables. PowerPoint presentations for each field serve as tutorials for students, who can use the presentations to review key concepts about each field. Instructors may wish to use these presentations in their lectures. A special video section with documentary film clips provides opportunities for students to view footage that has been carefully selected to illustrate important anthropological concepts. Many video clips serve as "lecture launchers." In addition, an interactive glossary organized alphabetically within each field provides key terms and definitions, many in written and audio format. Web links, organized within each field, provide students with easy access to helpful anthropology resources—ideal for students interested in taking more anthropology courses or considering a major in anthropology. Visit www.anthropologyexperience.com.

INSTRUCTOR'S MANUAL/TEST BANK   The Instructor's Manual includes for each chapter a summary, learning objectives, a lecture outline, suggested in-class activities, suggested assignments, and online and video resources. The Test Bank includes dozens of test questions for each chapter in five question types: multiple-choice, true/false, short-answer, fill-in-the-blank, and essay.

COMPUTERIZED TEST BANK   This computerized version of the test bank is available with Tamarack's easy-to-use TestGen software, making it possible for instructors to prepare tests for printing and for network and online testing. This software has full editing capability for Windows and Macintosh. Adopters may visit the online Instructor Resource Center at www.ablongman.com/irc to register for access to the computerized test bank.

POWERPOINT PRESENTATION AND USER'S GUIDE   This PowerPoint presentation for *Archaeology: The Science of the Human Past,* third edition, combines text and graphic images in teaching modules. Using either Macintosh or DOS/Windows, a professor can easily create customized graphic presentations for lectures. PowerPoint software is not required to use this program; a PowerPoint viewer is available to access the images. Adopters may visit the online Instructor Resource Center at www.ablongman.com/irc to register for access to this PowerPoint presentation.

RESEARCH NAVIGATOR™: ANTHROPOLOGY   This guide offers a general introduction to the Internet, a virtual tour of anthropology and its various subfields, and hundreds of anthropology Web links along with practice exercises. *Research Navigator™: Anthropology* gives students free access to Research Navigator™. Using this, students can search the ContentSelect database for the key words found in the ContentSelect section at the end of each chapter of *Archaeology: The Science of the Human Past,* third edition.

Acknowledgments

We acknowledge the contributors to this volume and the specific contributions they made. Their additions to our Highlights features and field reports enrich our introduction to archaeology. In addition to providing varied examples of archaeologists in action, the Highlights and first-person accounts give students exposure to geographic and cultural diversity.

Jack Broughton, Department of Anthropology, University of Utah, wrote Highlight 10.1, "Interpreting Animal Bones from the Emeryville Shellmound."

Jill K. Gardner, Statistical Research, Inc., San Diego, wrote the opening story in Chapter 3, describing how she became an archaeologist.

Duncan Garrow, Cambridge Archaeological Unit, University of Cambridge, UK, wrote the field notes that open Chapter 9, describing his experiences as a senior site assistant in excavations at the Neolithic site of Çatalhöyük in Turkey.

Brian E. Hemphill, Department of Sociology/Anthropology, California State University, Bakersfield, wrote these Highlights:
- 10.3: "City Planning and Sanitation in the Indus Civilization"
- 12.3: "Archaeology of the Silk Road: Ancient Mummies of the Tarim Basin"

Larry Bishop Lepionka, consultant for Archaeological and Other Cultural Resources, Beaufort, South Carolina, wrote these Highlights:
- 11.4: "Art and Archaeology in Africa"
- 12.2: "The Bantu Migrations and the African Iron Age"
- 13.1: "Sea-Level Rise and U.S. Coastal Archaeology"

Aren M. Maeir, Institute of Archaeology, Martin (Szusz) Department of Land of Israel Studies, Bar Ilan University, Israel, director of the Tell es-Safi/Gath Archaeological Project, provided Highlight 4.2, "Tell es-Safi: Goliath's Hometown."

Cynthia Van Gilder, Department of Sociology/Anthropology, St. Mary's College of California, wrote these Highlights:
- 9.3: "Island Geography and Subsistence Practices in Polynesia"
- 11.1: "Sex and Gender in Central European Burials"
- 12.1: "Archaeology of Proto-Polynesian"
- 13.3: "Janet Spector and the Archaeology of the Dakota"
- 13.4: "Heritage Management in Australia"

We also acknowledge the many reviewers of this book. Their critical comments and suggestions helped us to develop and craft this third edition. Previous edition reviewers were Mary C. Beaudry, Boston University; Karen Olsen Bruhns, San Francisco State University; Dr. Gary W. Burbridge, Grand Rapids Community College; Pamela J. Ford, Mt. San Jacinto College; Robert E. Fry, Purdue University; Robert G. Goodby, Franklin Pierce College; Randy McGuire, Binghamton University; Ann Morton, Finger Lakes Community College; Dr. Gordon C. Pollard, Plattsburgh State University; Cameron B. Wesson, University of Illinois–Chicago; Nancy Marie White, University of South Florida; and a number of anonymous reviewers. The reviewers for this edition were Anna Agbe-Davies, DePaul University; Randall H. McGuire, SUNY Binghamton; and Scott E. Simmons, University of North Carolina–Wilmington.

In addition, we very much appreciate the comments and contributions of a number of our colleagues on portions of the text, including Paul G. Chace, Jim Chatters, Nick Clapp, G. Dicken Everson, Jill K. Gardner, Brian E. Hemphill, Henry C. Koerper, Thomas E. Levy, Suzi Neitzel, Tom Origer, Richard H. Osborne, Max Pavesic, Fran Rogers, Sandy Rogers, Philip Silverman, Shelley Stone, Karen K. Swope, R. E. Taylor, Miriam Vivian, Linda Wells, Philip J. Wilke, Jim Woods, and Diana Yupe. We would not have been able to conduct the requisite research without the help of Janet Gonzales, Ariel Lauricio, and Kristi Khan of the CSU Bakersfield library. They contributed greatly to this project with their hard work in obtaining the many books and articles we ordered through interlibrary loan. Finally, we also appreciate the support we received from our department and the patience of our students while we were engrossed in this project.

TO THE STUDENT

What is archaeology, how is it done, and—most important—why is it done? Our basic goals are to answer these questions and to expose you to the real working world of archaeology by describing the research and experiences of archaeologists around the globe. We hope to convey the "flavor" of the discipline and spark your interest in learning about the experiences, technologies, successes, and failures of people in the past. If we are successful, we know that you will gain respect and admiration for other peoples and cultures.

Archaeology makes a practical contribution to society and is exciting, interesting, pertinent, great fun, and a wonderful career.

Special Features of Your Textbook

With you in mind, we have designed several features that appear in every chapter to capture your interest and help you master the content.

CHAPTER OPENING OUTLINE   Each chapter begins with an outline of the material covered in the chapter.

CHAPTER OPENING STORIES   A compelling story of a real archaeological adventure that expresses the main theme of the chapter follows the opening outline.

HIGHLIGHTS   Each chapter contains three or four Highlights—accounts of fascinating topics or sites related to specific sections of text. The Highlights focus on historical, classical, and prehistoric archaeology from diverse archaeological regions around the world. At the end of each Highlight are questions to stimulate your independent thinking.

LOCATION MAPS   Within each chapter is a map showing the location of regions and sites discussed in that chapter.

CHAPTER-ENDING PEDAGOGY   Each chapter ends with a summary, a list of key concepts, and an annotated list of suggested readings. There is also a ContentSelect feature with carefully selected search terms to encourage you to research articles from the ContentSelect online database, access to which is provided in the *Research Navigator™: Anthropology* booklet that can be packaged with *Archaeology: The Science of the Human Past,* third edition.

GLOSSARY AND INDEX   The glossary at the back of the book provides definitions of the key terms. The comprehensive index allows you to locate concepts and archaeological localities throughout the text.

Some Great Web Sites in Archaeology (just to start!)

Here are some of our favorite archaeology Web sites. Enjoy exploring the past!

- www.archaeologychannel.org
  Tour the Archaeology Channel Online. See videoclips on sites around the world at www.archaeologychannel.org/content/video.
- www.archaeology.org
  Sample *Archaeology* magazine.
- www.kv5.com
  Get continuous updates of excavations of the KV-5 tomb in the Theban Necropolis in Egypt. Also see a 3-D fly-through of the Valley of the Kings.
- www.pbs.org/wgbh/nova/lostempires
  In this five-part *Nova* series, "Secrets of Lost Empires," produced by PBS, see experimental archaeology in action: raising an Egyptian obelisk; constructing a medieval catapult.
- www.makah.com
  Find out about the Native American Ozette archaeological culture.
- www.smm.org/catal
  Take a virtual tour of the Neolithic city of Çatalhöyük in Turkey.
- www.maryrose.org
- http://refuges.fws.gov/generalinterest (click on Steamboat Bertrand)
  These sites explore maritime and underwater archaeology. Survey the archaeological excavation and reconstruction of the *Bertrand*.
- www.angkorwat.org
  Take a photo tour of the wonders of Angkor Wat.
- www.wam.umd.edu/~tlaloc/archastro
  Read about archaeoastronomy at the Web site of the Center for Archaeoastronomy.
- www.culture.gouv.fr/culture/arcnat/lascaux/en
  Take a virtual tour of the Upper Paleolithic rock art and cave art site at Lascaux.
- www.bnl.gov/bnlweb/pubaf/pr/1999/bnlpr092299.html
  Hear music played on the ancient bone flutes found in an archaeological site in China.
- www.saa.org
  Check out the site of the Society for American Archaeology.
- www.physanth.org
  Check out the site for the American Association of Physical Anthropologists.
- www.shovelbums.org
  Investigate this site for jobs in archaeology.

The Science of Archaeology

FOR DECADES, SCIENTISTS had studied the pottery of the Moche, an early civilization of farmers and fishers that thrived along the north coast of Peru between about 1,900 and 1,200 years ago. The Moche were superb artisans, working with metals (copper, gold, and silver), stone, and textiles. Their pottery (Donnan 1976, 1990) was finely made and depicted plants, animals, and people, some in three dimensions. Other pottery was simpler in form but was wonderfully decorated with scenes of elaborately dressed people engaged in interesting activities. Working diligently over the years, museum specialists had noted that a character depicted in a scene on one vessel was sometimes present in the scene on another vessel. As the decorations on more pottery were analyzed, scenes began to repeat themselves

and more links between different scenes were discovered.

By 1974, a series of scenes was linked together to identify a major chronicle, called the Sacrifice Ceremony. The characters were unearthly, their dress and decoration fantastically elaborate, and the activities astounding. Four major priests were identified: Warrior Priest, Bird Priest, Priestess, and an unnamed priest. The four are shown decapitating and mutilating war captives, then drinking their blood from a cup. The entire story and imagery were interpreted as depictions of the Moche gods conducting supernatural activities. The archaeologists working on the pottery thought they were learning only about Moche art and myth.

Although much work had been done to learn about the Moche, many of the sites had been vandalized and looted. In 1987, vandals discovered an intact royal tomb in a small mud-brick pyramid at the Moche site of Sipán (see-pan). Police caught the looters and were able to recover some of the materials stolen from the tomb, but other materials had already been sold on the black market. Archaeologist Walter Alva examined the confiscated materials and recognized some of the objects as having been depicted in Moche art. Alva realized the scientific value of the discovery and began an excavation to salvage whatever information might remain in the shattered site, knowing that it would be completely destroyed by looters as soon as he left (Alva and Donnan 1994).

Alva began to excavate into the pyramid and soon discovered, remarkably, the intact tomb (called Tomb 1) of a Moche lord (Alva 1988). As he painstakingly uncovered the burial of an adult male, Alva found many artifacts, some of which had never before been seen by archaeologists. Found were elaborate ornaments worn by the individual, many of which were seen in artistic depictions of warriors, suggesting that the person was a warrior. As the excavation of the main burial was completed, Alva discovered other burials surrounding it, people who appeared to have been sacrificed. Alva realized that he had discovered a person who had been buried with all of the ritual paraphernalia possessed by the Warrior Priest of the Sacrifice Ceremony (Donnan 1988).

A second tomb (Tomb 2) was soon discovered nearby and excavated.

This tomb also contained an adult male, but with different dress and ornamentation. Again, other people had been buried in association. A copper cup and a large copper headdress with an owl's head and large wings were found with the main burial. Amazingly, the individual in Tomb 2 seemed to correspond with another of the priests of the Sacrifice Ceremony, the Bird Priest.

A third tomb (Tomb 3; Alva 1990) was found deeper in the pyramid and dated to an earlier time than Tombs 1 and 2. The individual in Tomb 3 was buried alone but with spectacular clothing and ornamentation. Alva was not able to ascertain whether the individual was one of the priests of the Sacrifice Ceremony. However, the tomb of an individual identified as the Priestess of the Sacrifice Ceremony was later found in another Moche site (Donnan and Castillo 1992). Other similar tombs have been discovered at other Moche sites but were looted before they could be documented. However, they appear to have contained materials similar to those of Sipán, indicating that the Sacrifice Ceremony was widespread. There now seems little doubt that the fantastic Sacrifice Ceremony first identified on Moche pottery was actually practiced by the Moche. Warriors engaged in ritualized combat, and vanquished enemies were taken to Sipán as captives. They were stripped naked and bound, their clothing and weapons were bundled together, and they were brought before the Moche priests. There, they were sacrificed: decapitated, dismembered, their blood collected in cups and consumed in a ritual that was very important in Moche culture.

Christopher Donnan of the University of Californian–Los Angeles continued his explorations among the Moche ruins. He has uncovered additional tombs (Donnan 2001), gathering new information and details on materials discovered earlier. As work continues, a more complete understanding of Moche culture emerges.

For the location of Sipán and other sites mentioned in this chapter, see the map on page 4.

What Is Archaeology?

Before 1987, no one would have guessed that the ceremonies represented on Moche pottery were real, that the tombs of the Moche priests depicted in the art would be found, or that an understanding of the scenes represented on those vessels would be gained. Through archaeology, the realities of the past exceed the imagination of the present. To the average person, the word *archaeology* conjures romantic images of jungle adventures, lost treasure, and the romance of the ancient civilizations of Egypt and the Mediterranean. Some see archaeologists as traveling to exotic locales and snatching golden idols from the clutches of arch villains. Others believe that archaeologists are crusty old scientists in pith helmets who dig up dinosaurs or

LOCATION MAP: **Sites Mentioned in Chapter 1**

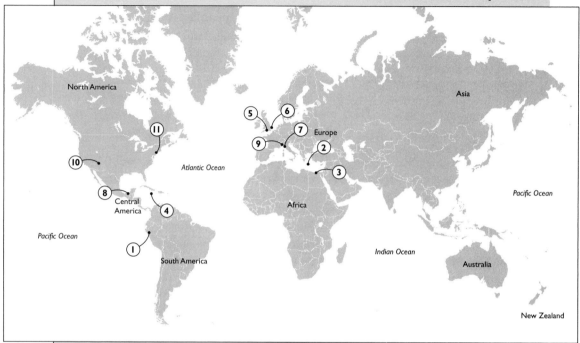

1 ■ Moche
   Sipán, Peru

2 ■ Minoan civilization
   Crete

3 ■ Cleopatra's Palace
   Alexandria, Egypt

4 ■ Port Royal
   Jamaica

5 ■ *Mary Rose* site
   Portsmouth, England

6 ■ Sutton Hoo
   Woodbridge, England

7 ■ Porto delle Conche
   Pisa, Italy

8 ■ Palenque
   Chiapas, Mexico

9 ■ Shroud of Turin
   Turin, Italy

10 ■ Pecos Pueblo
   Pecos, New Mexico

11 ■ New York Slave Cemetery
   New York City, New York

woolly mammoths (those scientists are not archaeologists but paleontologists). Neither image is correct, although the former has certainly served to popularize archaeology.

Archaeology is the study of the human past. In the United States, archaeology is considered a subdiscipline of **anthropology,** the study of people, whereas in Europe, archaeology is linked more closely to history. Archaeologists want to learn all about past peoples: where they lived, what they ate, how they were organized, what they believed, where they succeeded and failed, their language, their religion—everything. In a sense, archaeologists are detectives, finding clues to the past and trying to sort out what happened and why. Archaeologists do more than simply obtain facts about the past; they also interpret the information to create an understanding of the past.

Anthropologists who study living groups are called *cultural anthropologists* and have the same goals as archaeologists. The major differences between archaeology and cultural anthropology are in the methods used to obtain information. Cultural anthropologists can directly observe people doing things and ask them questions to get a detailed view of a culture. Because archaeologists deal with the past, they cannot directly observe behavior and must rely on what people left behind to infer what happened. The material remains with which archaeologists work are limited by preservation and recovery techniques, and as a result, it is very difficult to obtain a complete picture of a past society. However, archaeologists are able to detect change over long periods of time, can identify broad trends, and can examine transitions, such as the change from hunting and gathering to agriculture. In addition, archaeologists can detect the behaviors that might not be seen by a cultural anthropologist, such as foods eaten in secret (archaeologists would find the trash).

Humans have the unique ability to grasp the concept of their own past and can use this privileged stance to learn about our past through the study of archaeology in order to more clearly shape and direct our future. Archaeologists are interested in all aspects of the human past and are limited only by the kinds of questions they pose and their ability to find and recover information. Some of these questions seem esoteric, but all are ultimately practical, providing insight into where we came from, how we adapted to changing environments, and where we are going as a species. In addition, archaeology can enlighten us on social processes and social issues, such as nationalism and racism, by illuminating the present with the perspective of the past. Archaeology provides us with the album of our past, much like a family photo album, documenting where we have been, what adventures we have had, our high and low points, and where we may be going. It is a priceless treasure.

Archaeology is a growing and exciting science, encompassing a wide range of specialties and subdisciplines, that tries to foster an understanding of the global human experience over the span of human existence. This is a lofty goal but one that makes archaeology vibrant and ever changing. Although we do not yet know very much about the past, it is knowable: the material remains of the past do exist, they are recoverable, and we can understand them. To do so requires a great deal of work.

Archaeology and Anthropology

Anthropology is the study of humans and is holistic and comparative in its approach. Anthropology holds several core beliefs. The primary one is that of *cultural relativism*—that societies should not be judged by any standards other than their own and that no peoples are better or worse than others, although some specific cultural behaviors, such as genocide, are worse. It is also important to recognize that all societies are valid and important, being the product of many generations of knowledge and skills. The use of terms such as *primitive* to refer to a group is derogatory, and such terms are to be avoided.

Anthropology is a relatively new discipline, having been formalized within about the last 150 years. In Europe, Australia, New Zealand, Canada, and South Africa, archaeology originally developed from an early background of antiquarianism—collecting things merely for the sake of owning them—and later from classical studies and art history. In those places, archaeology and anthropology are considered separate disciplines. Being more closely aligned with history, the European system of archaeology has a greater emphasis on objects, art, architecture, and history.

American archaeology, in contrast, developed from anthropology. Although not denying its role in understanding history, American archaeology is more focused on the anthropology of past peoples. It has been said that "American archaeology is anthropology or it is nothing" (Willey and Phillips 1958:2). Although this statement should not be taken literally, the connection between archaeology and anthropology is very strong in the United States, and most archaeologists trained at most U.S. universities have degrees in anthropology. In the last few decades, however, it appears that European archaeology is becoming more allied with anthropology, while North American archaeology may be becoming less so (Gosden 1999:4–8).

From the anthropological perspective, discovering the age, history, and development of a past society is not the ultimate goal of archaeology but the beginning point for the inquiry of the past. Anthropological archaeology is more theoretically tied to science and the scientific method than is the approach concerned with history, although many of the actual techniques are the same. A separate discipline in Europe, archaeology is one of the four major subdisciplines of American anthropology, the others being cultural anthropology, anthropological linguistics, and biological anthropology.

Cultural anthropology (or *sociocultural anthropology*) focuses on the multifaceted aspects of human culture. **Culture** consists of a corpus of learned behaviors, such as language, territory, religion, and self-identity, that are learned and transmitted from generation to generation, and a *society* is a group of people who share a common culture. How a society raises its children, recognizes and names relatives, or practices religion are all learned behaviors that we call *culture*. Individual societies share specific patterns of this learned behavior, and these patterns may differ from one group to another. In the past, difficulties in transportation and communication tended to keep societies separate. This is less true in much of the world today; such barriers have largely been removed, and groups are no longer isolated.

Cultural anthropologists generally study extant (living) groups; the study of a particular group at a particular time is called *ethnography,* and the information obtained is called *ethnographic data.* Because anthropologists are interested in all groups, large and small, they may wish to study gang subcultures in east Los Angeles or the Aborigines in western Australia. The comparative study of culture and societies—similarities and differences—is called *ethnology.* More than one ethnography is needed to do ethnology, and it is through ethnology that we can learn about culture in general.

In a very real sense, archaeology is closely related to cultural anthropology and might even be considered the "ethnology of the past," in which archaeologists learn about individual past cultures and then compare and contrast what is learned about various past groups to form a broad understanding of human behavior. Archaeologists want to know the same things about a past society that a cultural anthropologist wants to know about a living one: what people ate, how they lived, how they were organized, what their religious beliefs were, and every other aspect of their lives.

Although the basic goals of cultural anthropology and archaeology are the same, the kinds of information available, as well as how such information can be obtained, are quite different. An ethnographer can travel to a group, live with them, observe, and even participate in their activities. The ethnographer can record what was observed and ask questions to fill in gaps in information. Ethnographers can gather a great deal of detailed information about a group in a relatively short period of time. Archaeologists cannot do these things, but they can investigate the past in great detail and over long periods of time.

Anthropological linguistics is the study of human languages, including the historical relationships between languages, syntax, meaning, cognition, and other aspects of communication. Archaeologists are interested in linguistics, especially historical linguistics, because certain aspects of language (and so groups) can be traced back in time (see Chapter 12).

The classification and distribution of languages are used by archaeologists to infer population movements in the past. For example, from the distribution of English around the world it is clear that Australia, New Zealand, much of North America, and portions of Africa were colonized by people from England in the recent past. Of course, we have historical records of these events, but the language distribution alone would also tell us. Such information is available for many regions, and prehistoric linguistics is a fascinating field that helps us understand where people and cultures originated.

The fourth major subdiscipline of American anthropology is *biological anthropology* (or *physical anthropology*): the study of human biology through time, focusing specifically on biological evolution and human variation. Within biological anthropology are a number of specialities. *Paleoanthropology* is the multidisciplinary study of primate and human evolution and hominid prehistory, as well as the various aspects of geology and biology that serve as the background to such studies (Tattersall et al. 1988). Anthropological geneticists study human variation and short-term (or micro) evolution. The study of our closest living relatives, the nonhuman primates, is called *primatology*.

Biological anthropologists also specialize in human osteology, the study of the human skeleton. Because many biological anthropologists have this training, they frequently use their skills in criminal cases or major catastrophes (such as wars and airplane crashes) in which human remains are badly decomposed, fragmentary, or skeletonized. Archaeologists who specialize in the collection of evidence from crime scenes or battlefields are called *forensic archaeologists* and were called on in September 2001 to contribute to the evidence recovery efforts at the sites of the World Trade Center and Pentagon terrorist attacks.

Archaeologists rely heavily on biological anthropology. In many cases, archaeologists recover the bodies or skeletons of past peoples and can record and analyze information on past nutrition and health. Analysis of wear and tear on the teeth and bones can tell us a great deal about how people worked and lived in the past, and their chemistry can inform us about diet and disease. Skeletal analysis can also tell us about the nature and direction of human evolution.

Archaeology and the Other Sciences

The field of archaeology is very broad, dealing with humans, their activities, and their environment over long periods of time. To understand all this complexity, archaeologists must rely on the expertise of other disciplines. In addition to cultural anthropology, archaeologists draw from a number of other social sciences, such as history, psychology, and sociology, to help provide a context in which to understand the cultural and social aspects of past human behaviors. As examples, studies of conditions in contemporary urban settings can be used to help understand the social situations of early cities, and a general understanding of the human mind can shed light on the thinking processes of early humans.

Other fields, too, provide information to archaeologists about things related to human activities. Botanists assist archaeologists in the identification of plants to help understand their evolution and use. Zoologists do the same thing with animals. Geologists study sites and their surroundings and provide information regarding erosion, deposition, age of deposits, and the like.

Finally, archaeologists rely on various specialists to help analyze what is found. Physicists and chemists actually perform most of the techniques used to date materials. Chemists also conduct other studies, such as residue analyses and geochemical sourcing. Mathematicians and computer scientists help in statistical analyses, mapping, and model building. Archaeology is truly an interdisciplinary science.

The Basic Goals of Archaeology

The basic and primary purpose of archaeology is to help us understand ourselves. To move toward that end, most archaeologists pursue three basic goals, each building on the other. As in all science, archaeology begins with the discovery of new information, which then must be described. Like newspaper reporters, archaeologists ask the five basic "W" questions: *who, what, when, where,* and *why.* The first four questions are answered by the discovery and description of archaeological materials, and once that task has been completed, archaeologists seek to explain the past by addressing the *why* question.

Archaeologists seek to reconstruct the lifeways of past people, their daily lives, where they lived, what they ate, what their tools were, how they interacted, and how they adapted to their environment. Ultimately, archaeology seeks to contribute to the development of a comprehensive understanding of human behavior. At any step along the way, the information and understanding derived from archaeological work can be applied to the management and conservation of the past and to the education of the public about the past.

DISCOVERY AND DESCRIPTION   The first goal of archaeology is to generate basic information—*baseline data,* the basic discovery, description, and classification of artifacts and sites. The greater the detail that can be found and recorded, the better the picture of the past will be. Sites are located and investigated, artifacts are described and classified, and regional chronologies are formulated. This basic work has to be done all over the world.

Once some basic idea of the prehistory of a region has been obtained, the information can be synthesized into definitions and a description—a **culture history**—of the past groups for that region. In conjunction, the delineation of **cultural chronology,** the description and sequences of groups through space and time, is also a major goal. These initial basic descriptions are often based on relatively few data and serve as foundations for future work. As such work gets done, the chronologies and culture histories will be rejected or revised as necessary. The advent of more accurate dating techniques has permitted much greater precision, and basic cultural chronologies are now much better understood. In spite of all this work, the basic cultural chronologies of most regions remain poorly known, and obtaining baseline data remains an important goal in much archaeological work today.

EXPLANATION   Once archaeological phenomena have been discovered and described, archaeologists seek to develop explanations for what was observed. Describing material is a relatively simple procedure; understanding why things are the way they are is a much greater challenge. To truly understand societies, one must understand how they operate, how they differ, how they change, and under what rules they do so. It is important to remember that one cannot seek an explanation of things that are not discovered or not described, so those two basic objectives remain critical.

UNDERSTANDING HUMAN BEHAVIOR   Finally, archaeology seeks to contribute to the comprehensive understanding of human behavior. By understanding the past, we can better understand ourselves, and archaeology can help to foster an understanding of the global human experience over the span of human existence. However, archaeology has yet to contribute significantly to the formulation of such knowledge, partly because of the difficulty in obtaining and analyzing appropriate information. As the discipline of archaeology matures, such contributions should increase.

The Branches of Archaeology

Archaeology can be divided into any number of specialties. Most such divisions are based on the time period or the geographic area being studied. Broadly, materials from the period before written history are considered "prehistoric," and materials dating from times after the advent of written records generally are considered "historical," although historical times are often given other names, depending on the region. Some archaeologists specialize in periods based on technology, such as the Stone Age, Bronze Age, and Iron Age. Some archaeologists specialize in all time periods for a particular region, such as North America or Southeast Asia. Others specialize in particular aspects of archaeology, such as *environmental archaeology,* the study of the effects that past people and the environment had on each other (Butzer 1982), or *geoarchaeology,* the study of the relationship between geology and geological processes and their impacts on archaeological interpretation (Rapp and Hill 1998).

Prehistoric Archaeology

Prehistory is the time before written records. Humans and their direct ancestors have been on the planet for about 5 million years, and approximately 99 percent of that time was spent hunting wild animals and gathering wild plants for a living. Most of prehistoric human activity falls within the **Pleistocene,** the geologic time period beginning about 1.9 million years ago and ending with the retreat of the glaciers some 10,000 years ago. Prehistory ends when history begins, so **prehistoric archaeology** can mean the archaeology before written records from any time and any place.

A number of other terms have been used to refer to more specific periods in prehistory. For example, in the Old World (Africa, Asia, Australia, and Europe), the term *Paleolithic,* or Old Stone Age, is commonly used to refer to the archaeology of Pleistocene hunters and gatherers. When the process of domesticating plants and animals began at the end of the Pleistocene, the *Mesolithic,* or Middle Stone Age, began. When farming became the primary mode of making a living, groups were classified as *Neolithic,* or New Stone Age. Each of these prehistoric periods is used to describe general adaptations in the Old World. In the New World (Central, North, and South America), all of the time prior to European contact is considered prehistoric.

Last, the archaeology of literate societies whose writing we cannot yet read is considered to be prehistoric. In some regions, writing was never developed and prehistory persisted until the arrival of other people who had writing, sometimes as late as the twentieth century.

Historical Archaeology

With the advent of writing, history and historical times began. This development occurred at different times in different places, beginning in the Middle East more than 6,000 years ago, later in other areas. Early writing was often in the form of simple records; the writing of narrative history developed later. In its most common usage, however, **historical archaeology** is considered to be the archaeology of the recent past (Orser and Fagan 1995:5). In most cases, this recent past is that of European colonialism, and the term *historical archaeology* is widely used to refer to the remains of intrusive, nonindigenous groups. For example, in North America the archaeology of the late entrants of the continent, including the Chinese, Dutch, English, French, Norse, Portuguese, Russian, Spanish, and later the Anglo-Americans, is considered historical archaeology (Paynter 2000).

The archaeology of historical times is important even when historical records exist. History records many things, including events, transactions, royal lineages, taxes, and trade. Some of the records are excellent, others less so; and for many activities, no records exist at all. All history is written by people, and all history contains some biases, sometimes unconsciously recorded. Some history is more obviously biased, written by people attempting to slant the historical record to serve their own interests. Even after records and accounts were made, later people sometimes would alter the records—that is, they would "rewrite history" to serve their own ends when they came into power. Thus, historical records and interpretations are suspect, for we know that much of what we take as history is incomplete, biased, and sometimes even false (and this is still the case).

As a scientific endeavor, archaeology can be employed to confirm, contradict, or correct historical records, to add depth to poorly recorded parts of history, and to elucidate the lives of those who were left out of recorded history, such as the Africans imported as slaves into the American colonies in the seventeenth and eighteenth centuries (Highlight 1.1). Such work can add much rich detail to what is already known.

HIGHLIGHT 1.1

The Archaeology of Enslaved Africans in the New World

Between about 1500 and the late 1800s, millions of people were kidnapped from Africa and transported in crowded ships to the New World, where those who survived the voyage were sold into slavery. (Slavery was abolished in the United States in 1863, persisted until later in some other countries, and, amazingly, is still practiced in some places.) Once in the New World, they were sold, lived, had families, and died. In many cases, they continued to practice many aspects of the cultures they had brought with them and so retained much of their cultural heritage. The casual observer would expect that, during the historical period, records would exist detailing the lives of these people. Although many records do exist regarding the transport and sale of slaves, very few records of their daily lives exist, and those that do are incomplete and biased. As a result, we know very little about how this large segment of the population lived.

What history cannot tell us about these people, archaeology can. Since about 1970, historical archaeologists have become interested in learning about the life of slaves, including where and under what conditions they lived, what they were given to eat, how they may have supplemented that diet, how they interacted with their owners, and many other questions for which there are few documents (Otto 1984; Ferguson 1992; Singleton 1995; Thomas 1998; Heath 1999). The African American community also is interested in the answers to these questions so that they can reconstruct their history and heritage.

Many of these archaeological investigations have been conducted in the eastern United States. Slavery was abolished in the northern states in the early 1800s but persisted in the southern states until the end of the Civil War. One of the better-known slave-period sites in the northern United States is the African cemetery in New York City.

In 1991, during the construction of a building for the federal government in lower Manhattan, a portion of an

The rediscovery of the "Negroes Burying Ground" greatly interested New Yorkers, historians, and members of the African American community. It is believed the cemetery originally contained between 10,000 and 20,000 people, sometimes buried three deep.

HIGHLIGHT **1.1** *continued*

eighteenth-century cemetery was discovered (Hansen and McGowan 1998). The cemetery, shown as "Negroes Burying Ground" on eighteenth-century maps of New York City, was located on a small plot of land then outside the city limits and was used from the early 1700s to about 1790. The area was eventually built over and the cemetery forgotten. After rediscovery of the site in 1991, construction was halted, and work to document and evaluate the site was undertaken.

Excavations have revealed almost 500 burials. Most of the interments were enslaved Africans, but other segments of the population, including the poor and indigent as well as prisoners held during the American Revolution, were also represented. Some of the findings include information about general health conditions and mortality. Nearly half of the bodies are those of children under age 12, and some of the adults showed the effects of being overworked, which may have led to their deaths. Many of the bodies were buried in traditional African ways (as evidenced by the kinds of grave goods present and the orientation of the body), attesting to the persistence of African cultural practices. A great deal was also learned about the demographics (sex and age at death) of the African

population. Of note was the realization that during the 1700s, slavery was as pervasive in the northern part of the country as in the South and that only South Carolina had more slaves than New York City.

After the excavations, the federal building was completed. The cemetery was designated a historical district by the city of New York and was named a National Historic Landmark by the federal government. A memorial to those interred in the cemetery was built on the site. Most of the human remains were transported to Howard University near Washington, D.C., creating a bit of a political problem (Harrington 1993). The remains will be reburied in the cemetery when the studies are complete.

CRITICAL **THINKING** QUESTIONS

1. What branch of archaeology and what related sciences were relevant to the excavation of the African burial ground?
2. What special function of archaeology does the story of the burial ground illustrate?
3. What was the impact of the excavation of the burial ground on people living today?

Archaeology conducted on early literate societies—even though they have written records—is often not considered to be historical per se but is seen as *text-aided archaeology,* "archaeology carried out with the aid of historical documentation" (Orser and Fagan 1995:4). The archaeology of certain early literate societies has been given specific designations. For example, the archaeology of the Middle East from the time of the Bible is called *biblical archaeology,* and the study of the time of the pharaohs in Egypt is called *Egyptology.* In Europe, post-Roman archaeology, that dating between the fifth and fifteenth centuries, is called *medieval archaeology;* all materials dating between the fifteenth and mid-seventeenth centuries in Europe are considered *postmedieval.* In Mesoamerica (Mexico and Central America), a number of groups had written records, but their archaeology is generally called *pre-Columbian archaeology,* referring to the time prior to the arrival of Columbus in AD 1492; more specific names have been given to certain times and regions.

A number of important texts, including religious texts, document people and events of the past, and many groups base their religion, philosophy, and other things on these texts. There has been a great deal of interest in whether these texts contain information that could be verified by archaeological work. A great deal of effort has been expended investigating the veracity of the ancient texts. In many cases, governments, religions, and some other entities have vested interests in the versions of history described in ancient texts, and there is often considerable resistance when archaeology, or any other science, shows them to be in error. This type of work is still an important part of archaeology.

One of the most famous historical texts is the Bible, a series of documents written over many hundreds of years and compiled into two major volumes, the Old and New Testaments. The Bible contains a number of historical accounts that deal with people and events. It has been demonstrated through scientific archaeology that many of the places, events, and people described in the Bible are, in fact, historical, while others may not be. However, showing that one part of a document is based in fact does not mean that all of the other information within it must also be true. Some things have been confirmed by science while others have not, and to believe in the things that are unconfirmed requires faith (Sheler 1999).

Classical Archaeology

Classical archaeology refers to the archaeology of the "classic" states that form the roots of Western culture, such as Greece and Rome, in the area of the Mediterranean Sea and surrounding regions (see Bowkett et al. 2001). Classical archaeology is related to these groups inasmuch as there are written records with which to interpret them. In the Mediterranean, classical (literate) times began about 4,000 years ago with Minoans on the island of Crete and ended with the fall of Rome about 1,500 years ago. Classical archaeologists spend a great deal of their time and energy studying architecture and art, the most visible and spectacular remains from the classical world. In addition, classical archaeologists seek to find sites related to historical events. As a result, classical archaeology requires different training, and many university classical archaeologists teach art history, rather than anthropology or archaeology.

Maritime Archaeology

Archaeology that has to do with anything related to the marine environment can be considered **maritime archaeology**, regardless of its age or geographic location (see Feulner and Arnold 2005). Maritime archaeology can be divided into at least two major fields, underwater archaeology and nautical archaeology. *Underwater archaeology* deals with sites of any kind that are located underwater. Many kinds of sites exist underwater, including shipwrecks, sunken cities, such as a portion of Alexandria in Egypt (La Riche 1996) or the pirate port of Port Royal in the Caribbean (Hamilton 1991; Pawson and Buisseret 2000), and sites occupied during times when sea levels were lower (Masters and Flemming 1983).

Nautical archaeology deals with ships, cargoes, harbors, anchorages, maritime technology, trade, and the influences that seafaring had on politics, social structure, and military events, along with anything else related to ships and their activities, even if the ships are now on dry land. Most known maritime archaeological sites are shipwrecks (Gibbins and Adams 2001), and tens of thousands of such sites are known, from the *Titanic,* to Viking ships, to wooden dugout canoes. One of the many famous ships recovered by maritime archaeologists is the *Mary Rose,* flagship of the English fleet in the sixteenth century under King Henry VIII (Highlight 1.2). Shipwrecks can provide detailed information about a specific moment in time (when the ship sank), such as crew life, trade and material culture, and ship technology.

HIGHLIGHT **1.2**

The *Mary Rose*

The *Mary Rose* was an English warship constructed between 1509 and 1511, during the reign of Henry VIII (McKee 1974; Bradford 1982; Marsden 2003). The ship, which was built in Portsmouth, England, displaced about 500 tons and was one of the first ships with its guns arranged so it could fire at broadside. The *Mary Rose* had a distinguished career and participated in

many campaigns. It was rebuilt twice, and its size was increased to 700 tons. The ship accidentally sank on July 19, 1545, off Portsmouth during a battle with the French, when water entered open gun ports. Some 385 of the crew drowned, and the ship settled on its starboard side into the muddy sea bottom. The English made a failed attempt to raise the *Mary Rose* a few weeks later, and the enterprise was abandoned. The mud created an anaerobic environment that preserved the keel and starboard side of the ship, but the port side eroded away.

The *Mary Rose* was rediscovered by a fisherman in 1836, and some items were removed before the location of the ship was again forgotten. In 1967 the ship was again discovered, this time with side-scan sonar. Repeated dives confirmed that about half of the ship

Excavations at the site began in 1968. In 1979 the Mary Rose Trust, with Prince Charles as its president, was created to preserve the ship. Excavators recovered some 20,000 items and skeletal remains of 179 crew members (see Stirland 2000; Marsden 2003).

Not all shipwrecks are found underwater. Some ships were moved onshore for a variety of reasons, including for use in burials, such as the famous Viking burial site of Sutton Hoo in England (Carver 1998) or the intact 4,500-year-old boats found entombed next to the pyramids at Giza in Egypt (El-Baz et al. 1989). Other ships sank in harbors that later became filled in, and the shipwrecks are now buried in dry land. For example, at least 17 Roman ships, many still containing their cargoes, were discovered in an old filled-in harbor in the Italian city of Pisa (Kunzig 2000).

The goals and techniques of maritime archaeology are not very different from those of other types of archaeology, although, as one might expect, it is especially difficult to find sites underwater and even more difficult to investigate them because of logistical problems and the physical limitations inherent in people working underwater. Nevertheless, since the development of lightweight diving gear after World War II, there has been an explosive growth in underwater archaeology. Ancient ships, their cargoes, and even

was in an excellent state of preservation and included intact decks, passageways, and cabins.

Because very little is known about ships or crews of that time, the recovery of the *Mary Rose* is important for a couple of reasons. First, the ship provides great detail on naval architecture at a time when shipbuilding and ship armament were rapidly changing. Many weapons were found, including large and small cannon, guns, swords, and knives. Guns and cannon represented relatively new technology. The most-feared weapon in the English arsenal at that time was the longbow, only a few examples of which have survived. However, 137 complete longbows, about 3,500 arrows, and other archery equipment were found on the *Mary Rose*, providing a much greater understanding of that weapon system.

Second, the daily lives of the ship's crew can be much better understood because many personal possessions were found, including clothing, games, and weapons. A great deal of food was found onboard, providing a clear picture of the diet of the crew. The surgeon's cabin was intact and contained a medical chest and medical instruments, including a razor, a syringe, medicine jars, and a mallet. The carpenter's cabin was also found and contained construction and repair materials, as well as tools.

Last, the recovery and analysis of the skeletal remains of many of the crew provide a great deal of information about the men on board the ship (Stirland 2000), including their occupations (archers, gun crews, etc.), health (many showed evidence of disease), and country of origin (about 25 percent came from countries south of England).

The ship was raised in 1982 and moved to a permanent display building in the Naval Museum at the naval base in Portsmouth, England. At that time, the *Mary Rose* was cleaned and reinforced, and today it is continually sprayed with a preservative that eventually will replace the water in the wood and preserve the ship. For more information on the *Mary Rose*, visit www.maryrose.org.

CRITICAL **THINKING** QUESTIONS

1. How does the story of the *Mary Rose* illustrate the special problems and rewards of maritime archaeology?
2. Why was the recovery of the *Mary Rose* important? How did the excavation of the *Mary Rose* help archaeologists learn about the past?

---

submerged land sites can be investigated in detail. One of the most interesting discoveries was the Swedish warship *Vasa*, which sunk on her maiden voyage in 1628. She was discovered mostly intact, raised in 1961, and is now on display in her own museum in Stockholm. Detailed treatments of maritime archaeology can be found in works by Muckelroy (1978), Dean et al. (1995), Delgado (1998), Gould (2000), and Green (2004).

Public Archaeology

The broad field of archaeology now involves much more than just the scientific quest to learn about the past. Archaeologists today work to preserve and protect the past and educate the public through the application of the various branches of archaeology. Archaeological sites and remains are fragile and once destroyed are essentially lost forever. This fact has long been recognized, and efforts have been made to preserve the remains of the past. For example, the National Museum of Denmark was formed in 1816 with the task of preserving Denmark's past. Since that time, many individual nations, and now the United Nations, have instituted programs to preserve archaeological sites when possible or to rescue or salvage sites threatened by development.

Today, most of the archaeology conducted around the world is related to the preservation and management of archaeological resources, a field known as *cultural resource management* (CRM) and sometimes called *heritage resource management.* Most CRM projects are funded by the government or by the organization doing the development that instigated the projects. Because so much development is occurring, a great deal of CRM-based archaeology is conducted. In fact, most practicing archaeologists today are employed in government or private industry doing CRM. In contrast, relatively few archaeological projects are undertaken as "pure" research. It is critically important that research be an integral objective of CRM projects so that the archaeology conducted can contribute to our understanding of the past. It is also important to educate the public about the past. Most people are interested in the past, and the past is an integral and vital part of the identity of some. There is a great deal to be learned, both of general value and of immense practical value.

Key Concepts in Archaeology

Archaeologists share a common understanding regarding the nature and manifestation of the past. This understanding is a series of basic concepts related to what things are, rather than how they are interpreted or what they mean. However, the concepts are not necessarily static and they, like interpretations, can change. These key concepts include the nature of the record of the past, the kinds of information present, the relationship between materials in the record, the age of things in the record, and the working assumption that societies of the past operated in the same basic manner as societies in the present.

The Archaeological Record

The evidence of the past exists in the **archaeological record**—the material remains and patterns of past human activities and behaviors. The archaeological record includes the physical remains of people and their tools, houses, foods, or any other materials lost, discarded, abandoned, and stashed by them, plus the geographic localities where these materials are found. The record also includes the various relationships between these materials and the patterns of those materials formed by their relationships.

Contained within the archaeological record is a variety of basic materials, including artifacts, ecofacts, features, and sites. **Artifacts** consist of tools, ornaments, or other objects manufactured or used by people to accomplish a specific task and come in a vast array of types and forms, from very simple to very complex. Most artifacts are portable. Artifacts contain a wide range of information about a group, including human skill, knowledge, symbolism, and activities. For example, a projectile point (commonly called "arrowheads" by the lay public) can tell us about warfare or hunting behavior, and a piece of painted pottery can tell us about vessel form, function, and symbolism.

Ecofacts are the unmodified (nonartifactual) remains of biological materials used by, or relating to, people and are common constituents of the archaeological record. Most ecofacts consist of food residues, such as the bones of animals or the seeds or other parts of plants. Pieces of charcoal from ancient campfires would also be ecofacts, as would pollen, whether the pollen was purposefully brought in by people as food or was natural and so could be used to help understand the environment at the time. **Features** are nonportable objects used or constructed by people (if the objects were portable, they would be artifacts). Examples of features include hearths, houses, walls, and other such facilities. Artifacts, ecofacts, features, and other aspects of the archaeological record are found in **sites,** specific localities where people lived, worked, or visited. Sites may range in size from very small (perhaps a single artifact) to huge (such as a city). Sites take many forms and reflect the full range of human behaviors.

Cultural Deposition, Stratigraphy, and Dating

As people live at a site, their cultural debris (trash, garbage, and other materials) begins to accumulate and build up, slowly burying materials in the soil and forming a site deposit. Some sites, such as those occupied for only a short time, may have no deposits; others may have extensive ones. Many of the artifacts, ecofacts, and features sought by archaeologists are contained within site deposits. If the activities occurring at a site change over time, the materials discarded into the site soils may also change and result in the formation of distinct soil layers, or strata. Natural strata, such as a layer of mud from a flash flood, may also be present. The various layers combine to form the stratigraphy of the site (Figure 1.1). Different strata in a site may indicate a variety of things, including periods of building, abandonment, destruction, or change in occupation, so archaeologists pay close attention to site stratigraphy. Alfred Kidder, an archaeologist in the early twentieth century whose excavations of Pecos Pueblo in northern New Mexico resulted in his seminal work, *An Introduction to the Study of Southwestern Archaeology* (1924), used cross-sectional stratigraphic drawings to analyze these sites.

To be able to document change through time, archaeologists must be able to determine how old things are. The ability to date things allows scientists to build chronologies and to track changes in material remains and behavior throughout prehistory and history. Thus, dating is of primary importance in archaeology. Much of the dating done in archaeology is *relative dating,* determining whether something is older or younger than something else. One of the main techniques of relative dating is through the use of the law of superposition—the idea that a layer, or stratum, as well as the materials in it, is older than the one deposited above it. Using relative dating, archaeologists can work out sequences of artifacts and sites and can provide a great deal of information. However, to really understand the past, *chronometric dating,* placing materials and events in real time, is necessary.

Using chronometric dating techniques, archaeologists are able to date things in actual number of years ago with reasonable certainty. Several techniques are used, but the most important one is *radiocarbon dating,* a technique that measures the amount of a radioactive isotope of carbon, ^{14}C, within a sample. Because the concentration of ^{14}C in living tissue is known and ^{14}C decays at a known rate, the residual ^{14}C in dead tissue can be measured, and the date of death of that tissue can be determined. Radiocarbon dating can be used to date nearly any organic material and has proved to be a huge benefit to

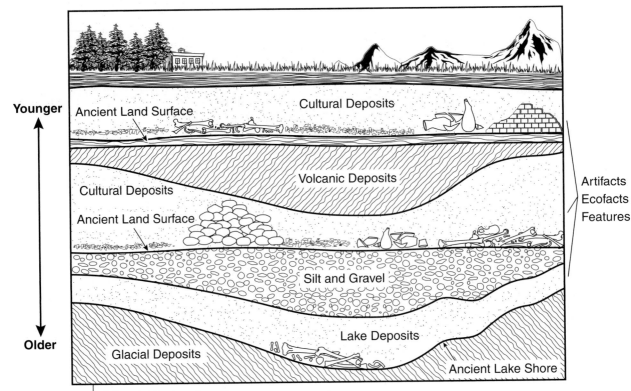

Younger

Older

Ancient Land Surface

Cultural Deposits

Cultural Deposits

Ancient Land Surface

Volcanic Deposits

Silt and Gravel

Lake Deposits

Glacial Deposits

Ancient Lake Shore

Artifacts
Ecofacts
Features

figure 1.1

Stratigraphy and the Law of Superposition. Here is an example of
stratigraphy with layers containing archaeological materials intermingled with natural
layers. Using the law of superposition, it is clear that the archaeological materials above
the volcanic deposits must be younger than those in the layer below.

Source: Adapted from Bernard Campbell and James Loy, 2000, *Humankind Emerging,* 8th edition
(Boston: Allyn & Bacon), Figure 5-1. Copyright © 2000 by Pearson Education. Reprinted by
permission of the publisher.

archaeology. The process was discovered by Willard Libby while conducting research on
the atomic bomb for the United States during World War II. The first radiocarbon dates
were reported in 1949, and the technique is now the backbone of most archaeological
chronology. Radiocarbon dating has been refined to the point where very small samples
can be dated. Other techniques based on radioactivity have been developed since, but
none is as widely used as radiocarbon dating.

Archaeologists use a number of reference points for time (Table 1.1). Many use the AD
and BC system, based on the Gregorian (Christian) calendar, which takes the birth of Christ
as its primary referent. The abbreviation AD refers to *Anno Domini*, Latin for "In the Year
of Our Lord"; BC means "Before Christ." Some Old World archaeologists use BCE ("Before
the Common Era") to mean the same thing as BC, but without the religious connotation. In
this system, a date of AD 700 is actually about 1,300 years ago and a date of 700 BC is actually

table I.I

Keeping Track of Time

SYSTEM	REFERENT	STATED AGE	ACTUAL YEARS AGO
AD/BC	Counting backwards and forwards from the birth of Christ	AD 700	1,308
		700 BC	2,708
Years ago	Counting backwards from the present	700 years ago	700

about 2,700 years ago. To avoid this confusion, others simply use a general time of "years ago" (sometimes using BP [Before Present] to mean years ago), where 700 years ago means 700 years ago, or roughly AD 1,300. However, BP is most commonly used to express radiocarbon dates (see Chapter 7), which are calculated from AD 1950. It can get confusing.

Archaeological Cultures

Archaeologists widely share the premise that behavior, present and past, is patterned and nonrandom; that culture consists of rules and expectations that shape behaviors; and that these behaviors, such as language, territory, religion, self-identity, and to a limited extent biology, are learned and transmitted from generation to generation. Furthermore, it is believed that these behaviors generate a material record that can be discovered, recovered, and interpreted validly and reliably. This general approach is called the *normative view* and forms the basis for much of the archaeology done today. Often included in the normative view is the basic working assumption that past behavior was rational and that people made "good" decisions. It is known that not all behavior was rational and that not all decisions were good, but this idea is used as the starting point for investigation.

Following the normative view, archaeologists work under the premise that past societies shared the same basic features of extant ones—that they were organized in some manner and shared a set of traits. In attempting to describe a past group, archaeologists actually create a model—a hypothetical cultural entity—to use as an analytical unit. Such a model makes it possible to organize archaeological data in space and time. Traits are plotted and combinations of traits are noted. When some sort of inclusive pattern is detected, the entity reflected by that pattern may be called a "culture." These **archaeological cultures** are essentially models that may or may not represent actual societies (although that is the goal), and, like any model, they are subject to testing, rejection, or revision.

As additional information is obtained on an archaeological culture, the model is rejected or refined. The greater the number and consistency of the traits assigned to an archaeological culture, the more confidence there is that it represents an actual society.

This tendency to treat archaeological cultures as real groups carries a danger: the archaeologist may come to uncritically accept the model as real and stop testing it. Nevertheless, archaeological cultures are very useful entities; they help to organize data, form models, and provide testable hypotheses.

The use of technological traits alone complicates the issue. For example, if you were to examine only the material culture of the last 200 years in the United States without the benefit of any historical background, it would be easy to create two major archaeological cultures: the horse and buggy culture and the automobile culture. In reality, neither of these "cultures" is real; they are just different technological developments within a single evolving culture. Such "ideal" and "real" cultures are a problem for archaeologists, who deal mostly with material culture.

Archaeology as Science

As individuals, we learn things through a variety of means—in school, by reading, through personal experience, and the like. Much of the knowledge we as individuals learn is new to us but is not actually new knowledge, being already known by others. We all question the veracity of what we learn (e.g., is the story in the newspaper actually true?) and employ methods to evaluate what we learn. We then make decisions to accept or reject what we see, read, or have been told.

Science is a formal system with which to learn new things, and it employs a number of premises, an organization of knowledge, and a specific method to evaluate new ideas. All societies have some sort of science, some more rigorous than others. Modern science (often called *Western science*) is based on several basic premises: that the universe is real, that reality is objective, that the universe operates according to certain constant laws, and that these laws can be discovered (Feder 2002:16–40). It is true that data are interpreted, that differences and biases arise in interpretation, and that two researchers can look at the same information and come to different conclusions. However, this does not mean that the past is not objective; it means only that there is disagreement within the scientific community. Through science, such disagreement ultimately gets worked out, although perhaps not in the lifetime of the researchers.

Science is **empirical** and objective, meaning that science can consider only those objects and patterns that physically exist and can be observed, measured, and tested. If something is not empirical or not testable, it is not science. Science requires that a specific

Archaeologist Margaret Conkey examines rock art at a paleolithic site in France. Dr. Conkey studies the images on the art to explore the structure of human thought patterns. She also studies the role of women in the past, including as depicted (or not) in rock art.

method, called the *scientific method*, be employed in scientific investigations, and scientists cannot ignore information that does not agree with their conclusions. Those things that are not empirical and not testable by means of the scientific method are not science and have to be considered through other means.

Science can be divided into three broad categories: (1) the physical sciences, such as physics and chemistry; (2) the natural sciences, such as biology; and (3) the social sciences, such as anthropology and sociology. The physical sciences are experimental and quantitative, classic examples of Western science. The natural and social sciences tend to be more descriptive, less quantitative, and less suited to experimentation, and their results tend to be less precise (Dincauze 2000:21). This does not mean that the natural and social sciences are somehow less scientific; it means only that they are more difficult. Archaeology employs elements of all three categories, the physical sciences through the description and analysis of artifacts and the like, the natural sciences in understanding environment, and the social sciences in its attempt to understand human behavior. Finally, like many sciences, archaeology suffers from incomplete and imprecise information, poor control of conditions (such as time), difficulty in experimentation, and too strong a reliance on inference.

The Structure of Scientific Knowledge

Scientists organize **data**—empirical and objective scientific facts—into coherent systems of understanding. These systems exist at levels of increasing complexity ranging from simple explanations of observable and measurable data to complex and overarching laws of behavior. Certain specific notions and terminology are employed in modern archaeology, and it is important to understand what these notions and terms mean. The following discussion generally follows that of Babbie (2001:51–52; also see Bell 1994b).

Archaeology generally operates within the **paradigm**, the philosophical framework, of Western science that assumes that the universe is real and knowable. Other, nonempirical frameworks have to be considered by other disciplines such as philosophy or religion. If the theoretical framework within which a discipline operates changes, a paradigm shift is said to have occurred. For example, for many centuries astronomy operated on the basic premise that the cosmos revolved around Earth. When it was discovered that Earth revolves around the Sun, a paradigm shift occurred and all of astronomy had to be rethought.

Laws are universal generalizations about classes of facts (Kaplan 1964:91). A classic example is the law of gravity: bodies are attracted to each other in proportion to their masses and in inverse proportion to the distance separating them. Laws must be truly universal, not accidental patterns found among a specific set of facts. Laws in and of themselves do not explain anything; they merely summarize the way things are. Explanation is a function of theory.

A **theory** is a systematic explanation for observations that relate to a particular aspect of the empirical world. Theories are grounded in fundamental assertions called *postulates* that are taken to be true. For example, for a scientist trying to understand past diet, a starting point could be the postulate that "everyone desires to satisfy his or her dietary requirements." From such a postulate, we might advance the general proposition that if procurement costs are the same, people should seek to optimize their diet by preferentially seeking foods of higher caloric content over foods of lower caloric content. It is from such general propositions that hypotheses are derived.

A **hypothesis** is a specified testable expectation about empirical data that follows from a more general proposition. Using the diet example once again, we could advance the hypothesis that in the Pacific Northwest, people would abandon root collecting when the salmon began to run up the rivers and streams, because salmon contain more calories per unit volume than roots. Research could be designed to test this hypothesis, and such research could support or fail to support the overarching theory (i.e., whether diet was optimized) only indirectly—by testing specific hypotheses that are derived from the postulates on which that theory was grounded.

Models are logically derived, interrelated constructs used to estimate reality. Scientists often employ them to operationalize and test theories by composing a set of interrelated hypotheses to measure the various propositions of a theory. Continuing with the diet example, a model of the theory that people in the Pacific Northwest optimized their diet might be constructed. Such a dietary model would include hypotheses regarding the caloric return of the various foods eaten by the people (including roots and salmon), hypotheses regarding what technologies were used to obtain the various foods, hypotheses about how to archaeologically detect the use of the foods, and hypotheses about any dietary restrictions the group may have had. The model would include a variety of aspects that can be empirically observed. Each of the hypotheses would be tested, and on the outcome of these tests, the model will be supported, revised, or rejected.

In developing hypotheses, models, and their tests, the scientist should seek the most direct and simple explanations, ones that do not require that improbable things be true. The postulate of Occam's razor states that the most simple explanation is the most likely to be true and that the most complex answer can be true only when less complex answers are shown to be false. However, one must also remember that correlation merely identifies association and association does not equal causation. Discovering a relationship between two things does not automatically mean they are causally related. For example, one could demonstrate that pollen is always present in the soils of archaeological sites. But, as it turns out, pollen is present in most soils and usually has no direct relationship to people.

The Scientific Method

To generate new scientific knowledge, scientists employ a specific method with rules and requirements designed to ensure an objective understanding of the nature of the universe. The **scientific method** generally encompasses the steps shown in Table 1.2.

In science, hypotheses, models, and theories are only rejected or supported; nothing is ever proven—in fact, the term *prove* is not even used in science (other than in mathematics). There are always more data, another test, and new hypotheses. Even well-known physical laws, such as the law of gravity, are constantly being tested and refined. Newtonian gravity provides a description that is adequate for most circumstances but does not hold up at the atomic level, so it had to be revised. Science is a never-ending, constantly evolving body of knowledge.

The two main methods of reasoning used in scientific endeavors are known as *induction* and *deduction*. Inductive reasoning moves from the observation of specific data to the development of a hypothesis to explain the data. In contrast, deductive reasoning moves from the general to the specific; if a hypothesis is true, then one should expect to see a set of specific results when the hypothesis is tested.

table 1.2

The Scientific Method

Data	All science begins with the observation and recording of some empirical and measurable phenomenon, collectively called *data.*
Hypotheses	Data themselves do not explain anything. To explain the data, a hypothesis must be developed that proposes some relationship between two or more variables. A hypothesis must be testable and refutable, with test implications being made, such as "If A is true, we will find B."
Test	To support or refute the hypothesis, a test with predictable results must be devised. To conduct the test, new or other data are required, applied against the test implications. The test and results must be able to be repeated by other researchers.
Retest	The test either supports or refutes the hypothesis. If the hypothesis is refuted, then the researcher will return to the second step and develop a new hypothesis to explain the data. If the hypothesis is supported, a new, perhaps more specific, test may be developed, more data gathered, and the hypothesis tested again. The process is then repeated, with the hypothesis being constantly refined.
Model building	If the hypothesis is part of a model constructed as part of a theory, the support or refutation of the hypothesis will influence the support or refutation of the model and, in turn, the theory. A refuted hypothesis may be dropped or refined and tested again.
Theory	Through the acquisition of new data, a reexamination of existing data, or the formulation of new hypotheses, new theories may be developed. Eventually, new laws may be proposed.

Scientists of all disciplines use the scientific method in the way outlined in Table 1.2. Phenomena of all types are observed, explanatory hypotheses are developed, and they are tested. Each test, whether the hypothesis is supported or rejected, creates useful knowledge, for it is as important to know what things *are not* as it is to know what they *are.*

Some hypotheses and models describe or explain things at single points in time and are called *synchronic.* All data are synchronic in that they reflect observations of human behaviors at points along a continuum. Other hypotheses/models are *diachronic*—that is, they deal with conditions through some period of time. Both synchronic and diachronic explanations are important to understanding the past.

We all use the scientific method in everyday life. If your car will not start, you will take that information and form a hypothesis: "It may be the battery." You test your hypothesis by checking the battery. If you reject the battery hypothesis, you will form another hypothesis: "I may be out of gas." You test that hypothesis by checking the gas gauge. Perhaps you solve the problem, or perhaps you call in an expert (your mechanic). You encountered a problem, formulated hypotheses, tested them, accepted or rejected them, and acted accordingly. The mechanic will do the same, but with more knowledge and experience. Science is everyday.

Archaeologists use the same logical thought process. When an artifact of unknown function is found, the archaeologist asks, "What was this used for?" The archaeologist formulates a hypothesis such as "It was used for cutting." An examination of the artifact would probably reveal evidence that would support or refute the cutting hypothesis, such as the presence or absence of a sharp edge. If no sharp edge was seen, the cutting hypothesis might be rejected and a "pounding" hypothesis formed. If there was evidence of pounding damage on the artifact, the pounding hypothesis may be supported. Further analysis of the artifact may continue to support the hypothesis, or a new one may be formulated.

Research Design

To conduct research, the scientist must develop a plan to do the work. This plan, or **research design,** includes a statement of the question (hypothesis or model) to be researched, a discussion of what is already known about the question, a detailed description of how the question is to be tested, and what data are expected if the question is to be supported.

Today, archaeologists must develop explicit research designs before going into the field. The hypotheses must be explicit, the ways in which they will be tested detailed, and the data expectations for accepting or rejecting the hypotheses explained. The research design can then be reviewed, refined, and improved prior to the work being done.

In some cases, simple questions may be asked to generate information for the development of a cultural chronology—for example, "How long did people occupy this site?" In other cases, much more complex questions may be posited, such as "What were the organization and subsistence preferences of various groups occupying a site throughout the term of its occupation?" Archaeologists can answer these questions only by studying the past in a systematic, scientific manner.

Pseudoscience

Science makes rigorous demands on data, testing, and acceptance of hypotheses and models. Lack of rigor or of adherence to the scientific method results in the rejection of the data or the hypotheses. In some cases, particularly in "popular" archaeology, people use scientific terms and phrases in an attempt to appear scientific when making their claims. In many of these cases, the data used to support such claims do not meet scientific standards, and many of the "hypotheses" are not testable. Science must reject these claims until and unless they meet scientific standards. Unfortunately, many laypersons are not aware of the unscientific nature of the claims and often accept the hypotheses as true. Such approaches are known as *pseudoscience* and do not generally follow the format of the scientific method (Feder 2006).

A well-known example of pseudoscience is the claim that extraterrestrials visited Earth and influenced a number of ancient societies, such as the Maya and Egyptians. In his book *Chariots of the Gods,* Erich von Däniken (1970) claimed to have irrefutable evidence that many of the mysteries of the ancient world, including the building of the Egyptian and Maya pyramids, could have been accomplished only through the guidance of ancient astronauts from another world. Von Däniken presented data and developed a series of hypotheses to support his claims. However, his data consisted mostly of questionable interpretations of rather ordinary things. For example, he presented a photograph of a sculpture from the Maya site of Palenque purporting to show a man in a spacecraft with flames coming out the back. The photograph had been cropped and tilted to show only what von Däniken wanted it to show. The full sculpture is of Pacal, a Maya ruler of Palenque, sitting in a chair or throne (the supposed spacecraft) amid the Maya version of the tree of knowledge, the leaves being the supposed flames.

That and other "evidence" reported by von Däniken fails any test of science because it is purposefully partial, perhaps even contrived, and its acceptance requires that a complex and untestable conclusion be accepted. This problem is worsened by the fact that other, much less complex, and quite testable hypotheses to explain the same data were not even considered. Logic dictates that the most complex answer can be true only when the less complex answers are shown to be false. To believe such a fantastic explanation as that proposed by von Däniken also requires the belief that the ancient Maya or Egyptians were not capable of building their own pyramids. It implies that these people were not creative, clever, intelligent, or capable, which is erroneous.

Frauds

Beyond pseudoscience, there are occasional instances of hoaxes in archaeology (Feder 2006), in which people purposefully fake data, "plant" objects in sites, or otherwise attempt to fool archaeologists. Such frauds have been perpetrated to embarrass, amuse, and bewilder both scientists and laypersons over the centuries. One of the more complex (due to its age) of these cases is the Shroud of Turin, long believed by many to be the burial shroud of Jesus of Nazareth. If the shroud were the burial shroud of Jesus, it would be about 2,000 years old. However, extensive radiocarbon dating of the shroud shows that it was manufactured about 700 years ago (an age also consistent with the cloth technology). It appears that the person(s) who made the shroud stained the linen in such a way as to represent the face, body, and even the wounds of Christ. Thus, the shroud is a fraud, although many still have faith that the shroud is genuine. Probably the most celebrated fraud is the Piltdown hoax, in which a human skull and an orangutan jaw were joined and passed off as a fossil hominid (Highlight 1.3). Because of the requirement of science that everything be tested, retested, and reexamined, both of these frauds were exposed. Although a fraud may fool people for a while, science ultimately is self-correcting.

The Importance of Archaeology

Archaeology is concerned with learning about the past, so the importance of archaeology is largely tied to the importance of the past itself. The past is important for a number of reasons (Figure 1.2), some esoteric and some very practical. Understanding ourselves is one of the most important of human goals, and archaeology contributes to this by helping us to understand the past. Humans are generally curious, and the past holds a great fascination for many. We are all tied to the past through our families, our politics, our religions, and our

HIGHLIGHT **1.3**

The Piltdown Hoax

Between 1908 and 1911, a Sussex lawyer and amateur scientist named Charles Dawson uncovered a mixture of fossil mammal and human skull fragments from Barcombe Mills Manor in the Piltdown region of Sussex, in southern England. Recognizing the importance of such a discovery, Dawson contacted Arthur Smith Woodward of the British Museum to inform him of his remarkable finds. Woodward knew Dawson to be a sincere and knowledgeable person and accepted his descriptions of his recovered material as genuine. The finding of the human remains with extinct hippopotamus and elephants was big news—it suggested that a fossil human of great antiquity had finally been found.

In 1912, when Woodward finally saw the human skull fragments brought to him by Dawson, all apparently from a single individual, he was convinced of the authenticity and antiquity of the remains. They were darkly stained and appeared to have old features. Further excavations by Dawson revealed a broken mandible (lower jaw) that was decidedly ape-like. The

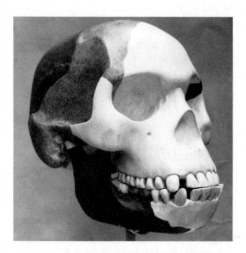

This reconstruction of the fraudulent Piltdown Man from skull fragments (darkest areas) resides in the Natural History Museum in London.

associations with the fossil mammals suggested that the "Piltdown Man" might be as old as 500,000 years. Both Dawson and Woodward claimed that this was the most important discovery of a human fossil to date, prompting the *New York Times*, in a headline dated December 19, 1912, to proclaim, "Paleolithic Skull Is a Missing Link" (Feder 2002:68).

But despite the enthusiastic claims, there were some concerns that the Piltdown Man (scientific name *Eoanthropus dawsonii*, or "Dawson's Dawn Man") was out of step with the growing human fossil record from Europe and Asia. By the 1920s, discoveries of early human fossils had suggested that the complete development of the brain did not occur until much later in human evolution, whereas Piltdown had a human-size brain and an ape-like face. Java Man and Peking Man (later called *Homo erectus*), believed to be of the same age as *Eoanthropus*, were decidedly different. Further fossil evidence from Africa of an early human ancestor known as *Australopithecus* showed that bipedalism (upright walking on two legs) was a human trait when the brain was still chimpanzee size. Before long, it appeared that the Piltdown discovery was an aberration rather than a "missing link."

Not until 1949 did a dating technique exist that could determine the true age of the Piltdown skull. This test, which determined the amount of fluorine absorbed by the fossil bones found at Barcombe Mills Manor, was undertaken that year at the British Museum. If the human remains were contemporaneous with those of the extinct animals with which they were found, then their concentration of elemental fluorine, absorbed from the surrounding soils, should be nearly the same. However, the analysis showed that the fluorine values were much lower in the human skull fragments and jaw than in the fossil mammals, indicating they were not the same age. Furthermore, the fossil mammals from Piltdown were found to be no more than 50,000 years old, not 500,000 (Feder 2006). Four

HIGHLIGHT **1.3** *continued*

years later, a more refined method of fluorine dating was applied to the skull and jaw fragments, which were determined to be from different animals entirely.

After the fluorine analysis, experts took a closer look at the specimens. It soon became obvious that the skull pieces were those of a modern human stained to look ancient, and the jaw was that of an orangutan stained to look old, with its teeth filed down to make them look less obviously nonhuman. The jaw also had been cleverly broken to make it impossible to align with the skull so that no one could tell that the jaw did not fit the cranium. The Piltdown skull had been a hoax from the start.

Who was responsible for the hoax? We may never know, although the finger has been pointed at everyone from Dawson to Sir Arthur Conan Doyle (author of the Sherlock Holmes stories). The latest suspect is Martin Hinton, curator of zoology at the British Museum at the time of the Piltdown discovery. He may be the true perpetrator of the hoax, because incrimi-

nating evidence was recently discovered in a traveling trunk tucked away in an attic of the museum (Gee 1996). Several "test pieces" of bone, looking strikingly similar to the Piltdown specimens and with the same artificial staining, were found. Arthur Smith Woodward may have been the target of the hoax, inasmuch as Hinton had significant salary disputes with Woodward when he worked for Woodward in the paleontology department. Whoever the perpetrator, Piltdown Man remains one of the greatest scientific hoaxes of the twentieth century. This somewhat embarrassing episode in anthropology nevertheless demonstrates the self-correcting nature of science.

CRITICAL **THINKING** QUESTIONS

1. How does the story of the Piltdown hoax illustrate the use of the scientific method in archaeology?
2. Do you think the discovery of the Piltdown hoax changed the way new finds are evaluated? How?

countries, and we could not function without some understanding of it. As people, we must be able to learn *from* the past; but in order to do that, we must first learn *about* the past.

The acquisition of fundamental knowledge is central to what scientists do. Basic research is critical because anytime something is learned, science expands and we all benefit. In some cases, the importance of discoveries may not be immediately recognized. New things can also be learned by making new connections between existing data. In addition, existing data may be used by future scientists to solve problems that we could not solve or that we never thought of. All of this holds true for archaeology. In addition, the range of possible human behaviors is vast and difficult to predict (as many sociologists and psychologists know too well). Any information that archaeology can provide regarding human behavior in the past may assist us in understanding current and future behavior.

Archaeology serves to enlighten people about the value of all societies, past and present, and stresses that they should be preserved. All peoples, worldwide, are ethnocentric; they believe themselves to be superior to all other people. It is an

- Learn from the past to help predict the future.
- Appreciate and preserve ancient traditional societies.
- Conserve cultural and biological diversity.
- Recover ancient knowledge and skills for adapting to the environment.
- Manage cultural resources and promote cultural tourism.
- Have an exciting and rewarding profession.

figure 1.2

The Importance of Archaeology

unfortunate truth of history that ethnocentrism has led to the subjugation and ultimate demise of many groups, all in the name of cultural superiority. For example, as Europeans began to expand across the globe after AD 1500, they felt justified in eliminating certain peoples they encountered, believing that the members of such "primitive" societies were not even human! When evidence of complex ancient societies was found, it was frequently attributed to past peoples of European ancestry, in the belief that native populations were incapable of such architectural and cultural accomplishments. Archaeology has since shown that in all cases these civilizations were the product of local peoples. Even today, these ethnocentric attitudes prevail in many places, as indigenous groups continue to face extinction at the hands of "modern civilization" (Bodley 1998). In addition, many groups that have survived the onslaught of Western culture have lost some or all of their cultural identities. Archaeology can help these people "rediscover" their past and thereby mutually benefit both outsiders and the people themselves by promoting and enhancing a better understanding of their traditional culture.

Archaeology also makes contributions to a number of contemporary political debates. By understanding the roles of gender, religion, power and politics, indigenous rights, and the like in past societies, we can engage in a more enlightened and informed discourse about these same things in today's world.

Dealing with the past, archaeology discovers the diversity of past peoples and societies and, to some extent, the past diversity of the natural world. The documentation and preservation of cultural diversity provide an understanding of how humans evolved and adapted, knowledge that will be useful to groups today. Archaeology also serves as a means of discovering and documenting the biological diversity of the past, an important task. An understanding of the genetic origin and diversity of maize (corn), for example, and the preservation of that diversity, could help prevent the loss of maize to some disease or other disaster.

Western culture frequently assumes that nonindustrialized (so-called primitive) peoples, today and in the past, cannot contribute anything significant to the industrialized societies of the world. What westerners fail to realize is that nonindustrial societies were highly successful for tens of millennia, and that these groups had a detailed knowledge of the natural world that allowed for this success. Nearly 50 percent of our major drugs are derived from plants and animals, many of which traditional peoples used as treatments for illnesses for thousands of years before drug companies and commercial laboratories existed. Unfortunately, as Western culture expands, this traditional knowledge, as well as their art, medicine, philosophy, and religion, is disappearing. Archaeology can help recover some of this lost information and document past traditional practices and use this knowledge to help the modern world. There is no reason to believe that there is only one successful response to a particular condition, and by understanding the responses of past peoples to various conditions, we can better anticipate and plan our own responses.

Another goal of archaeology is to study how people have interacted with the environment in the past. Archaeologists reconstruct past environments to understand how humans were influenced by their surroundings. This information may have significant applications today, especially with respect to long-term planning and understanding long-term change, such as global warming. For example, archaeologists are discovering evidence that El Niño events, the episodic warming of the western Pacific Ocean with its associated global weather fluctuations, have been occurring for thousands of years and have affected the course of civilizations, including ours (Fagan 1999; Van Buren 2001).

Archaeology provides the basis for cultural tourism, a major industry in many countries, such as Egypt, Greece, and Mexico, that are economically dependent on tourism. These countries focus on their cultural heritage and archaeological resources, and without archaeologists to discover and help interpret the remains, the economies of these countries would falter. The same is true in some parts of the United States where cultural tourism is important, such as the Southwest.

Archaeology is also of great commercial interest. Archaeological themes are widely used in advertising, generating large revenues. Archaeology also is widely used in Hollywood in films and television. Some movies featuring archaeologists have made hundreds of millions of dollars. The past provides considerable raw material for entertainment, but archaeologists first have to discover the past. Without the work of archaeologists, Hollywood could not use the past (even so, it does so poorly).

Finally, archaeology is just plain fun! It can be romantic, exciting, and fun to learn and discuss, and the discoveries can be thrilling. Archaeology is an excellent and rewarding profession or avocation. There is so much more to learn.

CONTENTSELECT

Search the ContentSelect database for articles using the following key words: *prehistoric archaeology, historical archaeology, classical archaeology,* and *maritime archaeology.* On the basis of your search, which brand of archaeology attracts you the most, and why?

Chapter Summary

Archaeology is the study of past peoples, developing from a base in history and anthropology within the past 150 years. Archaeologists work with the material record of past behaviors to reconstruct the past. Archaeology can be divided into a number of branches, including prehistoric archaeology, historical archaeology, classical archaeology, and maritime archaeology.

The goals of archaeology are (1) to generate information about the past through the discovery, description, and classification of artifacts and sites; (2) to synthesize information into culture histories and cultural chronologies; (3) to develop explanations for what was observed; and (4) to contribute to the comprehensive understanding of human behavior. Archaeological resources have to be managed, and the public has to be educated about both archaeology and the past. Archaeologists want to learn as much as possible about past peoples, including their subsistence, the size and complexity of their societies, how their settlements were organized, adaptations, technology, political organization, kinship, religion, symbolism, health, human genetic variability across time and space, and how and why groups changed over time. Answering these and similar questions is the ultimate goal of archaeology.

The evidence of the past exists in the archaeological record, which includes the material remains (artifacts, ecofacts, and features) of past human activities and behaviors, the geographic localities (sites) where these materials are found, the relationships between these materials (stratigraphy and distribution), and the patterns of those materials formed by their relationships. Knowing how old things are is critical to gaining an understanding of them, so dating is a central issue in archaeology.

Archaeology today is a science, empirical and problem oriented. To learn about the past, archaeology seeks to reconstruct and understand past human activities, to learn the *who, what, when, where,* and *why* of the past. To do this, archaeologists obtain data about the past, organize those data into a coherent system of hypotheses and models, and then continually test and revise them with the aid of research designs. This is not to say that archaeology is a cold science—in fact, much of archaeology is now done to put a human face on the past. Archaeologists are just as interested in the social and political aspects of the past as they are in objects and dates. Scientists generate data to test hypotheses, rejecting some and supporting others.

Archaeology is important for several reasons. First, it is useful to have a more complete understanding of ourselves, who we are, where we came from, and where we are going. Second, the conservation of cultural and biological diversity, past and present, is urgent. Third, we can recover ancient knowledge and skills for adapting to the environment. Fourth, the past has to be managed to preserve it from development. Last, archaeology is an exciting and rewarding profession and contributes to the well-being of humanity in general.

Key Concepts

anthropology, 5
archaeological cultures, 19
archaeological record, 16
archaeology, 5
artifacts, 16
classical archaeology, 13
cultural chronology, 8
culture, 6
culture history, 8

data, 21
ecofacts, 17
empirical, 20
features, 17
historical archaeology, 10
hypothesis, 22
law, 21
maritime archaeology, 13
model, 22

paradigm, 21
Pleistocene, 10
prehistoric archaeology, 10
research design, 24
scientific method, 22
sites, 17
theory, 21

Suggested Readings

If you want to learn more about the concepts and issues discussed in this chapter, consider looking at the following resources. (Some may be rather technical.)

Feder, Kenneth L. (2006). *Frauds, Myths, and Mysteries: Science and Pseudoscience in Archaeology* (5th ed.). Boston: McGraw-Hill.

This book explains how scientific knowledge is gained and provides a number of examples of frauds and pseudoscience, explaining the issues and problems with each. Very interesting reading.

Miller, Barbara D. (2004). *Cultural Anthropology.* Boston: Allyn & Bacon.

A basic introductory text in cultural anthropology, this book describes all of the major aspects of anthropology. Although it does not directly relate the concepts to archaeology, an understanding of anthropology is important for conducting research in archaeology.

2

Backgrounds
of Archaeology

I (MARK Q. SUTTON) first noticed it as a thin white stripe in the brown clay as I scraped the soil with my trowel. I am not sure how long it took for me to actually question the presence of the white stripe, but I do not think it was too long. Why was there a white stripe in the soil? As I cut back another thin vertical slice of clay, the stripe was still present, as if something extended horizontally into the clay. I decided to dig from the top, to come down on whatever was there. As I carefully excavated, a patch of white color emerged from the clay, a bit spotty at first, then about one-half square foot of pure white. I suddenly realized that the white background contained black spots, letters, in English, and the words of the handbill emerged into the sunlight for the first time in 120 years.

It was the spring of 1972 and I was one of the crew excavating at the Eagle Theater in Old Town Sacramento, that part of the city dating from the gold rush. It was my first historical excavation, although I had already been doing archaeology for a few years. The materials we were finding were different from what I had worked with before, and it was all new and exciting. The Eagle Theater was to be reconstructed as part of the city's Old Town renewal project. We knew roughly where the theater was, and we were to discover and map the foundations so that the reconstruction of the theater would be accurate.

I was working in an excavation unit toward the rear of the theater, in what had been an alley. I had discovered a pile of handbills advertising a sale at the hardware store that had been located next to the theater. The stack of ads had apparently been dropped in the alley and then buried in the clay brought in by one of the episodic flooding events of the Sacramento River, located 150 or so feet to the west. The paper had decayed, but the bleach in the paper had turned the clay white and the black ink of the letters had been preserved. As I excavated and exposed the pile of handbills, I made many errors, accidentally flicking away part of one sheet, but fortunately exposing the one beneath. After some four hours of work on that small chunk of clay, a portion of the ad was legible. I drew the piece, photographed it, and removed the entire block of soil in one piece, being careful not to break it or let it dry out. It was one of the best technical excavation efforts I have ever done, and my photograph of the flyer was used on the cover of the excavation report.

The hardware store had been owned and operated by Heinrich Schliemann, the man who would ultimately discover the famous city of Troy. When he began looking for Troy, he did so with the money he made in the hardware business in Sacramento and in other businesses in Russia. The discovery of a simple pile of advertisements greatly increased my interest in Schliemann, his work, and his search for Troy. I began to take an interest in classical Greece.

For the location of the Eagle Theater and other sites mentioned in this chapter, see the map on page 33.

In the *Iliad*, the Greek historian and narrator Homer wrote of the war fought in about 1400 BC between the Mycenaean Greeks and the Trojans. The story held that the war was

LOCATION MAP: **Sites Mentioned in Chapter 2**

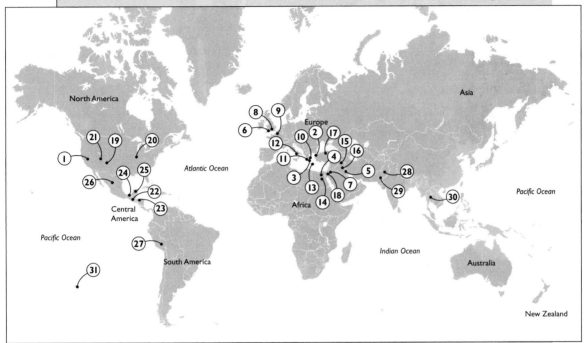

1 ■ Eagle Theater
   Sacramento, California

2 ■ Troy
   Hissarlik, Turkey

3 ■ Mycenae
   Argos, Greece

4 ■ Sphinx
   Cairo, Egypt

5 ■ Babylon
   Al Hillah, Iraq

6 ■ Glastonbury Abbey
   Glastonbury, England

7 ■ Petra
   Amman, Jordan

8 ■ Stonehenge
   Wessex region, England

9 ■ Somme River
   Abbeville, France

10 ■ Parthenon
    Athens, Greece

11 ■ Sparta
    Sparta, Greece

12 ■ Mt. Vesuvius, Pompeii,
    Herculaneum, Stabiae
    Naples, Italy

13 ■ Minoan civilization
    Crete

14 ■ Valley of the Kings
    Luxor, Egypt

15 ■ Assyrian civilization
    Northern Iraq

16 ■ Sumerian civilization
    Bagdad, Iraq

17 ■ Hittite civilization
    Turkey

18 ■ Jericho
    Palestine

19 ■ Folsom
    Folsom, New Mexico

20 ■ Mississippian civilization
    Cahokia, Illinois

21 ■ Anasazi
    Southwestern United
    States

22 ■ Tikal
    Flores, Guatemala

23 ■ Copán
    Santa Rosa de Copán,
    Honduras

24 ■ Palenque
    Chiapas, Mexico

25 ■ Uxmal
    Puuc Hills, Yucatán,
    Mexico

26 ■ Teotihuacán
    Mexico City, Mexico

27 ■ Machu Picchu
    Cuzo, Peru

28 ■ Harappa
    Multan, Pakistan

29 ■ Mohenjo-daro
    Sukkur, Pakistan

30 ■ Angkor Wat
    Siem Reap, Cambodia

31 ■ Easter Island
    Pacific Ocean

Heinrich Schliemann began to excavate at Hissarlik in western Turkey and was joined by Frank Calvert, who was working in the same area in search of Troy. Schliemann obtained permission from the Turkish government to dig, promising half of all the treasure he found. He and Calvert excavated a large trench through the center of the site, revealing a series of cities built one atop the other.

fought over Helen, a Mycenaean princess kidnapped by the Trojans. Helen was so beautiful that she inspired the Greeks to "launch a thousand ships" against Troy. The Trojans refused to return Helen, so the Greeks laid siege to Troy. After many years of stalemate, the Greeks pretended to leave, offering the Trojans a large wooden horse, the Trojan Horse, as a gift. The Trojans took the horse into the city, where Greeks hiding inside opened the gates and let the Greek army enter. Helen was recovered and Troy was destroyed.

For thousands of years, no one knew whether Homer's story was fact or fiction, but as interest in classical Greek civilization grew in the 1800s, several researchers began to investigate whether Troy actually existed. One of these was Heinrich Schliemann (1822–1890), who, after making his fortune (some of it, no doubt, from the hardware sale advertised in the handbill Sutton had discovered), traveled to Greece and began to research the archaeology of that region from the time of the *Iliad* in which Homer had told the story. In 1868, Schliemann began his search.

Schliemann was looking for Homer's Troy, the palace of Priam, and evidence that the Trojan War really happened. He found burned layers, walls, buildings, gates, many artifacts, skeletons, and a horde of silver and gold, which he dubbed "The Treasure of King Priam." He smuggled the treasure out of the country and declared that he had found Troy (Schliemann 1968). Schliemann continued to excavate at Hissarlik on and off and also worked at a number of other sites, including Mycenae, until his death. His fieldwork was very crude but improved greatly when he hired Wilhelm Dörpfeld, an experienced excavator, as his assistant. Despite the fact that fame and fortune were his major goals, Schliemann did make significant contributions to both the knowledge base and fieldwork techniques in archaeology.

Today, excavations continue at Hissarlik, and there is a wide consensus that the site is Troy and that the city was built, destroyed, rebuilt, and destroyed again several times. Many believe that the seventh city that was identified, Troy 7, is the city of Homer's tale, destroyed by the Greeks. Priam's Treasure (apparently too early to have belonged to King Priam) was taken to Berlin, where it disappeared after World War II. In 1993 the artifacts were discovered in the Pushkin Museum in Moscow. Turkey, Germany, and Russia all currently claim ownership of the artifacts, and the dispute is not likely to be resolved any time soon (Traill 1995; Morehead 1996; Allen 1999). On April 14, 2000, the artifacts were put on permanent display in the Pushkin Museum.

Ancient Archaeology

Interest in the past is almost as old as the past itself. It would not be hard to imagine that some Neanderthal 65,000 years ago would have come upon an abandoned cave with broken tools and discarded bones and wondered who had lived there, what they had done, and where they went—all basic questions in archaeology. However, we have no record of whether that Neanderthal, or any other, actually investigated those questions. Today, all societies have some mechanism to explain their origin and past, an explanation that is often codified in mythology, and it is possible that the Neanderthals had a similar belief. To many groups, the past was inhabited by powerful beings who created the sky, water, life, and land. People observing the archaeological remains of ancient structures and artifacts often believed that those things were also related to the powerful beings of the past. Thus, in this general view, the past was not human but mythical and supernatural.

Although it is possible that some sort of archaeology has been conducted from very early times, our record of archaeological investigation dates from only the last several thousand years. Perhaps the earliest known actual archaeological work was conducted by the ancient Egyptians themselves, when about 4,000 years ago they excavated and reconstructed the Sphinx, which had been built 500 years earlier. A bit later, about 2,500 years ago, the king of Babylon excavated the foundation of a ruined building in order to determine its age and, presumably, its relationship to Babylon. He also displayed in his palace some of the materials recovered, creating the first archaeological museum!

The ancient Greeks were interested in the past and collected some artifacts and visited some ancient sites. The Romans, however, were great antiquarians, and the collection of ancient art, especially Greek art, became a major pastime for the rich. The Romans even traveled to ancient sites as tourists (Casson 1994). During the Middle Ages in western Europe, little serious inquiry into the past was conducted. However, a few "excavations" were undertaken, primarily to recover religious artifacts and to "confirm" and empower certain leaders by linking them to the "heroic" past. For example, in AD 1191, the monks of Glastonbury Abbey in England conducted excavations at the presumed grave site of King Arthur, partly to validate the power of the church and partly to raise money by creating a shrine for visitors. The project was a success: a skeleton was found and declared to be the famous king.

Antiquarians

About 500 years ago, the intellectual climate of Europe began to change rapidly. The invention of the printing press in 1446 meant that books could be mass-produced, and as people became literate, information could be disseminated widely. In the fifteenth century, Constantinople (today called Istanbul) was a major center of knowledge, and with its fall to the Ottoman Turks in 1453, many scholars moved into western Europe. Later, in 1492, Columbus "discovered" the "New World," inaugurating the Age of Discovery. These and other events ultimately led to the Enlightenment, the development of scientific inquiry, and an explosion of knowledge.

European scholars began their inquiries by consulting the written knowledge of classical Greece and Rome, setting the stage for the great interest in those groups. Europeans became fascinated with classical art, and the rich began to collect this art, removing a great deal of material from ancient cities and stimulating the search for more cities and more art (following the pattern established by the Romans who collected Greek art). As these various places became known through books, a privileged few began to travel to them, and these tours became major events for the rich. By 1800, many of the cities of the ancient world, such as Petra in what is now Jordan, were known.

A few of these wealthy tourists became very interested in the past and began to do archaeology as a hobby. These people, mostly men, became known as **antiquarians.** Their interests were primarily history and the collection of objects. There were no trained archaeologists at that time, and the antiquarians were the only people making any inquiries into the past. In spite of their limitations, the antiquarians made many important discoveries and contributed to our understanding of the past.

A form of antiquarianism survives today in the guise of treasure hunting and artifact collecting. These people often vandalize and loot sites for their objects, unconcerned about the destruction they cause (Renfrew 2000). Much of this type of activity is now illegal throughout the world.

The Discovery of Prehistory

In 1640, Archbishop James Ussher of Ireland determined from the Bible that the date of creation was October 23, 4004 BC, meaning that humans had occupied Earth for only about 6,000 years. Because the Old Testament chronicled the creation and the subsequent general history of humans, Ussher's calculations left no room for any period of **prehistory**. Metal had been used by humans since creation, and there was no thought of an earlier technology based entirely on stone. However, discoveries of stones that looked like tools led eventually to the suggestion that there had been an earlier stone-based technology.

For centuries, many ancient materials, such as stone tools, simply were not recognized, and others were dismissed and explained as being the result of "thunderbolts" or other natural phenomena. The findings of some stone tools in association with extinct animals led to speculation that humans may have been present for longer than six millennia. This notion was dismissed, however, and the associations of bones and tools were ruled as accidental. Some of the more obvious prehistoric sites, such as the famous Stonehenge site in southern England, had been noted, and attempts were made to explain and understand them. However, no one was aware that a prehistory even existed, and as more and more sites and artifacts were discovered, it became a struggle to fit everything within the period of written history.

By the early 1800s, geological evidence was accumulating that suggested that Earth was much older than 6,000 years. Charles Lyell (1797–1875) argued that geological processes that could be observed were the same ones that had always occurred (the principle of uniformitarianism) and that a long period of time was necessary to explain Earth's complex geology. Lyell's evidence was powerful, and he altered the prevailing view that the Earth was young. In addition, the work of Charles Darwin (1809–1882) showed that the number, diversity, and distribution of plant and animals species had to be the result of change over a long period of time.

Among those arguing for early tools and humans was Jacques Boucher de Perthes, a French customs officer who conducted investigations along the Somme River in France in the early 1800s. He discovered stone tools in association with extinct animals and determined them to be antediluvian, or pre-flood, in direct contradiction to the Bible. Although he documented and published his results, he was ignored. However, de Perthes was able to persuade some prominent scientists, including Lyell, to visit the Somme River site in 1859, and they became convinced he was correct. Thus, by 1860, de Perthes was largely vindicated, and the authenticity of human remains and artifacts associated with extinct animals, prior to biblical times, was supported. This meant that humans had to be much older than 6,000 years. Also, in 1856 a new kind of ancient human, the Neanderthals, was discovered. Combined, these events required a complete rethinking of human antiquity and a realization that people had been around for a very long time (Grayson 1983; Van Riper 1993).

Some sort of a framework to place materials in chronological order was needed. After spending a great deal of time examining archaeological materials from western and northern Europe, the director of the Danish National Museum, Christian Thomsen, suggested (Thomsen 1848) that the past could be organized into three basic "ages": the **Stone Age,** the **Bronze Age,** and the **Iron Age.** At the time, however, all three ages were placed within the then-accepted 6,000-year span of human existence.

Later, when it was realized that the Stone Age had much greater time depth than the Bronze or Iron Ages, the Stone Age was subdivided into three periods: Old, Middle, and New, now generally called the **Paleolithic, Mesolithic,** and **Neolithic.** By the 1870s, some understanding of human antiquity was firmly established. The basic Paleolithic sequence in western Europe was proposed at that time and, though since refined, is still widely used throughout the Old World (Table 2.1).

Classical Civilizations

The Romans rediscovered the classical civilization of Greece and took a great interest in Greek art and architecture, but when Rome declined, so did knowledge of classical Greece. As Europe emerged from the Dark Ages, classical Rome and Greece were again rediscovered, along with ancient Egypt. Until 1829, Greece was occupied by the Ottoman Turks, who cared little for the Greek past and licensed collectors to remove Greek art.

One of the most controversial removals was conducted by the Englishman Lord Elgin. In 1802, he took roughly half of the marble sculptures decorating the outside of the Parthenon in Athens, shipped them to England, and sold them to the British Museum (for less than the cost of removal and shipping). The "Elgin Marbles" are still on display in that museum. The pieces were removed to "save" them from destruction, although most of the remaining sculptures survived the Turkish occupation and are still preserved on the Parthenon. For over 100 years, the Greeks have asked for the return of the Elgin Marbles, but the British Museum continues to decline these requests. The dispute remains an issue in Anglo–Greek relations to this day (Jackson 1992).

t a b l e   2 . 1

Basic Chronological Periods of the Old World

NAMED PERIOD	GENERAL TIME*
Iron Age	ca. 3,000 years ago to the present
Bronze Age	ca. 5,500 to 3,000 years ago
Stone Age	
Neolithic	ca. 9,000 to 5,500 years ago
Mesolithic	ca. 12,000 to 9,000 years ago
Paleolithic	
Upper	ca. 40,000 to 10,000 years ago
Middle	ca. 200,000 to 40,000 years ago
Lower	ca. 2.6 million to 200,000 years ago

*These dates are very general approximations and vary from region to region.

In many instances, the buildings and monuments of the classical civilizations decayed or were destroyed, damaged, or dismantled to construct new buildings, leaving only ruins. In other cases, however, preservation was good. For example, many of the buildings of ancient Rome, including some of the main public buildings, were later used for other purposes and had been maintained, resulting in their preservation. As genuine interest in learning about the past increased, more research-oriented work was undertaken.

Serious work on the ancient Greek civilization began in the mid-1800s, aided to a large degree by the surviving texts and histories from the period, such as the writing of Homer. Many of the famous city-states were rediscovered, and excavations began at Athens, Mycenae, and Sparta. Some amazing discoveries were made, such as the city of Troy, the royal tombs at Mycenae (Fitton 1996), and the cities buried below Mount Vesuvius (Highlight 2.1).

The Minoan civilization on the island of Crete, which preceded classical Greece, was brought to world attention by Sir Arthur Evans (1851–1941), who excavated at the major city of Cnossos in the early 1900s (Brown 1983). Evans showed that the Minoans controlled an economic empire encompassing much of the eastern Mediterranean between about 1900 and 1470 BC. Minoan society was severely disrupted in 1628 BC by the eruption of Thira in the Aegean that triggered a tsunami (commonly and erroneously called tidal waves) that devastated the coast of Crete. Work on the Minoan civilization continues (Hood 1971; Sakellarakes 1997), and there is still a great deal to learn. Even today, some of the writing used by the Minoans remains undeciphered.

HIGHLIGHT **2.1**

The Buried Cities below Vesuvius

On August 24, AD 79, Mount Vesuvius, located in western Italy on the Bay of Naples, erupted. Three Roman cities—Pompeii, Herculaneum, and Stabiae—were buried beneath dozens of feet of ash and mud. Thousands of people were killed, and the cities lay forgotten for centuries.

Pompeii (Maiuri 1958; Ward-Perkins and Claridge 1978; Connolly 1990; Etienne 1992; Slayman 1997) had been established in about 600 BC. It fell under Greek influence, became allied with the expanding Roman Republic, and was eventually conquered by Rome in 89 BC. The city and the surrounding region became a vacation spot for wealthy Romans, and many resorts and villas were constructed in the area. With a population of about 20,000, Pompeii flourished as a trading center and provider of luxury goods and services. The nearby smaller city of Herculaneum (Grant 1976) was a port and resort.

There were warnings of the coming disaster. A major earthquake badly damaged Pompeii in AD 62. In August of AD 79, small earthquakes began to occur, causing some wells and springs to dry. Damage was slight, and most people ignored the warning signs. The earthquakes became more and more severe, and on the morning of August 24, Vesuvius exploded, spewing ash, rock, mud, and poison gases down on the cities below. About one cubic mile of ash fell on the surrounding area. This event was witnessed by many, and it is the first major volcanic eruption for which detailed written accounts are available (Sigurdsson et al. 1985).

The people of Pompeii began to evacuate the city, taking most of their valuables with them. However,

some stayed, hoping to survive in sealed rooms. Thousands were killed by falling buildings, by poison gas, or by being buried in the rapidly falling ash, but most of the inhabitants escaped. The city was buried by 10 to 20 feet of ash. Soon after the eruption, many of the inhabitants returned to the city, dug into their former homes, and recovered as many of their possessions as they could. The city and its location were then forgotten. Thus, Pompeii contains few valuables.

Legend recorded the presence of a lost city, but its location was unknown. Pompeii had been noted in Roman history, and people occasionally found Roman-period artifacts in the area. Herculaneum was

Pompeii was inundated rapidly by a river of hot ash, mud, and gas that buried the city under as much as 100 feet of material. Some of the residents were unable to outrun the fast-moving volcanic flow, as casts of their bodies show.

HIGHLIGHT **2.1** *continued*

discovered in the early 1700s by a farmer digging a well. Looters destroyed a portion of the site, but in 1738, the king and queen of Naples sponsored more formal excavations, and work has continued since, although it has been interrupted from time to time. Looters have continued to ravage the site since its discovery.

Pompeii was discovered in 1594, only to be forgotten once more. The city was rediscovered in 1748, and this time, people knew what they had found. Excavations at the site began that same year and have continued sporadically ever since. Damage done to the city during World War II has been repaired, and excavations continue. To date, about two-thirds of the city has been excavated. Approximately 2,000 of Pompeii's former human inhabitants, including gladiators, as well as some of its animals, have been found. After the bodies were covered in ash, the ash solidified and the bodies, including the bones, decayed, leaving "hollows" in the ash. When found, these voids are filled with plaster, allowed to dry, and excavated to discover the shape of the body, foods, or other objects within the ash.

The architecture and art and many artifacts found at Pompeii and Herculaneum provide the most complete view of Roman life currently available (Zanker 1998). Many buildings, often even their second stories, have been preserved and span the full range of functions, from government buildings to shops to private homes. Some of the more interesting materials recovered at Pompeii are the human skeletal remains. Wealthy Romans generally cremated their dead, so skeletal remains are relatively rare in Roman sites and provide insight into the health and diet of the upperclass Romans themselves. Unfortunately, the excavations have left much of the city exposed to the elements and tourists, and much of the art and architecture is rapidly deteriorating.

CRITICAL **THINKING** QUESTIONS

1. How do the conditions of site deposition influence what we learn about the past?
2. In addition to their scientific value, what other values do the buried cities have?

Interest in the ancient civilizations of Egypt and the Middle East greatly increased after about 1800, when European powers began to enter and control those regions. In 1798, Napoleon invaded Egypt, then under the control of the Turks. He took some 200 scholars with his army, including some to document the antiquities they encountered. Although the French were defeated in 1801, the 21-volume *Description de l'Egypte* describing the scientific work done in Egypt by the French was published between 1809 and 1828 and created great interest in Egypt and other ancient groups.

One of the major discoveries by the French in Egypt was the Rosetta Stone, a tablet containing the same text written in Egyptian hieroglyphics, ancient Greek, and Egyptian demotic, the last two of which could be read. Using the Rosetta Stone, Jean-François Champollion deciphered the ancient Egyptian hieroglyphic writing in 1822.

With the decipherment of the hieroglyphic writing, interest in Egyptian archaeology increased greatly. Considerable work was undertaken to locate and map ancient cities and monuments, to document and try to understand pyramids, to discover the sequences of rulers, and to find royal tombs. This last goal was achieved with the discovery of the intact tomb of the pharaoh Tutankhamen in 1922 in the Valley of the Kings near Luxor, one of the most spectacular archaeological discoveries ever (El Mahdy 1999). Even today, work continues in the Valley of the Kings with the exploration of KV5, the largest tomb so far discovered, where it is thought 52 of Rameses the Great's sons were buried. Today, a great deal is known about ancient Egypt (Baines and Malek 2000; Shaw 2000), although there is still much to learn.

Europeans rediscovered the civilizations of the Middle East as early as the mid-1500s, and antiquarian interest in that region was high. By the mid-1800s, a great deal of work in the Middle East began as the cuneiform writing of the region was translated, making the thousands of clay tablets known from the various sites readable and greatly increasing interest in the area. Museums and private foundations in Britain, France, Germany, and the United States sent teams to work in the region as these countries competed for the pride of making discoveries.

Many of the major ancient groups of the region were discovered and excavations undertaken to document them starting in the mid-1800s, beginning with Assyrian sites in the 1840s, the Sumerians in the 1860s, and the Hittites in the early 1900s. Serious work in Palestine began after about 1860, with the goal of preserving the shrines of Christianity as related by the Bible. In more recent times, a great deal of work has been done in the Middle East on the transition from hunting and gathering to agriculture and the development of settled life. Some of the earliest evidence of agriculture in the region has been found in the lower levels of Jericho, a site occupied for some 10,000 years (Kenyon 1979; Bartlett 1982).

The Emergence of Professional Archaeology

Along with many of the other sciences, archaeology emerged as a distinct discipline with the scientific revolution of the second half of the nineteenth century. Before the mid-1800s, much of the work done to discover the past had been conducted by the antiquarians, whose work was all descriptive and their interpretations speculative and without much structure. In the early 1800s, museums began to be formed, and as more and more of them came into existence, they began to employ archaeologists, although their main tasks were usually obtaining objects for display.

As museums filled up with materials collected from all over the world, people began to realize that questions had to be asked to learn something about the past. Treasure hunting was replaced by more scholarly work, archaeology was added to university curricula, degree programs developed, and trained professional archaeologists began to appear. The serious work to learn about the past had begun.

As with many professions in the late 1800s and early 1900s, most archaeologists of those times were men. In the early to middle part of the twentieth century, female archaeologists were often viewed by their male colleagues as being "out of place," and their work was often not given the attention it was due. In spite of this drawback, a few women made important contributions to archaeology (Claassen 1994), with several doing pioneering work. Today, there are many more women archaeologists, and the opportunities to participate and contribute are much greater.

Most early archaeology was primarily descriptive, and relatively little interpretation was possible. However, by the mid- to late 1800s, some archaeologists began to place their information into larger interpretive frameworks, such as history, diffusion, and evolution. These efforts created an intellectual atmosphere in which the understanding of the past could grow.

A Historical Approach

The discipline of archaeology developed primarily from a base in history, and the early focus of archaeology was to learn when and where certain events happened. So little was known that the discovery, classification, and description of ancient materials was of major concern. This work formed the basis for the establishment of culture histories and cultural chronologies, both essential for the pursuit of more sophisticated questions about the past. The reconstruction of culture history and cultural chronologies became, in essence, the first major paradigm in the new discipline of archaeology and is still a very important aspect of most archaeology (Morris 2000).

Unilinear Cultural Evolution

Like many other disciplines early in their history, archaeology struggled to discover theoretical frameworks in which to place its information. Having very little theory of its own, archaeology turned to the concept of biological evolution, as championed by Darwin (1859). Like many scientists, anthropologists were inspired by the development of evolutionary theory in biology. By that time, there was evidence of a prehistory, an earlier stone technology, and even prior forms of humans. The idea that some sort of cultural evolution had also occurred seemed reasonable.

In the middle 1800s, two pioneering anthropologists, Lewis Henry Morgan and Edward B. Tylor, developed the theory that all societies evolved through a specific series of stages (see Morgan 1877), a theory later known as **unilinear cultural evolution** (UCE). Early in prehistory, they argued, all groups originally existed in a stage of "savagery." Over time, some of these groups progressed (evolved) "up the ladder" to the stage of "barbarism," and a few ultimately progressed to "**civilization**" (Table 2.2). In the eyes of many, the terms *hunter-gatherer, pastoralist,* and *agriculturalist* soon became synonyms for *savage, barbarian,* and *civilized.*

Though widely accepted at first, UCE was rejected when it became apparent that there was too much variation in cultural complexity and that groups did not evolve along a single line. For example, it was discovered that some societies, such as some of the groups on the Plains of North America, abandoned agriculture to become hunter-gatherers (thus moving "down" the ladder). It also was noted that several "stages" might coexist in a single group at the same time, such as hunter-gatherers, agriculturalists, and "advanced" townsfolk as segments of a single broader economy. In addition, some "simple" hunter-gatherers, such as those of the Pacific Coast of North America, were found to have complex social and technological systems. Interestingly, some of the basic concepts embodied in UCE are still used in anthropology, such as the term *civilization* to refer to preindustrial complex, state-level societies that emerged after the development of agriculture.

table 2.2

Simplified Version of Morgan's Stages of Unilinear Cultural Evolution

CULTURAL STAGE	CRITERIA	EXAMPLE
Civilization	Use of written records	"Modern" Europeans
Upper barbarism	Manufacture of iron	Early Greeks
Middle barbarism	Development of agriculture	Hopi
Lower barbarism	Invention of pottery	Iroquois
Upper savagery	Invention of the bow and arrow	Polynesians
Middle savagery	Speech and the use of fire	Australian Aborigines
Lower savagery	Before fire and speech	No extant examples

Archaeologists in the late 1800s widely adopted evolutionary theory. It was even argued (Lubbock 1865) that natural selection had created the differences in the various human cultures then being discovered throughout the world. Significantly, John Lubbock also argued that technological simplicity was equated with intellectual simplicity, both in the past and in the present—a false concept still held by many people. By the early 1900s, it was realized the societies changed because of many different factors, and the nineteenth-century unilinear view of "progress," with groups evolving "upward" along a single line, was dropped. A modified form of evolutionary theory would be reintegrated into archaeology in the latter part of the twentieth century.

Diffusion as an Early Explanatory Model

As evolutionary theory declined, some archaeologists adopted the belief that most cultural development could be explained by **diffusion,** the movement of traits from one place to another. Diffusionists argued that "civilization" developed in a few central places, such as Egypt, and spread to all of the other places, such as Mesoamerica, where civilizations later developed. The presence of pyramids in Mexico led many to accept this view, and some still do. Although diffusion does occur, researchers now realize that it provides only one possible explanation of cultural development, and evidence shows that civilizations arose independently in different times and places.

The diffusion explanation of culture encounters a number of serious obstacles. First, it requires contact between regions where contact is very difficult to explain. For example, if the civilizations of ancient Mesoamerica were the result of diffusion from ancient Egypt, there must have been some transatlantic contact thousands of years ago. There is no real archaeological evidence of such contact, although Thor Heyerdahl (1972) sailed an Egyptian-style boat, the *Ra II*, across the Atlantic to show it may have been possible. Second, the concept implies that most peoples were not intelligent or creative enough to have developed their own civilizations, a somewhat racist view.

Improving Field Methods

As archaeology developed from a hobby of collecting objects to a serious scientific inquiry of the past, archaeologists began to employ the scientific method in their work, and it became clear that more rigorous field methods were needed. Before the mid-1800s, only a few individuals made any efforts at systematic and careful excavation; most digging was little more than looting. However, by the mid-1800s, calls were being made for greater rigor in excavation and recording. The two pioneers in this transition were Augustus H. L. F. Pitt-Rivers and Flinders Petrie.

Pitt-Rivers (1827–1900) was an amateur archaeologist and an officer in the British Army. In 1880, he inherited a great deal of land and money and retired to do archaeology full time. Pitt-Rivers applied military rigor and discipline to his archaeological work, placing emphasis on recording the small details of excavation. He pioneered the development of **typology** beginning in the 1870s, which enabled the **cross-dating** of layers and sites.

At about the same time, Flinders Petrie (1853–1942) began almost singlehandedly to transform archaeological field methods from haphazard collecting to a rigorous and scientific undertaking. In 1880, Petrie went to Egypt to measure the pyramids at Giza, to test an earlier idea (by Charles Smyth) that they had been built according to divine specifications and held secrets about the future. Working under extreme conditions, Petrie made the first really detailed measurements of the pyramids between 1881 and 1883. He demonstrated that Smyth's ideas were based on inaccurate data and that the ancient Egyptian engineers had great skill and precision (the base of the Great Pyramid is almost perfectly flat, difficult to do even today). With this, and other work in the Middle East, Petrie set a new standard for fieldwork by pioneering the use of accurate measurements, recording context and stratigraphy, and using maps, photography, and field notes.

Another major innovation in archaeological field methods was the use of the grid system to keep track of where materials came from in a site, a system formally instituted by Mortimer Wheeler in the early part of the twentieth century. Grids are commonly used in archaeology today, both to record the location of materials and to allow for their comparison between different units of the grid.

As more sophisticated scientific methods became available, they were adopted by archaeologists, a practice that continues today. Aerial photography was first used in archaeology in 1906 and is now an invaluable tool. By the 1930s, archaeological excavations began to include studies of past environments, and specialists in other fields, such as botany and geology, were teamed together in archaeological research. Developments in the backgrounds of modern archaeology are summarized in Figure 2.1.

figure 2.1

Timeline: **Backgrounds of Archaeology**

PERIOD/ PARADIGM	DATE	PEOPLE, EVENTS, AND SITES
THE ANTIQUARIANS	1730s–1740s	Excavations begin at Pompeii and Herculaneum.
	1784	Thomas Jefferson excavates a trench through an Indian burial mound in Virginia.
	1785	James Hutton's *Theory of the Earth* published, presenting greater antiquity for Earth.
	1805	First professional excavations at Stonehenge, England.
	Early 1800s	Ancient Greek, Roman, Egyptian, and Mesopotamian cities become known, as well as prehistoric sites in Europe. Art and artifacts are removed from ancient civilizations to decorate European cities (e.g., Elgin Marbles, Egyptian obelisks).
	1822	Jean-François Champollion deciphers Egyptian hieroglyphs using the Rosetta Stone.
EARLY MODERN ARCHAEOLOGY	1833	Charles Lyell's *Principles of Geology* published, establishing the theory of uniformitarianism.
	1836	Christian Thomsen proposes Stone, Bronze, and Iron Ages.
	1841	Jacques Boucher de Perthes first publishes evidence of prehistoric stone artifacts made by humans.
	1852	Henry Rawlinson deciphers cuneiform writing of Mesopotamia.
	1856	Fossils of Neanderthals discovered in Europe.
	1859	Charles Darwin's *On the Origin of Species* presents the theory of evolution through natural selection.
	1865	John Lubbock's *Prehistoric Times* popularizes the concept of human prehistory in relation to theories of evolution.
	1870s	A. Pitt-Rivers and John Evans develop the scientific method of typology for classifying artifacts and cross-dating.
	1870	Britain's Archaeological Survey of India establishes a basis for later Indus Valley excavations at Mohenjo-Daro and Harappa.
	1871	Charles Darwin's *Descent of Man* extends the theory of evolution to humans.
	1877	Lewis Henry Morgan proposes the evolution of societies from a state of savagery to a state of civilization.
	1870s–1880s	Heinrich Schliemann excavates at Hissarlik, Turkey, in search of Homer's Troy. Flinders Petrie excavates in Egypt and Palestine, measures the pyramids at Giza, and develops seriation as a relative dating method.
	1886	Archaeological research on Easter Island culture begins.

T i m e l i n e :	**Backgrounds of Archaeology,** *continued*	

PERIOD/ PARADIGM	DATE	PEOPLE, EVENTS, AND SITES
CLASSIFICATORY/ HISTORICAL PERIOD	1894	Cyrus Thomas and others establish that Native Americans were the Moundbuilders.
	1892–1912	Max Uhle excavates in Peru, establishing baseline data for a cultural chronology. Archaeologists investigate Maya cities of Tikal, Copán, Palenque, and Uxmal.
	1906	Aerial photography first used in archaeology.
	1911	Machu Picchu discovered in the high Andes of Peru.
	1900s–1920s	Howard Carter excavates Tutankhamen's tomb, Arthur Evans discovers Minoan civilization on Crete, and Leonard Woolley excavates the biblical city of Ur in Mesopotamia. Alfred Kidder surveys the American Southwest and introduces research procedures for regional archaeology.
	1927	Folsom culture identified in the New World amid speculations on how the Western Hemisphere was populated.
	1929	Gertrude Caton-Thompson excavates Great Zimbabwe and proclaims that it is African in origin.
	1930s	Gordon Childe introduces the concept of artifact assemblages, surveys European prehistory, and postulates that civilization spread through a process of diffusion.
	1930s	Mortimer Wheeler develops the grid-square system for excavating sites.

Developing the Outline of World Prehistory

As trained archaeologists began to explore the various regions of the world, they obtained information with which to develop a broad outline of the prehistory of the world outside Europe and the Mediterranean. In many cases, the archaeologists were associated with colonial governments, a source of some bias and of some resentment among native groups of various regions (this is still an issue in some countries). Nevertheless, a great deal of work was done, and museums and archaeological programs were established in many countries.

Archaeology in the Americas

As soon as Europeans discovered the "New World," they asked questions about the age and origins of the native peoples. Initially, it was thought that the Indians were descended from one of the biblical "Lost Tribes" or from survivors from Atlantis. It soon became clear that they were physically related to populations in Asia, and the idea of a migration from northeastern Asia through Alaska took hold. In 1927, stone tools were found in association with extinct fauna at Folsom, New Mexico, and it was demonstrated that people had been in the New World at least since the Ice Age. The debate on when people first populated the New World continues to rage.

One of the major problems in North American archaeology was the question of who had constructed the many large earthen mounds found throughout eastern North America. This basic question prompted some of the first scientific archaeology, conducted by Thomas Jefferson in the 1780s (Jefferson 1787), who was unable to provide an answer. As in Africa, Europeans could not believe that the native peoples were capable of complex construction and so dismissed the idea that they had built the mounds.

The United States created the Bureau of Ethnology, later the Bureau of American Ethnology, in 1879, as part of the Smithsonian Institution. One of the bureau's first investigations was to solve the question of the Moundbuilders (Highlight 2.2), which was accomplished by Cyrus Thomas (1894), whose archaeological work conclusively demonstrated a native origin.

The ancient American Southwest was "discovered" in the late 1800s, when massive pueblos were studied and attributed to the Anasazi. These ruins were spectacular, and museums, institutes, and universities sent expeditions and competed for collections. As a result, researchers learned a great deal about the Southwest, and intense research in that region continues.

In Mesoamerica, the Maya and Aztec (or Mexica), among others, were noted by the Spanish, who made every effort to destroy them. The Spanish were very successful, and those civilizations were largely forgotten. The rediscovery of the ancient Maya in the early 1800s was due partly to government expeditions and partly to explorers who wrote travel books about Maya ruins. Serious work in the Maya area began in the late 1800s with the investigation of the great Maya cities, such as Tikal, Copán, Palenque, and Uxmal.

Archaelogists figured out the complex Maya calendrical system in the late 1800s, and the ability to precisely date monuments was a huge advantage in an era when few things could be firmly dated. Maya writing was not generally deciphered until the 1970s, and revisions and improvements to the translation are still occurring.

The other ancient complex Mesoamerican societies were rediscovered and investigated, beginning in the early 1900s in the Valley of Mexico and its largest site, Teotihuacán. Mesoamerica, with its complex civilizations, fabulous cities, and datable monuments, attracted a great deal of attention, a situation still true today.

Like the Maya and Aztec in Mesoamerica, the Inka (Inca) of South America were shattered by the Spanish and largely forgotten by Western scholars. The ancient Inka were rediscovered in the 1870s, and the "lost city" of the Inka, Machu Picchu, was discovered in the high Andes of Peru in 1911. Max Uhle worked in coastal Peru between 1892 and 1912, discovering many of the pre-Inka societies.

Archaeology in Sub-Saharan Africa

A number of ancient civilizations flourished in sub-Saharan Africa before 1500 but were generally unknown to Europeans. By the 1700s, Europeans began traveling through Africa and rediscovered many of the ancient societies. Although some Paleolithic tools had been

HIGHLIGHT **2.2**

The Moundbuilders

In the early 1700s, as European colonists moved west from the Atlantic Coast of North America toward the Mississippi and Ohio River valleys, they began to encounter earthen mounds that clearly had been constructed by humans. Many of these mounds were very large, and others were built in animal or geometric forms. Some were located in areas that were not then inhabited by Native Americans, and others were in areas where only small groups of Native Americans were living. The mystery of who the "Moundbuilders" were had begun (Silverberg 1968; Willey and Sabloff 1993:22–28, 39–45).

Speculation as to the identity of the Moundbuilders generally began with the basic premise that they could not have been native peoples. First, it seemed to the people at the time that there were too few Native Americans in those areas to have built such massive and complex structures (largely true, because of deaths from European-introduced diseases). Second, few Europeans or Americans believed that the Native Americans were intellectually or culturally capable of building the mounds (abjectly false). Many people held these racist views and felt that the Moundbuilders must have been "white"—perhaps an old and vanished group of Europeans or one of the Lost Tribes of Israel. If the mounds were built by members of some lost white race, their origin could be cited to provide some justification for white Europeans' claims to the land. Another view was that the Indians *were* the descendants of the people who built the mounds.

By the late 1800s, professional scientific archaeology began to take hold, and the Bureau of Ethnology, part of the Smithsonian Institution, assigned Cyrus Thomas to develop the necessary evidence to solve the problem. Thomas assembled all the data, undertook survey and excavation of some mounds, and based on the results of his work, concluded that Native Americans had built the mounds (Thomas 1894). The "lost race" model quickly died, and attitudes about the Native Americans slowly began to change. Today we know that the mounds were constructed by a number of different native groups at various times in the past, some as recently as the early 1700s. One of the Moundbuilder sites, Cahokia, is located near the city of St. Louis. This site covers more than 5 square miles and contains more than 100 mounds, including Monks Mound, the largest single mound in North America, measuring some 100 feet high and covering 16 acres.

CRITICAL **THINKING** QUESTIONS

1. Why was the identity of the Moundbuilders a problem for so long? How was the problem solved?
2. Are the issues illustrated in the Moundbuilder example still evident in the political climate of today? If so, where?

recognized in the 1860s and compared to the materials being found in Europe at that same time, serious work in sub-Saharan African archaeology was not undertaken until the 1920s. Many discoveries regarding the spread of farming, the development of iron working, and the development of a number of complex civilizations were made (Phillipson 1985; Vogel 1997). After 1925, Africa became the focus of the discovery of human origins.

Archaeology in Asia and Oceania

Although Europeans were vaguely aware of the great societies of Asia as early as the late 1200s, only a few Europeans, such as Marco Polo, had visited the region, and the reports of grand cities and civilizations, ancient and contemporary, were not generally believed. Many of these places were not rediscovered until the 1700s and 1800s.

By the mid-1700s, the British gained control over most of the region now occupied by India and Pakistan. Serious archaeological work did not begin, however, until the mid-1800s, when the Archaeological Survey of India was established. The survey located and recorded sites, conducted some excavations, explored India's Buddhist past, and discovered some Paleolithic materials. The 4,500-year-old Harappan civilization in the Indus River Valley (now in Pakistan) had been known since the early 1800s but was not investigated until the 1920s, with excavations at the major cities of Harappa and Mohenjo-daro.

Much of Southeast Asia was controlled by the Khmer Empire between AD 800 and 1400 from their capital at Angkor Wat, located in what is now Cambodia. The great Khmer civilization and Khmer cities, long under China's influence, were rediscovered by the French in the late 1800s. Though aware of their rich past, the Chinese themselves conducted very little archaeology before the 1920s, when European influence became significant. Political upheaval in China in the 1930s and 1940s prevented much archaeology from being done. By the 1950s, investigations were beginning to be undertaken, but until very recently, most archaeological discoveries in China had to be interpreted in a politically acceptable manner. Since that requirement was dropped, archaeological work in China has boomed (Loewe and Shaughnessy 1999).

Archaeology in Japan began in the late 1800s with the work of a few Western archaeologists who had moved to Japan. Some work was conducted to rediscover Japan's imperial past, along with its ancient agricultural roots, but this work was not generally acknowledged by the Japanese until the 1930s. Serious work on Japanese prehistory was not conducted until after World War II; since that time, a great deal has been learned (Aikens and Higuchi 1982).

In Australia there were questions about the origin and antiquity of the Australian Aborigines, and particular interest in the Tasmanian Aborigines, an island people who lacked boats and were thought to be of great antiquity because Tasmania was accessible only by foot during the last Ice Age (Cosgrove 1999). These groups were considered to be "surviving" ancient people and so attracted considerable anthropological interest; however, very little archaeological work was done before about 1950.

Most of the statues on Easter Island were toppled over. This one was restored to its platform. The statue itself was carved from a gray stone. The topknot was carved from a red stone quarried in a different location and placed on top of the head.

Very little work was conducted in the Pacific region before the 1920s. Easter Island was discovered in 1722, and the many large statues (called *moai*) on the island were a constant source of research. The first scientific work on Easter Island was not done until 1886. Since then, a great deal of work has been conducted on the people of ancient Easter Island (McCall 1994; Van Tilburg 1994).

Political Influences in the History of Archaeology

In theory, the field of archaeology is apolitical, with an interest in discovering the past, whatever that may be, rather than trying to "prove" certain things to advance a particular ideology (e.g., Bond and Gilliam 1994). However, like all fields, archaeology is influenced by politics, and many archaeologists—even well-meaning ones—operate with some sort of agenda. Political influences may affect the ability to conduct research, such as in areas of active warfare. Factors affecting the general political climate, such as racism and nationalism, can create biases and have an impact on the way the past is interpreted. The political environment at various times has affected archaeology, and although much of this influence occurred in the past, contemporary archaeology is still affected by it.

Colonialism

As Europeans expanded across the world, they took control of large regions and imposed their culture and values on the peoples living there. Most Europeans viewed native peoples as savages or barbarians and saw themselves as civilized. The archaeologists working in those regions were themselves part of the colonial regime and often took this same view. Thus, the ethnocentric view of living peoples held by Europeans was extended to the past groups of those same regions, and the past of those regions was likewise seen as inferior to the European past.

In many cases, European archaeologists could not believe that the native people of an area were capable of creating the archaeological remains that were found, so the materials were attributed to "lost" groups of "civilized" people. This racist view persisted well into the mid-twentieth century. The site of Great Zimbabwe in Zimbabwe (then the British colony of Southern Rhodesia) was discovered in 1871 (Pikirayi 2001). The site was so large and complex that the German geologist who found it thought that Africans could not have built it and perhaps the Phoenicians had done so (Highlight 2.3). Work at the site in the early 1900s demonstrated an African origin, but this conclusion was difficult for the colonial administrators to accept even as late as the 1970s.

Even though archaeology seeks to learn about and from the past, and not to make value judgments of it, it is possible that some archaeologists are still ethnocentric and view non-Western groups as somehow inferior to those from the West. Such ethnocentricity might manifest itself in subtle ways—for example, in descriptions of things as "primitive" or "unsophisticated."

HIGHLIGHT **2.3**

The Zimbabwe Problem

In 1871 a German geologist, Karl Mauch, discovered a massive stone fortress on the top of a hill in Rhodesia in southern Africa (McIntosh 1998). The structure was built from unmortared stone, and wooden frames were placed in doorways. Mauch knew that the site had to have been built by a complex and sophisticated group but never considered that it might have been built by native Africans. Looking for some other explanation, Mauch began to investigate. He discovered that the door frames were made from a wood that smelled like his cedar pencil and thought it was cedar from Lebanon, like the wood used by King Solomon. Mauch deduced that the site was the ancient city of Ophir, where the queen of Sheba had her palace, and announced his discovery to the world. Believing the site to be Ophir, treasure hunters looking for gold wreaked havoc, greatly damaging the site.

Further excavation was conducted at Great Zimbabwe in the late 1920s by Gertrude Caton-Thompson (Caton-Thompson 1931). She dated the site to about AD 1200 and attributed its construction to local Africans. The site was located in Southern Rhodesia, a British colony controlled by whites who wanted to keep the local black populations suppressed, so the interpretation that it could have been built by blacks was rejected. As late as the 1970s, some refused to believe that blacks could have had such a complex society, but it was eventually demonstrated that the site was African in origin (Garlake 1973) and that the Great Zimbabwe (*zimbabwe* means "house of stone" in the Shona language) was the capital of the Mwanamutapa Empire.

When Southern Rhodesia became independent in 1979, the name of the country was changed to Zimbabwe, to honor its past and recognize the site. The Great Zimbabwe site is a focal point for national

The idea that Great Zimbabwe was the city of Ophir eventually fell out of favor, but few believed that black Africans could have built it. Researchers variously attributed Great Zimbabwe to one of the "Lost Tribes" of Israel, the Greeks, the Romans, the Phoenicians, or the Portuguese.

pride and independence and was recognized as a World Heritage site in 1986. Today, mindful of the racism of the past, the black government of Zimbabwe is reluctant to have white archaeologists study the site.

CRITICAL **THINKING** QUESTIONS

1. How does the story of Great Zimbabwe illustrate the influence of political factors on the development of archaeology?
2. What beliefs and values in professional archaeology would guide the excavation of Great Zimbabwe today?

Colonialism continues to be an issue in contemporary archaeology. Modern archaeology was developed in the West, operates under Western rules of logic, and is practiced mostly by westerners trained in Western universities. As a result, archaeologists tend to look at things in particular ways, and not necessarily in the ways that the group under investigation (almost assuredly non-Western) meant things to be viewed. Thus, archaeologists tend to impose their own culture on the remains they study, a clear problem for interpretation.

In addition, many countries resent the fact that foreigners come to excavate their heritage, remove their artifacts, and interpret their national heritage. Some consider this activity a continuation of the colonial control of developing nations exercised by westerners. As a result, many countries now have stringent regulations to limit the activities of Western archaeologists—what they can do and what they can remove—and many countries now require that local archaeologists be involved in any project.

Nationalism

For the last 1,000 years, efforts have been made to relate what was thought to be a glorious past to the present, to confirm the rights of kings, the role of certain institutions, and the preeminence of nations. In this type of work, objective learning about the past was secondary to finding evidence to support the various nationalistic claims. This trend generally faded with the advent of a more scientific approach to archaeology in the mid- to late 1800s.

However, in the early to mid-1900s, the use of archaeology to support narrow nationalistic goals was renewed, particularly in Germany. Although most reputable archaeologists rejected these efforts, the Nazi government supported only efforts that demonstrated German claims to eastern Europe. Interestingly, the Nazis actually did make attempts to find the Ark of the Covenant and the Holy Grail, though not in the spectacular manner depicted in the Indiana Jones movies. Many other examples of the use of archaeology for nationalistic goals in Europe and elsewhere can be cited (Días-Audreu and Champion 1996; Kohl 1998).

A hallmark of nationalistic archaeology is its use as an aspect of national identity, a goal that does not necessarily conflict with the scientific goals of archaeology. Many people take pride in their past, a past illuminated by archaeology.

General Biases

Until fairly recently, most archaeology has been conducted by males, and their work emphasized the activities of males in the past. Hunting is commonly viewed as a male activity and gathering as a female activity, neither of which is actually true. Research on hunter-gatherers tended to emphasize the "hunting" aspect of the system; the gathering aspect was neglected. The title of the then-state-of-the-art treatise on hunter-gatherers, *Man the Hunter* (Lee and DeVore 1968), clearly communicated this bias. Soon afterward, the role of females in hunter-gatherer societies became a focus of research, as evidenced by the book *Woman the Gatherer* (Dahlberg 1981). Today, many more females are involved in archaeology, and there has been a great expansion in research on the roles of genders in the past.

All anthropologists and archaeologists are from agriculturally based societies—societies that tend to look down on and pity hunter-gatherers as people forced to wander about in an endless search for food. Contemporary hunter-gatherers live in regions, such as desert, not occupied by farmers, the very regions that farmers view as "harsh" or unsuitable to farming. However, throughout most of prehistory, people who made their living by hunting and gathering occupied the entire planet. About 10,000 years ago, plants and animals began to be domesticated, the areas suitable for farming were colonized by agriculturalists, and the resident hunter-gatherer groups were either expelled or assimilated. There is a tendency to forget that in the past, hunter-gatherers lived everywhere, including in very productive environments, and that many hunter-gatherer groups were large and complex, living in big, permanent towns, with complex economies and political systems.

On the positive side, archaeologists make every attempt to recognize their biases and to take action to lessen them. In addition to human biases, the kinds of information we gather and our abilities to analyze those data are limited by the youth of the discipline and our meager understanding of the past. As we do more archaeology, we get better at it, limit the biases, and understand more of the past.

CONTENTSELECT

Search the ContentSelect database using the key word *prehistory,* and survey the articles. On the basis of your survey, what does prehistory encompass, and why is professional archaeology important for understanding prehistoric peoples and cultures?

Chapter Summary

Human beings' interest in their past is quite old. Some early archaeology was done by the Egyptians and Babylonians, and other sporadic work was done during the Middle Ages, though primarily to validate claims and legends. During the Age of Enlightenment, interest in ancient societies grew and exploration of ancient ruins began, beginning the antiquarian movement. The antiquarians rediscovered and explored ancient Greece, Rome, and Egypt, emulating some of their traits, especially in architecture. Interest in the past grew dramatically.

With the rise of science in the 1800s, it was realized that human antiquity was much older than had been earlier believed. It was discovered that a prehistory existed, that humans had been present for a long time, and that most of the record of human existence was completely unknown.

By the mid-1800s, archaeology developed into a formal discipline. Serious work into the past began, and ancient civilizations throughout the world began to be rediscovered. Because almost nothing was known of the past, the development of basic culture histories and sequences became major goals in archaeology. Several interpretive approaches were applied to archaeological materials, including cultural evolution and diffusion, but neither proved sufficient. As field and analytical methods began to improve and more work was conducted, an outline of world prehistory began to emerge.

Ever since the beginnings of archaeology, political influences have greatly influenced it, and conclusions were often based on colonialism, racism, and political ideology. This situation persisted until the 1960s, when archaeology became more objective. However, such problems persist and archaeologists have to be cognizant of them.

Key Concepts

antiquarians, 36
Bronze Age, 37
civilization, 42
cross-dating, 44
diffusion, 43

Iron Age, 37
Mesolithic, 37
Neolithic, 37
Paleolithic, 37
prehistory, 36

Stone Age, 37
typology, 44
unilinear cultural
evolution, 42

Suggested Readings

If you want to learn more about the concepts and issues discussed in this chapter, consider looking at the following resources. (Some may be rather technical.)

Feder, Kenneth L. (2004). *The Past in Perspective: An Introduction to Human Prehistory* (3rd ed.). Boston: McGraw-Hill.

Fagan, Brian. (1999). *World Prehistory: A Brief Introduction.* New York: Longman.

Each of these books provides a general overview of what has been learned about the human past around the world and can point the reader to more detailed treatments of specific areas.

Trigger, Bruce G. (1989). *A History of Archaeological Thought.* Cambridge: Cambridge University Press.

Willey, Gordon R., and Jeremy A. Sabloff. (1993). *A History of American Archaeology* (3rd ed.). New York: W. H. Freeman.

These books provide a historical perspective of the development of the field of archaeology, particularly North American archaeology.

Van Riper, A. Bowdoin. (1993). *Men among the Mammoths: Victorian Science and the Discovery of Human Prehistory.* Chicago: University of Chicago Press.

Grayson, Donald K. (1983). *The Establishment of Human Antiquity.* New York: Academic Press.

Van Riper and Grayson provide detailed histories of the discovery of the antiquity and prehistory of humans and the process of having those ideas accepted in the eighteenth and nineteenth centuries.

chapter 3

The Development of Contemporary Archaeology

JILL K. GARDNER discovered archaeology by chance. She fell in love with the field, changed her career goal, and is now a professional archaeologist.

In 1990, I was attending a community college preparing for a career in business. One of the requirements at the college, of course, was a science class. I looked over the list and saw something called biological anthropology. I didn't know what it was, but it sounded intriguing (and easy for me as it turned out) and it fulfilled the requirement. So I signed up for the biological anthropology class. It was the best decision I ever made in my life. I took the lecture class and then the lab class, and I had a great time. The instructor—who later became a lifelong friend and colleague—made the class so much fun and so interesting that when it was over, I was really depressed. I thought it was too late to pursue a different career. After all, I was a business major.

A few months went by. Then I ran into this instructor on campus. He had always managed to get people to volunteer as student aides without ever having to ask,

but this quarter he was complaining because he didn't have any assistants. So I told him to give me a call if he needed any help, and that started a two-year apprenticeship with him while I finished my business degree. This chance encounter was a major turning point in my life, although I didn't know it at the time. After all, I was a business major.

Because he was an archaeologist, one day this instructor asked me if I was interested in going out with him to an archaeological site being excavated by a friend of his. I had never been on an archaeological site before, so I said sure, I'd love to. The site was a prehistoric village in Orange County, California, and covered about one acre. I did not know it was unusual at the time, but the artifact assemblage was quite impressive and contained many kinds of artifacts, including projectile points, fishhooks, and milling equipment, as well as a great deal of bone and shellfish. This wonderful site was my first experience in digging and screening. The soil from the excavation was being wet-screened, and by the end of the day I was wet, muddy, and smelly, but I was happier than I ever knew was possible.

I knew I had to find a way to change my career track. After I finished my community college work, I began attending a local university, taking anthropology courses while I worked full time in business, hating every minute my job took me away from my passion. I was not much impressed with the course offerings at the university but felt tied to it as my job was in the area. Then at the first professional conference I ever attended, I met an archaeologist from another university. I was recruited and transferred to the new school, where they had a good archaeology program. I got my B.A., then my M.A., then my Ph.D., and have never looked back.

For the location of sites mentioned in this chapter, see the map on page 57.

 ## Archaeology after World War II

Jill Gardner was the beneficiary of changes in professional archaeology following World War II. Most archaeological work around the world was interrupted by World War II,

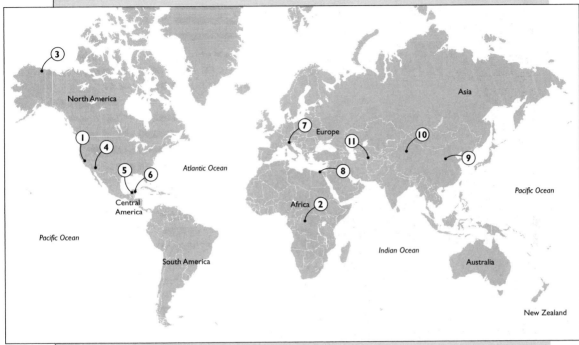

LOCATION MAP: **Sites Mentioned in Chapter 3**

1 ■ Lake Tulare
Tulare, California

2 ■ Aka people
Northeastern Congo, central Africa

3 ■ Nunamuit Eskimo
Barrow, Alaska

4 ■ Landfills
Tucson, Arizona

5 ■ El Mirador
Carmelita, Guatemala

6 ■ Nakbe
Carmelita, Guatemala

7 ■ "Iceman"
Bolzano, Italy

8 ■ Cleopatra's Palace
Alexandria Harbor, Egypt

9 ■ Qin terra-cotta armies
Shaanxi province, China

10 ■ Red-headed mummies
Tarim Basin, western China

11 ■ Oxus civilization
Mary (Margiana), Turkmenistan,
Central Asia

and many researchers entered the military service of their various countries. After the war, a new generation of archaeologists began to work, and the construction of culture histories and chronologies remained the primary goals in archaeology. Soon after the war, a number of developments took place that changed the way archaeology was done. A revolution in dating methods and other technical developments permitted archaeologists to begin asking *why* questions, in addition to the traditional *who, what, when,* and *where* questions. Over time, some archaeologists began to become dissatisfied with pursuing only culture history, setting the stage for a paradigm shift from description to explanation.

Before World War II, placing archaeological materials in time was a difficult and inaccurate task. In some cases, very accurate direct dating was possible but very limited, such as having inscriptions with dates or the use of tree-ring dating in a few areas. Most archaeological materials were indirectly dated on the basis of stratigraphy, general artifact types, and cross-dating estimates. Although it was known that some things were older or younger, actual dates could only be guessed. Developing sequences and chronologies consumed a great deal of archaeological energy.

A direct outgrowth of the wartime atomic bomb program was the development of the radiocarbon dating technique, easily one of the most important events in archaeology after World War II. The radiocarbon technique permitted the direct and accurate dating of almost anything organic, and it revolutionized the way in which sites and artifacts were dated. As it turned out, many of the chronologies so painstakingly constructed prior to radiocarbon were confirmed by the new dates. As radiocarbon dating became more and more routine, archaeologists were generally relieved of the demanding task of constructing chronologies through indirect means. As a result, they could begin to spend their time looking into other aspects of the past. Radiocarbon continues to form the backbone of most archaeological dating.

World War II also stimulated the computer revolution and the use of complex statistics. After the war, more sophisticated machines and programs were developed that could begin to deal with large sets of numbers. The use of modern statistical techniques was introduced into archaeology in the early 1950s, with the idea that statistical analysis of artifact attributes could be used to discover and define artifact types (Spaulding 1953). Formal sampling approaches for use in finding, excavating, and analyzing archaeological materials began in the 1960s, and the use of computers in archaeology began at about the same time. As the capabilities of the machines grew, efforts to develop statistical theory also increased. The ability to use quantitative methods in the sciences began to grow at an amazing rate, and the introduction of versatile and affordable computers after the 1970s made a huge impact.

Today, the use of statistical methods in archaeology is common and widespread. Probabilistic sampling and modeling are used in the analysis of past artifact and site populations. Most archaeological work now includes formal sampling and statistical approaches for survey, excavation, and artifact analysis (Ammerman 1992; Aldenderfer and Maschner 1996; Drennan 1996; Aldenderfer 1998; Orton 2000), and the use of computers in analysis is common as well (McPherron and Dibble 2002). A timeline for the development of contemporary archaeology is presented in Figure 3.1.

figure 3.1

Timeline: Development of Contemporary Archaeology

PERIOD/ PARADIGM	DATE	PEOPLE, EVENTS, AND SITES
RISE OF SCIENTIFIC ARCHAEOLOGY	1948	Walter Taylor calls for a broader, more anthropological approach in archaeology.
	1949	Willard Libby announces his invention of radiocarbon dating.
	1950s–1960s	Archaeological research in sub-Saharan Africa and Asia, including China and Japan.
	1952	After excavating Star Carr in Britain, Grahame Clark publishes *Prehistoric Europe: The Economic Basis*.
	1952–1958	Kathleen Kenyon excavates the ancient city of Jericho down to its Neolithic origins.
	1956	Anna O. Shepard, pioneer in petrographic analysis, publishes *Ceramics for the Archaeologist*. John Mulvaney establishes Australian antiquity.
PROCESSUAL ARCHAEOLOGY	1960s	Lewis Binford and others publish articles on the "New (Processual) Archaeology," applied, for example, by Richard MacNeish in Tehuacan Valley, Mexico, and Robert Braidwood in Iraq, focusing on a search for agricultural origins.
	1960s–1970s	Ethnoarchaeology established through works of Richard Gould among the Australian Aborigines, Richard Lee among the !Kung Bushmen, and Lewis Binford among the Nunamuit Eskimo.
	1972	Thor Heyerdahl makes a transatlantic voyage in *Ra II*, an early but unconvincing instance of experimental archaeology.
	1976	After recording rock art and excavating at Olduvai Gorge, Mary Leakey finds 3.7-million-year-old human footprints at Laetoli, Tanzania.
	1979	Anthropologist Marvin Harris publishes his influential book on cultural materialism.
POST- PROCESSUAL ARCHAEOLOGY	1980s–1990s	Ian Hodder, Mark Leone, and others publish criticisms of processual archaeology, calling for less concern with scientific method and more emphasis on the interpretation of symbolic, cognitive, and unique aspects of the human experience.
	1984	Archaeologist Marija Gimbutas calls for greater attention to the importance of women in prehistory. Margaret Conkey points out gender bias in the discipline of archaeology.
	1986	The first meeting of the World Archaeological Congress convenes amid political controversy about the role of archaeology in the real world.
	1993	Ian Hodder begins postprocessual reinterpretation of Çatalhöyük, where excavations were first undertaken by James Mellaart in 1961.

The Rise of Scientific Archaeology

By the late 1940s and early 1950s, the basic chronologies and culture histories of many regions had been developed and were being refined, and accurate and routine dating of archaeological materials and sites became possible. Some archaeologists began to ask *why* questions, and the focus of archaeological research began to change from mere description to include explanation. As early as 1948, Walter Taylor (1948) proposed that archaeology should be anthropological; it should do more than classify artifacts and try to understand past societies. Taylor's plea was echoed by some others, who recognized that "[t]oo often we dig up mere things, unrepentantly forgetful that our proper aim is to dig up people" (Wheeler 1955:4). But Taylor's call for archaeology to do anthropology rather than history was largely ignored, especially in Europe, where archaeology was firmly tied to history. It seems that in the 1950s, the discipline of archaeology was just not yet ready to move to the next level. However, a few younger archaeologists were greatly influenced by the need for archaeology to be explanatory, and the stage was set for a major change in the way archaeology was done.

Beginning in 1962, Lewis Binford published a series of papers (e.g., Binford 1962, 1964) that called on archaeology to become scientific. Binford argued that archaeology is a science, that the past is real and knowable, and that archaeology, like any science, should adopt the scientific method, using data to generate hypotheses to be tested by additional data. Archaeology, Binford argued, should make full use of scientific technology, quantitative techniques, and computers. Further, he contended that archaeology should not only list finds but also contribute to anthropology, the study of humans. Culture is tied together in a system in which all aspects are interrelated and changes in one aspect spawn changes in others, and the search for cultural processes is important.

Processual archaeology, sometimes called the "New Archaeology," was rapidly adopted by many archaeologists, especially in the United States, where archaeology was closely related to anthropology. It was not well received outside the United States and was particularly criticized in Europe because of archaeology's long-standing ties with history there. Nevertheless, some European archaeologists made major contributions to scientific archaeology (Clarke 1968). Processual archaeology represented a paradigm shift (from history to science) away from the earlier way archaeology was done, but it became the standard system employed by most archaeologists, even in Europe. Adopting the method of scientific inquiry meant that specific rules had to be followed, speculation and conjecture had to be testable, and explicit research designs had to be developed and implemented.

In spite of the shift to explanation as the main objective of archaeology, there still remains a critical need for the discovery, description, and classification of baseline data, and the development of culture histories and the determination of chronology remain major goals in archaeology. Some contemporary archaeologists consider this kind of basic work as "unworthy" of attention. However, as in all science, properly described and classified archaeological data are required before any hypotheses, theories, or models of the past can be constructed and tested.

Research Design in Archaeology

One of the central aspects of contemporary archaeology is the requirement for an explicit, written research design prior to conducting any work. All archaeologists operate under some general theoretical framework, and all have some idea of what questions they are researching when they conduct archaeological investigations. Until about the late 1960s, many research plans, goals, and justifications of methods were either poorly developed or nonexistent. Today, an explicit research design is an integral part of archaeology and of archaeologists' use of the scientific method.

A research design (Table 3.1) begins with the specific hypotheses, questions, or problems to be addressed, the theoretical approach to be used in the investigation, the biases of the investigators, the kinds of data sought to address the question, and the methods to be used to obtain the needed data. Many archaeologists develop explicit research designs prior to their work. The development of a research design forces them to focus on what they are going to do, what they are really looking for (you generally will not find what you are not looking for), and the best way to recover the necessary data. A written research design also allows other archaeologists to review the plan and to provide ideas and suggestions.

Actual conditions in the field may force changes in a research design. For example, if the research design calls for an investigation of architecture and a cemetery is discovered during the work, a rapid change in the research design may be necessary. Thus, a research design must remain flexible to adjust to changing field conditions. Also, the researcher has to be prepared to revise or reject hypotheses if they are not supported by the available data and to reformulate the research design for additional work.

Middle-Range Theory

Scientific archaeologists maintained that the past is past and that any evaluation of a dynamic past can be made only through the analysis of a static record in the present. No "direct" reading of the past is possible. It is possible to gain only an "indirect" understanding through the formulation of hypotheses and models to be tested against archaeological data. Thus, it is necessary to link the material archaeological record to past human behavior. This linkage is accomplished through the application of logic, analogy, and theory, collectively called **middle-range theory** (Schiffer 1995; Tschauner 1996).

The central element of middle-range theory is the use of **analogy,** an argument that if two things are similar in some aspects, they will be similar in others. A great deal of the reasoning employed in archaeology is based on analogy. Conclusions reached through the use of analogy, however, are themselves hypotheses and require testing. Thus, the scientific archaeologist continually tests and refines hypotheses and models generated by analogy.

Because the past is not directly observable in the present, archaeologists seek to generate or observe contemporary situations that they can study and link to the past. This work involves learning how the archaeological record formed and trying to understand how past human behavior created a material record. Much of middle-range theory has been developed through the use of ethnographic analogy, ethnoarchaeology, and experimental archaeology.

t a b l e   3 . 1

Constructing a Research Design

GENERAL STEP	ARE THERE BURIED PALEOINDIAN SITES AROUND TULARE LAKE, CENTRAL CALIFORNIA?
1. Formulate a general hypothesis from existing data.	It is known that Paleoindian people occupied North America by at least 12,000 years ago and that some of these early sites have been found on the surface of the shorelines of Pleistocene lakes, including Lake Tulare. Thus, it is hypothesized that buried Paleoindian sites also exist around Pleistocene Lake Tulare.
2. Explain the background of the hypothesis.	In the 1950s, a Paleoindian site was discovered at Lake Tulare, and some Clovis points were found. In the 1990s, more material was found in the same vicinity, suggesting a substantial Paleoindian occupation of the region. Unfortunately, all of the known sites have been damaged by agriculture and vandals.
3. Explain the theoretical approach to be used.	A standard scientific, processual, materialist approach.
4. Detail the specific hypotheses derived from the general hypothesis.	Some Paleoindian sites are exposed on the present surface whereas other Paleoindian sites lie buried beneath recent alluvium. These sites are undamaged and contain a detailed record of human occupation of the region during the Pleistocene.
5. List and explain the kinds of data needed to address the hypothesis.	To address the hypothesis, it will be necessary to determine the locations of buried shorelines, then locate buried sites on those shorelines, and then ascertain whether those sites are Paleoindian in age.
6. State the research methods to be employed in seeking the data to address the hypothesis.	To locate buried shorelines, GIS software will be used to analyze the elevation, slope, and angles of the terrain from existing map data to tease out possible locations of buried fossil shorelines. Backhoe trenches will be excavated at promising locations to locate buried sites. Archaeological materials exposed in the trenches will be collected for analysis.
7. Detail the methods to be used to analyze the data.	Recovered artifacts will be examined to determine whether they are Paleoindian in age. If possible, materials suitable for dating (e.g., organic material for radiocarbon dating) will be obtained and processed. Depending on the nature of the sites found, new questions and a new research design for excavation will be generated.

ETHNOGRAPHIC ANALOGY   Over the last several hundred years, anthropologists and others have gathered a great deal of information about living societies all over the world. Detailed information exists about the organizations, technologies, practices, social behaviors, and many other aspects of a large number of extant groups. Through the use of **ethnographic analogy,** archaeologists employ information about living groups to help construct models of past societies.

For example, technological adaptations of traditional seminomadic desert-dwelling peoples today include the construction of wells and cisterns for locating and storing water near seasonal settlements and along trade routes. The discovery of an ancient system of wells and cisterns might lead an archaeologist to hypothesize that the people who had constructed the system had semipermanent settlements and were engaged in trade with neighboring groups and that their material culture was based on adaptations to a generally arid environment. Other findings then would either support these hypotheses or suggest alternative explanations.

It is important to remember, however, that living groups are not past groups; they are different, living in different circumstances, with different people and histories (Testart 1988:1; also see Headland and Reid 1989:49–51). The behaviors and practices of contemporary societies can be used only to suggest hypotheses about the past, hypotheses that must be tested. If archaeologists keep this point in mind, ethnographic analogy can be a useful tool.

ETHNOARCHAEOLOGY   **Ethnoarchaeology** is the archaeological analysis of living peoples to gain insight into peoples of the past (Kramer 1979; O'Connell 1995; Longacre and Skibo 1994). In this approach, an archaeologist lives with a contemporary group and directly observes their behavior and the resulting material record of that behavior to learn through observation how the people's behavior formed the material record observed (Highlight 3.1). For example, an archaeologist might watch how a hunt is conducted, how game is butchered, what tools are used, which parts of the animal were eaten and which discarded, where debris is thrown, how debris becomes dispersed, and other behaviors. The archaeologist would carefully record the patterns of material remains and correlate them to the behaviors that resulted in them being formed. If similar patterns of material remains were found in a site, the archaeologist could develop working hypotheses that similar behaviors may have been practiced. The bulk of ethnoarchaeological research has been conducted among hunter-gatherer groups, but some work has been done with pastoralists. However, it is important to remember that contemporary traditional peoples do not represent past peoples unchanged through time and that the insights gained through ethnoarchaeology are only beginning points for research.

Between 1969 and 1973, archaeologist Lewis Binford (1978) spent time living with the Nunamuit Eskimo in Alaska, accompanying them on hunting trips and other activities. He observed and recorded how their activities resulted in a material record and how that record was patterned. He saw how animals were killed and butchered, where the tools were dropped, where the bones were tossed, how the small camps were organized, how the logistics worked, and the like. He observed contemporary hunter-gatherers so that he could gain an understanding of how ancient hunter-gatherers may have operated. Using the Nunamuit information as a basis, Binford later constructed models of how the Neanderthal hunters of the Middle Paleolithic of France may have operated.

HIGHLIGHT 3.1

Ethnoarchaeology among the Aka of Central Africa

Archaeologists interested in past diet often study the food remains (animal bones and plant parts) in archaeological sites to gain insight into what people ate and how they obtained their food. For example, archaeologists want to know what animals were hunted, how they were processed, what technology was used,

Jean Hudson lived with the Aka people specifically to observe their food-getting activities. What animals did they hunt, how did they butcher and cook game, where did they discard the bones, and how did dogs scatter the bones?

what parts were discarded, and what parts were cooked and eaten. Differences in these behaviors will result in different patterns of bone refuse in a site. However, it is known that bones in a site are disturbed, typically by domestic dogs who scavenge the bones, chew on them, and drag them away to cache them. Thus, it is logical to assume that some of the bone distribution patterns seen in archaeological sites may have more to do with dogs than with people. What does the original human pattern look like, and how does dog behavior alter that pattern?

To investigate these questions, Jean Hudson of the University of Wisconsin at Milwaukee, traveled to central Africa (Hudson 1990, 1993) to study the Aka. The Aka are a group of contemporary hunter-gatherers living in the Ituri Forest, and they make their living partly by hunting the game in the forest.

After the Aka abandoned a camp, Hudson excavated it as if it were an archaeological site, recording the size, damage to, and location of all the bones found. Through this analysis, she was able to determine how dogs damage and redistribute animal bone in an Aka camp, and she used those data to develop a model of bone distribution in prehistoric camps. She found that the damage done to the bones by dogs did not conceal the numbers of animals present or their relative importance in the Aka diet; this finding suggested that the same may be true in prehistoric sites as well.

CRITICAL **THINKING** QUESTIONS

1. How was Hudson able to develop a model of bone distribution in a prehistoric camp by studying living hunter-gatherers?
2. What other things could Hudson learn about the past by living with the Aka?

Believing that wasteful practices and lack of resource conservation through recycling contributed to the decline of many societies of the past, such as the ancient Maya, William Rathje excavated into modern landfills. He wanted to discover patterns and trends in what people discard and how garbage degrades in a landfill. He also wanted to investigate the effectiveness of landfills and issues of pollution.

Ethnoarchaeological work is not limited to other groups. Since 1971, William Rathje of the University of Arizona has been studying the modern garbage of Tucson for clues to human behavior (Rathje et al. 1992; Rathje and Murphy 2001). Rathje and his crew collected garbage directly from households and had the residents fill out questionnaires regarding what (e.g., food and other materials) they had consumed. The garbage record was then compared to the written records to determine the actual behavior of the people—comparing what they said to what they actually did. Rathje was hired by various companies, such as Kentucky Fried Chicken, to learn what consumers were discarding, how packaging might be improved, and other information that might improve performance.

EXPERIMENTAL ARCHAEOLOGY   **Experimental archaeology** attempts to understand past cultural processes through the controlled and directed replication of artifacts and features (Coles 1973). Experiments are conducted with ancient materials and techniques to discover how and why things might have been done in the past. It is natural to ask "How did they do that?" when examining past material, whether a pyramid or a projectile point. In some cases, ethnographic analogy can provide a starting point for investigation; in other cases, there is

To learn how much time and effort were required to make a stone mortar (a bowl-shaped object in which materials are crushed with the aid of a pestle), Richard Osborne of Porterville College, California, undertook an experiment to manufacture one (Osborne 1998). He took a small, flat granite boulder and used hand-size quartzite rocks with pointed ends to hammer out a depression (the mortar cup) into the granite rock. Osborne found it took eight hours (67,200 strikes with the stone hammer) to form a depression 11 centimeters in diameter and 3.5 centimeters deep. Clearly, past people put a great deal of effort into making their mortars.

little information available to form a hypothesis. One way to approach the problem is through experimentation, working with the material until the same result or form is achieved.

Most experiments so far have involved the replication or, in some cases, the actual use of flaked stone tools, but experimental archaeology can be used to investigate many other things. You could grind maize on milling stones to see what kind of wear patterns were produced on the stones and then compare the results with artifacts from archaeological sites. You could fire ceramic vessels at different temperatures to determine which technique matches the patterns seen in archaeological ceramics. Archaeologists have used the tools available to the ancient Egyptians to cut the kind of stone block used in the pyramids to see how long it took and to develop an estimate of the time and labor needed to construct a pyramid. Archaeologists have built replicas of reed boats to see how they may have been used for transport. To understand how people may have butchered a mammoth 12,000 years ago, you could use replicated stone tools to butcher a modern elephant. Some experiments involve creating an artificial (experimental) archaeological site and then observing effects, such as the effects of rain and rodents on the site over time.

Experiments provide clues to ancient technology, labor, effort, engineering, understanding of math and physics, and other information (Highlight 3.2). However, experimental archaeology demonstrates only that something *could* have been done in a particular way, not that it *was* done that way, for there may be other ways to achieve the same result.

Cultural Materialism

A common approach of processual archaeology is the use of **cultural materialism,** a theoretical framework based on the idea that "human social life is a response to the practical problems of earthly existence" (Harris 1979:ix). Using this approach, an archaeologist can

HIGHLIGHT **3.2**

Quarrying Limestone Blocks in the Yucatán

Many of the large buildings in the ancient Maya cities in Central America were constructed from limestone blocks. It was estimated (Adams 1991) that some 70 million cubic feet of cut blocks and fill were needed to construct the Danta Complex, a group of buildings and a platform at the Preclassic Maya city of El Mirador, Guatemala. It was previously not known how these blocks and fill were quarried, with what tools, how they were transported and placed in the buildings, how the mortar and stucco (made from the same limestone) were made, or how much time and effort it all involved. It was important to know how much labor and time were needed so as to be able to estimate the labor force, the overall population of the area, the resources Maya society committed to the project, and how the project may have impacted the environment.

James C. Woods and Gene L. Titmus of the Herrett Museum in Idaho undertook to investigate these issues (Woods and Titmus 1996). Working with the RAINPEG (Regional Archaeological Investigations in the Northern Petén, Guatemala) Project, they traveled to Nakbe, a Maya city located a few miles from El Mirador, to locate and excavate quarries where the limestone blocks had been cut and to examine the quarry debris. They found a variety of broken flaked stone bifaces associated with the ancient quarries, and they concluded that those bifaces may have been used to cut and shape the limestone blocks. Woods and Titmus replicated numerous bifaces, and then hafted them in different ways to see what would work. They began to cut limestone blocks themselves. They found that bifaces hafted on wooden shafts, like a spear, could be used to cut through the limestone rather easily. They also found that the resulting toolmarks in their experimental limestone quarry matched those in the ancient quarries. The replica bifaces that were broken during the experiment had the same breakage pat-

An experimentally quarried limestone block is removed from the quarry at the Maya site of Nakbe, Guatemala.

terns as the prehistoric examples, suggesting that they had been used in a similar manner.

Woods and Titmus found that a team of eight men could cut, remove, and shape four large limestone blocks in a day, and this information was used to calculate the time needed to provide materials for the large Maya buildings like those at El Mirador and Nakbe. Woods and Titmus calculated that a force of less than a thousand workers working half of each year over a period of four centuries could have been sufficient to provide the building materials for the Danta Complex. Some of the general quarry debris was used as fill; the rest was processed into mortar and stucco.

Woods and Titmus also noted that some of the quarries were located very near causeways (roads) that led to the city, making transport of the blocks easier than had been first thought. The experimental work at Nakbe provides valuable information regarding the

HIGHLIGHT **3.2** *continued*

time and effort required to build ancient Maya cities and gives us a glimpse at the ancient Maya themselves.

CRITICAL **THINKING** QUESTIONS

1. How was the Woods and Titmus study an example of experimental archaeology?

2. What was the research design? What hypotheses and propositions were being tested?

3. What are the most likely explanations of how architectural monuments were built in the ancient world?

investigate very basic and practical research questions centering on technology, economy (e.g., food), environment, and population. Cultural materialism has an unwavering commitment to the rules of Western science.

The cultural materialist approach begins with the idea (called *techno-environmental materialism*) that all cultural institutions can be explained by direct material payoff. To explain some cultural phenomenon, the researcher begins by looking for a specific direct material payoff, such as food. If the first payoff alone proves inadequate as an explanation, another material payoff, such as shelter, is considered and perhaps added to the first. If all material payoffs are eliminated or are inadequate as explanations, then research would move outside the realm of direct material payoffs and investigate psychological or sociological factors. Because many archaeological data are themselves material (e.g., tools, food residues, shelter foundations), materialism has proved an exceedingly useful research approach and is the basis of much processual archaeology.

The archaeological focus on dietary analysis offers a case in point. A great deal of what many archaeologists currently do is geared to understanding past diet through the analysis of food remains found in sites. Clearly, people must first meet some sort of minimum dietary requirements before they can do anything else, so an investigation into diet reflects a materialist approach. However, understanding diet is only a start in the task of understanding cultural systems.

Expanding Theoretical Horizons

Processual archaeology began with great fanfare and with the promise that all of the questions of the past would now be answered. However, by the 1980s, some archaeologists had become impatient with the apparent lack of results arising from this approach. One of the major goals of processual archaeology was to discover universal laws of human behavior, but none had been discovered in some 20 years of research. Further, many scholars found it difficult to explore issues beyond the narrow materialistic focus of processualism. To some, this suggested that processualism was inadequate, whereas others argued that archaeologists were still "working out the bugs." Whatever the case, the discipline moved forward, looking at the past in different ways and expanding explorations of alternative interpretations and issues such as gender, power, and cognition.

The dissatisfaction with processual archaeology came at a time when all of science, indeed, the entire modern world, was being questioned. These "postmodernists" were critical of all things modern and argued that science itself was flawed. Postmodernism took a very subjective and antiscientific stance in opposition to the objectivism of the modern world.

Some archaeologists, most notably Ian Hodder (e.g., Hodder 1991, 1999; also see Shanks and Tilley 1987), adopted this general postmodern view and began to question the merit of processual archaeology. A number of scholars, mostly from Britain, maintained that because archaeologists themselves were biased (a view also held by the processualists, who argued for research designs to mitigate this bias), any interpretations of the past were subjective. Thus, it was argued that there is no single truth of the past, only narratives of what the interpreter (the archaeologist) wanted to see. It was also argued that scientific archaeology was an "agent of colonialism" and viewed the past from a narrow, capitalist, male, Western perspective, ignoring the viewpoints of the people who had actually produced the past. This general approach came to be known as **postprocessual archaeology,** in which archaeological interpretations became narratives, stories told by the archaeologist about the past. Many view postprocessualism as a paradigm shift, away from an unemotional scientific archaeology and toward a more humanistic and democratic archaeology. Postprocessualists have explicitly recognized and embraced issues that deal with inequality, domination, gender, minorities, and the voices of the underrepresented.

Like processualism, postprocessualism has its critics. Some have described postprocessualism as being more interested in using interpretations, such as inequality and racism, to try to influence contemporary sociopolitical situations (Kuznar 1997:172). Postprocessualists would counter that traditional (processual) archaeology is part of a "conspiracy" to dehumanize and suppress non-European peoples and should be viewed with suspicion. Others (e.g., Renfrew 1994:3–4) see postprocessualism as actually being antiprocessualist, dismissive of the scientific approach and advocating a return to an intellectually simpler time.

Some of the underlying arguments of postprocessualism are difficult to accept. For example, the contention that science is dehumanizing and cannot be used to analyze humans implies that humans are above nature and so somehow above analysis. Yet, after declaring that people cannot be analyzed, postprocessualists proceed to analyze them. Postprocessualists suggest that all interpretations are equal and valid, but then reject some in favor of others. Interestingly, postprocessual archaeology is practiced in essentially the same way as processual archaeology (VanPool and VanPool 1999); field methods are the same, all of the available scientific tools are employed in the analysis of archaeological materials, and the same rigor is applied to the process of reporting the data.

Although it is clear that the past can be interpreted in different ways (in that there are different people interpreting it), it is the position of the authors of this book that an objective and knowable past does exist. We believe that postprocessual interpretations are, in fact, models, deserving of consideration and of testing like any processual model. Although it is true that science and scientific archaeology are practiced by subjective humans, we support the notion that the discipline of science is self-correcting and ultimately objective. We further believe that a careful reading of the postprocessual approach shows that the only fundamental difference from processual archaeology is in its use as social commentary (Kuznar 1997:159–172; VanPool and VanPool 1999, 2001), although there is significant disagreement on this point (e.g., Hodder 1999; Arnold and Wilkens 2001; Hutson 2001). We believe that postprocessualism is really a collection of perspectives added on to existing archaeology rather than an entirely new theoretical paradigm (e.g., VanPool and VanPool 1999), what Michelle Hegmon (2003:213) called "processual-plus."

Whatever the criticisms of postprocessualism, and whether it represents a paradigm shift, it has forced archaeologists to expand their consideration of the past to include issues of social stratification, minorities, suppressed peoples, ideologies, and the like. It could also be argued that these and other topics that are difficult to study employing processual archaeology can be better addressed by the broader approach of postprocessualism. All of this can only enhance our understanding of the past (Preucel 1995).

Gender and the Past

Until fairly recently, and with some notable exceptions, the field of archaeology was dominated by men. Thus, much archaeological excavation and interpretation emphasized men in past societies. The result was a depiction of a male-dominated past in which the roles, influences, and contributions of children (Baxter 2005), women, and other genders were often downplayed or ignored. In the last few decades, as more women have become involved in archaeology, the distinct emphasis on males has dramatically shifted, with a great deal more research being conducted on the roles of women and others in the past.

To research sex roles, it is necessary to understand the difference between sex and gender. In anthropology, *sex* is a biological classification, with individuals being male, female, or hermaphrodite (individuals with both male and female sex organs). **Gender,** however, is a culturally constructed category defined by the social role a person is expected to play in a particular society, regardless of their sex. For example, although we know that transvestites and homosexuals existed in the past and are reflected in the archaeological record, such individuals have been largely "invisible," perhaps because archaeologists rarely look for evidence of them.

Archaeologists are now aware of this gender bias in their interpretations of the archaeological record. Activities identified at a site are now sometimes assigned to males or females, often by means of ethnographic analogy. However, these assignments are simply working hypotheses and must be tested. As part of this testing, archaeologists need to formulate models describing gender roles and how these roles might be seen archaeologically. The study of past gender is now a major goal in archaeology.

The Archaeology of Power

Although archaeologists have always been interested in politics, the postprocessual climate stimulated the study of the past from a noncapitalist perspective of power, production, and the control of resources. Usually referred to as *Marxist archaeology* (McGuire 1992, 1993; Trigger 1993), this perspective has its roots in the 1930s, although it was not very popular until recently (perhaps due to the political connotation of the term *Marxist*). Interestingly, the Marxist approach is similar to processualism in that it is materialist. One of the major goals of Marxist archaeology is to understand the development of social and political inequality.

One recent outgrowth of Marxist archaeology is known as *critical archaeology,* which attempts to examine expressions of political ideology in the archaeological record. Mark Leone (1984) has used the critical approach to analyze the geometry and observer perspective of upper-class gardens in late eighteenth-century Annapolis, most specifically the garden of William Paca, one of the signers of the Declaration of Independence. Using critical analysis of the Paca garden layout and its use of the optical illusions of space, Leone argued that the garden reflected an ideology of strict adherence to rules and social control while giving the illusion of openness and mobility.

Cognitive Archaeology

Archaeologists want to learn about how people thought in the past, how they viewed their world, and what symbols they used to express meaning. The relatively new field of *cognitive archaeology* (e.g., Mithen 2001) seeks to discover past thought and belief systems through the analysis of symbols, styles, designs, and other expressive forms of culture. Belief systems can be reflected in cultural traits such as writing, rock art, decorations, and even architecture. However, hypotheses about past cognition can be difficult to test and, as a result, have often been avoided; as archaeological theory expands and becomes more adaptable, however, research in this field is increasing.

For example, the complex symbolism reflected in Moche art (see the opening story of Chapter 1) was thought to reflect purely supernatural beliefs. It was not until the discovery of the tombs at Sipán that archaeologists realized that the symbols in the art reflected actual behaviors and that the complex supernatural beliefs held by the Moche greatly influenced their life.

Evolutionary Archaeology

Evolutionary archaeology is a relatively new approach that studies the past from the perspective of Darwinian evolution (e.g., Leonard 2001). How humans adapt to their environments is part of **human ecology,** with cultural behavior being the primary mechanism of adaptation. One of the main approaches in human ecology is **evolutionary ecology,** in which the concepts of adaptation and selection are used to analyze cultural behaviors. A society can be viewed as having a collection of traits and practices its people use to adapt to their environment. As environmental conditions change, the selective pressures on traits would also change. For a society to adapt, it would be forced to replace deleterious traits with adaptive ones, patterns that would be reflected in the archaeological record by changes in a society's technology, where they lived, how they made a living, and so forth. Evolutionary archaeology developed as a central tenet of processual archaeology but for a variety of reasons was not pursued until fairly recently.

To illustrate, archaeologist David Rindos (1984) examined the origins and spread of agriculture from an evolutionary perspective. He argued that as the process of domestication began, each successive generation of people would have modified their existing agricultural tradition (including technological, social, and political traits), adding adaptive traits and dropping deleterious ones. This would have resulted in the expansion of both the number and quality of domesticated species used by people and in an increase in their geographic range. This approach helps archaeologists understand the adoption and spread of agriculture and the social and political changes that accompanied it.

Archaeological Frontiers

The practice of contemporary archaeology incorporates all three of the major paradigms: history, science, and humanism. None of these approaches precludes the application or pursuit of the others; in fact, together they combine to form a synergistic approach to understanding the past. It is probably true that pure scientific archaeology has tended to be a bit dehumanizing, emphasizing objects, systems, structures, and change, and rarely looking at the human side of the past, such as issues of social roles or power. In this regard, the postprocessual critique has been useful, if for no other reason than forcing archaeology to broaden its consideration of the past. Whatever the approach, all archaeologists employ the concepts of science and scientific thought, and archaeology, at its core, remains a science.

Contemporary archaeology is a sophisticated multidisciplinary approach in which the expertise of many professionals is employed to address questions of the past. Researchers rarely work alone and frequently rely heavily on the expertise of others. In the past, archaeology may have been an individual pursuit, but it is very much a team effort today.

As you read in Chapter 1, much of the archaeology done today falls under the general heading of public archaeology or cultural resource management. The majority of practicing archaeologists are engaged in the identification, preservation, management, and interpretation of archaeological sites and areas. However, none of this work could be accomplished without the basic understanding of the research results and values of the sites, and research remains the core aspect of archaeology.

Another important aspect of contemporary archaeology is the education of the public about the past and about the value of archaeological resources. Considerable effort is being made, with secondary education programs being established in some areas, the presence of many active nonprofessional societies, the establishment of parks and monuments for archaeological sites, and the proliferation of archaeological education programs on television. Still, much more needs to be done.

Archaeology is a young discipline with a very bright future. At various times, it has been claimed that we have found all there is to find and that we know all there is to know, but the truth is that we have only scratched the surface. There is still so very much to learn, and new and spectacular finds are still common, such as the "Iceman" (Fowler 2000), extensive new cemeteries in Egypt with thousands of mummies (Hawass 2000), the terra-cotta "armies" in China (Ch'in Ping 1996; Wenli 1996), Cleopatra's Palace submerged in the harbor of Alexandria (La Riche 1996; Goddio et al. 1998; Foreman 1999), and the red-headed mummies of the Tarim Basin in western China (Mair 1995a; Barber 1999; Mallory and Mair 2000). The list could go on. In addition to new discoveries, many old mysteries remain. Some ancient writing is still undeciphered; some civilizations, such as the Oxus civilization in central Asia, are still virtually unknown; and many fundamental questions are still unanswered, such as the date of initial colonization of the Americas and why and under what circumstances agriculture was adopted. We are also just beginning to learn about ordinary people in the past.

As you read at the beginning of this chapter, new techniques of analysis and interpretation are constantly expanding our understanding of the past. For example, the ability to analyze ancient DNA permits the reconstruction of family trees, from the pharaohs to humans in general, an achievement undreamed of only a few years before. Advances in medical imaging have permitted the examination of mummies and other materials in unprecedented detail without damaging them. Various other techniques of noninvasive and nondestructive investigation, such as ground-penetrating radar, are now beginning to be employed. As the power of computers increases, archaeologists will be able to use virtual reality to reconstruct ancient sites, be able to "walk" through them and gain insights by "being there." As we learn new things, our ability to learn increases, and we are on the verge of an explosion in archaeological knowledge. In addition, if there is life on other planets, we will want to know something of their history and prehistory as well (Highlight 3.3). In fact, archaeological sites now exist on our own Moon, and Tranquility Base, the first Apollo landing site, has been nominated to the National Register of Historic Places.

One of the new computer-based technologies used in archaeology is Geographic Information Systems (GIS) software to analyze spatially based information, such as sites and other archaeological data (Kvamme 1989; Limp 2000; Wescott and Brandon 2000; Gillings and Wheatley 2005). Using GIS, archaeologists can digitally map classes of information in a series of separate maps, called layers, that can be electronically overlaid on one another to show relationships. Unwanted or unrelated layers can be dropped, thus limiting the quantity of information to be examined at any one time. For example, all sites could be on one layer, all hydrological data on another, and soil types on a third. The relationship of the sites to the water sources could be seen and then compared to soil types. Information on current features (such as towns, roads, and farms) that are not archaeologically germane could be suppressed, making relationships between archaeological materials and geographic features more visible. A series of vegetation layers, each dating from a different period, might be imposed over the layer containing site information, giving the analyst an idea of how changing environments may have affected site types and locations.

Also, entire maps and their features can be digitized and viewed in virtual 3-D images (Gillings et al. 1999). This perspective has an advantage over the traditional two-dimensional view of most maps and gives the archaeologist an opportunity to see differences in the topography and elevation between sites. Used in conjunction with GIS, this can be a powerful tool. If Global Positioning System (GPS) is used to map the site locations, it is more precise and even more useful. The utility of GIS is not limited to large-scale phenomena; the same principles can be applied to mapping and analyzing materials found within a site.

With some GIS programs, archaeologists can conduct a statistical analysis of relationships, using existing information to model the probabilities that certain sites would be located in certain environments. Using such information, models to predict site locations can be made and tested, with important applications to both research and cultural resource management (Wescott and Brandon 2000). Further, GIS has a major practical

HIGHLIGHT **3.3**

Exoarchaeology

In 1890 the Italian astronomer Giovanni Schiaparelli noticed linear features on Mars and called them "channels"—*canali* in Italian. The American press excitedly announced that "canals" had been discovered on Mars, and an amateur American astronomer, Percival Lowell, claimed that these structures were the work of intelligent beings who had built a vast system of canals to move water about the surface of their dying planet. The polar ice caps were known to grow and shrink with the seasons, and large dark areas in the midlatitudes were also thought to grow and shrink, as might be expected of agricultural fields. Lowell mapped the "canals" and set out to prove the existence of the Martian civilization (Lowell 1906).

Many people believed Lowell, and there was a great deal of speculation about the nature of the Martians, their society, cities, engineering, and their efforts to survive their deteriorating climate. This work inspired H. G. Wells to write *War of the Worlds* and Edgar Rice Burroughs to write a series of books about the adventures of an Earth man, John Carter, on Mars. It was eventually realized that the Martian canals were natural features, such as canyons, and that no Martian civilization existed, but the study of *exoarchaeology* was born.

The archaeology of other worlds is a common theme in science fiction. The various *Star Trek* television series have featured a number of episodes dealing with archaeology. In addition, the starship *Enterprise* had a ship's archaeologist on the crew, and Captain Picard studied archaeology and gave papers at archaeological meetings.

The lack of knowledge about other worlds has not deterred the creation of other fields of study about other worlds. Work on exobiology and exopaleontology has begun (NASA has an exobiology branch).

The field of exoarchaeology, the study of past cultures on other worlds, does not formally exist because no exocultures are known, although humans have created archaeological sites in orbit and on the Moon (e.g., Rathje 1999). The archaeology of other planets is a common theme in science fiction, such as Ray Bradbury's stories about Mars and Stanley Kubrick's film *2001*, based on a novel by Arthur C. Clarke.

There is speculation about the origin, evolution, and nature of other life-forms throughout the universe, and this work is ongoing, some using computers to model what extraterrestrial life might look like. If and when societies on other planets are discovered, the field of exoarchaeology will be reborn. When other worlds discover us, our past will become their exoarchaeology.

CRITICAL **THINKING** QUESTIONS

1. What assumptions underlie exoarchaeology? How might they differ from those held in "regular" archaeology?
2. What special challenges and rewards do you think exoarchaeologists of the future could face?

application of managing archaeological data that exist in the form of site records and excavation reports (Limp 2000).

Careers in Archaeology

When first meeting an archaeologist, many people say, "Oh, I always wanted to be an archaeologist but I heard there were no jobs." This may have been generally true at one time, but since the 1980s, there has been a greatly increasing demand for archaeologists, although not all in well-paid positions (Patterson 1999). This demand has been fueled by the growing requirements to conduct environmental reviews for development and by the need for governments to manage the archaeological resources on their lands. Today, as you can see in Figure 3.2, there are many jobs available in archaeology, many for good pay, and archaeology is a great career choice.

Opportunities in archaeology at the undergraduate level include field classes, laboratory classes, internships, and volunteer projects. It is also important to attend regional and national archaeology meetings to learn things, meet people, and develop networks leading to future opportunities. There are jobs in archaeology for people without a college degree, but pay, benefits, and career advancement are limited. Thus, for most archaeological careers, a college degree is required. Jobs include teaching at the college or university level or working in a museum, each of which entails some research and administration. Further, many private companies now provide archaeological consulting services, and many opportunities are available with such firms, or you could start your own! Finally, national or regional government agencies now employ many archaeologists to manage the archaeological resources under their control.

Becoming an Archaeologist

What should you do if you want to become an archaeologist? The vast majority of archaeologists will need a college degree, perhaps even an advanced degree, depending on the type of job sought (see Figure 3.2). Most aspiring archaeologists should go to a college or university and major in anthropology (in Europe and Canada, you would major in archaeology because anthropology is often a separate discipline). You will receive training in all of the subfields, but you can tailor your program toward archaeology. There are many good minors to accompany archaeology, often geology or biology, but increasingly something involving computers. Make it a point to get involved in as much field or laboratory work as possible (you cannot have too much practical experience), and go to the state and regional archaeology meetings (meet and greet!) and give papers on your research (ask your professors for help with this). Get to know as many other archaeologists as you can; they will be the ones making hiring decisions later on.

If you want to specialize in a specific subfield of archaeology, such as classical archaeology, seek out a college or university that has such a program. You might major in art history or classical studies instead of anthropology or archaeology. You might want to minor in anthropology or history. The key is to ask for advice from the people at the school.

Career	General Duties	Education Needed[a]	Opportunities	General Salary Range
Teacher/Professor	Teaching, research, and administration	M.A. for community colleges, Ph.D. for universities	Relatively few jobs, but very good people can get them	$40,000 to $90,000+ plus benefits
Museum Specialist	Collections management, research, display preparation	B.A. to Ph.D., depending on position	Relatively few jobs	$30,000 to $80,000 plus benefits
Contract Archaeologist	Project planning and supervision, report writing	B.A. to Ph.D., depending on position	Some higher-level jobs with private companies, many lower-level positions	$35,000 to $80,000+ plus benefits
Cultural Resource Manager	Compliance, some fieldwork, contract writing	Usually an M.A. but some B.A.s	Many jobs with national or regional government agencies	$40,000 to $70,000 plus benefits
General Labor (field and laboratory)	Survey, excavation, and cataloging	Some college and appropriate experience	Many short-term jobs with private companies	$7.00 to $15.00/hr.

figure 3.2

Careers in Archaeology

[a]Ph.D. = doctoral degree; M.A. = master's degree; B.A. = bachelor's degree.

Most archaeologists will obtain jobs in Cultural Resource Management (CRM, see Chapter 13), government agencies (federal, state, or local), or private companies working in environmental studies. These positions are important to the field of archaeology. The majority of archaeological work conducted in the United States is done with CRM. It is our view that such managerial positions should be held by well-trained archaeologists rather than by managers who know little about archaeology.

CONTENTSELECT

Search articles in the ContentSelect database using the key words *processual approach* and *postprocessual approach,* and compare and contrast these theoretical orientations in archaeology. Where are the two approaches similar and different? What do you see as the chief issues in this debate?

Chapter Summary

World War II interrupted most archaeological research, and the deaths of some archaeologists in that conflict set back the field. However, after the war, a number of developments, most notably radiocarbon dating and the use of statistical analysis, substantially changed what archaeologists could learn. These new ways to look at the past were an outgrowth of new technologies and set the stage for a paradigm shift. There was a growing call for a more scientific archaeology, one that sought to learn about the people of the past rather than just to elucidate their culture histories and chronologies. This call was finally answered in the 1960s with the development of processual archaeology, which incorporated the scientific method into the discipline.

Processual archaeology incorporated research design, testable hypotheses, and the search for higher-level understandings of human behavior, and it used cultural materialism and human ecology as approaches. Processual archaeology also incorporated middle-range theory, a general approach by which static data could be related to a dynamic past through the use of analogy, including ethnographic analogy, ethnoarchaeology, and experimental archaeology.

By the early 1980s, some archaeologists had developed a dissatisfaction with processual archaeology, partly due to what was seen as a lack of results and partly to a general dissatisfaction with science by society. From this base, the postprocessual archaeologists argued that processual archaeology was too narrow, and they called for a less scientific archaeology with a greater emphasis on interpretation of previously unconsidered peoples and on symbolic and cognitive aspects of the past. Many see postprocessual archaeology as little more than an expanded version of processual archaeology because the goals and methods of the two approaches are essentially the same.

Archaeology today is a dynamic, sophisticated, multidisciplinary approach in which the expertise of many professionals is employed to address questions about the past. Much of the work done today is conducted as part of cultural resource management, and the conservation of sites and public education are now integral parts of archaeology. Research remains central to archaeology, for there is so much more to learn, and new materials and insights into the past are being discovered all the time.

Opportunities for involvement and careers in archaeology are many. There is a real need for well-trained, dedicated people in the discipline. Careers in teaching or with governmental agencies or private firms are available and rewarding.

Key Concepts

analogy, 61
cultural materialism, 66
ethnoarchaeology, 63
ethnographic analogy, 63

evolutionary ecology, 71
experimental archaeology, 65
gender, 70
human ecology, 71

middle-range theory, 61
postprocessual archaeology, 69
processual archaeology, 60

Suggested Readings

If you want to learn more about the concepts and issues discussed in this chapter, consider looking at the following resources. (Some may be rather technical.)

Hodder, Ian (ed.). (2001). *Archaeological Theory Today*. Oxford: Blackwell.

> This book includes a series of papers on various aspects of archaeological theory from a postprocessual perspective. Many interesting approaches are discussed in this book, many of which are at the cutting edge of archaeology.

Kuznar, Lawrence A. (1997). *Reclaiming a Scientific Anthropology*. Walnut Creek, CA: AltaMira Press.

> Kuznar provides a treatment of scientific archaeology with an unfavorable evaluation of the postprocessual approach. He maintains that the postmodern arguments against science in general have been addressed and that science is a valid method of investigation.

Longacre, William A., and James M. Skibo (eds.). (1994). *Kalinga Ethnoarchaeology: Expanding Archaeological Method and Theory*. Washington: Smithsonian Institution Press.

> Longacre and Skibo focus on ethnoarchaeology, one of the primary applications of middle-range theory. Using the Kalinga society of the Philippines as the common focal point, the ethnoarchaeological approach is explored in detail through the analysis of a variety of Kalinga material culture and behaviors.

Schiffer, Michael B. (1995). *Behavioral Archaeology: First Principles*. Salt Lake City: University of Utah Press.

Tschauner, Hartmut. (1996). "Middle-Range Theory, Behavioral Archaeology, and Postempiricist Philosophy of Science in Archaeology." *Journal of Archaeological Method and Theory* 3(1):1–30.

> These two publications deal with middle-range theory, providing in-depth discussions of its theoretical basis and application.

VanPool, Todd L., and Christine S. VanPool (eds.). *Essential Tensions in Archaeological Method and Theory*. Salt Lake City: University of Utah Press.

> A series of papers across the range of processual and postprocessual theory, including evolutionary archaeology. This book is the most recent general treatment of archaeological theory available.

chapter **4**

The Archaeological Record

YOU CAN USUALLY tell when you hit bone. It makes a very different sound from rock, pottery, or regular soil. It's hard to describe, but you can tell. The bone is always just slightly visible in the excavation at first. You have to carefully clear away the soil to determine what animal the bone is from. If human burials are already known from the site, you assume it is human so that proper care is taken in its excavation: shovels or trowels get replaced by brushes, and the excavation work slows considerably. You brush back the soil, seeing the bone clearly for the first time. The edges or ends of the bone are still obscured by the soil, but further brushing will expose it. Careful! If the bone is fragile, even brushing can severely damage it.

adult. Once you can expose the pelvis, you will usually be able to tell whether the person was male or female. Keep digging, but be very careful. Burial goods may be present, and only slow and meticulous excavation will reveal them. Careful!

There are few real opportunities to come into direct contact with the people of the past, and the excavation of burials is one of them. These are the actual people you are studying. You can look at them, see their faces, know whether they had arthritis, bad teeth, whether the women were mothers, get an idea of the state of their medical knowledge and treatment, know the care they gave their dead, and more. If grave goods are present, you can learn about their status, whether they were leaders, were wealthy, were specialized workers, and a great deal more. Analysis of their bone chemistry can reveal details about their diet, their environment, even their travels. Their DNA can be examined and family trees constructed. This detailed information, added to the other data obtained from the site, will be combined to form a more complete picture of the lives of the people who lived at the site those many years ago. The people were real, their lives were real, and their remains are real. Careful! In many cases, the descendants of the dead are also real and concerned. You have to be careful to consider the feelings and concerns of the living when dealing with the dead.

Once you know what the bone is, you will know where it extends into the soil, and it is easier to follow. You may not yet be able to determine whether it is human; you may need to see more of it. If the first bone articulates with another, it is likely that it is still in its original position. Look, you can now see the ends of two bones that articulate. Clearly human, no question. Someone goes to get a burial record form. The ends of the bones are fused, so you know that the individual was an

For the location of sites mentioned in this chapter, see the map on page 81.

The archaeological record contains the material remains of past human activities and behaviors. It consists of objects and materials (material culture), distributed in patterns

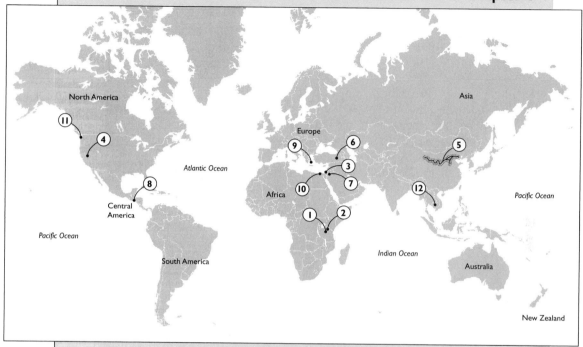

LOCATION MAP: **Sites Mentioned in Chapter 4**

1 ■ Laetoli footprints
   Laetoli, Tanzania

2 ■ Olduvai Gorge
   Arusha, Tanzania

3 ■ Tell es-Safi
   Gath, Israel

4 ■ Little Whisky Flat
   Hawthorne, Nevada

5 ■ Great Wall of China
   China

6 ■ Cappadocia region
   Cappadocia, Turkey

7 ■ Petra
   Petra, Jordan

8 ■ Joya de Ceren
   San Andres, El Salvador

9 ■ Thira
   Santorini Island, Greece

10 ■ Cleopatra's Palace
    Alexandria Harbor, Egypt

11 ■ Ozette
    Neah Bay, Washington

12 ■ Angkor Wat
    Siem Reap, Cambodia

across time and space and existing in varying degrees of preservation. The known record consists of all of the information obtained about the past, the location and condition of sites, all of the actual artifacts and ecofacts collected and removed from sites, and all of the records of the investigations, the results of the various analyses conducted on archaeological materials, and the published record of archaeological investigations. It is as important to conserve the records of past investigations as it is to conserve sites themselves.

Some consider the record to consist of only what is known by archaeologists, but here we define it as all of the data that exist, whether they have been found or not. Think of the archaeological record as a vast library of past human behavior described in a large number of books, some easier to read than others, some with pages missing, and others that need translation. Just because we have not yet seen or read a book does not mean it is not or could not be in the library.

The archaeological record consists of a variety of materials that form the record of past human behavior. Discrete localities of past human activity are called *sites* and come in a wide variety of forms. Sites can contain artifacts, ecofacts, features, and human remains, singly or in some combination. Sites and the materials within them form *patterns* that are also part of the record. Generally, things "enter the archaeological record" and become part of the pattern once they are discarded, lost, abandoned, or cached by past people.

The majority of materials present in the archaeological record were discarded after use. Thus, most of the materials found are broken, worn out, and no longer useful. Sometimes, however, complete and quite usable materials were lost or abandoned (such as at Pompeii). In some cases, caches or hordes of materials may be found—items that were purposefully stored but never reclaimed or were buried with the dead. To complicate the record, past peoples sometimes scavenged materials from earlier sites, reusing them before they again entered the record.

Archaeological Sites

A site is a geographic locality where there is some evidence of past human activity. To define a site, there must be some detectable evidence of activity, such as the presence of artifacts, features, or other materials. Sometimes a site can be defined on the basis of something less tangible, such as ethnographic accounts, historical records, or photographs. A site must have a geographic boundary that separates it from other sites, because sites are also analytical units—constructs that archaeologists use to keep the record of the past organized.

Material remains—the artifacts, ecofacts, and features within a site—are distributed nonrandomly across a site. They are concentrated in some areas and thinly distributed or absent in others. As you walk outward from the center of a site, you will encounter fewer and fewer remains until, at some point, no remains are present. If you keep walking, you eventually will encounter other materials, finding more and more of another concentration. Are those two separate sites? If so, how do you determine their boundaries?

Making this decision depends on a number of factors, including the distance between the two concentrations, the kinds of artifacts found, and the geography of the localities. If

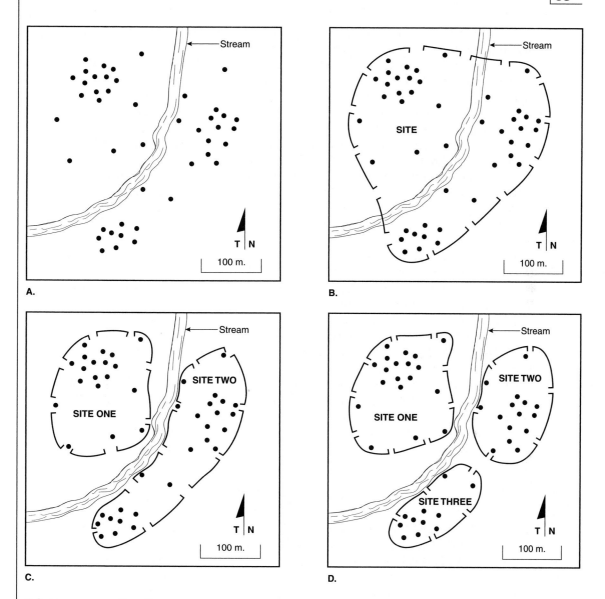

figure 4.1

Site Boundaries. When examining the distribution of artifacts (black dots) across the surface of an area (A), different archaeologists could come to different conclusions about how many sites are present and how large they are. One archaeologist might interpret the material as representing one site (B), another might see two sites (C), and a third might see three (D).

the concentrations are located close together, they may be lumped together as one site. If one concentration contains Roman material and the other is a modern trash dump, they may be split and recorded as separate sites. If the artifacts in the two concentrations were similar but separated by a stream, they might be recorded as different sites. As shown in Figure 4.1, individual archaeologists often define site boundaries differently, some preferring to lump concentrations into one site, others to split them into different sites. As important as it is to know where sites are, it is also important to know where sites are not. If we want to understand human land use and environmental adaptation, we must know where people did not go and what things they did not use.

Some sites may be small and fairly simple; others may be large and extend over broad areas. Large sites often contain distinct areas. Each area is called a **locus** (plural **loci**) and may be defined on the basis of function, such as a stone workshop locus or a plant-processing locus. Loci also might be defined on the basis of the ethnicity of the occupants. For example, a nineteenth-century mining town in the western United States may have had one locus where Euroamericans lived and a separate locus where Native Americans lived at the same time.

All archaeological materials in a site belonging to a particular cultural entity, whether an actual known group or an archaeological culture, constitute a site **component**. All sites contain one or more components; each component represents occupation by a specific group over a specific time. We might find site components arranged in simple or complex stratigraphy, or components might be contemporaneous if different groups occupied different parts of a site at the same time.

Because site components are generally defined in terms of their artifacts, the mixing of artifacts within the deposit can disrupt them, even to the point of making site components difficult to distinguish. If components cannot be recognized, the behavior represented in them cannot be analyzed, and comparisons with other components cannot be made. In many cases, simple single-component sites are very valuable because their deposits are not mixed with those of other components, making the analysis more straightforward.

If we either overlook or do not recognize the evidence of a site, we obviously cannot detect it. For example, if a person walked along a lakeshore 5,000 years ago and left footprints in the sand, that location would be a site (as an example, see Highlight 4.1). However, if the wave action of the lake washed the footprints away, the site would never be recognized and would not be found.

Types of Sites

Sites come in a bewildering array of types and can be classified according to any number of criteria. Three of the major classificatory criteria are (1) geographic context, (2) function, and (3) age. The descriptions of many sites combine characteristics from each of these broad categories.

Geographic context describes the situation of a site relative to its surroundings. Perhaps the first distinction is whether the site is underwater or on land. Underwater sites are generally classified not by geography but by form (shipwrecks are the most common). Most known sites are located on land and are classified by geography.

HIGHLIGHT 4.1

Ancient Footprints at Laetoli

Humanity's earliest beginnings appear to have oc-curred in Africa, as reflected in the rich fossil record discovered there over the last half-century. One of the important sites where the remains of certain early human ancestors (known as hominines, including the australopithecines) have been recovered is known as Laetoli (lye-toe-lee), located in northern Tanzania. Potassium-argon dates from the site indicate that it is at least 3.7 million years old. The search for early hominines began at Laetoli in the 1930s. Paleoanthro-pologist Louis Leakey found his first australopithecine fossil (a single canine tooth) there in 1935. This site, 30 miles south of the famous Olduvai Gorge, was re-investigated starting in 1974 by Louis Leakey's wife, Mary. Mary Leakey, also a respected paleo-anthropologist and the discoverer of the fa-

Sometimes ephemera—fleeting events, such as footprints in the sand—are preserved and are found. Consider these 3.7-million-year-old human footprints from Laetoli (lye-toe-lee) in eastern Africa.

mous australopithecine fossil *Zinjanthropus boisei* (now known as *Australopithecus boisei* or *Paranthropus boisei*) at Olduvai Gorge in 1959, found additional hominine fossils at the site, comprised mostly of jaw fragments and teeth.

However, in 1976, Laetoli revealed an unexpected scientific first (Leakey and Hay 1979). In a layer of vol-canic ash moistened by rain more than 3.7 million years ago was a record of animal tracks left in mud that had dried and hardened before being covered by another volcanic ashfall. Among the animal tracks was an un-usual footprint trail that clearly stood out from all the others: a 75-foot trackway consisting of the footprints made by two human-like bipeds walking side by side! The significance of this discovery was great, for these footprints represented the earliest irrefutable evidence of bipedalism. The makers of the tracks, probably two australopithecines of the species *Australopithecus afaren-sis* (whose fossil remains were those found at Laetoli), had been between 4 and 4½ feet in height. The size difference between the two individuals suggests that the tracks may represent a male and a female, perhaps the "first couple" to appear in the archaeological record.

CRITICAL **THINKING** QUESTIONS

1. How might archaeologists classify this site? Why is it unusual? What information can be inferred from this site?
2. How does this site illustrate the roles of preser-vation and discovery in conducting archaeology?

Most terrestrial sites are "open" sites—situated in the open and relatively unprotected from the effects of rain, wind, and weather. Some terrestrial sites are located in better-protected areas, such as in caves or rock shelters, and materials in such sites may be better preserved than they would have been in an open site. Many sites are located only on the surface; no materials are present below ground. Such sites are called "surface" sites and contain no deposit. If the site has a deposit, it may be shallow or deep, depending on conditions.

Another way to classify sites is by their function, such as where people lived or where they conducted specialized activities, such as burying their dead and conducting religious activities. A habitation site is a location where people lived, and it contains evidence of a large range of domestic activities. If more detail were known about the habitation site, the terms *camp, village, town,* or *city* might be used to describe it.

Special-purpose sites are places where specialized activities were conducted. Such sites may include localities where stone was quarried, where animals were killed and butchered, where ceramics were produced, where iron was smelted, where measures of the Moon were taken, where materials were stored, or where other, innumerable activities took place. Cemeteries are also specialized sites. Sometimes, small sites of unknown function may be called "special purpose" simply because the archaeologist does not know the site function.

Sites also are categorized according to their general age, such as Paleolithic sites, Roman-period sites, and historical sites. Little else may be known of a site other than its age. For example, if Roman pottery is found on the surface of a site, we know that the site dates from Roman times even if we do not know anything else about it.

Site Deposits

If a site is occupied for any length of time, the materials begin to accumulate, and a site deposit develops. Discarded materials become buried in the soil by being trampled, by soil washing or blowing in, and by walls and buildings collapsing and covering them. Many early cities were built entirely of mud brick. As the mud slowly dissolved and disintegrated, the buildings were leveled and rebuilt. The debris formed deposits of trash and melted brick that are sometimes hundreds of feet thick. In the Middle East, these huge deposits are called *tells,* and a number of modern cities, such as Tel Aviv, are the latest of many built on these ancient site deposits (Highlight 4.2).

Soils formed as the result of human activity are called **anthropogenic** soils. Many sites contain **middens,** site deposits that consist of a decomposed garbage pile (sometimes called "kitchen" middens). A midden contains broken tools, used-up artifacts, shell, plant materials, bones, grease, charcoal and ash from fires, and general household trash.

Site deposits accumulate at different speeds. Over time, the deposit can form layers that are visibly distinct based on color, soil type, obvious artifact content (such as a layer of pottery), or some other characteristic. Each visible layer is called a *stratum* (plural *strata*), and the collection of strata form the stratigraphy of a site (see Chapter 1). The strata may reflect natural events unrelated to the occupation of the site, or they actually may indicate separate occupations. Strata might be vertical, horizontal, or perhaps both. In some cases, site stratigraphy is not visible and has to be detected through the analysis of the different artifacts and ecofacts each stratum contains. Figure 4.2 shows an example of different kinds of site stratigraphy. If the strata are not disturbed, the strata that were laid down first are the oldest (following the law of superposition).

HIGHLIGHT **4.2**

Tell es-Safi: Goliath's Hometown

During the last 30 years, archaeological excavations have revealed much information about the Philistines during the Iron Age (sometimes known as the biblical period). The Philistines were one of the so-called Sea Peoples who appeared in the eastern Mediterranean at the end of the Late Bronze Age and the beginning of the Iron Age. The Philistines settled in portions of the area now encompassing parts of Israel and autonomous Palestine. Three Philistine cities have been excavated (Ashkelon, Ashdod, and Ekron), and many fascinating aspects of Philistine culture have been examined. One of the most recent finds is a monumental inscription discovered in 1997 at Ekron that lists the kings of the city during the Late Iron Age, a few years before the Babylonian destruction (603 BC).

From the biblical text it would appear that Gath was the most important of the Philistine cities during the early period of Philistine history, but little is know about Gath except that it was the hometown of Goliath, the fabled champion of the Philistines. It was the king of Gath, Achish, who reportedly played a role in the story of the young King David.

Although there is controversy over the exact location of Gath, most scholars believe it was located at the site known as Tell es-Safi. Situated between the modern cities of Ashkelon and Beth Shemesh, this tell is one of the largest Bronze and Iron Age sites in Israel. The photo shows Tell es-Safi in the 1920s, with herders in the foreground and their village on the hill in the background atop many layers of cultural deposits from thousands of years of settlement.

Settled almost continuously since the Chalcolithic period (fifth millennium BC) until modern times, Tell es-Safi is a veritable mine of archaeological evidence from all periods. Despite its size and archaeological promise, however, little research was conducted at the site until recently. Other than an exploratory excavation in 1899, only cursory visits and illicit robber excavations have occurred there. In 1996, to provide scientific knowledge about Tell es-Safi and contribute to the study of the history and cultures of the biblical period, a team of archaeologists led by Dr. Aren M. Maeir of Bar Ilan University in Israel initiated a long-term project at the site.

In the 1996 season, work at the site included an intensive exploratory surface-survey, detailed mapping, aerial photography, and airborne ground-penetrating radar imagery. Actual excavations were begun in 1997. Aerial photography had revealed an earthworks trench (2.5 km long, 8 m wide, and 3.5 m deep) surrounding the site on three sides. Probes dug in the backfill of the trench indicated that the trench can be dated to the Iron Age. This unique feature is believed to have been part of a siege system, set up by a besieging army to hinder escape from the city.

This 1920s photo shows the village of Tell es-Safi in Israel sitting atop an archaeological tell covering a time depth of more than 5,000 years of continuous occupation. Archaeologists working there in the 1990s believe they have identified the Philistine city of Gath, cited in the Bible as Goliath's hometown in the time of King David.

HIGHLIGHT **4.2** *continued*

During subsequent work (1998–2000) in the main excavation areas, archaeologists uncovered a stratigraphic sequence spanning the end of the Late Bronze Age until the Iron Age IIb (c. 1300–700 BC). Predominant among these strata was an occupation layer that was completely devastated by fire. In this level, archaeologists discovered houses that had collapsed during the destruction, sealing within them all the original objects the households contained. The rich assortment of well-preserved finds includes several hundred pottery vessels of various kinds, shapes, and functions, including those used for storage, cooking, serving, and cultic purposes, as well as various other objects, such as ivory decorations and metal weapons.

These finds provide a rich picture of daily life in the land of Israel during the ninth century BC, which, according to biblical text, was the period in which the kingdom of David and Solomon separated into two kingdoms, the Israelites to the north and the Judaeans to the south.

Although there is disagreement about the chronology and archaeology of this period, the finds discovered at Tell es-Safi appear to support other biblical and historical evidence about the history and culture of the Philistines. These finds now provide hitherto unknown data on the cultural development of the Philistine society. Find out more about Tell es-Safi and see photos of the site at http://faculty.biu.ac.il/~maeira.

CRITICAL **THINKING** QUESTIONS

1. What cultural formation processes are evident in a tell?
2. What processes might transform a tell, and how might transformation affect the archaeological record?
3. How is the site of Tell es-Safi an example of text-aided archaeological research, and what are some difficulties of using texts in prehistoric archaeology?

The stratigraphy of a site can be simple or complex. Generally, the stratigraphy of a site is vertical—that is, the layers are piled on top of one another, and earlier occupations are lower in the deposit. However, site stratigraphy can be horizontal—that is, the later occupation is adjacent to, rather than on top of, the earlier occupation. In some sites, the combination of vertical stratigraphy and shifting horizontal stratigraphy produces a more complex situation. Last, of course, is the site where the stratigraphy is very complex—many thin and hard-to-distinguish layers mixed with various disturbances.

At some sites, people may have removed their garbage to a particular location (such as a landfill), so the midden deposit may be located away from the habitation areas. In other cases, people may have thrown their trash into vacant places within the habitation area, such as nearby abandoned houses. In prehistoric sites, people often lived directly on middens, which continued to accumulate as people continued to live on them. If people lived on their middens, the middens may contain living floors, house foundations, burials, hearths, and other remains from everyday life.

Midden soils often are discolored and chemically altered by the materials within them. Many prehistoric middens are dark colored from charcoal and ash from fires, and greasy from decomposed animal fat in the soil. However, these organic materials will eventually leach out of the soil, so an "old" midden may be the same color as the surrounding soil. Archaeologists often look for, and excavate in, middens because the record of everyday domestic activities is contained within them.

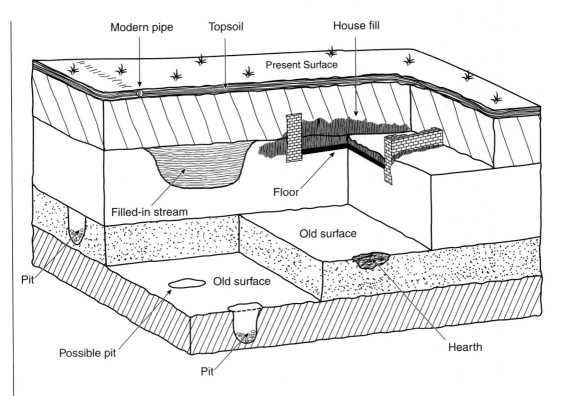

Modern pipe   Topsoil   House fill

Present Surface

Floor

Filled-in stream

Old surface

Pit

Old surface

Possible pit

Pit

Hearth

figure 4.2

Different Kinds of Site Stratigraphy.   This diagram shows a series of strata and examples of the various archaeological features that could be contained within them. Examples include several pits, a hearth, a masonry structure foundation with a floor, a filled-in stream, and a modern disturbance introduced into the site, such as a pipe.

Archaeological Evidence

Most archaeological data consist of the materials found within sites, including artifacts, ecofacts, features, and human remains. Although it is important to recover actual materials from sites, the real importance of these objects is in what they can tell us about the past. The archaeological record contains the material remains of past behaviors, remains that form patterns that are critical to the decipherment of the record. Knowing the location, or **context,** of materials relative to other materials is of critical importance in archaeology. Context ranges from the region something came from (which is very little information), to the site it came from, to about where in the site, to exactly where in the site it came from (the *in situ* context). The better the context of an item, the more information about the past it can convey.

Something in its original position, still lying where it was placed or dropped, is in **primary context.** Something that has been moved since it was deposited is in **secondary**

context. In many cases, materials in secondary context lose much of the information they could have provided, because they are no longer in a known relationship with other items, and the overall pattern of which they were a part was disrupted. The context of archaeological materials is of critical importance in their interpretation.

A simple example from today will illustrate. If detectives knew only that there was a dead person in a room and a knife was found, they would be unable to determine what had happened. They would have to know whether and how the body and the knife were associated. If they knew the knife was sticking in the body, they would know the direct association of the two in both space and time and would have evidence that a homicide had taken place. The contexts of the knife and the body are critical to understanding events. If the knife had been taken by a bystander, it would be more difficult to find the murderer. In the same way, the removal of artifacts by people making personal collections of items such as projectile points makes the job of the archaeologist more difficult.

Artifacts

Artifacts are portable objects made, modified, or used by humans for a specific task and the debris that results from their manufacture. Artifacts are the basic unit of archaeological analysis. To be recognized, an artifact must show evidence of its manufacture or use. This evidence can take the form of manufacturing marks, such as the flake scars present on many stone tools, the flakes themselves, or use-wear, such as the flattened surface of a stone used for grinding. Under certain circumstances, stones can be shaped by natural forces so that they appear to be artifacts but are not. These items are often called **geofacts,** and they can fool even experts.

It is sometimes very difficult to recognize use-wear on artifacts that were used only once or twice. For instance, if you use a stone to pound a tent stake during a camping trip, that stone is a tool, but an archaeologist 10,000 years from now probably would never recognize it as one. Such **casual tools** are present in the archaeological record but are rarely recognized or recovered by archaeologists.

Artifacts that consist of a single piece, such as a modern nail file, are called **simple tools.** Those that contain multiple parts, such as a knife with a metal blade and a wooden handle, are called **composite tools.** Artifacts include all portable objects made and used by people, not just tools. For example, a ceramic vessel made for a particular purpose such as storage or cooking is an artifact.

In addition, many artifacts are the debris left over from the manufacturing of tools or other objects. For example, to make a flaked stone tool such as a hand axe, one needs raw material and a hammerstone. The hammer is used to manufacture the axe; the flaking debris (debitage) falls to the ground, never to be touched again. Even though such debris are not tools and were never used, they are still the result of cultural activities and so are considered artifacts. In many cases, the only cultural material found at a site consists of debris.

As noted above, most artifacts in the archaeological record had reached the end of their **use-life** and were discarded. Some, however, enter the record intact, either lost or

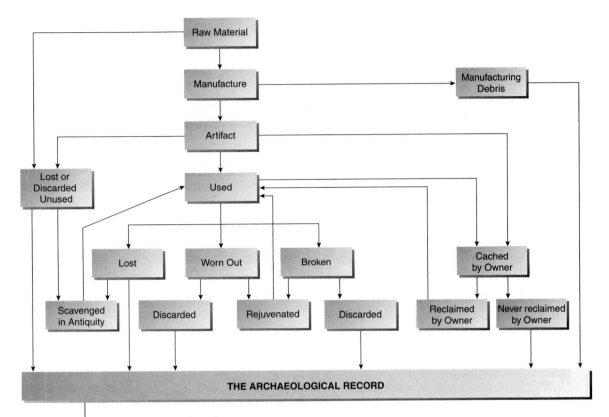

figure 4.3

Possible Use-Life of an Artifact. This diagram shows possible paths in the use-life of an artifact. Follow an artifact through the various possible paths and see how it can enter the archaeological record, be reused, be modified, enter the record again, only to be reused yet again. Some artifacts can have very complex histories.

cached by their owner. Archaeologists may recover artifacts in various stages of their use-life, a challenge for interpretation. An illustration of a possible use-life of an artifact is shown in Figure 4.3.

Some materials are clearly cultural in origin but are unmodified and so are not artifacts. For example, someone may have picked up an unusual stone from a distant source and taken it back to her or his village. This item would show no evidence of use or modification, but it was clearly brought to the site by people and would be called a **manuport.** Another example is the burned rock commonly found in many sites. Such rock, often called *fire-affected rock (FAR)* or *fire-cracked rock (FCR),* may have been used as a cooking stone or to construct a hearth and so burned, but it is not an artifact per se.

Ecofacts

Ecofacts are the unmodified remains of biological materials used by people. An analysis of ecofacts can provide a great deal of information about past human activities. As people processed animals, for example, they would eat the meat and discard the bones into the refuse. An archaeologist would classify these bones as ecofacts, unmodified but still representative of human activity. However, if one of the bones was made into a tool, such as an awl (needle or boring tool), it would be classified as an artifact. Most of the plant remains from a site also would be classified as ecofacts, including seeds, charcoal, and pollen. For example, corncobs would have been discarded after the corn was eaten or removed, and the cobs would be ecofacts, clearly cultural in origin but not artifacts. Though rarely found, human paleofeces are also ecofacts and contain considerable direct evidence of human diet and health.

Some ecofacts may be noncultural in origin but still relate to cultural activities. For example, clues to the environment in which people lived might be provided by the types of ecofacts at a site, such as the kinds of rodent bones or insect remains. Pollen is also a very important ecofact found at sites. **Palynology**—the study of pollen—can be employed to reveal a great deal about site environment, the identity of plants used, and whether those plants were wild or domesticated.

The analysis of ecofacts is employed to address a number of important questions. Archaeologists use most ecofactual data to try to understand questions of subsistence, what people ate. In addition, ecofacts can provide a great deal of information about past environments, a subject of great interest to archaeologists. Finally, ecofactual data can be used to reveal details about the domestication of plants and animals and to help understand the transition from hunting and gathering to farming.

Features

Features are constructions that people made for some purpose (Highlight 4.3). Features are not portable, almost always have many parts, and can rarely be moved without disturbing or compromising their overall integrity. Features occur in a wide variety of forms and sizes: hearths, roads, dams, rock art, and earthworks. Single sites can contain many features of various kinds.

A common feature encountered by archaeologists is hearths, also called fire hearths or campfires. Hearths were probably present at the vast majority of sites because fire was used for so many purposes—cooking, light, protection, warmth, and some manufacturing processes. Some hearths would be out of doors, such as in the center of a small camp, or inside houses. If a structure was large, several hearths might be expected. Most hearths would be small, some being in pits or surrounded with rocks to contain the fire. As the wood placed in the hearth burned and charcoal and ash filled the hearth, it would be cleaned out, and the charcoal and ash would be incorporated into the site soils. Any radiocarbon date from the hearth would probably be obtained from charcoal from one of its last fires, not one of its first.

Pits of various kinds are also common features in sites. Pits would have been dug to bury trash or to cache artifacts. In either case, when the contents of a pit are found, they and the pit generally date to the same time period, and that information can be very

HIGHLIGHT **4.3**

A Kill Site at Little Whisky Flat

During the 1800s, the Shoshone people of western Nevada hunted pronghorn antelope as a regular part of their subsistence system, and a few pronghorn hunts were actually observed by Euroamerican explorers (Steward 1938). Steward (1938:34–36) described the ethnographic information known about the hunts and recorded how the Shoshone drove the animals into traps. Some work had been conducted to identify these features in the archaeological record (Pendleton and Thomas 1983; Parr 1989; Arkush 1995), but few traps had been investigated and little detail about the hunts was known. It was also not known how far back in time such hunts were practiced. Archaeologist Philip J. Wilke of the University of California at Riverside became interested in the problem in the early

1980s and rediscovered the pronghorn trap at Little Whisky Flat, Nevada.

In 1845 a Euroamerican explorer, Edward M. Kern, observed and reported an "Indian corral" at Little Whisky Flat. Nothing further was done with that information until 1980, when a long linear feature was noticed on an aerial photo. The site was tentatively recorded and reported by Heizer and Baumhoff (1962) but was not investigated at that time. Wilke visited the site in 1983 and discovered the remains of a prehistoric pronghorn antelope trap. He returned to the area between 1984 and 1988 with several of his students (including both of the present authors) to record, map, and investigate the site.

Map of Little Whisky Flat, Nevada. The Little Whisky Flat site was constructed in the small valley to take advantage of the topography and natural features that allowed people to drive the animals, to corral them, and to kill and process them. The people lived nearby.

Source: Based on a map by Philip J. Wilke.

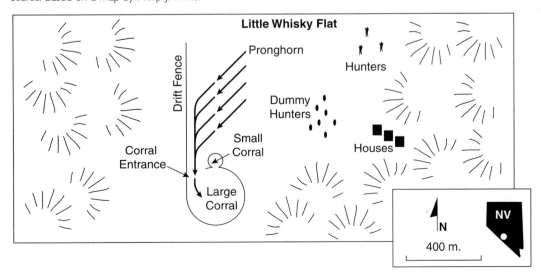

HIGHLIGHT **4.3** *continued*

Wilke traced and mapped a long (1,050-meter) fence extending across a small valley. The fence had been built with juniper posts placed about 0.5 meters apart. In some places, the posts had simply fallen over and were still lying on the ground; in other places, fire had burned the fence, and only the burned stumps of the fence posts were found. Where the ground was soft, the builders planted the posts in the ground; otherwise they were supported by piles of rocks. Sagebrush would have been stacked up along the fence, creating a visual barrier that the pronghorn would not readily cross.

At the southern end of the fence, a large corral (about 300 meters in diameter) was discovered, just below the crest of a small rise. The corral was built more sturdily than the fence. A small corral was found attached to the larger one, and a row of flagstones was found across the apparent opening of the large corral. Many projectile points, some dating from different time periods, were found in and around the corrals.

Further exploration of the area revealed a series of stone cairns along the southern edge of the valley. Several house structures were discovered next to a small canyon near the corral, and some rock art was found nearby. Excavations at the houses revealed evidence of projectile point manufacture and repair, some pronghorn bone, and a great deal of crushed large-mammal bone, probably also from pronghorn.

Throughout the last several thousand years, people constructed and maintained a light fence across the valley at Little Whisky Flat with a corral at its end to capture pronghorn (deer traps have to be much more substantial). The people drove small herds of pronghorn up the open valley toward the fence and corral, knowing that the animals would not venture into forested valley edges where they could not see long distances. Piles of rocks looking like humans ("dummy hunters") were placed along the edge of the valley to ensure that the animals stayed in the open. When the animals reached the fence,

they would not cross it even though it was lightly built and they probably could have walked through it if they wanted to. Instead, they moved along the obstruction and over a small rise. Before they realized it, they were inside the corral. They would have circled the perimeter of the corral and returned to the entrance, only to find it blocked by a large net stretched across the opening. Knowing that the animals would not jump over the net but would try to crawl under it, the people anchored the net to the ground with the flagstones.

The corral was large enough so that the now-panicked animals had some room to move about and would eventually settle down. Over the next few days, the animals could be killed at the leisure of the hunters. Some of the animals may have been isolated in the small corral for an unknown purpose, and others may have been released to repopulate the herd for another hunt another day.

For an unknown length of time during each hunt, people camped near the corral, but not close enough to agitate the animals. In camp, they processed the carcasses. The meat was removed (and perhaps jerked), and the bones were crushed and cooked to recover fats and other nutrients. The people also made and repaired their tools. The cycle of pronghorn hunting persisted for many centuries, until the arrival of Europeans and their cattle pushed both the Native Americans and the pronghorn out of the valley.

CRITICAL **THINKING** QUESTIONS

1. How was this archaeological site formed? What site features make up the archaeological record at this site?
2. What kinds of information on pronghorn antelope behavior were needed to fully understand this site?

A cache of stone artifacts, including charmstones (the long, thin specimens) and beads, was discovered at the Buttonwillow site (CA-KER-2720) in the San Joaquin Valley of California. Several hammerstones and abraders found with the cache indicated the presence of a tool kit for the manufacturing of charmstones and beads.

useful in the site analysis. Pits also may have been dug to obtain materials, such as clay for pottery, and so would not contain artifacts or ecofacts.

Architecture

The designing and building of structures (technically features), primarily those in which people lived or worked, is commonly called architecture, but the term is also often used to describe some particular style or method of construction. Some other structures, such as earthen mounds, fortifications, storage features, and tombs, may also be considered architectural. The presence of large-scale constructions, or monumental architecture, suggests that the group that built them had complex political and economic organizations.

Every society, past and present, has employed some type of architecture. Much architecture served the function of providing shelter and living space for people, from housing individual people and single families to groups of families in "apartment" structures. Other buildings include relatively small structures such as sweat houses, sheds, or storage facilities, and larger structures such as public buildings used for meetings, sporting or theatrical events (e.g., Roman coliseums and Maya ballcourts), or bathing. Other structures were produced for economic purposes, including dams, irrigation systems, aqueducts and canals, terraced or raised fields, and roads; for military purposes, such as walls (e.g., the Great Wall of China) and other fortifications (e.g., castles in Europe); and for religious purposes, such as cathedrals, tombs (e.g., some of the Egyptian pyramids), and shrines.

Architectural structures were made from a wide variety of materials, including brush, wood, bamboo, skins, bone (e.g., whale ribs, mammoth jaws or tusks), wattle-and-daub (a wooden frame covered with mud), adobe, mud brick, stone, or tile. Other buildings were made by excavating into solid rock, such as many of the structures at Petra, some of the Egyptian royal tombs, or entire underground cities, such as those in the Cappadocia region of Turkey.

Structures were built above ground, partly underground (semisubterranean), completely below ground (subterranean), or in some combination of these. Many structures have foundations, and many also have some sort of frame to support the walls and roof. In small, lightly built structures, such as tents, rocks may be used to help anchor the walls at the bottom. Many structures contain built-in decorations, such as frescoes (wall paintings), tile floor mosaics, or sculptures.

Ancient architects and engineers were often very sophisticated, designing and building huge structures such as massive pyramids, large and complex cities, and aqueducts that traversed hundreds of miles. Much of the preserved ancient architecture is of stone, and the ability of people to build in this medium is astounding (Highlight 4.4). Using relatively simple technology (but with a clear understanding of basic physics), people were able to move stones weighing hundreds or even thousands of tons over great distances and construct large buildings, from Stonehenge to the pyramids of Egypt and Mesoamerica. Among the finest stonemasons were the Inka of South America. The Inka were able to cut and place stones with such great precision that no mortar was needed to hold them in place.

The archaeological remains of buildings and structures depend on the materials used in construction and on a variety of preservation factors. Structures made from stone will generally preserve better than those made from brush. Aside from stone buildings, most architecture discovered consists of foundations for walls, rings of rocks used to hold down tents or brush structures, stones packed in around wooden posts as support (whether or not the post has preserved), floors of compacted soil, and pits dug into the floors of structures.

Structures of brush and wood generally do not preserve well. However, if the remains of such structures are burned,

Beginning in the sixth century BC, Nabataeans carved tombs and temples into solid rock, the soft sandstone cliffs of present-day Jordan. Their greatest architectural achievements are seen in the city of Petra, where this view first greets visitors.

How Were the Egyptian Pyramids Built?

The methods of construction of the three great pyramids on the Giza Plateau near Cairo in Egypt has long been speculated. Many people have had a difficult time believing ancient people could accomplish the feat, believing that a more "advanced" culture was responsible. Some believe that an extraterrestrial group was involved. However, there is no need for extraordinary explanations; it is clear that the Egyptians built the pyramids using the tools and techniques of the time.

Some find it difficult to see how the ancient Egyptians leveled the base to less than a few inches difference in height among the opposite corners of the Great Pyramid. However, it is not difficult at all. It was done by digging small trenches, filling them with water (which is self-leveling), then removing the rock to the level of the water. A neat trick.

The biggest mystery though, is how the large stones were quarried, moved to the construction site, and assembled. Experiments have shown that a block can be cut and shaped rather quickly by skilled workers. Once cut and shaped, the blocks had to be moved, but most of the stone came from nearby Giza and did not have to be moved far. Experiments have shown that a number of techniques for moving the stones could have worked, but the technique the Egyptians most likely used (as seen in some Egyptian paintings)

was placing the stone on a sled and pulling it up a ramp using ropes. Water on the soil in front of the sled allowed it to slide easily. It is true that long, shallow ramps would have been needed to use sleds, but dirt for ramp construction was plentiful and the Egyptians were not shy about expending labor. Other methods of moving the blocks, such as using special attachments to roll them up smaller ramps, are being explored.

The people that built the pyramids were a permanent staff of specialists: stone cutters, engineers, and architects working year-round. The primary labor was provided by farmers during the period of time they did not have to work in the fields. The farmers were paid by the Pharaoh. Thus, stone blocks could be cut, shaped, and stockpiled until the farmers came to move them. These people worked to please the gods and ultimately benefited everyone.

CRITICAL **THINKING** QUESTIONS

1. What are some of the ways stone blocks could have been transported over land and water? How has experimental archaeology contributed to answering this question?
2. Where did the workers building the pyramids live? What have we learned about them?

---

many of the architectural elements can be preserved. For example, you could discover burned support posts in the ground, some aspects of the collapsed superstructure, and even details of construction materials and techniques as impressions in burned and fired clay used in the construction.

Human Remains

The remains of humans themselves are often found in sites, may be present for various reasons, and can take a variety of forms. Some human materials, such as baby teeth or an occasional limb bone, represent parts lost during life and do not necessarily indicate the presence of burials. If the dead were actually disposed of in a site, their remains would generally occur as either inhumations or cremations.

Inhumation is the disposal of the dead by burial. Individuals would be placed in graves and covered with soil. The flesh usually decomposes, and the bones remain intact. If the soil conditions are good, the bones can preserve for some time. In some cases, the bones of individuals would be removed from the grave and moved for permanent burial in a central location, called an **ossuary.** Ossuaries can contain the bones of hundreds of individuals in a small area, inasmuch as the complete bodies decomposed elsewhere. Some groups disposed of their dead by **cremation,** burning the body. In a cremation, much of the bone is consumed in the fire, but many small fragments usually remain.

Human remains are often encountered unexpectedly, generally with the discovery of a single bone or fragment of bone. The excavator would carefully expose the bone, try to determine what animal it represented, and, if it is human, approach its excavation with great caution. The bones would be slowly and very carefully exposed, with the excavator paying close attention to whether any grave goods could be discovered.

Some human remains are neither buried nor cremated. Some bodies are placed in the open and left to decay, such as in the scaffold burials of the Plains Indians, or bodies are placed on hillsides, in crevices, or in caves. In some cases, if the body was placed in an area that was protected, the body might preserve as a mummy.

Site Formation and Transformation

The archaeological record and its parts, such as sites, are formed by a combination of cultural and natural circumstances (e.g., Schiffer 1987). All sites are initially produced as a result of some cultural action, such as the killing of an animal or the construction of a building, in which the actions of people resulted in some alteration of the natural environment. The cultural and natural variables that combine to shape the geography, geology, and environmental context of each site are unique; no two sites formed in exactly the same way.

It is easy to see how a small camp and a city would form differently, but even very similar sites have unique formation histories. For example, if a hunter shoots and kills a deer, the animal will fall onto the ground. If the hunter butchers the deer on the spot, evidence of that activity will remain in the form of bones and broken tools left on the ground, and a kill site is formed. If the same hunter kills a second deer, the second kill site will be unique. It will be at a different location, formed at a different time, contain the bones of a different deer, and include the remains of tools resharpened since their use on the first deer.

If a farmer builds a small hut to live in while near a field, a habitation site is created. The farmer may have leveled the ground for the hut, gathered rocks for its construction, and left a trash heap nearby. In any case, the natural environment is modified in some way, a site forms, and evidence of the activities that took place at the site is preserved in the record.

As cultural activities continue at a site, various materials are created and enter the record as part of the site. Tools are manufactured, broken, and discarded; features are constructed and torn down; ecofacts accumulate; garbage and other debris accumulate; and midden deposits form. In some cases, natural soil may be brought to a site by people, either purposefully (e.g., as fill dirt) or as mud on shoes. These cultural processes often are augmented by and combined with natural processes, such as the deposition of soil onto a site by wind and water.

Through time, the archaeological record is subject to **transformation processes**—actions that change the record from its original form. This transformation can reach the point where the archaeological record is obscured, masked, unrecognized, or difficult to decipher. The many formation and transformation processes acting on the archaeological record are summarized in Table 4.1 and are discussed in the rest of this section.

Geology and Hydrology

The natural forces that affect site formation are primarily those that involve the deposition of materials, generally through the action of water—**hydrology**—and wind. Water and wind erode and deposit soil. A severe flood can suddenly bury a site and lead to its abandonment. Repeated small flood events can result in the slow accumulation of alluvium while the site continues to be occupied, and the deposits in such sites can become very thick. Soil deposited by wind can have much the same effect. Wind-borne (aeolian) soils can accumulate by being trapped by plants and by features such as walls.

Other natural actions can result in the sudden deposition of materials, such as ash falls from volcanoes, and many sites have been buried beneath them, such as the famous site of Pompeii (see Highlight 2.1 in Chapter 2). Other examples include the Maya village of Ceren in El Salvador, buried by ash from a volcanic eruption some 1,400 years ago and discovered in 1976 (Sheets 1992). Another good example is the island of Thira (also called Thera or Santorini) in the Aegean Sea. After the island exploded in 1628 BC, only a crescent-shaped remnant remained above water. Sites on Thira not destroyed by the explosion, such

table 4.1

General Formation and Transformation Processes

PROCESS	FORMATION		TRANSFORMATION	
	Natural	*Cultural*	*Natural*	*Cultural*
Various kinds of deposition and erosion	X		X	
Earthquakes and tsunamis	X		X	
People living/working on a site in the past		X		X
Decomposition			X	X
Taphomonic processes			X	
Bioturbation			X	X
Modern development				X
Vandalism and looting				X

as the famous site of Akrotiri, were buried in ash. It is likely that the destruction of Thira was the basis for the legend of Atlantis.

Earthquakes can result in the destruction and abandonment of sites. In some cases, sites "sink into the sea" as a result of an earthquake. Such an event apparently happened about 2,000 years ago in the Egyptian port of Alexandria, where the palace of Cleopatra sank into the harbor. The remains of that palace were only recently discovered (La Riche 1996; Goddio et al. 1998; Foreman 1999). Tsunamis also can demolish and bury coastal sites.

Mud slides can also rapidly and suddenly bury sites. A classic example is Ozette, located in northwestern Washington State. The site was a Makah Indian village lying along the shore of the Pacific Ocean next to a large hill. The site had been occupied for about 2,000 years. Then one evening about 250 years ago, the rain-soaked hillside above the site gave way, and mud buried the village. The movement of the mud was slow enough for the people to escape but too fast for them to take their possessions (Samuels 1991). Unusual depositional events such as rockfalls, cave-ins, and avalanches also may damage sites while burying them.

Some geological conditions remain stable through time, in that they are not subject to either deposition or erosion. Thus, materials dropped on the surface at some time in the past are still lying on that surface. Other actions, such as exposure to cold or heat, may be affecting those materials, but they are not being buried or eroded. Thus, stable surfaces could contain archaeological materials still in original position.

Some surfaces and deposits are not stable and get eroded. Materials are affected or removed through the action of wind and water. If the erosion is severe, entire sites can be washed away only to be deposited again in other locations downstream. In this case, all the accumulated materials are removed from their primary context, broken up, and mixed with other materials, or are lost. The site would often be considered "destroyed." If the erosion is less severe, only parts of the site may suffer damage. In some cases, erosion can remove the soil of a site deposit, mixing artifacts of different ages onto one surface.

Water can affect sites in ways other than erosion. Over time, water leaches the organic and chemical materials from site soils, changing them from their original form. For example, old sites rarely contain charcoal because over time the charcoal is broken into smaller and smaller pieces and the pieces eventually become small enough to be leached by water seeping though the soil. Water may also cause compaction of the soil as it settles over time. Thus, some site soils can be very dense and hard, difficult for burrowing animals to penetrate but even harder for archaeologists to excavate. Rising sea levels, lake levels, or water tables may engulf sites, radically changing preservation conditions and causing erosion.

Taphonomy

Once biological materials (ecofacts) enter the archaeological record, they are transformed from their original state by a number of factors. The study of these processes is called **taphonomy** (e.g., Lyman 1994). Preservation of biological remains is an important consideration in taphonomic studies because they will decompose, become fragmented, get scattered, and eventually reach the point of not being recognized by archaeologists. Thus, only a portion of the materials that enter the record are recovered by archaeologists (Figure 4.4).

The other important aspect of taphonomy is to understand the condition and distribution of the materials that are recovered. Each of the many biological materials recovered from a site exists in some state. How did that piece come to be in that state? If it was burned,

figure 4.4

General Taphonomic Processes. You can follow an item down both sides of this chart to discover the many paths it can take before it is recovered in an archaeological excavation.

Source: Mark Q. Sutton and Brooke S. Arkush, 2002, *Archaeological Laboratory Methods,* 3rd edition (Dubuque, IA: Kendall/Hunt), Figure 99.

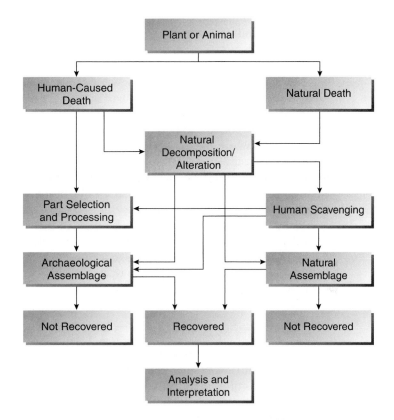

was burning the result of a natural fire, cooking, or disposal in a campfire? The answer to that question has a great deal to do with the interpretation of human behavior.

Ethnoarchaeology and experimental archaeology aim to increase understanding of taphonomic processes. Using these approaches, archaeologists can formulate and test hypotheses about site formation processes and the origin, preservation, and movement of archaeological remains in a site. For example, considerable broken bone is often found in archaeological sites. How did this bone get broken? Did it get broken by people, animals, or other means? Experiments (e.g., Jones 1986; Butler and Schroeder 1996) have been conducted on what happens when animals chew, break, consume, and digest bones, carefully noting the kinds of damage and breakage patterns on the bones themselves. Other experiments (e.g., Lyman 1994) have been conducted on how people break bone during food processing. It turns out that animal and human breakage patterns are different and can be distinguished. Thus, archaeologists can usually tell whether bones were broken through human processing or through animals scavenging them after people had discarded them.

Bioturbation

Materials may be affected by **bioturbation,** the disturbance or movement of deposited materials by organisms. The major agents of bioturbation are burrowing animals, primarily rodents but also including badgers, coyotes, hyenas, ants, and earthworms. These animals live underground, excavate tunnels and dens in the soil, and often prefer the relatively soft soils of archaeological sites. Old burrows collapse, and subsequent generations of animals dig new ones. These burrowing activities can be so extensive that the deposit in a site could be completely remodeled. All of the artifacts and ecofacts could be moved vertically from their original positions; horizontal displacement seems to be less of a problem (Bocek 1986).

Even nonburrowing animals may affect a site, digging into it for roots, trampling materials on the surface, and breaking, dislodging, and moving them. Animals also create wallows, areas where they gather, rest, stomp around, and form depressions that may fill with water, causing erosion or other impacts. Animal wallows might even be misinterpreted as cultural features, such as house pits. Animal dung on a site could alter its soil chemistry, masking the chemical signatures of cultural activities and making the work of the archaeological chemist more difficult.

Plants also can bioturbate sites. The roots of plants penetrate the ground, often to great depth, break up and move materials, and alter the chemical and organic content of the soil. Roots are particularly ruinous to features such as walls. If a tree dies and falls over, it can move materials many feet laterally, expose buried items, and create depressions that might be misinterpreted as house pits.

Human Agency

Probably the most dynamic force in the alteration of the archaeological record is human action. As we already noted, some human action is required to create an archaeological site. As soon as most sites form, humans begin altering them. People dig pits into old deposits, burying their dead, building their houses, or disposing of their trash in the pit and disturbing and displacing the earlier materials.

Materials also get reused and recycled by past people who may have found discarded materials they could use, scavenging those materials from earlier sites, reusing them, and then depositing them in later sites. For example, if someone discarded a large broken tool 1,000 years ago, another person could have found that tool 500 years later and made it into a smaller tool. The smaller tool was made from a larger 1,000-year-old tool, and that single tool was evidence of the activities of two different groups separated in time.

Such activities are still ongoing. For example, contemporary people in Siberia occasionally discover a frozen mammoth, remove the ivory tusks, and manufacture things from them. Thus, we have modern things made from 25,000-year-old mammoth ivory. Sorting out this type of activity is difficult. In addition, building materials were also scavenged and reused. In the southwestern United States, people building a pueblo took timbers from an earlier pueblo, mixing old and new timbers in the construction of the new pueblo. The reuse of stones was common in many of the ancient civilizations, such as in Egypt, Rome, and Mesoamerica.

 # Preservation

In archaeology, preservation is of paramount importance, for we can recover and analyze only what we can find. **Preservation** refers both to physical objects and to their context in a site. All material things decompose and break down at a speed that depends on conditions. Most stone decomposes slowly and preserves very well; archaeologists generally expect to find stone tools even if they are millions of years old. Other materials, such as pottery, glass, and fired clay bricks, are sturdy and can be expected to preserve for many millennia. Under the right conditions, bone preserves well but eventually decomposes and must be fossilized (mineralized) to preserve for a long time. More fragile materials, such as flesh, wood, and textiles, usually decompose very rapidly but may be preserved under unusual conditions. Thus, the older a site is, the fewer materials are likely to be preserved in it. Very old sites may contain only stone and fossilized bone.

Preservation Conditions

Decomposition has two basic causes: biological activity and inorganic action. Biological activity is probably the major cause of decomposition. Various organisms, such as termites, bacteria, and fungi, literally eat organic materials. Consider a wooden bowl manufactured and used and protected during its use-life by its owner. Once the bowl is discarded and enters the archaeological record, it has no real protection and is assaulted by wood-eating organisms. The wood is consumed, and archaeologists are not even aware that the bowl existed, much less able to recover it from an excavation. Some of the inorganic compounds from the wood might remain, perhaps even staining the soil where the bowl lay, and an observant archaeologist might discover and recognize the stain. This process applies to most organic materials, few of which are found by archaeologists.

Inorganic action also affects preservation, often in conjunction with biological activity. In the case of the wooden bowl, alternate cycles of wet (winter) and dry (summer) conditions might crack and fragment the bowl, making it easier for organisms to consume. If the bowl were lying on the surface, wind action might erode it and quickly break it up. Erosion can damage and decompose rock as well, often to the point where the evidence of its use by people is removed, such as by stream action or sandblasting. Although it would take many millions of years for wind and sand to erode the hard stone of the Giza pyramids, the nearby Sphinx, made of soft sandstone, has been badly eroded in the last few hundred years and requires protection from further damage.

Thus, under normal conditions, stone preserves the best. Next best are materials such as pottery and iron, followed by bone, shell, and nonferrous metals. Most other organic materials preserve very poorly (Table 4.2). However, if conditions are not "normal," preservation can be quite different. Materials tend to preserve in unusual situations, where the normal biologic and inorganic actions that break them down are limited or absent. Such situations include the alteration of the physical condition of an item and materials being in locations of extreme environment.

Preservation and the Environment

The environment in which an item is found is a critical factor in preservation. Materials tend to preserve in extreme environmental conditions—those that are very dry, very cold, very wet, or anaerobic (lacking oxygen)—where the biological agents that consume organic materials cannot thrive. These extreme conditions have to remain fairly constant, such as being always cold or always wet. Variation in conditions fosters decomposition.

t a b l e   4 . 2

General Preservation Conditions

MATERIAL	NORMAL TIME OF PRESERVATION	SOME CONDITIONS THAT PROMOTE PRESERVATION	SOME CONDITIONS THAT HASTEN DECOMPOSITION
Stone	Millions of years	Most	Exposure in erosional environments
Bone	Hundreds to many thousands of years	Rapid burial, slight burning, alkaline soils, fossilization	Disturbance, breakage, exposure to sunlight, acidic soils
Shell	Thousands of years	Rapid burial, alkaline soils	Disturbance, breakage, acidic soils
Ceramics	Thousands of years	Most	Disturbance, breakage
Perishables (e.g., wood, textiles, and fibers)	A few months to a few years	Where bacteria do not live, either very dry, very cold, or anaerobic	Moisture and warm temperatures
Flesh (soft tissue)	A few weeks to a few months	Where bacteria do not live, either very dry, very cold, or anaerobic	Moisture and warm temperatures
Glass	Thousands of years	Most	Disturbance, breakage
Ferrous metals (e.g., iron)	Tens to hundreds of years	Not many, absence of oxygen	Moisture, presence of oxygen
Nonferrous metals (e.g., copper and bronze)	Thousands of years	Many	Moisture, presence of oxygen
Gold	Thousands of years	Most	Few

The most common environment for good preservation is warm and dry regions or localities. Most organisms that eat organic materials need water. So the less water there is and the faster things dry out, the better are the chances of preservation because most organisms do not consume dry material. Deserts and other regions that receive little rainfall and have low humidity have environments favorable for preservation. In desert areas such as Egypt, coastal Peru, and central Asia, it is so dry that human bodies buried in the open mummify naturally, and tissue and even burial clothing are preserved.

Dry conditions can exist in regions that receive rain if there are locations that do not get wet and if the humidity is low enough. If people lived in a cave in which rain or other water did not penetrate, organic materials could preserve. Also, artifacts collected by a packrat and incorporated into its protected nest might preserve there for hundreds or thousands of years. Archaeologists often seek dry caves because they know that perishable items may be present there.

If the environment is continuously cold, things preserve well because of two factors. First, most of the biological agents that decompose materials cannot operate in cold conditions. Second, water, being frozen, is unavailable to organisms and thus conditions tend to be dry. In such situations, decomposition is slow or absent, and natural mummification can easily occur. Such conditions exist in regions that remain cold throughout the year, such as in high mountains, in much of the Arctic and Antarctic, and even in ice caves. The discovery of the "Iceman" in the Alps, found with many of his belongings, and the intact dwellings of ancient Eskimo peoples in the Arctic are examples of this type of preservation.

In most situations, water fosters decomposition. However, if conditions are right, preservation can occur when materials are waterlogged. In cases where the water was open, such as many shipwrecks, very cold water would prevent the organisms that cause decomposition from operating. Also, in cases where archaeological materials repose in soils that were continually wet, the presence of water might create an environment in which decay-causing organisms cannot operate, such as the highly acidic peat bogs in northwestern Europe, where some fairly well-preserved bodies have been found.

Preservation can occur in fine mud, an anaerobic environment—one that contains no oxygen—where decomposing organisms cannot live. In these conditions, even the most fragile organic materials can be well preserved. Many examples of such preservation are known, including entire 5,000-year-old lakeside villages in Switzerland, the Ozette site in northwestern Washington mentioned earlier, and numerous ships such as the *Mary Rose* (see Highlight 1.2 in Chapter 1).

Recognizing and Recovering Evidence

Whatever the condition of an item or its state of preservation, the archaeologist has to recognize the material before it can be recovered and analyzed. Preservation is really a matter of recognition, inasmuch as most identification and recovery of materials is done visually. Materials eventually become too small or altered to be recognized. If something is completely intact, it is easily recognized and the preservation is considered excellent. As things decompose, they become more and more difficult to identify, eventually breaking down and fragmenting to the point where they are not recognized.

We can follow an artifact as it deteriorates into smaller and smaller pieces, as depicted in Figure 4.5.

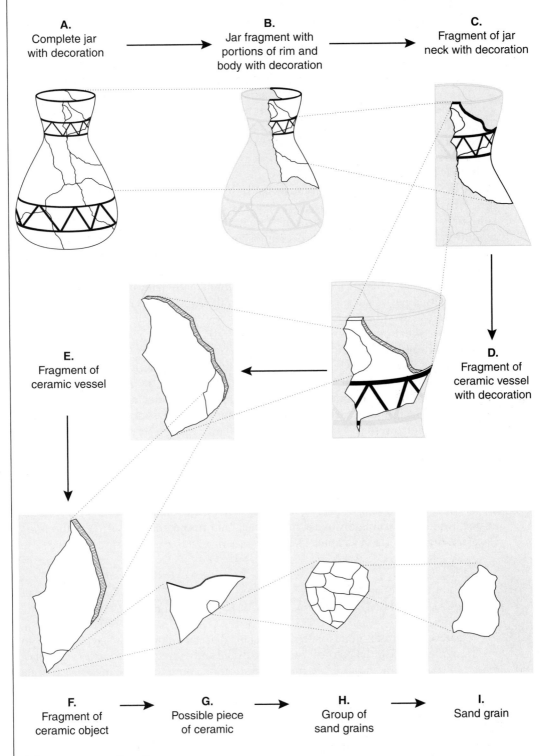

A.
Complete jar
with decoration

B.
Jar fragment with
portions of rim and
body with decoration

C.
Fragment of jar
neck with decoration

E.
Fragment of
ceramic vessel

D.
Fragment of
ceramic vessel
with decoration

F.
Fragment of
ceramic object

G.
Possible piece
of ceramic

H.
Group of
sand grains

I.
Sand grain

figure 4.5

Size Reduction, Recognition, and Preservation of a Ceramic Jar. At what
point would an archaeologist no longer be able to recognize the ceramic jar?

A. We find a complete, decorated ceramic jar—an artifact that few would miss. Because the jar is complete, the size, capacity, and method of manufacture are easily determined. All of the decoration is present, so we have complete information about the design.

B. We find a large fragment of the rim and body with decoration. The artifact is easily recognized as a decorated jar. Enough of the jar is present so we can estimate its size, capacity, and method of manufacture. But some of the decoration is missing, along with whatever of its information it would have conveyed.

C. We find a small piece of the jar neck with decoration. We can tell that it comes from a jar and that the jar was decorated, and we can identify the method of manufacture. But the piece is so small that we cannot estimate the size and capacity of the vessel, and we have little information on the decoration.

D. We find a still smaller piece. We recognize it as a fragment of a decorated vessel, but it is too small for us to determine the form of the vessel. No estimate of size or capacity is possible, and the method of manufacture cannot be determined.

E. A fragment of that piece lacks decoration and must be listed as a fragment of some sort of ceramic vessel.

F. A smaller fragment is recognized as ceramic but from an unknown object.

G. A still smaller piece might not be recognized as ceramic but might be listed as "possible" ceramic.

H. A fragment of that piece consists of what appears to be a group of sand grains somehow held together. Someone might spot it and think it unusual, but it will not be recognized as an artifact.

I. A single isolated sand grain from the jar is not even noticed, much less recognized as an artifact.

Recognition is a prerequisite for recovery. As the pieces get smaller, more and more information is lost. At some point in their decomposition, all archaeological materials cease being recognizable.

In theory, all of the materials from the past still exist in the archaeological record (we must at least adopt that philosophical position), with their state of preservation influencing our ability to discover them. Whether or not something is "preserved" is related to the environmental and taphonomic processes that govern its size and form, to the ability of archaeologists to recognize it, and to the methods used to recover it. As our detection abilities improve, we will "find" more and more things because we will be better able to recognize them. Unfortunately, many field techniques (see Chapter 5) are designed to find relatively large objects, and many small things are not collected. However, some special techniques are being used to discover things not visible to the naked eye, such as special chemical techniques for recovering preserved proteins or DNA.

Ongoing Impacts on the Archaeological Record

Archaeological sites are nonrenewable resources: once formed, sites and the materials in them can only degrade, and the record slowly becomes more and more difficult to interpret. Sites are affected by a variety of natural actions, such as erosion. Although there are probably millions of sites worldwide, the ongoing and cumulative naturally occurring damage to the archaeological record is considerable.

Humans, however, pose the most serious threat to the archaeological record. As development occurs, sites are damaged or destroyed by the construction of buildings, roads, and facilities such as dams. Another major impact on the archaeological record comes from the practice of large-scale agriculture. By its very nature, agriculture continually modifies the land through plowing, leveling, augmentation by fertilizer, and the like. Each of these activities damages and alters archaeological sites, often severely. Even casual and recreational use of land can damage archaeological sites, such as off-road vehicles driving over sites, breaking artifacts, damaging features, and causing erosion. In addition, the archaeological record is affected by warfare, which damages or destroys archaeological sites and museums either accidentally or by design.

One of the most detrimental impacts to the archaeological record comes from looting, sometimes called pothunting (Renfrew 2000; Brodie et al. 2001; Brodie and Renfrew 2005). Looters dig into sites and remove artifacts or objects of art for their own personal collections or for sale on the black market (Highlight 4.5). Looters dig up burials, collect the skulls and artifacts, and discard the rest of the body in fragments across the site. Many artifacts are destroyed to obtain a few "pretty" ones for a collection. Even the collection of arrowheads from the surface, legal in the United States, is very destructive to the archaeological record because such marker artifacts are often used by archaeologists to date sites.

Looting is a huge problem all over the world. Some people make their living by looting. In many countries, looting is illegal, and the United Nations has strict regulations about the sale and transport of antiquities. Nevertheless, a great deal of this type of illegal activity occurs even in the United States because few law enforcement officials bother to enforce the existing laws.

Looting is not limited to materials actually in sites. When coalition forces entered Baghdad in April 2003, the National Museum of Iraq was left unprotected between the time Iraqi forces left and coalition forces took control. During those few days, the museum was ransacked and tens of thousands of priceless items were looted. Fortunately, many of the looted items have since been recovered, and the museum has reopened.

An often overlooked contemporary impact on the archaeological record comes from the activities of archaeologists themselves. When a site is excavated, it is literally dug up and dismantled. The amount of information recovered during the excavation depends on the skills of the excavators and the efforts they expend to record what was found and where it was found. In theory, if the artifacts and ecofacts from a site are properly recovered, the information from, and value of, a site are preserved even if the site itself is razed. Unfortunately, the theory differs from the practice: we never recover all of the potential information from a site, and site destruction, even after excavation, results in a loss of information. Even the most careful excavation is destructive.

The archaeological record is fragile, nonrenewable, and suffering from considerable impacts. This realization has prompted efforts to preserve and manage archaeological sites.

HIGHLIGHT **4.5**

The Looting of Angkor Wat

Angkor Wat, the great capital city of the Khmer Empire in Cambodia (now called Kampuchea), was occupied between the 800s and 1432. The site covers nearly 400 square miles and has vast complexes of temples, palaces, canals, and living areas. The main temple at Angkor Wat alone covers a full square mile. The city was built from stone and decorated with sculpted reliefs and much statuary, some of which were very large. It is not clear why the city was abandoned. Some believe that the cost of maintaining the city became too great, others think that the Thai invasion and sacking of the city in 1432 was the reason, and some now believe that the silting in of the city's canals and waterways (an issue related to maintenance) was the cause. For whatever reason, the city was abandoned in the mid-1400s.

Although the ruins were never really lost, they became famous when described in 1860 and investigated by the French (Cambodia was part of French Indochina until 1954), beginning in 1898. Work continued at Angkor Wat for many years, interrupted by World War II and the subsequent conflict in southeast Asia. When Cambodia was taken over by the Khmer Rouge in the mid-1970s, much of the art at the site was looted by the government to generate cash, and no archaeological work was allowed. Not until quite recently have archaeologists been allowed back. Much of their work is focused on assessing the damage done.

In 1992, Angkor Wat was simultaneously designated as a World Heritage Site and placed on the list of World Heritage Sites in Danger. Today a major international effort is under way to conserve the art remaining at the site, to establish meaningful protection from looting, and to develop long-range plans for research and conservation.

CRITICAL **THINKING** QUESTIONS

1. What does this story illustrate about the nature of looting and the problems of preserving the archaeological record?
2. How does looting destroy the information that archaeologists seek in order to learn about the past?

C O N T E N T S E L E C T

Search articles in the ContentSelect database using the key words *site formation* and *taphonomy*. What are some examples of taphonomic processes described in these articles? How are the formation of a site and the transformation of a site similar?

Chapter Summary

The archaeological record contains the material remains, known or unknown, of past human activities and behaviors—materials distributed in various patterns and existing in varying degrees of preservation. The known record consists of all the information obtained about the past, the location and condition of sites and their contents, the records of the investigations, results of analyses, and the published results of archaeological investigations.

Most information on the human past is found within sites—discrete localities that contain artifacts, ecofacts, features, and human remains. Sites are classified by geographic context, function, and age. Many sites contain anthropogenic soils, which formed as the result of human activity, and contain a combination of broken tools, used-up artifacts, plant and animal materials, grease, charcoal and ash, and household trash. Many sites exhibit stratigraphy, layers of soils deposited at different times.

Once formed, archaeological sites are continually transformed through natural and cultural processes, including taphonomy, bioturbation, and human agency. The recovery of archaeological data is dependent on the degree of preservation of the materials, the degree of transformation, and the ability of the archaeologist to recognize materials.

Key Concepts

anthropogenic, 86
bioturbation, 101
casual tool, 90
component, 84
composite tool, 90
context, 89
cremation, 98
geofact, 90

hydrology, 99
inhumation, 98
locus (loci), 84
manuport, 91
midden, 86
ossuary, 98
palynology, 92
preservation, 102

primary context, 89
secondary context, 89
simple tool, 90
taphonomy, 100
transformation processes, 99
use-life, 90

Suggested Readings

If you want to learn more about the concepts and issues discussed in this chapter, consider looking at the following resources. (Some may be rather technical.)

Brodie, Neil, Jennifer Doole, and Colin Renfrew (eds.). (2001). *Trade in Illicit Antiquities: The Destruction of the World's Archaeological Heritage.* Cambridge, UK: McDonald Institute Monographs.

The papers in this volume detail the scope and impact of vandalism of archaeological sites and the illegal trade in looted archaeological materials. The authors paint a very bleak picture.

Lyman, R. Lee. (1994). *Vertebrate Taphonomy.* Cambridge, UK: Cambridge University Press.

Lyman examines the various processes that affect bone after it enters the archaeological record. Many of these taphonomic principles also apply to other biological materials.

Schiffer, Michael B. (1987). *Formation Processes of the Archaeological Record.* Albuquerque: University of New Mexico Press.

The processes involved in the formation and transformation of the archaeological record are outlined in detail by Schiffer. Each of the various factors, from natural to cultural elements, is considered and discussed.

chapter 5

Conducting Fieldwork

EXCAVATION CAN GENERATE a huge amount of information. Although the data are recorded and mapped, they sometimes are so overwhelming that interpretation is difficult. Conventional mapping methods involve hand-drawing maps for every surface exposed during the course of excavation. Everything has to be mapped because during the excavation it is often difficult to tell whether an object, such as a rock, is important archaeologically. Further excavation might reveal that it is a random rock or that it is part of something else, such as a wall. A great deal of time and energy goes into laborious mapping, and some maps contain too much information.

The archaeologist Thomas Levy and his colleagues (Levy et al. 2001) faced such a situation when working at an Early Bronze Age

Researchers at the University of California–San Diego Jabal Hamrat Fidan (JHF) Project work with a total station (TS) and ranger data collector in the Jordanian desert.

Levy used a "total station" (a computerized laser surveyor, or transit) to map the location of each artifact. He then downloaded the digital locational data to the GIS program (paper records also were kept). All the features (mostly rooms in a small town) were also photo-mapped and tied to the GIS grid. This information was then loaded into a laptop computer and combined to create a 3-D map of the site, its features, and its artifacts. Through GIS, all of the information from the site was linked together and could be updated on a daily basis.

Different classes of Early Bronze Age artifacts, such as molds for ingots of copper, molds for finished copper products, and hammerstones, also were placed in separate GIS layers so they could be compared. Each digitally photographed artifact had a "pop-

metal "manufactory" site of Khirbet Hamra Ifdan in Jordan—the largest metal production site from the period in the ancient Middle East. In an area of some 1,200 square meters, Levy's team discovered more than 10,000 artifacts within six major soil strata. To make sense of this huge data set, Levy turned to Geographic Information Systems (GIS) software, which enables the researcher to create maps electronically and put information about specific materials, such as artifacts or features, on separate overlays, which can be combined and analyzed as desired (see Chapter 3).

The University of California–San Diego team rewrote the software for the data collector so that TS data could be directly downloaded into ArcView, a Geographic Information System (GIS) program, shown here. (Courtesy of Thomas Levy.)

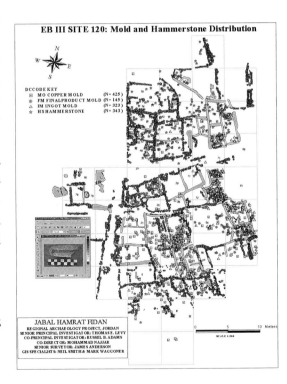

up" photo encoded into the GIS layer, so an image of each artifact was available at a click of the mouse.

These precise spatial data enabled Levy and his colleagues to view the results of their work in ways not possible prior to computer technology. These data influenced both their interpretations of the site and their plans for future work. By using GIS, they were able to identify the production process by which past peoples turned raw metal into finished products, a task that would have taken the researchers years without the aid of GIS.

For the location of Khirbet Hamra Ifdan and other sites in this chapter, see the map on page 114.

The only real way to learn about the past is to locate, recover, examine, and analyze the patterned material remains of past behaviors. Although one can formulate hypotheses, develop predictions, create models of the past, and so forth, the only way to test these models is by using archaeological data gathered from the field. Ultimately, all data have to be gathered from the field—by finding sites and by excavating them.

In most cases, a research design (see Chapter 1) is needed before fieldwork can be carried out. The research design sets out the research questions, identifies the kinds of data needed to address those questions, and selects the field methods necessary to recover the desired data. In addition, the research design includes the necessary background research, such as detailing ethnographic data for use in analogy and conducting literature searches to locate pertinent historical records.

Finding Sites

One of the most fundamental tasks in archaeology is locating and documenting sites, a process called *survey* or *inventory*. There are, no doubt, millions of archaeological sites in the world, and archaeologists ultimately want to know as much as they can about each of them. Some sites, such as the pyramids in Egypt, are easy to find, but most are much less obvious. Archaeologists also want to know where sites are *not* present, so that a better understanding of why they are located where they are can be gained. Archaeological survey data can be used to address certain kinds of questions regarding settlement patterns, demographic patterns, relationships between sites and environmental parameters, and how these things may have changed over time.

Accidental Discoveries

Many archaeological sites are accidentally discovered by members of the public who are out and about in the landscape. Sites are found by hikers, farmers, ranchers, landowners, real estate agents, amateur archaeologists, and construction workers, among others. Some

LOCATION MAP: **Sites Mentioned in Chapter 5**

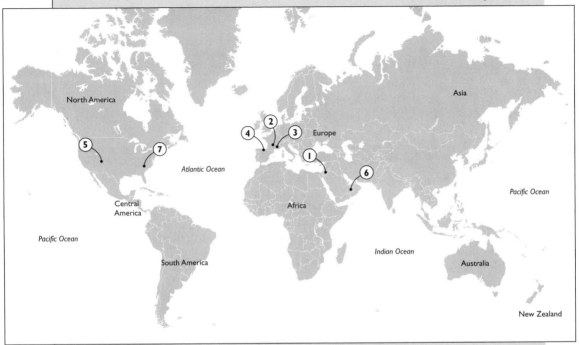

1 ■ Khirbet Hamra Ifdan
  Greig'gra, Faynan district, Jordan

2 ■ Lascaux Cave
  Moutignac-Lascaux, France

3 ■ La Grotte Chauvet
  Ardèche, France

4 ■ Altamira caves
  Santander, Spain

5 ■ Mesa Verde National Park
  Cortez, Colorado

6 ■ Ubar
  Southern Oman

7 ■ Little Tennessee River
  North Carolina

of these discoveries are reported to local archaeologists, who will record the information about the location and nature of the site and file a formal site record; however, most accidentally discovered sites are never reported and so remain unrecorded. Because of a lack of time and other resources, most accidentally discovered sites are recorded but not investigated in detail. If the site is somehow threatened (e.g., by development or erosion), an effort may be made to salvage as much information as possible before the site is destroyed, but often little can be done: too many sites, too few archaeologists.

Some discoveries are made in unexpected ways. For example, in 1962 an avid sailor tacking along the coast of Massachusetts in his sailboat noticed a strange whitish deposit in a sandy cliff on the shore. This deposit was being exposed and eroded by waves and wind. He reported his observations to environmentalists at a local university. They recognized cultural debris and called in the university archaeologists. The feature proved to be an Early Eastern Woodland Indian shell midden (refuse pile of discarded clam, oyster, and mussel shells), which also contained broken implements and a few human teeth. Because the site contained important sources of information and was being destroyed, the decision was made to investigate further. Because of the location of the midden, some of the excavation had to be done laterally by workers on platforms suspended over the side of the cliff.

Some accidental finds might be so important that local archaeologists drop what they are doing to work at the site, local archaeological societies provide some assistance, and granting agencies provide emergency funds. Occasionally, an accidentally discovered site assumes monumental importance, both as a source of information about the past and as a tourist and educational facility (Highlight 5.1).

Project-Related Discoveries

Most of the sites that are actually recorded are discovered by archaeologists conducting formal archaeological surveys. A great deal of the archaeological survey work conducted is done as part of the environmental work associated with development projects, generally called cultural resource management (CRM). Some CRM projects are large and may involve the survey of thousands, even tens of thousands, of acres. Most, however, are relatively small projects involving a few acres to a few hundred acres. Ideally, in CRM projects the area of development is the area surveyed, and any sites discovered within that area are researched and evaluated as part of the development.

Some survey projects are done as part of academic research projects. In such cases, the decision about where to survey is based on research questions rather than on the requirements of a development project. This type of research is the ideal because the science directs the project instead of the project directing the science. In a modern survey project (Hester et al. 1997; Roskams 2001), a research design is developed first. The research design details all pertinent information on the project area, including previous archaeological studies, models, and predictions; historical information; knowledge of past and present environment; and any other important data. Background studies include, in addition to previous studies in the site area, any ethnographic information and historical records or texts that might be relevant. All the information is then integrated into a plan for conducting the actual fieldwork.

HIGHLIGHT 5.1

The Discovery of Lascaux

On a fall day in 1940, four teenage boys living in southern France decided to explore a deep "hole" in the woods above Lascaux Manor. Years earlier, a pine tree had fallen over, its roots moving a large clump of soil to expose a crevice leading to an underground cavern. The original entrance had long since been covered. The boys entered the hole, found a cavern, and discovered on the walls hundreds of remarkably preserved paintings of animals. They had accidentally discovered one of the most famous archaeological sites in the world (Ruspoli 1987).

The boys knew they had stumbled on an important archaeological discovery and told their schoolmaster. A few days later, the eminent French archaeologist Abbé Breuil was informed, and he soon visited the cave. He, too, understood the importance of the discovery. As word spread, increasing numbers of people visited the cave, and the boys spent much of their time as tour guides. Archaeologists later determined that the cave art had been produced around 17,000 years ago by the Magdalenians, Upper Paleolithic people living in Europe at the time.

After World War II, the entrance of the Lascaux cave was enlarged and the interior modified to allow the approximately 1,200 daily tourists to move through the cave. By 1955 there were signs that the

Painting of an aurochs in Lascaux II.

Conducting Archaeological Surveys

The goal of an archaeological survey is to discover sites and record the details of their location and content. Most surveys are conducted by archaeologists physically walking over a tract of land and looking for visual evidence of sites. Such indications may be artifacts or ecofacts on the surface of the ground; telltale features such as mounds, walls, ditches, or rock outcrops; discolored soil (dark midden); different patterns of vegetation (middens often have different soil chemistries that attract certain plants); or places that "look" like sites should be there (this comes with experience).

paintings were beginning to deteriorate. The high levels of carbon dioxide and moisture produced by the many visitors were causing the cave walls to erode, allowing the growth of algae and moss. Although a system was put in place to monitor carbon dioxide levels, the deterioration continued, and the site was closed to the public in 1963. In just 23 years, paintings that had survived for thousands of years were nearly destroyed. Today the cave is stabilized and monitored daily, and access is still allowed to researchers.

In 1980, authorities decided to build a replica of the cave, complete with its art, for public visitation. A steel and concrete structure was constructed, and the main portions of the site were copied, down to the finest detail of the rock texture and color. Lascaux II was buried near the original site and opened in 1983.

Paleolithic cave art has been known for hundreds of years, and some 150 sites have so far been discovered in western Europe (Clottes 2001). The recent discovery of La Grotte Chauvet in Ardèche, France, may surpass the discoveries of Lascaux and Altamira (in Spain), the two most famous cave art sites in Europe. Most of the European sites date to between about 30,000 and 10,000 years ago. The animals represented in the paintings at Lascaux include bison, reindeer, horse, ibex, aurochs (ancestors of oxen), rhinoceros, and lion—

animals present in the region during the Upper Paleolithic. The figures were painted with pigments of red ochre, charcoal, and other minerals mixed with animal fat or blood. The artists used scaffolding to reach the upper parts of the cave walls and fat-burning lamps for light (many of which were found in the cave). The exact purpose of the cave paintings—instruction, art, magic, graffiti—is still debated.

Lascaux and Lascaux II are prime examples of the role of accidental discoveries in archaeology, the problems of conserving archaeological finds, and the challenges of making archaeological sites accessible to the public. Cave art and rock paintings worldwide also highlight the essential challenge of how to interpret archaeological evidence in terms of human motivation.

CRITICAL **THINKING** QUESTIONS

1. Lascaux was found accidentally. What are the other principal ways that sites are located?
2. Would Lascaux have been discovered by modern remote sensing technology?
3. What conditions at sites might influence the decision about whether to excavate? What factors might affect decision making about how to treat a site after excavation?

When archaeology first emerged as a discipline, little formal or systematic survey work was done. Researchers recorded only sites that were large, obvious, or thought to contain "treasure." Early surveys concentrated on finding large sites to excavate, with very little systematic coverage of areas or regions. For example, in the Middle East much of the early survey work focused on locating mounds (tells), and most of the smaller sites were ignored (Wilkinson 2000:226). In Mesoamerica, until fairly recently most sites found contained buildings large enough to protrude above the jungle canopy, resulting in the discovery of cities but relatively few towns and villages (which are much smaller). Most survey work is now done in a systematic manner to make sure that all portions of an area are examined. Individual archaeologists will walk back and forth across the survey area at a regular interval—for example, 10 meters apart—depending on conditions. Anything of interest will be examined and, if it is archaeological, recorded.

Such survey work requires that the surface of the ground be visible so that the archaeologist can actually see what is there. However, the surface of the ground is sometimes obscured by vegetation, dead leaves, or pine needles (duff). In these instances, the archaeological survey is conducted by systematically digging small holes (postholes or shovel pits) at regular intervals through the duff and into the soil. The soil is then examined for indications of a site. Although this is not a very good method for finding sites, it is the only practical one in those circumstances. If the duff should burn off, however, the surface of the ground would be exposed and a traditional survey could be conducted. In fact, a number of agencies in the United States have adopted a specific policy to conduct surveys in forests after fires, when the ground is more visible. To illustrate this point, archaeologists conducted a survey of an area of Mesa Verde National Park, Colorado, that burned in 1999 and, in spite of the area having been previously surveyed, discovered some 1,000 new sites. This forced a reevaluation of settlement and population models for the region.

Today, archaeologists have greater awareness of the need to find and record all types of sites so as to be able to reconstruct a complete picture of a past society. A modern survey project (Hester et al. 1997; Roskams 2001) is accomplished in several phases. First, a research design will be developed for the study. The research design will detail whatever pertinent information on the project area is available and integrate that information into a plan developed to conduct the actual fieldwork, detailing field methods, what kinds of sites are expected, and the like. Once the research design and background work are complete, the fieldwork can begin.

Background Studies

Before conducting fieldwork, archaeologists must do background research on the area in which they intend to work. First, they must determine what other archaeological work has been done in the area, what was found, and how the findings may relate to the current project. A number of other sources, including ethnographic data, historical records, and any other available information, may also be consulted.

To help understand the prehistory, particularly the late prehistory, of an area, archaeologists will conduct research on the ethnographic groups known to have occupied that area or similar areas. Such research can provide a great deal of information that could be used to build models of past behaviors. For instance, if one were working in a desert, one would want to know how contemporary people lived in such environments, how they adapted, what they ate, how they were organized, and so forth, so that such information could serve as a starting point, an analog, for research into the archaeology of the area in question. Much of this type of information would be used as ethnographic analogy (see Chapter 3), but some other information would be more directly applicable.

Historical records may contain a great deal of information about the archaeology of an area. Such information might be found in the written records and accounts of the culture under investigation. For example, those working on ancient Egyptian materials would use any pertinent hieroglyphics. Ancient narrative texts, such as the Bible, may also be useful. Historical accounts and narratives might provide an outline of what happened in the past and might serve as a basis for further research, as was the case with the English colony at Jamestown.

In some cases, there may be historical records on or about nonliterate peoples who were encountered in a region. Some of these records may relate directly to the people, such as the diaries of explorers describing native people. Other records may be less descriptive of native cultures but still useful to researchers, such as birth, marriage, and death records at missions.

Remote Sensing Techniques for Finding Sites

Another important way of locating sites is through the use of **remote sensing,** a group of techniques that permits the detection of phenomena, unobserved or unnoticed by the human eye, in a nondestructive manner from above the surface (Sever 2000; Kvamme 2005). Remote sensing techniques range from aerial photography to space-based laser imaging and mapping. Information generated using remote sensing techniques, in combination with the precision of GPS systems and GIS analysis, allow for the integration of data sets for computer analysis (Limp 2000; Levy et al. 2001). Remote sensing technology is revolutionizing the ways sites are discovered, how they are recorded, and even how they are investigated.

The primary remote sensing technique is aerial photography, first used in 1906 to photograph Stonehenge. From the air, the observer can see many ancient features that cannot be seen from the ground, such as roads, footpaths, buried features, fortifications, fields, and crop marks. Natural features, such as ancient river channels, old shorelines, and undisturbed landforms, can also be detected. For instance, patterns in the growth of grass in a field can be seen from the air as areas of lush growth that contrast with areas of poor growth. Areas of poor growth might indicate a buried wall that is interfering with the growth of the plants above it.

Until recently, standard black-and-white or color film was used in most aerial photography. Today, multispectral (e.g., infrared) photography is also used and can distinguish minute differences in vegetation, elevation, soil type, moisture, and other characteristics that delineate ancient features. Morever, film is being replaced by digital imaging systems. Most archaeological aerial photography is conducted from manned aircraft, but some is now being done from space and some from remote-controlled model airplanes flying at less than 500 feet in altitude.

Other aerial remote sensing techniques include the use of airborne lasers, such as the Airborne Oceanographic Lidar (ADI), which can map terrain, including cultural features, with great precision. Airborne radars can also be employed. For example, Synthetic Aperture Radar (SAR) sends multiwavelength radar signals to the ground and measures the radar energy returned. Different materials and features return different wavelengths, which are then mapped. A space-based version of SAR was used to locate the ancient city of Ubar (Highlight 5.2).

More recently, satellites are being used to locate sites. In Egypt, Sarah Parcak of the University of Alabama, Birmingham, has used photographs taken from satellites to identify hundreds of previously unknown settlements and to further map locations.

A number of other remote sensing techniques are employed underwater. Magnetometers and side-scan sonar are used to locate materials on the ocean floor, such as

HIGHLIGHT **5.2**

Ubar: The Atlantis of the Sands

The legend of a lost city in the Arabian peninsula had been passed down for some 1,700 years. This city, Ubar, was purported to have been a prosperous trading center dealing in frankincense, a highly valuable incense manufactured from the sap of the frankincense tree, which grows in the region. In great demand all over the ancient world, frankincense was used for fragrance, medicinal purposes, and funeral pyres. It was said that Ubar became very rich from the trade. Then, the story goes, the residents of Ubar became decadent and wicked, and the city was destroyed by Allah, buried, and lost in the sand.

Over the years, the Ubar legend intrigued a number of explorers and archaeologists, who made several attempts to locate the city. The city was thought to have existed in the Empty Quarter, a vast region of the southern Arabian peninsula so named because of its extensive sand dunes. Every attempt to find the city, called the "Atlantis of the Sands" by T. E. Lawrence (Lawrence of Arabia), failed.

In the early 1980s, Nick Clapp, an amateur archaeologist from Los Angeles, researched the various records, maps, and accounts of Ubar and concluded that the city was in the region of southern Oman. He deduced that well-worn caravan trails must have led to the city and that those trails might still be visible from above. Clapp obtained the cooperation of NASA and was given access to ground terrain imaging (SAR) radar data taken from the space shuttle. Some trails and roads, most of modern origin, were apparent on the images. The wavelengths reflected by ancient caravan tracks are different from the wavelengths of vehicle tracks, so the modern roads could be electronically removed from the photos. The resulting image showed one ancient caravan track crossing the desert: the road to Ubar.

Two expeditions to Oman to find the city were undertaken in 1990 and 1991. The expedition members followed the caravan track to an oasis called Shisur, located near the eastern edge of the Empty Quarter in southern Oman. An archaeological site was found there, and test excavations were begun to determine whether the site was Ubar. In 1992, evidence uncovered at Shisur indicated that it was indeed Ubar.

shipwrecks. The devices are towed behind ships to map the ocean floor. Anomalies are recorded and promising contacts are later investigated by divers or robots carrying cameras. NASA is planning to send a remotely operated vehicle (ROV) to explore the ocean of Europa, one of the moons of Jupiter. Europa's ocean is cold and covered with ice; to test the cameras under similar conditions, NASA is photographing the ships of a whaling fleet trapped and sunk by pack ice off northern Alaska in 1871. Still other remote sensing techniques can be used to explore below the surface of a site once it has been discovered.

Sampling

The goal of an archaeological survey is to detect and record sites. Background research and remote sensing data are helpful tools in this task, but an on-the-ground examination is always necessary. When the area to be surveyed is small and the entire project area can be examined for sites, the result is a complete or 100 percent survey. When the area is

NASA photo of the ancient caravan road (see arrow) to Ubar.

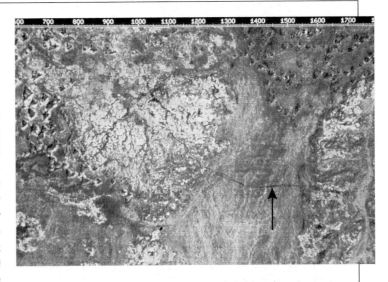

Ubar was revealed as a small walled city, built around the oasis well, that flourished from about 4,800 to about 1,700 years ago. Frankincense was processed in the city and then shipped across the ancient world by caravan. As the city drew water from the well, the water table dropped and the land adjacent to it became more and more unstable. At some time between 1,700 and 1,500 years ago, part of the city fell into the well. Ubar was then abandoned, and its remains were consumed by the desert (Clapp 1998).

A television program on the discovery of Ubar, called "Lost City of Arabia," was made by public television. Excavations at the site by Juris Zarins were completed after four years, and you can get information on the progress of this project on the Web by using the key word *Ubar*.

CRITICAL **THINKING** QUESTIONS

1. What was the role of background information in the quest for Ubar?
2. What was the role of remote sensing in the discovery and excavation of Ubar?

too large to be completely surveyed, some sort of sampling must be done. A number of sampling approaches are possible. The approach the archaeologist chooses depends on environmental conditions (vegetation and terrain), project specifications, background information, remote sensing data, or other factors (Orton 2000).

A **judgment sample** (or *nonrandom selected sample*) is based on the archaeologist's judgment or special interest—his or her experience and previous understanding of the region. For example, the archaeologist may make a brief reconnaissance of an area and select a few likely locations to examine. To further define sample boundaries, the archaeologist may divide the project area into structured units, such as 1-by-5-kilometer transects or 1-kilometer squares, which the researcher carefully lays out using surveying equipment. Alternatively, the selection of sample units to survey may be intentionally biased, such as concentrating along a river where sites are thought to be located. Judgment samples offer flexibility, but inferences drawn from a judgment sample cannot be generalized to a statistical model of the whole area.

A **statistical sample** is one in which sample units are chosen randomly: each sample unit has the same mathematical chance of being chosen to be surveyed as any other. The units in a statistical sample can be used to predict characteristics of the whole study area. Thus, statistical sampling allows the researcher to survey a portion of an area and be able to construct a predictive model of sites and their locations within the total survey area. An advantage of random sampling is that it forces an objective examination of the entire area: the researchers survey everywhere, even in places they may think are not likely to contain sites. It is often important to know where sites do not exist. Many archaeologists use a combination of judgment sampling and statistical sampling in their work.

Sampling approaches and survey methods influence what types of sites are found and recognized. For example, if a few people survey a large area quickly, they may locate large sites but miss small ones. The topography (landscape) of the survey area also may be a factor. Steeper, more overgrown, less visible, and less accessible places may contain sites that remain undiscovered.

Sometimes, archaeologists may suspect that buried sites are present, even in areas where ground visibility is good. In such cases, archaeologists may dig small test pits at intervals to look for sites. To look deeper, a backhoe may be used to cut a trench into the soil to see whether a buried site is present. Some sites are buried so deep, however, that they are missed and remain undiscovered.

Recording Sites

Once a site is located, information about it is recorded. The archaeologist gives the site a name or number, describes the site, establishes its boundaries, identifies surface finds (artifacts, ecofacts, and features), and analyzes its environmental context (vegetation, hydrology, geology, etc.). A map of the site will be made, initially often just a sketch map produced with the aid of a compass and measuring tape, and the location of the site will be plotted on a regional map using topographic features and GPS readings.

In many cases, a formal record of the site is prepared on government forms and submitted to a regional site-record clearinghouse for assignment of a permanent site number and entry into the regional site database. In the United States, site-record databases are maintained by each state, and sites are assigned permanent site numbers based on state, county, and number. For example, the 103rd site recorded in Kern County, California, would have the permanent number of CA-KER-103 (some people use the number 4-KER-103, with "4" referring to California, the fourth state in an alphabetical list). Future researchers searching the site-record database would find a site indicated on a map and be able to retrieve the record describing the site, its contents, location, and references to any work that had been conducted there.

Excavating Sites

A great deal can be learned from the process of finding and recording sites. Various kinds of information can be obtained from sites without excavating them. Artifacts and ecofacts observed on the surface of the site can provide information about age, function, and size of a site, and its geography (e.g., along a river, on a mountain slope) would be recorded. In some cases, the archaeologist would collect some of the materials from the surface of the site for later analysis. All of these data can be used to construct and test models about settlement pattern, resource use, change over time, and the like. However, to obtain detailed information, excavation is required.

Ideally, sites are chosen for excavation because they are thought to contain information that addresses particular research questions. The following account, for example, describes finds at an excavation designed to understand the purpose of a prehistoric site in Africa:

> Along one edge of the cemetery we found a small row of pots just below the surface, each containing an infant burial, the tiny bones caked or sprinkled with red ochre pigment. Why were these remains in pots when others interred in the cemetery were not? And why were the pots placed in a separate area apart from other burials, including other infants? Forensic analysis revealed that the infants were preterm or less than one month of age and appeared to have died natural deaths. We hypothesized that these pot-burials represented a special-purpose prehistoric graveyard for the miscarried, the stillborn, and infants who may have died too soon to have full status as family members.
>
> By analogy with local historic cultures, we wondered if babies were expected to survive for one month before being presented to the moon as a family member and named. In this graveyard, what African limbo did the pot-burial infants occupy? Had their mothers suspected sorcery? Had they believed that the souls of these babies would reenter them in their next pregnancies? But these were questions we could not answer. Many more sites would have to be excavated just to establish the frequency, range, distribution, and time frame of pot-burials as a pattern of behavior in African prehistory.

Often, however, particular questions do not guide the research. Instead, sites are excavated to rescue or salvage the information they contain before they are destroyed by some development. The decision to excavate is based on the nature of the development and the funding and time available.

In either case, information from the site survey is used to determine whether excavation is warranted. The archaeological record is a nonrenewable resource, and excavation is destructive. Thus, excavations should be undertaken only when necessary, so as to preserve the archaeological record. Even when a site is excavated, a portion is left unexcavated, if possible, so that future generations of archaeologists with improved field methods and analytical tools can obtain additional information.

Mapping the Site

One of the first tasks of an archaeologist working at a site is to make a detailed map of the site (the map made by the person who first found the site is usually not detailed enough and has to be redone). This map has to record the surface manifestations of the site, its extent, the location and detail of features, its topography, and its natural setting.

Detailed site mapping is done with the aid of an instrument, such as a standard transit, theodolite, plane table, or laser transit. The instrument is set up on the main reference point on the site, called the site **datum,** and all of the mapping shots are taken from that point. The distance, azimuth, and elevation of each shot are recorded so that all of the items and features can be mapped in three dimensions and elevation included in the site map. Using the site datum, a grid is usually established over the site so that the location of materials on the surface of the site and excavation units can be plotted. As excavation proceeds, the subsurface materials discovered will be added to the map.

Many archaeologists are now using total stations—laser transits with an onboard computer that records the data from each shot—or GPS-based surveying systems. These data can be downloaded into a computer and, with the aid of a mapping program, the computer can quickly and easily generate a map of the site and its contents (Figure 5.1).

In addition to mapping the surface of the site, ground-based remote sensing techniques, called **geophysical survey,** may be used to map below the surface (Clark 1990; Herz and Garrison 1998; Heimmer and De Vore 2000; Roskams 2001:51). Geophysical survey methods consist of various noninvasive and nondestructive techniques to discover buried features within sites, such as walls, trenches, floors, pits, burials, and hearths. These

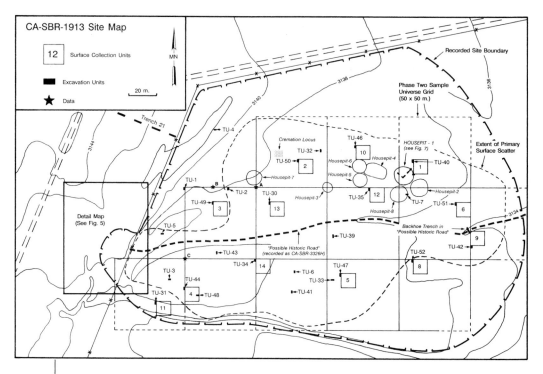

figure 5.1

A Site Map. Map of the late prehistoric site of Guapiabit (CA-SBR-1913), San Bernardino County, California. Notice the various details, including the site topography and hydrology, location of modern features (fences and roads), house pits, and location of surface collection and excavation units.

Source: Based on Mark Q. Sutton and Joan S. Schneider, 1996, "Archaeological Investigations at Guapiabit: CA-SBR-1913," *San Bernardino County Museum Association Quarterly* 43(4), Figure 4. Used by permission of the San Bernardino County Museum Association.

techniques can help archaeologists determine where and where not to excavate. Geophysical survey instruments measure the fluctuations, alterations, or responses of an electrical or magnetic field. Data from these measurements distinguish "normal" soil from disturbed soil and identify other anomalies that might be archaeological in nature.

The simplest geophysical instrument is a metal detector, used to locate metal objects buried in the soil. Metal detectors are used in sites thought to contain metal, such as historical sites or Bronze Age sites in the Old World, or evidence of modern materials intrusive in older sites. Another instrument is the *magnetometer,* which measures variations in the strength of the earth's magnetic field. Measurements are taken at points on the site grid to create a map of the magnetic field strength across the site. Two other techniques, *electrical resistivity* and *electrical conductivity,* are used to measure the electrical properties of the soil. Both instruments pass an electric charge through the soil and build a picture of the subsurface according to the degree to which it resists or conducts electric current (Figure 5.2).

Another geophysical survey tool is **ground-penetrating radar** (GPR). An active radar signal is beamed into the ground, reflects off materials in the soil, and returns a signal (Watters 2001; Conyers 2004). As in other geophysical techniques, signal data are used to create a map showing anomalies. The GPR device is placed on a small sled and dragged across the surface of the site. About 4,000 square meters in a day can be covered using a GPR unit.

Deciding Where to Dig

After mapping the site, the next step is deciding precisely where to excavate. Excavation plans have to be flexible to accommodate time and weather and the unexpected. Information from background research, mapping, testing, and surface collections is used to decide on an excavation plan.

The extent of the site may already be known, and there may already be some understanding of the surface distribution of artifacts and the location of features. In some cases, information may already exist about the extent and depth and condition of the deposit, the nature and location of features, and artifact concentrations. In addition, it is possible that some geophysical exploration was already done, providing a picture below the surface of the site. All this information would be used in formulating an excavation plan.

Decisions about where to dig also may be guided by a **surface collection**—the materials found lying on the surface of the site. Archaeologists might collect only certain materials, such as temporal types of artifacts, or may elect to collect everything from the surface of the site. Any materials collected from the surface are mapped, and the distributions of the materials are used as a guide to what may be below the surface. Because the process of collection creates materials that must be stored, some archaeologists attempt to analyze surface finds without collecting them (Beck and Jones 1994). The main drawback of this procedure is that the artifacts are not readily available for further study in the future.

Another way to examine the subsurface portion of a site is to conduct limited **test-level excavation.** Guided by the results of surface features or collections and any geophysical information, archaeologists may dig one or more test pits in a site. The goal is to gather information to help determine the content and importance of the site and to

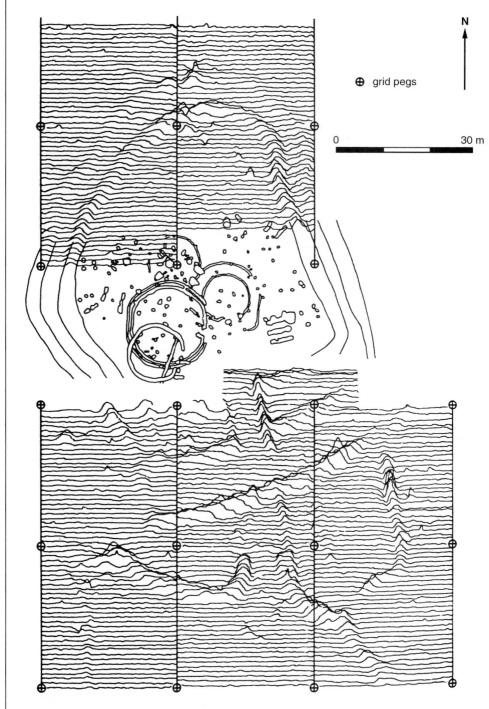

⊕ grid pegs

0　　　　　　　　　　　30 m

figure 5.2

Magnetometer Results.　A magnetometer can be used to locate anomalies under the surface, which can then be targeted for excavation to reveal the archaeological materials beneath.

Source: Anthony Clark, 1996, *Seeing Beneath the Soil: Prospecting Methods in Archaeology* (London: Batsford), p. 138. Used by permission of B. T. Batsford Ltd.

guide further excavations, if any. Often the testing effort is enough to recover the desired information, or it may reveal that the site does not contain the kinds of information the researchers expected to find. Even if no further work is done, the data from testing still add to our understanding of the past.

Finally, decisions about where and how much to dig are based also on the sampling methods to be used, described earlier in this chapter.

Digging

All excavation involves actually digging into sites, removing soil; locating, recording, and recovering various archaeological materials found; and keeping records of any other important information discovered, such as soil types and layers. Excavation "holes" are typically called *units* or *pits* and vary in size and number, depending on the type of project and the kinds of information sought (Figure 5.3). Unit types and sizes include small postholes,

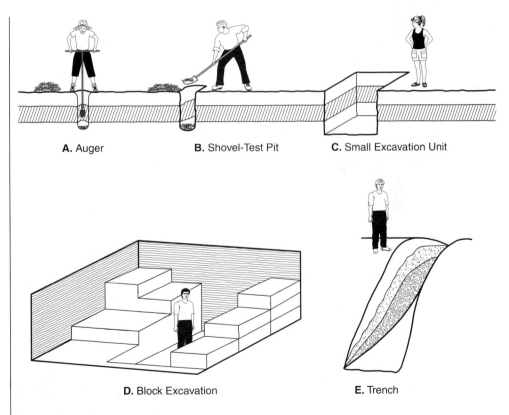

A. Auger   **B.** Shovel-Test Pit   **C.** Small Excavation Unit

D. Block Excavation   **E.** Trench

figure 5.3

Types of Excavation Units. Shown here are (A) an auger hole, (B) a shovel-test pit, (C) a small (1-by-1-meter) excavation unit, (D) a block excavation, and (E) a trench. Units differ according to the volume of soil moved, the degree of control used in removing the soil, and the amount of stratigraphic detail visible in the deposit.

or auger probes (e.g., 10 to 30 cm in diameter), shovel-test pits (about 50 cm square), **standard excavation units** (1 to 2 meters square), **block excavations** (2 to 10 meters square or larger, often a series of connected standard units), and **trenches** (1 to several meters wide and as long as necessary). Each type of unit typically is excavated to the bottom of the cultural deposit and into the natural soil. If the deposit is too deep, special safety measures, such as shoring, are necessary. In some cases, *balks* (narrow pillars of soil) are left between units to retain a record of the stratigraphy across a site. The soil profiles exposed in the walls of units and trenches also show stratigraphy.

Whatever methods are employed, excavations must be tied into the site datum so that the location, or **provenience,** of the materials recovered can be recorded accurately. To accomplish this, units are mapped on the site grid and assigned a unique number—Auger Hole 13, Test Unit 5, Trench C, and the like. Materials coming from these units then can be tracked as the excavation progresses.

Most excavation is done by hand with small tools such as trowels and paintbrushes. Workers typically scrape the entire surface of a square a few centimeters at a time, repeating the process. Shovels are used to move excavated soil or to remove any natural soils covering a site. When fragile artifacts, floors, or burials are found, work with larger tools stops, and field hands switch to smaller, more precise tools, even dental tools. In some cases, a skiploader, bulldozer, backhoe, or other heavy equipment may be used to remove natural deposits, dig trenches, move large objects such as columns or statues, or backfill completed excavations.

In mapping and excavation, the location of the unit provides the "horizontal" (x- and y-axes) context of any materials found. It is also important to know how deep materials were below the site surface—the "vertical" context. Archaeologists therefore excavate in "levels" of some standard depth, one level at a time. For example, if the level were arbitrarily set at 10 centimeters, the unit would be excavated from 0 to 10 centimeters, then from 10 to 20, then from 20 to 30, and so forth. In most cases, archaeologists use the metric system (meters and centimeters) to measure unit size, levels, and dimensions of artifacts. Most historical archaeologists use the English system (feet and inches), because it is known that the makers of most historical materials used that system.

An advantage of using standard levels is that the volume of soil from each level is the same and materials from each level can be more easily compared. Other "vertical" controls may be based on recognized stratigraphy (see Figures 1.1 and 4.2), with separate strata being excavated separately. Whatever the method, the purpose is to record precisely where things were found so they can be compared with other materials.

Unique features found in a unit or level, such as hearths or burials, are excavated separately. Other examples of unique features are caches, postholes, walls, floors, mosaics, and architectural sculptures. Separate excavation of features keeps together materials deposited at the same time, even when they happen to spill over into different levels.

Excavation projects can become very complex and can involve more than one site. For example, a multisite project conducted by researchers at the University of North Carolina in the 1960s had the aim of reconstructing and comparing Cherokee life just prior to and during contact with European settlers. Researchers wanted to try to assess the changes in the way Cherokee people lived and the overall rate of change in material culture that occurred following first contact. Many other questions arose, such as the movement of native peoples after contact and changes in their nutrition and health. Work on each site was guided by a research design and an excavation plan that would address particular key questions.

Consider, for example, the excavation of a feature in a site that a farmer discovered in his cornfield along a branch of the Little Tennessee River (our description is based on a student's field report). The farmer called the university after his plow turned up stone tools. The tools were Cherokee of a known type and period, and a survey and test pit identified a buried feature to be excavated—a mound, postholes, and floor of a dwelling. This feature hinted at a story that careful excavation could reveal. There proved to be two houses, one atop the other.

First the Cherokee had carried sand in baskets from the river to create a low mound. The impression of the basket weave was preserved in the wet sand. Experienced diggers with fine brushes exposed this evidence, and a photographer, cartographer, and artist recorded it.

The Cherokee drove posts into the mound to form the circular walls of their house. Using mathematical principles, archaeologists were able to infer the height of the house from the circumference and depth of the "postholes," which actually were just discolored soil from where the posts had decomposed in the earth.

On the framework of posts, drawn together at the top to form a smoke hole over a central hearth, the Cherokee wove in branches to create a wall that they then plastered with clay. Archaeologists found the source of this clay nearby, along the Little Tennessee River. The hearth was made of the clay also, and artifacts were found in the hearth—a good place to look because people often do not try to retrieve objects they drop in the fire. Artifacts from the hearth at this level of the excavation revealed a traditional, precontact, inland Cherokee tool assemblage.

At some point during the occupation of their fine large house, the Cherokee had to deal with a flood. Evidence of a flood could be seen in the reconstruction of the original landscape and the condition of the house mound, which showed an area of sudden subsidence. A low rough wall of river rocks showed where the Cherokee had tried to shore up their mound to protect their house from the flood.

They were successful, but evidence also showed that the house ultimately had burned down. There was a large quantity of burned clay, and the color and texture of the clay revealed that both the inside and outside surfaces of the house walls had been daubed with clay. The inside clay burned black, and the outside clay burned red because of the different exposure of the two surfaces to air during the fire. (Clay fired in the absence of oxygen is darker colored; clay burned in the open air is red.)

After the fire, the Cherokee raked the burned clay rubble into small piles off

Cherokee house feature A: double ring of postholes with hearth and burned clay daub.

Cherokee house feature B: shoring of the house mound against river flooding.

to the side of the mound, and then right away they built another house on the same spot. The second house was much smaller, clay-daubed only in spots and only on the outside, and the hearth was much smaller, too. Clearly, fewer people were living there. Why had the Cherokee taken less care with this house?

In the second hearth, archaeologists found artifacts associated with European contact, such as manufactured kaolin clay pipes and glass beads. They also excavated tool types more typical of coastal Cherokee, such as worked sharks' teeth. Had patterns of trade changed? Did the same family rebuild the house, or were the occupants from farther to the east?

Burials were associated with the feature, all linked to the second, more recent, occupation. Most of the deceased were children ages 4 to 12, buried on their sides in a flexed position in shallow graves. The skeletal remains showed signs of malnutrition. Uncharacteristically for the Cherokee, the dead were buried without grave goods, and, also uncharacteristically, the graves were right in the mound not far from the door of the house. Analogical reasoning based on ethnographic information about the Cherokee from the historical period led researchers to wonder why this house door did *not* face east and why the burying had been done so close to the house. What did the differences in burial practices mean? The archaeologists felt that all signs pointed to a native population under stress, and that events related to contact with European settlers were the most likely cause.

The second house also had burned down, and whoever was left had then abandoned the site. The hard burned clay lay over the house floor and covered the postholes and hearth. It was this burned clay that archaeologists initially had to jackhammer away after removing the surface soil from the farmer's cornfield.

After the excavation was completed, the archaeologists restored the surface soil to the site and even helped the farmer replant his corn. Other sites in the area confirmed these findings or addressed other questions, such as the extent of Cherokee farming at the time of contact. Could it be that an ancestor of this farmer learned how to grow corn from the Cherokee living here on the Little Tennessee River?

So, how should one proceed to excavate a site? Which methods should be used and which should not? To select the appropriate methods, one has to go back to the research design. Archaeologists have a variety of possible field methods at their disposal and choose particular methods to accomplish specific tasks. If the goal is to look for the remains of houses, the use of an auger would probably not work well, but if the goal is to find the extent of a charcoal layer, the auger would be a good choice. Such decisions have to be made on a daily basis, and the more experienced the archaeologist is, the better the decision making.

Recovering and Cataloging Data

In the course of excavation, archaeologists discover artifacts and ecofacts in the soil **in situ** (Latin for "in place"). Materials found in situ are carefully exposed, excavated, mapped, often photographed, and then collected and separately labeled and bagged. Many archaeology students have spent many hours washing individual potsherds (or shards—pieces of broken pottery) and labeling them with unique identifying numbers in India ink or permanent marker. Special samples, such as charcoal from a hearth for radiocarbon analysis or soil for pollen analysis, would be mapped and bagged separately. Workers in each unit maintain a record of all the information from each level. All the information is recorded on unit and level records that are maintained by the workers in each unit. When the units are completed, all of the records are placed in a central location for easy accounting and access.

Often, workers miss very small items, such as flakes or beads or small bones, while digging. Most excavations practice **screening** (or *sieving* or *sifting*) of the excavated soil to recover missed items. Buckets of soil may be dry-screened by hand or in a mechanical sifter or wet-screened using water to wash away soil to reveal artifacts and ecofacts. Probably the mesh size most commonly used by archaeologists is one-quarter inch. However, smaller mesh sizes may be used to rescreen soil to capture very small objects, especially dietary evidence. Some artifacts and many ecofacts, including entire taxa of

Typical handwork in an excavation unit.

Screening excavated soil for minute objects.

small animals, are too small to be caught in quarter-inch mesh. Thus, only the bones of larger animals are found, greatly confusing the interpretation of the dietary evidence at a site (Thomas 1969; Grayson 1984; Shaffer 1992; Shaffer and Sanchez 1994; Gobalet 1989; Gordon 1993). Thus, many archaeologists are shifting to one-eighth-inch mesh as the standard.

When all the desired materials and samples have been removed from the excavation unit, it is photographed again, a final mapping of the unit is done, and typically a soil profile map of one or more walls of the unit is drawn. Usually the unit is then filled in with the soil that was removed. Sometimes, however, the excavation may be left open for public viewing or other special purposes.

Laboratory processing of artifacts and ecofacts is the first step in classification and analysis (see Chapter 6). Materials are brought to the archaeological laboratory at the sponsoring institution or to a temporary field laboratory set up near the site. There, materials are sorted, cleaned, measured, and classified, and a catalog of the materials is compiled (Banning 2000; Sutton and Arkush 2006). Artifacts might be sorted, for example, as pottery, stone, or metal, and then each of these general categories is sorted and classified into types. After being sorted and classified, each item is cataloged with a record of its attributes and provenience (original location). This record becomes part of a computer database.

Working with Specialists

Archaeology is a team effort because most archaeological field projects involve much more than archaeology. Archaeologists need to know about many other subjects, including past environments, hydrology, geology, geomorphology, biological anthropology, zoology, and botany. No one can be an expert in all of these other disciplines, so archaeologists seek the assistance of specialists.

Specialists often are members of the field research team. While a site is being excavated, a geologist might examine the region for clues to ancient landscapes, a biologist might inventory all the plants and animals in the region, a hydrologist might map water courses and springs and, with the geomorphologist, indicate which sources of water might have been available to the people inhabiting the site. In the laboratory also, specialists work with samples of recovered materials. Pollen samples go to the palynologist, flaked stone to a lithic (stone) technologist, and human skeletal remains to an osteologist. The archaeologist incorporates the findings of specialists into his or her interpretations of the dig. Table 5.1 gives an idea of the interdisciplinary nature of archaeology.

t a b l e 5 . 1

Specialists Assisting Archaeologists

SPECIALIST	WHAT THEY DO
Geologist/geomorphologists	Assist in the identification of rock and soil materials. Examine and interpret geological structures, such as stratigraphic layers, lakeshores, springs, and landforms.
Palynologists	Process and analyze pollen from archaeological sites, primarily for use in environmental reconstruction.
Osteologists	Examine human skeletal remains to determine age, sex, and stature of the individual. Look for evidence of injury and disease.
Chemists	Conduct various chemical analyses of archaeological materials.
Physicists	Assist in the application of dating methods, such as radiocarbon.
Botanists	Assist in the identification of plant remains.
Zoologists	Assist in the identification of animal remains.
Molecular biologists	Identify ancient DNA in archaeological specimens.
Computer scientists	Assist with statistical analyses, mapping, and model building. Often conduct the GIS work.

Practical Aspects of Fieldwork

To conduct any fieldwork, it is necessary to plan the work, obtain personnel and equipment, actually do the work, manage the information collected, and produce a report on the findings. Whatever the scale of the project, these issues have to be addressed. If the project is small, perhaps involving only one or two people, they are relatively minor. Some projects, however, involve dozens, sometimes even hundreds, of people and require formal administration.

Many archaeologists are employed by government agencies, colleges and universities, large companies, and other organizations that already possess various sorts of administrators. In these cases, a personnel department already exists to deal with time sheets, payroll, benefits, accounting, insurance, travel claims, and the like. Archaeologists who operate their own small companies, however, have to do all the administrative work themselves—a task few are specifically trained for. Some projects use volunteers and thus avoid the pay and benefits side of personnel, but logistical matters will still have to be dealt with.

Funding and Staffing

Funding an archaeological project, even a small one, is always an issue. If the project is related to some sort of construction activity (either private or government), the funding for archaeology generally is included in the budget for the organization's environmental impact study. Other archaeological work conducted by a government agency, such as the building of an interpretive center, would be proposed and funded by the agency on a case-by-case basis.

Obtaining funding for archaeological work not related to some development or public works project is more difficult. In many small projects, volunteers pay their own expenses for the privilege of participating. Archaeological field schools and classes operate in a similar manner: the school pays some of the costs, and students pay their own expenses. Archaeologists also seek funding from granting agencies, including universities, local companies, and foundations, and national agencies such as the National Science Foundation and the National Endowment for the Humanities. Large research grants, though difficult to obtain, are excellent sources of long-term support.

Any project requires a crew of trained and experienced people organized in an efficient manner (Figure 5.4). As members of the crew gain experience, they are promoted to supervisory positions and may eventually lead their own projects. The overall project is directed by the principal investigator (PI). Generally, the PI is the lead archaeologist who planned the work, wrote the research design, and is in charge of the project administration, personnel, and research. The field crew is supervised by the field director, and the field laboratory is supervised by the lab director, each of whom reports to the PI. Any work done on the project after the fieldwork is completed also would be supervised by the PI, who is also responsible for the completion of the project report.

In the field, there has to be some system to keep track of the data coming from the site, both records and materials. In large projects, this can consume a great deal of time, and a person might have this responsibility full time. Space for the storage of equipment and

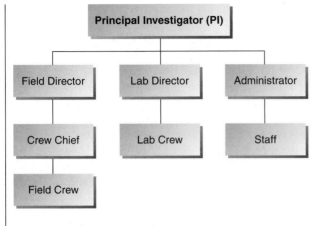

f i g u r e   5 . 4

Organizational Chart for an Archaeological Project. Archaeological projects may be administered through a formal organization chart such as the one shown here.

materials is always required—in tents, trailers, or permanent buildings. There also may be a need for facilities for the crew and for a field laboratory. In some cases, a camp supervisor and cook are needed.

Security is always a concern, for it is necessary to protect the excavations, equipment, personnel, and data at a site. Looters sometimes target sites where archaeologists are working, believing that valuable materials must be present. A site left unguarded at night may be looted even while the project is ongoing. After archaeologists complete their work, a site may be at the mercy of vandals, art thieves, or souvenir hunters. Police or army units may be needed to guard sites with commercially valuable materials, such as gold. Even ordinary curiosity seekers can cause problems if not managed during their visits, so a site guide may be needed to deal with the public. Popular sites may warrant the construction of a visitor center, and some sites have become parks managed by governmental agencies. Most archaeological parks (see Chapter 13) receive a constant flow of tourists.

Curation

Data collected from the field have to be managed in some systematic manner. Computerization facilitates records storage, but artifacts and ecofacts must be cataloged, analyzed, and conserved. Conservation might involve stabilizing fragile materials or storing perishables at a certain temperature and humidity. A temporary laboratory at the site during excavation might accomplish this, or materials might be sent to a professional lab for later processing. The process of conserving material, preparing it for storage, and then storing it is called **curation** (Kenworthy et al. 1985).

Curation often poses a challenge because of space limitations and the need to protect stored collections from damage from pests, flooding, fire, and theft. In addition, archaeological collections, along with the associated records, must be accessible to other researchers. As new analytical methods and technologies are developed, and as more sites are destroyed, stored collections will become increasingly important as a source of new data.

For many archaeological projects, it is legally mandated that collections and records be permanently stored in a formal curation facility. Unfortunately, few such facilities exist and these are often full. Therefore, many collections get stored in temporary facilities where they can be neglected, lost, or even discarded due to lack of space. This "curation crisis" is a major problem in archaeology all over the world.

Occupational Hazards in Archaeology

Archaeological fieldwork can be hazardous (Poirier and Feder 2001), another reason why good project management is so important. In addition to accidents associated with working outdoors, such as falls, bruises, sprains, and strains, fieldworkers may face lack of water, poor food, harmful animals, and inadequate sanitation. Injured or sick workers may experience delays in receiving medical care.

Some sites are more dangerous than others. For example, the fungal disease coccidioidomycosis (Valley Fever) is endemic in the American Southwest and parts of California and can be contracted by breathing the dust generated by excavation. Old buildings and animal dung can harbor other problem fungi. Hantavirus, a very serious disease, can be contracted from working in old buildings, dry caves, and other places where infected mice might be present. Rabies can be contracted by breathing in vapors that contain urine from infected animals, such as bats living in caves. In some environments, mosquitoes and ticks may carry harmful diseases. Museums and the specimens in them may be affected by rodent, insect, mold, and fungal infestations that can cause related health problems in workers. It is remotely possible for disease pathogens to remain viable in archaeological specimens recovered from sites for laboratory analysis, especially human and animal remains. Workers at historical sites where mining and industrial activities took place may risk exposure to harmful chemicals such as lead, mercury, arsenic, beryllium, and petroleum. Archaeological work on military bases raises concerns about fieldworkers encountering live ordnance.

A *nonhazard* worth mentioning is the famous "Mummy's Curse"—the notion that angry supernatural forces act against those who dare to disturb remains of the past. This myth originated in the untimely coincidental deaths of a few people involved in the excavation of the tomb of Tutankhamen in 1922 and subsequently was popularized by Hollywood in movies about the vengeful mummy. However, there is no scientific evidence of any such curse or of any other supernatural sanction against those doing archaeology (Nelson 2002). It is true that all the people who worked on the Tutankhamen project 80-plus years ago have died, but so have most people who were alive at the time!

Ethics in Archaeological Fieldwork

Archaeologists have to consider a number of ethical issues, from dealing with vandals to publishing results in a timely manner. Many potential ethical problems are related to doing fieldwork. Archaeologists try to conduct their work in an ethical manner, but there are areas of conflict. For example, in the United States there has been conflict between archaeologists and Native Americans over the ownership of sites, artifacts, and remains (see Chapter 13).

A prime professional principle is that of basic science and scholarship in general: the archaeologist will remain objective and honest, will not falsify data, and will use the best methods and practices available (Highlight 5.3). Archaeologists also must remain sensitive to the work of others, consult with others working in the same area or on the

HIGHLIGHT **5.3**

Scandal! Planting Artifacts in Japan

For decades, a Japanese archaeologist, Shinichi Fujimura, exhibited an uncanny ability to locate sites and artifacts dating from the Middle and Upper Paleolithic in Japan. Fujimura's work pushed back human antiquity in Japan by hundreds of thousands of years and illuminated details about the settlement patterns, trade networks, and technology of the Paleolithic people of Japan. In late 2000, however, it was discovered that Fujimura had planted many of the materials he "found" (Magnier 2000; Normile 2001; Romey 2001). The finds he discovered were fake!

Fujimura was an "amateur" archaeologist with no formal training. He educated himself, became involved in archaeological projects, and began to discover many important sites and artifacts. He gained a great deal of field experience, became well known, won many awards, and rose through the ranks to become the senior director of the Tohoku Paleolithic Institute in Japan.

Over the years, some archaeologists privately questioned Fujimura's luck, but archaeology in Japan is a pursuit of "gentlemen" not inclined to scrutinize scientists or their finds. No one really investigated. Eventually, the private concerns of some came to the attention of several investigative newspaper reporters, and a "sting" operation was set up. Fujimura was videotaped planting artifacts in a site early in the morning and "finding" them a few days later. He had made some of the artifacts. Others were real, stolen from museums or other sites. He may have faked data at some 300 Paleolithic sites (Ikawa-Smith 2001).

This deception has created serious problems. All interpretations based on information from the sites with fake data have to be discarded, and understanding of the Paleolithic in Japan has been set back by many years. Books in which the sites are mentioned have to be rewritten, and any materials that Fujimura came in contact with are now suspect. A huge effort will be needed to repair the damage. Also, the reputations of all archaeologists, and all scientists, in Japan have been undermined. Science relies on the honesty of its practitioners, and any violation of that trust is a serious matter. It will be many years before archaeology in Japan can recover.

Still from video surveillance footage of Shinichi Fujimura planting artifacts.

CRITICAL **THINKING** QUESTIONS

1. Fujimura was dismissed from his post following his confession, and he was hospitalized soon after. He later admitted to planting artifacts at more than 40 other sites in Japan. In archaeology, why is this kind of fraud more than just a crime?

2. Which of the ethical issues in archaeology described in this chapter is relevant to the Fujimura case? With what other kinds of ethical issues must archaeologists be concerned?

same problem, not steal the work of others, and make the results of their work available to others within some reasonable time.

Because archaeology is a destructive enterprise, it is important that the archaeological record be conserved. Archaeologists should not excavate a site unless necessary (as prescribed in a research design) and should never excavate the entire site (unless it was to be completely destroyed by some other means), so that at least part of the archaeological record is saved for the future when there may be better methods. Archaeologists conduct research into the past; they do not merely collect objects for display. Therefore, collection without proper record keeping, analysis, and reporting is destructive and unethical.

The archaeological record is continually impacted by the vandalism of sites and the theft of antiquities, ranging from the casual person collecting *arrowheads* to commercial operations destroying sites to gather artifacts to sell. People involved in these acts should be considered criminals, as well as the people who buy looted materials. The past belongs to all people, and for this reason all citizens—not just professional archaeologists—have an ethical obligation in archaeology. This obligation centers on preserving the archaeological record by not destroying or damaging sites, not collecting artifacts for personal use, and respecting the cultural heritage of other peoples.

Legal Issues

Legal issues must be addressed before the start of any fieldwork. The country in which the work is to be done may require permits and have other rules and regulations that must be followed. Permits may be difficult to obtain. Few countries allow the removal of artifacts from the country, even for study. Others allow it for a limited time. In these cases, laboratory work must be carefully planned.

In the United States, federal laws and state statutes regulate archaeology in every state. Most apply only on federal or state property. A permit must be obtained to conduct work if the land is owned by the government. If the land is privately owned, permission to work must be obtained from the owner. In some states, a state permit is required even if the land is privately owned. Some types of sites, including known cemeteries, cannot be excavated without a special permit. If an unknown cemetery or burial is found, special permission must be obtained to continue the work. In most states, human burials are protected by law whether on public or private lands. The federal Native American Graves Protection and Repatriation Act of 1990 reflects the concerns of indigenous peoples about the treatment of the dead by archaeologists, biological anthropologists, and museums. Other laws that affect archaeology are the Abandoned Shipwreck Act and the National Historic Preservation Act. These issues are discussed further in Chapter 13.

Humanistic Issues

Archaeologists work to discover the past, but sometimes the search leads to living peoples. In such cases, it is the responsibility of the archaeologist to consult with contemporary peoples, such as native people in a region who may have some connection with the archaeological materials. Some native groups are very interested; others are opposed to any archaeological work. Local descendants may object to further excavation of a site if a burial is found, or materials recovered from a site may be regarded as too sensitive culturally to display in a museum. In some circumstances, science must defer to the feelings, wishes, and desires of the people involved. When such conflicts have arisen in the United States, the government has tended to side with contemporary groups, denying or withdrawing archaeological permits and preventing further work. Often, however, archaeologists are able to work with the people, take their feelings into consideration, and involve them in the research. Cultural respect and close communication are the keys to handling humanistic issues in archaeology.

Professional Obligations

After a project is completed, it is the researcher's obligation to report the results of the work (see Zimmerman 2003). Sites must be recorded, artifacts cataloged and analyzed, and a report published and distributed as widely as possible. In many cases, survey and excavation reports are submitted to the agency that issued the permit for, or funded, the work and are placed on file with that agency. Obtaining these reports is sometimes difficult. Ideally, reports are published as monographs or books by the institution that did the work or by specialized publishers. Summaries of the work also may be published in professional journals. Attendance at professional meetings, both to inform others of your work and to learn about theirs, is also an important obligation. It is also important that archaeologists educate the public about what has been learned. After all, it is the public, in one form or another, that pays for archaeology. Most important, researchers must take proper care of artifacts and ecofacts from their projects and make them accessible to other researchers for examination and reanalysis. These materials represent the evidence of the human past.

CONTENTSELECT

Search articles in the ContentSelect database using the key word *remote sensing*. What are some examples or remote sensing technologies described in these articles? Why are these technologies beneficial in archaeological fieldwork? How are they transforming the way archaeology is done?

Chapter Summary

Fieldwork is necessary to locate, examine, recover, and analyze the patterned material remains of past behaviors. Fieldwork involves finding sites and digging them. Some sites are found accidentally, but most are located during some archaeological project, either a CRM project or a research project.

An archaeological survey begins with the development of a research design that integrates into a plan the important information and results from any previous work. The research design details the sampling method, field techniques, and expected outcomes of the project.

A survey usually is done on foot by team members walking across the project area. Another survey technique is remote sensing by means of aerial photography, airborne and spaceborne lasers, radar or sonar mapping, and geophysical methods. Some sites are easy to recognize; others are more difficult. Invariably, some sites are missed in a survey. Once located, sites have to be recorded and evaluated.

Further work is conducted on some sites to address research questions. This work may include sampling and mapping the site, surface collection of artifacts, and excavation. If excavation is undertaken, the results of any geophysical survey work, such as magnetometer readings and ground-penetrating radar waves, are used to help determine where to dig. If possible, portions of the site are saved for future research.

Some excavations are small-scale efforts to test and evaluate the content of sites. Larger-scale excavations may be undertaken on promising sites. Judgment sampling or statistical sampling may be employed to get the most from the site. Excavation involves removing soil and locating, recording, and recovering finds. Excavation units include small auger probes, shovel-test pits, standard units, block excavations, and trenches. Units generally are excavated to the bottom of the cultural deposit. Most excavation is conducted by hand with small tools, but power equipment is sometimes used. Often, soil is passed through screens to recover small objects.

Many specialists are involved in archaeological projects, such as biological anthropologists, chemists, biologists, osteologists, and palynologists. Archaeological teams include people responsible for project administration, security, logistics, supply, data management, and the management of risks stemming from field conditions.

Like all scientists, archaeologists must adhere to a strict ethical code of conduct. Their ethical concerns include humanistic and legal issues as well as professional obligations to disseminate information about their work.

Key Concepts

block excavation, 128
curation, 135
datum, 123
geophysical survey, 124
ground-penetrating radar
   (GPR), 125

in situ, 131
judgment sample, 121
provenience, 128
remote sensing, 119
screening, 131
standard excavation unit, 128

statistical sample, 122
surface collection, 125
test-level excavation, 125
trench, 128

Suggested Readings

If you want to learn more about the concepts and issues discussed in this chapter, consider looking at the following resources. (Some may be rather technical.)

Hester, Thomas R., Harry J. Shafer, and Kenneth L. Feder (eds.). (1997). *Field Methods in Archaeology* (7th ed.). Mountain View, CA: Mayfield.

Roskams, Steve. (2001). *Excavation.* Cambridge: Cambridge Manuals in Archaeology.

Stewart, R. Michael. (2002). *Archaeology: Basic Field Methods.* Dubuque, IA: Kendall/Hunt.

Surprisingly, there are relatively few books on archaeological field methods. These three titles are the only ones currently available. Each of these books covers most of the aspects of fieldwork, but the Stewart book is the best for beginning students.

Classification and Analysis of Artifacts

THE LITTLE CHERT stone was first picked up by a person at the Rorhi Hills quarry in central Pakistan about 10,000 years ago. Looking for a particular type of rock, the person broke off a corner to see whether the color of the stone was what he or she wanted. It wasn't, and the stone was dropped back onto the ground. A thousand years later, it was picked up again, but this time it met the needs of the finder. The stone was put in a pouch and taken back to his or her camp. Some flakes were removed and each flake was made into a tool. What was left of the stone, now a core (a stone from which flakes are removed to make tools), was traded to visitors who took it far to the east, into what is now China. The new owners lost it in a small valley near the coast. About 6,000 years ago, a

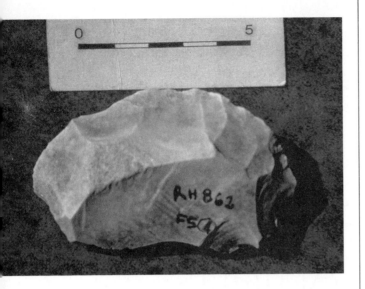

farmer noticed the core in one of his fields and recognized that the stone was not local. He picked it up and decided that it could be used as a hammer. Over the years, the edges of the stone were battered until they became dull. One day, someone decided to throw it away, and it ended up in the village trash area. About 1,500 years ago, the village expanded and the traditional trash area was moved. Someone noticed the stone, decided it was attractive, and took it home. The house where the stone was displayed burned down some 750 years ago, and the stone was again lost and forgotten.

In 1983, archaeologists began investigations at the ancient village. Upon discovering the burned house, they decided to excavate it in the hope that materials were preserved by the fire. Eventually, they found the little core, flaked, battered, and burned, in a corner of the house. The diggers recognized that it was not local and put it in a bag to be shipped to the laboratory for analysis. The laboratory analyst recorded the artifact as a core that had been used as a hammerstone, made from an exotic stone, perhaps brought in from the west. Chemists eventually were able to determine that the stone was from the Rorhi Hills in central Asia. Examination of the artifact revealed a weathered and clearly old flake scar. Other flake scars were less weathered, so it was obvious that the tool had been flaked at different times, probably thousands of years apart. No flakes of the material of the core were found in the village, however; so the archaeologists believed that those villagers had not used the stone as a core. It seemed clear that the tool was first a core and was then used as a hammer, brought in from the west long ago. It had gone through a complex history and passed through many hands. Today, the chert core from Pakistan is on display at the Natural History Museum in Beijing, China, testament to the long, continuous, and complex human occupation of central and eastern Asia.

For the location of the Rorhi Hills and other sites mentioned in this chapter, see the map on page 143.

Once discovered, recorded, collected, excavated, or observed, the materials recovered from the archaeological record, like the Asian core, have to be analyzed. The first step in analysis is **classification,** the placing of materials into categories of types that can be used for identification and comparison. Indeed, **typology**—the recognition and definition of

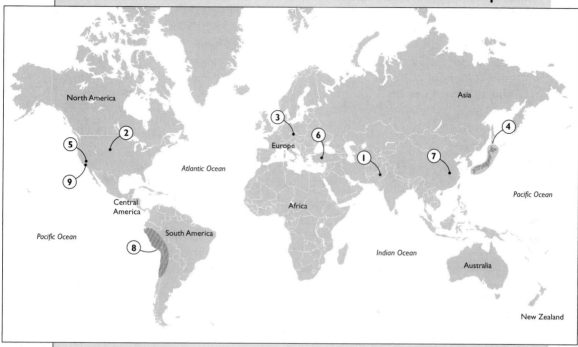

LOCATION MAP: **Sites Mentioned in Chapter 6**

1 ■ Rorhi Hills
   Central Pakistan

2 ■ The *Bertrand*
   Blair, Nebraska

3 ■ Dolni Vestonice
   Czech Republic

4 ■ Jomon culture
   Japan

5 ■ Coso Volcanic Field
   California

6 ■ Funeral feast
   Central Turkey

7 ■ Jiahu site
   Henan province, China

8 ■ Inka
   Peru

9 ■ Riverside Chinatown
   California

shared similarities between artifacts—is central to archaeology. Classification sometimes can be difficult because archaeologists often are dealing with materials designed and made by members of other cultural systems and because experts sometimes disagree on how things should be classified. Nevertheless, all recovered material comes from some past cultural practice, and all is relevant to our understanding of the past. Nothing is insignificant or too small to consider, and all things, even a fragment of rock, have the potential to inform us about the past. Tools can inform us about technology and economic activity, and the distribution of tools can inform us about social organization. In some special circumstances, such as burial practices, tools can inform us about people's cultural beliefs and their roles and status in society.

Classification and Typology

Archaeologists generally classify materials by **attributes,** or sets of characteristics, believed to be culturally significant, following the principle that past groups and their material remains are patterned (this is the normative view explained in Chapter 1) and that these patterns can be discovered. Major characteristics used in classification are **morphology** (form or "style") and function. For example, tools of stone and tools of metal would be classified separately, as would tools used for grinding and tools used for cutting. No classification or typological scheme is perfect, but such schemes allow archaeologists to communicate through shared terminology and nomenclature for describing and naming the objects under study (Adams and Adams 1991).

The classification of material culture is also important for documenting and explaining changes in types, forms, and functions over time. Even small changes in archaeological remains could reflect major changes in a society. For example, the change from the use of the atlatl (spear thrower) to the bow and arrow, a major technological shift that affected whole economies, can be seen in a decrease in the overall size of projectile points, so the placement of projectile points into proper size categories is important. The same is true for classification of sites. For example, a shift from temporary camps to permanent camps might indicate major changes in the economy and social and political organization, making accurate site classification essential in detecting and understanding such shifts.

Attributes

Archaeological sites and artifacts are classified according to particular attributes, such as size, content, color, material, and shape. Archaeologists select attributes that they believe are important for understanding the thing being classified. Attributes relevant to the archaeologist, however, may not be attributes that the maker or user of an object or site regarded as important. Those attributes have to be inferred. Often it is difficult to know what the makers were thinking or what was important to them. Therefore, archaeological classifications are somewhat arbitrary. As we learn more about the past, classificatory systems are continually refined and revamped.

Attributes selected for use in classification must be objective and measurable, and archaeologists use both quantitative and qualitative attributes to describe artifacts. *Quantitative attributes*—the most common are length, width, thickness, weight, and the numerical dimensions of elements such as perforations or decorations—are characteristics that can be described through metric measurement. Other quantitative attributes include angles of edges, the number of specific items within a certain space (e.g., threads per inch of textile), and ratios (e.g., length to width). Together, quantitative measurements describe a site, feature, or artifact.

Qualitative attributes—such as what material an artifact was made from, whether architecture is present, whether an artifact is broken, whether a pot was painted, or whether a bone has a healed fracture—describe the presence or absence of a descriptive characteristic or trait. For instance, flaked stone artifacts might be classified as projectile points, bifaces, blades, or *debitage* (stone waste or debris) made out of flint, chert, quartzite, felsite, obsidian, rhyolite, or other material.

Most materials from the archaeological record fall into already established types based on morphology, function, and other attributes, but new types of sites and artifacts are continually discovered and defined. Through classification and delineation of attributes, archaeologists seek to discover **style,** the particular way things were done or made (Hegmon 1992). Style reflects someone's conscious choice to do something in one way rather than another. The discovery of style can enlighten us about the importance of some things over others and about how people may have thought. Also, style can be used to distinguish between societies of the past.

Temporal Types

As technology changes over time, people introduce new material culture, abandon old material culture, and retain objects but change their morphology, function, or style. As archaeologists learn more and more about the past, it is clear that many specific types of artifacts and other remains, such as architecture, occur only within specific periods of time. **Temporal types** are artifacts tied to specific times and can be used to date the sites in which they are found and the activities with which they are associated.

Sites, too, can be temporal types. In ancient Egypt, for example, the first royal tombs were rectangular mud-brick platforms, called *mastabas,* built over underground pits, cross-dated through inscriptions to the kings of the First and Second Dynasties.

Artifacts found in association with these structures can be dated by temporal type. In ancient Egypt, rectangular stepped tombs predated smooth-sided pyramids in a well-known sequence. Artifacts can be analyzed in relation to changes over time in morphology (shape or form), function (use), style (method of manufacture), or quantitative and qualitative attributes (number and appearance).

The tomb was built as a replica of the royal occupant's home. Then, during the Fourth Dynasty of the Old Kingdom period, the mastaba became a series of mastabas, one atop the other, forming a stepped pyramid. Only later did people build the gigantic smooth-sided stone pyramids so well known to tourists today. Because the tombs could be dated, artifacts found in association with them also could be dated.

Materials that do not change in morphology over time are poor temporal markers. For example, Paleolithic hand axes made throughout Eurasia remained largely unchanged for hundreds of thousands of years and are not very useful for dating. Conversely, the presence of datable artifacts cannot always be used to determine the age of a site. For example, an implement made of mammoth bone in a North American site likely would have been fashioned before mammoths became extinct about 10,000 years ago. However, a mere thousand years ago, a person may have found the mammoth bone and worked it. Anyone who relied solely on the mammoth bone to date the site would be off by at least 9,000 years! When analyzing artifact types, archaeologists use as many temporal markers as possible.

Assemblage Types

All the artifacts and ecofacts collected from a site constitute an **assemblage,** a representative sample of the evidence for all the activities that took place at the site at a particular time. Archaeologists classify assemblages for purposes of site-to-site comparison. Comparisons of site assemblages, or of categories of material within site assemblages (subassemblages), can reveal similarities and differences in people's technological and economic adaptations in different times and places.

An example of classifying assemblages comes from the excavation of the steamboat *Bertrand.* During the mid-nineteenth century, thousands of steamboats operated on the waterways of North America. A few of the vessels that sank in these waters have been discovered and excavated. Among the first to be found was the *Bertrand,* which sank in the DeSoto Bend of the Missouri River in 1865. It was a 250-ton, 161-foot, shallow-draft stern-wheeler designed to carry passengers and cargo.

According to historical records, the steamboat *Bertrand* was bound for the Montana gold fields with cargo intended for general stores there. The remains of the vessel were located in 1967 and excavated between 1968 and 1969 (Petsche 1974; Switzer 1974). The lower portion of the hull was intact, and much of the cargo was well preserved in the ship's hold. An assemblage of some 2 million artifacts was discovered, including a wide range of foodstuffs, clothing, building supplies, household items, tools, hardware, books, and personal articles. The *Bertrand's* material culture assemblage is representative of the North American frontier economy and mining technology at a specific moment in time.

Classifying Types of Artifacts

Recall from Chapter 1 that artifacts are portable tools, containers, and other objects manufactured or used by people to accomplish some goal or task. The types of artifacts are very diverse. Artifacts convey both functional and symbolic information about a group.

They can tell us a great deal about subsistence and economic activities; about social and political systems, because people of different roles and status tended to use different tools for different activities; and about belief systems, because some artifacts are associated with religious practices. Artifacts can also inform us about human skill, knowledge, and symbolism. They generally are classified first into broad types based on objective descriptions of qualitative attributes, especially form and material. (The exact functions of artifacts are harder to interpret and often disputed.) Major artifact types include stone, ceramics, metal, glass, shell and bone, and perishables such as wood, textiles, and paper.

Stone

Stone tools may be ground or flaked. *Ground stone tools* were used primarily for grinding, smashing, or crushing various plant, animal, and mineral resources (Schneider 2002). People manufactured ground stone tools by a process of percussion followed by pecking, grinding, or polishing. Some ground stone artifacts were ground and polished through use; others were ground or polished intentionally during manufacture. Either way, specific wear patterns develop through friction of stone on stone, or stone on worked substances such as hides, shell, clays, and plant fibers. Examples of stone objects ground and polished through use include milling implements such as grindstones, querns, bowls, mortars, and

Some of the many types of ground stone tools. On the left is a metate with a mano lying on top. These tools were mostly used to grind various foods. A bowl is shown in the upper right and a broken grooved axe in the lower right.

pestles; anvil stones; abrading or scraping tools for working shell, bone, wood, hides, and stone; and tools used in processing fibers. Examples of stone objects ground and polished intentionally through manufacture include palettes, pipes, beads and pendants, figurines, and balls. Some tools, such as shaft straighteners, axes, and hoes, are ground through both manufacture and subsequent use.

Milling tools usually were made from coarse-grained stones, such as granite, for durability. Other ground stone tools were made from fine-grained stone, such as slate or steatite (soapstone), so the surface finish would be smooth and fine. In either case, people obtained stone from trade or from special quarry sites, often located at great distances. Quarrying also provided stone for flaked tools.

In many cases, items within a ground stone subassemblage have been assigned to gender-specific tasks, such as milling stones being used by females. It is increasingly clear, however, that such gender assignments are problematic, for many ground stone tools were used for many purposes by both males and females. Interpreting sex roles and gender characteristics from artifact assemblages is a challenge.

Flaked stone tools were manufactured primarily by chipping off pieces rather than by grinding or polishing, a process called *tool stone reduction* or **flintknapping** (Yohe 2002). Flaked tools were made of fine-grained stone, such as volcanic glass (obsidian), chert, calcedony, flint, basalt, or quartzite, and had sharp edges that could be used for piercing, cutting, and scraping. Flaked tools dull easily through use and often were reworked to restore their edges. Obsidian was traded over great distances because it easily flakes to produce sharp edges. Obsidian is especially useful to archaeologists because it can be dated and geochemically sourced. Thus, trade in obsidian can be reconstructed across space and time.

Some of the many types of flaked stone tools. The tool in the upper left is a 2-million-year-old flake tool from Bed II at Olduvai Gorge. In the lower left is a 400,000-year-old hand axe from a site near Paris, France. In the center is a replicated large biface, similar to ceremonial bifaces common to parts of California. Just to the upper right of the biface is a replicated Clovis point with a replicated arrow point to its right. Below the scale is a replicated small blade core with a number of blades from it.

People made flaked tools by reducing the mass of a stone until the desired result was obtained. In some cases, such as in the manufacture of a hand ax or hammerstone, the flakes knocked off were discarded and the remaining *core* was used. For other tools, such as projectile points and thumbnail scrapers, the flakes were used and the remaining core was discarded once it was no longer useful. Thus, the stones that archaeologists identify as cores are stones from which flakes were removed, and they may have served as tools or as a source of flakes.

People used two methods for stone reduction (Figure 6.1). *Percussion flaking* involves striking the stone either directly with a hammerstone, or indirectly by striking a chisel or

A.

B.

C.

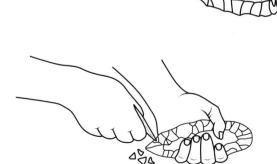

figure 6.1

Flintknapping Techniques Used in the Past and in Experimental Archaeology.   The upper drawing depicts *direct percussion:* the material is struck by a hammer such as a quartzite cobble. The center drawing shows *indirect percussion:* a bone punch is struck by an antler hammer, removing a flake from the core. The lower drawing depicts *pressure flaking:* a small antler tine is used to "push" flakes off a biface.

Source: Mark Q. Sutton and Brooke S. Arkush, 2002, *Archaeological Laboratory Methods,* 3rd edition (Dubuque, IA: Kendall/Hunt), Figure 10. Reprinted by permission of Kendall/Hunt Publishing Company.

punch placed against the stone. *Pressure flaking,* best for detail work and retouching edges, is accomplished by using a small tool, even a fire-hardened stick, to apply pressure to the edges of a flake until it breaks.

The original production of a completed tool is not necessarily the end of the use-life of the tool. Like the stone tool described at the beginning of this chapter, a tool may break, be reworked, break again, and be reworked again into a tool with a different function before finally entering the archaeological record as discarded material.

Types of flaked stone tools include cores (stone remaining after flakes were struck off),unifaces and bifaces (flakes worked on one or both sides), blades (flakes struck from prepared cores for a kind of mass production), and utilized flakes (naturally flaked stone). To remove flakes of the proper size and shape to make finished tools, cores of specific shapes were manufactured, resulting in cores that were unifacial, bifacial, or multifaceted. Some cores were also later used as choppers or hammerstones, taking advantage of their relatively sharp edges (called *arrises*) resulting from the removal of flakes.

Bifaces are tools flaked on both sides. The functional types of bifaces include projectile points (for spears, atlatl darts, and arrows), some knives, drills, and some scrapers. Another form of biface is an eccentric, an artifact flaked in unusual ways to create very unusual forms, often for functions unknown to us. *Unifaces* are flaked on one side only and include functional types such as some knives, burins (used for engraving), and some scrapers.

Blades are flakes manufactured in particular shapes and sizes (generally at least twice as long as wide), often for use in specialized composite tools (see Chapter 4), such as a sickle, where a number of sickle blades would be set into the working edge of the sickle and then used to cut grasses. Often, stones were hafted (tied or otherwise attached) onto wooden handles or shafts, creating composite tools, such as arrows, sickles for cutting grasses, javelins, and harpoons. Some flakes, called *utilized flakes,* were simply found, picked up, and used as casual tools.

Discarded material, especially manufacturing debris, can tell us a lot about how tools were made and used in the past. The manufacture, use, reworking, and resharpening of flaked stone tools generates debitage, which enters the archaeological record. Analysis of debitage often makes it possible to infer the exact methods by which people produced stone tools.

Ceramics

Ceramics are objects made of clay and other organic and inorganic materials that are fired usually at temperatures above 1,100 degrees Fahrenheit (600 degrees Celsius). Ceramic artifacts come in a vast array of utilitarian and decorative forms and are among the most durable objects in the archaeological record (Orton et al. 1993). Most ceramic artifacts are containers (commonly called *pottery*), but a variety of other items, such as tiles, pipes, clay tablets, and figurines, also have been found.

Throughout the world and especially in North America, ceramic technology is relatively recent and serves as an important dating tool. Different types of ceramics are known to be associated with specific time periods. Thus, the analysis of ceramic potsherds (clay vessel fragments) can provide important information about site chronology as well as technology, culture, and prehistoric trade patterns.

Some of the ceramic vessels found in Tomb 4, Cemetery II, at Morgantina, a city in Sicily. The family-owned chamber tomb contained five burials dated between 550 and 475 BC. The grave goods included 247 objects, including 160 vases, 21 of which were imported from Athens, Greece.

The development of pottery seems to be related to the appearance of domesticated plants and animals, and in many cases the mere presence of pottery implies an increasingly sedentary way of life and an economy based on concentrated and secure resources. The earliest known pottery was made by the Jomon hunter-gatherers of ancient Japan between 10,000 and 12,000 years ago. In the Middle East, the earliest known ceramic vessels were made in Anatolia (Turkey) between 10,000 and 10,500 years ago. In the New World, it appears that people independently developed pottery in several different places between about 4,500 and 5,000 years ago, beginning in South America along the coast of Ecuador and spreading to coastal Colombia, Pacific coastal Mexico, and the southeastern United States.

In both the Old and the New Worlds, pottery was first crafted by hand. The potter modeled a mass of clay into the shape of a vessel. Techniques included using a paddle to slap a pot into shape (the paddle-and-anvil technique) or joining together a series of clay coils (the coiling technique) to form a container. Sometimes people carved simple decorative patterns onto the paddles, which then transferred to the pot during manufacture. In the Old World around 5,500 years ago, the potter's wheel was invented, which led to standardization of vessel forms and sizes and decreased the time needed to manufacture vessels.

Archaeologists generally classify ceramics into four basic types: terra-cotta, earthenware, stoneware, and porcelain, depending on firing temperature. *Terra-cottas* are made from coarse clays fired at a relatively low temperature so that the grains do not melt together (vitrify). Terra-cottas usually were made into bricks, flowerpots, tiles, and statues. *Earthenwares* also are made from relatively coarse clays but are fired at higher temperatures and are more vitrified. Earthenware is the most common ceramic type used in prehistory. *Stonewares* are made from finer clays fired at higher temperatures and are partially vitrified. First produced in Europe beginning about 400 years ago, stonewares eventually were used for fine tableware. *Porcelains* are made from fine clays and are completely vitrified (very glassy) from firing at high temperatures. Porcelains were first made in China about 1,000 years ago and are widely known as chinaware or simply "china."

Ceramics can be decorated by scratching, incising, or punching some design onto the surface of the clay or by adding appliqués and other clay elements before the piece is fired. Paints and glazes can be applied either before or after firing. Styles of decoration are important in the analysis of ceramics. Decorative styles are unique to cultures, periods, or even certain individuals and can be used to determine where and when and by whom certain pieces were made.

Another major aspect of ceramic analysis is vessel form and function. Forms include bowls, jars, scoops, plates, ladles, cups, beakers, and pitchers, used most often for storing, cooking, serving, and eating foods or for storing or displaying other products for other purposes. The ancient contents of a pot can provide important clues about its function. Residues may be present in the porous inner surfaces of pots or in vessels where charring has preserved portions of the original contents. Organic remains in pots often can be identified. Animal fats and vegetable oils are the most common materials collected for chemical analysis. Techniques of infrared absorption, mass spectrography, and gas chromatography can identify fatty acids, lipids, cholesterol, triglycerides, and other organic components (Rice 1987:233; Heron et al. 1991; Heron and Evershed 1993:250; Evershed and Tuross 1996).

Metal

A broad array of metal artifacts occurs all over the world. Some metals, such as copper and gold, are easily obtained and used in natural form. Native gold and copper can be cold-hammered into the desired shape, annealed (heated and then hammered), or cast (melted and poured into molds). These and other metals also occur in impure forms (ores) and have to be smelted (melted and refined by separating the metal from impurities) to produce purer metal. Copper, silver, iron, and lead were all smelted and widely used by peoples of the past. Some metals were alloyed (combined with other metals) to form new materials, such as brass, an alloy of copper and zinc.

The most common method of metal casting involves pouring molten metal into a mold. As the metal cools and resolidifies, it assumes the shape of the mold. Ingots, symbolic objects, and coins were among the earliest cast objects. Casting freestanding three-dimensional objects in metal was a more complex process involving several alternative techniques. Whatever the technique, casting permitted the mass production of durable objects of standardized manufacture and stimulated the rise of the ancient civilizations. The casting of iron, for example, led to a new age in the history of technology.

Metallurgy is the science of extracting metals from their ores and creating useful things from metal. Peoples with metallurgy-based economies—peoples familiar with the technologies involved in making metals, such as mining, smelting, forging, and casting—tended to replace or absorb peoples who depended only on tools of stone and wood. In developments that led ultimately to an industrial revolution based on steam-powered metal machines, people throughout the ancient world found ways to extract metals and make them more useful, harder, stronger, and more durable. Thus, for instance, iron hoes and plowshares came to replace digging sticks and wooden plows, and steel machetes replaced stone knives.

First came bronze, an alloy of copper and tin or arsenic. Much harder and more useful than pure copper, bronze became so valuable that it stimulated a huge trade in metals and manufactured metal goods. It is the marker material for the Bronze Age, which developed independently in China and in Europe. The earliest and most complex use of bronze occurred in China some 5,000 years ago, where it was cast into elaborate decorative objects.

Iron, much harder and stronger than bronze, largely replaced bronze and marked the Iron Age. Ironwork required much higher temperatures than bronzework and greater knowledge of chemistry. Steel (a strong low-carbon iron) was made in Europe in Roman times but was first produced in sub-Saharan Africa many centuries earlier (Vogel 1997).

As archaeological artifacts, metal objects may be difficult to identify, recover, and conserve. Different metals preserve differently and deteriorate at different rates, depending on conditions. Iron-based metals, for example, are susceptible to deterioration through oxidation (rust). A deteriorated metal artifact might survive only as a discoloration or stain in the soil, hard to discern during an excavation.

Glass

Glassmaking is a recent technological development dating from Mesopotamia about 4,500 years ago, although a glass-like substance (faience) was produced in Egypt more than 5,000 years ago. By about 3,500 years ago, both Egyptian and Mesopotamian artisans were producing glass beads and small glass vessels (Munsey 1970:6). Some of the earliest bottle-like containers were produced in Syria around 2,100 years ago, when artisans discovered that they could form hollow vessels by blowing air through a tube into a blob of hot molten glass (Munsey 1970:30).

Glass is a substance manufactured by melting sand (silica) and then letting it cool rapidly. However, sand has a high melting point, and the technology to produce high enough temperatures developed along with metallurgy. People increased firing temperatures by using bellows to blow air on the fire. Glassmakers also soon discovered that adding soda and lime to silica allows it to melt at lower temperatures and produces a better quality of glass. By Roman times, glass production was common, and a large number and variety of glass artifacts were produced. Interestingly, however, glass is uncommon in the archaeological record before the last several hundred years, not because it did not preserve but because often it was collected, melted down, and recycled into new glass (Renfrew and Bahn 2004:345). Although dating glass is difficult, it preserves well except in waterlogged soils.

Glass manufacturing is a conservative industry. There was little change in manufacturing techniques until recent times, so it is hard to date glass by the way it was

HIGHLIGHT 6.1

Historical Material Culture: A View from Riverside's Chinatown

Historical archaeology is the marriage of two disciplines that study the past, one based on historical documents and the other on the material remains that are found in the ground. The beauty of historical archaeology is that it can help fill in the gaps that all too frequently exist in written histories, especially of those groups who may have been misrepresented or not represented at all in the historical record. Disenfranchised populations or groups have often not fared well in history; one typical example is the Chinese immigrants who came to North America during the middle of the nineteenth century. Political and social problems in China at the time resulted in a large influx of Chinese people, mostly men, who worked primarily as laborers. Small Chinese communities began to pop up at the edges of the larger cities of the American West, especially in California. Following the gold rush of the 1850s, many Chinese stayed to work as agricultural laborers, especially in southern California, with its burgeoning citrus industry. Unfortunately, many Americans at the time were anti-Asian in sentiment (leading to two "exclusion acts," one in 1882 and another in 1915), so Chinese Americans were largely marginalized and not considered favorably by many historians, who often excluded them completely from local histories (Lawton 1987).

One such Chinese community was the Riverside Chinatown in southern California east of Los Angeles.

Between the 1880s and the 1940s, Riverside's Chinatown was a bustling community of up to a few hundred residents serving a much broader community of agricultural workers. During this 60-year period, as the population of Riverside and the surrounding areas increased, the population of Chinatown waned, due in part to the diminishing role of large-scale agriculture toward the middle of the twentieth century. Unfortunately, the few early historical accounts about Riverside Chinatown were written by Euroamerican historians, many of whom were biased against the Chinese living there. By the 1970s, Chinatown had only one resident, George Wong, who had lived there for many years, possessed considerable knowledge about the town, and was the source of much of what we now know about the last several decades of this community (the site was named Wong Ho Leun in his honor). On his death in the 1980s, the remaining buildings were torn down, and the site was threatened with further destruction in anticipation of the building of a parking lot. Much of what Chinatown had to offer with respect to understanding this community stood to be lost.

In the mid-1980s, a campaign to save Riverside's Chinatown was launched by local history buffs and archaeologists. Funding became available, and the Great Basin Anthropological Foundation (GBAF) initiated an archaeological investigation at the site. Although bottle hunters and relic collectors had dug into parts of the

made. Also, making dating difficult is the fact that many fragments of glass do not retain diagnostic attributes and often are categorized simply as flat, curved, brown, or blue, without regard to function. In historical sites, however, glass bottles are important dating and function markers because they can be dated by their manufacturing attributes, such as mold form, seam type, color, and lip designs. Embossed labels in the glass can reveal country of origin. Functional types include service pieces; storage glass, such as canning jars; wine, liquor, and ale bottles; beverage bottles for beers, mineral water, and

site, archaeologists had hope that a small parking lot put in by George Wong had served to seal important trash deposits and structural foundations. This hope was realized, and many incredibly well-preserved dumps with whole bottles, ceramic vessels, plates, opium pipes, and various metal objects were recovered by the GBAF scientists.

The various artifact types help to paint a clearer portrait of daily life in Riverside's Chinatown. The common ceramic vessels included a mixture of traditional Chinese food storage containers such as soy pots, pickled meat and vegetable jars, and liquor bottles, all imported from China. Having a wide range of complete jars and bottles made the task of identifying fragmentary vessels and individual potsherds much easier, allowing researchers to determine the minimum number of containers of each type. This, in turn, provided information about which foods or other items stored in these containers were most frequently used by the inhabitants of Chinatown at different times during its occupation. The use of traditional, imported Chinese food items continued to be an important part of Chinese American culture during the occupation of Chinatown; we know this because of the recovery and analysis of material culture, such as ceramic food containers, that corresponds with botanical and faunal remains of nonlocal species. When taken in combination with the few historical accounts and photographs, oral histories, and other material artifacts recovered from the site, our knowledge of late-nineteenth-century Chinese America is greatly enhanced.

Archaeologists excavating undisturbed pile of soy sauce and pickled vegetable jars discarded at the Riverside Chinatown.

CRITICAL **THINKING** QUESTIONS

1. What are the types of problems faced by historical archaeologists interested in studying nineteenth-century ethnic communities in North America?
2. What can the archaeological record of Riverside Chinatown tell us about acculturation into more mainstream American society during the history of its occupation?

soda; pharmaceutical glass; window glass; and lighting devices, such as candle chimneys and lanterns.

The general objective of glass analysis is to determine the approximate number of each type of bottle represented in an assemblage, the approximate age of items, the companies that made them, and their likely source of distribution. Determining the original contents of bottles provides insight into the economic patterns and personal habits of site occupants (see Highlight 6.1). As with many other artifact types, people often used bottles for other purposes after consuming the original contents, especially in regions far removed from centers of glass manufacture. The analysis of glass vessels can inform archaeologists about trade networks, individual and ethnic preferences for specific products, and even the health of individuals (Switzer 1974; McDougall 1990).

Glass beads were widely traded all over the world and often provide the first evidence of contact with Europeans. In North America, glass beads have received a great deal of scholarly attention, for they are important indicators of early historical Native American culture change. The beads are common throughout the continent, are well preserved, and can be used to date components. Glass beads also are important behavioral indicators; often they provide the only evidence of native peoples modifying their material culture in response to contact. From the eleventh century to the mid-1800s, most glass beads traded around the world were produced in factories in Venice, Italy (Deagan 1987:158). Other centers included Bohemia, France, and later the Netherlands.

Shell and Bone

Shell and bone (and antler) are sturdy materials easily carved and shaped into artifacts and easy for people to obtain. Shell was made into ornaments, beads, pendants, sequins or appliqués, and tokens of exchange (money). Shell also was used for fishhooks, cups, and bowls. Although shell is present throughout the world, most freshwater shell is too thin for the manufacture of artifacts, and the thicker marine shell is needed. Groups that did not have direct access to marine shell had to obtain it through trade. Identifying the species of marine mollusks used in shell artifacts helps to determine their source. People in Africa also made beads from the thick shells of ostrich eggs.

Artifacts made from bone included needles, awls (tools for poking holes), scrapers, beads and ornaments, and tubes for smoking pipes and musical instruments (Highlight 6.2). Bone punches could be used in flintknapping by pressure-flaking the edges of tools to resharpen them. In less acidic soils, bone preserves well in the archaeological record, and bone artifacts are relatively common in prehistoric sites. People manufactured most bone tools by cutting the bone to the desired shape and then polishing it smooth. The analysis of bone includes identifying the species of animal and determining how it was butchered and processed and how products were made from it.

Perishables

Perishables are artifacts made of organic material—such as wood, fiber, bark, and seeds—that decomposes rapidly. Perishables seldom preserve well and are only rarely recovered from the archaeological record (see Chapter 4). Bone, antler, and shell, though also organic, are more substantial than most perishables and preserve for a comparatively longer time.

Perishables include basketwork, textiles, wood, and leather and hide. Basketry consists of baskets and other things hand woven from grasses, rushes, and twigs. Grass baskets, matting, woven fencing, and weirs woven from twigs to trap fish are examples. Even people with ceramic technology used basketry for many purposes, especially storage. Baskets also were devised for carrying water, and people cooked in them, steaming grains

HIGHLIGHT **6.2**

The Flutes of Jiahu

Excavations at the Early Neolithic site of Jiahu, located along the Yellow River in Henan Province, China, have been ongoing for a number of years (Zhang et al. 1999). By 1999 about 5 percent of the site had been excavated, and numerous houses, cellars, kilns, graves, and many thousands of artifacts and ecofacts had been revealed. The site is dated to between 9,000 and 7,700 BP. Among the artifacts, archaeologists recovered six complete bone flutes and fragments of some 30 others, found in strata well dated to about 9,000 years ago (Zhang et al. 1999).

The flutes were made from the ulnae (wing bones) of red-crowned cranes. Each flute contains between five and eight holes. Several of the instruments are still playable, and the best-preserved specimen (containing seven holes) was played and analyzed for its tone. The instrument can produce multitones, rather than just single notes. Musicologists determined that the seven holes produce sounds very similar to the eight-tone scale used in contemporary Western music. The Jiahu flutes are the earliest multitone musical instruments so far discovered (older flutes found in Neanderthal sites are too fragmentary to play or analyze for tone). Hearing the tones of the instruments helps us to imagine the prehistoric musicians who played them, but we do not know how musical compositions were performed or precisely what they meant to the players and listeners.

Bone flutes of Jiahu, China.

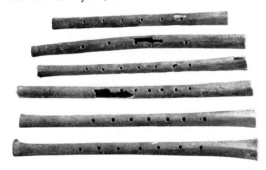

CRITICAL **THINKING** QUESTIONS

1. In what sense is even music recoverable from the archaeological record?
2. Is it surprising that bones worked by people tens of thousands of years ago were preserved in the archaeological record? What kinds of finds would be more surprising, and why?

and vegetables and making soups and porridges. People also made ceremonial objects, hats, and cloaks from basketry. Basketry sometimes can be analyzed on the basis of basket-weave impressions left in deposits in house floors or in burned clay (Adovasio 1977).

Evidence of sewing dates to the Upper Paleolithic. Materials woven from plant fibers, such as flax and cotton, or from animal hair, such as wool, are called *textiles*. Textiles are more flexible than basketry. Most clothing, plus blankets, tent coverings, sails, and many other items, were made from textiles (Highlight 6.3). Cordage (string, twine, or rope) also is classified as a textile; people used it for bowstrings, nooses, snares, fasteners, and seines and nets. People used nets for bags and for traps to capture game such as deer, rabbit, wildfowl, and fish.

The Fabled Fabric of the Inka

The Inka, warriors who conquered a vast empire in South America, were above all weavers. Their weavings included everything from bridges to roofs to items for recording history and numerical accounts. Inka weavers produced an extraordinarily fine cloth fabric from the fleece hair of a particular line of alpacas, animals related to the llama. This cloth rivaled cashmere in its quality. People prized it and commonly used it as a kind of currency. The cloth was stored in government warehouses and distributed as payment and tribute, forming a mainstay of the Inka economy (Pringle 2001b).

After conquering the Inka Empire, the Spanish looted the Inkas' gold and silver and ignored the cloth, the greatest of the Inka treasures. In their ignorance, the Spanish bred the special alpacas with other llamas as livestock for meat and labor. As a result, the genetic purity of the wool-bearing species

was lost and along with it the very fine fleece. The villages that produced the cloth fell into a poverty that has lasted 500 years.

In the early 1990s, archaeologist Jane Wheeler was asked to analyze some mummified alpacas found buried in the floors of Inka houses. The animals were mostly young males that had been killed, probably sacrificed, by a heavy blow to the neck. Wheeler found that the fine fleece of the animals was completely intact. The fibers of the fleece were remarkably uniform in both size and color and were consistently much finer than the finest modern alpaca fleece. The consistency of the material could have come only from purposeful selective breeding of the animals for that trait, an indication of the sophistication of the ancient textile industry.

Wheeler reasoned that if the genetic line of the special alpacas could be reconstructed, the fine fleece restored, and the ancient skills resurrected, the ancient textile industry of Peru could be revived. The special textiles could possibly contribute to a revitalization of the Peruvian economy and restore the prosperity of the villages. With this goal in mind, Wheeler began looking for purebred alpacas, established a DNA bank to try to isolate the genes for the fleece, and began a breeding program to reconstitute the Inkas' alpacas. In time, it is hoped, people will again be able to wear the fabric that powered the Inka Empire.

Inka textiles.

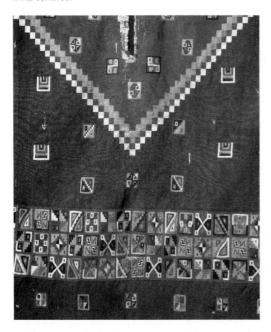

CRITICAL **THINKING** QUESTIONS

1. What attributes of the textiles did the archaeologist use in her classification and analysis of the remains?
2. What are some other examples of perishables in the archaeological record, and what kinds of analysis could aid in their interpretation?
3. How is this story about the Inka textile industry and the alpacas an example of the practical application of archaeology?

Numerous examples of animal-trapping nets have been recovered archaeologically, one in North America dating to as early as 8,600 BP (Frison et al. 1986). The oldest known woven cloth dates to some 27,000 years ago and was found as impressions in clay in sites in the Czech Republic (Soffer et al. 2000). Woven cloth clothing discovered with the red-headed mummies in western China was manufactured from materials and with techniques that link the textiles to eastern Europe. This find indicates active trade or contact between the two regions (Mair 1995a; Barber 1999; Mallory and Mair 2000).

Past peoples all over the world used artifacts of wood and cane. Wooden artifacts include bowls, buckets, scoops, digging sticks, tool handles, gaming sticks, bows, arrow and dart shafts, musical instrument parts, carvings, masks, figurines, and trap parts such as triggers. Wood also is found as features or parts of structures, such as hearths, fireplace wood, posts, planks, architectural embellishments, and boats. Wood perhaps is the most versatile resource. A fire-hardened stick could do many of the same things that a stone implement could do. A chunk of tree trunk could yield both a toothpick (or a replacement tooth) and a totem pole or statue of a god.

It is likely that the majority of objects made and used by past peoples were made from perishable materials that archaeologists do not recover. When perishables are recovered, they enrich our understanding of material culture, technological adaptation, art, and ritual.

Analyzing Artifacts

After classification, artifacts are further analyzed. Meaningful analysis requires good contextual information—that is, accurate records of where each item and feature was found. Other types of analysis relating to dating, sites, and ecofacts are taken up in Chapters 7 and 10. Figure 6.2 gives an idea of the sequence of questions that an archaeologist might ask when conducting an artifact analysis.

Whereas standard analysis of artifacts can reveal a great deal about the past, other information about archaeological materials requires special analyses, such as use-wear, geochemical sourcing, residue analysis, and DNA analysis. Specialists' analyses contribute to a more detailed picture of artifacts and their use.

Use-Wear Analysis

Use-wear analysis can tell the life of a tool. When a tool is used, it develops a wear pattern on its surface, revealed in alternations of microscopic striations (linear scratches) and plain or polished areas. Wear patterns provide information about what a tool was made from and what it was used on (Semenov 1964; Yerkes and Kardulias 1993). Specific types of microscopic wear patterns on the surfaces of many ground stone tools, for example, indicate on what kind of materials the tool was used to process.

Since the 1950s, experimental archaeologists have used replicated stone tools for a host of subsistence tasks, such as cutting meat, extracting marrow from bones, cutting fibrous plants, and grinding tubers or grains. Experimenters have discovered particular

1. *Overview:* What kinds of artifacts were found at the site? How do they indicate what technology was used and in what ways? What hypotheses about activities that may have taken place at the site will guide the analysis?
2. *Descriptive Analysis:* What types of tools were present? What types of tools were absent? How many tools of each type were found, and what are their forms and measurements? What are their associations with other artifacts, ecofacts, or features?
3. *Determining Tool Kits:* What tools were used for what specific tasks? What tools go together for certain related tasks? What tools found together in caches or burials could help in the reconstruction of tool kits?
4. *Functional Analysis:* What activities are suggested by the tool kits? What was the function and use of the site? Was there more than one use? Does the evidence support the hypotheses? How many people used the site? What were their characteristics, such as age and sex?

figure 6.2

Questions for a Standard Analysis of Artifacts

patterns of wear for particular processing activities, and these patterns of wear can help support hypotheses about the particular functions tools served. In particular, microscopic examination of wear patterns on the edges of stone tools can reveal whether the tool was used for cutting, scraping, or piercing; in what directions the tool was moved during use; and possibly even whether the user was right- or left-handed. Care must be taken, however, because wear patterns can be simulated through taphonomic events such as artifacts being trampled by livestock or damaged in a landslide.

Geochemical Sourcing

Analyzing artifacts includes finding out where the source material for making them came from. Many natural inorganic materials used by past peoples contain unique chemical compositions. If the chemical composition of an artifact can be determined, it establishes a kind of "fingerprint" that can be compared with known sources of the material. This kind of analysis, called **geochemical sourcing,** is especially useful with stone such as obsidian, jade, and turquoise; with some metals, such as copper, tin, silver, and gold; and with the clay in ceramics. A match can place a tool with the location of its specific source, just as a crime lab can source evidence such as fibers or bullets. If projectile points of red chert found in a Massachusetts site were sourced to a particular quarry in western New York State, that would indicate a pattern of east–west trade between Eastern Woodlands Indians.

Another example is obsidian, a natural volcanic glass used for many stone tools and traded extensively in Mesoamerica, North America, and the Middle East. Obsidian is produced in volcanos when magma cools very rapidly and forms a natural glass. Each magma pool has a different chemistry, so the chemistry of each obsidian flow is unique. Thus, using techniques such as x-ray fluorescence, neutron activation, or laser ablation, archaeologists can match the chemical fingerprints of obsidian artifacts with their sources. For example, in southeastern California, the Coso Volcanic Field was the main source of high-quality obsidian in artifacts from the southern Sierra Nevada to the Pacific Coast. Archaeologists determined that Native Americans quarried and traded obsidian from the Coso Volcanic Field about 2,000 years ago, which resulted in the distribution of obsidian throughout southern California (Ericson 1982; Gilreath and Hildebrandt 1997).

Residue Analysis

In some cases, unknown materials are preserved on artifacts, either as visible chunks of matter or as chemical residues. Residues include dried food in a pot, wine stains in a jar, embalming material in a mummy, resin on a basket, adhesive on a stone knife, and proteins such as blood on a tool. Various techniques are used to identify unknown material. Identification is important to discover not only what material was being used but also under what circumstances and with what technology.

Some materials can be identified visually with a conventional, infrared, or scanning electron microscope. In studies of mummies, infrared scanning has revealed (otherwise invisible) dyes used to tattoo the skin. Other materials can be identified by means of chemical techniques such as analyzing the carbon, hydrogen, and nitrogen (CHN) or more complex chemical compounds in the sample. *Gas chromatography (GC)* and *gas chromatography/mass spectrometry (GC/MS)* are techniques using devices that measure unknown archaeological materials chemically and compare them to the "fingerprints" of known substances (Figure 6.3).

Chemical analysis of residues have been used to recreate the original substances. In one such example, residues from 2,700-year-old pottery found in a funeral feast in central Turkey (thought to be associated with King Mita, the person that gave rise to the King Midas legend) were identified and used to brew the beer originally consumed at the feast (Gallagher 2005). Other work has been done to trace the origin of winemaking (McGovern and Mondavi 2007).

Protein residue analysis detects proteins, such as those from blood or saliva, that have survived on the surfaces of tools or other artifacts, in the feces of animals or humans, and even in soils (Newman et al. 1997; Shanks et al. 1999). Proteins can survive on tools for long periods and can be detected and identified. For example, stains of grass on a sickle or of deer blood on an arrowhead can contribute to archaeological interpretation.

Common techniques used for protein residue analysis in molecular biology are based on knowledge of enzyme reactions and immunology. For example, in crossover immuno-electrophoresis (CIEP), solutions of recovered proteins are tested against certain proteins (antisera) from known plants and animals. Immune reactions, like those occuring in a series of allergy tests, differentiate the related proteins from the incompatible ones, permitting identification.

DNA Analysis

DNA, a molecule that contains the genetic code of an organism, is a special kind of chemical residue found in organic substances. **DNA analysis** is another important new tool in archaeology from molecular biology. DNA can be recovered from the cutting edges of tools as well as from preserved tissues of plants, animals, and people. A recent study (Hardy et al. 1997) may have successfully recovered mammalian DNA from Middle Paleolithic butchering tools dating to between 35,000 and 65,000 years in age.

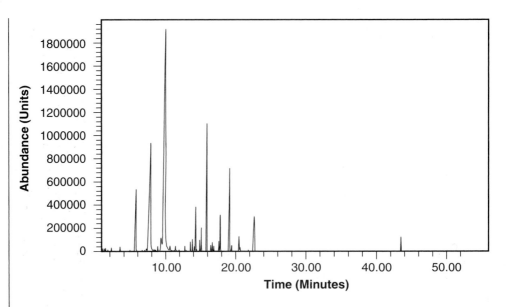

figure 6.3

A Gas Chromatography/Mass Spectrometry Fingerprint. This GC/MS graph identifies an insect resin used by native people in western North America for a variety of purposes, including making baskets watertight and repairing ceramic vessels.

Because ancient DNA molecules are normally so fragmented, and because preserved soft tissues are so rare, scientists had little hope of finding and analyzing these proteins until recently. Breakthroughs that made DNA analysis possible included the polymerase chain reaction (PCR), a method for copying any fragment of DNA, and the successful recovery of DNA from preserved hard tissues, such as bones and teeth. Preserved hard tissues are durable and relatively abundant in the archaeological record.

DNA can be used to understand the evolution of modern humans, trace migrations of people, identify individuals, and determine the origins of domestic plants and animals. People's subsistence activities led to alterations (and sometimes to domestication) of the DNA of the plants and animals they used, and the history of those changes can be traced through DNA analysis. The use of DNA analysis in the interpretation of human remains is discussed further in Chapter 8.

CONTENTSELECT

Search articles in the ContentSelect database using they key words *temporal types* and *tool assemblages*. What are some examples of these classes of artifacts described in the articles? What are some issues in classifying artifacts in terms of temporal types and assemblages?

Chapter Summary

All materials recovered from archaeological collection and excavation must be cataloged, classified, and analyzed as a basis for interpretation. Classification of artifacts can be a challenge because it is difficult to know the intentions and cultural values of the prehistoric makers.

Even small changes in artifacts can reflect major changes in technology and society. In classification, attributes are defined, measured, and described quantitatively or qualitatively. Artifacts generally are classified into types according to their morphology and sometimes also according to their function and style.

Artifacts limited to certain time periods establish temporal types. All the materials from a site, representing all the activities that took place there at a particular time, are called an assemblage. Artifact categories include stone (flaked and ground), ceramics, metal, glass, bone and shell, and perishables such as textiles.

Basic artifact analyses begin with descriptive analysis, in which archaeologists determine the associations among the materials and identify tool assemblages. More specialized analyses include evaluating use-wear, sourcing raw materials, identifying inorganic or organic residues on artifacts, and performing special studies such as protein residue analysis and DNA analysis.

Key Concepts

assemblage, 146
attributes, 144
classification, 142
DNA analysis, 161

flintknapping, 148
geochemical sourcing, 160
morphology, 144
protein residue analysis, 161

style, 145
temporal types, 145
typology, 142
use-wear analysis, 159

Suggested Readings

If you want to learn more about the concepts and issues discussed in this chapter, consider looking at the following resources. (Some may be rather technical.)

Banning, E. B. (2000). *The Archaeologist's Laboratory: The Analysis of Archaeological Data*. New York: Plenum Press.

Balme, Jane, and Alistair Paterson (eds.). (2006). *Archaeology in Practice: A Student Guide to Archaeological Analysis*. Malden, MA: Blackwell Publishing.

Rice, Patricia. (1998). *Doing Archaeology: A Hands-On Laboratory Manual*. Mountain View, CA: Mayfield.

Sutton, Mark Q., and Brooke S. Arkush. (2006). *Archaeological Laboratory Methods: An Introduction* (4th ed.). Dubuque, IA: Kendall/Hunt.

These are the four guides to general laboratory procedures. As with field methods, there are few general guides to the analysis of archaeological materials. However, a fairly large number of works on the study of very specific materials, such as lithics, faunal remains, and botanical materials, are available (see references in text).

chapter 7

Determining Time

GRADUATE STUDENTS IN archaeology at the University of California at Riverside had the advantage of a radiocarbon laboratory, not only on campus but also in the anthropology department itself. We also had the good fortune to have as one of our professors the director of the radiocarbon lab, Dr. R. E. Taylor, one of the world's foremost authorities on **archaeometry** (the science of archaeological measurement). My dissertation topic dealt with the chronology of the western Great Basin in eastern California, so I was going to need to have a large number of radiocarbon dates "run" from my excavations at the Rose Spring site. Back then, in the mid-1980s, archaeologists were required to pay as much as $250 per radiocarbon sample. As a poor, starving graduate student, I (Robert Yohe) was horrified at the prospect of paying for up to 20 radiocarbon samples. Fortunately, Dr. Taylor was very willing to work with students on their projects, and he struck a simple deal with me: if I learned how to become a radiocarbon laboratory technician and prepared my own samples, I would not have to pay for my dates. I was more than happy to accept the deal. I had always enjoyed working in labs (I started out as an undergraduate in biology) and was looking forward to learning the ins and outs of a working research radiocarbon laboratory.

My first visit to the interior of the laboratory had occurred when I was considering entering the Ph.D. program at Riverside a couple of years prior to my agreement with Dr. Taylor. The gas production line (used to turn archaeological samples into carbon dioxide) took up most of the smaller of the two laboratory rooms devoted to the radiocarbon equipment. It was a strange amalgam of the lab of Dr. Frankenstein and something out of a Tim-Burton-meets-Rube-Goldberg nightmare, with networks of plastic and glass tubing tracing the walls and ceilings, connected to glass containers with bubbling brown liquid (which I would later discover was potassium dichromate, a gas-cleaning fluid). Several glass cylinders submerged in insulated containers of liquid nitrogen overflowed, the resulting mist cascading to the floor several feet below. "Wow," I said to myself at the time, "Wouldn't it be great to actually work in a place like this!" Some years later, I got my wish and spent many hours over many months in that same

Robert Yohe in the radiocarbon lab at UC Riverside.

laboratory, preparing and dating my charcoal samples from ancient fire hearths that had once warmed hands and roasted jackrabbits for people who had camped in eastern California long ago.

Many archaeologists who have not had the good fortune of working in a radiocarbon laboratory tend to look at radiocarbon (^{14}C) dating with a "black box" mentality: you send your charcoal or other organic sample to the dating lab, they do their magic, and out the other end pops a date! In other words, they do not recognize the multiple steps of "running" a radiocarbon date. Each step is vital to producing an accurate, uncontaminated date. After preparing and dating more than a dozen samples, I came to fully appreciate the wonder of what I was doing.

Although the pretreatment and sample preparation for the charcoal was fairly "cookbook" in its technique, each of the samples I prepared was

165

slightly different because it had a separate, individual, and unique history that had special meaning to me because I had collected the samples myself. I approached the preparation of every sample with a sense of anticipation and excitement because each one would provide yet another important date that would help me understand the history of my site. As it turned out, the samples from my archaeological project varied in age from little more than 100 years old to nearly 6,000 years of age. Because I was so closely involved in the process of running my own dates, I developed a profound and lasting appreciation of archaeometry and the scientists who make this discipline their lifework.

For the location of the Rose Spring site and other sites mentioned in this chapter, see the map on page 167.

What Is So Important about Time?

When people discuss archaeology, you generally hear references to time, such as "2000 BC" or "50,000 BP," that seem to have profound importance. Why is time so important to archaeologists? Because archaeology is the study of all aspects of the human past, it is critical to know *when* the particular archaeological phenomenon we are observing occurred in order to relate it to other things that are either older or younger. We view the past as a sequence of temporal events that constitutes a **chronology**. If we want to track how human behavior changed over time and across geographical space, we need to establish a time frame or chronological context for our artifacts, ecofacts, and features. In other words, we need to control for time in order to understand change—for example, change in the types of animals people ate, in the types of dwellings they built, or in the designs on the pottery they made. Recall from Chapter 1 that there are two main approaches to the dating of archaeological materials: relative dating and chronometric dating.

Older or Younger?
Relative Dating in Archaeology

Relative dating gives the relative age of an artifact, feature, or stratum in relation to other cultural items found in archaeological deposits. What this means is that the archaeologist can say that item A is older than item B, which is younger than item C, where item A is at the highest point in the deposit, item C is at the bottom of the site, and item B is between the other two. With relative dating, you may be able to determine the age of items in relation to one another, but you cannot determine the number of

LOCATION MAP: **Sites Mentioned in Chapter 7**

1 ■ Rose Spring site
   Olancha, California

2 ■ Hogup Cave
   Southwestern Utah

3 ■ Danger Cave
   Wendover, Utah

4 ■ Thasos
   Greece

5 ■ Olduvai Gorge
   Tanzania

6 ■ Shroud of Turin
   Turin, Italy

months, years, decades, or millennia that separate the objects or features. Relative dating allows archaeologists to arrange artifacts, ecofacts, and features in a chronological sequence without knowing exactly when these events occurred or for how long. Table 7.1 summarizes the relative dating methods that archaeologists have used to determine whether groups are older or younger than one another. In the remainder of this section, we describe each one.

Stratigraphy and Superposition

Before the discovery of radiocarbon dating and other radiometric techniques for measuring time, it was difficult to construct a meaningful temporal context for archaeological materials. In the early days of archaeology, sites that lacked historical documents or

table 7.1

Relative Dating Techniques

METHOD	REQUIREMENTS	EXAMPLES OF USE
Stratigraphy (law of superposition)	Undisturbed, clear geological deposition of soils, gravels, lava	Dating of material relative to underlying or overlying strata; used in developing temporal types/index fossils
Index fossils/biostratigraphy	Fossils of known relative age	Use of vertebrate fossil forms to date sites with poor or inverted stratigraphy (used the same way as temporal types)
Temporal types	Artifact types that are specific to dated strata	Use of certain projectile point types or decorated pottery shards to date surface sites or sites with poor stratigraphic context
Seriation	Artifact styles in a stratified context	Uses similar to temporal types; also measures changes in popularity of certain styles over time
Fluorine, uranium, nitrogen (FUN) dating	Bones in an uncertain stratigraphic context	Determining whether human and extinct animals are contemporaneous in a site

features (such as hieroglyphics or inscribed stelae) required some method of dating that could reliably differentiate between groups that were obviously separated by centuries if not millennia. Archaeology owes a debt of gratitude to the earth sciences, particularly to Charles Lyell for his work *Principles of Geology,* written in 1830. It was here that the concept of superposition (defined in Chapter 1) was first popularized. This simple law states that under most circumstances, items found in strata (rock or soil layers) above a particular fossil or stratum are more recent in age than those found below. Archaeologists facing the problem of deciphering cultural strata frequently use stratigraphic analysis to differentiate materials that are older or younger.

Index Fossils and Biostratigraphy

Geologists and early paleontologists realized that fossils of certain extinct species of animals and plants were found only in certain strata, which could be placed in a chronological sequence based on the presence of these **index fossils.** Knowing the position of time-sensitive species in the stratigraphic sequence gave geologists a powerful tool with which to "date," at least in a relative sense, strata of unknown age separated by great distances from known sequences or stratigraphic deposits with significant discontinuities. Using evolutionary changes in well-known groups of animals as a dating tool is known as **biostratigraphy** (or *faunal correlation*).

Sometimes the human bones and artifacts with which fossil animals are associated can be dated at least relatively to certain epochs of time by reference to the time-sensitive species. This is using index fossils archaeologically in the same way that paleontologists use them for dating extinct faunas. In eastern Africa, for example, certain species of extinct pigs of the genera *Notochoerus* and *Nyanzachoerus* serve to place fossil humans of the genus *Australopithecus* in the correct temporal sequence. This sequencing is possible because it is well established in the paleontological record when particular species of pigs (as well as other types of animals, including elephants, antelopes, and rodents) existed. The presence or absence of particular time-sensitive species is helpful when other dating techniques cannot be applied.

Archaeologists adopted the concept of the index fossil and applied it to artifact types that appeared to be commonplace only during specific periods. Certain styles of pottery, certain types of material (such as stone, bronze, or iron), and certain forms of projectile points became known as *temporal types* because they seemed to be time-specific. Although archaeologists could not be certain of the actual length of time each artifact type was used, the concept of temporal types (defined in Chapter 6) allowed them to develop an ordinal scale of time-marking changes in aspects in material culture.

Temporal Types

Recall from Chapter 6 that temporal types are archaeological materials that can be tied to specific earlier or later periods of time. An early example of the use of temporal types was the development of the **three-age system** of chronology (Stone, Bronze, and Iron Ages) in Europe by Christian Thomsen, who in 1816 was appointed curator of the Danish National Museum of Antiquities (see Chapter 1). After studying and organizing the archaeological materials in the collections under his charge, Thomsen noticed that certain types of artifacts and certain types of burials seemed to occur together in excavated sites in Scandinavia. Stone cutting tools were found with pottery, glass beads, and stone-chambered tombs. Bronze tools were found with glass beads, pottery, stone cist (coffin) graves, human cremations, cinerary urn (urn with ashes from cremation) graves, as well as objects made from copper and silver. Iron tools were found associated with bronze tools, chamber tombs in barrows (burial mounds), and horses, but lacked stone-chambered tombs and stone cist graves.

These groupings of finds suggested at least three separate chronological periods in northern Europe (Graslund 1987) and served as temporal markers. Assuming that stoneworking preceded the production of metals, and relying on accounts from historical sources relating to the Romans and the Celts, Thomsen recognized that the age of forged iron tools was the most recent. In his book, *Guide to Northern Archaeology* (1848), he described the archaeological collections of the Museum of National Antiquities and first proposed the three-age system that is still in use today. Thomsen's recognition of time-sensitive artifacts allowed him to develop a rudimentary chronology without ever seeing direct stratigraphic relationships in the ground. A more recent example of temporal types is stone projectile points from the Great Basin of western North America (Highlight 7.1).

Seriation

The use of temporal types allows archaeologists to see specific changes in certain artifact styles over time and gauge their popularity at any point in the past by observing stratigraphic changes in stylistic frequencies. The tracking of such frequencies over time is called **seriation.** By examining the various percentages of types of artifacts that occur stratigraphically, and plotting these percentages as horizontal bars on a graph, one can easily see stylistic popularity change over time. What emerges are seriation frequency curves, also known as "battleship" curves because of their similarity in configuration to a battleship seen from above (Figure 7.1).

Many humans seem to enjoy frequent change. Today, in contemporary Western culture, we want to wear the latest styles in clothing, drive the newest cars, or engage in the latest craze in body adornment, all of which will change within a matter of months. Historical archaeologists can use seriation of objects such as clay pipe stems, tin cans, and grave markers to give precise measurements of time, because we have records that tell us specifically when certain styles changed or when new manufacturing techniques were adopted.

One advantage of seriation is that it allows the archaeologist to "date" nonstratigraphic sites to particular periods of time based on the occurrence of known temporal types. For example, pottery styles—both vessel form and decoration—can be used for purposes of seriation. Seriation can be either contextual or frequency based. Context-based seriation uses groups of artifacts of a particular type (such as pottery) that shift through time. Frequency-based seriation looks at the change in a particular type of artifact (such as a change in decoration). An illustration of how seriation can work as a dating method is seen in the analysis of design or style changes in ancient coins (Highlight 7.2).

Temporal Markers in Great Basin Archaeology

Projectile points are the sharp tips of spears, darts, or arrows, all weapons that the inhabitants of the New World used at various times in the past. Based on the excavation of hundreds of archaeological sites, archaeologists noted that certain types of projectile points seem to occur within limited time spans in the archaeological record.

At the bottoms of deeply stratified archaeological sites such as Danger Cave and Hogup Cave in northwestern Utah, large, lanceolate (narrow leaf-like) projectile points or shouldered-stem points occur. Midway up into the cultural deposit, large corner- or side-notched projectile points, such as Elko Corner-notched and Northern Side-notched points, are found. At the

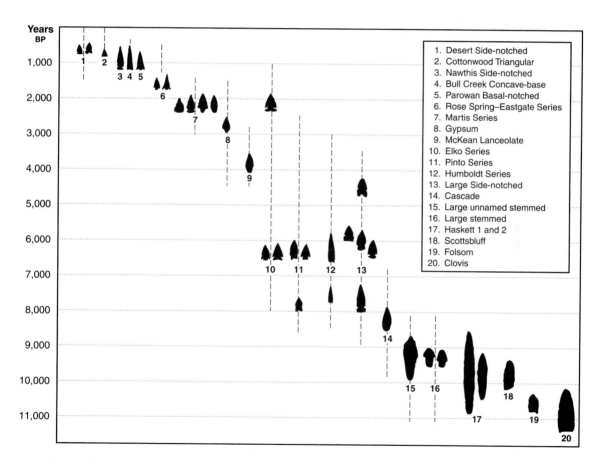

1. Desert Side-notched
2. Cottonwood Triangular
3. Nawthis Side-notched
4. Bull Creek Concave-base
5. Parowan Basal-notched
6. Rose Spring–Eastgate Series
7. Martis Series
8. Gypsum
9. McKean Lanceolate
10. Elko Series
11. Pinto Series
12. Humboldt Series
13. Large Side-notched
14. Cascade
15. Large unnamed stemmed
16. Large stemmed
17. Haskett 1 and 2
18. Scottsbluff
19. Folsom
20. Clovis

Great Basin Projectile Point Sequence. These projectile points are temporal types for the sequence of material culture in the Great Basin area of western North America.

Source: Adapted from Warren L. d'Azevedo, ed., 1986, *Handbook of North American Indians,* Vol. II (Washington, DC: Smithsonian Institution), Figure 3. Used with permission.

top of the cave deposits are small points with notches in their sides called Desert Side-notched points. None of the large lanceolate points are found with the small, side-notched points, nor are the large corner-notched points found with the small side-notched points at the top of the deposit.

These patterns of vertical distribution of points recur in archaeological deposits throughout the American West, and, although there is overlap in the usage of the various types, many seem to be specific to limited spans of time. Even without the assistance of radiocarbon dating to give a more precise range of time for these various projectile points, lanceolate points indicate an early occupation, and small side-notched points represent the most recent period of time in the Great Basin.

CRITICAL **THINKING** QUESTIONS

1. What is a vertical distribution? How do vertical distributions help to determine temporal types?
2. Why are temporal markers a relative dating method rather than a chronometric dating method?
3. Why would it be important to determine the horizontal distribution of temporal types?

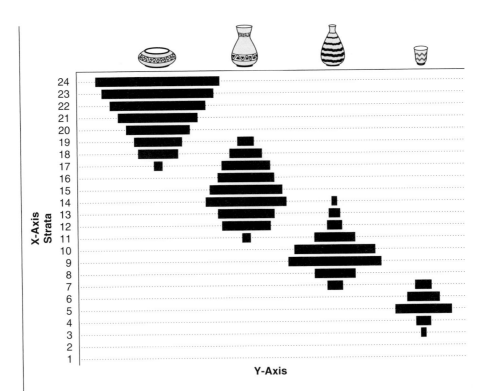

figure 7.1

Seriation Frequency Curves. The x-axis represents time, and the y-axis represents frequency. This format offers a quick means of immediately recognizing the popularity of style of certain artifacts over time. You can see why these plots are called "battleship" curves.

HIGHLIGHT **7.2**

Seriation in Ancient Greek Coins

Consider the development of the satyr and nymph motif (theme) from the Archaic to the Classic periods in Greek coins from the island of Thasos in the northern Aegean Sea (Koerper 1999). As you can see, there is clear evidence of stylistic changes in coins with satyr and nymph images from the Early Archaic (ca. 530 BC) to the High Classic (411 BC) periods, a relatively short period of time in archaeological terms. According to ancient texts, the people of Thasos were subjugated by the Athenians about midway through this period.

Applying the assumption that stylistic changes are both gradual and lineal, an archaeologist can arrange the coins in a sequence from the presumed earliest (number 1) to the latest (number 10) based on changes in hairstyle, facial detail, and body proportions. This sequence, or series, then can be used diagnostically to help date coins and artifacts found in association with coins in archaeological sites throughout the ancient Mediterranean world.

Seriation in motifs in ancient Greek coins. (Courtesy of Henry C. Koerper.)

CRITICAL **THINKING** QUESTIONS

1. Is the Thasos sequence an example of context-based or frequency-based seriation? Under what circumstances might the Greek coins represent both types of seriation?

2. What are the advantages and limitations of seriation as a dating method?
3. How could you use the Thasos sequence to date events in the archaeological record such as contacts among peoples of the Aegean?

Fluorine, Uranium, and Nitrogen (FUN) Dating

Measuring the quantities of fluorine, uranium, and nitrogen (FUN) in bone provides a useful relative dating tool that became available to scientists in the first half of the twentieth century. The longer bone is buried in the ground, the more nitrogen it loses. At the same time, it gains more fluorine and uranium from the surrounding soil. Suppose you are trying to determine the contemporaneity of human bone with extinct fauna found in the same stratum. The values for fluorine, nitrogen, and uranium in the human bone and in the extinct animal bone should all be similar if the bones are of like age. Without giving a specific age, **FUN analysis** tells whether the human bone is as ancient as the associated animals.

Since the advent of radiocarbon dating, this method has been used infrequently. The highest-profile case featuring fluorine dating was the infamous Piltdown case (see Highlight 1.3 in Chapter 1), in which fluorine analysis of bone fragments showed that the remains were not contemporaneous with the fossil mammals found with them.

Real Time: Chronometric Dating

Chronometric (sometimes called *absolute*) dating provides a specific temporal assignment in terms of years (with, in most cases, an error factor included). Thus, chronometric dating gives a specific age of both prehistoric and historic materials rather than indicating simply that one object is older or younger than another. It puts the past in more of a "real time" context. Chronometric dating techniques include cross-dating, dendrochronology, and radiometric methods, such as radiocarbon dating and potassium-argon dating. Table 7.2 summarizes chronometric dating techniques and their potential limitations.

Cross-Dating and Dendrochronology

Cross-dating uses some common indicator to link objects of known age to similar objects of unknown age. Examples of cross-dating are the use of ancient texts of known age to date similar texts of unknown origin as well as events to which the texts refer. Cross-dating is a feature of tree-ring dating—**dendrochronology**—in which archaeological remains are linked to growth rings in trees that represent specific calendar years.

Dendrochronology was the first consistently accurate means of providing specific absolute dates for archaeological materials (Stokes and Smiley 1996). The annual production of tree rings was a phenomenon first described by the ancient Greeks, and the first reference to the use of tree rings as a possible means of dating the antiquity of humanity in Europe was made in the early 1800s (Baillie 1982). Andrew Ellicot Douglass (1867–1962), an astronomer from Flagstaff, Arizona, is credited with the direct application of tree rings to archaeological concerns of time.

While working at the Lowell Observatory in 1901, Douglass developed an interest in sunspots and how their climatic influence might be reflected in the annual rings of trees. Tree rings reflect tree growth, which is influenced by weather and hence by solar activity, so it seemed plausible that trees could provide a long-term record of sunspots. Tree rings tend to be wide in years with warmth and high rainfall and narrow when these are absent. This tendency yields a recognizable sequence of ring widths. Douglass recognized that by looking at a series of trees from within a specific area but cut at different periods, he could cross-date the trees by matching up the tree-ring sequences. Once ring-width variation was recognized, tree-ring sequences could be matched up with logs cut from trees of the same species, decades after they had been cut (Figure 7.2).

In 1914 the archaeologist Clark Wissler asked Douglass about the possible application of his cross-dating technique to logs recovered from prehistoric ruins in the Ameri-

table 7.2

Chronometric Dating Methods

METHOD	MATERIAL REQUIRED	AGE RANGE	EXAMPLE
Dendrochronology	Large pieces of wood with visible ring structure	0 to 12,000 years	Use of wooden beams from Viking ship to date its construction
Radiocarbon	Organic material: wood, bone, shell, leather, hair, plant remains	300 to 50,000 years	Charcoal from an ancient fire hearth
Potassium-argon	Volcanic rock or ash	100,000 to several billion years	Lava flows covering fossil-bearing beds
Uranium series	Bone, shell, calcite	10,000 to 500,000 years	Fossil bone from a limestone cave
Thermoluminescence	Fired clay, pottery	0 to 100,000 years	A fired-clay vessel
Electron spin resonance	Tooth enamel, calcite, bone	1,000 to 1 million years	A tooth from a fossil hominid
Archaeomagnetism	Pottery, clay, soil, rocks	0 to 30,000 years	Burned clay house floors
Obsidian hydration analysis	Obsidian	0 to 500,000 years	A thin section from a projectile point

can Southwest. Soon after, samples of wooden beams from various ruins were submitted, and over the next 15 years Douglass began to build a sequence. After many collecting expeditions and analysis of hundreds of prehistoric wood beams, by late 1929 Douglass had succeeded in pushing the sequence from the modern era back to AD 700. In following years, the chronology was extended to the beginning of the Christian era (Nash 2002). European dendrochronologists soon were developing dendrochronological sequences for parts of Great Britain and northern Europe.

Dendrochronology is the most accurate of the dating techniques, but its limitations are obvious. Only rarely and only in certain areas are timbers well preserved in the archaeological record. Also, trees that do not produce annual tree rings cannot be used for

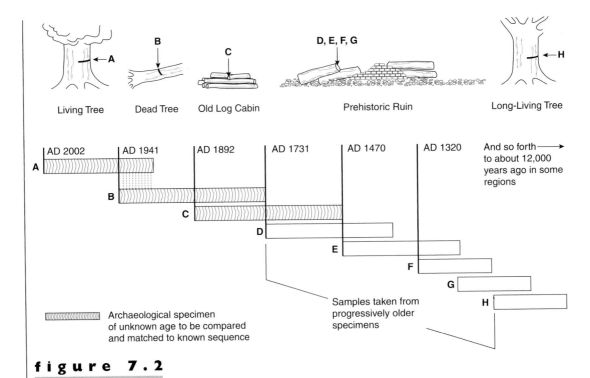

figure 7.2

How Dendrochronology Works. Cores are taken from woods of different ages, beginning with a living specimen, and the unique ring distributions are matched up to form a continuous sequence, called a *skeleton plot.* The rings of an archaeological specimen of unknown age can be matched to the skeleton plot, and its age can be determined.

dating even if they are preserved. Additionally, there are geographic limitations to the method. For instance, dendrochronology sequences for the American Southwest work only in that area and nowhere else. Further, the technique works best in areas where tree growth is determined primarily by annual rainfall rather than river flow.

Radiometric Techniques

Radiometric dating is based on the principle of atomic decay. Not until the mid-twentieth century and nuclear research spawned by World War II did archaeologists have at their disposal chronometric dating methods applicable to most archaeological sites everywhere. These methods—radiometric techniques—can give specific dates with a margin of error of only a few decades—a very small margin when one is looking at an event that took place more than 25,000 years ago. Reliable radiometric dating revolutionized archaeology (even so, archaeologists usually use several dating strategies simultaneously to establish or test the accuracy of both relative and chronometric dates).

Some elements ("parent" elements), such as carbon, have naturally radioactive isotopes and can decay over time to become some other element ("daughter" elements), such as nitrogen. If we can determine the rate of decay, and can measure accurately the ratio of the original, "parent" element to the "daughter" element (the product of decay), then we can reliably determine how much time has passed since the original element first started to decay. Fortunately, there are certain decay pathways of common elements that we can use for determining the age of archaeological materials. The decay process functions like an ancient clock, marking time with each decay event. What starts the ancient radiometric "clock" ticking? What events or circumstances allow us to use radioactive decay to measure prehistoric age?

Each method of radiometric dating has its own clock-starting mechanism. For radiocarbon dating, which is used to date organic items (things that once lived), death (the point at which the plant or animal stops taking in any new radioactive carbon) starts the clock. For potassium-argon dating, the clock starts ticking with the creation of volcanic rock: the molten state of rock drives off the accumulated daughter product, argon, thereby allowing for the buildup of new argon gas as the radiopotassium decays.

RADIOCARBON DATING   Perhaps the most commonly used and most important method of radiometric dating in archaeology is **radiocarbon dating.** This method can be successfully applied to most archaeological sites that contain organic materials, including charcoal, bone, shell, wood, and other plant and animal remains. In some cases, even soils and pottery (when they contain shell or charcoal fragments), mortar (which may contain atmospheric carbon), and iron (when it contains carbon from forging) can be dated with this versatile method, developed after World War II by an American physicist (Highlight 7.3).

How Radiocarbon Forms   Research and refinements have made radiocarbon dating an indispensable technique to modern archaeology. To appreciate this technique and its limitations, it is important to understand how ^{14}C becomes integrated into living organisms and how it "behaves" in the natural world.

Carbon occurs as two stable isotopes (^{12}C and ^{13}C) and one radioactive form (^{14}C), or radiocarbon. Radiocarbon is formed in the upper atmosphere as a by-product of cosmic-ray bombardment and ultimately is incorporated into carbon dioxide (Figure 7.3). Between 0.01 and 5 percent of the carbon dioxide in the biosphere contains radiocarbon. Most of it is absorbed into the ocean, and the rest mixes with the general atmosphere. The radiocarbon that is left in the atmosphere is taken up by plants during photosynthesis, thereby integrating itself into the structure of all plants. Plant-eating animals and the animals that eat them ultimately incorporate ^{14}C into their bodies, reaching a level of equilibrium with atmospheric ^{14}C.

When an organism dies, it ceases to take in radiocarbon, and the radiocarbon that has been integrated into its structure begins to decay and disrupt the equilibrium. The death of the organism starts the radiometric clock. The known decay rate allows us to estimate the age of remains from the amount of radiocarbon remaining. Radiocarbon's **half-life** (the time it takes for one-half of the total amount of a given sample to decay) is known to be approximately 5,700 years, so in about 5,700 years, only half of the original amount of radiocarbon will be left in the remains of an organism. By convention, however, the **Libby half-life** (5,568 ± 30 years) is used in all radiocarbon determinations (it is based on an earlier estimation of the half-life).

HIGHLIGHT **7.3**

Willard Libby and the Beginnings of Radiocarbon Dating

One of the by-products of the development of the atomic bomb was the establishment of specific decay rates for many radioisotopes. Among the young physicists participating in the Manhattan Project (the brain trust of the United States' best scientists working on the development of the atomic bomb) was Willard Libby, who developed a particular interest in determining the actual half-life of the commonly oc-

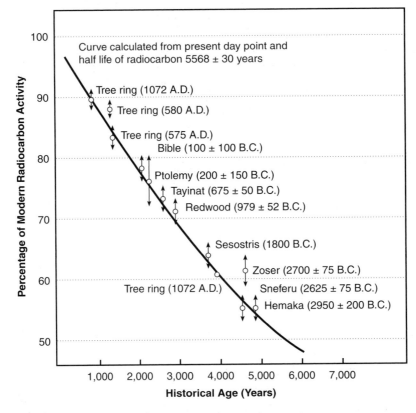

Libby's Curve of Knowns. By radiocarbon-dating objects of known ages, from historical contexts (such as the item labeled "Bible," representing the linen wrapping of one of the Dead Sea Scrolls) and from tree rings, Libby was able to demonstrate the reliability of this form of dating.

Source: R. E. Taylor, 1987, Radiocarbon Dating: An Archaeological Perspective (Orlando, FL: Academic Press), Figure 2.3. Used with permission.

Willard Libby.

curring (and the only naturally occurring) radioactive isotopes of carbon, ^{14}C. At the end of World War II, Libby was hired as the youngest full professor at the University of Chicago and continued to pursue one of his pet projects—the use of radioactive carbon to date archaeological materials.

At the time, Libby feared that his idea would be viewed with such skepticism that he would be considered mad, so he kept his research in this area very low-key (Taylor 1987). New research suggested that the half-life of ^{14}C was about 5,000 years, and in a paper published in *Physical Review* in 1946, Libby proposed that the amounts of "radiocarbon" found in fossil carbon (e.g., in ancient plant or animal remains) would differ from the amounts found in modern biological carbon. Experimentation successfully showed that the half-life that Libby proposed for radiocarbon was correct and that carbon older than 50,000 years was devoid of ^{14}C. It became apparent that radiocarbon dating could become a reality.

The true test of the method was acquiring archaeological specimens of known ages and seeing whether the remaining amounts of radiocarbon really could be used to determine how old they were. This first radiocarbon analysis involved the sampling of four tree rings of known age and artifacts that could be specifically dated back to nearly 3000 BC by using the historical record. Much to the joy of all involved, the radiocarbon dates and the historical age of the items were nearly identical, and the resulting graph of the relationship became known as the **Libby Curve of Knowns** (Taylor 1987). The face of archaeology was to change forever in light of the development of a technique that could be used to date archaeological carbon younger than 50,000 years of age.

CRITICAL **THINKING** QUESTIONS

1. Why is radiometric dating using ^{14}C especially useful for the dating of archaeological remains?
2. What are some limitations of ^{14}C dating?
3. How is Willard Libby's story an example of the use of the scientific method in archaeology?

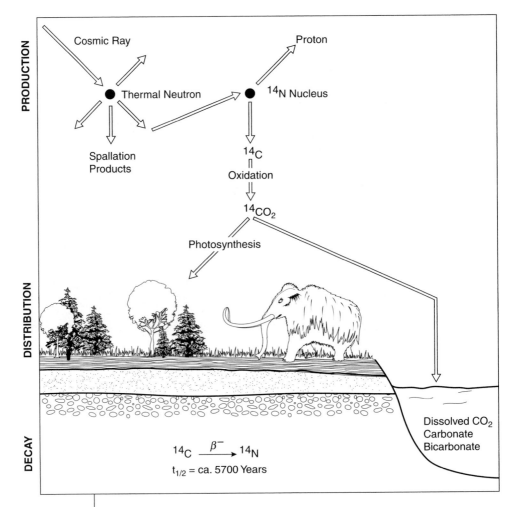

figure 7.3

Formation of Radiocarbon. This classic diagram illustrates the chemical process by which radioactive isotopes of carbon are formed. What is the half-life of radiocarbon? What kinds of remains can be dated with radiocarbon analysis? How do measurements of radiocarbon yield chronometric dates?

Source: R. E. Taylor, 1987, *Radiocarbon Dating: An Archaeological Perspective* (Orlando, FL: Academic Press), Figure 1.1. Used with permission.

Assumptions about Radiocarbon   The use of radiocarbon as a method of dating archaeological samples rests on certain assumptions (Taylor 1987):

1. The concentration of ^{14}C on Earth (both present in the atmosphere and dissolved in the ocean) has remained the same over time.
2. ^{14}C, as it is produced, mixes rapidly throughout the atmosphere and ocean.

3. The amounts of ^{14}C in samples used for radiocarbon dating have been unaltered other than by natural radioactive decay.
4. The half-life of ^{14}C is accurately known.
5. Natural levels of ^{14}C can be accurately measured.

Those assumptions are known to be basically correct, with the exception of the first. We now know that slight variations in the amount of radiocarbon produced in the upper atmosphere occurred in the past. Periodic fluctuations in Earth's magnetic field influence the cosmic-ray flux and resulted in periods of lesser and greater ^{14}C production at different times in the past.

As radiocarbon measurement became more sophisticated and sensitive, discrepancies between some of the known-age materials and the calculated radiocarbon dates became apparent. Radiocarbon studies of tree rings, for example, have demonstrated fairly consistent variation in both short-term and long-term radiocarbon production over the past 8,000 years. What this means to the archaeologist is that **radiocarbon years before present** (RCYBP) are not equivalent to calendar years.

This is not as great a problem as one might initially assume. The dating of tree rings—particularly those of the ancient bristlecone pine *(Pinus longaeva)* of eastern California, with a continuous 8,700-year record—and uranium series dates on corals have allowed for the development of calibration curves back to about 20,000 years (Taylor and Aitken 1997). Calibration curves allow for the conversion of radiocarbon dates to calendar-year equivalents. For example, 4,000 RCYBP is equal to approximately 4,400 calendar years ago (or 2400 BC). Figure 7.4 summarizes how to read a radiocarbon date. It is important to be aware that "present" is defined as AD 1950, which marks the beginning of radiocarbon dating.

Collecting Radiocarbon Samples in the Field The first step in radiocarbon dating is the collection of an archaeological sample suitable for analysis. The material must be organic and must be from a meaningful stratigraphic context or association with artifactual materials that one wishes to date. A field archaeologist is unlikely to date random pieces of bone or charcoal but is likely to choose charcoal from specific features, such as ovens or hearths, or human bone from a burial in primary context. It is important that the sample for dating is cultural and not some item naturally introduced into the deposit. Rodent burrowing and natural fires can account for the presence of some bone and charcoal that is out of context.

1. A published radiocarbon date always appears in the same format, for example:
     4,572 ± 60 RCYBP (UCR-4957)
2. The "plus-or-minus" value after the age means that the date is a statistical statement about the "average" age of the sample within a certain margin of error, rather than an actual age. In the example, the date 4,572 is the mean or statistical average of the calculated date of the sample, give or take the standard deviation of 60 radiocarbon years. Thus, the sample ranged from 4,512 to 4,632 radiocarbon years (RCY) before the present (BP).
3. The last part of the radiocarbon date is the designation of the laboratory where the sample was run, in this case the University of California at Riverside (UCR), and the laboratory number (4957). The laboratory number is reported so that researchers who have questions about a date or sample can contact the appropriate laboratory.

f i g u r e   7 . 4

How to Read a Radiocarbon Date

This archaeologist is collecting a carbon sample in the field. What are some likely sources of this carbon? What are the steps in collecting the sample, and what precautions must be taken? How will the sample be processed in the radiocarbon laboratory? How will an absolute date for the sample and its associated site feature be determined?

Once material is chosen for ^{14}C dating, care must be taken to avoid contamination. The sample is collected with a clean trowel and is placed in a sterile, sealable container. Often aluminum foil packets are custom-made in the field for the purpose and are then placed in paper bags with the appropriate provenience information. Storage of the samples away from heat and humidity is another precaution to prevent or delay possible fungal or bacterial growth on samples before they are sent to the radiocarbon laboratory for analysis.

Preparing Samples for Radiocarbon Dating When radiocarbon dating was first developed, required samples were huge (sometimes weighing more than a pound), not an easy selling point for archaeologists at the time. Datable artifacts are often one-of-a-kind, and radiocarbon dating is by its very nature a destructive technique. Smaller samples later became possible as techniques for assessing radiocarbon age improved. Even so, sample size still can be a problem for archaeologists because dating labs still prefer fairly large samples, ranging from 2 grams for charcoal to over 100 grams for bone.

Samples of archaeological material must first be "cleaned" or pretreated. For example, charcoal recovered from fire hearths frequently is full of contaminants, such as dirt, fungus, insects, and fine plant rootlets that literally grow through the pieces of charcoal. The first thing to do with such a sample is to separate the charcoal from the dirt and other materials under a microscope. Once the sample is visually clean, it is weighed, boiled in a strong basic (high pH) solution to remove base-soluble contaminants, washed in distilled water several times, and then boiled in a strong acid (hydrochloric acid) to remove carbonates. Then the sample is boiled in distilled water to remove the acid absorbed by the charcoal, and finally it is dried in a drying oven.

The sample, now presumably clean, is ready to be converted to gas. This is done by burning the sample at high temperatures using pure oxygen. The resulting carbon dioxide gas goes through a series of copper furnaces, cleansing solutions, and desiccants (drying agents) into gas collection containers, which are submersed into containers of liquid nitrogen. The liquid nitrogen captures the purified carbon dioxide as "dry ice" by freezing it to the sides of the container. This dry ice is thawed and stored in canisters for a minimum of 23 days to eliminate any radon—a radioactive gas with a short half-life—that may have been introduced during sample processing and could produce false readings.

Methods of Radiocarbon Dating   The most common technique for assessing radiocarbon age is known as *decay counting* and relies on the measurement in a modified Geiger counter of the number of decay events of any remaining ^{14}C over a specific period of time. This information is used to infer the concentration of ^{14}C in the sample and thus the age of the item being examined.

In gas decay counting, once the sample is prepared and is devoid of possible radon contamination, it is placed in a Geiger counter–type device. This device measures the number of decay events of any ^{14}C that remains in the carbon dioxide gas. The number of decay events during a specific period allows for the calculation of the amount of ^{14}C present. The amount of ^{14}C then can be used to calculate the age of the original sample of charcoal and of the hearth from which it was collected.

In liquid scintillation decay counting, the sample is converted to a carbon-rich liquid that uses a specialized decay detector. This technique, unlike gas decay counting, does not result in the formation of radon, so there is no delay in counting.

The recent development of ion counting has been a tremendous advance in radiocarbon dating. It eliminates the need to estimate the amount of ^{14}C remaining in a sample. Radiocarbon atoms are counted directly by means of **accelerator mass spectrometry (AMS)**. AMS employs a particle accelerator and measures the exact number of remaining isotopes of radiocarbon in a sample. Ion counting has reduced sample size to milligrams. Basically, if something is big enough to see, it is big enough to date.

Limitations of Radiocarbon Dating   Radiocarbon dating is likely one of the greatest boons to archaeology of all time, but it is a technique that cannot be used in every situation. Generally, only objects that were once alive (organic material)—animal bones, shell, charcoal, skin or leather, wood, grass, seeds, and so on—can be radiocarbon dated. The one exception is the direct dating of iron tools by extracting carbon introduced to the metal alloy during forging. In archaeological sites where organic preservation is poor, such as areas with highly acidic soils, there may be no collectable samples to submit for radiocarbon analysis.

Another limitation is that radiocarbon dating presently is accurate only for dates ranging from 300 to 50,000 years ago; it is not very good for dating older or younger

HIGHLIGHT **7.4**

Dating the Shroud of Turin

The Shroud of Turin, for centuries believed by many to be the burial shroud of Jesus Christ, has had its share of skeptics over the years. Housed in the Cathedral of St. John the Baptist in the rural countryside town of Turin, Italy, it has been an object of veneration and pilgrimage for much of Christendom. It was first documented in texts in 1353. Is this cloth really the burial sheet that covered the body of Jesus after his crucifixion?

The rectangular cloth appears to have bloodstains in appropriate places—the palms of the hands and tops of the feet and at the wound site in Jesus' side, reported in the New Testament to be the result of the thrust of a Roman spear. The ghostly, smoky image seemingly burned into the fabric depicts a bearded man with long hair who looks very familiar to all faithful Christians who gaze on it. Why, however, was such an extraordinary religious relic not written about prior to the mid-fourteenth century?

Until the development of accelerator mass spectrometry, determining the true age of the shroud simply was not possible. Conventional gas decay counting would have required too large a piece of the relic, and

the Catholic Church would not allow such a desecration. However, the development of direct ion counting through the use of a mass spectrometer meant that sample sizes could be small. Individual threads weighing milligrams could be used instead of large swaths weighing hundreds or thousands of grams.

After much discussion and negotiation, the church allowed the removal of approximately a dozen threads to be dated by three separate laboratories: one in Tucson, Arizona; another in Oxford, England; and a third in Zurich, Switzerland. The test was simple: dating a known-age piece of Egyptian linen of approximately the same age as the recorded death of Christ (in this case, the linen had previously been dated to 2,010 ± 80 RCYBP) and several samples from the Shroud of Turin. If the shroud was genuine, then the specimens from both sources should date to about the same time. If the shroud was not genuine, then the dates from the shroud should all be significantly more recent than the expected 2,000 years.

The results from all three labs were consistent: the shroud was a fake, albeit an impressive one. The mean

---

samples. Recent samples often are contaminated by carbon from the burning of fossil fuels since the beginning of the Industrial Revolution and from radiocarbon released into Earth's atmosphere during the above-ground testing of thermonuclear weapons in the 1950s. Nevertheless, radiocarbon dating stands as one of the most useful, relatively inexpensive, and accurate dating methods available to archaeologists today (Highlight 7.4).

A variation of radiocarbon dating called **oxidizable carbon ratio** (OCR) has been developed as a new dating technique. Using OCR, one can measure the amounts of organic and oxidized carbon in a sample (thus, obtaining a ratio of the two) to determine how long the sample material had been in the soil. Although OCR is still an experimental method, it holds great promise as an easy and inexpensive alternative to radiocarbon dating.

POTASSIUM-ARGON DATING   Another radiometric technique that has made it possible to date truly ancient archaeological sites, as well as our earliest ancestors, is **potassium-argon**

age of the known-age specimen of Egyptian linen was calculated as 1,964 ± 20 RCYBP (statistically the same as the original date). The twelve samples from the Shroud of Turin all turned out to be much younger. The average age of the shroud was determined to be 689 ± 16, calibrated to AD 1260 to 1390. Interestingly, the first mention of the shroud, in 1353, occurred within this range of dates.

Many of the faithful believe that modern science is simply in error and that the Shroud of Turin really is the burial cloth of Christ. After all, the scientific testing has not revealed how the image got on the cloth. In spite of many efforts by several scientists to explain how the image on the shroud was produced, no clear consensus has been reached. Many mysteries still surround this intriguing holy relic.

CRITICAL **THINKING** QUESTIONS

1. How might the supporters of the biblical age of the shroud argue that the radiocarbon dates were wrong?
2. How can experimental archaeology be used to determine how the image on the shroud was made?

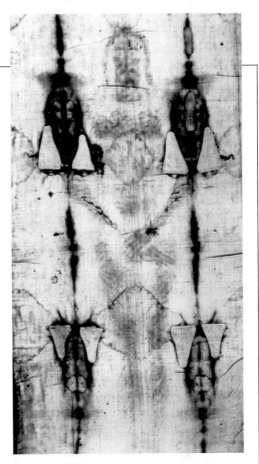

The Shroud of Turin.

(K/Ar) dating (also known as *radiopotassium dating*). Potassium, one of the most common elements on the planet, is found in nearly every object on Earth. It is particularly common in Earth's crust, especially in basalt. A certain amount of the potassium found in rock is the radioactive isotope of potassium, radiopotassium, or ^{40}K. Radiopotassium decays to form argon (Ar) and calcium (Ca). Whenever rock is melted, any accumulated argon gas in the rock is driven off, thereby resetting the radiometric clock and allowing new argon gas to accumulate. Scientists can measure this gas. Just as radiocarbon dating requires some event to start the radiometric clock (the death of an organism), potassium-argon dating requires the melting of rock to remove accumulated argon gas. By comparing the ratio between remaining potassium and the accumulated argon, the age of the rock can be determined.

The half-life of ^{40}K is around 1.3 billion years, so this dating method is useful for any volcanic rock that is older than 100,000 years of age. Potassium-argon dating has been used to determine the age of Earth—about 4.6 billion years. This technique has been particularly useful in dating truly ancient fossil hominid sites in eastern Africa, where there is a long history of volcanic activity. Here fossils or archaeological materials sandwiched between K/Ar-datable volcanic layers can be said to date between the two ages of the lava. For example, K/Ar dating indicates that the two lowermost volcanic layers at the Olduvai Gorge site in Tanzania date to 1.7 million and 2.1 million years ago; therefore, any materials found between these two layers are between 1.7 million and 2.1 million years old. At Olduvai, what was being dated was the eruption of the volcano, not the actual prehistoric sites. The findings of archaeological materials between the dated layers was fortuitous.

A limitation of the use of this technique is that the range of error for K/Ar dates is generally much higher than for radiocarbon dating (even though the detectable time depth is much greater). Margins of error can range from 10 to 50 percent. Even so, potassium-argon dating remains the best available method for determining the age of the very earliest archaeological sites.

URANIUM DATING A dating technique that bridges the gap between the upper limits of radiocarbon dating (50,000 years) and the lower ranges of potassium-argon dating (500,000 years) is the use of isotopic uranium. It has been used to date archaeological deposits in limestone caves ranging from 5,000 to 500,000 years of age. Two common isotopes of uranium (^{238}U and ^{235}U) decay into "daughter" elements, thorium (^{230}Th and ^{234}Th) and protactinium (^{231}Pa), which further decay at known rates into a variety of other elements. **Uranium-thorium (U/Th) dating** is applicable only to limestone (calcite) cave deposits, because what is actually being dated is the age of the formation of calcite, which contains water-soluble uranium but not thorium (which is not water soluble). Because ^{235}U (which decays into ^{231}Pa) is less common than ^{238}U (which comprises 99 percent of all uranium isotopes), protactinium is not particularly useful for measuring the age of archaeological samples. However, ^{238}U decays into daughter element ^{230}Th over time, so the archaeologist can measure the ratio of ^{238}U to ^{230}Th to determine when the cave limestone was deposited. Fortunately, ancient peoples commonly used caves for habitation purposes, so archaeological deposits under limestone deposits can be dated with this technique. Uranium series dating of fossil bone is not accurate, however. Natural bone contains no uranium but does absorb environmental uranium through groundwater.

FISSION TRACK DATING Another dating method based on the decay of ^{238}U is known as **fission track dating.** This method can be applied to volcanic glass, ancient manufactured glass, and even crystalline minerals found in ceramic artifacts. The radiometric clock is started by the formation of the natural glass or the production of the manufactured glass. Naturally occurring ^{238}U sometimes undergoes spontaneous decay or fission (splitting in half), breaking apart with such energy that it causes considerable damage to the internal structure of the glassy material. This damage is known as *fission tracks,* and when a glass surface is etched with acid, these tracks become visible under magnification.

In fission track dating, the amount of ^{238}U in the specimen is determined and the fission tracks are counted, based on a statistical sampling of the acid-etched surface of the glassy material. Because the rate of decay of ^{238}U is known, the total number of fission tracks reveals how many years have passed since the material was formed. The dating range for naturally formed materials is generally between 300,000 and several billion years. Human-produced glass less than 2,000 years of age can also be dated with this method.

THERMOLUMINESCENCE **Thermoluminescence (TL) dating** is a radiometric technique commonly used to date pottery, burned clay features (such as clay-lined fire hearths), and cave formations ranging from 50 to 500,000 years of age. Museums and antiquarians frequently employ this method to determine whether certain fired-clay artifacts are forgeries, and the technique is useful to archaeologists trying to date archaeological sites during that difficult temporal period between 50,000 and 500,000 years ago. Thermoluminescence dating is based on the fact that certain minerals (such as quartz and feldspar) entrap energy (in the form of electrons) from the decay of naturally occurring ^{238}U, ^{235}U, and ^{232}Th in the surrounding soils. The energy is caught in irregularities that exist in the crystalline lattice of the mineral microstructure. The entrapped energy can be freed only by heating the sample, which then releases the energy in the form of measurable light. The older the sample, the more light is released during heating.

What starts the radiometric clock for this method is the heating of the minerals, presumably from a cultural activity such as firing a clay pot or other ceramic object. The object then releases any energy that may already have been stored in the mineral crystals, freeing up space in the crystals to store new energy. Because clay contains such minerals in abundance, and people of the past manufactured many clay artifacts and fired-clay floors and hearths during daily activities, these artifacts or features can be used to date these cultural events. Also, stone tools made from crystalline stones, such as flint, can be dated by this method if they were heated in a fire at some time in their use-life.

Thermoluminescence dating is complicated. It is necessary to measure the amount of radioactivity in an object being dated as well as in the surrounding soils. It also is necessary to measure irregularities in the crystal lattices of the minerals in the object, which affect the amount of stored energy. Using the information, archaeologists can determine how much exposure the sample has had as well as how much it gets on average in a year. The ratio of the annual rate of exposure (or annual "dose") to the all-time exposure ("archaeodose") is equal to the actual age of the specimen in calendar years. When the sample is reheated and the released energy is measured, it is then possible to determine an age.

ELECTRON SPIN RESONANCE A related dating technique that is less commonly used (and is less sensitive) than thermoluminescence is **electron spin resonance (ESR)**. This technique is based on the same principle of trapped electrons in mineral crystals, but instead of heating the sample to release trapped electrons as light energy, ESR dating uses microwave radiation to cause the entrapped energy to resonate (continuously vibrate). This resonance is a function of microwave absorption, which can be measured. The technique seems to work best on fossil tooth enamel but has been used on bone and cave calcite. ESR dating also has been applied to the estimation of the maximum temperature to which past people heated certain materials (such as ancient preserved seeds or grain). As a dating method, it remains less accurate than thermoluminescence and is limited in age determination to less than a million years.

Archaeomagnetism

Archaeomagnetism (or *paleomagnetism*) is a nonradiometric dating technique based on the fact that the position of Earth's magnetic poles is continually changing. We have good historical records of these changes over the past several hundred years, and earlier geologic history shows evidence of frequent magnetic-pole shifts, including complete pole reversals in which north became south and south became north. Figure 7.5 shows examples of pole positions in the past. However, much like dendrochronology, these maps of magnetic direction are regionally specific, and only a few areas (such as the American Southwest and Great Britain) have well-developed archaeomagnetic sequences.

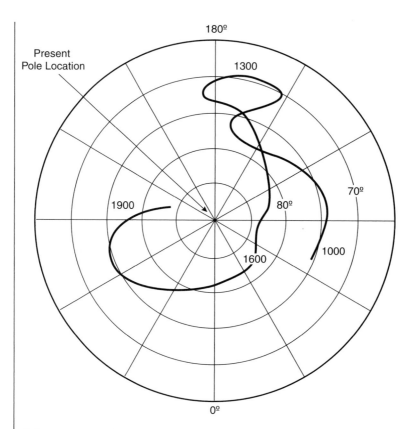

f i g u r e   7 . 5

Shifts in the Magnetic Poles.   The shifting of the position of magnetic north over time that is the basis for archaeomagnetic and paleomagnetic dating. This example represents the position of the north pole over the past 1,000 years from the perspective of Great Britain.

Source: Adapted from P. A. Parkes, 1986, *Current Scientific Techniques in Archaeology* (New York: St. Martin's Press), Figure 4.2.

Interestingly, when certain objects (pottery, clays, soils, stones) are heated to 700 degrees Celsius, the iron particles within these objects align with the north pole, very much like a needle in a compass. If the position of the object collected in the field excavation is carefully recorded, the current position of the north pole can be compared with the position of the north pole indicated by the object. The calculated variation in degrees between the two positions can be linked to specific time periods with the aid of ^{14}C dating.

Obsidian Hydration Analysis

Early peoples worldwide sought out volcanic glasses, especially obsidian, to use in the production of stone tools. Obsidian is common in archaeological sites located near volcanic sources. **Obsidian hydration analysis** is a nonradiometric dating method that is limited to volcanic glasses and is still in development as a consistently useful dating method.

Obsidian adsorbs (or hydrates) water from the surrounding environment over time—that is, water is absorbed into the matrix of the stone. When a fresh surface of the glass is exposed, it begins to absorb water, forming a *hydration front* (or rim or band) as the water soaks in deeper. To measure this hydration rim, the obsidian is cut, ground thin enough to transmit light, and then observed under a microscope. In theory, the thicker the rim is, the longer the surface of the glass has been exposed. When a piece of obsidian is broken and flaked into a tool, a fresh surface is exposed, which starts the clock for new water absorption and the development of a measurable hydration rim. The hydration process is very slow, and the thickness of the hydration rim is typically measured in microns (millionths of a meter).

How do we know how long it takes for a hydration rim to develop, and how much older is an artifact with a 5-micron-thick rim than an artifact with a 2-micron rim? Using obsidian artifacts from the same volcanic source, taken from known-age contexts from well-dated archaeological deposits (frequently calibrated by using radiocarbon dates), archaeologists can develop estimates. The rate of water absorption depends on the composition of the obsidian, which varies from lava flow to lava flow. Recall from Chapter 6 that x-ray fluorescence and mass spectrometry can identify specific sources of obsidian. Unique "fingerprints" quantify the trace elements common to specific volcanoes and lava flows. The rate of absorption also depends on local temperature and humidity, which are more difficult to estimate.

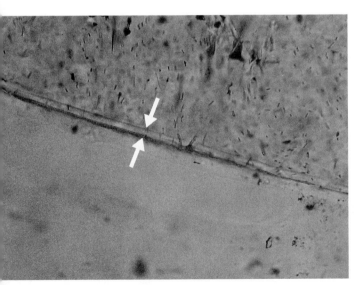

As water penetrates newly flaked obsidian, it forms a hydration rim (see arrows) that can be measured and used to estimate the amount of time that has passed since the obsidian was flaked.

ContentSelect

Chapter Summary

Accurately dating sites and their contents is critically important for establishing the chronology of people and events of the past. Two general methods of doing this are relative dating and chronometric dating.

Relative dating establishes relative age—whether something is older or younger than something else. Relative dating methods include stratigraphy and superposition; index fossils and biostratigraphy; temporal types; seriation; and fluorine, uranium, and nitrogen dating.

According to the law of superposition, finds in lower layers are older than finds that overlay them, assuming the layers are undisturbed. Index fossils tie archaeological finds to periods when certain plants or animals are known to have existed, and biostratigraphy establishes the relative age of flora and fauna and, by extension, of associated archaeological finds.

Temporal types tie archaeological finds to periods when certain artifacts, features, or sites are known to have been made. Style changes within a temporal type permit dating by seriation. FUN dating chemically establishes the relative age of bone.

Chronometric dating establishes actual age—how many calendar years ago something lived (or died) or was made. Chronometric dating techniques include radiometric methods (radiocarbon dating, potassium-argon dating, uranium-thorium dating, fission track dating, thermoluminescence, electron spin resonance) and nonradiometric methods (dendrochronology, archaeomagnetism, obsidian hydration analysis).

Radiocarbon dating, first developed by Willard Libby in the 1950s, is based on counting the decay of radioactive carbon (^{14}C) and is used to date remains of organic origin of more recent age. K/Ar dating and U/Th dating, based on the same principles, are used to date older organic remains and inorganic remains respectively. Fission track dating and TL dating are based on measurements produced when archaeological materials are heated, and ESR dating is based on measurements produced when archaeological materials are subjected to microwaves.

Dendrochronology dates objects and events by linking them to annual tree-ring growth. Archaeomagnetism dates objects and events by linking them to known-age shifts in Earth's magnetic poles, and obsidian hydration analysis provides estimates of when tools of glassy stone were made.

Chronology is so important that archaeologists typically use several methods simultaneously to establish and test dates, rigorously debate or replicate proposed dates, and retest dates as new technologies become available.

Key Concepts

accelerator mass spectrometry (AMS), 183
archaeomagnetism, 188
archaeometry, 164
biostratigraphy, 169
chronology, 166
dendrochronology, 174
electron spin resonance (ESR), 187
fission track dating, 186

FUN analysis, 174
half-life, 177
index fossils, 169
Libby Curve of Knowns, 179
Libby half-life, 177
obsidian hydration analysis, 189
oxidizable carbon ratio (OCR), 184
potassium-argon (K/Ar) dating, 184

radiocarbon dating (^{14}C), 177
radiocarbon years before present (RCYBP), 181
seriation, 170
thermoluminescence (TL) dating, 187
three-age system, 169
uranium-thorium (U/Th) dating, 186

Suggested Readings

If you want to learn more about the concepts and issues discussed in this chapter, consider looking at the following resources. (Some may be rather technical.)

Nash, Stephen Edward (ed.). (2000). *It's about Time: A History of Archaeological Dating in North America.* Salt Lake City: University of Utah Press.

> This book provides an excellent background to the history of archaeological dating methods by providing separate sections on both relative and chronometric dating techniques practiced in the United States. Each chapter is written by recognized specialists such as Jeff Eighmy and R. E. Taylor.

Nash, Stephen Edward. (1999). *Time, Trees, and Prehistory: Tree-Ring Dating and the Development of North American Archaeology, 1914 to 1950.* Salt Lake City: University of Utah Press.

> An in-depth and easily digestible history of the discovery and subsequent progression of dendrochronology and its archaeological applications in the American Southwest and elsewhere. Chronicles the significant changes in archaeological thinking shepherded by the first absolute dating technique available to archaeologists.

Taylor, R. E. (1987). *Radiocarbon Dating: An Archaeological Perspective.* Orlando: Academic Press.

> The seminal work on the topic of radiocarbon dating written by one of the world's leading authorities on this subject. This work provides detailed information on the history of the development of radiocarbon dating that could only be written by an insider.

Taylor, R. E., and Martin J. Aitken (eds.). (1997). *Chronometric Dating in Archaeology.* New York: Plenum Press.

> Provides the student with clear explanations of the important commonly used and experimental chronometric dating techniques, including dendrochronology, radiocarbon, potassium/argon, and thermoluminescence.

chapter 8

Bioarchaeology: Human Remains

THE COLD AUTUMN air was still as I (Robert Yohe) crouched in the frigid muck, carefully but quickly scraping moist soil from the interior of the coffin with my trowel, my stiff fingers protesting each time my progress was abruptly interrupted by a fragment of soggy yet immobile wood. It was already past 7:00 PM. Darkness had fallen sometime a few hours before, but I had been caught up in a whirlwind of activity since the first human bones had been found earlier that day. Floodlights plugged into a portable generator illuminated the brown bones and black coffin wood directly beneath me. Between dealing with television news reporters and cell phone conversations with the coroner, and trying to keep the progress of the excavation of the historic burial on course, I had lost track of time.

Earlier that day, I had been contacted by an archaeologist from the Boise National Forest who was monitoring excavations of a flood retention pond by the city of Boise in southwestern Idaho. The excavations were near the site of Fort Boise, a military installation established during the Civil War. Garbage deposits dating to the latter part of the nineteenth century associated with the fort had been encountered during earlier excavation work, and the archaeological significance of these features required the presence of archaeologists for documentation. During the monitoring, it was noticed that a human femur and several planks of wood had tumbled out of one of the bulldozer dump piles.

I was the Idaho state archaeologist at the time, so I was contacted whenever human skeletal remains were found anywhere in the state. Idaho state law requires that law enforcement officials be contacted in the event the remains are modern or the result of a homicide, and that the appropriate Native American group be contacted in the event that the remains represent one of their ancestors. I arrived on the scene, followed shortly by the local police. After a quick look around, it was clear that the remains were from another time and did not fit the category of modern homicide or prehistoric burial. Several outlines of graves were visible, and part of a human skull in a fragmentary coffin was protruding from the shallow water in the bottom of a retention basin. When the fort cemetery was moved in 1907, some burials were missed.

The Fort Boise soldier burial during excavation. The open mouth is visible at the top of the photo, and the dark patches are fragments of the coffin.

In all the confusion of the earlier part of the day, the local press had caught wind of a good story and now swarmed around the gravesite. The story was going to be on the six o'clock news, and I knew that if the burial was not removed before the weekend, it would be looted within hours of our departure. Several of my staff from the State Historic Preservation Office and colleagues from the Idaho Historical Museum joined forces to do a professional archaeological excavation of the one complete human burial in a collapsed coffin that we had found by the end of the night.

193

As we carefully removed the mud from the skeleton, we could see that the remains were likely male and that he had suffered from a severe bacterial infection of the lower limb bones. Was it syphilis? It is estimated that nearly 50 percent of the enlisted men in the military who were stationed in the West after the Civil War had some form of venereal disease, and the later stages of syphilis frequently settle in certain bones of the body. Also, he was buried in a plain pine box, and there was no evidence that he had been clothed in anything but a shroud. Had he died in the infirmary and been buried quickly in only a shroud?

After several hours, we successfully extricated the remains from the coffin. The coffin itself had been badly damaged through a combination of collapse and decomposition. Samples of the wood were taken to determine construction techniques and wood type. The skeleton was removed to my laboratory, where I analyzed it and the remains of two other extremely fragmentary individuals. The skull and several elements of the body were x-rayed to check for skeletal anomalies. This was an adult male around 40 years of age, an unknown soldier who, interestingly, had received good dental care during his life. He had gold fillings, indicative of wealth—the common poor foot soldier would not have been so lucky. But if he was wealthy, he likely would have been an officer. So why was he wrapped only in a shroud and buried in a plain pine box? And what about the bone disease? If it was syphilis, it would have been unremarkable at the time because it was so common. Was it some other disease? Was he buried rapidly after dying in the infirmary because there was fear of whatever disease he had? And who was he?

My search of the archival records to put a name with this forgotten man proved futile.

Further studies are being conducted to help address these and other questions about this mysterious soldier. With the use of mass spectrometry, I plan to determine whether this person had received heavy doses of mercury, a common nineteenth-century cure for syphilis. I also will check for other heavy metals, such as lead, commonly used to solder food cans during this period and a source of lead poisoning to many people who ate a lot of canned products. Analysis of his dental calculus (tooth tartar) indicated that he had a diet rich in wheat and other grains and likely used a toothpick a great deal. The results of this study were presented at the annual meeting of the Society for American Archaeology to share with colleagues the importance of dental calculus studies (Yohe and Cummings 2001). Bit by bit, more information about this individual is coming to light. All of this information helps us to understand medical treatments, disease, and health on the frontier during the last half of the nineteenth century.

On May 26, 1998, the remains of the three soldiers were reburied in three separate pine boxes appropriate to the period in the "new" Fort Boise cemetery, established at the turn of the twentieth century. As a light rain fell, Idaho Civil War reenactors in military garb fired black powder rifles three times in honor of the dead. Although questions remain, some insight into this period of American history has been gained.

For the location of Fort Boise and other sites mentioned in this chapter, see the map on page 196.

The Study of Human Remains: Getting to Know Past Peoples

In previous chapters, we looked at the discovery and analysis of the things that people leave behind: their refuse, their constructions, their things. **Bioarchaeology,** in contrast, attempts to look directly at the people themselves and to learn about their individual lives by studying and interpreting their mortal remains. We can learn about the composition of ancient populations—**paleodemography**—by establishing the age, sex, stature, and health status of prehistoric peoples. Through the study of human remains, we also can markedly enrich our knowledge of ancient warfare, trauma, and health practices, including surgery. We can even get some idea of what ancient peoples looked like through both artistic and computer reconstructions of facial features from human skulls.

Preserved Bodies

The way remains are preserved often dictates the degree to which we are successful in reconstructing the life history of an individual. Preservation of remains ranges from the exceptional, such as frozen intact bodies (such as the Ice Princess described in Highlight 8.1), to the scant, such as the ashes of cremated human bone. Most remains, however, fall in between and consist of parts of human skeletons. Much of what we know today about past populations is based on studies of human skeletal materials recovered from archaeological contexts.

Our best information about the biology of prehistoric and early historic peoples comes from preserved human soft tissues (hair, skin, connective tissue, muscle, and organs) in addition to the more sturdy and enduring hard tissue (bone). Soft-tissue preservation is the rarest form and includes frozen bodies and mummies (both natural and cultural).

Frozen Bodies

Frozen human bodies have been discovered in northern Italy, Greenland, British Columbia, Russia, and the mountainous regions of Peru. The most celebrated of these bodies is the "Iceman" (now affectionately referred to as "Ötzi"), discovered in the Italian Alps in 1992 very near the Austrian border. Ötzi's nearly complete preservation for more than 5,300 years has provided the best glimpse yet of an individual from the European Late Neolithic. The preservation was so exceptional that the body was originally thought to be the remains of a recently deceased hiker or skier. The Austrian coroner's investigator from Innsbruck (the city closest to the site of the discovery) began to wonder about this

LOCATION MAP: Sites Mentioned in Chapter 8

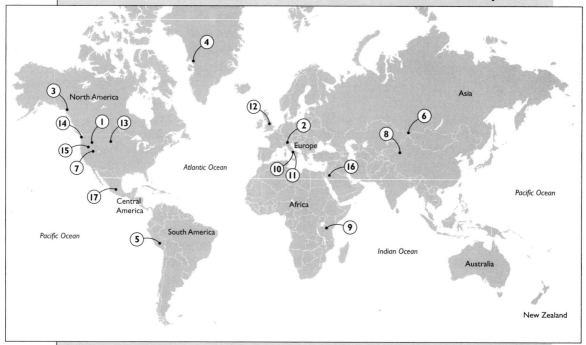

1 ■ Fort Boise
Fort Boise, Idaho

2 ■ Ötzi the Iceman
Otztal Alps, Italy

3 ■ Kwaday Dan Sinchi
Tatshenshini-Alsek Provincial Wilderness
Park, British Columbia, Canada

4 ■ Qilakitsoq (Qllakitsoq)
Qilakitsoq, Greenland

5 ■ Juanita
Mt. Ampato, Peru

6 ■ Ukok Plateau
Altai-Sayany region, Russia

7 ■ Spirit Cave
Reno, Nevada

8 ■ Tarim Basin
Xinjiang, China

9 ■ Laetoli
Northern Tanzania

10 ■ Pompeii
Naples, Italy

11 ■ Herculaneum
Naples, Italy

12 ■ Towton
Tadcaster, North Yorkshire, England

13 ■ Crow Creek
Chamberlain, South Dakota

14 ■ Kennewick
Benton County, Washington

15 ■ Braden site
Southwestern Idaho

16 ■ El-Hibeh
Egypt

17 ■ Teotihuacán
Mexico

HIGHLIGHT **8.1**

The Ice Princess

In 1993 a striking archaeological discovery was made in Russia near its far eastern border with China in Gorno Altai. Deep in the permafrost of the Ukok Plateau, the archaeologist Natalya Polosmak discovered a wooden tomb containing the incredibly well-preserved remains of a young woman still clothed in felt, silk, and leather. A combination of ice and ancient embalming techniques had resulted in the remarkable preservation of this woman for more than 2,500 years. Still visible were elaborate images of animals and flowers tattooed on various parts of her body. Still adorning her head when she was discovered was a three-foot-long felt headdress. Still intact were her silk blouse and soft leather riding boots. Wooden ornaments depicting fanciful beasts and snow leopards and covered in gold leaf adorned her remains. Accompanied by other fabulous grave goods, including the fully regaled remains of six sacrificed horses, this ancient Scythian "princess" apparently was a high-status individual who was buried more than two millennia ago in a kurgan, a log tomb mounded with dirt and stone.

The so-called Ice Princess was not the first such discovery in this region. In 1948 the archaeologist Sergei Rudenko found a kurgan containing the remains of a robust male chieftain around 50 years of age, also mummified and bearing vivid tattoos of wild game including rams and deer. This individual and the Ice Princess (found nearly 45 years later) had been embalmed in a similar manner: their organs were removed, and their body cavities were stuffed with tannin-rich peat. Other mummies have been recovered from kurgans dating to this same period, but none as well preserved as the chieftain and Ice Princess.

Little is known about the peoples represented by the mummies from these Russian tombs. They are believed to be Pazyryks, a Scythian group of nomads who dominated the steppes of this region for hun-

dreds of years until their disappearance sometime around 400 BC. Fortunately, some historic information about these people exists. Herodotus, the fifth-century BC Greek historian, described their "fierce nature" and "war-like tendencies" in great detail. Among their predilections was the creation of the elaborate tombs now being investigated, which have proved to be a boon to archaeologists trying to understand these Eurasian warriors.

CRITICAL **THINKING** QUESTIONS

1. How were the Russian kurgan mummies preserved? In what other ways can soft tissues be preserved in the archaeological record?
2. What kinds of information can the Ice Princess yield about herself, her people, and her life and time?
3. What methods can be used to date the Ice Princess and warrior chieftain?

The Ice Princess of the Russian steppe was buried with her headdress, gold-covered ornaments, horses, and other symbols of her high status.

interpretation of the discovery only when unusual artifacts were found with the remains. These artifacts included a copper ax and a stone knife hafted to a wooden handle.

Radiocarbon dating showed that the remarkable body was indeed ancient, more than five millennia in age. The unique preservation of the Iceman allowed scientists to conduct a formal autopsy and a whole battery of special analyses of soft tissues—such as skin, hair, and muscle—rarely done with ancient remains. New evidence now suggests that Ötzi had been in a fight and was killed by an arrow shot from behind. Before he died, he stumbled to the low spot on the mountain where he was preserved under an advancing glacier for so many years. Further studies on the Iceman (e.g., Cullen 2003) and an analysis of his bone metrics and densities suggest (Ruff et al. 2006) that he lived a very mobile life, perhaps as a shepard. The Iceman is now housed at the South Tyrol Museum of Archaeology in Bolzano, Italy.

North America's own version of Ötzi, though much more recent in time, was discovered in 1999 eroding out of a glacier about 1,000 miles north of Vancouver, British Columbia. The partially preserved body (one arm, one leg, and the pelvis) suggests that the man, recently named "Kwaday Dan Sinchi" (Southern Tuchone for "long ago person found") fell into an ice crevasse, probably while hunting. The partial body was dressed with leather clothing, and several artifacts were found in association, including a spear thrower (atlatl) and a walking stick. Archaeologists originally believed the remains to be between 3,500 and 12,000 years in age, but radiocarbon dating showed that Kwaday Dan Sinchi died in the first half of the fifteenth century AD. The discovery is so recent that many of the details have yet to be reported.

Other frozen bodies include the Greenland mummies—eight Inuit villagers who died around AD 1475 near the coastal settlement of Qilakitsoq, Greenland (Hansen et al. 1991). In 1972, two hunters discovered the remains of six women and two children, the youngest about six months of age at death. Studies on the bodies revealed information about last meals and diseases. One of the women had a malignant tumor at the base of her skull. From the high mountains of Peru have been discovered the frozen bodies of ritually sacrificed children of the Inka. The most famous body has been named "Juanita," a young girl left on the mountain after being intentionally struck on the head more than 400 years ago.

Purposeful Mummies

The word *mummy* conjures images of the ambulating, bandage-swathed undead that inhabit late-night classic horror films found on cable television. The origin of the word we use today is the Arabic term *mumiya*, which refers to an embalmed body. The most commonly known examples of mummies are the human and animal bodies purposefully desiccated (dried out) and preserved by the ancient Egyptians, but, as you will see, nature also engages in **mummification** through the rapid drying of soft tissues.

Many cultures, past and present, have a complex view of the afterlife that calls for elaborate ceremony surrounding the preparation and disposal of the dead. In ancient Egypt (from 2,800 BC through the Roman period), mummification was practiced not only on the god-king pharaohs but also on all but the poorest of the common people. According to the Egyptian *Book of the Dead,* the body of the deceased must retain the physical attributes it possessed in life in order to continue in the afterlife. Therefore, the ancient Egyptians took great pains to preserve the body for its journey after death.

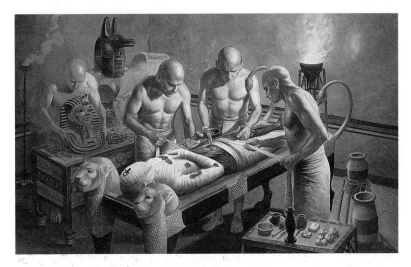

Artist's rendition of the processes of mummification described in this section. What are the steps in this method of preservation, and why was it so successful?

Egyptian mummification, undertaken by priests specializing in this art, involved a combination of organ removal, chemical drying, and treatment with various antimicrobial preparations (alcohol and resins). The first order of business was to wash the body with palm wine and quickly remove the brain and viscera, which are particularly prone to rapid decomposition. Several organs, including the heart and liver, were put into *canopic jars,* special urns that were interred with the body in the tomb. The brain was liquefied using a long hooked probe, then poured out through the nostrils. The internal organs were removed through an incision in the side. The body cavity was rinsed with palm wine and rubbed with powdered resins. The corpse was dried to further arrest decomposition. Drying was accomplished by means of *natron,* a blend of natural salts that drew out any moisture remaining in muscle tissue, a process that took several weeks. Once drying was completed, the body cavities were stuffed with cotton, and the body itself was wrapped in resin-soaked linen strips (the so-called bandages). The deceased was then ready to face the challenges of the afterlife.

The preservation of Egyptian mummies is so good, and the Egyptian desert so dry, that many bodies have lasted as long as 5,000 years (Highlight 8.2). Purposeful mummification also has occurred in other parts of the world. Eight-thousand-year-old mummies have been found in coastal Peru and Chile. These are the "black" and "red" Chinchorro mummies, named for their treatment with manganese or red ochre. Other examples are the Guanche mummies of the Canary Islands, the Kabayan mummies of the Philippines (made between 2000 BC and AD 1500), and the mummies of Melanesia, who were smoked and dried over a fire. In each instance, organs were removed, the skin was deliberately dried, and body cavities, faces, and limbs were stuffed with clay, wood, or fiber. In the late 1990s, a 500-year-old cemetery containing more than 100 Inka mummy bundles with incredible preservation was rediscovered on the outskirts of Lima, Peru (Cock 2002). This is an excellent example of how arid environments can naturally preserve human remains.

HIGHLIGHT **8.2**

The Roman Mummies of Tell El-Hibeh

As a specialist in North American archaeology, I (Robert Yohe) never would have dreamed that I would be working on an Egyptian tell along the Nile River in the summers of 2003 and 2004. But life is full of surprises, and occasionally some of them are life changing, as my recent trips to Middle Egypt have proved to be. After being told by a friend and colleague about a wonderful project in Egypt she had worked on the previous year, I asked the project director, Dr. Carol Redmount, if she would be interested in the assistance of a zooarchaeologist (a person who looks at animal remains from archaeological sites) and/or a human osteologist (someone who looks at human bones), both of which are specialties of mine. Dr. Redmount, an associate professor at the University of California, Berkeley, and the curator of Egyptian Archaeology at the Phoebe Hearst Museum, said yes, and I was on the team.

The site at the center of this project is El-Hibeh (also El Hiba), a large town mound, or tell, that appears to have been founded around 1070 BC during the Twenty-Second Dynasty at the beginning of what is known in Egyptian history as the Third Intermediate Period. The most notable extant structure at the site is a limestone temple built in honor of the god Amun by Sheshonq I, the first pharoah of the Twenty-Second Dynasty (who is mentioned in the Bible as attacking Israel in the time of Rehoboam). The site of El-Hibeh, also called Teudjoi in Egyptian or Ankyronpolis in Greek,

appears to have had its heyday during the Third Intermediate Period (between 1070 to 664 BC), but continued to be occupied for all of the first millennium BC and at least the first half of the first millennium AD. During late Roman and Coptic times, parts of it appear to have been used primarily as a necropolis, or burial site.

My first season at the site, I documented vandalized mummies and tombs. Two mummies from a limestone burial chamber on the top of the tell, believed to date from Ptolemaic times to the late Roman period (332 BC to AD 392), had been severely mangled over the course of the past couple of years. One of the mummies, an adult male, had been completely unwrapped down to the tops of the thighs, the bandages strewn for many meters beyond the burial crypt. Another mummy, that of a child, had been crushed, and the contents of the head bandages had been removed from the head. Several additional mummies, all severely disheveled, were observed in the back of the tomb. Other mummies were observed nearby eroding from a large looter's pit believed to date to the Late Roman/Byzantine period (also called the Coptic period) (AD 393 to AD 641). These burials were earmarked for salvage the following season because there were justifiable concerns about their safety.

In 2004 we returned to address both the limestone burial chamber and the looter pit mummies through salvage excavation. We recovered partial mummies of at least five individuals, plus numerous skeletal remains,

Natural Mummies

The work of a skilled embalmer was not always necessary to preserve the remains of ancient peoples. Extreme aridity or water chemistry sometimes works to preserve bodies by inhibiting microbial activity through profound soft-tissue desiccation or through chemical alteration of the skin and flesh (natural "tanning").

The drying of soft tissue in arid environments seems to be the most common means of natural mummification. From the American Southwest to the beaches of coastal Peru and the arid steppes of western China, the placement of the dead in natural grottos and

Late Roman mummy recovered from looter's pit during the 2004 field season at El-Hibeh.

shattered stucco mummy masks, *cartonnage* (plastered and painted linen), Greek and Roman coins, and ceramic amulets. Whereas the burial chamber mummies appeared to be at least middle-class people, those recovered during the excavation of the looter pit appeared to be of a lower social class, with bodies literally stacked one atop the other. However, unlike the burial chamber mummies, these individuals were completely intact because they lacked the burial goods so attractive to grave robbers. It also appears that the six mummies we recovered from this locality (and those we left, carefully backfilling to conceal their presence from tomb robbers) were buried all at one time in a large trench, perhaps the victims of a major epidemic.

In 2005, two additional Byzantine mummies were salvaged from the looter pit. One exhibited evidence of preservation by being packed in natron (the salt used in mummification) and the other was buried with elaborately decorated tunics (this latter burial likely dates to the seventh or eighth century AD).

There is much work to do at El-Hibeh. There is still more damage assessment as well as additional rescue and salvage work to be done. Other shattered burials may still provide a brief glimpse into the past and the people who lived there. Although perhaps not as romantic as finding a pristine crypt full of golden burial goods and fully encased mummies, this work is noble and no less important.

CRITICAL **THINKING** QUESTIONS

1. What might we be able to determine about changes in religious beliefs and views of the afterlife by studying mummies from several different time periods?
2. What can we learn from studying mummies of several different social classes? How do archaeologists determine which mummies belong to which social class?

dry caves has resulted in uncanny preservation. One of the oldest of these desiccated bodies is the Spirit Cave mummy from northwestern Nevada, found with exceptionally preserved fiber artifacts and radiocarbon dated to 9,400 years ago (Kirner et al. 1997). Some of the best examples of natural mummification through desiccation are the fully clothed mummies from the Tarim Basin in extreme western China. The so-called Chärchän Man has a face that appears only recently deceased even after the passage of 3,000 years, and he is still dressed in colorful woolen clothes and white deerskin boots.

Because the organs of naturally dehydrated mummies have not been removed, these mummies provide more information about ancient people's internal anatomy than do purposeful mummies. Modern imaging technology, such as computer-assisted tomography (CAT) and magnetic resonance imaging (MRI), makes possible "virtual autopsies" to locate organs and assess their condition. Imaging lessens the need for invasive tissue sampling by coring organs with special probes.

Preserved bodies in other environmental settings are much rarer. Among these are the "Bog People"—remains of partial bodies preserved in the peat bogs (waterlogged ground rich in peat moss and organic compounds) of northwestern Europe. Organic acids (such as tannins) and other organic compounds in the soggy peat literally "tan" the skin of long-dead people and keep decomposing bacteria and fungi at bay. Sometimes skin and organs are preserved while the bones of the skeleton are dissolved away. Many of the bog bodies were purposefully interred, but other individuals appear to have met violent ends. They were drowned, knifed, or garroted, perhaps as punishment for crimes or as religious sacrifices. The age of these remains ranges from as early as 8000 BC to medieval times.

Other Evidence of Soft-Tissue Anatomy

Although it is unusual for human bodies to preserve, the imprints or casts of body parts are sometime left for scientists to study. Handprints are silhouetted in cave paintings, fingerprints and fingernail prints sometimes are left in fired pottery, and footprints occasionally are found during careful excavation of certain archaeological sites. As you read in Chapter 4, the intriguing 3.7-million-year-old footprint track at Laetoli in eastern Africa has provided insight into early hominid gait as well as foot anatomy. And as you read in Chapter 2, unusual representations of ancient human bodies come from the volcanic ash molds of Pompeii. When excavators were exhuming the doomed city during the early nineteenth century, they frequently encountered odd voids. It soon became clear that these blank spaces within the hardened ash had once contained human remains and were actually the molds of the bodies. Excavators filled the molds with plaster and then broke the molds to reveal the macabre visages and positions of people dying under horrible circumstances. Important information about soft-tissue anatomy can be derived from such casts.

Skeletal Remains

Unfortunately, archaeologists rarely find frozen bodies or dehydrated mummies. Bone is by far the most commonly recovered form of human remains by virtue of its partial mineral composition and resistance to decomposition. Although not as likely to provide as much information as a complete body, the human skeleton contains much more information about the living individual it belonged to than one might initially imagine. Each skeleton retains a history of the life of its owner, including a record of past accidents or disease, certain habitual behavior (such as handedness), and dietary preferences. The bioarchaeologist can also usually determine within an acceptable range of accuracy the person's sex and age at death, his or her stature, and sometimes characteristics of the population in which the person shared genes. Human remains can tell a great deal about subsistence activities and other aspects of culture. For instance, wear patterns in the front teeth of European Neanderthals tell us that they used their teeth as tools to soften hides. In addition, the way that remains are buried can inform us about the status of individuals in their society and people's view of the afterlife. What exactly are skeletal remains, and what do they tell us?

Components of the Human Skeleton

The details of human skeletal anatomy are beyond the scope of this text, but here are some basics. The human skeleton comprises 206 bones and 32 teeth (Figure 8.1). The skeleton is usually divided into two major, closely associated groups of bones. The **axial skeleton** forms the core of the human skeletal system; it includes the skull, the vertebral column, the ribs and sternum (breastbone), the bones of the shoulder girdles (collar bones and shoulder blades), and the pelvic girdle. The **appendicular skeleton** includes the bones of the arms, hands, legs, and feet.

The skull is made up of 29 separate bones, many of which fuse together as the individual ages, plus six small bones of the inner ear. Some bones of the skull occur singly, such as the lower jawbone (mandible); others occur in pairs, such as the upper jawbones (maxilla) and cheekbones (zygoma). The spine is composed of 24 vertebrae, of which there are 7 neck (cervical) vertebrae, 12 upper-back (thoracic) vertebrae, and 5 lower-back

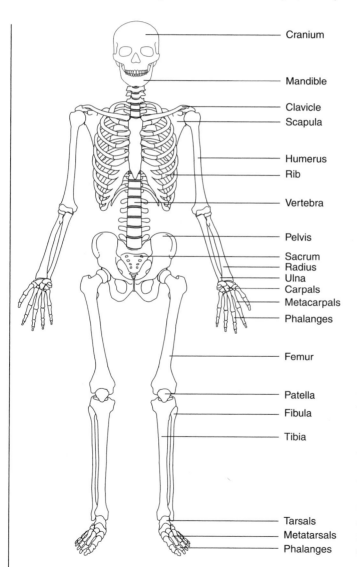

Cranium

Mandible

Clavicle
Scapula

Humerus
Rib

Vertebra

Pelvis

Sacrum
Radius
Ulna
Carpals
Metacarpals
Phalanges

Femur

Patella
Fibula

Tibia

Tarsals
Metatarsals
Phalanges

figure 8.1

The Human Skeleton. The human skeletal system is organized around the protection of internal organs and functions and the enabling of movement. Thorough knowledge of the human skeleton is the basis for osteological studies of skeletal remains. What kinds of information can osteologists gain through these studies?

(lumbar) vertebrae. At the base of the vertebral column is the sacrum (several fused vertebrae) and the coccyx, a remnant of our remote tailed ancestors. Humans have 12 paired ribs connected by cartilage to the sternum, forming a rib cage that protects the lungs and heart. The shoulder and pelvic girdles provide for the attachment of muscles vital to the movement of the upper and lower limbs. Bioarchaeology, like forensic anthropology, requires a thorough understanding of human bones. In archaeological fieldwork, the discovery of people who died and were buried is not uncommon. The study of bones is called **osteology.**

Inhumation and Cremation

Our ancestors appear to have begun the process of inhumation (formal interment of the dead) at least 40,000 years ago. It has been suggested that once the human intellect developed to the point of recognizing the inevitability of death, humans developed the concept of an afterlife. Burials were accompanied by funerary objects varying in elaboration from simple personal effects—a woman's jewelry, combs, makeup supplies, and spindles for spinning fibers—to massive tombs and monuments encompassing several acres—such as a queen's royal resting place containing symbols of power and the remains of sacrificed servants and horses. In most instances, intentional human burials provide important cultural information.

As you read in Chapter 4, burials can be in primary context or, if moved to another location, in secondary context. In some cases, for example, bodies were left on the surface or placed on platforms to decompose prior to burying the bones or placing them in caves or constructed mortuary chambers called *ossuaries*. Although **secondary burials** usually contain the relocated remains of only one individual, ossuaries contain the remains of many individuals (in some cases thousands). In some cultures, ossuary bones were sorted by type—femurs stacked in one pile and skulls in another, for example—which makes it difficult to reconstruct significant information about individuals.

Many cultures past and present have practiced cremation, the burning of bodies. From the suburbs of ancient Rome to deserts of the American West, burned human remains, or **cremains,** present an additional challenge to the bioarchaeologist trying to reconstruct the life of an individual from his or her bones. The condition of burned bone ranges from simple charring to complete combustion of the bone protein. Although cremains are much more difficult to study, they still provide important information about past people.

Disasters, Accidents, and Battles

Occasionally, the deposition of human remains is the result of a natural disaster, such as the eruption of Mount Vesuvius. The skeletons of nearly 300 people buried in volcanic lava and ash from that eruption were found on the beaches adjacent to Herculaneum. Earthquakes, floods, and hurricanes also can kill quickly and rapidly bury bodies that archaeologists may discover at some point in the future. Accidental deaths often can be inferred from the location and position of bones that are not the result of intentional burial.

Natural disasters include disease epidemics, which result in mass death and mass graves. The Black Plague of fourteenth-century Europe produced mass graves, sometimes

A view of a mass grave at Towton, England. What can archaeologists learn about people of the past from mass graves at battle sites?

called "plague pits." In Britain, plague pits contain as many as 400 individual skeletons, and bodies are stacked five deep (Hawkins 1990). Battlefields and mass graves resulting from conflict can be especially challenging for the bioarchaeologist because it is sometimes difficult to recognize specific individuals: bodies may be mutilated, dumped into burial trenches, or carelessly reburied.

One of the best examples of a mass grave resulting from conflict was discovered in England, near the site of the Battle of Towton (Fiorato et al. 2000). In 1996, workers constructing a private garage at Towton Hall accidentally discovered the remains of 36 soldiers who had died on Palm Sunday, AD 1461, during one of the bloodiest battles of the War of the Roses. According to historical records, the Battle of Towton resulted in the deaths of an estimated 28,000 men. The rectangular grave was packed with bodies arranged in a "sardine can" fashion. Most were placed in a west–east orientation, the traditional burial custom in fifteenth-century Christendom. The skeletons found within the tightly packed grave all bore the wounds of brutal hand-to-hand combat, primarily to the skulls.

An example of a difficult mass grave analysis for the archaeologist and osteologist is the Crow Creek Massacre site in south-central South Dakota (Willey and Emerson 1993). The jumbled remains of 483 Native Americans were dumped into a mass grave after the massacre of a village by unknown assailants sometime around AD 1325, hundreds of years before European contact. Men, women, and children were scalped, decapitated, and dismembered, left where they fell, and then buried sometime later. As a result of exposure, the bones were skeletonized, scattered, and gnawed on by carnivores before burial.

Another form of human bone deposition resulting from violence is battered and burned remains in food middens. Cannibalism in the archaeological record has been the source of some controversy, but evidence for this practice has been found among diverse ancient cultures from Neanderthals to Aztecs (Turner and Turner 1999). Convincing evidence of cannibalism comes from the American Southwest. At least 286 individuals from 38 Puebloan archaeological sites, dating between AD 900 and AD 1200, bear evidence of butchering and cooking and were mostly mixed in with other food bones in trash middens (Turner and Turner 1999). The skeletal remains of the men, women, and children possess the same cut marks, breakage patterns, and burn patterns as in the associated food animal remains.

Analytical Approaches in Bioarchaeology

When human skeletal material is recovered, the main goal of analyzing the remains is to understand as much as possible about the biology and life history of that individual. Analysis permits a clearer view of the actual people who lived in the past. The basic approach is to create an **osteobiography**, a life story inferred from bone evidence, including information about an individual's appearance, health, age at death, sometimes cause of death, and characteristics in relation to population, including other populations across time and space. Bioarchaeologists or biological anthropologists accomplish this task through a combination of both qualitative and quantitative analyses, employing skills that frequently involve artistic as well as scientific prowess. How do we construct osteobiographies? What can the bones tell us about their former owners that can help us in our quest to understand the past?

Constructing an Osteobiography

The first step toward putting flesh on the bones of ancient skeletons is to look at a wide range of indicators on the bones that provide basic information about the person under study. Certain parts of the skeleton can tell us about the age, sex, stature, and certain population characteristics of the individual.

SKELETAL SEX   The sex of a skeleton is most accurately determined by assessing the morphology of the pelvic bones. The female pelvis has unique features to accommodate the birth of a full-term baby. The opening in the pelvic girdle, for example, must be large enough to permit passage of the baby's comparatively large head. Correct sex assessment is achieved about 90 percent of the time with the pelvis alone. A summary of **skeletal sex** traits is provided in Table 8.1.

Attributes of the skull serve as a good indicator of biological sex, including the prominence of the brow ridges. Also, the bones of males usually are larger and have more pronounced muscle attachments than those of females. Today, males are generally more robust than females, and it is assumed that this also was the case in the past. However, robusticity alone is not a sure means of determining sex because of individual variability. Variability is another reason why it is important to look at as many traits as possible.

table 8.1

Examples of Sex Traits Observable in the Human Skeleton

SKELETAL TRAIT	TYPICAL MALE	TYPICAL FEMALE
Areas of muscle attachment (entire skeleton)	More pronounced	Less pronounced
Forehead	Slanted	Globe-like, projecting
Upper-eye orbits	Rounded	Sharp
Chin	Square	Rounded or pointed
Brow ridges of the skull	More pronounced	Less pronounced
General robusticity of the skeleton	Greater	Lesser
Pelvic outlet (open area in center of pelvic girdle)	Narrow	Wide
Sacrum	Small, narrow, curved	Large, wide, straight

SKELETAL AGE The estimate of the age of a person at the time of his or her death is based on the analysis of several possible **skeletal age** traits (Table 8.2). Even with well-preserved skeletons, one rarely can determine successfully a person's exact age at death. By looking at several traits in mature adults, it may be possible to narrow the range to a five- or ten-year period. Because the majority of known-age skeletal samples come from recent or historic human populations, calculations are based on the assumption that people in the past aged at rates similar to those of today.

Determining the age of the skeletons of infants and children relies on the condition of the skull, the degree of bone development and fusion of bones, and the eruption sequence of the teeth (Figure 8.2). The state of the bones of the skull and the types of teeth present (deciduous or "baby" teeth versus permanent teeth) can be assessed together to help determine the age of the infant or child.

In the fetus, the skeleton begins as a cartilaginous material that is slowly replaced with calcium phosphate, which hardens the cartilage to bone. The bone formation process is called **ossification**. By the time the child is born, much of the cartilage has been replaced by minerals and has become bone. Bone grows from ossification centers in the middle and ends (epiphyses) of each bone. As the child ages, the ossification centers grow toward each other and eventually fuse, so the degree of fusion helps to determine the age at death. For example, long bones, such as the femur, completely fuse end-to-end by the late teens or early twenties. The rate at which this **epiphyseal fusion** takes place is different for each bone of the body and is also affected by variables such as nutrition. Within a margin of error, and considering other age-estimating factors such

table 8.2

Indicators of Human Skeletal Age

TRAIT	ELEMENT NEEDED	RANGE OF ACCURACY
Dental eruption	Teeth in skull	2 months to 3 years
Epiphyseal union	Long bones with epiphyses	3 to 6 years
Pubic symphyseal surface morphology	Pubic bones of pelvis	10 to 50 years
Distal rib morphology	Sternum end of rib	2 to 10 years
Skull sutures	Intact cranium	10 to 50 years
Bone microstructure (osteon abundance)	Thin section of any long bone	10 to 50 years
Vertebral osteoarthritis	Vetebral column or vertebrae	Used with other age indicators
Dental wear	Teeth	Used with other age indicators

as tooth development and bone sizes, epiphyseal fusion can help determine the age of the infant, child, or young adult at death.

The degree of fusion of the cranial sutures, tooth length and wear, and distinct morphological changes to the surfaces of certain bones where they articulate (connect) also help to determine age. For instance, surface changes between the rib tips and the breastbone and between the pubic bones of the pelvis indicate greater age. Conditions such as osteoarthritis of the spine, which becomes more pronounced in midlife, also indicate greater age. Microscopic techniques of age determination include looking at the annual layers of the material that keeps teeth in place (called cementum).

Osteologists look at as many of these indicators as possible to achieve the most accurate age estimate of an individual skeleton. Because variations exist in each person, and certainly between populations over time, any one indicator alone could lead to an estimation that is either too young or too old.

SKELETAL STATURE   Like estimates of skeletal age and sex, stature estimates are based on **skeletal stature** traits of historical and modern populations that we attribute to peoples in the past. Measurements of known height, body proportions, and the length of long bones in different populations are expressed in mathematical formulas that can be applied to bones collected from the archaeological record (Table 8.3).

RACIAL DETERMINATION   *Race* is a biological term that has become politically charged when applied to humans, and many anthropologists shun usage of the concept altogether.

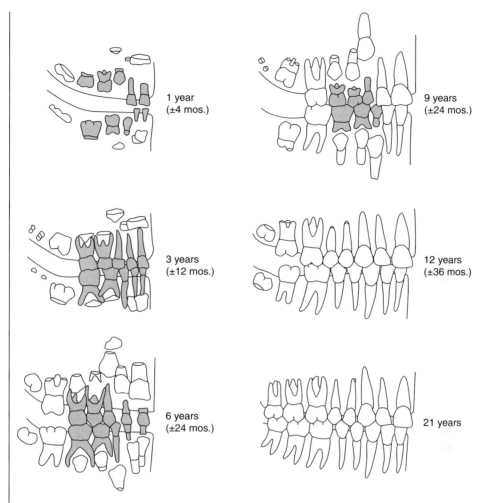

figure 8.2

Eruption Sequence of Teeth According to Age among American Indians.
These infant skulls and teeth show the general changes that occur at different ages ("baby"
teeth are shaded). What characteristics of the skull and teeth help to determine skeletal age?
What other characteristics of skeletal anatomy contribute to determinations of skeletal age?

Source: Adapted from Jane E. Buikstra and Douglas H. Ubelaker, 1994, *Standards for Data Collection from
Human Skeletal Remains* (Fayetteville, AR: Arkansas Archaeological Survey), Figure 24.

However, populations that maintain at least some level of reproductive isolation from
other populations may possess traits that make them somewhat distinctive from other
populations. Some skeletal traits seem to be statistically significant for specific geographically isolated populations because, like all biological characteristics, skeletal traits are inherited and follow the rules of human population genetics. Among living populations,

table 8.3

Calculation of Living Stature from Measurements of Skeletal Elements

RACE/SEX	BONE*	STATURE FORMULA
African male	Femur	$2.10 \times$ femur length (cm) + 72.22 cm
African female	Femur	$2.28 \times$ femur length (cm) + 59.76 cm
Asian male	Femur	$2.15 \times$ femur length (cm) + 72.57 cm
European male	Humerus	$2.89 \times$ humerus length (cm) + 78.10 cm
European female	Humerus	$3.36 \times$ humerus length (cm) + 57.97 cm
Mexican male	Radius	$3.55 \times$ radius length (cm) + 80.71 cm
Mexican female	Tibia	$2.72 \times$ tibia length (cm) + 63.78 cm

*Several different bones can be used for each race/sex; these are just a few examples of specific regression formulas.

Source: Adapted from Trotter and Gleser 1952, 1977; Genoves 1967.

for instance, the bones of East African Masai and the bones of Inuit of the Arctic would never be confused in the laboratory, assuming enough specimens were available for study to account for individual variability. Forensic anthropologists use a combination of metric (measurable) and nonmetric (observable) skeletal traits to help them determine the "racial" affiliation of skeletal remains.

Extrapolating "races" into the past can be both challenging and problematic, especially in situations where sample sizes are very small. To begin with, characteristics of populations typically associated with racial variation, such as blood group, skin color, eye shape, and hair form, cannot be determined presently from the fossil record or skeletal remains (though possibly in the future through DNA analysis). The best we can hope for is to characterize these ancient populations both quantitatively and qualitatively through the analysis of metric and nonmetric traits. If we have a particularly large skeletal database for a certain region, we might be able to make statements about prehistoric population movements across great physical space over time (e.g., "The Native Americans share skeletal characteristics with the current Siberian populations, further supporting the idea that the earliest Americans migrated from eastern Asia").

What People Looked Like: Soft-Tissue Reconstruction from Skeletal Data

Although racial characteristics can be problematic when we are dealing with ancient peoples, an individual's appearance often can be inferred from features of the bone. The size and location of ridges on the bones show where muscle tissues attached to the bone and how

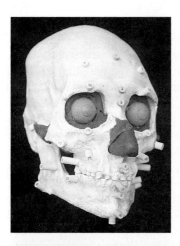

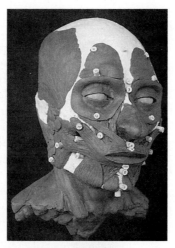

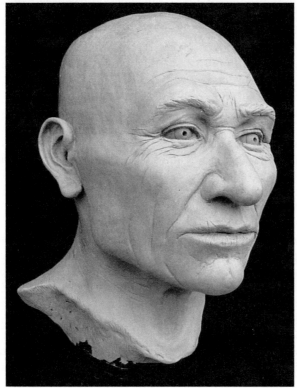

These three photographs illustrate progress in the techniques of facial reconstruction, which are based on knowledge of muscle attachments on bone and the average measurements, such as length or thickness or density, for tissues such as muscles, cartilage, tendons, and skin. In this case, the result is a representation of the likely general appearance of Kennewick Man. To what extent can racial attributes be assigned reliably on the basis of skeletal evidence?

large the muscles were. With a well-preserved skull and the help of established techniques of facial reconstruction, a biological anthropologist or forensic artist can re-create the appearance of the face as it appeared in life. Using modeling clay to reconstruct muscles, fat, and skin, artists trained in human anatomy can use the clues of muscle attachments, known

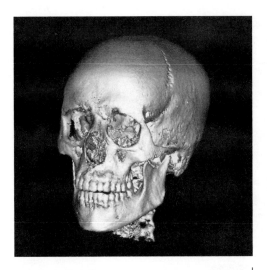

The skull of an Egyptian mummy was digitally scanned and replicated using rapid prototyping, allowing for its study without damaging the mummy.

mean tissue depths, and known effects of aging to rebuild a person's face. Although characteristics such as skin color, amount and color of hair, eye shape and color, and "personality" or expression cannot be known (and attempts to portray them always lead to controversies), facial reconstructions can give reasonable approximations of the appearance of humans long past. The accompanying photos show the reconstructive process of the 9,300-year-old Kennewick Man (see the opening story in Chapter 14), based on modeling of the facial musculature and overlaying skin.

New technology now enables the creation of solid objects by scanning the original and producing a plastic copy (a method called rapid prototyping). This method has been used to create an exact copy of the Kennewick skull (see photo on page 211) and of the projectile point in his hip. It has also been used to digitally extract and create a copy of the skull of an Egyptian mummy (see accompanying photo).

Tracking Skeletal Variability in Early Human Ancestors

Variation is more obvious early in the fossil record of humans, their ancestors, and other primates. In addition to determining age, sex, and stature from skeletal remains, paleo-anthropologists identify marker traits of fossil skulls and teeth. In combination these marker traits are seen as diagnostic of certain species. In Pleistocene sites, for instance, the cusp pattern on a tooth can instantly identify the individual as an extinct monkey, ape, or human.

Marker traits of the bones and teeth also are diagnostic of geographic populations that lived during the course of human evolution, and newly found fossils are classified in terms of these traits. For example, "robust" australopithecines (cf. *Paranthropus* spp.) of southern Africa, which became extinct about a million years ago, had a wide, "dished" (concave) face; a low forehead; a small cranium with a bony ridge (sagittal crest) and flared cheekbones (zygomatic arches) that would have anchored large chewing muscles; pronounced bony ridges over the eyes (supraorbital ridges); and a massive U-shaped jaw with small eyeteeth and front teeth (canines and incisors) and huge grinding teeth (molars), indicating a mainly vegetarian diet (Campbell and Loy 2002). Other australo-pithecines, living contemporaneously in northern and eastern Africa, had measurably different traits of the skull and teeth, and it was these "gracile" australopithecines who continued the line toward modern humans. Other measurable traits of skeletal anatomy distinguish varieties of *Homo erectus* from one another and from the australipithecines, and still others distinguish varieties of *Homo sapiens* from one another and from varieties of *Homo erectus*.

Physical anthropologists working in archaeological excavations of such great age must rely on small numbers of scarce and fragmentary fossil finds. Although new finds may be made each year, paleoanthropologists lack large samples on which to base interpretations. New species have been proposed on the basis of bones from a single individual and even on the basis of a single bone. As you can imagine, having a population to study instead of an individual fossil is important, for just as no two people today are exactly alike, so no two australopithecines were alike. Drawing conclusions from measurements of single specimens is risky because the individual may not be typical. Only when a large number of specimens is available can variation be taken into account. Because of the limitations of their data, paleoanthropologists frequently disagree on precisely how fossils should be classified. In reconstructing the story of human evolution, as in creating an osteobiography for the Civil War soldier in the story at the beginning of this chapter, making bones speak is both a science and an art.

Determining Nutrition, Health, and Disease

Once age, sex, and stature are determined, the basic information of the osteobiography of an individual has been put into place. But how did the person die? What accidents or other misfortunes befell this person when he or she was alive? Did the person have good nutrition? What was the general status of his or her health? These questions are important in the quest for understanding the people who lived in the past.

PATHOLOGY   Osteologists examine bones to look for **skeletal pathology,** indications of ancient disease or trauma in skeletons. Through training and experience, these specialists have to be able to differentiate between characteristics of the skeleton that indicate the degradation of bone from natural causes, such as rodent or carnivore gnawing, weathering, or root "etching," from characteristics that are the result of accidents or illness. Is the gash in the head the result of prehistoric warfare? A run-in with a predator? Or did it occur after death? Pathology that originated during life is called **antemortem** and that which originated after death is called **postmortem.**

Evidence of trauma in skeletons may range from a series of small cut marks on the cranium resulting from the removal of the scalp to massive battle-inflicted injuries such as those seen in the prehistoric Crow Creek Massacre (described previously). Not all traumatic injuries are fatal (even in prehistory), and the way they heal can reveal ancient healthcare practices. The healing of a fracture may indicate splinting, for instance. Evidence of prehistoric surgical practices has been found in both the Old and the New World. **Trephining** (or *trepanning*), for example, involved cutting a hole into the skull of an individual while the person was still alive, presumably to relieve pressure on the brain. Amazingly, many patients survived their treatment, as indicated in the archaeological record by their healed skulls.

Many human diseases leave traces in bony tissues of the body, such as the pitting caused by bacterial infections like syphilis. Infectious diseases such as yaws, tuberculosis, and leprosy can damage bone in identifiable ways. Viruses, parasites, and fungi can also inflict damage. Noninfectious disorders leave their mark on bone in more subtle ways— by robbing bone of nutrients, for example, or interfering with growth. Abnormalities

HIGHLIGHT **8.3**

Origins of Syphilis and Archaeological Evidence

Crucial evidence to settle the debate about where syphilis came from would be the recognition of syphilitic lesions on skeletons from clear archaeological contexts with good dating. Making the job especially complex, however, is the fact that other diseases caused by *Treponema* bacteria, such as yaws and bejel, can also affect the skeleton in severe forms of infection.

If archaeologists could differentiate the various treponemal ailments skeletally and could find evidence of one or the other in the New World prior to the arrival of Columbus, or in the Old prior to New World contact, the debate should be settled. Various claims have been made about skeletal syphilis in both

Superio-frontal view of modern human cranial vault (top portion) ravaged by late-stage syphilis. This characteristic scarring resulting from a severe infection by the *Treponema pallidum* bacterium is recognizable in prehistoric skeletons in parts of both the New and the Old Worlds. This type of damage and other bone pathology caused by different diseases can be used by bioarchaeologists to better understand the status of human health in the past.

cases, but no large, systematic analysis of such skeletal remains had been undertaken until recently. Then two American paleopathologists, Bruce and Christine Rothschild, examined more than 1,600 skeletons with good chronological data and said they could differentiate between yaws and syphilis by looking at the characteristics of the lesions (Rose 1997).

In examining 687 skeletons from the New World dating to between 400 and 6,000 years in age, the Rothschilds found that North American individuals had yaws and those of Mexico and Central and South America had clear evidence of syphilis. In contrast, an examination of 1,000 Old World skeletons dating to pre-1500 exhibited no evidence of syphilis. Based on these data, the investigators suggest that yaws, which first appear in skeletons as early as 6,000 years ago, probably mutated into venereal syphilis between 800 and 1,600 years ago when the first evidence of this disease appears in the skeleton populations.

The controversy, however, still rages. In May 2001, a British archaeologist, Dr. Simon Mays, insisted that the skeleton of a woman dating to between AD-1296 and 1445 from an Essex cemetery shows classic skeletal evidence of syphilis, suggesting that venereal syphilis was present in the Old World prior to Columbus's voyages. Further analysis of the skeleton, including DNA studies to identify the presence of *Treponema* bacteria, need to be undertaken.

CRITICAL **THINKING** QUESTIONS

1. How can paleopathology contribute to explanations and interpretations about peoples of the past?
2. What issue is at the heart of the debate about the origins of syphilis, and what hypothesis is best supported by evidence to date?

such as osteoporosis, dwarfism, gigantism, tumors or cancers, and inflammations of joints from arthritis are clearly visible.

Both yaws and syphilis are caused by a spirochete bacterium of the genus *Treponema*, and it has been argued that yaws, a nonvenereal disease, may have been the precursor of the more infamous syphilis. For nearly 500 years, scholars have argued about where in the world syphilis originated: in the Old World or the New? Did Columbus's men introduce the dreaded disease to Europe after 1492, or did his men spread it to the New World natives (Highlight 8.3)?

NUTRITION   Nutritional deprivation, such as vitamin deficiencies, and other nutritional stress also leave evidence in the skeleton. Starvation as a cause of death can be diagnosed from bone, for instance. **Harris lines**—thin, bony horizontal lines representing periods of arrested growth—can be seen in the X rays of long bones of individuals who experienced times of starvation during their childhood and adolescence (see photo on page 262). Vitamin D deprivation causes rickets, seen especially in weakened, bowed leg bones. Vitamin D synthesis depends mainly on exposure of the skin to sunlight and is believed to have contributed to variations in skin color in different geographic regions during human migrations. (See Chapter 10 for further discussion of these analyses.)

Chemical Analysis of Bone

It is true that you are what you eat. Various chemical elements and compounds that you take into your body from food, water, and even the air that you breathe ultimately become incorporated into your body tissues, including your bones (see Lambert 2005). For example, the element strontium, which is richer in plants, nuts, and mollusks than in animal protein, generally occurs in higher concentrations in people living in agricultural communities than in hunters and gatherers. Concentrations of toxic metals, such as lead, mercury, or arsenic, may indicate certain cultural practices, environmental hazards, or health problems during life. Chemical analysis of bone is an important tool of bioarchaeology.

A prime example of the possible effects of heavy metal toxicity is the fate of Sir John Franklin's doomed expedition to the Arctic in 1845. The frozen bodies of the sailors were found to contain high levels of lead in their tissue, probably as a result of eating foods from lead-soldered cans (Kowal et al. 1991; Farrer 1993; Beattie 1995; Keenleyside et al. 1996). Lead poisoning can result in lethargy, mental disturbances, neurological problems, and death. It has been suggested that lead toxicity resulted in poor decision making and erratic behavior, ultimately contributing to the demise of everyone in the Franklin expedition.

STABLE ISOTOPE ANALYSIS   Many elements exist in a number of isotope states, either stable or unstable (which are radioactive). Stable isotopes tend to be absorbed into tissues differentially, due to differences in molecular weight. Different types of plants tend to take up different isotopes and animals that eat those plants will absorb those isotopes. Humans will absorb the isotopes of the plants and animals they eat and those basic isotopic ratios will be reflected in human tissues. The stable isotopes within a tissue sample can be measured, plotted, and used to deduce the diet of the person from whom the sample was taken, although there are some problems with isotopic degradation that can distort the analytical results (e.g., Hedges 2003). Of the stable isotopes, ten are of biological interest. Carbon and nitrogen are the most commonly used (e.g., Ambrose and Krigbaum 2003).

Isotopic analysis can be used in a number of ways, including to determine the ratios of terrestrial to marine foods in a diet, (e.g., Bocherens et al. 2007), the ratios of plant to animal resources consumed (e.g., Lillie and Jacobs 2006), the types of animals that were eaten (e.g., van der Merwe et al. 2000), whether the animals that were consumed were raised locally or imported (e.g., Klippel 2001), the role of dairy resources (e.g., Boucherens et al. 2006), group mobility (e.g., Bentley et al. 2004), social and economic status (e.g., Honch et al. 2006), diets based on age (e.g., breastfeeding and weaning; Turner et al. 2006), and the food changes evident in the transition to agriculture (e.g., Hu et al. 2006).

One of the most important stable isotopes is carbon. Measuring the ratios of the two stable isotopes of carbon, ^{12}C and ^{13}C, in human bone can provide information on the types of plants eaten by both humans and their animal prey. The variations are the result of the different **metabolic pathways** that plants use to convert carbon dioxide into energy and tissue. The most common food plants rely on one of two metabolic pathways: the *Calvin cycle (C3),* common to trees, shrubs and grasses in temperate climates; and the *Hatch-Slack pathway (C4),* used by high-temperature tolerant grasses, the most important of which is maize. Diets high in maize should result in a measured value suggesting a C4 plant diet. However, sometimes measurements are misleading. For instance, a mixed diet of C3 plants and seafood can yield the same values as a diet of predominantly C4 plants. (For application of this process to studies of ancient nutrition, see Chapter 10.)

Like carbon, nitrogen has more than one stable isotope: ^{14}N, representing 99.63 percent of naturally occurring nitrogen; and ^{15}N, which composes the remaining 0.37 percent. Nitrogen isotopes derive mostly from protein in the diet and are found in abundance in well-preserved bone. Measurements of the ratio of ^{14}N and ^{15}N can provide specific dietary information because nitrogen values of marine-based and land-based diets differ dramatically. For example, a marine-based diet will result in a mean ^{15}N value of 14.8 parts per thousand, whereas an exclusively land-based diet will yield a mean value of 5.9 (Parkes 1986:133) (Figure 8.3).

One example of the utility of stable isotope analysis was the recent study of a 7,000-year-old skeletal population recovered from the Braden site along the Snake River at the Oregon–Idaho border (Yohe and Pavesic 2000). Salmon, a fish that runs from salt to fresh water to spawn, was once abundant in the Snake River and is known to have been an important food resource to later prehistoric Native American populations. Did earlier populations also rely heavily on this resource? Skeletal isotopic studies were undertaken to address this question. An analysis of the ^{15}N for 17 individuals resulted in a mean value of 16.7 parts per thousand, a strong indicator that salmon was a significant component of their diet.

Another example of stable isotope analysis is the tracing of population movements through the measurement of strontium isotope ratios (^{87}Sr/^{86}Sr) in bone and tooth enamel recovered from burials. Strontium is present in food, and foods grown in different regions will have different ratios of strontium. By measuring the ratios of strontium in bone (set about the time of death) and tooth enamel (set at the time of birth), Douglas

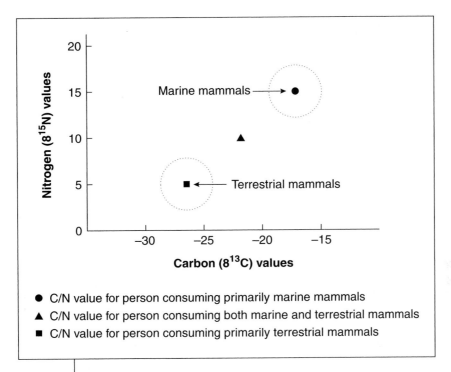

figure 8.3

Isotope Clusters Showing Dietary Regime. This diagram shows how isotope clusters indicate diet. One cluster shows the carbon/nitrogen isotopic signature for people whose diet consists mainly of land mammals. The other cluster shows the carbon/nitrogen isotopic signature for people whose diet consists mainly of sea mammals. Stable isotope analysis is one of the tools used in the archaeological reconstruction of past diets.

Price and his colleagues (Price et al. 2000) were able to determine that a number of individuals buried in the city of Teotihuacán in central Mexico had been born elsewhere and immigrated to the city. In the future, such data may be coupled with other information to understand how the city grew, what regions it controlled, what its economic influence was, and the overall political situation in central Mexico at the time.

TRACE ELEMENT ANALYSIS   Trace elements are those that occur in very small amounts in tissues, generally due to being ingested with food or from environmental exposure. The primary elements are barium and strontium (see Burton and Price 2000). Although most of the archaeological work has been conducted on bone, with hair (and nails) and tooth enamel being the most preferred, (e.g., Hoppe et al. 2003), the majority of work on trace element analysis has been performed on soft tissues.

Archaeological interest in trace elements centers on issues of diet, health, and behavioral correlates (Aufderheide 1989:240–241), and trace element concentrations in human tissues may be employed to investigate a variety of issues, such as the relative contribution of plant and animal foods (e.g., Little and Little 1997), similarity of diet by sex (e.g., Cook and Hunt 1998), social status (e.g., Schutkowski et al. 1999), the contributions of marine resources (e.g., Baraybar 1999), migration and mobility (e.g., Ezzo et al. 1997), identification of group affinity (e.g., Safont et al. 1998), residence patterns (e.g., Baraybar 1999), and even whether a woman might have been pregnant or lactating (e.g., Blakely 1989). In addition, some aspects of pollution can be measured through trace element analysis (e.g., Bresciani et al. 1991:164–167). For example, Pyatt and colleagues (2000) measured copper and lead concentrations in various samples from the area of a copper mine used during Nabatean, Roman, and Byzantine periods in southern Jordan and discovered not only that heavy metals polluted the area during those times, but continue to do so today.

Electroanalysis, MS, and neutron activation analysis (e.g., Pollard and Heron 1996) may be employed to measure elements. A new method for such analysis is Inductively Coupled Plasma-Mass Spectrometric (ICP-MS) analysis.

ANALYSIS OF ANCIENT DNA   The cells of all organisms contain DNA, deoxyribonucleic acid, the genetic code for that organism. Fortunately for science, DNA can preserve over long periods of time and has even been extracted from insects trapped in amber over 100 million years ago. In archaeological contexts, nuclear and mitochondrial DNA may be present in human remains in bone and mummified tissue. This DNA can be recovered and replicated by polymerase chain reaction, and the sequence of genes can be read to determine hereditary relationships between populations and even between individuals (Kolman and Tuross 2000; Mulligan 2006). The analysis of ancient DNA (aDNA) holds the potential to revolutionize archaeology, and its recovery in ancient specimens could be used to address many research questions, including the identification of pathogens in human remains (e.g., Likovsky et al. 2006), population migrations (e.g., Kaestle and Smith 2001), ethnicity and lineage (e.g., Dudar et al. 2003), the sex of human remains (e.g., Mays and Faerman 2001), the identification of species in food remains (e.g., Newman et al. 2002), the identification of species processed on stone tools (e.g., Shanks et al. 2005), and the identification and tracking of domesticates (e.g., Bar-Gal et al. 2002). The testing of DNA is also used in a variety of forensic applications such as the identification of war casualties (Holland et al. 1993), including those from the American Civil War (Fisher et al. 1993).

Obtaining samples for DNA analysis is difficult (see DeGusta and White [1996] for protocols in using skeletal materials in aDNA analysis) because contamination is a major problem. The best samples are those taken from places that are most difficult to contaminate, such as the dentin of teeth. In taking samples, the archaeologist must be exceedingly careful both in the field and in the lab (Richards et al. 1993:19–20).

Preservation and contamination are also major issues in aDNA analysis (see Kolman and Tuross 2000; Mulligan 2006). While it is clear that some aDNA survives over time, even over millions of years (e.g., DeSalle et al. 1992), it is not clear in what form the molecules survive, if they have been altered, and whether they can be correctly identified (e.g., Gilbert et al. 2006). Even if well preserved, aDNA samples can be easily contaminated by a variety of organisms, especially bacteria and fungi, and of course, by the researcher.

However, the analysis of aDNA also has the potential to provide information on the hereditary relationships among ancient groups. For example, using tissue from mummies, scientists have attempted to trace the heredity of ancient Egyptian pharaohs and to identify individuals in relation to their dynasties. In 2000, molecular biologist Scott Woodward's DNA analysis of dozens of mummies, including King Tutankhamen, confirmed that brother–sister marriages were common among members of the Eighteenth Dynasty's royal line. Sibling incest was practiced in the belief that it kept the royal line pure. Efforts to determine the relation of Tutankhamen to Amenhotep III, believed to be the father of Akhenaten, founder of early monotheism (belief in one god), have proved controversial, however, because of political concerns about possible relationships between the ancient Egyptians and the ancient Hebrews.

Meanwhile, in 2001, scientists at Emory University's Center for Molecular Medicine began the DNA study of mummies in Canadian museums, including a mystery royal mummy believed to be Rameses I, who ruled Egypt more than 3,000 years ago. Rameses I has been missing since the mid-1800s and remains the only royal mummy outside of Egypt. In Egypt lie the mummified remains of Seti I, the son of Rameses I, and Rameses II, his grandson. An analysis of Y chromosomes from each will help establish their relationship. Canada's mummies, 10 in all, will have CT scans and X rays to reveal how they lived, what illnesses they suffered from, and how they died.

In 1997, DNA extracted from Neanderthal fossil bone established that there are significant enough differences between modern humans and Neanderthals, which became extinct by around 30,000 years ago, to classify them as separate species (Campbell and Loy 2002). The discovery that fossils can yield biochemical data such as DNA is revolutionizing paleoanthropology in much the same way that the discovery of radiocarbon dating revolutionized archaeology. As the fossil record is reassessed by means of DNA analysis, new knowledge will come to light about past populations, including their ancestry, migrations, adaptations, relationships, and classification. And as with other scientific advances, our understanding of the story of human evolution will change in light of new information.

Is Studying Human Remains Ethical?

There has always been some question about the ethics of digging up or disturbing burials. In fact, it is illegal nearly everywhere in the world to disturb historically modern graves in recognized and maintained cemeteries. Is it right to "desecrate" an ancient grave, even if the intent is to gain important knowledge about the past? There has been considerable debate over this issue, especially during the past two decades, as indigenous peoples throughout the world have gained more political clout and have decried the removal of human remains and burial objects from their primary resting places. This issue has led to the development of specific legislation in many countries, including the 1990 Native American Graves Protection and Repatriation Act in the United States (see Chapter 13).

However, many archaeologists feel that very ancient remains that cannot be directly linked with specific groups of modern people can and should be studied. The recent Kennewick Man case (this chapter and Chapter 14) illustrates the recent debate over whether ancient remains (in this instance, over 9,000 years old) can be attributable to living peoples. The Umatilla, Colville, Yakima, and other related tribes believe that because their creation stories state that they have always been in what is now eastern Washington,

Kennewick Man must be an ancestor and, according to tribal beliefs about the dead, should be returned for reburial without scientific analysis. Although most archaeologists sympathize with traditional concerns, many believe that the scientific knowledge to be gained by the study of such truly ancient remains that cannot be directly linked to living groups is not only appropriate but also necessary, as long as the process is carried out in a respectful manner.

In the majority of cases in the United States and several other countries, indigenous peoples are consulted prior to archaeological excavations, and the treatment of human burials is negotiated before the initiation of fieldwork. In those situations where known burial areas are identified, they are usually avoided unless the graves are endangered by impending development or other ground-disturbing activities. When human remains are encountered, they are treated with respect and dignity during the process of excavation, removal, and analysis. Many remains that are being studied today will ultimately be repatriated on request by indigenous peoples for reburial.

CONTENTSELECT

Search articles in the ContentSelect database using the key words *paleonutrition* and *paleopathology*. What is the focus of archaeological research in these areas? How are diet and disease apparent in ancient human remains?

Chapter Summary

The best way to learn about the people themselves in the past is to look at their remains, the study of which is known as bioarchaeology. Sometimes we are fortunate, and complete bodies are frozen or mummified, preserving soft tissues such as skin, hair, and organs. Most commonly, however, human remains are skeletal. Bioarchaeologists are frequently trained as biological anthropologists, who have specific training in the study of human bones, or osteology.

Skeletal remains are frequently found as intentional inhumations, such as complete burials, which are often accompanied by grave goods that can give indications of social status. Sometimes bones were removed from primary inhumations and buried elsewhere as secondary burials or were placed in ossuaries. Some groups cremated the dead, and the resulting burned, fragmentary remains (cremains) provide a challenge to the osteologist. Human remains can also enter the archaeological record as a result of natural disasters, such as floods or volcanic eruptions, or the end result of battles and massacres. Cannibalism represents another form of skeletal deposition, often in trash heaps or midden deposits with other food remains.

Once human remains are recovered, they are analyzed in an effort to produce osteobiographies that tell us details about individuals during their lives. Using a combination of qualitative and quantitative techniques, bioarchaeologists determine age at death, sex, stature, and health status. Forensic facial reconstruction techniques are used to flesh out the faces of ancient peoples to give us an idea of how they may have appeared in life. Chemical and isotopic analyses can provide information about ancient diet, and the extraction of DNA from human bone can give us a look into ancient pedigrees as well as human migration patterns.

Key Concepts

antemortem, 213
appendicular skeleton, 203
axial skeleton, 203
bioarchaeology, 195
cremains, 204
epiphyseal fusion, 207
Harris lines, 215

metabolic pathways, 216
mummification, 198
ossification, 207
osteobiography, 206
osteology, 204
paleodemography, 195
postmortem, 213

secondary burial, 204
skeletal age, 207
skeletal pathology, 213
skeletal sex, 206
skeletal stature, 208
stable isotope analysis, 215
trephining, 213

Suggested Readings

If you want to learn more about the concepts and issues discussed in this chapter, consider looking at the following resources. (Some may be rather technical.)

Barber, Elizabeth Wayland. (1999). *The Mummies of Urumchi*. New York: W. W. Norton.

> This book weaves an engaging story of discovery, study, and explanation of some of the best preserved human remains and textiles known to archaeology.

Bass, William M. (1995). *Human Osteology: A Laboratory and Field Manual* (4th ed.). Columbia: Missouri Archaeological Society Special Publication No. 2.

> Indisputably the best field manual and quick reference for human osteology available to archaeology students. This spiral-bound, small-format book is perfect for putting in your field pack.

Cockburn, Aidan, Eve Cockburn, and Theodore A. Reyman (eds.). (1998). *Mummies, Disease, and Ancient Culture* (2nd ed.). Cambridge: Cambridge University Press.

> An in-depth examination of the mummies, both natural and intentional, from around the world and what they can tell us about ancient disease and cultural practices. There are particularly good sections on Egyptian and Peruvian mummies.

Powell, Mary Lucas, Patricia Bridges, and Ann Marie Wagner Mires (eds.). (1991). *What Mean These Bones: Studies in Southeastern Bioarchaeology*. Tuscaloosa: University of Alabama Press.

> A collection of papers on bioarchaeological research in the American Southeast that focuses on prehistoric health, mortuary practices, and cultural change. This compilation provides good examples of how bioarchaeological research is conducted, and the questions asked here could be applied to any archaeological population in the world.

White, Tim D., and Pieter Arend Folkens. (2000). *Human Osteology* (2nd ed.). San Diego: Academic Press.

> For the student who is serious about learning human skeletal anatomy, this book will be a necessity. This is the only skeletal anatomy book that contains full-sized photographs of human bones at every important angle, complete with labels of important bone features.

chapter **9**

Environment and Adaptation

ON JULY 19, 1999, Duncan Garrow wrote:

Since last time, we've been digging ovens/fire installations/hearths. The dirty area in the south-east corner seems to have been a long-term thing, with hearth upon hearth . . . all nicely associated with ashy/charcoal spreads and occasionally floors. After three clearly different features, we met a thick layer of grey silt mixed with loads of oven demolition material. We took that out to reveal . . . another "hearth," which looks very nice so far. Best of all, though, the layer had a whole figurine within it!!! It exactly matched the head found (in screening) a few days earlier from the same context. The depth of the deposit, and what we can see so far of the stratigraphy, suggests that this is an earlier phase, so we've left it there. It's interesting to play games: the destruction of houses and the burial of people under the floor coinciding with our destruction of the hearths and the deposition of person-like figurines—the head was separated from the figurine body; the hearth was followed in the next few phases by other hearths on top of each other; the unit as a whole reminded me slightly of the unit of demolition rubble we'd taken out from above

the floors of the room; and so on. . . . Unless of course they were toys and got there by chance! Everything seems to have "had its place" (as Mark would say) though, at Catal, things were definitely done in very specific ways, so its being there still would mean something. We've now started on the features around the room—the big upstanding oven in the SW corner and the bins in the NE. It's going to be hard to tie everything in together, as they're all separate features standing alone, but interesting, a good challenge. We'll see.

Duncan Garrow's diary entry describes some of his experiences in the 1999 season of excavations at Çatalhöyük, a famous early Neolithic settlement in present-day Turkey. His discoveries of house floors with ovens and storage bins and "hearth upon hearth" are clear indications that the people who lived there were sedentary and had food surpluses. Their economy was based on the domestication of plants and animals, a way of life that began at the end of Pleistocene about 10,000 years ago. During the next 6,000 years, people all over the world domesticated millet, rice, chickens, and dogs in eastern Asia; wheat, barley, pigs, goats, and sheep in the Middle East; cotton in Egypt; squash, beans, chiles, millet, and maize in Mesoamerica; lima beans, potatoes, cotton, llamas, and alpaca in South America; and sunflowers and sumpweed in North America.

Why did people make this change at this time? Humans had been in intimate contact with plants and animals for millions of years, so why did domestication suddenly develop in different places? Archaeologists are still seeking answers to this question. One answer is that a major environmental change occurred at the end of the Ice Age, beginning about 10,000 years ago. Earth began to warm and the ice sheets melted and retreated north, raising sea levels and dramatically altering climate. Some areas that had been wet became drier, some became desert (the Sahara is still expanding). Other areas became wetter—some hotter, some cooler. Many plants and animals became extinct, others were able to adapt, and the geographic ranges of others changed. Wherever humans were and whatever the details, humans were faced with a new environment to which they had to adapt.

Humans, however, had faced this situation before. The last Ice Age was the most recent of four such events within the last several

223

hundred thousand years, and no domestication or agriculture had developed at the end of the previous three. Although environmental change could not have been the only cause, it may have been the catalyst. Modern humans (*Homo sapiens sapiens*) and their complex cultures were fairly recent. Their sophisticated Upper Paleolithic tool kits included prerequisites for the development of the Neolithic, such as grinding tools adaptable to process seed crops and blade technologies adaptable for sickles used to harvest grains. Perhaps environmental change, coupled with increasing population pressure, compelled people to intensify their relationships with certain plants and animals in ways that led inexorably to agriculture (Richerson et al. 2001).

Domestication initially developed in places where domesticable plants, such as grasses, and animals, such as those living in herds, existed. Farmers and their crops eventually spread across much of the globe, absorbing or replacing hunters and gatherers. This agricultural expansion is still going on; agriculture-based economies affect hunters and gatherers even today. The economic changes that began at the end of the Pleistocene resulted in fundamental changes in human culture, changes to which we are still adapting. Archaeologists seek an understanding of small- and large-scale changes in environments and of how humans adapted (or not) to those changes. Understanding past environmental adaptations helps a great deal in understanding how we can adapt to environmental changes today.

For the location of various centers of domestication and other sites mentioned in this chapter, see the map on page 225.

Human groups have to adapt to their environment through the decisions and actions of their members. Because many cultures became "extinct" in prehistory, an understanding of the relationship between the environment, people, and adaptation is necessary to understand what happened in the past (Butzer 1982; Dincauze 2000). The study of the relationships between humans and their environment is called *human ecology* (Kormondy and Brown 1998; Sutton and Anderson 2004).

The relationship between culture and environment is complex. It was first believed that environment determined culture. Eventually it was realized that culture was the primary factor in adaptation. Julian Steward (1938, 1955) first articulated the concept of cultural ecology when he argued that (1) cultures in similar environments may have similar adaptations; (2) all adaptations are short-lived and are constantly adjusting to changing environments; and (3) changes in culture can elaborate existing culture or result in entirely new cultures through cultural evolution. Steward is frequently referred to as the father of ecological studies in anthropology.

LOCATION MAP: Sites Mentioned in Chapter 9

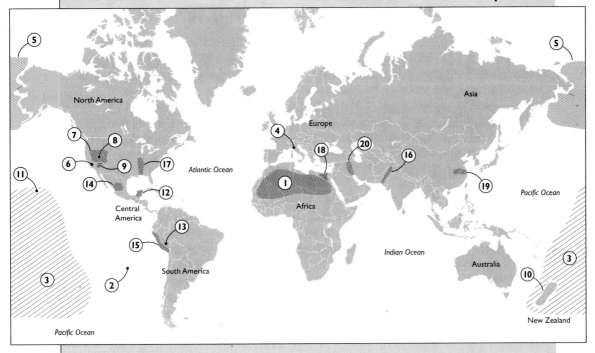

1 ■ Sahara Desert
North Africa

2 ■ Rapa Nui (Easter Island)
2,000 miles west of Chile, Pacific Ocean

3 ■ Polynesia

4 ■ Pisa
Pisa, Italy

5 ■ Bering Strait (Land Bridge)
Alaska

6 ■ Guapiabit site (CA-SBR-1913)
San Bernardino, California

7 ■ Great Basin
Western United States

8 ■ Lakeside Cave
Southwestern Utah

9 ■ Hohokam
Southern Arizona

10 ■ Aotearoa
New Zealand

11 ■ Hawai'i Archipelago
Hawai'i

12 ■ Yucatán Peninsula
Mexico

13 ■ Colca Valley
Peru

14 ■ Central Mexico

15 ■ Coastal Peru

16 ■ Indus Valley

17 ■ Mississippi Valley

18 ■ Nile Valley

19 ■ Yangtze Valley

20 ■ Tigris-Euphrates River

The map shows the sites and archaeological regions mentioned in Chapter 9. The shaded areas show the river valleys in which people first domesticated plants and animals and practiced intensive agriculture.

The Environment

The **environment** consists of living and nonliving systems interacting within a bounded geographic unit called Earth. The *biotic* (living) part of the environment consists of all living things—fungi, bacteria, plants, and animals, including humans. The *abiotic* (nonliving) part of the environment consists of things such as air, water, soil, rock, heat, sunlight, landforms, and processes such as weather and the passing of time. The environment of the prehistoric past is called **paleoenvironment.**

Earth's environment is commonly divided into zones, such as *biomes*, large-scale divisions incorporating large areas of similar environment, such as "tropical rain forest" or "grassland." A biome might contain several **ecozones**—each a distinct geographic area containing a specific group of interdependent living species. Most ecozones are defined by major plant species, such as pine forest or marshland; others are defined with a geographic designation, such as lake. Within a particular biome or ecozone, biotic and abiotic elements of the environment operate as an integrated unit called an **ecosystem** (Odum 1953; Golley 1993).

In addition to the natural environment, a cultural environment also can be defined as consisting of the interactions of people within a culture and between cultures. Thus, a cultural environment consists of the culture of the group plus all the surrounding groups that exerted influence. The place where two ecozones meet and overlap is called an **ecotone.** Because ecotones contain resources present in both ecozones, ecotones are highly productive localities—a good place for people to be. The place where two cultures meet, a kind of cultural ecotone, could also be a very productive place because of the exchange of ideas and goods.

Each organism occupies both a habitat and a niche within its environment. *Habitat* is the geographic place where an organism lives. *Niche* is the role an organism plays in its environment: what it eats, how it reproduces, and what it does. In some places, farmers and hunter-gatherers were able to share portions of the same habitat because they occupied different specific niches.

Humans occupy and dominate most terrestrial places on the planet and so have a huge habitat. Humans also are omnivores—they can eat and digest just about anything (except cellulose) and therefore occupy a broad general niche (Barth 1956:1088; Hardesty 1975:71). Through the use of technology, humans modify their habitat to suit their needs and even create artificial habitats, such as cities or space stations. Having such a broad niche and huge habitat, humans compete with most other species and often drive them to extinction.

A *resource* is a commodity actually used by an organism. Some resources, such as water, are used by all organisms; other resources are used only by some. Natural resources include land, water, air, time, firewood, minerals, and fossil fuels. Resources manufactured by humans include commodities such as tools.

The limited number of organisms that an environment can support at any one time under a given set of circumstances is called the **carrying capacity** (Glassow 1978; Baumhoff 1981; Dewar 1984). As conditions change, carrying capacity also changes. There is always one factor—often a resource such as water, food, or land—that limits carrying capacity. For example, let us say that the carrying capacity of a small valley is 100 people who hunt and gather wild plants and animals for a living. Under the same conditions, the valley could support 1,000 people who farm for a living. In this example, the natural environment does not change; what changes are the technology and subsistence practices of the people living in the valley. But if the rainfall in the area decreases by 50 percent, agriculture may not be possible at all, and the carrying capacity may drop to only 60 hunter-gatherers.

All organisms, including humans, affect their environment to some degree. As people become more numerous and as technology becomes more complex, the scale of human impact on the environment increases. It is true that the scale of impact was generally less in the past, but there are many instances in which past people severely, even disastrously, affected the carrying capacity of their environment (Highlight 9.1).

Environmental Archaeology

With the development of a more scientific archaeology after the 1960s, archaeologists realized that documenting and understanding changes in environment are necessary to comprehend and interpret changes in human adaptation. Information on the environment is needed as a starting point for formulating economic models, and it is important to determine whether changes in environment were caused by people. Archaeologists now routinely include the study of past environments in their work and use that information, derived through observational or experimental data, to develop models of the relationship of past peoples and their environments—that is, **paleoecology** (Dincauze 2000:497).

Environmental archaeologists want to discover the environmental conditions under which people of any particular place and time lived. To understand human interaction with the environment, we have to know what the environment was, which resources people had available, what they did and did not use, what organizations and technologies they used to adapt (what worked and what did not work), how successful they were, and how their culture was affected. Conversely, we also want to know how cultures and their practices affected environments through people's technology, practices, and contacts. The introduction of new plants and animals, for example, often resulted in a significant alteration of the environment. People also had major impacts on populations of animals (Grayson 2001), which can help us understand similar impacts today.

Archaeologists work to reconstruct past environments by formulating and testing models of human adaptation in those environments. Initial investigations establish the general climate and environment of a region. Researchers then investigate the more specific conditions at particular sites. As the scale of space and time becomes smaller, precise dating becomes more critical.

Reconstructing Past Landforms

Any environment exists within a landform consisting of various abiotic elements, including its geology and hydrology. All landforms change through time, and the study of how they change is called **geomorphology**. Archaeologists also are interested in how geological and geomorphological processes affect archaeological sites, including site formation and transformation—a field called **geoarchaeology** (Rapp and Hill 1998). The reconstruction

HIGHLIGHT **9.1**

Easter Island's Ecological Disaster

When discovered by Europeans in 1722, Easter Island (Rapa Nui), remotely located in the southeastern Pacific Ocean, was a rather barren place with relatively few trees and a small population of Polynesians barely getting by. Yet the archaeological record of the island contains many deserted settlements and abandoned agricultural fields. In addition, there are almost a thousand moai on the island, some of which weigh as much as 270 tons, and many of which were abandoned during manufacture or transport. These remains bear witness to a time when there were many more people, a thriving economy, a more complex technology, and a much more complex political and social system. What happened?

Explorers from Polynesia discovered and settled Easter Island about 1,600 years ago. They brought with them a variety of domesticated plants and animals, quickly established a prosperous farming and fishing economy, and the population grew. People began to quarry and erect moai, which were placed on elaborate platforms. The transport of the statues would have required considerable rope and lumber, obtained from trees and other plants that did not exist on the island in 1722. Could it be that the island was not so barren in the past?

Pollen analysis showed that prior to the arrival of people, Easter Island supported an extensive forest containing trees, shrubs, and other plants, some of which were quite suitable for use in making rope and lumber for moai transport. Analysis of animal bones in the sites showed that Easter Islanders ate a large number of porpoises (caught in the open sea from large canoes), fish, and many species of both sea and land birds. In addition, they ate the domesticated foods they had brought with them. All in all, the islanders enjoyed a bountiful and diverse food supply, cooked using firewood from the forest.

People began to cut down the trees to make canoes, to obtain wood for moai transport, to make rope, to clear land for fields, and to obtain firewood. As the forest began to shrink, plants and animals that depended on the forest (and were eaten by the people) began to disappear. The once-ubiquitous seabirds were eaten almost to extinction. Eventually, no trees large enough to make canoes were left, and the supply of porpoises and some fish vanished. Moai, the status symbols of powerful men, could no longer be moved, statue production ceased, and warring factionalism replaced centralized government. As food supplies dwindled and people began to starve, the

of landforms is an important aspect of understanding where people may have lived and what resources they may have had access to (see Butzer 2005). Also, certain landforms may serve as temporal markers, such as terminal moraines dating from the end of the last glaciation.

Landforms are modified in a number of ways. Mechanisms of change include human activity, plate tectonics, vulcanism, earthquakes, valley formation by rivers or by glacial activity (which leaves distinctively shaped valleys), erosion and deposition by water or wind, and isostatic lift—the rebounding of depressed land after the weight of glaciers is removed. Shorelines, a landform important to many human groups, are also dynamic. Changes in the levels of lakes over time may produce fossil

Megalithic statues, called *moai,* are testimony to the Polynesian culture that once thrived on Easter Island. How does environmental archaeology help explain what happened to the people who occupied Easter Island long ago?

last remaining source of protein, human flesh, began to be exploited, and cannibalism became common.

Finally, the forest was gone, the island was barren, and the surviving population struggled to survive

(McCall 1994; Van Tilburg 1994; Diamond 1995; Rainbird 2002). It is speculated that rats, brought to the island in canoes of the Polynesian colonists, contributed to the devastation of the island's forests (Hunt 2007).

It seems ingrained in popular belief that prehistoric and native, or traditional, peoples somehow lived in harmony with their environment, not harming the land or overexploiting resources (e.g., Grinde and Johansen 1995; White 1997). However, it is abundantly clear that past peoples did impact their environments, sometimes overexploiting resources and disrupting ecosystems, albeit on a smaller scale than today (Diamond 1992; Lewis 1992; Krech 1999; Rowley-Conwy 2002). Diamond (1995:63) underscored the practical importance of understanding the Easter Island problem when he wrote, "In just a few centuries, the people of Easter Island wiped out their forest, drove their plants and animals to extinction, and saw their complex society spiral into chaos and cannibalism. Are we about to follow their lead?"

CRITICAL **THINKING** QUESTIONS

1. What other scenarios that could lead to an environmental disaster can you think of?
2. What environmental conditions are likely to amplify the effects of the overexploitation of resources?

lakeshores and wave-cut terraces around the edges of a lake. Sea levels also fluctuate; modern coastlines generally are not the same as ancient ones. River systems, too, can change shorelines. For example, the river system running through the Italian town of Pisa silted in several thousand years ago, burying the Roman port and preserving a number of Roman ships (Kunzig 2000). Pisa is now located some six miles from the ocean.

Sea-level changes were sometimes substantial, such as the 300-foot drop during the Late Pleistocene due to the vast quantities of water being locked up in glacial ice. Large tracts of land were exposed all over the world (Figure 9.1), including the Bering land bridge between Asia and North America used by people migrating into the New World

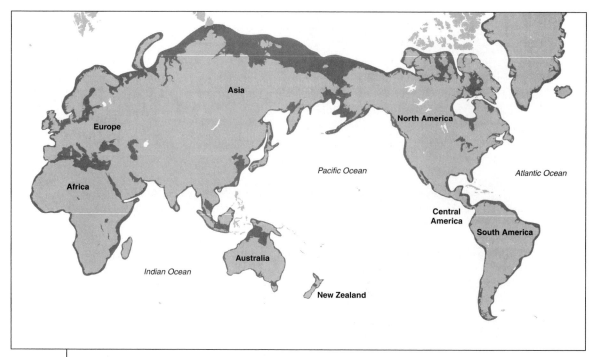

figure 9.1

Global Sea-Level Map.   During the Ice Ages, the expansion of the glaciers resulted in a worldwide sea-level drop of about 300 feet, exposing large regions *(shaded)* along coastlines around the world. The sea-level drop exposed the Bering Strait land bridge between Asia and North America, and this route may have been used by the first people entering the New World at the end of the Pleistocene.

some 15,000 years ago. As the glaciers melted, sea level rose again, covering Late Pleistocene archaeological sites located near ancient shorelines.

In addition to landforms, the abiotic environment also includes the atmosphere. Analysis of past air samples, such as those from sealed tombs or bubbles trapped in ice, can reveal the gas composition of the atmosphere. These measurements reveal the rise in atmospheric carbon dioxide over the last few hundred years. Air samples also provide evidence of pollution, such as the high levels of copper in the atmosphere during Roman times caused by the production of copper (Hong et al. 1996; also see Pyatt et al. 2000).

Reconstructing Past Plants and Animals

Reconstructing the record of plants and animals in an environment indicates which of these were available for people to use, as well as the nature of the general environment. Archaeologists use the reconstruction of past vegetation to model ecozones, which then are used to infer animal populations. A forest ecozone, for example, would be expected to contain deer. Models of the human economy and adaptation are based on the ecozone models.

Pollen, phytoliths, and macrofossils (remains visible to the naked eye) can be used to reconstruct vegetation. Pollen is the sperm cells of plants, and as you may recall from Chapter 4, the study of pollen is called *palynology* (Pearsall 1989:245–310; Fægri et al. 2000). Pollen from many plants, especially trees, is distributed by wind, so pollen "rains" onto archaeological sites and other exposed surfaces and is incorporated into sediments. Pollen from flowering plants often is distributed by insects and so has a different pattern. Palynologists recover pollen from soils, including soils from archaeological sites. The analysis of the pollen record reveals the types of plants present in an area over time—data critical to environmental reconstruction (Figure 9.2).

Phytoliths are microscopic silica bodies that form when the silica in solution in water precipitates out within the individual plant cell (Rovner 1983; Piperno and Pearsall 1993). When the plant dies and decomposes, phytoliths enter the soil in large numbers. Researchers are just beginning to learn how to properly recover, process, and identify these remains. Like pollen, phytoliths could help us understand what plants were present and which ones people may have used.

Macrofossils include charred seeds or other plant parts found in sites that can be used to infer the nearby presence of those plants or their acquisition through trade. Charcoal from wood burned in campfires can be identified to learn what plants were used for fuel and undoubtedly grew nearby. Plant macrofossils sometimes are found in packrat nests that have been occupied for thousands of years. Because materials incorporated into a packrat nest come from within a few hundred feet of the nest, they can be dated to reconstruct plant communities over time.

Likewise, the remains of animals, typically bones, also can be used in environmental reconstruction. The animals found can indicate types of vegetation near a site. Mammoths, for example, were grazers, and if mammoth bones are found at a site, there must have been grasslands in the vicinity at the time.

Reconstructing Past Climate

Climate is the long-term (on the scale of centuries) pattern of temperature and precipitation in a given region. *Weather* is the short-term (on the scale of days or months) manifestation of actual conditions of temperature and precipitation. Thus, climate is the long-term average of weather. Researchers reconstruct long-term patterns of past temperatures and precipitation, or **paleoclimate,** to study changing adaptations to changing environments (Figure 9.3). Weather is more difficult to study because it requires precise dating of events. Nevertheless, some actual weather can be seen in the archaeological record, such as flash-flood deposition evident in soil profiles.

Investigations of paleoclimate may begin by addressing broad questions such as average global or regional temperature, ice coverage, and sea level. As more detailed and specific data are obtained, the climate of smaller regions can be reconstructed. As the paleoclimate is refined through detailed information about temperature and precipitation, archaeologists can construct models of the biotic elements of the environment. Models of human interactions with those biotic elements can then be constructed and tested.

A major source of information about paleoclimate is cores—long cylindrical plugs of material removed by hollow drills from ocean or lake sediments and from glacial ice. Samples can be removed from different layers in the cores, dated, and examined and

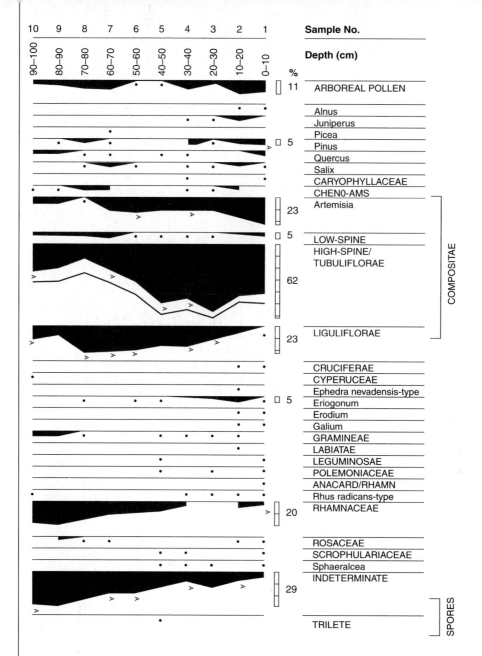

figure 9.2

Pollen Profile of the CA-SBR-1913 Site. This pollen profile identifies the proportions of different types of plants in an environment over time—the Guapiabit site in southern California (CA-SBR-1913). The profile suggests that the area supported a larger woodland plant community prior to occupation by people and that the plant community changed to sagebrush scrub near the site people occupied. From this kind of information, what can be inferred about people's adaptations to and impacts on their environment?

Source: Linda Scott Cummings, 1996, "Pollen Analysis of CA-SBR-1913, California," Appendix 6, in Mark Q. Sutton and Joan S. Schneider, "Archaeological Investigations at Guapiabit: CA-SBR-1913," *San Bernardino County Museum Association Quarterly* 43(4). Used by permission of the San Bernardino County Museum Association.

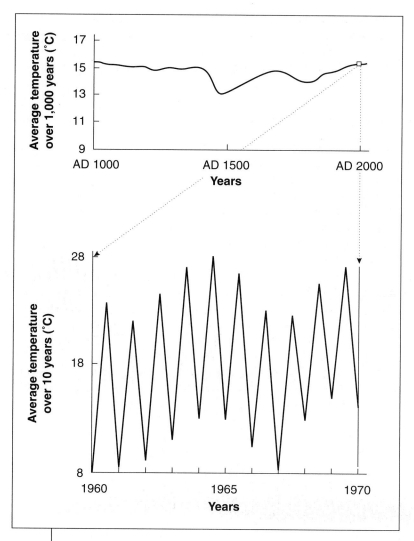

figure 9.3

Scale of Climate and Weather. This graph showing average global temperatures over the last 1,000 years exhibits a rather smooth line but with significant cooling evident in the 1400s. The graph showing temperatures in the 1960s exhibits considerable seasonal variation. Small-scale variations in weather are averaged together to create a picture of climate.

tested for relevant information. Data from cores have been employed to reconstruct climate over millions of years.

Cores can contain a great deal of information. Most ocean sediment cores contain the fossils of microscopic animals (foraminifera) that are temperature sensitive, and the distribution of specific species of these fossils throughout the core can be used to infer ocean temperature. The rate of sedimentation may also be apparent in a core, and slower or faster rates may be used to infer the amount of sediment reaching the ocean as a result of rainfall and erosion.

Cores taken from some lakes can reveal *varves,* a precise annual record of sediment deposition. Varve records were first employed in glacial lakes to determine the rate at which glaciers melted. However, varves also can be found in lakes deep enough that bottom-dwelling organisms are not present to mix the deposits. In these cases, the varve record can be used to reconstruct annual rainfall.

Cores taken from glacial ice can often be detailed enough to reveal the yearly deposition of snowfall (much like tree rings) so that a precise record of precipitation at that locality can be obtained. The ratio of oxygen isotopes ($^{18}O/^{16}O$) can be measured in the various ice layers to reconstruct ocean temperatures at the time the ice was deposited. Finally, air trapped in bubbles in the ice can be studied to reveal the concentrations of atmospheric gasses over time. In fact, recent work has revealed that greenhouse gasses began to increase some 8,000 years ago, probably as a result of farmers clearing forests and raising more livestock (Ruddiman 2003).

Archaeological data also can be used in paleoenvironmental and paleoclimatic reconstruction. For example, a number of rock art sites in the Sahara of northern Africa contain depictions of giraffes and other animals that no longer reside in that region. This implies that at the time the rock art was made, those animals were present and the climate was wet enough to support the kind of vegetation on which they feed.

Finally, remote sensing techniques can be used to map ancient landforms shaped by different climates. Spaceborne radar, for example, has detected ancient riverbeds buried by sand in the Sahara, demonstrating that the climate was very different at some time in the past.

Human Biological Adaptation

Like all species, humans have to adapt to changing environmental conditions. Successful adaptation depends on finding workable solutions to environmental challenges. A successful adaptation allows an organism (or culture) to reproduce itself and survive from generation to generation. Humans adapt biologically through both short- and long-term means. Interestingly, human culture and technology are making human biological adaptation less important.

Physiological adaptations are short-term changes in the body in response to rapid changes in the environment. Primary responses take place within hours or days; secondary responses may take months or even longer. Common conditions that stimulate physiological adaptations include exposure to sun, high altitude, cold, heat, high activity, malnutrition, and even disease (Kormondy and Brown 1998:162–226). Physiological adaptations affect evolution only to the extent that they affect survival or reproduction.

Anatomical adaptation involves long-term genetic alteration to anatomy and physiology as a result of selective pressures brought about by long-term changes in the environment. Such change is manifested over generations rather than in the lifetime of an individual, so the selective pressure for a particular change cannot be too rapid or extreme if the organism is to survive long enough to adapt. Like all organisms, humans are under constant selective pressure and have undergone a number of anatomical changes over the millennia, as can easily be seen in the fossil record of human evolution.

Evolutionary Ecology

Evolutionary ecology is the application of the principles of biological selection to the understanding of how organisms adapt. Archaeologists begin with a few assumptions: that cultures function like organisms; that varying cultural practices are the equivalent of biological variation; and that cultural behaviors, like biological traits, are selected for or against depending on conditions. Selection then acts on cultures, depending on whether cultural behaviors are adaptive (Richerson and Boyd 1992). Most evolutionary ecologists study the efficiency of diet, a biological aspect of adaptation. The **diet** of a group consists of the long-term patterns and trends of foods that are and are not eaten, how and when foods are obtained and processed, their nutritional value, their overall role in the diet (the focus of many ecological studies), and how those patterns change over time.

Most cultures devise more than one possible solution to changing environmental (natural or cultural) conditions. The greater the number of solutions a culture possesses, the more likely the culture is to adapt successfully. Some solutions work well; others do not. If a solution to a situation does not work, whether because of poor decision making or factors beyond people's control, a culture could disappear. Successful solutions are often seen as somehow being "optimal"; but, in reality, they only have to be "good enough."

If two groups find themselves in competition within the same environment, one group eventually outcompetes the other in some way, such as in the control of land or resources. According to general ecological theory, the most efficient adaptation ultimately prevails. Following this approach, archaeologists Robert Bettinger and Martin Baumhoff proposed that the ethnographic Numa peoples of the Great Basin outcompeted and replaced the earlier pre-Numa occupants of the region largely because the Numa possessed a more efficient technology for gathering and processing grass seeds (Bettinger and Baumhoff 1982). People, however, often do not follow the rules of the ecological game. A group with a much less efficient overall adaptation could win a competition by simply conquering or killing all or most of the members of the competing group.

Optimization Models

In the study of evolutionary ecology, **optimization models,** or *optimal foraging models,* are used to explain aspects of behavior related to the use of resources (Jochim 1983:157). Originally developed by economists, optimization models were borrowed by biologists to study animal behavior and then were borrowed again by anthropologists and applied to humans (Winterhalder 1981; Smith 1983). The basic assumption is that people attempt to maximize their net efficiency and minimize their risk (Jochim 1998:14–20)—that is, people spend the least (in time, energy, or resources) to get the most (in food, materials, or land). An example of one of the optimization models is given in Highlight 9.2.

HIGHLIGHT 9.2

Using the Diet Breadth Optimization Model

The diet breadth model is perhaps the most commonly used optimization model. Using diet breadth, the researcher ranks resources by net return rate (almost always in calories) and constructs the diet that the group under study should have adopted if they were behaving optimally. To construct such a model, the researcher needs to know the full range of resources available, the caloric value of each resource, and the caloric costs of finding, obtaining, transporting, and processing each resource. The researcher ranks the resources and constructs a model of the optimal diet.

People (as measured in the United States) need about 2,500 calories a day (Whitney and Rolfes 1996: Table G-3). Strictly from the standpoint of calories, people should first exploit the highest-ranked resource, for it can provide the most calories with the least effort. Once the highest-ranked resource becomes unavailable, the breadth of the diet should expand to the second-ranked resource, then to the third, and so on, until the requirements of the diet are met.

Some issues become readily apparent. First, the ranking of resources is based on estimates. As we learn more, these rankings are likely to change. Next, calories are not the only concern. People in prehistory knew something about basic nutrition and made efforts to design their diets to include the full range of other needed nutrients, such as vitamins, even if the needed foods did not rank high in calories. Also, the availability of any particular resource would depend on season; during certain seasons, the resources included in the diet would change. Finally, some nonfood items, such as tobacco, were obtained and used in ceremony and recreation. Tobacco is a costly resource, but people with a good diet could "afford" to get it. Also, if people believed that tobacco was a necessary item in ceremonies intended to ensure the productivity of other resources, getting it could be critical, whatever the cost.

The next issue is gathering and analyzing archaeological data so the model can be tested. Sites in the area and time under investigation have to be found and excavated with field methods designed to recover the kinds of data needed. If field techniques are not properly designed, some data may be missed, as is often the case with insect remains (Sutton 1995). Estimates of the number of other resources at a site depend on how well the botanical and faunal remains are identified and how they are analyzed. Finally, an analysis of the recovered technology also has to be made to see whether it was used in processing the resources. As you can see, problems in recovery and analysis could make testing the model difficult.

If the model is not supported, there is the question of why (the same question would be asked if the model was supported). It certainly is possible that the model was just plain wrong, in which case a new model is needed. It also is possible that the diet of the people under investigation was not optimal, perhaps because of cultural beliefs and practices. In that case, the model has to be revised to take those factors into consideration. Finally, if the model is correct but the testing was poorly designed or executed, the next investigator will have to try to improve the model.

If the diet met the needs of the people, the culture would be successful and would endure. If the diet was somehow deficient, or became deficient because of changing conditions, the culture would have to modify the diet or become extinct. If another culture entered the area, the one with the most efficient adaptation (or diet, in the case of optimization modeling) would be selected for, and the other culture would be replaced. In most cases, however, the dietary needs of a culture are easily met. Most cultures operate at a "profit" and so are able to afford tobacco, other luxuries, and leisure time.

HIGHLIGHT **9.2** *continued*

This example from the Great Basin of western North America illustrates some of the issues. Researchers developed information about many of the resources that they thought were used by prehistoric peoples in the Great Basin and did not model other resources (e.g., Simms 1984; Madsen 1986). Subsequent excavations at Lakeside Cave, Utah, demonstrated that grasshoppers, a resource thought to be of minor importance, were very significant (Madsen and Kirkman 1988).

Initial excavations at Lakeside Cave resulted in the recovery of a few fragmentary grasshopper parts in the site deposit. When a smaller mesh screen was used on some other site soils, the presence of a larger number of grasshopper parts led the researchers to consider the possibility that grasshoppers were a resource used at the site. The use of still finer mesh resulted in the recovery of a large number of grasshopper parts, forcing a reconsideration of the role of those animals in the overall subsistence system. It was discovered that grasshoppers could be obtained nearby from the shore of the Great Salt Lake. They occasionally washed up on shore, naturally dried and salted. It was determined that the return rate for collecting grasshoppers at Lakeside Cave was somewhere between 270,000 and 7 million calories per hour, far higher than the return of any other resource (the next highest were deer, sheep, and antelope at about 30,000 calories [Simms 1984:Table 4]) and making grasshoppers by far the highest-ranked resource in the region. Grasshoppers, however, were not always available in such quantities right next to where people were living.

It was later determined (Jones and Madsen 1989) that if the grasshoppers were transported to other localities (and if the caloric cost of carrying the grasshoppers from place to place were counted), their return rate would be much lower: about 3,500 calories. However, the new calculations were based on the transportation of whole grasshoppers and did not allow for the likelihood that at least some of the grasshoppers may have been processed prior to transport, allowing a person to carry many more grasshoppers and lowering transport costs.

In sum, we do not know the ranking of grasshoppers in the Great Basin. It appears to have been very high, at least in places where they could be collected in abundance (e.g., Madsen and Schmitt 1998). A determination of whether the animals were processed prior to transport, whether they were stored, and other factors must be made before the return rate, or rates depending on conditions, can be calculated. In the meantime, a model of the optimal diet of the prehistoric people in the area cannot be determined until the grasshopper issue is resolved.

CRITICAL **THINKING** QUESTIONS

1. What parameters other than calories might be important to consider in formulating models of diet?
2. What cultural needs or desires might "override" a strictly optimal diet?

Thus, in theory, people who make optimal use of available resources (calories) will be most successful. For example, if 100 calories of food cost 150 calories to find, kill, and prepare, a person depending on that particular food would quickly starve even if the food was abundant. It would be much better to eat 100 calories that cost only 50 calories to produce. Humans, however, frequently make decisions based on many factors other than calories, thereby weakening researchers' ability to model human behavior on calories alone. Optimization models can help answer some questions about past cultures but, like all models, have only limited utility for answering other questions. One of the major strengths of optimization models is that they get researchers thinking about a variety of issues, different approaches, new problems, and new questions to ask.

Human Cultural Adaptation

The primary mechanism by which humans adapt to their environment is culture. Technology and social organization, including the structure of economic, political, and social behavior, are cultural responses to adaptive pressures. Compared with biological adaptation, culture is an extremely flexible and rapid adaptive mechanism because "behavioral responses to external environmental forces can be acquired, transmitted, and modified within the lifetimes of individuals" (Henry 1995:1). The study of cultural adaption to the environment is called **cultural ecology.**

The Aka hunter/gatherers of central Africa practice a subsistence strategy that may be thousands of years old. Net hunting enables the Aka to meet dietary needs through the cooperative capture of game. A division of labor by sex and age makes men the "drivers" of wild game and women and children the "catchers" at the nets. Decisions about which animals to kill are based on cultural preferences as well as optimization values, such as meat preservation. Even today the Aka generally lack the technology for preserving meat. In these photos, a division of labor is shown by women and children sorting seeds and a man with an animal captured in a snare.

Individuals are born into a cultural system operating in a particular way within a particular environment. In past groups, the cultural system one was born into tended to be influenced by the "natural" environment: geography, local resource distributions, climate, and the like were critical factors. In industrialized cultures, the important environment tends to be much more socioeconomic, and class and income (access to resources) are the major environmental differences between individuals.

All environments are dynamic (even if the changes are small). Therefore, a culture must make constant adjustments to maintain some sort of equilibrium, and there is a constant interplay between cultural practices and the environment. Cultural practices can lessen the impact of environmental change and so level out environmental differences. Mitigating and leveling mechanisms might be seasonal adaptations to differences in food availability between the spring and winter, or longer-term adaptations to climatic fluctuations. Culture chooses from a variety of solutions to various problems. As some solutions become unavailable, others present themselves. If the solutions are adequate, the culture survives. There may be multiple sets of solutions. A particular culture might choose one; a different culture might choose another.

The Hohokam people living in the arid Sonoran desert of Arizona between 500 and 1,700 years ago developed a complex system of water control to adapt their agricultural system to a desert region with sporadic rainfall (Haury 1976; Reid and Whittlesey 1997; Bayman 2001). The Hohokam constructed reservoirs and irrigation canals to utilize the seasonal flow of the Salt River and to store rainwater when it became available. They used this stored water during dry periods, mitigating the seasonal availability of water.

People respond to environmental pressures and opportunities in many ways. These include economic organization, such as division of labor; social organization, such as kinship; political organization, such as resource allocation or redistribution; and religious organization, such as seasonal ceremonies or calls for supernatural intervention in environmental forces—for rainfall, for instance, or for the return of a migrating animal resource. Adaptations may also include adjustment such as growing different crops in different areas, as shown in Highlight 9.3. Economic, social, political, and religious organizations are all closely interconnected and mutually reinforcing in the cultural system.

Cultures respond to environmental stress in more concrete ways. For example, a simple technique to alleviate seasonally uneven resource distributions is the use of storage to save resources when they are abundant for times when they are not (Testart 1982). Agriculturalists, in particular, utilize storage on a massive scale. Technology plays an important role in storage. Resources often are processed by grinding, drying, smoking, or parching to make them storable for long periods, sometimes years. In addition, people often construct special facilities, such as granaries, cairns, silos, cisterns, and warehouses—features that are fairly durable in the archaeological record—to store resources. Living resources, such as domesticated animals, also can be "stored" for later use. Another way to "store" resources is by controlling access to an area where resources are found, preventing their exploitation by others and saving the resources for later use (Ingold 1987:207).

Different groups may use the same space in different ways, reflecting the organization of their culture. Basic economics has a major influence on land use. For example, hunter-gatherers use a valley floor very differently than agriculturalists. Resource exploitation, in both kind and scale, is also a major factor in land use: some groups have iron mines, oil

Island Geography and Subsistence Practices in Polynesia

Polynesia, from the Greek for "many islands," is a name given by European explorers to a region of the Pacific inhabited by many different contemporary cultural groups all descended from a common ancestral culture known to archaeologists as Lapita. The Lapita people first colonized the archipelagoes of Samoa and Tonga by about 1200 BC, bringing with them from Melanesia a broadly developed subsistence system. This subsistence system included the farming of tubers (taro and yams), fruit trees (bananas and breadfruit), and domesticated animals (pigs, dogs, and chickens). With their tremendous double-hulled sailing canoes and highly developed navigation skills, Polynesian peoples colonized over 300 islands of the Pacific from as far south as Aotearoa (New Zealand), as far east as Rapa Nui (Easter Island), and as far north as Hawai'i. Among these islands spanning 80 degrees of latitude, they encountered a wide variety of geographical diversity, each time adapting their suite of subsistence methods to their new homes, as well as developing new strategies along the way.

Archaeologist Patrick Kirch has studied the role of different forms of agriculture in the social and economic development of the islands (Kirch 1977, 1984, 1994; Kirch and Sahlins 1992). His book *The Wet and the Dry: Irrigation and Agricultural Intensification in Polynesia* (Kirch 1994) explored the biological and cultural dynamics of wet and dry environments in Polynesian lifeways. Kirch drew not only on his extensive archaeological experience throughout the Pacific but also on ethnographic research undertaken on the islands of Futuna and 'Uvea, where the inhabitants still practice traditional subsistence strategies.

Although Kirch explored the dynamic of wet and dry adaptations throughout Polynesia, he elaborated the case of agriculture in the Hawaiian archipelago. The Hawaiian Islands, classed by geographers as "high islands" because of their significant landmass above sea level, were formed by tectonic-plate movement over a volcanic "hot spot" on the ocean floor. Because of the time needed for the breakdown of lava into farmable soil, one finds much broader, more fertile valleys on the older islands of the chain. Rainfall is carried to the islands primarily by the trade winds, which blow out of the northeast, but the height of many of the volcanic peaks creates what are known as rain shadows. Low-flying, moisture-laden clouds reach the islands on their northern and eastern sides, bump into the mountains, and release most of their rainfall before traveling over the peaks to the southern and western sides of the islands. This weather system can create tropical rain forests on one side of the islands and deserts on the other, giving most of the islands a wet side and a dry side.

When it comes to growing plants, the difference between 400 and 4 inches of rainfall a year is enormous, and the Polynesians had crops in their repertoire that could be grown in either circumstance. On the wet, windward sides of the islands, Hawaiians developed extensive systems of irrigated pondfields called *lo'i*, used for the growing of *kalo* (or taro). On the dry, or leeward, sides of the islands, where streams ran seasonally and rainfall was scarce, the primary crop was *'uala*, sweet potato. This meant that the wet portions of the islands could more easily support larger populations, produce larger and more reliable surpluses of agricultural products to support chiefs and their courts, as well as consistently provide pigs and taro to be used as offerings in state temples (Kirch 1994).

In the case of Hawai'i, as local chiefs tried to consolidate power, both the quantity and the transportability of surplus depended on whether they held lands on the wet or the dry side of an island. In fact, one of the long-term recurring dynamics of Hawaiian political history is that the strongest and most powerful chiefs have consistently risen to power in the dryland areas and then have launched successful raids of conquest on their wetland neighbors. This historical pattern can be seen archaeologically as well as in oral tradition.

The recognition of this historical pattern of power and conquest has in some ways challenged accepted anthropological logic, which predicts that the strongest, most centralized polities arise in the areas with the greatest productivity. In fact, in other parts of the world, prehistorians have argued that the development of large-scale community projects such as irrigation systems directly led to increasing sociopolitical complexity as the need for coordination of building and maintaining such a system became necessary for the group's survival. In Hawai'i, however, it would seem that coveting such systems was an even more powerful impetus to social change! When the islands were finally united under a single high chief and king in 1795, seventeen years after the first European contact, it was under the rule of Kamehameha I, an upstart lower chief originally from the drylands of the Big Island of Hawai'i.

Although increased productivity of agricultural resources might be reason enough for dryland chiefs to want to conquer their irrigated neighbors, in Hawai'i the significance of taro went beyond its ability to efficiently feed many mouths. Symbolically, taro was the most important food in Hawaiians' lives. In their understanding of the creation of the world, taro was humankind's brother, a beloved relative who nourished them all and brought them closer to the gods. This cultural importance was retained in the dry areas. Thus, even though sweet potatoes and yams likely made up more of the people's everyday diet, taro was still thought of as the sustainer of life.

In the case of Hawai'i, the symbolic importance of taro was known to archaeologists through ethnohistoric sources, but it is evidenced in the archaeological record as well. Kirch undertook a large project of settlement pattern survey and accompanying excavation in the district of eastern Maui known as Kahikinui (Kirch 1997). This area, with only a few inches of rainfall a year and intermittent streams, was once the home of thousands of people living primarily on ocean resources and dryland crops of sweet potato and yam. Among the many thousands of domestic structures mapped on the landscape, a small percentage stand out as

Traditional Polynesians still create pondfields for planting taro. What has been the historical relationship of taro to the people's subsistence, social organization, and symbolic culture?

likely to have been the homes of local chiefs. Behind one of these stands the stone outline of the one and only attempt at building a lo'i (a pondfield for taro) found so far. The one-of-a-kind nature of this site, its proximity to an elite residence, and its inherent impracticality on this dry landscape suggest to archaeologists that it might have been symbolically important. Only by exploring the complex relationship between culture and environment does the true significance of past subsistence systems become evident.

CRITICAL **THINKING** QUESTIONS

1. What is the significance of geography for human subsistence patterns? How is the case of Polynesia an example of the significance of geography for subsistence?
2. What is the archaeological significance of subsistence patterns for interpreting social stratification and political culture? How can Hawaiian social stratification and level of political organization be inferred from subsistence patterns?
3. How do archaeologists know that taro was important symbolically in Hawaiian culture of the past?

fields, and reservoirs, and other groups do not. Of course, different groups may use the same space in the same way. For example, many of the transportation corridors now used follow ancient trade routes.

The use of technology is a major factor in adaptation, so the more we know about technology, the more we can learn about how a culture adapts to its environment. Technology has changed over time, and some of those changes have had profound effects on the relationship between culture and environment. The impact of some contemporary technology on the environment (such as bulldozers) is obvious, but there are many instances from the past as well. As Neolithic farmers spread across Europe, for example, they brought with them stone axes. With that technology, they were able to clear vast stretches of forest and turn that land into fields. Stone axes profoundly affected the environment of Europe, changed the primary subsistence system of the people living there, and left a very different place for future generations. Similar deforestation impacts were seen with the introduction of metal axes in North America and with chainsaws in Amazonia.

Controlling the Environment

All groups make some effort to control the environment on which they depend, through social, political, economic, and religious activities or organizations. Groups attempt to exercise both indirect and direct control of their environments with different degrees of success. *Indirect control* involves the use of religion and ritual to influence weather, animal behavior, and other things beyond the direct control of people. For example, the ancient Mesoamericans, Egyptians, and Chinese constructed extensive facilities for ceremonial functions and devoted great energy toward ensuring that the Sun would rise, the rains would come, the crops would grow, animals would reproduce, and the supernatural would remain happy. Understanding the activities conducted in these facilities is one goal of the research now undertaken at those archaeological sites. *Direct control* is the actual, physical management or manipulation of resources or landscapes.

ENVIRONMENTAL MANIPULATION   Large-scale, active alteration and management of landscapes, such as building dams, cutting down forests, or burning large areas, is called *environmental manipulation.* Controlled burning probably was the most widely used method of environmental manipulation in the human past (Lewis 1973, 1982). Fires clear away debris, reduce competition between plants, and encourage new growth, which may attract animals for hunting and reduce weeds in stands of economically important plants. Burning also may be conducted as part of ceremonial activities. In Australia, Aboriginal groups employed a number of renewal ceremonies (Eliade 1973:60–63), such as the use of fire to remove old plant growth and encourage the renewal of life (Lewis 1982:59–62).

Much of the world's plant cover was burned repeatedly by hunter-gatherers and early agriculturalists who actively and constantly modified and managed their landscapes. European farmers coming to North America saw vast areas of "untamed wilderness," but in reality most of those areas had been manipulated and managed by native peoples for over 10,000 years. Even in the dense rain forest of the Yucatán of southern Mexico, the ancient Maya manipulated the distribution of plants and the flow of water.

Some landscapes were actually constructed. The most common example of this type of manipulation is changes associated with agriculture—alterations made to adapt the land to farming. Changes included clearing of vegetation, leveling of land, removal of rocks, reduction of geological features such as rock outcroppings, construction of walls, digging of irrigation and drainage ditches, and the construction of terraced field systems. For example, the Colca Valley of Peru is terraced from river to mountaintop over hundreds of square miles, and some of the terraces are thousands of years old (e.g., Guillet 1987).

Irrigation systems can have thousands of miles of canals, ditches, and other facilities, such as those built by the Hohokam in Arizona (Haury 1976; Bayman 2001). Most prehistoric dams were relatively small, but some flooded large areas, created lakes and swamps, and eliminated portions of rivers and valleys. In addition, water from irrigation systems transformed landscapes from arid regions to lush agricultural areas. Other large-scale and lasting constructions that transform landscapes include cities, with their housing, transportation, water, and waste management systems. Cities then become the dominant factor in the landscape and the focus of social, political, and economic power.

RESOURCE MANAGEMENT   Much active management is of individual resources. This smaller-scale resource management can take a number of forms, from pruning individual plants to make them more productive to managing herds of wild deer. An example of active resource management comes from the western United States, where native people managed juniper trees to produce wood for the manufacture of bows (Wilke 1988). Juniper is a naturally twisty and knotty wood unsuited for bow making, but the people selected a seedling and then groomed and pruned the tree to grow a straight trunk, a process that took decades. When the tree was large enough, the outline of the bow stave was cut into the trunk but not removed until a few years later when it had cured and dried on the tree. The bow tree eventually formed new wood in the scar left by the removal of the stave. People monitored the growth in the scar to ensure that

For Native Americans living in the western United States, managed juniper trees were valuable resources. The wood of these trees was the source of bow staves, and bow trees were monitored, maintained, and reused over hundreds of years. This 12-foot-tall juniper tree was carefully pruned to have a straight trunk. This resource management process continued until the repeated regrowth of the staves caused them to become too short for use as bows. The location of this bow tree in western Nevada remains confidential even today.

no branches grew in the stave area. Then, in a decade or so, a second bow stave could be removed.

Domestication and the Agricultural Revolution

In some cases, the active management of individual resources became intense, leading to the genetic control, or **domestication,** of a species. In the Middle East between about 10,000 and 12,000 years ago, people began to keep wild sheep and goats (feeding them in captivity and moving them to feeding grounds) and to focus their gathering efforts on a few plant species, such as wheat and barley (Bar-Yosef and Meadow 1995). The herding and feeding of animals in captivity led to nonrandom mating, which altered the genetic characteristics of the animals (Highlight 9.4). Similarly, intensive exploitation of certain grains altered the ability of the plants to reproduce.

In wild stands of wheat and barley, the seeds usually fall off the plant during the normal process of seed dispersal. Sometimes, however, the seed heads are tough and the seeds do not drop. The tougher seed heads with the seeds staying on the plant longer would be attractive to human collectors, who would collect a higher proportion of the tougher seeds. If humans then planted some of those tough seeds, the subsequent generation of seeds would be a bit tougher, with even fewer falling off and more remaining on the seed head for people to collect. This process of human selection for tougher seeds continued for many seasons, and eventually the plants reached the point where they all had tough seed heads and were unable to reproduce by themselves because the seeds could not fall to the ground naturally to self-sow. The humans increased the number of seeds they could collect, gained control of when and where the plants could grow, and so "domesticated" the plant. At the same time, such intensive manipulation and management of these species required constant attention, forcing the people to focus on those species and eventually become dependent on them. Thus, agriculture was born.

Until about 10,000 years ago, all humans were hunters and gatherers, living in relatively small social units and using generally simple technologies. Their impact on the environment, while certainly apparent, was relatively minor. At the end of the Pleistocene, however, there was a major climatic change in a number of places—such as central Mexico, coastal Peru, the Indus Valley, the Mississippi Valley, the Nile Valley, and the Yangtze Valley—that began a process that led to the formal domestication of plants and animals and the development of agriculture. As plants and animals were domesticated, the cultures involved began a radical transformation of lifeways called the **agricultural revolution.** How and why this happened are fundamental research questions in archaeology.

Hunter-gatherers and farmers utilize their environments in fundamentally different ways. Hunter-gatherers exploit a diversity of resources over relatively large areas in an extensive exploitation of the environment. Farmers utilize the environment intensively, even creating artificial landscapes for themselves and their domesticated species (Price and Gebauer 1995b:3–4). Farmers use fewer species, but use them much more intensively.

HIGHLIGHT **9.4**

Detecting Animal Domestication

People began domesticating animals in the Late Pleistocene, and it seems likely that the first domesticated animal was the dog. The ancestor to the dog was the small southwest Asian wolf, which was something of a scavenger and, presumably, was familiar around human settlements. Families probably kept young ones as pets. The most docile animals eventually began to breed in captivity, and "man's best friend" emerged. These animals began to appear in the archaeological record, as did evidence of their bone-gnawing activities. They were smaller than their wolf ancestors, were present in site deposits, and were sometimes even buried with their human hosts. Later, humans began to domesticate other animals, ones used primarily for food (meat and milk) or materials (hides or hair). Detecting the process of animal domestication in the archaeological record—knowing which species were domesticated, where, when, and for what purpose—provides information on cultural development, changing economic systems, technology, and even social systems.

To detect domestication, archaeologists look for various patterns in the skeletal remains of the animals (Davis 1987:133–152; Crabtree 1990:162–166). First, if people began to concentrate their efforts on a few animals, one would expect the record to reflect a reduction in the number of species exploited and an intensification of those still used—that is, one should find many bones of a few species and few bones of others. Second, individuals tend to get smaller when first domesticated. Thus, the archaeological record should show a progressive reduction in the size of individual animals early in the process of domestication. Later, the animals should get larger as people undertake selective breeding to increase their size.

Third, the natural defenses of the animals would be bred out. For example, wild sheep are smart, fast, and tough, have large horns, and defend themselves well, whereas domesticated sheep are relatively helpless. In the archaeological record, one should see a reduction in horn size, and the bones of domesticated animals should reflect less stress (less activity and less strenuous activity) than the bones of wild ones.

Fourth, the sex and age profiles in domesticated populations should be quite different from those in wild populations (see diagram). In domesticated populations, only a few males are needed to breed with the females, and many of the young males are killed for their meat and hides, and females are retained for breeding and milking purposes. Therefore, the age and sex profiles in the skeletal materials from a site should show many young males, a few old males, a few young females, and many old females.

Fifth, archaeologists would expect that other aspects of the archaeological record would reflect intensive animal exploitation. Such aspects include animal husbandry

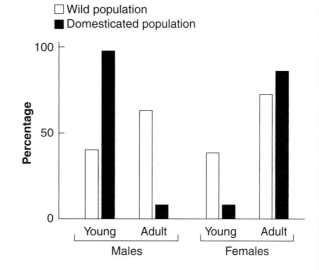

HIGHLIGHT **9.4** *continued*

technologies, such as dairy-related tools, and facilities such as pens, pastures, and processing sites associated with domesticated animals. Also, a settlement pattern, social structure, and political system adapted to herding animals would be evident in other archaeological evidence. For example, most pastoral groups would have had a settlement pattern of relatively permanent villages and a complex series of temporary stock camps. They probably would have been organized in patrilineal households and have had a tribal political organization.

CRITICAL **THINKING** QUESTIONS

1. What prerequisites are needed before animals can be domesticated? Would you expect that hunters were the first humans to domesticate animals? Why or why not?
2. What kinds of archaeological field and laboratory methods would be required to find animal bones and analyze them to detect domestication?

Farmers also increase the scale of intervention in their environment and the ritual management of resources.

There are a number of possible explanations for the development of agriculture (Rindos 1984; Harris and Hillman 1989; Price and Gebauer 1995a). People had been dependent on wild plants and animals for millions of years. Why did some people abandon a relatively stable and productive hunting and gathering way of life to take up a new subsistence system? To what extent was the process unintentional or even accidental? How and under what conditions all this happened is still unclear, but there are a number of models. Inasmuch as domestication occurred in at least several different places at the same general time, there may be a variety and combination of causal factors, including environmental change, population expansion, and organizational changes (Table 9.1).

Based on his work in the Middle East, V. Gordon Childe (1936, 1942) proposed the **oasis theory.** Childe suggested that as the environment became drier, people, plants, and particularly animals were forced into close association in areas of remaining permanent water, or "oases." He argued that this geographic association led to a close symbiotic relationship between people and certain species and eventually led to the domestication of some of those species. Later, Robert Braidwood (1960) proposed the **hilly flanks theory.** Braidwood argued that the earliest evidence of agriculture in the Middle East was along the hilly flanks bordering the Tigris-Euphrates River Valley. He saw no evidence in his excavations of the kind of severe climate change proposed by Childe, and he maintained that the wild grasses that would become wheat and barley thrived in the prime grass habitat on the hillsides that surrounded the valley. Braidwood suggested that people's living in the midst of dense stands of grasses eventually resulted in the development of harvesting technology, which in turn led to the domestication of those species and the spread of the practice to other regions.

Other archaeologists (Binford 1968; Flannery 1969) argued that domestication probably first occurred in marginal environments where resources were less abundant. According to this theory, people living in such places had to pay especially close attention to the species on which they depended and had to manage them carefully. The eventual result was domestication. Also, it was suggested (Cohen 1977) that the mass extinction

table 9.1

Some Theories of Agricultural Origins

THEORY	MAJOR ELEMENTS	REFERENCES
Oasis	At the end of the Pleistocene, the environment changed, forcing people into close association with certain plants and animals, leading to domestication. Farming led to population expansion and to increased dependence on some species.	Childe 1936, 1942
Hilly flanks	People began to exploit the native grasses, such as wheat and barley, that thrived along the hilly flanks of the Tigris-Euphrates River Valley, eventually domesticating them.	Braidwood 1960
Marginal environment	People in marginal environments would have been forced to better manage their plants and animals. The eventual result would have been domestication.	Binford 1968; Flannery 1969
Food crisis and population expansion	The loss of many species at the end of the Pleistocene created a food crisis, forcing people to depend more heavily on remaining species. Population growth forced even more reliance, leading to domestication.	Cohen 1977
Scheduling changes	Changes in scheduling in the exploitation of wild resources created an overreliance on some resources, eventually leading to domestication.	Flannery 1972

of large animals at the end of the Pleistocene caused a "food crisis" that led to a diversification of economic activities, including agriculture. In an argument related to the **food crisis theory,** Mark Cohen (1977) said that by the end of the Pleistocene, human groups occupied all of the terrestrial habitats, and population growth had reached a critical point that "required" a larger and more stable food supply. Cohen argued that agriculture offered the only way to support the growing populations (also see Richerson et al. 2001). Now, however, many archaeologists believe that population growth and pressure may have been an effect, rather than a cause, of the development of agriculture (Price and Gebauer 1995a:7).

Another theory about why domestication occurred is that simple changes in the schedule of collecting wild resources could have sent a group of humans down the road to overdependence on a specific resource and ultimately to the domestication of that species (Flannery 1972). It may also be that agriculture arose in ecologically complex areas in the central parts of large regions where trade was active (MacNeish 1992). Under those conditions, agriculture may have developed out of the need to produce increasing quantities of products for trade or exchange. Ultimately, it probably will be shown that agriculture developed in different areas through different mechanisms.

Understanding how people adapted to their environment is fundamental to most of the other questions that archaeologists ask. Technology, social and political organizations, settlement patterns, and other aspects of culture are intertwined with environment. After about 10,000 years ago, people began taking a more active role in shaping, modifying, and even creating their own environments, and this process is still ongoing.

CONTENTSELECT

Search articles in the ContentSelect database using the key words *paleoclimatology, geoarchaeology,* and *paleoecology*. On what research questions do these articles focus? Why are those questions important to answer for understanding the human past?

Chapter Summary

Ecology is the study of the relationships between organisms and their environment. Adaptation to the environment is necessary for all organisms, including humans, who have to adapt over time both as biological entities and as cultural groups. Archaeological understandings of human ecology are central to an understanding of the humans of the past, present, and future.

The environment consists of abiotic and biotic elements interacting within a system. Humans and their cultures are part of that system. Environments can be divided into large-scale segments, biomes or ecozones, in which ecosystems operate. Ecosystems contain niches and habitats occupied by various organisms. Humans fill a very broad niche and occupy most terrestrial habitats. The human carrying capacity of a habitat depends on the subsistence system and technology of the group occupying it. An understanding of paleoenvironment through environmental archaeology is critical to understanding past human adaptations.

Archaeologists reconstruct the paleoecology of regions to learn how people interacted with, adapted to, and modified their environments and how those environments changed over time. Reconstructions of landforms, plants and animals, and climate are combined to create models of past environments. These models are incorporated into models of human adaptations to learn about the past.

Humans adapt both biologically and culturally to their environment. Through evolutionary ecology and the use of optimization models, archaeologists can study the processes by which cultures adopt different diets based on environment.

Culture, however, is the primary mechanism by which humans adapt. Each culture possesses particular organizations and technologies that it uses to develop a successful adaptation. Cultures employ a variety of techniques, such as trade and storage, to deal with resource needs and also construct landscapes to fit their needs. Cultures also employ large-scale methods to manipulate their environment and smaller-scale methods to manage individual resources. Intensive management of certain resources can lead to domestication.

Domestication took place in a number of places around the world within the last 10,000 years. Farming was a radical departure from the way people had previously used the environment. Several theories have attempted to explain the change to agriculture, but no one theory seems sufficient to explain all of the occurrences. Various interrelated factors gave rise to domestication and to the development of agriculture, and much work is needed to understand them.

Key Concepts

agricultural revolution, 244	ecotone, 226	hilly flanks theory, 246
carrying capacity, 226	ecozone, 226	oasis theory, 246
cultural ecology, 238	environment, 226	optimization model, 235
diet, 235	food crisis theory, 247	paleoclimate, 231
domestication, 244	geoarchaeology, 227	paleoecology, 227
ecosystem, 226	geomorphology, 227	paleoenvironment, 226

Suggested Readings

If you want to learn more about the concepts and issues discussed in this chapter, consider looking at the following resources. (Some may be rather technical.)

Dincauze, Dena F. (2000). *Environmental Archaeology: Principles and Practice.* Cambridge: Cambridge University Press.

As one of the foremost experts on the subject, Dincauze covers the basic principles of the kinds of information used by archaeologists to reconstruct past environments. She also discusses the various ways in which archaeological data are used to discover past environments and how that knowledge is used to generate understanding of past human adaptations.

Redman, Charles L. (1999). *Human Impact on Ancient Environments.* Tucson: University of Arizona Press.

Humans constantly impact their environment, and Redman reviews the various ways in which humans have affected past environments, from hunting and gathering to agriculture. Redman mostly deals with North America, but his discussion is valid worldwide.

Sutton, Mark Q., and E. N. Anderson. (2004). *Introduction to Cultural Ecology.* Walnut Creek, CA: AltaMira Press.

This book provides a basic introduction to the concepts of cultural ecology, defines the terminology, and provides numerous examples of different adaptations. It is not a book about archaeology per se, but the same concepts are used by archaeologists.

chapter 10

Understanding Past Settlement and Subsistence

WHEN PEOPLE FIRST migrated to Tasmania some 35,000 years ago, they carried with them technology and a knowledge base adapted to exploit the resources in southeastern Australia during the Late Pleistocene. When Tasmania was isolated from Australia by rising sea levels at the end of the Pleistocene, the people there became isolated (until contacted by Europeans some 10,000 years later) and focused on the exploitation of marine resources, such as fish, shellfish, and sea mammals. The abrupt disappearance of fish bones from the archaeological record in Tasmania about 3,500 years ago indicates that the people suddenly stopped fishing (White and O'Connell 1982; Jones 1995). Bone tools disappeared from the archaeological record at about the same time. In addition, the ethnographic record showed that the historic Tasmanians did not eat fish. What happened?

Why would people stop using fish? There does not seem to be any ecological reason, such as climate change. Could it be that the long isolation of the Tasmanians had resulted in some sort of cultural "decline" (Jones 1978)? According to this model, Tasmanian society, technology, and even intellect evolved into a simpler, less sophisticated form. But perhaps fishing was never all that important to the Tasmanians. At the time fishing stopped, a systematic change in shellfish exploitation also occurred (Bowdler 1982). Species of shellfish living in shallow water were dropped from the diet, and species (including crayfish) living in deeper water where diving was necessary to obtain them were added. Thus, the dropping of fish from the diet was part of a larger subsistence change. Still, why did this happen?

Was it more efficient (optimal) to take certain shellfish rather than fish? Was there a shift toward foods, such as seals, that contained more fat than fish? And what about ethnographic analogy? Ethnographic data in-

dicated that Tasmanian women were tasked with providing food from the ocean and men were tasked with providing food from the land. If this division of labor was established by 3,500 years ago, it could account for the loss of fish from the diet because women specialized in diving for shellfish and crayfish.

It is clear that the Tasmanians dropped fishing about 3,500 years ago, but it is most likely an adaptive change rather than some sort of "decline" in Tasmanian culture. As you read in Chapter 9, subsistence systems are complex and continually changing in response to conditions and needs. The study of subsistence patterns can provide much information about past cultures.

For the location of Tasmania and other sites mentioned in this chapter, see the map on page 252.

How Did People Make a Living? Subsistence

Subsistence—making a living—is a more complex undertaking than one might think. Most subsistence activities revolve around food: getting, processing, storing, distributing, cooking, and eating food. The purpose of other subsistence activities is to obtain the other

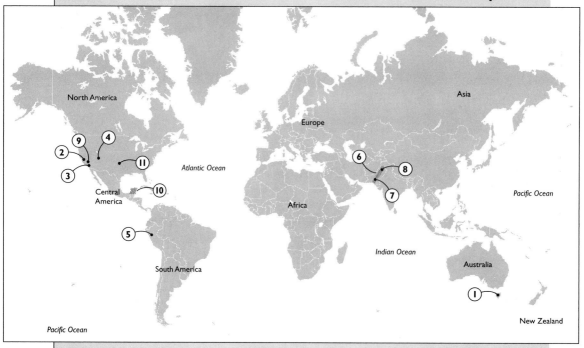

LOCATION MAP: **Sites Mentioned in Chapter 10**

1 ■ Tasmania

2 ■ Emeryville Shellmound
   San Francisco, California

3 ■ Lake Cahuilla sites
   Indio, California

4 ■ Cowboy Wash
   Southwestern Colorado

5 ■ Virú Valley
   Northern Peru

6 ■ Indus Valley
   Pakistan

7 ■ Mohenjo-daro
   Sind province, Pakistan

8 ■ Harappa
   Sind province, Pakistan

9 ■ Guapiabit site (CA-SBR-1913)
   San Bernardino, California

10 ■ Yucatán Peninsula
   Mexico

11 ■ Uncas site
   Kaw Lake, Oklahoma

necessities of life, including shelter, fuel, and basic raw materials. For members of a group to obtain and process the resources they need, they must have particular technologies, live in or move to areas where the resources can be found, and be organized to get food effectively. In addition, people need to share beliefs and values about their interactions among themselves and their interactions with the resources they seek. Thus, subsistence and subsistence activities form an intricate system embedded in all aspects of culture.

Archaeologists investigating past subsistence want to identify and analyze three basic elements of subsistence: diet, technology, and organization. As you read in Chapter 9, the study of diet includes reconstructing patterns of which foods people ate and their overall role in the diet, how and when people obtained and processed food, and how those patterns changed over time. Diet also includes the study of *cuisine,* how foods are prepared, in which combinations (meals), and short-term (daily or seasonal) patterns of consumption. Also, people have food preferences, taboos, tolerances, and requirements that affect their diet. Because the evidence of food (e.g., bones and seeds) is common in sites, archaeologists focus a great deal of attention on diet.

The technology recovered from sites reveals much about subsistence, as you have seen. Organization, the third element of subsistence, is a cultural characteristic. Political organization reflects the necessities of controlling and managing resources such as agricultural lands, water supplies, and herd animals. Social institutions such as family and kinship are organized to facilitate food sharing and other economic functions. Settlement patterns reflect political, economic, and social organization in diverse ways. For example, a farming settlement might reveal social stratification: families with more wealth and power have fields in better locations, privileged access to irrigation water, and larger households containing more goods. Settlements in which fields have been repeatedly subdivided over time suggest kinship systems calling for the equal inheritance of land by children in each generation.

In subsistence analysis of historical materials, dietary remains include fewer species of domesticates, and text-based information may exist to aid in interpretation. For example, documentary evidence might explain the use, care, and cost of subsistence items and related technology. Records may exist to show where and to whom higher-priced and lower-priced goods were sent. Such records aid in the interpretation of differential access to subsistence goods on the basis of gender and social status.

The Four Primary Subsistence Systems

The four primary subsistence systems are hunting and gathering, horticulture, pastoralism, and intensive agriculture. **Hunters and gatherers,** or **foragers** (Kelly 1995:xiv), make their living predominantly from wild foods. In most hunter-gatherer groups, plant foods are the mainstay of the diet; animals compose a smaller, though no less important, part. Until plants and animals were domesticated beginning about 10,000 years ago, all people subsisted as hunter-gatherers. A popular misconception is that hunter-gatherers were "nomadic," wandering around aimlessly in an endless search for food. Aimless wandering, however, is not a normal subsistence activity. Even highly mobile hunter-gatherer groups such as the Inuit in the Arctic do not simply wander around: they know where to find resources, and they move around to utilize them on a regular basis.

Prehistoric hunter-gatherers had a diverse range of structures, forms, and adaptations (e.g., Price and Brown 1985; Thomas 1986; Bettinger 1987, 1991; Burch and Ellanna 1994; Kelly 1995). Many groups had small populations of only a few hundred members; others were much larger. Thousands of individuals lived in single settlements in some parts of Europe between 7,000 and 12,000 years ago. Social and political systems varied in complexity and expression, and in many cases, religion, literature, art, and music were quite sophisticated.

Horticulture is a low-intensity system of food production using domesticated plants, such as yams, grown in small fields or gardens. Horticulturalists also raise small numbers of domesticated animals, such as pigs. Most members of a horticultural group tend plants using hand labor (rather than draft animals). Horticultural societies rely on wild resources as well. Hunter-gatherers sometimes practice small-scale horticulture on a part-time basis as a secondary mode of subsistence. Archaeologically, habitation sites of horticulturalists are relatively small, occupied year-round, and contain evidence of farming tools and the use of domesticated and wild species.

Pastoralism is a subsistence system based on the herding, breeding, consumption, and total exploitation of domesticated animals in captivity. Pastoralists usually specialize in two or three species—such as cattle, horses, sheep, goats, pigs, camels, or reindeer—that can be semiwild and free-ranging. Many pastoralists also engage in limited horticulture and exploit a few wild resources. Pastoralists may be sedentary, or they may move with their animals to different grazing locations and water sources during the year. The latter pattern is called *pastoral nomadism.* Archaeologically, pastoralist habitation sites tend to be small, scattered, and occupied seasonally. They contain evidence of domesticated animal use but little evidence of domesticated plants or wild species.

Intensive agriculture is the large-scale production of domesticated plants, often with animal labor, equipment such as plows, and irrigation or other water diversion techniques. Intensive agriculturalists may keep herds of animals and have gardens and may utilize a few wild resources. Intensive agriculture–based populations are larger, occupy urban centers, and have more differentiated political and social systems. Archaeologically, the primary habitation sites of intensive agriculturalists indicate permanent settlement and contain abundant evidence of agricultural activities and resources.

Archaeological Evidence of Subsistence

Data relating to diet; artifacts used in procurement, preparation, and consumption of foods; and aspects of material culture from which subsistence practices may be inferred constitute archaeological evidence of subsistence. Information on subsistence also may be found in depictions of crops or hunted animals, in stories of food getting, and in documents shedding light on the trade of items. Human skeletal material (see Chapter 8) also provides evidence of past diet, such as in tooth wear and in the chemical signatures of certain classes of foods contained in bone. Most archaeological inquiry into subsistence centers on discovering the general diet, primarily from the ecofactual remains of animals and plants used for food. Because most food remains are deposited in an archaeological site as mixed garbage, it is very difficult to identify individual meals or to gain a clear understanding of cuisine.

Most subsistence information is based on *indirect* evidence of what people ate, in the form of assumptions (working hypotheses). For example, most bone from a site is assumed to be cultural in origin, although it is possible for natural bone to enter a site deposit. If corncobs are found at a site, it is assumed that the corn kernels were eaten even if the corn kernels are not actually found. If charred seeds are found around a fire, it is assumed that they were lost during the preparation or consumption of other seeds of the same plant. Stone tools similar to ones known to have been used to grind maize are assumed to have been used that way even if the tools lack maize debris.

Materials that provide *direct* evidence of diet are primarily paleofeces and human remains. Maize kernels found in preserved feces and pollen or phytoliths incorporated into the tartar on teeth are examples of direct evidence of diet.

FAUNAL REMAINS   The primary **faunal remains** are bone and shell, but sometimes hair, hides, scales, chitin, and even proteins and DNA (see Chapter 8) are found. The study of faunal remains is called **zooarchaeology** (*zoo* is Greek for "animal"), and many reviews of faunal studies are available (Crabtree 1990; Reitz and Wing 1999; Redding 2002). People used animals mainly for food but also for tools, clothing, and shelter.

In most sites, the majority of faunal remains is bone. Vertebrates share a common general skeleton that is bilaterally symmetrical (the same on both sides). Many of the bones—called *elements*—of different animals share a basic shape, look similar from species to species, and have the same names. For instance, the femur (upper leg bone) of a mouse closely resembles the femur of a deer but is much smaller.

Some bones are difficult to identify. For example, turtles and tortoises have bony shells that if fragmented can be confused with the skulls of some large mammals. Some bones are relatively thin and fragile and do not preserve well, and many fish skeletons contain a great deal of cartilage, which does not preserve easily. Other materials from vertebrates may be found, such as eggshell fragments from birds and reptiles, otoliths (ear stones), gastrolithis (gizzard stones), and fish scales.

Invertebrates—animals without backbones—are vastly more numerous than vertebrates in nature; 97 percent of known species are invertebrates (Powell and Hogue 1979). The major types of invertebrates include mollusks (Waselkov 1987) and insects (Sutton 1995). Mollusks are soft-bodied animals, often living in shells, such as clams, oysters, snails, slugs, squids, and octopi. Insects are six-legged animals with exoskeletons made of chitin. Lobsters, crabs, shrimp (marine and freshwater), spiders, scorpions, and worms are also invertebrates. All of these animals may be found in archaeological sites and must be considered in any faunal analysis.

When analyzing faunal remains, archaeologists want to be able to answer several basic questions (Lyman 1982; Brewer 1992):

1. What was the diet, and how were animals used as food?
2. Which animals were eaten, in what quantities, and with what other foods (cuisine)?
3. Who (e.g., males, females, young, old) was involved in the procurement of food animals, and was there differential access to certain foods based on age or gender? For example, the Tasmanians (as you read at the beginning of this chapter) employed a

strict sexual division of labor in animal procurement, a recognizable pattern in the archaeological record.

4. What technologies and behaviors were associated with the diet, and how were other aspects of culture influenced?
5. How were animals used for purposes other than subsistence, such as religion, entertainment, or transportation?

Finally, because certain animals live only in specific environmental conditions, faunal data can guide an understanding of past environments. For instance, turtle remains found in a site located along an intermittent stream would indicate that the stream was permanent at the time the site was occupied. Consider, for example, the interpretation of faunal remains from the Emeryville Shellmound, described in Highlight 10.1.

BOTANICAL REMAINS   The remains of plants, from whole logs to pollen, are called **botanical remains.** Several other terms are also used, including *archaeobotanical, paleobotanical, phytoarchaeological,* and *floral remains* (although *floral* technically refers only to flowers). Like faunal remains, most botanical remains are ecofacts, although some artifacts, such as baskets, were made from plant materials. Specialists called *paleobotanists* analyze this material (Hastorf and Popper 1988; Pearsall 1989; Fritz 1994; Miller 2002).

Most botanical remains are fragile and are recovered from archaeological sites only if they have been carbonized to some degree. Botanical material that is too carbonized, however, turns to ash. In dry caves and other sites where preservation is very good, uncarbonized plant remains can be common. Such remains probably are recent in origin; otherwise, they would have decomposed. Nevertheless, even recent plant remains can be useful in learning something about a site, such as the extent of disturbance.

The basic goals of botanical analysis are to reconstruct diet and the use of plants as foods, to determine who was eating and processing which plants, to ascertain patterns of access, and to identify the technologies involved in procurement and processing. Archaeologists also want to understand the use of plants for purposes other than food (such as for construction) and to gain an understanding of past environments.

Most plant remains recovered from sites are macrobotanical remains, visible to the naked eye. Specialized methods also allow the routine collection of microremains, such as pollen and phytoliths. The analysis of chemical remains, such as protein or DNA, is still uncommon. Macrobotanical remains are primarily seeds and charcoal—the burned woody parts of plants. Archaeologists assume that most charcoal in a site resulted from human activities such as campfires, cooking fires, and kiln fires.

PALEOFECES   Preserved ancient human fecal matter—**paleofeces**—is sometimes recovered from archaeological sites (Fry 1985; Sobolik 1990; Reinhard and Bryant 1992). Paleofecal specimens contain the residues of food and other materials ingested by the individual and so constitute direct evidence of what was consumed. Materials were ingested for primary food, as condiments (Trigg et al. 1994; Sutton and Reinhard 1995), and as medicine (Sobolik and Gerick 1992; Trigg et al. 1994). Paleofeces also can be used to investigate general health and nutrition, food processing, and food preparation (Callen 1967a, 1967b; Robins et al. 1986; Reinhard and Bryant 1992:270–272; Rylander 1994). In addition, paleofeces

HIGHLIGHT **10.1**

Interpreting Animal Bones from the Emeryville Shellmound

Patterns in faunal remains recovered from stratified middens can reveal changes in ancient human foraging behavior and the causes of that behavior. Archaeologist Jack Broughton analyzed the fauna from the Emeryville Shellmound to investigate these issues (Broughton 1999). Before it was demolished in 1924, the Emeryville site was located on the east shore of San Francisco Bay. The mound itself was huge, measuring about 100-by-300 meters in area and extending to a depth of more than 10 meters. The mound was made up of shells, soil, rocks, animal bones, ash, charcoal, and artifacts—all trash, debris, and tools left by the people who once lived there. Before the mound's destruction, parts of the mound were excavated stratigraphically—layer by layer. Archaeologists found ten major strata. As the strata were peeled back one at a time with shovels and trowels, workers sifted

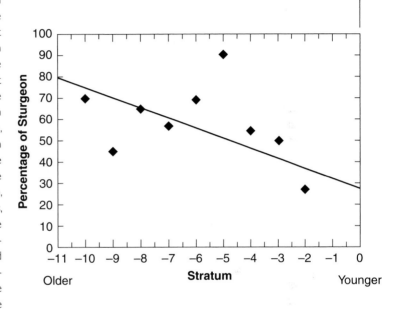

The number of sturgeon bones recovered from the Emeryville Shellmound (upper chart) suggests that as time passed, fewer and fewer fish were taken. An analysis of the size of the fish taken, as measured from the size of their dentary bones (lower chart), suggests that smaller and smaller fish were taken. Together, these data suggest that the inhabitants of the site overfished the sturgeon population, taking fewer and younger fish.

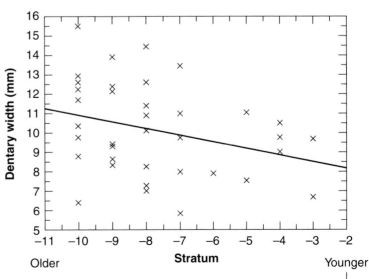

HIGHLIGHT **10.1** *continued*

the loosened soil and debris in screens to retrieve artifacts and animal bones. Subsequent radiocarbon dating indicates that the site was occupied between 700 and 2,600 RCYBP.

Over time, the remains of large animal species at Emeryville became less abundant. The upper graph shows the trend for the decline in the percentage of sturgeon bones in the various strata of the Emeryville midden. The bones of large animals—such as sturgeon, elk, and geese—were prevalent in lower, older strata of the site; their remains are scarce in the upper, more recent strata. Why was this the case?

Studies of local pollen and other evidence from paleoclimatology indicate that the progressive decline in the numbers of sturgeon and other large prey was not caused by changes in climate. Instead, the decline most likely reflects reductions in numbers of large prey species because of human hunting. Because large animals usually provide more calories for the amount of time it takes to catch and prepare them for consumption, people who hunt and fish for a living tend to pursue large prey animals whenever they find them. Therefore, large animals are more susceptible than small animals to population declines caused by human patterns of subsistence.

Other faunal data from the site, especially the age structure of the exploited prey, support this interpretation. Modern studies of fish and game species have shown that increased hunting or fishing places species under such pressure that the average age of animals in those populations declines. The proportion of younger individuals in the population increases as more and more adults are caught and killed. The average age

of trout in lakes that are heavily fished, for instance, is much younger than in lakes that are barely fished at all, and the average size of trout in heavily fished lakes is smaller.

So if the decline through time in the abundance of sturgeon bones at Emeryville was a result of overfishing, we would expect the average age and size of sturgeon also to decrease. And that is exactly what happened, judging by changes in the size of the lower jawbones of the fish, called the "dentary" bones. The width of these bones indicates the size, and by inference the age, of the individuals. The lower graph shows the trend for a decline in the dentary width (size and age) of the sturgeon population, which corresponds with the decline of sturgeon overall from overfishing by prehistoric hunters.

The decline in sturgeon dentary size reflects a decrease in the age of individuals and in the size of the overall population. Thus, midden records such as at Emeryville show that even ancient foragers could have substantial impacts on the animal species they used.

CRITICAL **THINKING** QUESTIONS

1. What model do archaeologists use to study people's choices of prey and patterns of consumption? How does that model work? How does the story of the Emeryville Shellmound reflect that model?
2. What factors might cause hunters, fishers, and foragers to change their choices of prey and the amounts of prey they consume? How are these choices reflected in the archaeological record?

may contain body fluids, chemicals, cellular elements, and bacteria. Paleofeces are rarely recovered from sites, however, because of poor preservation, sampling choices (latrines were located away from living areas), and failure to recognize the specimens when found.

Paleofeces take the form of coprolites, gut contents, or cess (Greig 1984:49; Holden 1994:65–66). *Coprolites* are specimens that are individually distinct and are found either singly or in concentrations that probably represent latrine features. They usually are not associated with particular human remains, so they contain much less information on sex and age, health, other meals, and so on, than is available from the gut contents of specific people. Gut contents are materials preserved and recovered from the intestinal tract of an intact human body, usually a mummy or otherwise preserved body. Gut contents can be associated with specific people of known age, sex, general health, and sometimes even social status, allowing a correlation of these factors with diet (Reinhard and Bryant 1995; Reinhard 1998b). For example, an analysis of the gut contents of Lindow Man, the 1,500-year-old body of an executed man found preserved in a peat bog in England (Hillman 1986; Holden 1986), showed that his last meal consisted of a number of grains, suggesting that he had eaten bread just prior to his death. The lack of evidence of psychotropic drugs, as in some other bog bodies, suggests that Lindow Man was not drugged before his execution. *Cess* is a deposit formed by a mixture of numerous feces, such as would be found in a cesspit or privy, and often includes other debris, such as discarded materials. Dietary remains recovered from cess cannot be used to reconstruct individual diet but are useful in reconstructing the diet of a group.

Paleofecal specimens are soaked in a mild solution of trisodium phosphate (Callen and Cameron 1960), which allows the items within the fecal matrix to gently rehydrate with little damage. The specimens are then broken apart and their contents removed and identified. Faunal remains may be present in paleofeces, including bone, feathers, hair, eggshell fragments, shell fragments, insect fragments, fish and reptile scales, and the bone fragments of some large animals. Macrobotanical remains may be present in paleofeces because some do not get digested completely and others are undigestible. Microbotanical remains, such as pollen and phytoliths, also may be present, sometimes in large quantities. Highlight 10.2 describes the analysis of coprolites at La Quinta, California, in the reconstruction of diet and cuisine.

Other materials found in paleofeces include fungi, bacteria, viruses, and endoparasites, primarily round, flat, and thorny-headed worms (Reinhard 1998a). The analysis of endoparasites in paleofeces can be used to infer a variety of conditions and behaviors, including health, disease, population movement, trade, and changing nutritional and social conditions associated with the transition to agriculture (e.g., Faulkner 1991). For example, the presence of hookworms suggests both a health danger and unsanitary conditions, and the presence of pinworm eggs suggests unhygienic conditions (Reinhard and Bryant 1992:254).

The chemical analysis of paleofeces can identify hormones (Sobolik et al. 1996), lipids (fats), carbohydrates, minerals, and trace elements. Work to recover and identify human DNA from paleofeces has recently been undertaken (Sutton et al. 1996) and has been used to determine the sex of the person. Protein residue analysis can identify materials that are not visible, such as meat (Yohe et al. 1991; Newman et al. 1993). In an interesting application, Marlar et al. (2000) identified direct evidence of prehistoric cannibalism at the Cowboy Wash site in the southwestern United States by chemically detecting the human muscle protein myoglobin within human coprolites. The only way that specific protein could have been present in fecal material is if the human flesh had been eaten. The practice of cannibalism in the Southwest had long been suspected (White 1992; Turner and Turner 1999), but the paleofecal analysis conducted by Marlar et al. (2000) was the first to confirm the actual consumption of human flesh.

HIGHLIGHT **10.2**

Diet and Cuisine at Lake Cahuilla

Archaeologists investigating subsistence employ a number of lines of evidence, including the kinds and amounts of plants and animals eaten, indications of seasonal use, and the technology employed in the food quest. However, many of the data come in the form of lists of resources, without information on which resources were used in combination with which other resources. Thus, archaeologists often have an idea of the components of the diet but little knowledge of the cuisine. A delineation of cuisine would add a great deal of information to our understanding of subsistence. Such a study was conducted in southern California.

In the mid-1970s, archaeologist Philip J. Wilke of the University of California at Riverside investigated the Myoma Dunes and Wadi Beadmaker sites located along the northern shoreline of ancient Lake Cahuilla. He was looking for information on human diet and adaptation to the lake (Wilke 1978). These sites dated to the last stand of the lake, about 500 years ago. Wilke recovered numerous ecofacts from the site deposits and from paleofeces. The data revealed a general diet that consisted of two major fish species—bonytail chub (*Gila elegans*) and razorback sucker (*Xyrauchen texanus*)—rabbits, a few reptiles, and marsh plants.

In 1985, excavations were undertaken at the nearby La Quinta site (CA-RIV-1179) by Wilke and Mark Q. Sutton (Sutton and Wilke 1988). The site consisted of a fairly large open camp dating from the same time and contained numerous artifacts, ecofacts, cremations, and paleofeces. Again, the ecofactual data revealed a diet similar to diets found 10 years earlier by Wilke, but other resources were also identified.

In 1993, additional analysis of the coprolite data from the La Quinta site was undertaken by Sutton (1993). The objective of that study was to search for patterns of resource utilization by conducting a statistical hierarchical cluster analysis of the various coprolite constituents (the contents of each specimen were identified, quantified, and compared to one another to establish patterns). Although the La Quinta paleofecal data might appear to be relatively homogeneous (e.g., "fish in every sample, cattail in most"), it was thought that cluster analysis might reveal patterns of food combinations delineating dietary preferences, habits (e.g., meals), and differences in the seasonal use of resources. The faunal and botanical materials recovered from the general midden were then compared to the coprolite data in an attempt to detect additional patterns between the two data sets.

The analysis of 30 paleofecal specimens from the site revealed several patterns. The diet was not uniform but varied, likely on a seasonal basis. The importance of fish and other aquatic resources appears to have changed seasonally, in spite of the presumed constant availability of fish. Several specific combinations of resources were found, perhaps constituting the remains of meals (see table). Cattail appears to have been consumed largely alone. Terrestrial animals were apparently not consumed in meals with cattail, although some fish was included. In addition, bulrush often was identified in specimens containing bonytail. Bonytail seems to have been the preferred fish, although razorback occasionally was obtained. The two fish species were not identified together, and that finding suggests a differential use or preparation of these fish.

Three other observations were made from the analysis. First, fish, generally viewed as an everyday staple (e.g., Wilke 1978; Farrell 1988), appear to have

Paleofecal Constituent Clusters from the La Quinta Site (CA-RIV-1179)

CLUSTER	*n*	PRIMARY CONSTITUENTS	CULINARY INFERENCE	SEASONALITY INFERENCE
1	13	Abundant cattail, few fish	Meals of cattail	Spring, summer
2	7	Abundant unidentified fish, some mammals and reptiles, few plants	Mixed meals; fish unidentified due to processing; other resources included in meals	Late winter/ Early spring?
3	8	Abundant bonytail and unidentified fish (mostly charred)	Meals of bonytail	Summer?
4	2	Abundant razorback and unidentified fish (cattail is abundant in one specimen)	Meals of razorback	Summer?

Source: Sutton 1993, 1998: Table 2.

not been a staple at certain times—specifically during the portion of the year when cattail was consumed. Terrestrial animals may have been more important at lakeside sites than previously thought. Second, it seems that cattail was very heavily exploited when available, perhaps to the exclusion of other resources for that short time. Third, the midden at La Quinta contained abundant razorback bone, sometimes found articulated, suggesting that those fish had been subjected to some processing technique, such as filleting.

The analysis of the various lines of midden- and paleofecal-derived ecofactual evidence revealed a much more detailed picture of the diet and cuisine of the people who inhabited the shoreline of Lake Cahuilla some 500 years ago. This sort of analysis will allow archaeologists to construct and test more sophisticated models of subsistence than were possible before.

CRITICAL **THINKING** QUESTIONS

1. How might the methods applied to the analysis of paleofecal constituents be used in the analysis of other archaeological materials?
2. What other kinds of archaeological data could be used to test the competing models of settlement and subsistence around Lake Cahuilla?

HUMAN REMAINS As you read in Chapter 8, human remains contain a great deal of information about past diet and nutrition, visible in some pathologies (Larsen 1997, 2000; Aufderheide and Rodríguez-Martín 1998) and in bone chemistry. Living conditions, cultural interactions, population movements, and change in nutrition and health over time can all be inferred from skeletal remains (see Huss-Ashmore et al. 1982; Larsen 1987, 1997; Mays 1998; Larsen 2000), as well as from changes in subsistence systems—from general hunting and gathering to specialized hunting and gathering (Lambert 1993) and from hunting and gathering to agriculture (Cohen and Armelagos 1984).

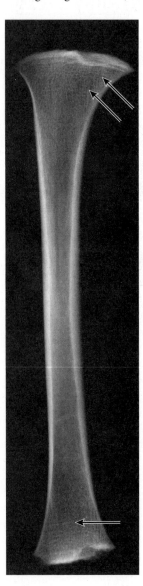

Bones preserve a record of nutritional stress. The two most common pathological indicators of nutritional stress are evidence of anemia (porotic hyperostosis) and Harris lines. *Anemia* is a blood deficiency that stimulates the production of red blood cells, resulting in an expansion of marrow and a thinning of the outer layer of the bone, exposing the spongy interior. Lesions may be visible in thin bone, including the eye orbits and cranium. It is commonly assumed that iron deficiency anemia was the result of dietary deficiencies (Kent 1992:3), although females are more susceptible than males to the condition (Stuart-Macadam 1998).

Harris lines form during times of nutritional stress when the normal

This radiograph of a human tibia (lower leg bone) of a child from the Cross Mountain site (CA-KER-4619) in the southern Sierra Nevada of California shows periods of nutritional stress in the individual's childhood. This stress might have been caused by periodic prolonged famine or chronic malnutrition. The evidence is in the Harris lines—the thin striations visible at the ends of the bone indicating restricted bone growth (*arrows*). In the archaeological record, nutritional stress is also evident in the growth characteristics of teeth.

bone growth of young individuals is interrupted. They indicate the formation of layers of alternately thinner and denser mineralization in the growth areas of the bone (Larsen 1997:40–43) and may be visible either by radiograph or in cross section. Harris lines appear most frequently in leg and arm bones. As a person ages, Harris lines fade. Harris line data can be used to study the nutritional status of populations over time.

Teeth also record nutritional stress during their growth (Hillson 1986, 1996; Larsen 1997). In times of nutritional stress, tooth enamel stops growing. If the nutritional event is short-lived, very small bands of thin enamel—**Wilson bands**—form. If the event is longer, larger bands form. The record in teeth is permanent, so the "biological adequacy of childhood diets [by age and sex] can thus be inferred from the dentition of adults" (Rose et al. 1985:282). In addition, the microstructure of bone can provide a partial record of past nutritional events (Martin and Armelagos 1986) and vitamin-related nutritional deficiencies, such as the bent and distorted (e.g., bowed) limb bones that result from vitamin D deficiency (rickets) (Huss-Ashmore et al. 1982; Stuart-Macadam 1989).

Bone also can be analyzed for both stable isotopes (as discussed in Chapter 8) and trace elements (Katzenberg and Harrison 1997), which can provide insight into past subsistence. Isotopes such as carbon, nitrogen, and strontium are taken up by plants, and when animals consume the plants, the isotopes are incorporated into their tissues, enriching the existing ratios. Thus, all animal (including human) tissue contains an isotopic signature that reflects, at least in part, the food consumed. Measuring the isotopes in tissue allows archaeologists to deduce a number of attributes of the diet. For example, the carbon/nitrogen signature of people who consume terrestrial mammals is very different from the signature of people who eat marine mammals (see Figure 8.3 in Chapter 8). Trace-element data have been used to investigate similarity of diet by sex, social status, contributions of marine resources to the diet, migration and mobility, identification of group affinity, residence patterns, whether women might be pregnant or lactating, and weaning patterns.

Subsistence Technology and Organization

Nearly all subsistence practices require the use of some technology—hunting implements, basketry for gathering, hoes for weeding, and the construction of storage facilities, for example. Thus, an understanding of the various technologies used by the group under study informs archaeologists about how group members made their living. For example, mortar and pestle technology appears in the archaeological record of coastal California beginning about 5,000 years ago. In historic times, acorns (from oak trees) formed a major staple for many native California groups, and acorns were processed with mortars and pestles. The appearance of acorn-processing technology in the archaeological record at 5,000 BP suggests that acorns became an important resource at that time. The adoption of acorns as a food staple seems to have stimulated a significant growth in population and an increase in the social and political complexity of California groups.

Every culture is organized so its subsistence system can be successful. Political structure reflects the necessities of controlling and managing resources. For example, the development of unified states may be tied to the increasing need to control agricultural resources such as water. Social structures also are organized to facilitate necessary economic functions. For example, kinship systems identify relationships in which reciprocity and cooperation are expected in food getting and food sharing. Subsistence organization is reinforced through cultural practices such as food taboos, which may be reflected in the archaeological record.

Recovery and Identification of Ecofactual Evidence

The methods used in the recovery of plant and animal remains from sites are probably the most important issue in any analysis. Until about 1960, archaeologists did not systematically collect ecofactual materials from sites, and these remains were recovered only incidentally. Today, ecofacts are commonly saved when found during routine excavation, and specialized soil samples are frequently taken to recover ecofacts, particularly small botanical remains. For example, soil samples might be taken from around fire hearths and examined to recover seeds for dietary information and charcoal for dating. When analyzing ecofactual data, it is important to know what recovery methods were used, to determine whether the data were reliable.

The preservation of ecofacts is always an issue. Most bone is tough and preserves well, but in some cases the chemistry of the soil causes bone to dissolve and it cannot be recovered. Botanical remains often decompose and are not recovered. Even charred or otherwise preserved remains are often lost. To ensure recovery, samples of soil may be taken and processed by *flotation,* a technique that has revolutionized botanical studies. The archaeologist places the soil sample in water (Bodner and Rowlett 1980) and gently agitates the water. Lightweight botanical remains "float" to the surface and are poured off into fine screens; heavy materials, such as bone and rock, settle to the bottom of the container.

Once recovered, ecofacts have to be identified with as specific a taxon (e.g., genus and species) as possible (see Chapter 6). This multistep process involves sorting materials into general categories of remains and then identifying each specimen's genus and, if possible, species. Some charcoal can be identified by a specialist examining the microscopic structure of its cells. Animal bone is first sorted by the size of the animal (small, medium, and large), then by element (e.g., skull, humerus), and then by taxon. Identification is done by experienced people with the aid of comparative collections of known plants and animals.

Once identified, material is examined to determine whether it originated from human (cultural) or natural (noncultural) sources. Materials directly associated with features (hearths or storage pits) are considered cultural; those associated with animal nests are considered natural. Most burned bone and botanical remains are considered cultural in origin. Bone with butchering marks is considered cultural, as are the remains of species found outside of geographic context, such as fish bones at a site on top of a mountain.

Once material is identified, it is important to learn which parts of the plants or animals are represented. For example, if all the head elements of the fish at a site were in one location and the body elements were in another location, a pattern of fish-processing activities within the site could be deduced. Artifacts connected with those activities could also be identified by their associations with the concentration of fish elements. Knowing which elements are *not* present at the site can also be useful. Large animals may have been killed and butchered at a distant hunting camp and only certain parts brought back to the site. In such a case, only the limb bones of the animals may be found in a village because the rest of the skeleton was left at a hunting camp. Butchering often results in cut marks or fractures to the bone or shell (Lyman 1987, 1994; Fisher 1995). Bones may be smashed, ground, or broken open to obtain marrow. If marrow extraction was the goal, one or two blows with a hammerstone may have been sufficient to break open a bone, resulting in large bone fragments. If boiled for marrow or grease, the bone may have been systematically crushed, resulting in highly fragmented remains. Some small animals, such as rodents, may have been processed whole, smashed, then ground bone and all, resulting in the further fragmentation of the already small bones.

Many animals were cooked prior to consumption, a process that may have involved roasting over a fire, baking in an oven, or boiling. However, this does not necessarily mean that the bone was exposed to fire or heat, for flesh may have been removed from the bone before cooking, and the unburned bone may have been discarded or cooked separately for the marrow. Bone exposed to fire or heat often is modified in color or distorted in shape. Patterns of burning may be seen on bones, and such patterns can reveal prehistoric cooking practices. For example, if rabbit legs are roasted over a fire, much of the bone is protected by muscle tissue, but the ends, with little flesh covering them, are exposed and burned. The resulting bone would show burning only on the ends, and the archaeologist would know how the rabbit was butchered and cooked.

Quantifying Ecofactual Remains

Once identified and classified, ecofacts are quantified—counted to measure abundance and to gain an understanding of what plants and animals people were using. Quantification depends on good field techniques for recovering remains so that the numbers will reflect what the people of the past actually used.

Botanical remains can be measured in two basic ways: qualitative and quantitative (Pearsall 1989). Compiling a descriptive list of the plants identified as present or absent at a site is a qualitative method. Quantitative methods include (1) absolute counts and weights; (2) rankings based on absolute counts; (3) various ratios; (4) estimates of species diversity from counts and weights; and (5) *ubiquity,* a measure of how frequently materials are found in samples. Statistical techniques can be used to compare the results of these methods. For example, a basic qualitative list of botanical materials might show the presence or absence of types of seeds; a more complex tabulation would also show the distribution of seeds in the various samples, revealing how ubiquitous the specimens were—whether present in every sample or concentrated in a few.

For faunal remains, the two most commonly used measures of quantification are *number of identified specimens (NISP),* how many specimens of a particular taxon are present within an analytical unit, and *minimum number of individuals (MNI),* how many identified individuals of a particular taxon are present. Each measure has its strengths and weaknesses (Marshall and Pilgram 1993), but both may be quite informative when computerized and used together (Cruz-Uribe and Klein 1986). Quantification methods used in analyses of mollusk remains are slightly different from those used for vertebrates: weight is often the primary measure (Waselkov 1987:158). NISP also is sometimes used in the analysis of botanical remains.

NISP numbers tend to overestimate the actual abundance of a species. For example, if a single complete rabbit humerus was recovered from an analytical unit, the NISP would be 1. However, if that same bone had somehow been broken in two prior to analysis, both parts would be identified as rabbit and the NISP would be 2. Thus, due to an accident (known as the *fragmentation effect*), the NISP would double—as would the estimation of the importance of rabbit—creating a problem in interpretation.

The minimum number of individuals (MNI) is determined by counting the most abundant element. Because of bilateral symmetry in most vertebrates, either the right or the left elements of a species must be used. For example, if you find that the left mandible is the most abundant element for bison, and there are four left mandibles in the unit, the MNI for bison must be 4. You cannot get four left jaws from only two or three bison. Although there may be more than four bison in the unit, the *minimum* number is determined. If there are four mandibles but five left femora, the MNI is 5—the minimum number of animals needed to account for the five left femora. If you have five femora but do not know whether they are left or right, the MNI would be 3: because each animal has two femurs, the elements must represent at least three bison.

Although MNI does provide some idea of how many animals are represented in an analytical unit, there is the possibility of overlap with other units and thus an overestimation of MNI. Suppose an excavation unit was dug in 10-centimeter levels (the level is the analytical unit), and three left rabbit femora are found in the first level and three right rabbit humeri are found in the second level. The rabbit MNI is 3 for the first level and 3 for the second level—a total of 6. However, because the element used to calculate the MNI was different from level to level, there is a chance that the humeri and femora are from the same individuals and that the "actual" MNI is 3. This example indicates one reason why many people use NISP rather than MNI. However, for unmixed deposits within a site, or for single-event sites, MNI can be very useful.

DETERMINATION OF AGE, SEX, AND SEASONALITY   Archaeologists also want to determine the age, sex, and seasonality of the ecofacts from a site. For plants, age and sex are rarely issues (although the age of a log might be important in dendrochronological studies). Seasonality often is an issue. Many plants produce seeds only during certain seasons, and the presence of such materials at a site could be used to deduce season of plant collection or site occupation.

Determination of the age, season of capture, and sex of the animals identified at a site can be important to studies of prey selection, seasonality, dietary stress, and domestication. The age of the animal at death can provide information about hunting patterns and the demographics of the prey species. In some cases, age at death can imply certain technologies, such as the use of nets to capture small, young fish. As you read in

Chapter 8, archaeologists use several indicators to determine age—degree of bone fusion and dental eruption in many vertebrates and annual growth rings in some of the structures of vertebrates (e.g., fish otoliths, scales, and vertebrae) and invertebrates such as mollusks.

It is possible to determine the season in which some animals were obtained. Such information can shed light on hunting patterns and when a site was occupied. Waterfowl may be in an area only during certain times of the year, so the presence of waterfowl in a deposit may indicate season of capture. The season of capture also can be determined by examining rates of bone fusion and dental eruption. However, the researcher must always remember that food was often stored and that season of capture does not necessarily indicate season of use.

A determination of the sex of an animal can provide insight into faunal utilization, especially with domesticated species. It is often difficult to determine sex unless specific elements are present. For example, the humerus of a deer generally is larger in a male than in a female, although one cannot be sure of sex on the basis of one bone, given the range of variation that exists in all organisms. However, if you have a deer skull, you can use the presence or absence of antlers to determine sex. A combination of sex and age data can be quite informative. For example, if only adult males are found in a site, you could infer that female and young animals were not hunted, perhaps as a conservation measure.

ASSESSMENT OF DIETARY CONTRIBUTION   Once number and types of food remains are identified from a site, efforts are usually made to understand the relative importance of the various resources in the economy. Simple estimates of abundance, such as NISP or MNI, may not alone provide such information. For example, if a particular faunal collection has an MNI of 5 rodents and 1 deer (assuming both were used as food), which species was more important to the diet in prehistory? A simple numeric calculation would show a 5-to-1 ratio in favor of the rodents. However, if the rodents each contributed 1 pound of food (a total of 5 pounds) and the large mammal contributed 100 pounds, the ratio would favor the deer by 20 to 1. Thus, abundance must be converted to relative contribution before the role of the various resources in subsistence can be understood. Some studies have been done to calculate such figures for animals. The live weight, available meat (live weight minus bone and hide), and usable meat (what people might actually eat) have been determined for some species. Some of these numbers are shown in Table 10.1.

It is more difficult to estimate dietary contributions of plants to the diet. Less work has been done on this issue with plants, and there is a greater possibility that many botanical remains in a site may not be related to diet. For example, most of the charcoal in a site is likely related to firewood rather than to food residues. Although firewood is related to subsistence and even to diet, it does not represent actual food remains. In addition, many seeds may have found their way to a site on plants used for firewood, for building material, or for making items such as mats or baskets. If those items burned, many nonfood burned seeds could enter the archaeological record. The reseacher has to exercise caution in analysis.

table 10.1

Estimated Edible Meat for Some Animal Species

COMMON NAME	SCIENTIFIC NAME	TOTAL EDIBLE MEAT (G)
Canada goose	*Branta canadensis*	2,089
Mallard duck	*Anas platyrhynchos*	653
Ringed seal	*Phoca hispida*	64,774
Elephant seal	*Mirounga angustirostris*	1,305,500
Eastern grey squirrel	*Sciurus carolinensis*	440
Woodrat	*Neotoma* spp.	261
Cottontail rabbit	*Sylvilagus audubonii*	653
Mule deer	*Odocoileus hemionus*	37,300
Bison (male)	*Bison bison bison*	335,700
Bison (female)	*Bison bison bison*	147,200
Armadillo	*Dasypus novemcinctus*	2,798

Sources: White 1953; Stewart and Stahl 1977.

Where Did People Live?
Past Settlement Systems

The places where a group lived, worked, played, worshiped, and obtained various materials at any time form a system of interrelated sites. Because ways of living change, a group may have different settlement patterns at different times. As the natural and cultural environment, people, and technology change, people's needs change, and the way they occupy an area also changes. Archaeologists strive to discover and understand land-use patterns, systems of settlement, the reasons a certain settlement structure is used, and the causes of changes in systems and structures over time.

The first actual study of a settlement system was conducted by Gordon Willey in the 1940s in his landmark examination of the settlement system in the Virú Valley, Peru (Willey 1953). In ecological analyses and aerial photographs of the Virú Valley in the Andes Mountains, Willey observed a pattern of permanent prehistoric settlements around sources of water with landforms suitable for the expansion of maize agriculture and for defense. Settlements often were defended by fortification of the natural terrain with

Today, a few groups of San hunter-gatherers live in much the same way as did peoples of the past. Throughout prehistory, people were foragers; the other modes of subsistence—horticulturalism, pastoralism, and intensive agriculture—are very recent in the archaeological record. If preserved as a site, the faunal remains and subsistence technology from the activity shown in the photo could be used to interpret the people's environment, mode of subsistence, diet and cuisine, and even their social organization.

earthworks. Areas of settlement were dominated everywhere by ceremonial centers large and small. As subsequent work in settlement archaeology has shown, settlement patterns can provide key insights into the ways of life of past peoples (Chang 1968; Binford 1982; Billman and Feinman 1999; Brück and Goodman 1999).

Settlement Archaeology

The manner in which a particular group organized its settlements and occupied its geographic space is called its **settlement pattern.** People, their activities, facilities, transportation, resources, sacred places, and everything else are distributed across the landscape in a culturally significant way. The settlement pattern of a group includes all the sites that the group used at a certain time and for any purpose, plus an understanding of the relationship between them. An understanding of settlement pattern also must include some comprehension of how a group conceptualized the use of space (Highlight 10.3).

HIGHLIGHT 10.3

City Planning and Sanitation in the Indus Civilization

In the mid-nineteenth century, British colonial authorities were in the midst of constructing a railway network to link the disparate regions of India. In 1856, Alexander Cunningham, director of the recently established Archaeological Survey of India, toured railway construction in what is now Pakistan. There he encountered brick ruins, some pottery, pieces of carved shell, and a badly damaged steatite seal decorated with a unicorn and inscribed with symbols in some unknown language. Cunningham believed these artifacts could be attributed to nearby Buddhist temples from the seventh century AD, but the objects proved to be from a vast ancient civilization known today as the Indus Civilization.

During its height from 2,600 to 1,900 BC, the Indus Civilization brought unprecedented cultural and technological uniformity to some 280,000 square miles of the Indian subcontinent surrounding the Indus and Saraswati river systems. Archaeologists have identified over 1,500 Indus Civilization settlements from hamlets to small cities. The center of Indus culture was concentrated in a handful of large cities scattered throughout the Indus Valley, including Mohenjo-daro and Harappa to the north. Though unlike the well-known contemporaneous civilizations of Egypt and Mesopotamia (Wheeler 1968), the Indus Civilization was an economic powerhouse that featured the world's first planned cities and a level of sophisticated sanitation that remained without parallel until 300 years ago!

Recent excavations at Harappa suggest that this great urban center began as a humble farming village around 3,300 BC. Good land and a reliable food supply allowed villagers to thrive as farmers and stockbreeders. Because of Harappa's strategic location at the crossroads of several major trading routes, the city grew to encompass some 370 acres and had a population of nearly 80,000.

Ancient cities such as Harappa may have served as hubs for a vigorous trading network that extended far beyond the Indus Valley (Kenoyer 1998:49). Archaeological evidence reveals that these cities served as conduits for the flow of copper and tin from the west; gold, silver, lapis lazuli, and timber from the north; and semiprecious stones and shells from the south. The flow of such exotic commodities allowed some residents of these cities to specialize as artisans and traders.

The ancient cities of the Indus Civilization were carefully planned and characteristically divided into several areas or neighborhoods. Each area was surrounded by a large, sturdy wall made of mud brick with massive, red-brick gateways. Early scholars, such as Sir Mortimer Wheeler (1947, 1968) and Stuart Piggott (1950), assumed that these walls and gates were constructed for defensive purposes, but recent researchers have developed an alternative theory. Kenoyer (1998:55) points out that a single wall with no moat and no sudden turns to lead enemies into an ambush would have been poorly suited for defense. Rather, recent excavations of the main gate at Harappa suggest that these walls were created with an economic purpose—to control the flow of goods into and out of the city. The main gateway is only 9 feet across, just wide enough to permit one oxcart at a time to pass in or out. Standardized cubical weights recovered at these gates are believed to have been used to levy taxes on goods coming into the city as well as on goods going to markets outside the city. Thus, great managerial skill is exemplified by the city planning that characterizes all Indus Valley urban centers (Menon 1998).

Unlike Mesopotamian cities, arranged in a haphazard way, Indus Civilization settlements follow a basic plan. Streets and buildings are oriented toward the cardinal directions. Kenoyer (1998) emphasizes that the grid-like arrangement of streets and houses within these planned cities reflects a cultural template for the organization of space. This template also is apparent in the symmetric division of space that underlies house plans, painted motifs on pottery, diagrams on stamp seals, and even the symbols used in Harappan script. Although some archaeologists (Chakrabarti 1995) disagree, Kenoyer says that the template cuts across status divisions within the population. The distinctive urban planning is evident in large public buildings, marketplaces, craft workshops, small residences arranged around a central courtyard, and large residences surrounded by smaller units for servants (Kenoyer 1998:52).

The Indus Civilization template for urban planning features remarkable skill in the control of water and an unparalleled sophistication in urban sanitation. Well-laid-out streets and side lanes equipped with sewer drains are prominent features of Indus cities. The fact that even small hamlets and towns had impressive drainage systems suggests that removal of polluted water and sewage was an important daily concern. Indeed, many scholars have suggested that these drains reflect cultural values based on concepts of ritual purity and calling for a ritual devotion to sanitation. The presence of latrines and bathing platforms in or adjacent to almost every house, regardless of neighborhood, supports this interpretation.

Nowhere is the cultural emphasis on sanitation and control of water more exquisitely demonstrated than by the "Great Bath" at Mohenjo-daro, the earliest known public water tank (Kenoyer 1998). This tank is approximately 12 meters long and 7 meters wide. Two wide staircases, one from the north and one from the south, lead down into the tank. The floor and sides of the tank are sealed with finely fitted bricks, plaster made from gypsum, and a thick layer of bitumen (a natural tar). Rooms are located along the eastern edge of the Great Bath, and in one room there is a well that may have been used to replenish the tank. Most scholars agree that the Great Bath was

The carefully laid-out grid of streets and lanes in prehistoric Mohenjo-daro—along with the complex system of water supply, drainage, and sewerage—is evidence of urban planning. Other cities, such as Harappa, also exhibit these hallmarks of Indus Civilization.

most likely used for special religious functions in which water was used to purify and renew the well-being of the bathers.

CRITICAL **THINKING** QUESTIONS

1. How has archaeological evidence at Harappa and Mohenjo-daro been interpreted to shed light on the beliefs, values, and customs of the people of the Indus Civilization?
2. How can evidence in cities of the Indus Valley be interpreted to suggest the functional and ritual uses of site features for controlling the flow of water as well as controlling the flow of people and goods?

The settlement pattern depends on many variables, including the basic subsistence system, resources, ideology, technology, and environment. Archaeologists typically work with a relatively small number of sites at any given time and work to place each site into a settlement pattern. Small-scale societies have a relatively small number of sites organized in a relatively simple manner; groups with larger populations have more complex and expansive systems. As environmental conditions change, settlement patterns also change. For example, hunter-gatherers are organized differently, emphasize different resources, and have different patterns of movement from farmers even within the same geographic space and basic environment.

When farmers enter areas occupied by hunter-gatherers, a shift in the settlement pattern is easy to see. In an area with seashore, valleys, and mountains, for example, precontact foragers with their diverse subsistence system might use all three ecozones. After contact, however, farmers tend to plant their crops in river valleys and move their herds seasonally to hillsides, displacing hunter-gatherers into marginal environments. Areas used by both groups might include river deltas and sites with critical subsistence resources. Settlement patterns such as these are preserved in the archaeological record.

To determine the settlement pattern of a group, archaeologists must determine the complete range of activities and sites of that group. They find the sites, identify the components, and determine their age, their functions, the seasons of occupation, and who the occupiers were. The settlement pattern then can be determined to the extent that the information is complete or can be predicted from models. The difficulty of accurately dating sites often makes the reconstruction of settlement patterns difficult.

Settlement can be viewed in large or small scale: from how overall landscapes are organized (Anschuetz et al. 2001) and sites are located within landscapes, to how households and activities are patterned within sites. Landscapes are shaped through continual management, even if people are not actually living in all parts of them, and so become cultural entities (Anschuetz et al. 2001:160–161; Thomas 2001). People created concepts of space, territoriality, landownership, and established boundaries, all of which influenced the actual location and function of settlements. In archaeology today, landscapes are in the forefront of settlement pattern studies, to understand how people considered and interacted with their environment (Ashmore and Knapp 1999).

The location of prehistoric sites in the landscape was based on a variety of factors. In many cases, the availability of resources was a major factor, but other requirements, such as social needs, transportation, and defensive considerations, often played a role in site placement. Areas where multiple resources could be obtained, such as an ecotone, generally yield more sites.

Some groups—hunter-gatherers or pastoralists—were quite mobile and moved around the landscape to take advantage of the seasonal availability of resources. The timing and movement of groups across the landscape is called a **seasonal round.** A seasonal round might be relatively simple or very complex, depending on the size of the group and nature of the resources being exploited (Figure 10.1). Other movements are based on changes in the size and distribution of a group. Groups may routinely split into several smaller groups that separate from the larger group (this process is called *fission*) and then may rejoin (*fusion*). Some groups practice splitting and joining as a regular

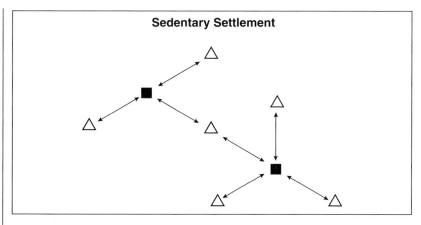

Sedentary Settlement

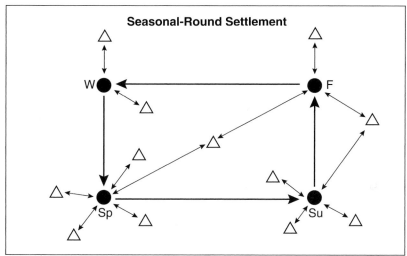

Seasonal-Round Settlement

■ Permanently occupied site   ←——→ Short-term trip

● Short-term camp   ——→ Settlement movement
    (Sp = Spring, Su = Summer,
    F = Fall, W = Winter)

△ Seasonal camp

figure 10.1

Sedentary and Seasonal-Round Settlement Patterns. The top diagram represents
a sedentary settlement system. The area contains two permanently occupied sites, plus other sites
used on an occasional basis by people from both permanent settlements. The bottom diagram
represents a seasonal-round pattern. This population moves to new camps every season. At certain
times of the year, seasonal camps serve as base camps for forays into short-term camps in the
surrounding area. In this example, some short-term camps are used during more than one season,
and during the winter the people's subsistence activities are largely restricted to the base camp.

part of their seasonal round. This **fission–fusion pattern** may have served to alleviate seasonal resource shortages or to resolve disputes between members of a social unit. For example, some Inuit populations split into small family groups and disperse for winter subsistence, coming together again as larger communities in summer. Changes in economic and social activities between the two times and places can be discerned in settlement pattern analysis.

Farming groups generally are sedentary and live year-round in cities, towns, or villages located close to their fields, and in smaller sites located near important resources. Pastoralists have mobile settlements and a seasonal round. The pattern in which only one segment of the population, such as the herders, moves with their animals seasonally while the rest of the population stays in one place is called **seasonal transhumance.** Many hunter-gatherer groups also had a seasonal round, although in some cases where the environment would support it they had large sedentary populations.

Within sites, people were organized by household, gender (Price 1999), work group, and social unit. The study of households (family units or domestic groups) is done through the analysis of house size and contents. Household archaeology often is used to infer population size, as well as the structure of social (e.g., kinship), economic, and political systems (Wilk and Rathje 1982). Households also relate to other aspects of settlement, such as land availability, control of resources, and management of landscapes. The study of households democratizes archaeology by ensuring that common people, not just the elite, are studied.

Understanding Site Components

Settlement pattern analysis rests on an understanding of sites occupied contemporaneously within a landscape. Sites contain one or more components that, in turn, contain features, artifacts, and ecofacts. Single component sites represent one archaeological culture. However, many sites are multicomponent, containing materials reflecting occupation by different cultures, usually at different times. In essence, then, components form the primary analytical unit within sites. Important analytical elements of components include their age, structure, function, and season of occupation, each of which is determined through the analysis of artifacts and ecofacts.

AGE   Recall from Chapter 7 that sites and components are dated through a variety of means, including the stratigraphic position of components and of individual items within components and the use of temporal markers. Archaeologists obtain dates of things, such as the radiocarbon date of a hearth. Based on the sum of information from the various dating methods, the site usually is dated to within a range of time, such as between 800 and 1,000 years ago. If possible, each component is dated separately.

SITE STRUCTURE   All sites have some internal structure: certain activities are conducted at certain locations within a site, called *activity areas* (Figure 10.2). A site may contain houses, cooking areas, places where garbage or other discarded material was thrown,

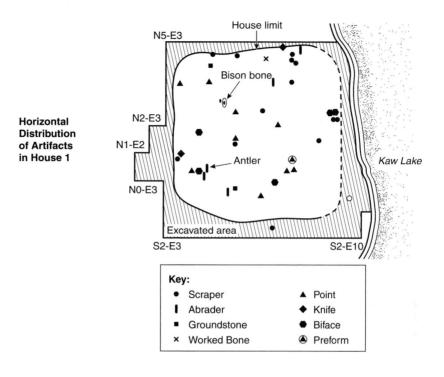

Horizontal Distribution of Artifacts in House 1

House limit

N5-E3

Bison bone

N2-E3

N1-E2

Antler

N0-E3

Kaw Lake

Excavated area

S2-E3   S2-E10

Key:
- ● Scraper
- I Abrader
- ■ Groundstone
- × Worked Bone
- ▲ Point
- ◆ Knife
- ⬢ Biface
- ◮ Preform

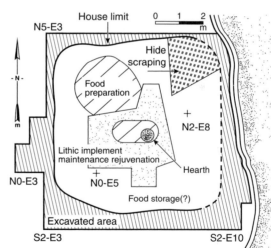

Reconstruction of Activity Areas in House 1

House limit

0 1 2 m

N5-E3

Hide scraping

Food preparation

+ N2-E8

Lithic implement maintenance rejuvenation

Hearth

N0-E3

+ N0-E5

Food storage(?)

Excavated area

S2-E3   S2-E10

figure 10.2

Examples of Activity Areas. The top diagram shows the horizontal distribution of artifacts in a unit of analysis (a layer) in House 1 at Uncas, a late village site on the southern Plains of North America (Galm 1979). The bottom diagram shows the reconstruction of activity areas in the house based on artifact distribution and other evidence. For example, the concentration of scrapers in the upper right quadrant suggests that hide scraping was the dominant activity in that area of the house. The concentration of abrading tools in the lower left quadrant suggests that people customarily used that area to grind and sharpen stone tools.

Source: Jerry R. Galm, 1979, *The Uncas Site: A Late Prehistoric Manifestation in the Southern Plains* (Norman, OK: Archaeological Research and Management Center), Figure 13. Used by permission of the Archaeological Research and Management Center, Department of Anthropology, University of Oklahoma.

areas where foods were processed, community places, latrines, and many other possible activity areas. Each area leaves a unique archaeological signature. Even a very simple site, such as a place where a person stopped for five minutes to sharpen a stone knife, has a structure: the debitage fell to the ground in relation to where and how the person was sitting or standing. An understanding of how people and activities were organized across a site requires the analysis of the distribution of artifacts, ecofacts, features, and soils.

Materials are distributed across a site *horizontally;* and if the site has any deposit, materials also are distributed *vertically.* In theory, artifacts lying on the same horizontal plane, or living surface, were deposited at the same time and are associated with the same occupation. In sites with clear, intact stratigraphy, the living surface or "floor" used at any one time can be isolated. Materials on that surface are then analyzed to discover patterns in the artifact distributions so that activity areas can be delineated. When more than one living surface is present, the structure of each is analyzed separately. The archaeologist can then compare two living floors to determine how the structure, function, or seasonal occupation of the site may have changed over time, taking into account all the ways that the internal structure of a site can be transformed through the various forces described in Chapter 4.

FUNCTION   Knowing the function of a site or component is necessary to place it within the larger settlement system. The greater the number and variety of activities evident in a site assemblage, the more numerous or complex were the functions of the site. If a site contains structures, burials, a diverse artifact assemblage, and a well-developed midden, it likely is a habitation site, such as a village or town, where people lived for some time. Temporary camps typically are smaller and contain fewer types of artifacts because they were not occupied throughout the year and so do not contain materials generated throughout the year. Sites such as a quarry or fortification contain specialized tools relating to function; ceremonial sites may contain few or no artifacts. The assignment of function to a site depends on the assignment of function to materials recovered from that site. Therefore, accuracy in artifact classification is important in determining settlement pattern.

SEASONALITY   Some sites were occupied all year long, others only during certain seasons, and others only when necessary, regardless of season. Artifacts and ecofacts at a site may be related to the season of its occupation. Some artifacts are associated with the procurement of seasonal resources, and the presence of those artifacts could be used to infer the season of their use. For example, sickle blades found in a site could suggest that the site was occupied during the spring, when grass seeds were harvested with sickles. Ecofacts also indicate seasonality. If waterfowl migrated through an area only during the fall, the presence of their bones in a site would indicate a fall occupation. The more data that are brought to bear on the question, the stronger is the case. For example, a site that is located next to a river where salmon run during the fall, and that contains artifacts related to fishing and the bones of salmon, probably was occupied during the fall fishing season and functioned as a fishing camp.

Analyzing Population

Settlement pattern analysis establishes a basis for determining past population size, distribution, and density at archaeological sites and regions. For instance, a maize- and legume-farming settlement with house floors of four extended-family dwellings, each sleeping as many as 20 people—in an environment with an estimated carrying capacity of 80 people—probably contained 80 people. As you read in Chapter 8, data from bioanthropology also are used to analyze ancient populations. Paleodemography is the study of prehistoric populations—their number, distribution, density, sex and age structure, mortality, and fertility (Meindl and Russell 1998). Much of the information on paleodemography is derived from skeletal materials, which are identified as to age and sex and compared to other known populations, past and present.

Paleoenvironmental data for an area are used in estimating the potential resources available and the carrying capacity of the land, based on the subsistence practices of the group. With this information as a starting point, researchers use skeletal and nonskeletal data to model the population present. Nonskeletal data include the number, type, structure, and contemporaneity of habitation sites. The physical size of a site may have some relationship to the number of people who lived there (or to the length of occupation), for large sites are not formed by only a few people. As you have seen, in a site containing structures such as houses, their number and size can be used to estimate the population. Population figures generated by site are combined to produce an estimate of the overall population of an area. Then, a model of population is constructed and tested. As additional archaeological data become available, the various demographic estimates would be revised. The model of prehistoric demography could also be tested by analogy by using ethnographic data.

Catchment Analysis

Another type of site analysis in the study of settlement patterns is **catchment analysis**—the study of where the materials found in a site were obtained, how much of an effort was necessary to procure them, and how that procurement affected settlement patterns (Flannery 1976; Roper 1979). The catchment area of a site is divided into geographic zones based on distance from the site itself. The *primary* catchment zone is within about a 5-kilometer radius from the site, approximately the distance a person could walk in about two hours (Vita-Finzi and Higgs 1970). The *secondary* catchment zone is at some greater distance from the main site; people would go there for a short time, perhaps a few days, to obtain resources. This distance influences settlement patterns because new sites are formed by people staying overnight. A *tertiary* catchment zone is at a still greater distance from the main site; people going there had to be away from the main site for extended periods, perhaps to trade for materials obtained by others from distant places. Catchment analysis, whether predicted as part of the research design or based on excavated materials, can help in understanding how group members interacted with their environment.

table 10.2

Resources by Catchment Zone at the Guapiabit Site CA-SBR-1913

RESOURCE	ZONE 1	ZONE 2	ZONE 3
Water	x		
Materials for ground stone tools	x		
Materials for flaked stone tools	x		
Quartzite	x		
Silicates		x?	x?
Quartz	x		
Igneous stone	x		
Obsidian			x
Silicified tuff			x
Firewood	x		
Pond turtles	x		
Eagles	x		
Deer	x		
Lagomorphs (rabbits and hares)	x		
Felids (e.g., bobcats, mountain lions)	x		
Various seeds	x		
Pronghorn antelope	x?	x	
Pottery	x?	x?	x
Green slate for ornaments			x
Shell beads from the Pacific Ocean			x
European glass bead			x

Source: Mark Q. Sutton and Joan S. Schneider, 1996, "Archaeological Investigations at Guapiabit: CA-SBR-1913," *San Bernardino County Museum Association Quarterly* 43(4), Table 29. Used by permission of the San Bernardino County Museum Association.

To illustrate, in their excavations at a late prehistoric Guapiabit site (CA-SBR-1913) in the San Bernardino Mountains of southern California, Sutton and Schneider (1996) identified a variety of resources used by inhabitants of the site (Table 10.2). The location of the source of each resource was determined and mapped in terms of one of three catchment zones (Figure 10.3). Using this analysis, the archaeologists were able to reconstruct

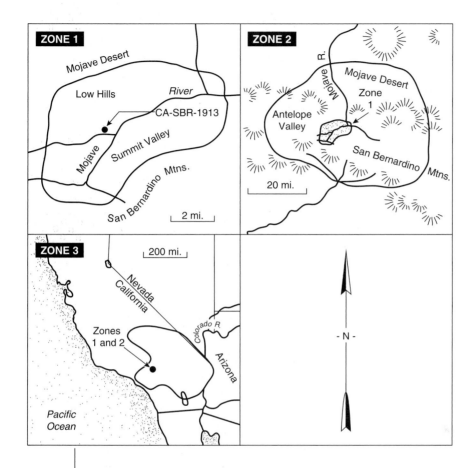

figure 10.3

Catchment Zones of the CA-SBR-1913 Site. This catchment diagram for CA-SBR-1913, a late prehistoric site in southern California, identifies the three principal locations where people went to obtain the materials and resources found at the site. As you can see from Table 10.2, most resources, especially food resources, came from nearby in Zone 1, and materials such as obsidian, green slate, and beads were obtained at greater distances over a larger geographic area.

Source: Mark Q. Sutton and Joan S. Schneider, 1996, "Archaeological Investigations at Guapiabit: CA-SBR-1913," *San Bernardino County Museum Association Quarterly* 43(4), Figure 35. Used by permission of the San Bernardino County Museum Association.

which materials were obtained locally, which had to be obtained by small groups away from the site for a few days, and which had to be obtained at substantial distances from the site, probably by trade. They discovered that most of the resources used by the site occupants were easily obtainable from zones 1 or 2, close to the site, and that only nonessential materials were obtained in trade.

The Interplay between
Subsistence and Settlement

Subsistence and settlement systems are closely related and often are considered together (as in this chapter). It is difficult to understand a subsistence system in the absence of settlement data because site type and location reveal a great deal about how an economic system was structured, how it functioned, and how it changed over time. Also, the distribution of sites is hard to comprehend without some idea of the function of each site within a subsistence system.

The unfolding understanding of ancient Maya settlement/subsistence systems illustrates this relationship (Coe 1999). Among the first ancient Maya sites to be recognized and investigated were some of the large stone pyramid complexes discovered in the jungles of the Yucatán. These sites were heavily overgrown and difficult to clear and map. As more of them were found and investigated, they were seen as ceremonial centers containing complexes of temples and facilities to support priests/rulers and workers. Smaller sites found away from the ceremonial centers suggested that a relatively small population dispersed in the countryside supported the local ceremonial center. The settlement pattern was seen as individual farms associated with a village, a number of villages linked to a small ceremonial center, and a number of small ceremonial centers aligned with a large ceremonial center. The subsistence system was seen as having been primarily horticulture augmented by some hunting.

In the 1980s, this picture began to change when evidence was found of large numbers of houses at the ceremonial centers. Unlike the public buildings made from stone, Maya houses had been made from wood on small earth foundations, and the small house mounds, engulfed by the jungle at the large sites, had gone unrecognized for decades. At about the same time, much more extensive agricultural facilities were discovered. Researchers began to realize that the large sites they had thought were ceremonial centers with small populations were actually cities with large urban populations. Suddenly, the view of the Maya changed because of a major shift in the understanding of their settlement pattern.

Cities require extensive logistical support systems. A reexamination of the regions surrounding the Maya cities resulted in the discovery of a much more extensive and complex settlement and agricultural system than had previously been recognized. It soon became apparent that the Maya had a complex, diverse, and productive agricultural system that combined hunting, gathering, and horticultural and intensive agricultural techniques. Their irrigation systems and sophisticated land management policies were able to support far more people than anyone had imagined. Our understanding of this system is still developing.

The early view of Maya settlement resulted in certain assumptions about subsistence, and that view of subsistence reinforced the view of settlement. As additional data were obtained, the view of settlement began to change, forcing a reevaluation of subsistence;

Interpretation of prehistoric Maya culture has been changing because of advances in understanding the relationships between subsistence systems and settlement patterns. Many previously undiscovered houses, like the one under excavation here, indicate a much larger population surrounding ceremonial centers than was previously thought. At the same time, previously undiscovered evidence of large-scale subsistence technology indicates a much more extensive agriculture-based economy than was previously thought. Maya prehistory has been rewritten as a consequence.

as more information became available on subsistence, the view of settlement was altered even more. The overall model of Maya settlement and subsistence changed and became more accurate as its components became better understood.

Subsistence and settlement systems also affect other aspects of culture, such as technology and religion. Further, the biology of the people themselves may also be affected by changes in subsistence and settlement, as illustrated in Highlight 10.4.

ContentSelect

Search articles in the ContentSelect database using the key words *settlement* and *subsistence*. What specific examples of settlement and subsistence do these articles offer? On what research questions do the articles focus, and why are those questions important for understanding the human past?

The Impacts of Agriculture and Urbanization on Health and Nutrition

The interplay between subsistence and settlement can be seen in the impact of agriculture and urbanization on health and nutrition. Before about 10,000 years ago, nobody practiced agriculture; today, almost everyone does. The process of the development and adoption of agriculture as the primary economic system of most people brought about some major changes in the way cultures were organized, how they operated, their populations, their subsistence systems, and their settlement patterns. The adoption of agriculture also had profound effects on the natural environment (Goudie 1994; Meyer 1996; Redman 1999).

What were the consequences of adopting agriculture? First of all, as the table suggests, agriculture involves the intense management (domestication) of certain plants and animals and the manipulation of landscapes to allow for their production. Hunter-gatherers did similar things, but on a much smaller scale. Agriculturalists take an ecosystem containing many different plants and animals and convert it to a much less diverse system by raising only a few plants and animals in the same space, thus dramatically reducing biodiversity (Matson et al. 1997; Vitousek et al. 1997:495), a process still ongoing in the rain forests of the world. Other associated impacts are the diversion of water from natural to agricultural systems (Pimentel et al. 1994:204; Vitousek et al. 1997:494), the progressive loss of topsoil and an associated decline in soil fertility (Pimentel et al. 1994:203), and the alteration of landscapes and natural habitats (Vitousek et al. 1997:495). Such alterations bring short-term benefits to farmers, but the long-term effects are not good.

The adoption of agriculture also produced changes in human cultures. Farming is difficult work and requires a great deal of labor, putting a premium on having many children. Population began to grow dramatically (now at a rate of 2 percent a year). In addition, farmers generally had to work longer hours and do more difficult labor than hunter-gatherers.

Farmers are tied to their land. As population grew, people began to coalesce, first in small towns and then in larger and larger urban centers. Political systems became more complex to deal with the increased numbers and densities of people. Resources such as land and water became more valuable, and warfare to control these resources began. Farmers began to clear more and more land for farming, expanding their territories, and absorbing or killing the hunter-gatherers in those areas.

As urban centers developed and grew, people became packed ever more tightly, and stress and violence increased. Sanitation and the availability of clean water became serious problems. Diseases that rely on unsanitary conditions to infect people thrived, and outbreaks of "crowd diseases" became common. Between 1346 and 1350, some 25 million people died from the bubonic plague, the "Black Death," in Europe. These same diseases swept through the New World after 1500, killing tens of millions of unprotected natives (Stannard 1992:268). Another 20 million people across the world died from the flu in 1918.

The diversity of foods used by humans decreased from hundreds or thousands of species to a few dozen. Today, wheat, rice, maize, potatoes, sugar, soybeans, and cotton account for most of the world's agricultural production, and a handful of other grains and legumes account for most of the rest. Animal raising depends primarily on cattle, pigs, chickens, and sheep. The reliance on so few foods is a dangerously narrow base, and periodic crop failures result in famines with millions of deaths. In addition, there are nutritional consequences from the reliance of so many people on only one or two plants for their food: complete and adequate nutrition is difficult to achieve in many cases.

One could argue that agriculture provided the food necessary to allow humans to develop the complex cultures seen in the archaeological record of the

Summary of the Impacts of Agriculture

CATEGORY	GENERAL IMPACTS
The Natural Environment	
General	Overall loss of biodiversity and habitat, pollution by chemicals
Plants	Loss of habitat for most species, extinction of some species, domestication and proliferation of a few species
Animals	Loss of habitat for most species, extinction of some species, domestication and proliferation of a few species
Water	Overall loss of fresh water for natural habitats, pollution of most water sources
Soils	Overall erosion of topsoil in agricultural lands, exhaustion of soils
Landforms	Alteration of landforms resulting in habitat loss
Atmosphere	Pollution
Climate	Long-term global warming
People and Cultures	
Population	Huge long-term increase in population, subsequent sedentation and urbanization
Resource dependence	Ongoing trend of reliance on a fewer number of resources, populations more frequently subjected to famine due to crop failure
Workload	Increase in workload for most, decrease for some (elite or rich)
Disease	Dramatic increase in crowd diseases affecting millions but with a recent general decline in a number of diseases
Health	An overall increase in general health for many people, little change for others, generally longer life expectancy
Warfare	Overall increase in scale of warfare, with increasing effects on population and environment
Knowledge	General loss of traditional knowledge, increase in specialized agricultural knowledge, explosion in overall knowledge

last 10,000 years, to pursue science and art, and to improve the quality of life for all humanity. Although it is true that the quality of life has improved, that benefit is enjoyed by only a minority; most people still live in poverty and in conditions worse than the hunter-gatherers they replaced. In sum, it seems that agriculture is like an addictive drug: it seems good at first but has devastating long-term effects. However, it is too late: we are addicted and cannot go back.

CRITICAL **THINKING** QUESTIONS

1. How are you personally affected by your subsistence system? Do you actually farm, or are you only a consumer? How do you think agriculture and urbanization have affected the health and nutrition of you and your family?
2. How might current agricultural techniques be altered to have less impact on the environment? Would you be willing to pay a bit more for food to lessen the impact of agriculture?

Chapter Summary

Subsistence, how people make a living, is a major avenue of archaeological research. The investigation of past subsistence involves the identification and analysis of three basic subsistence elements: diet, technology, and organization. An understanding of diet rests on knowing what foods were eaten, how food was obtained and prepared, its contribution to nutrition, and its role in cuisine. The technology employed and the way cultures organize themselves to conduct subsistence activities are other important topics of subsistence research.

Although there are seemingly infinite variations, four basic subsistence systems can be identified. Hunter-gatherers utilize wild foods. Horticulturalists use small-scale farming plus some wild foods. Pastoralists emphasize the herding of domesticated animals but also use some wild foods and small-scale farming. Intensive agriculturalists utilize large-scale farming plus all of the other methods as well.

Most of the archaeological evidence of subsistence is indirect—that is, it is assumed that the bones and seeds found in a site represent animals and plants that were eaten. Direct evidence of consumption is relatively rare but can be found, for example, in the analysis of paleofeces. Much of the evidence found is in the form of faunal remains (bone, shell, chitin, etc.) and botanical remains (seeds, pollen, phytoliths, etc.), and the recovery of these types of data is an important goal of most archaeological work. Other evidence is recovered in the form of human remains, the technologies people used, and the way sites are distributed and organized.

After subsistence data have been recovered, they have to be identified, quantified, and analyzed as to their contribution to the diet or to other aspects of the culture. Each of these tasks can be difficult and requires the help of specialists.

Archaeologists have had a long-standing interest in how people organize themselves through space and how that pattern changes over time. The settlement pattern of a group is a manifestation of their organization, involving the placement of all of their sites and reflecting all of their activities. Thus, the settlement pattern of each group is unique. Settlement pattern is dependent on many variables, such as the basic subsistence system, resources, ideology, technology, and environment. As conditions changed, the settlement pattern also would have changed. To determine the settlement pattern of a group, archaeologists must locate the sites, identify the components, and determine their age, their functions, the seasons of occupation, and who the occupiers were.

Some groups were mobile and practiced a seasonal round; other groups were much more sedentary. The sites of such groups would have different spatial organizations. Within sites, too, unique organizations of households and activity areas would exist.

To understand a settlement pattern, one must first understand the sites that compose the system. Sites contain one or more components that, in turn, contain features, artifacts, and ecofacts. The age, structure, function, and season of occupation of each component are determined and fit within a model of a settlement pattern. This model can be tested and refined as necessary.

In addition to information on the distribution and organization of settlements, data on the paleodemography—the size and makeup of the population—of the sites are also sought. Through the use of site type, number, density, size, and distribution, populations can be estimated. With the addition of burial data, demographic information on population structure (age, sex, mortality rates, etc.) can also be modeled.

Subsistence and settlement systems are interrelated. Once information about settlement has been obtained, it can be used to create a preliminary model of subsistence, a model that can be tested. Subsistence data, in turn, can be employed to build initial models of settlement, which can then be tested. These models are continually refined as more information becomes available.

Key Concepts

botanical remains, 256
catchment analysis, 277
faunal remains, 255
fission–fusion pattern, 274
foragers, 253

horticulture, 254
hunters and gatherers, 253
intensive agriculture, 254
paleofeces, 256
pastoralism, 254

seasonal round, 272
seasonal transhumance, 274
settlement pattern, 269
Wilson bands, 263
zooarchaeology, 255

Suggested Readings

If you want to learn more about the concepts and issues discussed in this chapter, consider looking at the following resources. (Some may be rather technical.)

Brück, Joanna, and Melissa Goodman (eds.). (1999). *Making Places in the Prehistoric World: Themes in Settlement Archaeology.* London: UCL Press.

This book consists of a variety of articles that explore many of the ways in which archaeologists study ancient landscapes and how people distribute themselves across them.

Kelly, Robert L. (1995). *The Foraging Spectrum: Diversity in Hunter-Gatherer Lifeways.* Washington, DC: Smithsonian Institution.

Humans were hunters and gatherers for most of their existence, and much archaeology is done to understand them. Kelly explores the vast diversity of hunter-gatherer forms and adaptations and is an excellent starting point in the study of them.

Meindl, Richard S., and Katherine F. Russell. (1998). "Recent Advances in Method and Theory in Paleodemography." *Annual Review of Anthropology* 27:375–399.

Understanding the structure of a population is as important as understanding its distribution. Meindl and Russell explore how archaeologists learn about demography, the structure of a population by sex, age, gender, mortality, fertility, and the like. This information is then used to help understand all the other aspects of a past society.

Redding, Richard W. (2002). "The Study of Human Subsistence Behavior Using Faunal Evidence from Archaeological Sites." In *Archaeology: Original Readings in Method and Practice,* Peter N. Peregrine, Carol R. Ember, and Melvin Ember, eds., pp. 92–110. Upper Saddle River, NJ: Prentice Hall.

Miller, Naomi F. (2002). "The Analysis of Archaeological Plant Remains." In *Archaeology: Original Readings in Method and Practice,* Peter N. Peregrine, Carol R. Ember, and Melvin Ember, eds., pp. 81–91. Upper Saddle River, NJ: Prentice Hall.

These two papers provide a brief but thorough explanation of how archaeologists use animal and plant remains from archaeological sites to help understand past subsistence systems. If more detailed information is desired, see Elizabeth J. Reitz and Elizabeth S. Wing's book, *Zooarchaeology* (1999, Cambridge: Cambridge Manuals in Archaeology) for faunal remains, and Christine A. Hastorf and Virginia S. Popper's book, *Current Paleoethnobotany* (1988, Chicago: University of Chicago Press) for botanical remains.

Interpreting Past Cultural Systems

THROUGHOUT TIME, AS the relationship between people and their environment became more complex, people's efforts to influence the supernatural powers they believed to be in control of that environment became evident and possibly more important. For agricultural groups, totally dependent on weather (rain, frost, wind, etc.) for the success of their crops, control of the environment became paramount, and considerable effort was expended to communicate with, and satisfy, the gods.

Many groups believed that the world functioned properly only by the good graces of the supernatural powers. It was commonly felt that the gods required compensation for their services in maintaining the world, so people offered payments of many kinds, such as offerings

of tobacco, goods left on altars, and the sacrifice of animals. In some cases, the sacrifices were of people, a widespread practice in Mesoamerica and South America.

Probably the best-known group practicing human sacrifice was the Mexica (or Aztec) of central Mexico. The Mexica believed that a number of gods residing in the sky completely controlled the world and that some of the stars were demons that might someday descend and eat people. In addition, the gods controlled the movements of the Sun, and if they were angry, the Sun would not rise and the world would be plunged into permanent darkness. Appeasement was required, and the Mexica believed offerings of human blood were necessary.

The Mexica generally sacrificed non-Mexica, mostly prisoners of war. Because the Mexica had an expanding military empire, there was a constant supply of war prisoners. Eventually, the demand for prisoners became so great that the Mexica and some adjacent groups who also sacrificed prisoners held prearranged battles (called "flowery wars") to generate prisoners for each side. At such events, victims of the Mexica were taken to the top of one of the high-stepped pyramids in their city of Tenochtitlan. There a priest cut out the heart of the still-living victim, and the heart and blood were offered to the sky. The body was then cast down the front of the pyramid, to be removed by special workers. At one particularly large sacrificial event held by the Mexica over several days, some 20,000 victims were killed.

There is evidence suggesting that the Mexica butchered the bodies and consumed the meat from at least some of their sacrificial victims as a normal part of their diet. However, the importance of human flesh in the Mexica diet is unclear, and there are ongoing debates as to whether such cannibalism was solely the result of ritual or addressed a general shortage of protein in the Mexica diet (Harner 1977; Ortiz de Montellano 1978; Winkelman 1998). Whichever the case might be, the impetus behind these sacrifices was political and religious, and the practice demonstrates the power of belief systems in the operation of culture.

For the location of Tenochtitlan and other sites and cultures mentioned in this chapter, see the map on page 290.

How Can Archaeology Answer Anthropological Questions?

Anthropological questions ask what it means to be human, to live in human societies, and to participate in human cultures. How is human behavior motivated, mobilized, patterned, regulated, and transmitted by members of a society who share a cultural system? As anthropologist Edward B. Tylor wrote in 1871 in his classic definition, *culture* is "that complex whole which includes knowledge, belief, art, morals, law, custom, and any other capabilities and habits acquired by man as a member of society." These are some of the "components" of culture through which a society defines the identity and expectations of the people who share it. Thus, culture is more than behavior; it includes cultural beliefs, values, symbols, and ideas.

Society refers to the actual people, individually and in groups, who live together and share aspects of culture. The relationships that hold a society together—the system of roles and statuses—are known as its *social structure*. Kinship systems and systems of social stratification, for example, are expressions of social structure. The activities and groups that accomplish the work of living in a society—through systems of affiliation, rules, and procedures—are known as its *social organization*. Families or households, political systems, and economic systems are examples of social organization.

As you have seen in previous chapters, elements of society, culture, social structure, and social organization leave signatures in the archaeological record that contribute to interpreting peoples of the past. Elements may be as straightforward as inferring the art of spinning fibers from the discovery of spindle whorls for that purpose, or as sophisticated as inferring divine kingship or specific religious beliefs from ceremonial objects and structures. But how does archaeology make these links? For instance, understanding which species of plants and animals people consumed is a long way from understanding their beliefs, values, and customs about food consumption. Yet the presence of food taboos, unequal distributions of food in a community, and ritual offerings of food—the stuff of culture, social structure, and social organization—can be detected in the archaeological record.

Social Archaeology

The study of social archaeology involves more than simply taking basic archaeological data and reconstructing a social system. Models of cultural systems are integral to this process of reconstruction. To create and test models of past societies and cultures, researchers decide what kinds of data to seek, how to obtain them, and what kinds of questions to ask. As in all scientific work, archaeological models and data are mutually reinforcing in the development and planning of further investigations.

Archaeologists begin with the assumption that past cultures operated in the same basic manner as contemporary ones. Then, as now, components of culture were learned by individuals, existed within their minds, and were reflected in the empirical world through material remains. Thus, the behavior that resulted in the formation and content of the

LOCATION MAP: **Sites and Groups Mentioned in Chapter 11**

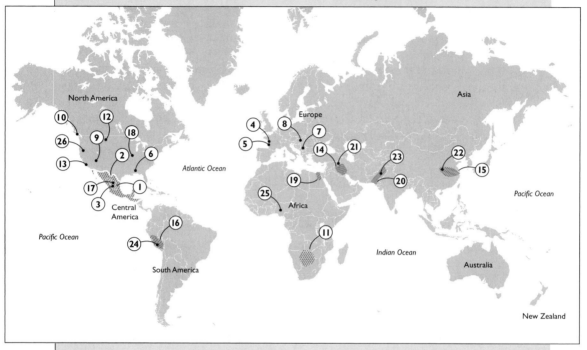

1 ■ Mexica Central Mexico	10 ■ Kwakiutl British Columbia, Canada	19 ■ Early state Egypt
2 ■ Mesoamerica Mexico and Central America	11 ■ San Southern Africa	20 ■ Early state Indus River
3 ■ Tenochtitlan Mexico City, Mexico	12 ■ Cheyenne Montana	21 ■ Shanidar Cave Iraq
4 ■ Téviec Brittany, France	13 ■ Chumash California	22 ■ Terra-cotta army Xianyang, China
5 ■ Hoëdic Brittany, France	14 ■ Early states Mesopotamia	23 ■ Harappa Pakistan
6 ■ Moundville Alabama	15 ■ Early state China	24 ■ Nasca Valley Peru
7 ■ Mokrin Serbia	16 ■ Early states Peru	25 ■ Kingdom of Benin Nigeria
8 ■ Basatanya Hungary	17 ■ Teotihuacán Mexico City, Mexico	26 ■ Virginia City Nevada
9 ■ Hopi Arizona	18 ■ Monk's Mound Cahokia, Illinois	

archaeological record first originated in the minds of past peoples and was then materialized through action.

Figure 11.1 offers an archaeological model of culture. It differs from anthropological models of culture by emphasizing four cultural domains that often are evident or can be modeled from archaeological data. These data come from (1) technology and material culture, (2) settlement and subsistence patterns, (3) information about cultural systems, including inferences about social structure and social organization, and (4) cognition—how people think—and symbol systems. These four domains are embedded in a matrix of time and place—that is, people's physical, cultural, and temporal environments form the context within which societies and cultures develop and change. Starting with this general model, archaeologists can begin with material remains and their patterns in the archaeological record and then construct models of past cultures: how people thought, how they organized themselves, and how they communicated with others both within and outside their communities.

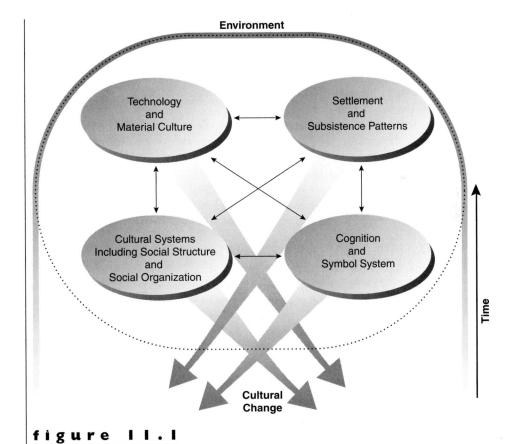

figure 11.1

An Archaeological Model of Culture

Source: Adapted from Renfrew and Bahn 1996:194.

Cognitive Archaeology

A recent emphasis in interpreting past cultures attempts to understand the cognitive systems on which those cultures were built. Cognitive systems include how people thought in the past and how that thinking was reflected in the content and patterning of their material culture (Mithen 2001). **Cognitive archaeology** is "the study of past ways of thought as inferred from material remains" (Renfrew 1994:3). For example, the designs, forms, styles, characteristics, and techniques of technology can reflect the priorities and values of the maker and user (Stark 1998). Other expressive forms of culture, such as art, writing, and other symbolic systems, also have designs and patterns of form that constitute a system of meaning. Working back from material remains to thought processes, archaeologists seek to reconstruct the **worldview** of past peoples—their assumptions and beliefs about how the world works and should work. Knowledge of the worldview of a culture, in turn, can be used to better understand the archaeological record.

The human capacity for culture has changed since the beginnings of the genus *Homo*. These changes can be traced in the fossil record through elaborations of the brain and in the archaeological record through elaborations of technology and culture. It is generally believed that modern human abilities can be traced back to the appearance of anatomically modern humans (*Homo sapiens sapiens*) at least 50,000 years ago. Human mental capabilities prior to that time are a matter of debate (e.g., Mithen 1994), but most archaeologists assume that past modern humans had the same basic mental abilities that humans have today.

Some researchers use their imaginations to try to "become" the ancient persons and so to enter their minds. The goal is to achieve insights or leads into people's motives and values, much as a detective might try to enter the mind of the perpetrator of a crime to determine how and why the crime was committed. Critics of this approach point out, however, that it is fundamentally "subjective, idealist, [and] interpretationalist" and thus not scientific (Renfrew 1994:6). Also, archaeologists operate within the cognitive systems of their own present-day cultures and may be mistaken in imposing these systems on other cultures of the past. A more scientific approach relies on models of cognitive patterns built on artifact typologies, much as a detective might focus on the physical evidence at a crime scene to deduce what happened.

Much of the cognitive aspect of culture is communicated to others through the use of **symbols**—icons, writing, art, and other material expressions of meanings and ideas. Symbols are used to communicate, organize, and regulate social relations among people, as well as between people and supernatural entities, such as spirits, ghosts, or gods. Archaeologists are divided on the question of whether symbol systems of the past can be known and understood. Some believe that symbols are arbitrary and subjective and that past symbolic systems are not knowable. However, we believe that past symbol systems are knowable, however difficult their decipherment may be (Bell 1994a).

Understanding symbols and their complex role in culture cannot be accomplished by simply identifying specific symbols that mean specific things, for the deeper meaning of any symbol may go far beyond its literal meaning. As an analogy, words can be defined in a dictionary, but an English-speaker can take the individual words and combine them in an infinite number of ways to express complex meanings well beyond the literal meanings of the component words. To understand a language, we must understand not only the meanings of the words themselves, but also the grammar, syntax, context, and other components of the language (Robb 1998:341). To understand past cognitive systems, we must first understand that material culture is intertwined with its underlying cultural context and meanings within the system under study; thus, it is necessary to understand both to understand either (Robb 1998). This formidable task is critical to our understanding of the past.

Symbols may directly convey information, such as certain shapes (e.g., crosses, stars, crescents) for a religious affiliation, a ring on a particular finger for marital status, or jewels or purple robes denoting the power of a monarch. Beyond transmitting basic information, symbols may generate intense feelings, such as a national flag invoking patriotic sentiment.

In archaeology, categories of symbols that can be inferred from artifacts include values related to design, planning, measurement, social relations, relations with the supernatural, and representational art and writing. For example, a lizard motif on pottery might signify the desirability of lizards as a resource, or it may identify a clan. Hatch marks on an axe handle might symbolize the number of kills its owner claimed; a schematic diagram scratched into soft rock might be a navigational or celestial chart; grave goods might signify social rank as well as belief in an afterlife; wedge shapes stamped into clay might be writing, and so on. Table 11.1 shows some archaeological correlates for the presence of symbol systems.

Most material culture recovered from the archaeological record contains some symbolic expression of cultural meaning. Artifacts, features, and sites were created by means of techniques, methods, materials, and forms that relate to particular worldviews. To discover symbols, archaeologists analyze attributes that do not appear to be directly utilitarian—that is, the shape, context, or raw materials of items suggest some function beyond a specific utility. A button made from bone, for example, might be interpreted as a common utilitarian item, whereas a button made of gold might be interpreted as a symbol identifying higher political and social status. As another example, for an arrowhead to be effective, it must be small and have a pointed end and sharp edges. After those functional criteria are met, the specific style or decoration of the arrowhead may convey some other cultural information, or information about its maker. If the functional criteria are *not* met, however, then the object is nonutilitarian. It may be a ceremonial object, or perhaps the maker was a child lacking the knowledge and skills to produce an adequate arrowhead.

During the Bronze Age, trumpets made from bronze, silver, or other metals, such as this drawing of one from northern Europe, were used as hunting horns in large communal hunts. In addition, they identified the user as a member of the aristocracy because such instruments are found associated only with the wealthiest people or in the wealthiest houses.

table 11.1

Some Archaeological Correlates of Cognitive Systems

SYMBOL SYSTEM	HUMAN MOTIVATION OR VALUES	MATERIAL CORRELATES	ARCHAEOLOGICAL EXAMPLES
Design	E.g., repetition, symmetry, color, form, interest	Repetitive elements or embellishments in artifacts or sites	Pot styles; brickworks; decorative motifs
Planning	E.g., organization, preparation for future activities	Evidence of preplanned sites; production lines	Preserved layouts or schematics; urban planning
Measurement	E.g., keeping count, keeping track	Measuring devices; objects conforming to measurements	Weights; objects that vary by size; calendar; star chart
Social relations	E.g., affiliation, role and status, social inequality	Objects denoting identity, wealth, power, rank	Heads on coins; royal architecture; slave quarters
Supernaturals	Explanation/ control of the world and life: origins, nature, disasters, death	Ceremonial objects and architecture; objects of worship; treatment of the dead	Embalmed remains; nonutilitarian/rare objects of great size or value
Representation	E.g., describing the world, communicating experience	Art objects/artistic representations; written language	Cave/rock paintings; sculptures/figurines; written texts

Source: Adapted from Renfrew 1994:6.

As you read in Chapter 10, the organization of space may also be reflected symbolically in the settlement pattern of a group, including their use of the environment, modification of landscapes, and site organization. As noted in Chapter 1, archaeologists use these consistent patterns of symbolism and styles of archaeological materials to construct models of archaeological cultures.

Much of the work in understanding past cultural systems is the struggle to recognize the political and social boundaries that distinguish groups (Stark 1998). Without distinguishable boundaries, different groups cannot be recognized, and the reasons for their differentiation cannot be explored. In many cases, symbols embedded in material culture were used to publicize boundaries between groups, such as uniforms used to distinguish military personnel from civilians or the specialized clothing and paraphernalia separating royalty from commoners.

Interpreting Past Social Structures

All societies have some kind of social structure—the way in which people are identified and classified in relation to one another; in other words, their roles and statuses. Social structure sets the stage for social organization, the actual interactions and relationships between people. For example, all cultures have kinship systems with rules for descent, reciprocity, marriage, residence, and inheritance. These rules, in turn, are the structural basis for the organization of family groupings and residential units.

All societies assign roles and statuses on the basis of age, sex, and gender. More stratified societies may assign roles and statuses on the basis of ethnicity, occupation, and caste or class. The more roles and statuses there are in a society and the more differentiations there are in the system of social stratification, the more "complex" a society becomes overall. At the same time, people in "simple" societies can have very complex elements of social structure. Aborigines of Australia, for example, lived as hunter-gatherers in essentially nonstratified societies, yet their kinship system is among the most complex known to anthropologists.

Kinship

Through the study of households, archaeologists can discover how large the social groups were within a household, how those groups were organized, and how they were related to groups in other households. Sometimes the kinship system can be deduced from the evidence. For example, among people with a *moiety system*—a kinship system in which people are organized into two separate descent groups with a common ancestor—the division into two groups might be detected in the physical distribution of houses as well as in typological distinctions in artifacts, such as house or pottery styles.

Marriage patterns also can be discerned in the archaeological record. For example, archaeologists in Great Britain (Schulting and Richards 2001) conducted a stable isotope analysis on the bone from burials at the Mesolithic sites of Téviec and Hoëdic along the coast of France and found that young women had consumed fewer marine resources over their lifetimes than had the men in the same communities. This suggested that the women had been raised at sites in the interior and had moved to the coast later, probably as marriage partners to the men raised on the coast. *Exogamy*—marrying outside one's group—is a common feature of hunter-gatherers.

Social Stratification

Some social groups within a society may maintain differential access to important resources, such as water, food, weapons, information, or supernatural power. When one social group uses that access to control or influence the actions of other groups, inequality between the two groups is created (Paynter 1989:369–370; also see Brumfiel 2002). As a result, social, economic, and political inequality, as well as gender inequality, may emerge. The degree of stratification and inequality in a society is one dimension of its social complexity.

Nonstratified societies often are referred to as "egalitarian." In egalitarian groups, no one is significantly wealthier, more powerful, or higher status than others, although a clear division of labor by age and sex always exists. For instance, elders may have the authority to resolve disputes, and females may have dominion over hut building. The economy of the group might support part-time specialists, such as an artisan, shaman, or medicine woman. Otherwise, social standing may be based on individual skill or accomplishment, called *achieved* status. In **stratified societies,** in contrast, social roles and statuses are many and diverse, formally defined, inherited (*ascribed*) as well as achieved, and often institutionalized through the creation of castes or classes.

The status of individuals and of social groupings can be observed in the archaeological record in a number of ways. A common approach to the study of social status is through **mortuary analysis,** the study of burial data, which is based on the model that the status an individual held in life is reflected in the differential treatment he or she received at the time of death. Recall from Chapter 8 that individuals recovered from burial contexts often can be identified as to age, sex, and general health. In addition, some individuals have been interred with grave goods while others have not. The presence and type of grave goods can be associated with demographic information such as sex, age, location of burial, and orientation of the body. People may be buried with the items they used in life, providing insight into their activities and roles in that culture as well as their individuality.

The way a person was interred and the location of the interment also may reflect social status. For example, in early imperial Rome the rich typically were cremated and people of lower status simply were buried. Cremation was preferred, but it was expensive and only the rich could afford it. Thus, in most cases, the wealthy and the poor of Rome can be differentiated by method of interment.

Using this general approach, archaeologists Christopher Peebles and colleagues (Peebles and Kus 1977; Peebles and Black 1987) examined the sex, age, location, and grave goods data from 2,053 burials from the Moundville site in Alabama, occupied by the Mississippian culture between 750 and 500 BP. Twelve separate clusters of individuals were identified on the basis of the grave goods and location, and the differences among them clearly indicated the presence of a stratified and ranked society. The highest-ranking individuals were buried in or near artificial mounds and had copper artifacts buried with them. The larger and more complex dwellings, presumably of the elite, contained the same material culture as the burials thought to be of high status, reinforcing the model of a ranked society (Peebles and Kus 1977:439; Peebles and Black 1987).

Table 11.2 shows the ranking of individuals at Moundville based on the burial data. The highest-status individuals were buried in mounds, tended to be males, and had rich grave goods, including copper objects. Individuals with low status were buried away from mounds, in groups of mixed age and sex, and were buried only with ceramic vessels. The great majority of low-status burials had no grave goods at all.

The mortuary data from Moundville and other sites might be viewed from a different perspective. Perhaps grave goods did not signify the actual status of an individual but rather reflected the social environment at the time of death. Perhaps the family of

table 11.2

Burial Clusters and Ranking from the Moundville Site

GENERAL RANK AND PERCENTAGE OF SOCIETY	CLUSTER	NUMBER OF INDIVIDUALS	AGE AND SEX	BURIAL LOCATION	GRAVE GOODS
High (10.6%)	IA	7	Adult males	All in mounds	Copper axes, copper beads, pearl beads
	IB	43	Adult males and children	Mostly in mounds	Copper ear spools, copper gorgets, stone disks, bear-tooth pendants, and various minerals
	II	67	All ages and sexes	Near mounds	Copper gorgets, shell beads, and stone cubes
Middle (12.7%)	III	211	All ages and sexes, but many children	Near mounds	Effigy ceramic vessels, shell gorgets, stone celts, and animal bones
	IV	50	All ages and sexes	Near mounds	Projectile points, discoidals, and bone awls
Low (76.7%)	V	55	Mostly adults, but many children	Away from mounds	Certain types of ceramic bowls or jars
	VI	45	Mostly adults	Away from mounds	Certain types of ceramic bowls or jars
	VII	55	Mostly adults	Away from mounds	Certain types of ceramic water vessels
	VIII	70	Mostly adults, but many children	Away from mounds	Certain types of ceramic water vessels
	IX	46	Mostly adults	Away from mounds	Certain types of ceramic water vessels
	X	70	Mostly adults	Away from mounds	Ceramic shards
	XI	1,256	All ages and sexes, but many children	Away from mounds	None

Source: Based on Peebles and Kus 1977:439, Figure 3.

the deceased, the mourners, and the social context were more important than the dead person's status in life. Thus, it has been suggested that the power and inequality seen in the archaeological record could reflect the status of the living rather than that of the dead (e.g., McGuire and Paynter 1991).

The Archaeology of Gender

As you read in Chapter 3, genders are social categories of behavior, role, and status. These roles are typically "male" or "female" but also include transvestites, homosexuals, and the like. Though culturally defined, gender is typically self-assigned or socialized. Gender concepts change over time in a culture, and some cultures attach greater importance to gender differences than do others. The gender of an individual is recognized by others in a society through appearance (clothing, hairstyles, and adornment), activities ("male" and "female" work), and styles of social interaction.

Archaeologists seek to identify genders in past cultures, to determine their importance in the group under study, and to interpret the meaning of gender within the worldview of that culture. In recent years, there has been a great deal of interest in gender as an issue in archaeology (Conkey and Spector 1984; Wright 1996; Conkey and Gero 1997; Schmidt and Voss 2000; Claassen 2002; Nelson 2004) and in the theoretical aspects of past gender (Wylie 1992; Little 1994; Hill 1998). Archaeologists have paid attention to gender in both prehistoric (Ehrenberg 1989; Gero and Conkey 1991; Price 1999) and historical contexts (Scott 1994; Wall 1994; Spencer-Wood 2006; Wilkie and Hayes 2006). Increasingly, archaeologists are turning their attention to homosexuals in antiquity, *queer archaeology* (e.g., Dowson 2000). The study of queer archaeology includes an attempt to understand how archaeologists who are homosexuals influence gender studies of the past.

To investigate gender in the past, archaeologists commonly use evidence from ethnographic analogy, historical texts, dietary data, skeletal data (e.g., differential pathology, such as arthritis), mortuary data, and representational art (Costin 1996:116–117; 2002). In ethnographic analogy, gender roles observed in the present are projected into the past. For example, in most hunter-gatherer societies, women obtain the majority of the plant resources and prepare most of the food; thus, the technologies associated—digging sticks, collecting bags, firewood carriers, tongs for moving coals, cooking vessels, and the like—are viewed as "female." An archaeologist who finds these artifacts in a hunter-gatherer site may then argue by analogy that they were part of a tool kit used by females. The danger of this line of reasoning is that without proper evaluation and testing, such assumptions may become self-fulfilling. However, if females commonly are buried with food preparation tools, one can conclude that females used those tools to prepare meals. If a male were found with those same tool types, it could suggest that he took a female gender role.

Differences in diet may also shed light on sex and gender roles. Although most dietary data cannot currently be linked with specific individuals, it is now possible to identify whether paleofeces were male or female in origin using DNA (Sutton et al. 1996) and hormonal evidence (Sobolik et al. 1996). As you read in Chapter 10, once sex is determined, the specifics of the diet can then be detailed; thus, differences between male and female diets and cuisine can be observed. A recent chemical residue and DNA analysis of a glass syringe recovered from an archaeological excavation at the historic silver mining boomtown of Virginia City, Nevada, indicates not only that the syringe was used for morphine injection, but also that the needle was shared by at least four individuals, both males and females, one of whom may have been of African descent (Powell 2002). Such data hold the promise of shedding light on differential access to various foods and medicines, indicating power and prestige relationships between the sexes. Highlight 11.1 explores the process of interpreting gender roles from mortuary analysis.

Other evidence of gender relationships can be seen in human bone pathology. For example, arthritis, the inflammation and destruction of the joints, is a condition generally associated with aging but also correlates with workload and activity, which may be defined by gender. Evidence of arthritis is often visible in skeletal materials as polished bone surfaces from direct bone-on-bone wear, the formation of bone along the edges of the joint (lipping), or bone spurs (exostoses) in and around the joints.

In his study of hunter-gatherers in the Great Basin of North America, bioarchaeologist Brian Hemphill discovered that females tended to have greater arthritic affliction in their hands and knees and males suffered more in their shoulders and arms (Hemphill 1999). Further, males exhibited evidence of a higher overall workload and greater mobility throughout their lifetimes than did females. These data suggest that females knelt and used their hands in a repetitive motion more than males did, and males used their upper bodies more than females did. Males seem to have been more mobile than females, perhaps as the result of spending a great deal of their time walking through rugged terrain looking for game.

Artistic representations also provide information on gender in the past. In much ancient art, animals and men are portrayed in hunting scenes, but depictions of other activities of hunters, other men, females, and children are uncommon. However, some small human figurines portraying adult females (made of bone, ivory, and clay), dating from the Upper Paleolithic, have been discovered in Europe, North Africa, and the Middle East. These female figures, commonly called *Venus figurines,* often are depicted naked with large breasts and buttocks and sometimes with large abdomens (suggesting pregnancy). Various interpretations of these figurines suggest they may have been symbols of fertility, "mother goddesses," social status markers, and even erotica.

In addition, some figurines are depicted with clothing, and several clothing types and styles, including hats, belts, and decorations, have been identified (Soffer et al. 2000). Clothing on female figurines may suggest roles and values associated with women's labor, as in the production of textiles. Perhaps women were highly skilled and valued laborers in Upper Paleolithic society, manufacturing and wearing garments indicating social prestige. It has also been suggested that different types of figurines may represent separate symbolic meanings for the roles of females (Gvozdover 1989).

The Archaeology of Ethnicity

Ethnic groups can be defined as self-identified groups who are differentiated from other groups on the basis of cultural attributes (Jones 1997:xiii). These attributes may include language, customs, religion, and territory, and they can be recognized through symbols, signs, and beliefs (Hodder 1982:139; Royce 1982:7), such as the use of style in clothing, tools, housing, and settlement. In most contemporary industrial societies, different ethnic

HIGHLIGHT 11.1

Sex and Gender in Central European Burials

Although archaeologists use many different methods and theoretical tools to explore gender relations in the past, one area of study that remains of primary interest is mortuary remains, or burial sites. This is one of the rare instances in the archaeological record in which specific individuals can be definitively associated with material remains. Through the study of skeletal remains, the sex of mature adult humans can be determined with varying degrees of accuracy, depending on preservation and the individual's physical characteristics (no one knows precisely how many tall women with strong jawlines have been sexed by archaeologists as men!). Nevertheless, there is a long way to go theoretically from sexing individuals to understanding how gender may have structured social relationships in the past. To examine how archaeologists approach this process, let us consider the example of burial remains in two central European cemeteries.

Mokrin, located in present day Serbia near the Romanian and Hungarian borders, is a cemetery site from the Early Bronze Age culture known as Maros. The site yielded calibrated radiocarbon dates between 2100 and 1500 BC (Rega 1997:231). Although Maros was originally excavated from 1958 to 1969, archaeologists have continued to work with the materials, asking new and different questions from those pursued by the original excavators. Elizabeth Rega examined 268 skeletons from the site and was able to assign 146 of them to a specific biological sex (Rega 1997:231). Once this was accomplished, patterns in the burial treatment became evident: "The females in the cemetery are generally oriented with their head to the south or southeast, on their right side facing east. The males are oriented with their head to the north or northwest on their left side, also facing east" (Rega 1997:213).

In addition, some artifacts appear to have strongly gendered associations. Multiple coil bracelets, bone needles, and stone maces were found only in the graves of adult female skeletons (Rega 1997:233). Copper daggers and knives were found only with adult male skeletons (Rega 1997:235). Such facts oversimplify the picture, however, because the vast majority of graves contained a mix of items, such as bowls, that were exclusively associated neither with female nor with male burials. Thus, we find that although biological sex—and its social significance in the form of gendered identity—clearly played a role in some aspects of burial practices (such as the orientation of the body), others (such as grave goods) appear to have been mediated by gender roles but not exclusively determined by them.

What does all this mean, and what can archaeologists do with this information? The true interpretive potential of most archaeological assemblages becomes apparent only in the light of comparison. Mortuary site information such as sex, age at death, and burial treatment can be greatly enriched when considered in the context of habitation site information for the same population. For example, is there any correlation in the orientation of Maros graves (bodies facing east) and the orientation of Maros houses or other significant structures? Where else are the objects found in the graves? Do living spaces show similar distributions of artifacts that might be explained by gendered activities? Another source for comparison can be temporal variation, or change over time.

In the modern country of Hungary, a few hundred miles north of Mokrin, lies another mortuary site, Tiszapolgar-Basatanya, which dates to an earlier period known as the Copper Age. At Basatanya, 67 graves were identified from the Early Copper Age and 87 from the Middle Copper Age, spanning the period between 4500 and 3600 BC (Chapman 1997:138). Although there is no clear chronological break between these two phases, archaeologists distinguish between them in terms of the emphasis of the participants' subsistence strategies. The transition from the Early Copper Age to the Middle Copper Age is distinguished by a change in the importance of the production of so-called primary products (e.g., meat) to that of secondary products (e.g., wool and dairy foods) (Chapman 1997:136–137). Habitation practices also changed: Early Copper Age people lived primarily in close quarters on a tell; Middle Copper Age people moved into dispersed farmsteads (Chapman 1997:136).

Researchers would assume that with such drastic changes in lifestyles would come some changes in the relationships between and among men and women. Cemetery data from Basatanya confirm that with changes in subsistence and habitation came changes in materials associated with social identity. As the accompanying table indicates, for adult male skeletons, only one grave inclusion stays constant between the two periods: snails. For females, bone spoons and pebbles remain constant. It seems clear that in the Middle Copper Age, there is an increased emphasis on items made by humans as important grave goods. Also, in the case of the males, there is an exclusion of wild animal bones and an inclusion of domesticated animal bones (cattle), which may reflect a change in the importance of hunting in defining manhood (Chapman 1997:141). In the case of the females, one change that can be seen is the decline in deer teeth and the rise in items such as spindle-whorls, associated with processing wool (Chapman 1997:141). What is most clear is that significant changes in the material representations of maleness and femaleness were occurring in this period. Almost certainly these bear a relationship to changes in the daily lives of Copper Age peoples. By documenting these kinds of correlations, archaeologists can begin to pry open the door to gender relations in the past. Each new data set leads to more correlations and, inevitably, to more questions.

Associated with Adult MALE Skeletons Only	Early Copper Age	Wild animal bones, snails, complete dog, limestone disc, loom weight, ochre lumps
	Late Copper Age	Tusk, snails, cattle bones, antler artifacts, ground stone, clay funnel, fire, copper awl, copper pin, copper dagger
Associated with Adult FEMALE Skeletons Only	Early Copper Age	Deer tooth, bone spoon, pebble
	Late Copper Age	Shed antler, mussels, fish bone, bone awl, bone spoon, pebble, polished stone plate, polished stone hammer ax, spindle-whorl, clay stud, copper bracelet, copper ingot

Diagnostic Nonceramic Artifacts from the Tiszapolgar-Basatanya Cemetery by Associated Skeleton's Sex.

Source: Adapted from Chapman 1997.

CRITICAL **THINKING** QUESTIONS

1. How did evidence of sex and gender at the sites of Mokrin and Basatanya compare? Why is site comparison important for interpreting aspects of culture such as social identity?
2. What can associations between sex and material culture tell archaeologists about the economic and social organization of past societies?
3. What can associations between sex and material culture tell archaeologists about gender concepts and gender relations among people of the past?
4. What can material representations of maleness and femaleness tell archaeologists about social and cultural change?

groups exist within the overall culture. However, in the past, most societies were smaller and more homogeneous. Basic to the idea of recognizing ethnic groups or cultures in the archaeological record is the premise that they can be defined through the identification of unique sets of attributes, traits, and symbols. For example, the arrival of Europeans in North America is easy to detect because their material culture, architecture, spatial organization, and land use is so different from that of the native peoples who preceded them.

Individuals may belong to more than one social entity, each of which might differentiate itself from the others through the use of symbols. As the size and social complexity of a society increase, opportunities for multiple memberships (plurality) in different groups also increase. Membership in a specific group can be used to reward certain individuals, to maintain status between groups, or to maintain political and economic contacts with other groups. The presence of different ethnic groups may illuminate other issues as well, such as the presence of an enslaved population pointing to political and social stratification.

In constructing past ethnic and cultural identities, archaeologists need to exercise care, for it is easy to confuse archaeological cultures for actual ones. There is also the danger that archaeologists may "create" ethnic groups, either by error or through some desire to construct an alternative past for political purposes, such as a newly formed contemporary group's creating a cultural identity to legitimize an ancient claim (Jones 1997:2–3). Thus, the symbols, signs, and beliefs by which groups distinguish themselves become criteria for studying such groups (Royce 1982). In most cases, however, single traits are rarely sufficient to identify an actual past ethnic group, and archaeologists know that a combination of traits is required in the analysis of past ethnicity. The more idiosyncratic the traits, the better. For example, there are only a few basic ways to make a pottery vessel, but there are many ways to decorate one, so construction traits would be less informative of ethnicity than decoration techniques.

If an archaeological site contains Roman pottery, researchers could assume that the site was occupied by Romans. However, it is possible that the occupants of the site were not Roman but had traded for the pottery. If further excavation at the site revealed Roman architecture, the case for a Roman presence would be strengthened, but it is possible that the site occupants copied Roman house styles and traded for Roman pottery. If Roman-style personal artifacts and burials also were found, the coincidence would become more difficult to explain, and many researchers would then argue for an ethnic Roman presence at the site. Nevertheless, it is still possible that people from some other ethnic group emulated the Romans even down to their burial practices. Anthropometric evaluation of the burials could help determine whether the bodies were biologically Roman, and DNA studies ultimately could settle the matter.

One method commonly employed to determine the ethnic identity of some archaeological materials is the **direct historical approach.** Using this method, archaeologists assume that the earliest ethnographic or historically known group in an area is the direct descendant of the latest archaeological group in that same area (Lyman and O'Brien 2001). For example, the Hopi were contacted by the Spanish in 1540 and have lived in the same location since that time. By examining known Hopi traits and comparing them with the archaeological materials found in the area, archaeologists have shown that the same suite of traits that characterize the Hopi, including architecture, pottery, subsistence systems, settlement patterns, and religious activities, was also present several thousand years ago. To many archaeologists, this demonstrates continuous occupation of the area by the Hopi for at least the last 2,000 years and supports the same claim made in Hopi oral history (Brew 1979:514).

Interpreting Past Political Organization

Political organization is a specific type of social structure that allocates and distributes power and authority in a society. Power and authority may come from acquisition of inherited statuses or from individual characteristics. Examples of political offices—defined or formal positions of power and authority—are chiefs, warlords, and monarchs. Ritual offices, such as shamans and priests, also are political offices. A group that has an independent political organization is called a **polity.**

The exercise of power eventually leads to institutionalized inequality. One of the major goals in the study of past political systems is to examine the interaction between political and social units, to understand the "struggles among members of society over the exercise of social power" (Paynter and McGuire 1991:1). Some groups dominate others, and there often is resistance to such domination, resulting in culture change.

Four Types of Political Organization

The American anthropologist Elman Service (1962) developed a classification of levels of political complexity. Service identified four major types of political organization: **band, tribe, chiefdom,** and **state.** These four types describe the scale and complexity of political organization as well as other aspects of culture. Although quite general and descriptive, this classificatory scheme is still used by archaeologists and anthropologists in the study of how past polities were structured and organized, how they functioned, and how they changed over time.

In constructing models of past political systems, archaeologists estimate the size and scale of the society and culture, including population, settlement pattern and size, and basic subsistence system. These factors correlate with different levels of political organization. For example, a site with public works or trade networks that may have required some sort of supervisory control would have required a more complex political organization. Likewise, status differentiations discovered in mortuary data would indicate a more complex political organization based on social stratification. However, archaeologists must be cautious in classifying archaeological cultures in terms of political organization because bands, tribes, chiefdoms, and states are ideal types, and actual societies might combine the features of two or more types. Small-scale societies dominate the archaeological record; the development of larger-scale societies, with significant social stratification and more complex political systems, has occurred only within the last 12,000 years or so.

BANDS   Small-scale, nonstratified societies with hunting and gathering as their primary subsistence system are typically organized as bands. Bands are organized through kinship and have informal leaders who lead by persuasion and consensus. Band settlement patterns are characterized by temporary habitations and seasonal mobility. The material culture of bands reflects a mobile lifestyle, such as the use of easily transportable basketry in lieu of more cumbersome pottery. A good ethnographic example of a band is the San people of southern Africa (Lee and DeVore 1976).

TRIBES   Tribes have larger populations than bands, up to a few thousand people. Tribes also tend to have more formal leaders, commonly called *chiefs*. Tribes have mixed economies, larger and more permanent settlements, and some social segmentation based on criteria other than kinship, although kinship is still very important. Tribes remain egalitarian to the extent that they remain small and nonstratified. In stratified societies, individual and group status is formalized. Although achieved status is still important, ascribed status plays a more substantial part in social organization. The Cheyenne people on the Plains of North America are an ethnographic example of a tribal society (Moore et al. 2001).

CHIEFDOMS   Chiefdoms are polities with populations of up to tens of thousands of people. Most chiefdoms are based on agriculture and have large, permanent settlements, a centralized political structure, a formal leader authorized to use force, and formal ranking (usually based on heredity). The economic system of a chiefdom may also be stratified, with specialists in a number of areas, such as trade. Many ethnographic examples of chiefdoms can be cited, such as the hunting and gathering Kwakiutl of the Northwest Coast of North America (Codere 1950, 1990; Boas and Codere 1966).

Archaeologically, large tribes and chiefdoms are recognized through the size and complexity of their sites and the community structures within them, although both would continue to occupy many smaller sites as well. There should be evidence of large populations, economic specialization, control of important resources, and differential status within the population. In chiefdoms, community religious activities may be at the forefront of the political structure, and the political leader may also be the religious leader (a *theocracy*). Evidence of the mobilization, support, and management of community labor should also be apparent, as seen in the construction of public buildings, irrigation systems, and the like.

Another measure of social and political organization within a chiefdom is the degree of craft specialization. A society able to support full-time, non-food-producing specialists is producing surpluses and has the elaborate exchange networks and complex political system necessary to control the economy. Craft specialization can be detected in the archaeological record through the discovery of large numbers of items of standardized manufacture, through the presence of manufacturing localities and specialized tools, and even through the identification of repetitive patterns of motion in skeletal remains.

For example, in studying the prehistory of coastal southern California, Jeanne Arnold argued that after about 1,000 years ago, the Chumash Indians of that region had developed a highly complex, ranked society, probably a chiefdom (Arnold 1992, 2001; Arnold et al. 1997). The hunter-gatherer Chumash lived in a very productive environment and established large sedentary villages of more than 1,000 people. Village-based chiefdoms probably were linked together in a loose confederacy and cooperated in alliances of marriage, trade, and defense. There is also evidence of extensive craft specialization for the production of shell beads and plank canoes, a monetary economy, and a network of long-

View of the large pre-Columbian city of Teotihuacán looking north up the "Avenue of the Dead" from the "Pyramid of the Moon." Note the numerous buildings in the city and the large "Pyramid of the Sun" on the left side of the photo.

distance trade. The development of craft specialization, and the political control of that labor, combined to increase the complexity of the Chumash system.

STATES   State-level political organizations are of a qualitatively different scale from tribes and chiefdoms. Early state-level societies (analytically separate from contemporary, industrialized states) were all based on intensive agriculture. They were complex societies with a large population (up to millions), the presence of cities, some form of formal record keeping (e.g., writing), monumental architecture, and specialization (Adams 2001). All early states had a set of codified laws and central authority, or a ruling elite with sole authority to enforce laws and make war (e.g., Childe 1942; Steward 1955). Early states also had full-time administrators, a full-time military, controlled storage facilities, defined citizenship, and a system of taxation. Many early states had an official religion and standardized temple architecture visible in the archaeological record.

The criteria used to define a state demonstrate the sociopolitical complexity of the society and the ability of the rulers to mobilize labor, calling on the populace to accomplish important tasks such as road building and military campaigns. States have complex infrastructures—bureaucracies that can serve and control the population, sufficient resources to feed the many people who are not food producers, and other complex organizations. All known early states were based on a system of grain agriculture that produced surpluses sufficient to support the political and social organization. In Mesopotamia, the grains were wheat and barley; in China, rice; and in Mesoamerica and Peru, maize.

The labor required to construct facilities for public or ritual use can serve as a measure of social and political organization. Consider, for instance, the labor needed to construct barrows (a Neolithic burial mound), henges (above-ground stone monuments), irrigation systems, and stone building blocks. Estimates of labor requirements can be used to make hypotheses about the organization and logistics required to support the labor force and their projects, which reflect the complexity of the political system. As an example, a small barrow requiring 10,000 hours to construct could be completed in about 10 days by 100 people working 10-hour days, well within the capabilities of many nonstratified societies. However, Monk's Mound at the Cahokia site in North America required some 3 million hours to construct and would have required a much more complex, stratified sociopolitical system.

Some Theories of the Origin of States

Questions about the origin and development of early states are among the most enduring in archaeology. Archaeologists want to know when and where states formed and under what circumstances. Also important are questions about the operation and diversity of early states (Feinman and Marcus 1998). Making the task difficult is the fact that early states had few or no written records, although it is generally known where and when early states in various regions of the world formed. The early states of Egypt, Mesopotamia, China, the Indus River, Mesoamerica, and Peru, for example, appear on the Location Map on page 290. However, the causes underlying state formation are not yet clear. A number of theories regarding the conditions under which early states formed have been advanced and fall into three basic explanations: irrigation, warfare, and multicausal models. Table 11.3 summarizes the three main theories about the cause of state formation and some elements of each explanation.

table 11.3

Some Theories of State Formation

THEORY	MAJOR ELEMENTS
Irrigation	The competition for and need to control water for irrigation of fields led to the need for complicated management and eventually the need for a state-level sociopolitical organization to manage and protect water.
Warfare	Highly productive and prosperous agricultural systems became targets for conquest, leading to the necessity to create and maintain a military to defend and to conquer, leading to a state-level organization.
Multicausal	State formation was the result of a number of factors, including the need to control water, warfare, and trade. Each state would have had its own developmental trajectory.

In 1957, Karl Wittfogel proposed the *hydraulic theory.* According to this theory, water for irrigation was such a critical resource that state-level organizations emerged to ensure its control (Wittfogel 1957). In some instances, Wittfogel argued, competition for water led to the development of irrigation management systems and even military organizations to protect water sources. Many researchers have rejected the hydraulic model (e.g., Hunt 1988); others (e.g., Price 1994) have argued that it still has utility.

A second general model of state formation is warfare, in which competition or outright warfare is seen as a powerful incentive to organize. Warfare between political entities, particularly over critical resources, may have had a major influence on the development of complex organizations (Carneiro 1970; Cohen 1984). According to this theory, highly productive and prosperous agricultural systems would have become targets for conquest, necessitating the creation and maintenance of a military to defend and to conquer, leading to a state-level organization. For example, spectacular finds near Xianyang, China—the tomb of an early emperor guarded in death by a huge army made of clay—have identified military organization and warfare as key factors in the formation of early states and empires in Asia (Highlight 11.2).

Last, some researchers (e.g., Adams 1966; Butzer 1976) have suggested state formation probably was due to several factors, rather than a single cause. Warfare, irrigation, trade, and demographic factors would have interacted to stimulate the development of the complex social and political organizations that characterize the state. According to this multicausal model, each state would have had its own developmental trajectory unique to its environment and history.

Empires—states that dominated other polities—formed later. Many empires were the result of military expansion to control the resources, raw materials, labor, goods, and services of other groups. Some empires were less militaristic but still controlled the resources of, and exercised political power over, other groups.

Interpreting Past Belief Systems

As noted earlier in this chapter, each culture has its own worldview, the shared framework of assumptions about how the world works. Worldview forms a system of beliefs about all aspects of culture, including the nature and role of the supernatural in human affairs, the proper structure of the human-controlled world, and the way the culture should be organized. Belief systems contain a number of components, including religion, art, cosmology, iconography, and philosophy.

Religious Organization and Expression

Religions are coherent systems of shared beliefs in supernatural powers, beings, and forces, based on faith. Religions function in part to explain the world, to prescribe values, to assert social control, and to ensure harmony between humans and the supernatural. Learning about the religious beliefs of a past culture helps us gain a better understanding of people's basic relationship with their environment, their value system, their treatment of others, and justifications for their actions and activities.

HIGHLIGHT **11.2**

The Terra-Cotta Army

In 1974 a farmer digging a well in central China discovered a life-size statue of a soldier made from terra-cotta, a type of ceramic. The farmer called local officials, who contacted the local archaeological authority. The initial archaeological investigation revealed a large number of these soldiers, standing in military formation (Ch'in Ping 1996; Wenli 1996). A major excavation was undertaken, and some 7,000 life-size, fully armed statues of soldiers and horses were eventually discovered. Each soldier had a weapon, and accompanying the army were terra-cotta horses pulling some 100 wooden chariots. Each of the statues has unique individual features, thought by some to represent the individual soldiers of the emperor's actual army. The figures represent a complete military force—infantry, archers, cavalry, and chariots.

The site is located about 20 miles from the ancient Chinese capital of Xianyang and about a mile from the tomb of Qin Shi Huangdi, the first emperor of China, who united the country in 221 BC and died in 210 BC. The emperor is buried beneath a huge earthen pyramid that has never been excavated, so its contents and condition are unknown. Nearby are associated tombs, burials, structures, and other features. The scale of this tomb complex, with all of its associated features, attests to the enormous power wielded by the state and the emperor, who commanded and supported a huge force of skilled artisans, architects, engineers, soldiers, and laborers. The resources devoted to the construction of this project must have been enormous.

Several other groups of terra-cotta warriors have been found. During construction of the airport used to bring tourists to the original find, archaeologists discovered a second terra-cotta army of thousands of 2-foot-high warriors, this one belonging to the fifth emperor of the Han Dynasty. Yet another terra-cotta army, with some 40,000 statues, was later found near the tomb of Emperor Jingdi and Empress Wang (157 to 141 BC). Most recently, a new army of many thousands of 1-foot-tall soldiers in battle formation has been discovered in a Han Dynasty tomb 300 miles south of Beijing and is currently being excavated (Lobell 2003). More such armies undoubtedly await discovery.

CRITICAL **THINKING** QUESTIONS

1. What level of political organization can be inferred from the terra-cotta army? What are the characteristics of that level of political organization?
2. How can the origins of political unification be interpreted on the basis of finds like the terra-cotta army? What are some alternative explanations for the origin of the state?

Terra-cotta army at Xianyang, China.

Many belief systems include concepts of generalized impersonal supernatural power, such as luck, fate, or mana. Many religious systems also contain beliefs in spirit beings, deities, and objects of worship. In *animism,* deities take the form of things in nature, such as wind, rocks, trees, and animals. Bands and tribes typically have animistic belief systems. Religions of the ancient Egyptians, Greeks, Romans, and others involved a whole society of deities (*polytheism*)—gods and goddesses in human form. Formal religion and temple building for deities became a characteristic of agricultural societies. Religion based on a single deity (*monotheism*) is a recent development in human history. Some religions included the belief that living human rulers or spiritual leaders were the incarnations of gods, the basis for divine kingship.

Religious practitioners, such as priests and shamans, possess specialized knowledge and ritual paraphernalia and conduct the ceremonies necessary for the religion to function. Religious practitioners and facilities are generally separated from the secular aspect of culture through the use of symbolic dress, objects, art, and architecture. Archaeology, therefore, can contribute to the understanding of the belief systems of people of the past.

The earliest archaeological evidence of religious beliefs is deliberate burials with grave offerings. The act of intentionally burying someone, especially with offerings, is thought to demonstrate a belief in some sort of an afterlife. Of course, it is possible that the dead were buried just to dispose of the corpses in a sanitary manner, but the presence of grave goods implies that they were intended to be used by the deceased in some other existence. Other early evidence of religious beliefs may be present in rock art where the art appears to function as a way to communicate with or influence supernatural forces or deities.

The earliest known intentional burials are Neanderthal, dating from the Middle Paleolithic. Many see them as evidence of religious or ritualistic activities; others (e.g., Gargett 1989) view the "burials" as just corpse disposal. One of the best known Neanderthal burials is that of a man found in Shanidar Cave, Iraq, dating to about 50,000 years ago (Solecki 1971). Pollen analysis of the soils associated with the skeleton suggested that the man had been covered or decorated with masses of colorful flowers, such as hyacinth, bachelor's button, and hollyhock (Campbell and Loy 2002), implying that some sort of ritual was involved in the interment.

RITUAL OBJECTS AND SACRED PLACES   *Ritual* is the performance of formalized, repetitive acts that others identify as meaningful. Rituals are enacted during ceremonies that involve the use of ritual objects and places. As nonutilitarian items, ritual objects are rare, even one-of-a-kind, and so are rarely recovered from archaeological contexts. Such artifacts may have been made from unusual or valuable materials and are frequently associated with features or architecture thought to be ceremonial in purpose. Archaeologists must be cautious about assigning ceremonial value to an object simply because its function may be unclear. Examples of ritual objects include the magical wand of a shaman, the crown of a king, and sacred texts of a religion.

Places with ritual and religious significance (also referred to as sacred places) occur frequently in contemporary cultures and were certainly also important in the past. Many of these places occur as natural features on the landscape, such as mountains, groves of trees, springs, caves, and rock formations. Such sacred places figure prominently in creation and culture hero stories, like the rock formation in northern Idaho referred to by the Nez Perce Indians as "the heart of the Monster" that is believed to represent the remains of the heart that was cut out of a giant monster by the culture hero Coyote during the creation of the Northwest tribes. These features are difficult to physically identify in the archaeological record unless they were modified in some manner or local oral traditions describe and pinpoint such places. Other places, such as Stonehenge or the pyramids at Giza, were constructed by humans and contain features designed to dramatize and facilitate human goals (Stonehenge for celestial observation and ritual, the pyramids as monuments to god-kings). Modern cultures, too, have similar important sacred sites; examples could include such places as St. Peter's Cathedral in Rome, or the Grand Mosque in the city of Mecca in Saudi Arabia. Cemeteries also are important sacred places and may have been maintained, evidence of which can be observed in the archaeological record (e.g., reinterment of disturbed burials, repair of burial facilities).

Ritual may be recognized in archaeology as natural places that were altered by repetitive ritual activities or by the construction of some special architecture. Some sites exhibit symbolic and repetitive art, perhaps representing supernatural beings or events. Ritual artifacts, such as Native American power crystals, Mongolian prayer beads, or the remains of food offerings or incense burnings, may also be present at such places.

THE ARCHAEOLOGY OF BIRTH AND DEATH   The birth and death of individuals are among the most meaningful events in human experience. These events represent a passage from one state to another, from unborn to born, from living to dead. These events, along with puberty and marriage, generate religious ceremonies called *rites of passage*. Ritual activity associated with the birth of an individual may be reflected archaeologically in rock art thought to be associated with pregnancy or the birthing process.

In some cases, religious or ceremonial items may have been cached or deposited in sacred places. A classic example of this type of behavior is the use of large, natural wells—*cenotes*—in Mesoamerica, some of which have contained numerous ritual items. Human remains believed to be the result of sacrifices rather than burials have been found in cenotes (Coe 1999). To underscore their importance, cenotes were incorporated as important places within the settlement plans of some Maya cities.

Ritual behaviors also may be observed in mortuary patterns. Mortuary patterns are linked with status but also may have religious connections. For example, the orientation of the individual bodies in a burial place—let us say facing west—may have significance and may serve to differentiate populations in terms of religious values.

Beliefs about the dead can sometimes be quite intriguing. Some burial practices, such as erecting tombstones, call attention to the presence of an individual's body. In shaft-and-chamber burials, however, the underground location of a body is concealed. A narrow shaft is dug, and then a chamber is hollowed out to the side at some depth. The body is interred headfirst through the shaft and pushed in by the heels until it curls into the chamber. The very small entrance is then easily concealed. This practice is consistent with beliefs in sorcery calling for an individual's remains to be protected from an enemy's negative magic.

In Europe the bodies of some saints, most dating from the fourteenth century, are amazingly well preserved. The bodies of these individuals, known as "the Incorruptibles," were thought to have been preserved through divine intervention; thus, the state of preservation of a body was a criterion for the petition to consider the individual as a candidate for sainthood. Recent scientific studies (Pringle 2001a) of these bodies, sponsored by the Vatican, showed that in most cases the preservation could be explained by natural environmental conditions, such as unusual pH or temperature. In some cases, it was discovered that the bodies had been artificially mummified immediately after death, but records of those procedures had been overlooked or lost. As a result of the study, the Vatican no longer considers the state of preservation of the body in applications for sainthood.

Cosmology, Philosophy, and Oral Tradition

All cultures possess a system of knowledge about the origins of things, about what is right and wrong, and about what is good and bad. All cultures also have some system of communicating that knowledge to others. **Cosmology** is the understanding of one's universe, including how and why it originated, how it is organized, and how it works. Philosophical thought—the part of worldview that deals with ethics, aesthetics, values, morality, and epistemology—also is a core component of any culture. Cosmology and philosophy often are based on empirical knowledge intertwined with religious beliefs. Among peoples of the past, cosmology also was expressed in the use of astronomical symbols (Highlight 11.3) and record keeping.

Oral tradition is information that is transmitted from generation to generation through the narration of stories. Oral tradition serves to convey not only the beliefs, values, and morals of a group but also history—what happened in the past. Research into oral history can be useful in generating and testing archaeological models of the past.

In all of human history, writing has been independently invented no more than six times—in Egypt, Mesopotamia, India, the Indus Valley, China, and Central America. Law codes, warehouse inventories, temple records, business receipts, tribute tallies, tax and tariff lists, royal chronicles, and other written records constitute evidence of centralized authority and the development of states. Before 5,000 years ago, records consisted mainly of pictures drawn or carved on stone, bone, or shell. These pictures functioned much like historical paintings or newspaper photos, telling a story. Ideograms came into being when these images became simplified and generalized to stand for ideas. A palace, for instance, might be symbolized by a house with a crown over it. In some places, ideographic writing replaced simple picture writing. Ideograms became further simplified and abstracted as writing systems—first cuneiform and later *hieroglyphics,* a combination of abstracted pictures and symbols, such as the writing system used by the ancient Egyptians—developed. Pictographs, ideograms, cuneiform, hieroglyphics, scripts, and runes are all examples of written expression found in the archaeological record.

Iconography, Art, and Expression

Iconography is the use of artistic images to represent information and aspects of belief systems. The house-with-crown ideogram to represent a palace, for example, is also an icon symbolizing royal authority. Iconographic symbols express many aspects of culture, including religion, cosmology, politics, and history. Iconography is readily apparent in

HIGHLIGHT 11.3

Archaeoastronomy

From earliest times, the movements of the Sun, Moon, planets, and stars have prompted people to ask questions about the origin of the universe, and all cultures have provided explanations for the workings of the cosmos. These understandings are rooted in celestial observations and religious traditions and form the basis of how cultures view their world, as well as how ancient groups precisely measured and tracked celestial cycles and the movements of heavenly bodies. The study of ancient astronomical knowledge, practices, oral tradition, and cosmology is called **archaeoastronomy** (Aveni 1981, 1993; Williamson 1981; Heggie 1982; and Krupp 1983, 1984).

The cosmos has always been of great importance for a variety of reasons. In a practical sense, precise measurements of the annual movements of celestial bodies are necessary to create an accurate calendar; it is not just a matter of counting days. Our own calendar system contains 365 days a year. We know

that it is inaccurate by about a quarter of a day, so it is necessary to insert an extra day into the calendar every fourth year, called the "leap year." The ancient Mesoamericans kept an elaborate and complicated calendar system that coordinated solar and lunar patterns with the cycles of the planet Venus; in some respects, their calendars were more precise than our own.

Navigation is another practical application for celestial knowledge. Pacific Island navigators mastered the patterns and rotational movements of the stars. This knowledge enabled them to sail their canoes for thousands of miles over the open ocean without instruments, confident that they would arrive safely at their destinations. Western navigators did not surpass this level of skill until the invention of precise instruments such as chronometers and sextants.

To many, supernatural powers inhabit the sky, often appearing as planets or stars. To the Romans, Mars was the god of war. To the Pawnees, Venus as Morning Star in the east is a powerful male creator deity, and Venus as Evening Star in the west is his counterpart, a primordial female creator. To the Maya, Venus was a fierce and ominous god who played an instrumental role in the destiny of nations. To the ancient Egyptians, the constellation Orion was Osiris, god of the dead. To the Mexica, also known as the Aztec, the stars were feared demons who might one day descend to Earth and eat people. Religious leaders have always watched the skies carefully, with good reason!

Reading the heavens requires much more than glancing skyward, so throughout antiquity,

Mexica calendar.

astronomers and astrologers devised many techniques for conducting their observations. The horizon itself serves well as an instrument for tracking the seasonal cycles of the Sun to pinpoint the solstices and equinoxes, important occasions for agricultural societies and crucial dates for keeping calendars in order. The heliacal rising (first annual appearance in the east) and setting (final annual appearance in the west) of stars similarly served to mark important calendar dates or to announce the arrival of particular annual events. In ancient Egypt, for example, the heliacal rising of the star Sirius heralded the annual flooding of the Nile.

Many archaeological sites around the world seem to commemorate horizonal alignments to important astronomical azimuths, such as solstice and equinox sunrise and sunset positions, the rising and setting points of prominent stars, and extreme angles of the Moon. Such features can take many forms, from simple rows of rocks pointed toward a solstice or equinox horizon point to entire buildings constructed and oriented to incorporate risings, settings, and culminations (highest point or arc in the sky at transit) of the Sun, Moon, planets, and stars. It has been suggested that certain ventilation shafts in the great pyramid of Khufu at Giza align with the culmination of Orion as it was 4,500 years ago and with Thuban, the "north star" at the time the pyramid was built. We know from their own writings that the Maya focused their attention on Venus, and the evidence is strong that the Palace of the Governor at Uxmal was oriented toward the southernmost rising position of that planet a thousand years ago. Perhaps the most famous of all such features is Stonehenge in England, which was aligned with the summer solstice sunrise as it was some 4,000 years ago. The possibility that more sophisticated celestial calculations could have been undertaken in that part of the world continues to generate lively debate.

Many archaeologists discount the study of ancient astronomy. Some note that the association of some feature with an astronomical entity does not demonstrate that such an association was intentional. Others argue that because these associations do not fit the perspectives of Western science, they cannot be established empirically. In addition, the rising and setting positions of celestial bodies change over time, so an alignment in antiquity, even if it could be established, would be in a different position today and difficult to reconstruct convincingly.

Although these criticisms have considerable merit, it remains clear that some sites are astronomical in nature. Computer programs available today can easily compensate for changes in celestial position, allowing rapid and accurate reconstructions of the sky as it was when particular features were built. In any case, regardless of whether Western science finds merit in these heavenly associations, they do represent the worldview and religious beliefs of peoples from the past and are cultural elements of great interest to archaeologists.

CRITICAL **THINKING** QUESTIONS

1. How would you determine whether an ancient alignment was related to an astronomical phenomenon? What measurements should be taken? How would you account for the passage of time in the location of stars today?

2. Is it necessary for the astronomy of past peoples to "agree" with contemporary scientific astronomy? Why or why not?

3. What examples in this Highlight would be classified as examples of iconography?

Upper Paleolithic cave art, carved figurines, and decorated artifacts. The stick figure, for instance, is an icon for human.

Some iconography is complex and conveys substantive information. Some of the first writing systems, such as those developed by the Egyptians and the Maya, were hieroglyphics based on the use of icons. Icons remain important tools, part of an increasingly global system of communication conveying messages of power, functionality, direction, identity, and the like.

Numerical systems are iconographic. Most cultures have developed systems of measurement for time, for weights and measures, and for the value of materials. Archaeologists often discover evidence of standardized weights and measures used in commerce, manufacturing, and urban planning. At the site of Harappa in present-day Pakistan, for example, transportation and trade patterns can be reconstructed from street dimensions, wheel ruts in the pavement, and features of gateways in and out of the walled settlement. It is clear that wagon axles uniformly were made a particular length, and wheels a particular size, to pass through the city's few gates. Also, special platforms and large counterweights at gateways suggest that traffic was regulated. Perhaps officials admitted travelers, examined and weighed wagon loads, and collected tolls, tariffs, or customs duties.

Calendric systems apparently are quite ancient and may have been depicted on Paleolithic rock art. The movements of the Sun and Moon, the changing seasons, solstices, and other astronomical events were tracked by ancient peoples, and archaeologists have found that some natural features, such as caves, were modified as observatories for tracking the sky. In other cases, archaeologists have discovered that constructed facilities were aligned to mark astronomical events and so measure time (see Highlight 11.3).

Iconography and art are related and easily confused. **Art,** the creation of aesthetic objects, is both expressive and symbolic, both abstract and representational. Art may be ruled by conventions and be highly stylized, such as the art of ancient Egypt, or art may be very individual in form and style. All art of a society reveals a great deal of cultural information, however, including cultural values and concepts of aesthetics (e.g., Gosden 2001). Nevertheless, as an accessory in the explanation of human culture, art often is enigmatic (Highlight 11.4).

Most visible in the archaeological record is **representational art,** primarily paintings, inscriptions, and sculptures. Representational art is classified descriptively in terms of its dimensions and portability. *Two-dimensional art* refers to pictorial representations on "flat" media or surfaces, such as pottery, paper, wood, cloth, plaster, basketry, and stone. *Three-dimensional art* refers to sculpture showing all sides of the subject. Representational art may be part of a permanent installation or may be small and portable enough to be carried about by an individual or otherwise transported. Portable art also may include jewelry and other items made for personal adornment. Such personal art may entail cosmetic body modifications, such as tattoos, filed teeth, removed fingers, and scarification. In many instances, body modifications served functions beyond art or decoration and may have involved aspects of ritual and religion.

Commonly studied rock art consists of designs and depictions on rock surfaces (e.g., Chippindale and Taçon 1998; Whitley 2001). Most rock art is in the form of *petroglyphs,* depictions pecked into stone, or *pictographs,* depictions painted onto the stone surface.

HIGHLIGHT **II.4**

Art and Archaeology in Africa

We have difficulty explaining the meaning and intent of our own art in our own time, so it is not surprising that our difficulties increase when the art objects are artifacts of bygone ways of life. Some simple conclusions certainly can be drawn. Here are a few examples. South African rock art clearly depicts hunters with simple curved bows identical to the tools that the San of recent times use to power arrows and drills and to make music. In contrast, North African rock art indicates that hunters in the Saharan culture (about 5000 BC) used more powerful double-recurved bows. Also, South African rock art suggests a fascination with the eland, and this interest is confirmed by the complex of tales associated with this species of antelope in San folklore. Saharan art indicates that the people were at one time pastoralists, herding cattle. The artists' renderings of cattle and wild animals inform us of a period in which the area that is now desert was extensive grassland.

More recent sub-Saharan art can yield similar information, but it is difficult to carry interpretations beyond the obvious. Traditional African art comes in many media—wood, ivory, eggshell, ceramics, metals, pigments, cloth, glass, stone, horn. Factors of preservation in tropical climates result in the loss of most of these materials over time, so we have a truncated view of the full artistic repertoire of archaeological cultures. However, even in recent cultures, full interpretation usually is not possible. We can understand the function of a ladle, but what do we say of that ladle when its bowl is the downturned head of a woman and its long, thin shaft is a representation of the female body?

Contemporary traditional African art is, in a very general sense, "functional." Spoons, stools, and neck rests (used as "pillows") have obvious functions, but most such objects are also used in ritualistic proces-

Bronze heads and tusks in Benin shrine.

sions, in shrines, or as protective icons. The artists make them, and remake them, following traditional patterns that validate their ritualistic function, and the creation of the art becomes part of the larger ritual. In many cases, the artist's own explanation is "That is just the way it is done"; there is no active knowledge of the detailed meaning of the traditional symbolism.

It must be emphasized, however, that the African artist was not a mere traditionalist—one who copies. African art is replete with variation. Although there were "canons" of art—general patterns that artists followed—individuals were capable of unique fluidity, treating the human form in a completely plastic way by expanding or contracting body parts to emphasize what they desired to show. Africa has yielded beautiful "realistic" art—the sculpted heads of Ife, for example, which must be portraits—but African artists also created abstractions of the human form

HIGHLIGHT **11.4** *continued*

that inspired Western art to take new directions a century ago.

Art permeated African societies. The kingdom of Benin, renowned for its royal art, is an excellent example. The Oba, or king, was served by three sets of chiefs. Of these, the "palace chiefs" directly served the king and his family. One group of palace chiefs, the Iwebo chiefs, were responsible for protecting and maintaining the royal regalia and the shrines to ancestral kings. These shrines, decorated with stylized bronze heads and ornately carved elephant tusks, are major repositories of royal art (Willet 1993).

The Iwebo chiefs also supervised the craft guilds that produced the royal art, and they administered trade as well. A major function of trade was to obtain artistic materials, such as red coral and cowrie shells. There were 68 craft guilds in all, founded by past kings, and membership in a guild was hereditary. Specialties included ironworking, bronze casting, ivory and wood carving, and leather working.

The organization of art in Benin society reflected a state-based social and political organization (Willet 1993). The presence of royal art and guild activity areas in Benin and other archaeological sites has helped researchers to interpret the prehistoric development of early African kingdoms.

CRITICAL **THINKING** QUESTIONS

1. What kinds of information can we confidently infer from art in archaeological contexts?
2. What kind of information is more difficult to infer from archaeological evidence of art alone, and why?
3. Why might the concepts of functional art, representational art, and abstract art not apply in African art or in the art of prehistoric peoples anywhere?
4. How can "art" objects help archaeologists to interpret the culture of peoples of the past?

Geoglyphs—large-scale images or designs made by removing soil or by piling rocks to create lines or designs—are less common but can be spectacular. The famous geometric lines in the Nasca Valley of Peru are an example. Identifying and recording geoglyphs is a challenge for archaeologists even in the best of circumstances.

The images, or individual elements, carved or painted on stone are natural animal and human forms (zoomorphs and anthropomorphs, respectively) and abstract designs. These images may have served as boundary markers, family markers, important place

What does this pictograph from the Teddy Bear Cave site (CA-KER-508) in California show? What was its purpose? What did it mean to the people who made it? Analyzing and interpreting the function and meaning of artistic representations is part of the archaeology of symbol systems. Interpreting the iconography and art of people of the past is also a concern of cognitive archaeology, which emphasizes reconstructing the motivations and intentions of ancient peoples. How might a pictograph like this be made into ideograms—the forerunners of written language?

markers, magical symbols for hunting or other purposes, religious images, historical narratives, or simply art for art's sake. Some designs may represent images seen by people during trances or under the influence of hallucinogens. Some rock art may be graffiti.

Rock art can be difficult to date, but it is possible to radiocarbon date the organic materials used to make the paint. Petroglyphs can be dated relatively from the patina that formed on the surface of the rock after the elements were pecked. Some images may relate to known dates, as in the case of horse elements on rock art from the Plains of North America. Images of horses must postdate AD 1700 because horses were not in that region of North America until after that time.

A great deal of attention has been given to cave art dating from the Upper Paleolithic in Europe. A history of interpretation of this art shows how thought on the archaeology of symbols has evolved (Robb 1998:335–336). When first discovered, cave art was seen as having a magical purpose, to increase success in hunting and fertility, or as band or clan symbols. Some believed that the paintings were art for art's sake. Later interpretations were that the paintings represented relationships between male and female animals, possibly as a model of human or animal behavior, possibly as instructional materials for young hunters. More recently, it has been suggested that shamans may have produced at least some of the paintings during trances.

Remembering the Individual

Although art is a cultural manifestation, it is made by individual artists with their own intentions and techniques. The creation of certain artifacts and styles of decoration can be attributed to individuals. In addition, many technological items, such as projectile points, were manufactured by individuals. Analyses of such items can reveal a great deal about individual craftsmen, their skills, handedness, and beliefs and values.

Archaeological sites contain other evidence of the behaviors of individuals, including how they interacted with one another within a group. Much of the analysis in archaeology deals with average group behaviors, and from such evidence researchers construct models of past cultures. Thus, a great deal of archaeological interpretation is biased toward the group. However, there also have been many efforts to learn about actual individual people (e.g., Hill and Gunn 1977), their behaviors, lives, families, and beliefs.

One of the difficulties in this line of investigation is distinguishing individual behaviors from the behavioral patterns of the overall group. The most direct approach is through the analysis of burials, the remains of actual people. The analysis of skeletal material can tell us about individual health, disease, diet, status, and occupation. DNA analysis even makes it possible to determine biological relatedness between individuals. In addition, paleofeces can produce information about the diet, cuisine, and health of an individual. Further, the fingerprints of individuals are sometimes found in sites (e.g., in clay) and can be used to differentiate children from adults (Kamp et al. 1999) and to associate specific individuals with specific activities (Åström and Eriksson 1980). As archaeologists learn how to identify material culture (e.g., toys), symbols, and how children use space, the ability to detect children in the archaeological record is improving (Kamp 2001; Baxter 2005).

Some archaeologists seek to empathize with past individuals and what their lives must have been like. These archaeologists combine their knowledge of human nature, knowledge of the society and culture under study, ethnographic analogy, and material evidence in the archaeological record as a basis for imagining the individual behavior that produced that evidence. The result may be mere speculation or a model that can be tested or verified through further study. The following field note from an archaeological site in Botswana is an example of remembering the individual in this way:

This is clearly an activity area for making ostrich-shell beads. Shards of ostrich eggshell form a kind of midden and the concentrations of beads in different stages of manufacture is terrific. I think the person brought the ostrich eggshells to this area already broken—the contents would have been prepared as food in another place. The association with food makes me think this was a woman. The people here don't make beads of any kind today, although sewing is man's work and stringing beads might have been regarded as a form of sewing. But as the chief foragers, women probably found the ostrich eggs in the first place, and only the women wore these beads, so in lieu of other evidence, I'm going to say "she." She and her children and perhaps a sister would have found the eggs a few miles from their winter camp, assuming ostrich came to breed there as they do now. The people wouldn't have had to walk as far then—the region was wetter and would have supported ostriches better. So they brought the eggs home, cooked them, and cleaned out the shells. Then they carried the shells here to this bead making area in their summer camp. The woman would have had some leisure to make beads then.

She punched out disks for beads from the eggshell shards, using templates to get uniform size. It looks like there were three sizes, intended to be strung with the largest pieces in the center and the smallest at the ends, much as beads are strung everywhere today. Interesting! Either there is a near-universal aesthetic at work here or else the comparative size of the beads on a string has some functional advantage. Anyway, judging by the distribution of beads in the area, she must have established a production line, and she certainly would have had company or helpers, including her younger children.

The woman punched out a bunch of the roughly circular disk-like forms first and made a pile of them before going on to the next step. Then she and her helpers punched a hole in the center of each form, although we didn't find the tools for this here. Probably a bone punch was used or an animal tooth, rather than stone, because of the delicate material.

Beads that broke in the process of being holed were immediately discarded into another pile, and it looks like this happened a lot, especially with thinner parts of the shell. I wonder if the woman's children broke a lot of beads trying to learn how to make holes. There's also a small cache of discarded beads where in every one the hole is off-center! But in the few necklaces found elsewhere more or less intact, the beads all have neatly centered holes, so clearly a standard of manufacture was applied. It looks like as many as one in three or four beads didn't make the cut.

There are a lot of small flat and curved palm-sized stones in the activity area. I think they were used as surfaces against which to punch out and hole the beads, and I'll bet the woman experimented with different stones to try to reduce the wastage. In my own experiments I get the best results (still bad by any standard) punching holes with a very small flat stone on a firm but pliable surface like my palm.

Some of the stones in the area also have wear from abrasion. So after she accumulated a pile of forms with acceptable holes the woman then switched to finishing the beads, grinding their edges to make them perfectly smooth and circular. Beads that broke in this production process were discarded on top of the beads that broke before when the holes were being made.

And, I realize, because of the strong likelihood of breakage, it made perfect sense to make the holes first before attempting to round out and finalize the forms.

Interestingly, there are no perfect beads anywhere in the area! So the enterprise must have been successful. Nor is there evidence of stringing activity. Maybe the beads were carried away to be strung in another area or were distributed in reciprocity or trade for stringing by others. Maybe the beads themselves were multifunctional and served as objects of wealth or value. The woman and her helpers would have used processed animal sinews for stringing, and she would have had to negotiate for this from the men. The men butchered the animals, cleaned the hides and sinews, cured them with milk, and pegged them out to dry. And typically the men and their sons kneaded the hides to soften them and make them pliable.

For sewing, the sinews would have been stiffened again with bee's wax. If the beads were strung in the bead making activity area, I would expect to find a tiny awl or two for punching the wax-coated sinew through the holes and working the small knots between each bead. But there are no tools other than the platform stones—just little piles of shell shards, bead blanks, bead rejects, and broken beads, leaving me to wonder if the woman and her daughters laughed together here, punched their palms by accident like I did, and walked away from this place wearing necklaces of the beads they made.

CONTENT SELECT

Search articles in the ContentSelect database using the key word *archaeology of gender*. How do those articles define archaeology of gender? What are some examples of ways that sex and gender are evidenced in the archaeological record? Why might it be important in archaeological intreperation to consider characteristics such as sex, gender, age, social status, race, and ethnicity?

Chapter Summary

All past cultures had a social system—a structure and organization for social, economic, and political purposes—that leaves a signature in the archaeological record. Interpreting past cultural systems and their varied expressions is an important step in understanding human behavior. Culture includes the worldview of people of the past, reflected in their artifacts and the patterns of their activities in the archaeological record.

Cognitive archaeology interprets how people thought, what their motivations and expectations were, and how that thinking was reflected in the content and patterning of their material culture. People used symbols to communicate and to organize and regulate their relations with others and with supernatural forces and entities. Most materials recovered from the archaeological record are utilitarian, but many are also symbolic and reflect the worldview of the culture that produced them. The same is true of the organization of a society—how people used space and time and established social institutions such as religion.

Social systems include kinship and the social groupings that result. Patterns of marriage, residence, and household organization in social systems can be investigated. Individuals and groups have roles and statuses, however obtained, and all societies are stratified to some extent by age, sex, and gender. Egalitarian societies have little social inequality compared with highly stratified societies. Gender roles and ethnic identity also can be investigated in archaeology.

In small-scale, egalitarian hunter-gatherer societies, political organization commonly is at the band level. As the economic base enlarges and population size and social complexity increase, political organization tends to become more complex, leading to the formation of tribes, chiefdoms, and states. Intensive agriculture was accompanied by the rise of states, although the origin of states remains an important archaeological question. Early states feature extensive division and specialization of labor, organized religion, monumental architecture, and the use of armies.

Religion and ritual are important in all cultures, to explain the physical world, to establish control, and to maintain relationships with the supernatural. Religious practitioners from shamans to priests control knowledge and retain the paraphernalia for conducting ceremonies and cures. Sacred objects and places are common in the archaeological record, although recognizing them and determining their significance is difficult.

Art contains a great deal of information about a culture, and much evidence of art is present in the archaeological record. Most such evidence comes from representational art, including painting, inscription, and sculpture. Rock art is a common art form in the archaeological record, as are some sculpture and objects for personal adornment. The interpretation of iconography embedded in art is an important goal in archaeology. Archaeologists also are interested in learning about other belief systems of past cultures, including cosmology and philosophy. Such beliefs were commonly encoded into oral tradition and later in written form.

The individual behaviors of actual people in the past often are difficult to detect, for the interpretation of much of the archaeological record focuses on the activities of groups and larger populations. Nevertheless, individuals are important and can be studied through a variety of means, including analysis of the craftsmanship of artifacts, paleofeces, DNA, and the skeletons of the people themselves.

Key Concepts

archaeoastronomy, 312
art, 314
band, 303
chiefdom, 303
cognitive archaeology, 292
cosmology, 311

direct historical approach, 302
iconography, 311
mortuary analysis, 296
nonstratified society, 296
oral tradition, 311
polity, 303

representational art, 314
state, 303
stratified society, 296
symbols, 292
tribe, 303
worldview, 292

Suggested Readings

If you want to learn more about the concepts and issues discussed in this chapter, consider looking at the following resources. (Some may be rather technical.)

Claassen, Cheryl. (2002). "Gender and Archaeology." In *Archaeology: Original Readings in Method and Practice*, Peter N. Peregrine, Carol R. Ember, and Melvin Ember, eds., pp. 210–224. Upper Saddle River, NJ: Prentice Hall.

Claassen briefly discusses the progress made in investigating gender in the past. She also deals with the ongoing process of engendering the profession of archaeology—that is, increasing the number of women participating in archaeology.

McGuire, Randall H., and Robert Paynter (eds.). (1991). *The Archaeology of Inequality.* Oxford: Blackwell.

This book contains a series of papers that deal with social organization, domination, resistance, and inequality between Native Americans, blacks, and Europeans in North America during historical times. This book helps readers understand many of the inequality-based issues people are still faced today.

Nelson, Sarah Milledge. (2004). *Gender in Archaeology: Analyzing Power and Prestige* (2nd ed.). Walnut Creek, CA: AltaMira Press.

Nelson, Sarah Milledge (ed.). (2006). *Handbook of Gender in Archaeology.* Lanham, MD: AltaMira Press.

In the last few decades, the study of gender, and of others such as children, in past societies has exploded, and there are many books and articles on the subject. These are some of the most recent state-of-the-art discussions of the various issues and problems in gender studies.

Price, Neil (ed.). (2001). *The Archaeology of Shamanism.* New York: Routledge.

Price brings together a collection of papers that deal with the difficult subject of archaeological investigation into religion and cognition. The papers address issues such as the material record left by shamanistic activities, social perception of animals, rock art, and cognitive neuroscience. Another interesting article in this area is "The Archaeology of Symbols" by John E. Robb (1998, *Annual Review of Anthropology* 27:329–346), where it is proposed that cognitive systems be broken down into components that can be approached by archaeologists in a systematic manner. Both of these works provide insight into how cognitive archaeology is investigated.

Schmidt, Robert A., and Barbara L. Voss (eds.). (2000). *Archaeologies of Sexuality.* New York: Routledge.

The book deals with the investigation of sex in the past, including sexual practice, the representation of sexuality, and the roles of gender in both prehistoric and historic societies. Examples are taken from medieval and prehistoric Europe, the ancient Maya, ancient Egypt, and convict-era Australia.

Scott, Elizabeth M. (ed.). (1994). *Those of Little Note: Gender, Race, and Class in Historical Archaeology.* Tucson: University of Arizona Press.

For those interested in the study of gender and others from the perspective of historical archaeology, start with this book.

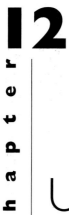

Understanding Culture Change

FOR AT LEAST 12,000 years, native peoples have lived in the interior of western North America. These people were dependent on the hunting and gathering of plants and animals, including grass seeds, various roots, rabbits, deer, and bighorn sheep. A particularly arid portion of this region is the Mojave Desert, where small groups lived for millennia with relatively simple technology. Important among their tools were hunting implements, which for many thousands of years were dominated by a weapons system called the atlatl and dart. The dart, which is similar to a large arrow or spear, is thrown with the aid of the atlatl (Figure 12.1).

At some point in time, the bow and arrow generally replaced the atlatl and dart in North

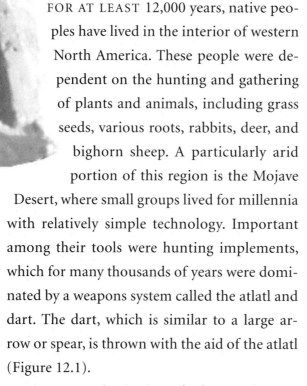

America. We know this because bow and arrow technology was being used when the first Europeans arrived in the 1500s, although some groups, such as the Mexica, were still using the atlatl. What is not known is when the replacement took place. Most of the components of these weapons were constructed of wood, bone, feathers, or sinew, materials not commonly recovered from archaeological sites. Thus, dating the weaponry—and therefore the change—has been difficult. What have been recovered are the flaked stone projectile points used on darts and arrows, which can provide dating through stratigraphic and typological analyses.

The question of the timing of the introduction of the bow and arrow depends on two things: (1) being able to recognize the change in technology from dart to arrow and (2) being able to date that change. Because the analysis of known darts and arrows consistently indicates that dart points are larger than arrow points (as darts are larger than arrows), the idea that stone points found in archaeological sites can be typed by size forms a working hypothesis. From the study of other archaeological sites throughout the Americas, it is known that dart points tend to be earlier in time and arrow points tend to be later. Therefore, to researchers investigating the timing of the introduction of the bow and arrow in a particular area, a clear shift from large projectile points to small ones should be evident.

To test this hypothesis, it would be necessary to locate and excavate a site with a cultural deposit containing both large and small points, and the transition between

Robert Yohe at the Rose Spring site.

the two point sizes would need to be dated. The site would need to be one where people lived for a long time, so that evidence for the change would be detectable. In addition, datable materials from the site, such as organic matter suitable for radiocarbon dating, would be needed.

Based on work conducted in the 1950s and 1960s, the Rose Spring site in eastern California, shown in the chapter opening photograph, was known to contain such a record. To investigate the question of the introduction of the bow and arrow, additional excavations were undertaken at the

323

site by archaeologist Robert M. Yohe II (Yohe 1992). He found an obvious change in projectile point size from large to small in a layer at the site that dated to about 1,600 years ago. This date was consistent with inferences made from observations and analyses of other sites in the region, so the hypothesis was supported. Because much of the site remains unexcavated, future researchers could return to replicate the test.

What changes in people's way of life resulted from the shift from the atlatl and dart technology to the bow and arrow? An increase in food supply and hence in population was an immediate result. The bow and arrow is a more efficient and productive means of killing game over greater distances using fewer resources. And, as you will see, there are long-term results as well.

For the location of the Mojave Desert and other sites mentioned in this chapter, see the map on page 326.

The Archaeology of Change

Change is universal, and considerable archaeological effort is exerted to document and explain cultural change. The study of change can take at least three basic approaches: The study of culture history concentrates on changes in traditions. The study of *cultural ecology* (see Chapter 9) emphasizes changes in the relationship between a society and its environment. The study of *political and social systems* (see Chapter 11) stresses changes in the relationships between social groups (Paynter and McGuire 1991:1).

Change occurs at various speeds. Sometimes it is very rapid, such as when a new political system is imposed virtually overnight by invaders. Rapid change also occurs by means of new technology (such as automobiles or computers) that radically alters how a society operates, perhaps within a single generation. Sometimes change is very slow and cultures are very stable. The archaeological record of Australia over the last 40,000 years or so demonstrates that relatively little technological change occurred during that time, although it is not yet clear what social changes may have taken place. Periods of a hundred thousand years or more with little technological change apparent to archaeologists are not uncommon in the archaeological record of early humans. People generally have always tended to be conservative culturally and to react to agents of change more than they initiate change.

Change can be viewed across space as well as over time. **Synchronic** change is change that occurs at the same general time across geographic space and can be seen in the various environments, languages, economies, and cultures that exist in different places at that time. A contemporary example of synchronic change is the global spread of technologies such as vaccination against disease, a process that involves an idea, a complex of manufactured equipment and materials, and a method. Archaeologists of the thirty-first century

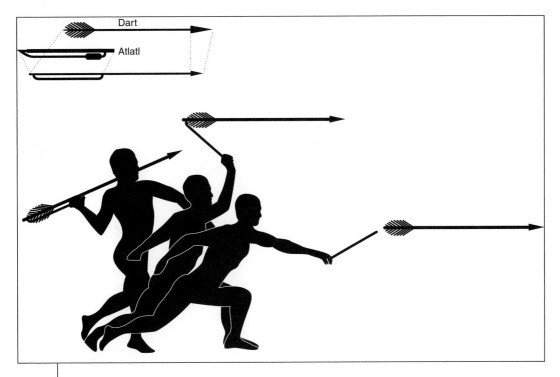

f i g u r e   1 2 . 1

Atlatl/Dart System.   The atlatl is a device used to throw a dart that resembles an over-size arrow. The atlatl affords the thrower greater leverage, speed, and accuracy than would be possible by hurling the dart by hand like a spear. The smaller and more versatile bow and arrow system replaced the atlatl and dart.

investigating people of the twenty-first century might find simultaneous evidence of this technology—syringes, hypodermic needles, traces of synthetic and organic medicinal compounds, and so on—in sites all over the globe.

Change that can be observed over time is **diachronic** change. To detect change over time, it is necessary to have information on the pattern being studied from at least two time periods. Comparisons then can be made between the various expressions of the pattern under investigation in order to detect change and to propose an explanation for that change.

The absence of change in a particular system can be just as interesting: some explanation is required to understand that as well. For instance, why did prehistoric peoples of southeast Asia lack the horse and related technologies when the ancient Chinese to the north with whom they were in contact (and who traditionally dominated them) had well-established horse-based economies? Hypotheses tend to focus on environmental factors, such as soils and vegetation in ancient southeast Asia being unsuitable for horse fodder,

L O C A T I O N   M A P :   **Sites Mentioned in Chapter 12**

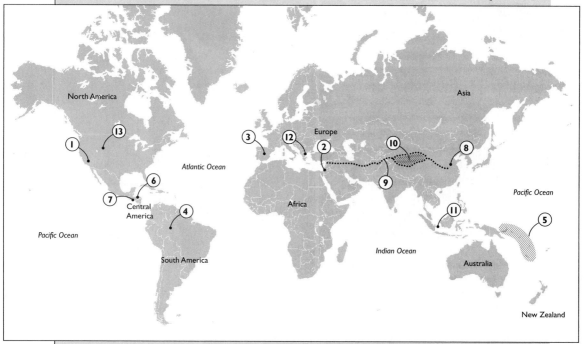

1 ■ Rose Spring
  Olancha, California

2 ■ Tell es-Sultan
  West Bank, Jordan

3 ■ Brivet River
  France

4 ■ Caverna da Pedra Pintada
  Brazil

5 ■ Lapita culture
  Pacific Islands

6 ■ Puerto Escondito
  Honduras

7 ■ Ceren
  El Salvador

8 ■ Lion Mountain
  Jiangsu, China

9 ■ Great Silk Road
  Asia

10 ■ Tarim Basin
  Xinjiang Vygur, China

11 ■ Belitung Island
  Malay peninsula, Indonesia

12 ■ Thermopylae
  Greece

13 ■ Little Bighorn battlefield
  Wyoming

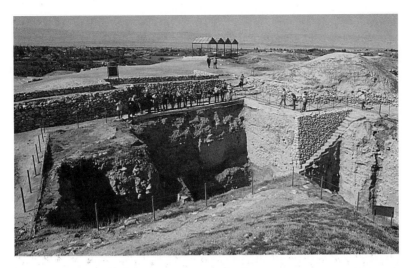

The Book of Joshua in the Old Testament mentions the fall of the walls of Jericho in Israel's conquest of Canaan over 3,500 years ago. According to archaeologist Kathleen Kenyon, the walls of Jericho (Tell es-Sultan) actually were constructed and destroyed seventeen times—by erosion and earthquake as well as by warfare. The site was inhabited and abandoned discontinuously numerous times during Stone Age, Early Bronze Age, Middle Bronze Age, and Late Bronze Age occupations. Today, Tell es-Sultan in Jordan continues to reveal the secrets of culture change in the prehistory of the region.

not to mention tropical heat and disease pathogens that might have been unfavorable to horses. There are many instances in history and prehistory when people did not adopt a technology because they lacked either the opportunity or the basic prerequisites.

Archaeologists seek to document change, place it in context, and attempt to explain it—tasks that are often difficult. Change can be viewed at many levels, from changes in single items or particular events, to short-term patterns of events, to long-term transformation (Renfrew and Bahn 2004:470–471). Short-term change is usually the most difficult to recognize in the archaeological record because the material record of change is often masked by the mixing of archaeological deposits and by the difficulty of precisely dating materials and events. Thus, most archaeological models of change deal with relatively long-term change.

Consider one of the more dramatic changes in prehistory: the shift from hunting and gathering to agriculture. Excavations at Tell es-Sultan, better known as Jericho (see the Location Map on page 326), revealed an occupation of the site beginning in late Mesolithic times (ca. 11,000 BP) and spanning the development of agriculture and the growth of cities and urban life (Kenyon 1957, 1979; Bartlett 1982). At Jericho, more than 20 distinct layers have been identified. The earliest inhabitants (called the "Natufians") hunted near the oasis at Jericho, but as plants and animals became domesticated, people settled near the oasis and began to construct permanent dwellings. They eventually developed pottery and fortifications against attack. The early town was not planned out, so the structures were scattered about. By the Bronze Age, a well-planned community had emerged. Jericho contains some of the earliest evidence in the region for agriculture, permanent architecture, pottery, fortifications, and urban life, all within a single site.

Systems Theory

One traditional approach to the study of change is **systems theory** (Flannery 1968). As you read in Chapter 11, cultures have various subsystems, such as economy, politics, and settlement, that are interrelated and articulate with one another in complex ways. The complete cultural system operates in a kind of equilibrium under a set of rules influenced by cultural and noncultural conditions at that time. As conditions change, the way a particular subsystem operates may also change, disrupting the equilibrium and necessitating change in other subsystems to reach a new equilibrium. In other words, change in one subsystem has a ripple effect on all of the other subsystems, resulting in a new cultural condition. Thus, "culture change comes about through minor variations in one or more [sub]systems which grow, displace or reinforce others and reach equilibrium on a different plane" (Flannery 1967:120).

Using systems theory, archaeologists can study change by examining each of the various subsystems, determining the change in each, and then analyzing how that change influenced or altered the overall system. For example, the introduction of the bow and arrow undoubtedly had profound effects on the culture of the people in and around the Rose Spring site. Assuming that bows and arrows increased hunting efficiency, researchers can draw several inferences: Hunters killed more animals, thereby increasing the food supply as well as the carrying capacity of the area. As a result of the abundance of food, human populations grew dramatically, placing a greater demand on other resources, such as plant foods and living space. The technology for acquiring and processing plant food then became more complex or more efficient, such that the settlement pattern changed to accommodate the different plant and animal procurement needs. Ultimately, the increase in population may have necessitated changes in social and political organization. A model of such relationships could be constructed to predict these changes, and the various subsystems could be analyzed to test it.

Evolutionary Approaches

In biological evolution, traits possessed by a population of organisms may be selected for or against, depending on whether they are adaptive to particular environmental conditions. Traits selected against will eventually be deleted from the population in favor of traits that are adaptive, and the overall group of traits that characterizes the population changes over time. In a general sense, a trait in an organism can be equated with a trait in a culture—such as a technology, an organizational structure, or a food choice—and an organism may be equated with the culture itself. Thus, given this evolutionary analogy, cultural traits could be subjected to selective pressures ultimately resulting in change in—or even the extinction of—human cultures.

As you saw in Chapter 2, early anthropologists, including archaeologists, embraced the concept of biological evolution, applying it to cultures. Although the early model of unilinear cultural evolution ultimately was abandoned, it remains clear that cultures do evolve—that is, they change over time through adaptation. Precisely how and why this happens is not clear, and these continue to be important questions.

Archaeologists have adopted and applied the basic tenets of evolutionary theory in an attempt to understand how cultures adapt and change. One line of investigation is evolutionary ecology, discussed in Chapter 9. A more narrow approach is **evolutionary archaeology,** the study of the human past from the strict perspective of Darwinian evolution (Maschner 1996; O'Brien 1996; O'Brien and Lyman 2000; Leonard 2001; Shennan 2002). Evolutionary archaeology attempts to explain cultural change as the result of direct selective processes on the variation of artifact types and frequencies, resulting in the change of those types and frequencies over time.

For example, in 1996 archaeologists excavated about 50 dugout canoes built by Late Bronze Age people in central France along the Brivet River. The canoes show great variety in shape, size, and length. Some were dug from whole logs, and some were crafted from several pieces of timber from different trees. Some had rope holes for mooring and anchoring and showed traces of repair; others contained net weights, oars, or paddles, suggesting a variety of uses. One can only speculate about the conditions or events that caused the people to abandon their boats, which were quickly covered by river silt and preserved. In any event, to an evolutionary archaeologist the variation in the "population" of boats represents the variety on which evolution operates. Studying the changes in the boats over time would show which styles, methods, and materials were most successful in the "competition" to be selected as a boat. In its extreme form, evolutionary archaeology ascribes all change to these selection processes, with little or no consideration of the role of human behavior (Boone and Smith 1998:141).

Within archaeology there has been considerable debate about how closely the strict biological model of selection can be applied to the study of past cultures (e.g., Spencer 1997; Boone and Smith 1998; Lyman and O'Brien 1998; Neff 2000; Flannery 2002). Culture is a powerful force in adaptation, and any evolutionary explanation must include the role of culture, such as behavior, decision making, and political and social factors. Mechanisms of change include invention and diffusion, social and political movements, and migrations and diasporas.

Invention and Diffusion

All the technologies, ways of doing things, and systems of organization employed by people ultimately originated through either invention or innovation. **Invention** is the creation of a new type of technology, often in response to a need to accomplish some task. All technology is invented and reinvented, such as by the widely scattered individuals who first picked up stones to use as hammers; but invention also includes the combining of existing technologies in new ways, such as by hafting a stone hammer onto a wooden handle to make a more efficient tool. Closely related to invention is **innovation,** thinking up new ways of doing things by using already established methods, systems of organization, or technologies. The use of clay to make receptacles was an invention. The transfer and elaboration of that technology to other uses are examples of innovation. Basic pottery technology, for example, was applied to make plaster masks, waterproof walls, and ceramic roofing tiles.

Once inventions or innovations are developed, useful ones are adopted and ineffectual ones are dropped. Useful inventions and innovations adopted by one group may also be adopted by other groups through the process of diffusion. New technologies or ideas may be traded from one culture to another. In many cases, the recipient culture may reproduce the item or idea, perhaps in a slightly different form or by using slightly different materials. For example, we have seen that agriculture initially developed in a number of centers and then spread into other regions. As agriculture diffused, various inventions and innovations made it more efficient, new species were domesticated, and new technologies and cultural organizations developed.

Early in the twentieth century, diffusion became an easy and convenient way to explain particular phenomena, and many archaeologists believed that diffusion was the prime instrument of change. Early diffusionists argued that civilization developed in only one or two central places, such as ancient Egypt, and then spread to all of the other locations where civilizations later emerged. Subsequent research has demonstrated that this was not always the case, so diffusion is no longer an automatic explanation for the distribution of cultural traits.

Today, diffusion is but one of the possible explanations for the movement of materials and ideas. Research has also indicated that technologies, methods, and systems were sometimes developed independently in different regions through the process of **independent invention**. For example, ceramic technology was invented in both the Old and the New Worlds, and both the Maya and the Egyptians constructed pyramids. Therefore, archaeologists must always consider the possibility of independent invention when studying the distribution of traits.

Social and Political Movements

Cultures are clearly responsive and adaptive to changing external conditions, but change can also be the result of internal stimuli. In many cases, people purposefully alter their practices to achieve some social or political goal, creating a "movement" of some kind that is expressed in material culture. All social and political movements change the cultural landscape to some degree, and powerful social movements can cause substantial change. One example of this is the spread of Christianity, which radically altered the Roman Empire and changed the course of Western history. An example in prehistory is the spread of market economies using tokens of economic exchange such as cowrie shells, iron ingots, woven or knotted cloth, or coins.

Migrations and Diasporas

The movement of people from place to place is a major mechanism of change. People move for many reasons, including response to environmental, social, or political stresses, as well as population pressure. **Migration** is the actual movement of a population, such as an ethnic group, from one locality to another. Migrating people generally carry their culture with them and frequently replace, are absorbed by, or blend with an existing population. Because it is known that migrations have occurred in the past, migration must be considered a possible mechanism for major change and a possible explanation for changes in the archaeological record (Anthony 1990).

For example, in the 1990s archaeologist Anna Roosevelt, working in the Amazon River basin of Brazil, discovered evidence of a Paleoindian culture unlike others known in the Western Hemisphere, including the Andean culture to the west and the Clovis culture to the north. Those early hunters of 11,000 years ago lived in open, temperate lands where they hunted large game with stone-tipped spears. The Paleoindians of Brazil, however, had adapted to a humid tropical environment. They lived along rivers and gathered fruit, seeds, and nuts and hunted fish, birds, reptiles, amphibians, and shellfish. They also used pigments in cave art, such as the now-famous paintings in Caverna da Pedra Pintada. The evidence all points to a more extensive migration in the peopling of South America than anyone had previously thought, perhaps even a migration separate from those that led to the settlement of other parts of South America. Another good example of a migration that is evident in the archaeological record is that of the Polynesian migration, as described in Highlight 12.1.

A **diaspora** is the breaking up of a population into smaller segments that disperse into different areas without replacing the existing population. Diasporas are caused by some force or circumstance, such as war or famine. The word also refers to a forced population movement for a particular purpose, such as labor or trade (Cohen 1997). A good example of a diaspora is the forced movement and dispersal of African people in the New World as slaves.

RECONSTRUCTING POPULATION MOVEMENTS   There is no question that people moved around in the past, that they colonized new regions, that new populations replaced older ones, and that small groups of individuals moved from culture to culture. Archaeologists attempt to detect these population movements in the archaeological record and then determine when, where, how, and why they happened.

Population movements can be detected in the archaeological record through various means (Harding 1974; Rouse 1986; Clark 2001). A basic assumption is that a population (a culture) possesses a unique cultural assemblage, that it carries that assemblage with it as it moves, and that the assemblage can be identified and traced in the archaeological record (e.g., Rouse 1986:3–13). Given this reasoning, when a new ethnic group enters an area, they should bring with them (1) a new language and symbolic system, (2) new burial patterns, (3) new artifact types, (4) new settlement types, and (5) a new settlement pattern. In addition, the people themselves should be biologically (genetically) distinct. With the exception of distinct biology, each of these categories could also be explained by diffusion, and archaeologists must use caution to distinguish migration from diffusion. The greater the number of trait changes present, the stronger the case for a population movement. Finally, historical records may exist that document the population movement.

In theory, migrations of people into previously unoccupied regions should be relatively easy to detect because the earliest archaeological sites in an area would represent the initial colonization of that region. However, actually determining when the first colonists

Archaeology of Proto-Polynesian

When Captain James Cook of England explored the Pacific in the eighteenth century, he found that the languages spoken on the islands of Polynesia were so similar that even he, with his rudimentary knowledge of Tahitian, could communicate on islands separated by thousands of miles of sea. Linguists, starting with this simple observation of similarity, have used comparative techniques to illuminate the shared history of these languages. By studying historically known languages with written sources, historical linguists have developed analytical tools that help them to reconstruct languages that must have existed but have never been recorded. For example, we know that French and Spanish share many similar words because Gaul (France) and Iberia (Spain) were both part of the Roman Empire for several centuries and Latin influenced their local languages. Even though the Gauls and Iberians never wrote down the languages they were speaking before Roman occupation, we can reconstruct many aspects of their languages through careful comparison and peeling away of the Latin overlay.

Some of the changes that languages go through can be linked to specific events such the Roman conquest, but others occur naturally over time, often with systematic patterning. In theory, if these patterns can be documented, they can be reversed and an earlier language will come to light. In the history of Polynesia, one of the most common sources of change was the colonization of a new island or archipelago. Historical linguists are untangling a complicated web of degrees of contact and separation among the many islands to lead them back to Proto-Polynesian, a language spoken by the ancestors of all modern Polynesians. Proto-Polynesian is a purely reconstructed language that scholars estimate was spoken approximately 3,000 years ago in the Polynesian homeland.

Some archaeologists reject the idea of using linguistic analyses to augment their research. They may work in an area where linguists have not studied the languages, where there is no well-understood historical continuity between modern languages and the archaeological record they are studying, or where the linguistic data have previously been used poorly by archaeologists. For example, in Europe, where many Indo-European languages are spoken, Nazi attempts to use linguistic data to guide archaeologists to the remains of the "racially pure" Indo-European homeland discouraged many archaeologists from using historical linguistics data.

In Polynesia, however, many archaeologists have embraced historical linguistics as a welcome source of supplemental data against which they can cross-check models and derive inspiration. While linguists were fine-tuning their language family trees in the latter half of the twentieth century, archaeologists were systematically exploring the record of Oceanic culture history for the first time. A culture called Lapita in Melanesia, for example, left behind a distinctive archaeological pattern of dentate-stamped pottery, unique fishhooks and adzes, as well as stilt-house habitation sites dating from approximately 1600 BC. Most archaeologists now believe that members of the Lapita cultural complex arrived in Samoa, Tonga, and other nearby islands by approximately 1200 BC and that it was here they evolved from Lapita into a distinctive group that can be recognized as Polynesian. This archaeologically known culture is called Ancestral Polynesian Society (APS) (Kirch 1984).

In theory, members of the APS were speaking Proto-Polynesian, but comparing reconstructed linguistic data and archaeological data can be like comparing apples and oranges: you know you've got fruit, but what exactly does that mean? Linguistic and archaeological data can most easily be fit together in two ways. One is dating. For example, archaeologists might find a site they consider to be part of this earliest Polynesian culture and radiocarbon date the remains to AD 200. Linguists would be able to say, "Keep looking for something earlier, because Samoan and Hawaiian must have been separated by then to account for all of the differences." In the case of Proto-Polynesian and APS, the fit between archaeologically derived dates and historical linguists' dates is remarkable and has enabled archaeologists to move on to fitting their data together in the second way: through vocabularies.

One of the ways in which language ancestors are reconstructed is through vocabulary comparison. Many of the very widely shared words that can be traced to Proto-Polynesian refer to objects that can be found archaeologically. For example, most of the known modern Polynesian languages have a version of the Hawaiian word *ko'i*, which refers to a woodworking tool called an adze that is made from stone. In Tahitian the word is *to'i*, and in Tongan it is *toki*. Linguists have reconstructed a word **toki* for Proto-Polynesian. Archaeologists find adzes at APS sites, thus confirming the consistency of the model of early Polynesian lifeways.

Confirming that Polynesians were making adzes before they colonized many islands and separated linguistically may not seem like big news, but consider how this technique might be used on more complex material culture. For example, there does not seem to be a deeply held common word for *irrigation system* in Proto-Polynesian. By looking at when such a word does come into a language, archaeologists can build hypotheses about where and when such technology was invented and test the hypotheses through excavation and survey.

Reconstructed vocabularies can also give archaeologists clues about aspects of culture history that are more challenging to document directly in the archaeological record. For example, all Polynesian languages have a version of the word *ali'i*, which is Hawaiian for "chief" or "elite." In Tongan the word is *'eiki*, in Tahitain *ari'i*, in Nanumean *aliki*, and in Mangaian *ariki*. Linguists have reconstructed the word **qariki* for Proto-Polynesian. Although one cannot

Lapita culture, or APS, featured adzes. An adze is an ax-like woodworking tool with a curved blade set at right angles to the handle.

indiscriminately project modern definitions of chiefliness into the past, this reconstruction suggests that a notion of social hierarchy existed in the APS. Similarly, the ethnohistorically known concepts of "mana" and "taboo" (or sacred power and prohibitions associated with it, respectively) seem to have very deep roots in Polynesian culture history. The ability of linguists to project such fundamental aspects of the Polynesian mind-set into the past illuminates for archaeologists aspects of the APS that would be very difficult for archaeologists to otherwise discern in the archaeological record, thus greatly enhancing understanding of this fascinating period.

CRITICAL **THINKING** QUESTIONS

1. Why is comparing archaeological data with linguistic data like comparing apples and oranges?

2. In what ways can archaeological data and data from historical linguistics reinforce each other? How was this the case with Proto-Polynesian?

3. How can dating and vocabularies in historical linguistics contribute to archaeological reconstructions of ancient cultures such as the Ancestral Polynesian Society?

of a region arrived, where they came from, and why they moved into the region can be difficult. The continuing heated debate over the timing of the first entry of people into the New World is a good example of how difficult an issue this can be.

It can be much more difficult to detect migrations of new people into areas already occupied by other people. A new ethnic group that moves into an area brings their culture with them, either displacing or absorbing the existing population. Thus, the archaeological record should reflect new organizations and technologies "suddenly" replacing earlier ones. The appearance of a few new traits, however, is not enough to clearly demonstrate a migration; such an argument requires that a series of related new traits be discovered.

In a 3,100- to 2,900-year-old village site in Honduras called Puerto Escondito, for example, archaeologists found pottery in the style of the Olmec civilization, which flourished 400 miles to the northwest beginning around 3,200 years ago. Also found in the village site was pottery in the style of the Pacific Coast peoples, who lived a hundred miles farther west of the Olmec heartland between 3,000 and 2,500 years ago. The puzzle for archaeologists was to determine whether the evidence pointed to a migration of people from the Olmec heartland, a migration of people from the Pacific Coast culture, or a pattern of trade between contemporaneous peoples whose ancestors had parted company a longer time ago. These questions are still being answered, but neutron-activation analysis of the sources of clay used in the pottery supports the hypothesis that the Honduran site does not represent a population migration. That and other evidence suggests that the people were part of a long-distance trading network in which Honduran cacao beans and obsidian were traded for Olmec pots.

The immigration of individuals, or small groups of individuals, into an already populated area is even more difficult to detect given the small scale of the population movement and the likelihood that the immigrants would be absorbed by the resident population. Nevertheless, immigrants tend to retain some aspects of their original culture, and immigration can be inferred when such traits are discovered in relative isolation within the host culture. Recall from Highlight 1.1 in Chapter 1, for example, that the African population in eighteenth-century New York retained many of their burial practices and much of their religion, as evidenced by excavations at the slave cemetery.

LANGUAGE, GEOGRAPHY, AND GENETICS   One of the major traits that archaeologists examine to investigate population movements is language (Nichols 1997). Although there is currently no known way to directly recover spoken language from the archaeological record, the study of contemporary languages can reveal much about the past. An examination of the structure and content of languages can show their relatedness, much like a family tree (Figure 12.2). The structure can reveal how languages developed, where they may have originated, and when they moved, presumably along with the peoples who spoke them. This field is called **paleolinguistics.**

Archaeologist Colin Renfrew (1987) examined the structure (oral and written) of the many diverse Indo-European languages, traced the origins of that broad language group back through geographic space and time, and suggested that it originated some 8,000 years ago in what is now Turkey. Renfrew argued that one main branch of Indo-European spread west and north across Europe when farming moved into those regions,

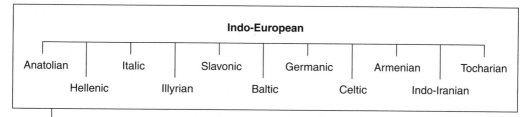

Indo-European

| Anatolian | Italic | Slavonic | Germanic | Armenian | Tocharian |

| Hellenic | Illyrian | Baltic | Celtic | Indo-Iranian |

figure 12.2

Indo-European Language Tree. The Indo-European language family contains many language groups, spread over a wide geographic area. English is one of the languages of the Germanic branch, located in northwestern Europe.

Source: Adapted from Renfrew 1987:74.

and then split into the various languages now spoken throughout most of Europe. Renfrew's critics point to reconstructed evidence that Proto-Indo-European (the ancestor of Indo-European languages) predated the advent of farming and may have had a heartland farther to the east than Turkey. In any event, the other main branch of Indo-European, according to Renfrew, spread east to India and beyond. Thus, Sanskrit and Greek share an ancestral language. As speakers of Indo-European languages spread, they displaced or absorbed many of the native peoples they encountered, leaving pockets of more ancient languages, such as the forerunners of Basque in Spain and Burushaski in Pakistan. Another example of the movement of languages and people in prehistory is that of the Bantu in Africa, as outlined in Highlight 12.2.

Studies of the geographical distribution of contemporary languages can also reveal considerable information about the movement of people in the past. For example, even a casual examination of the distribution of English would suggest that English-speakers migrated to North America, Australia, and India. A more detailed examination of the available information, including written records, would show that actual population replacements took place in North America and Australia but not in India, for elite English-speakers moved to India and took political control of the population but did not replace it. The archaeological record in the former two regions demonstrates that new technology (systems of subsistence and settlement) and a new biological population (the Europeans) suddenly appeared. In India the archaeological record shows continuity in the native archaeological pattern and a small, intrusive, and intensive European incursion epitomized by the network of British railways across India.

The study of linguistic prehistory is now being aided by *molecular biology,* the study of population genetics. Using DNA groupings, basic genetic profiles can be obtained from living individuals, and a picture of relatedness to other, geographically separate populations can be produced. From these results, a model of population movement over time can be developed. The genetic model can then be compared to a linguistic model to test and refine both.

This technique is being used to address population movements in a number of regions. Until recently, the evidence, including the languages and biological attributes of

The Bantu Migrations and the African Iron Age

The linguistic unity of much of Africa has long been recognized. With the exception of the indigenous Khoisan languages of South Africa and a diversity of Afro-Asiatic and Nilo-Saharan languages in East Africa, Bantu languages dominate the continent from the Congo River south. Languages of this family so much resemble one another that it is evident their dispersal must have been both recent and rapid, with little time for diversity to develop.

Such dispersals argue for a cause—some kind of cultural "driving force" that enabled speakers of Bantu languages to achieve success both in rapid adaptation

This map shows the six routes of Bantu groups' migration from their homeland.

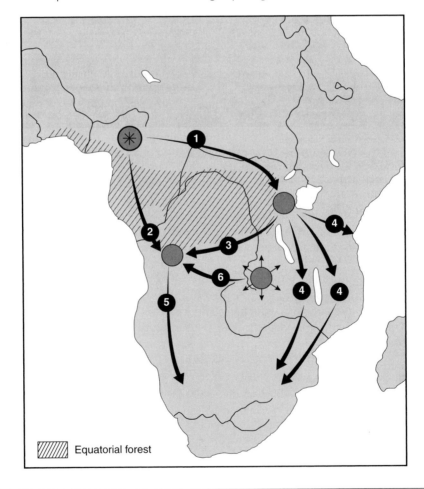

Equatorial forest

to new environments and in competition with previous inhabitants of these regions. Iron metallurgy is the usual answer to the question of what factor powered the Bantu success. According to this hypothesis, the production and use of iron tools and weapons gave Bantu populations the impetus they needed. The complete answer is far more complex.

The Bantu homeland was in the Cameroon region (see map) at the northwest extreme of the present distribution of the Bantu language family, on the fringe of early centers of agriculture and pastoralism. Proto-Bantu peoples had a lithic (stone) technology, probably herded goats, and may have farmed. Between 3,000 and 2,400 BP, these Bantu ancestors dispersed along the northern edge of the Congo forest (Route 1) and from northern neighbors absorbed knowledge of cattle, sheep, and sorghum cultivation, as well as knowledge of iron metallurgy. Other Proto-Bantu peoples moved southward across the Congo River (Route 2), apparently without acquiring the use of iron. These movements set up the ancient linguistic split between Eastern (Route 1) and Western (Route 2) Bantu.

These earliest Bantu were recipients of knowledge from other peoples, and movement was away from settled agrarian areas and toward territory thinly occupied by hunters and gatherers. Route 1 migrants settled in East Africa, where the basic components of the Early Iron Age culture were stabilized around 2,300 years ago. Later migration out of East Africa reestablished contact with Route 2 populations in the west (Route 3) and brought Bantu languages and the Iron Age into South Africa (Route 4). Western Bantu populations moved into southwest Africa (Route 5, about 1,900 BP) and, by 1,500 BP, moved toward the east (Route 6), reestablishing a broad zone of contact with Eastern Bantu populations. This junction of Eastern and Western Bantu formed a new center of dispersal from which developed the significant cultural changes and more complex societies of the Late Iron Age, broadly established throughout the African subcontinent by a thousand years ago.

Some Bantu remained in the original homeland; others eventually adapted to the forest environment, and the "arrows" of migration left populations all along their track. As a result, a large portion of Africa now speaks languages of the Bantu family. Migration was not always easy. Some early Southern Bantu (Route 4) evidently lost their cattle in the tsetse fly–infested areas through which they passed, reacquiring cattle herding from indigenous peoples (influenced by Route 5 Western Bantu) in South Africa.

Obvious major factors in Bantu expansion are the influences of non-Bantu peoples on the overall development of the Iron Age culture. Without those sources of information, the course of Iron Age development would have been greatly altered. Second, interaction among diverse Bantu groups was vital to overall development. Particularly notable were the Route 3 movement that established the Iron Age among the Western Bantu, and the Route 6 influences that led to the reformulation of Iron Age cultural patterns that were expressed in the more complex societies of Late Iron Age Africa (Phillipson 1977). The diffusion of ideas was probably a more important factor in culture change than actual population movements. Nevertheless, such movements did occur, well into historic times, such as during the Zulu wars of the nineteenth century and their aftermath.

CRITICAL **THINKING** QUESTIONS

1. Why does the greatest diversity within language families occur in the earliest-occupied areas?
2. How might historical linguistics and archaeology interrelate in efforts to reconstruct population origins and movements during prehistory?
3. What kinds of artifacts do you think would be most important for tracing cultural relationships during population dispersals? Why?
4. How might cultural diffusion take place without migration?

contemporary New World native peoples, suggested that people had migrated into the New World from Asia in two or three separate waves beginning about 15,000 years ago. Recent comparative studies of blood groupings now suggest that there may have been four separate migrations into the New World, the first perhaps as early as 40,000 years ago (e.g., Brown et al. 1998; Torroni 2000; also see Meltzer 1995). To date, however, there is little archaeological evidence to support such an early entry. This very interesting problem remains unresolved.

Interpreting Evidence of Change

Detecting change involves the discovery and plotting of differences in traits across space and over time. In both cases, archaeologists require multiple data points from which to judge whether any change occurred. Traits are described, plotted, and compared in an attempt to detect differences that indicate change. Archaeologists begin by reconstructing synchronic events, activities that took place at a specific time. These events are then compared to others of different times to document evidence of change. The ability of archaeologists to track and explain such changes depends on the quality of the archaeological information available to them.

Reconstructing Events

The archaeological record consists of the accumulation of evidence of innumerable individual events. In many cases, the evidence of these events is stacked up and becomes mixed in archaeological deposits. Separating the remains of one event from another is often difficult. Therefore, archaeologists generally lump together evidence of several events to describe patterns of "average" behavior.

Sometimes, however, individual events and behaviors can be distinguished. An archaeological site may consist of the remains of a single event, and all of the materials at that site reflect that event. When studying such a site, archaeologists can learn considerable detail about a specific behavior. For instance, if a person walking through the landscape stops to camp for the night, the resulting site will contain discrete synchronic evidence of site function and organization, individual diet, and other information. Unfortunately, many single-event sites are quite small and tend to be missed or considered insignificant.

Evidence of individual events and behaviors also is present in larger sites. Features such as hearths, living floors, activity areas, and caches contain information about individual behaviors and events, and many such features can be dated with radiocarbon analysis or other methods. The interment of a body is a specific event that can provide a great deal of information about biology, religion and ritual, social status, and worldview. As discussed in Chapter 11, burial data from the Moundville site were used to reconstruct status and rank within a complex society.

Even materials from mixed deposits can be reconstructed to recover details about individual behaviors and events. One example is the refitting of flakes to reconstruct the core or other tool from which they came. Such reconstruction provides information on tool form, lithic technology, the movement of materials within the site, and activity areas. Similar analysis of faunal remains provides information on animal utilization, butchering patterns, and processing. In some cases, materials from different sites can be refitted and used to reconstruct the specific movements of people (Close 2000).

Catastrophic events can sometimes result in the preservation of a site and its activities at a moment in time. Sites such as Pompeii, Herculaneum, and the ancient Maya town of Ceren were buried by volcanic ash. Others, such as Ozette (in Washington, on the Pacific Coast), were buried by mud. Shipwrecks also are excellent time capsules, for a ship, its equipment, and its cargo are "frozen" at the time of the sinking. In each case, detailed evidence of specific activities can be discovered.

Sometimes called the "Pompeii of the New World," Ceren, in present-day El Salvador, was suddenly buried by ash from a volcanic eruption some 1,400 years ago. A complete and intact small town was sealed beneath the ash (Sheets 1992). The site was found in 1976 when a house feature was exposed in a bulldozer cut during the construction of a grain silo. Using ground-penetrating radar, a team of archaeologists from El Salvador and the United States discovered structures, agricultural fields, and other features.

Excavations revealed that as the volcano erupted, people quickly evacuated Ceren, leaving most of their possessions where they lay. Many things, including casts of perishables, were preserved very well in the ash. Multiple households were discovered, showing differences in construction, features, and artifact assemblages. Among the other items recovered were complete tool kits, specific artifacts in direct association with specific features (e.g., pottery in association with hearths), and storage features still containing corn and other materials. Archaeologists also found the actual agricultural fields of the inhabitants, with casts of corn and other plants still remaining in furrowed rows near the houses. This discovery will shed much light on the agricultural practices of the common people. The maturity of the corn plants indicates that the eruption took place in August.

Reconstructing Patterns and Trends

Despite many instances of evidence of specific events being found in sites, most of what is recovered from archaeological sites is mixed, making it difficult to differentiate the material remains of individual events. In these cases, archaeologists describe general patterns of remains in order to reconstruct general patterns of behavior. In the same way that archaeologists can track specific change over time, they can also track changes in average behaviors over time. As the specific behaviors that produced a particular pattern of material culture change, the overall pattern of material culture also changes and can be detected even if no specific event was delineated.

The change from the use of the atlatl and dart system to the bow and arrow system, mentioned at the beginning of this chapter, should have resulted in the adoption of smaller projectile points. This change can be seen in the size of the points found at a site, but it also could be detected through analysis of debitage from the manufacturing process. An examination of the average size of the individual waste flakes could reveal the shift from large to small points even if no actual points were found.

Cultural Contact and Conflict

Individual cultures never exist in total isolation for very long, although some large regions (e.g., Australia) containing many cultures were isolated from other regions for long periods of time. All cultures eventually come into contact with others, and there is a constant interplay between groups. Among the outcomes of this **cultural contact** are the diffusion of technology and ideas, immigration, emigration, and the exchange of mates.

Direct contact between cultures also can lead to **acculturation,** an exchange of cultural features between two groups or societies in which aspects of both cultures change but each group remains distinct. Acculturation is evident in the development of mixed languages that arise to facilitate communication between different cultures in direct contact. Swahili, for example, originated as a mixture of East African languages and Arabic as a language of trade in ancient Indian Ocean commerce. In the archaeological record, acculturation is evident in adjacent groups that have different features but nevertheless share some core technology. The blending of cultures, called **syncretism,** also can be detected in archaeological sites. An example is the combination of animistic imagery and Christian iconography in early German art. When cultural differences disappear, **assimilation** has occurred. When groups maintain their distinctiveness within a merged culture, **cultural pluralism** is the result and cultural differences often are visible in artifact assemblages.

When groups in direct contact are disproportionate in size or are culturally very different—having different modes of subsistence or different levels of political organization, for example—the larger and more complex groups tend to prevail, and the smaller and less complex groups tend to be driven out and replaced, assimilated, or enslaved, peacefully or through colonization or conquest. **Cultural conflict** most often occurs between groups that compete for territory or access to other resources. The history of contact between peoples sometimes includes all these consequences, such that people in a trading network later engage in warfare and ultimately are destroyed or absorbed by a more dominant group. The history of contact between Euroamericans and native cultures of the Americas followed this pattern.

The Archaeology of Trade

Understanding exchange and trade is an important goal in archaeology (Figure 12.3). Trade reflects many aspects of culture, including commodities and systems of measure, internal social systems and politics, and interaction and power relations with external groups. Trade is a primary mechanism by which the diffusion of traits can take place, and control of trade is an important source of the power of chiefdoms and states. Some trade or exchange also takes place within a culture, such as the reciprocal exchange of food, gifts, and offerings. Internal exchange can be an important factor in understanding how a culture operates, such as when a redistribution system becomes part of the political structure.

When archaeologists discuss **trade,** however, they are generally referring to the exchange of goods and services between different cultures. Such trade is generally conducted

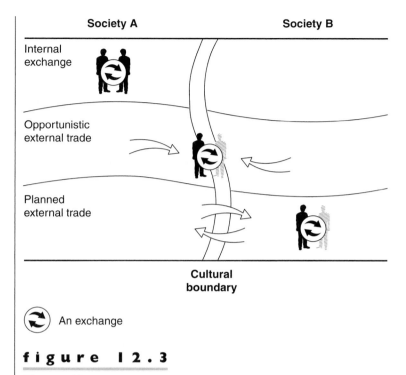

Society A   Society B

Internal
exchange

Opportunistic
external trade

Planned
external trade

**Cultural
boundary**

⟳ An exchange

figure 12.3

Types of Trade. Trade can occur in a number of ways, such as internal exchanges between members of the same group, opportunistic exchanges when people happen to meet, and planned trips where people travel to other places to conduct trade.

by means of barter and market exchange systems, sometimes with the aid of money. Systems of exchange tend to focus on obtaining materials not readily obtainable locally. Desirable nonlocal, exotic materials might include gold, silver, copper, gems, some kinds of shell, feathers, skins, ivory, and items of fine craftsmanship.

For example, in 1996 Chinese archaeologists discovered the body of a king buried 2,170 years ago in a tomb carved into the rock of Lion Mountain in eastern Jiangsu Province. Liu Wu, the third king of Chu during the Western Han Dynasty, was buried in a jade shroud—thin jade plaques sewn together with gold thread—along with coins, official seals, jade weapons, and some 1,500 other objects made of gold, silver, copper, bone, and lacquer. Comparing these artifacts with artifacts from other Chu sites of the period helped archaeologists identify exotic items and important trade goods. The king's belt, for example, contained a 13-ounce gold button engraved with two bears tearing at a galloping horse, not a part of Chu culture. Archaeologists hypothesized that nomadic peoples on China's northern and western borders made the belt. Perhaps it was paid as tribute to an overlord king or as an emblem of alliance.

Trade goods were sought as prestige items or for use in the manufacture of particular tools. Obsidian, for example, is easy to manufacture into tools and has a very sharp edge useful for many purposes. Therefore, for many groups obsidian was a preferred material, and extensive networks of obsidian trade existed in various areas, including Mesoamerica and the Middle East.

Some trading was opportunistic, conducted on the spur of the moment when groups happened to meet. However, most trade was planned, carried on by trading expeditions organized by individuals or groups. In some cultures in which trade was extensive, professional traders and merchants emerged. Some trade was conducted over long distances and involved large-scale networks. By the Bronze Age, for example, extensive trading networks, with integrated economic structures and related political structures, linked most of the Mediterranean region.

Trade networks and systems are reflected in settlement patterns in a number of ways. For instance, materials must be moved from their source to their destination. If ships are used, ports will exist. Land transport requires trails and roads, plus support settlements along the way, some of which could grow to be major centers and cities as people move to the centers as a result of the trading activity. In some cases, a trading center exists for the sole purpose of trade, and if the trade disappears, so does the center (recall the example of Ubar, in Highlight 5.2 in Chapter 5). In many cases, contemporary trade routes and transportation corridors follow ancient ones. One of the most extensive trade networks in the ancient world was that of the Silk Road between China and the Middle East (Highlight 12.3).

In some cases, a group might prefer to control resources rather than rely on trade to obtain them. Southern Mesopotamia, where the first cities developed, lacked many of the raw materials needed to support cities. Some of these early cities, such as Uruk in what is now Iraq, established colonies or outposts in what is now Turkey, Syria, and Iran to secure and control sources of raw material (Oates 1993). Thus, these cities dominated not only southern Mesopotamia but also an extensive area to the north, controlling trade and access to raw materials and so expanding their own power. Colonization and conquest are both important sources of cultural change.

Archaeologists can document the distribution and movement of traded materials in the archaeological record by identifying the source of the materials. Some materials, such as some types of building stone, are unique and their sources can be visually identified. Other materials, such as certain metals, must be identified through the use of chemical sourcing (discussed in Chapter 6). Certain types of rocks and ceramics can be identified petrographically by examining thin sections under a microscope. In some cases, materials manufactured by single individuals can be tracked in the archaeological record, such as Roman ceramic storage vessels (*amphorae*) that have been traced to a particular maker by the potter's mark. Materials must also be dated (e.g., by radiocarbon or artifact styles).

With this information, archaeologists can reconstruct trading systems and interpret other aspects of past cultures, including social and political interaction. Near Belitung Island in Indonesia, archaeologists recently discovered a sunken ship dating from the ninth century AD (Flecker 2001). The ship was loaded with Chinese porcelain being

HIGHLIGHT **12.3**

Archaeology of the Silk Road: Ancient Mummies of the Tarim Basin

Gold, silver, rare spices, silk, and glass passed between East and West along the Great Silk Road linking Europe to China. People often believed that the Great Silk Road opened with the pioneering west-to-east journey of Marco Polo to the court of Kublai Khan in the thirteenth century AD. But, there is good reason to suspect that Marco Polo *never* went to China—although other Europeans did—and that initial contacts between East and West occurred long before the thirteenth century AD (Mallory and Mair 2000:71). Written evidence of an east-to-west expedition led by Zang Quian from China to Central Asia in 138 BC shows that the earliest contacts predated Polo's "journey" and went in the opposite direction. Two troublesome finds, however, cast doubt on this scenario.

The first find came from a series of expeditions to Xinjiang Province in western China around the turn of the twentieth century, which led to recovery of ancient texts dating to the earliest centuries AD. Most were written in known eastern Indo-European languages (Iranian, Indo-Aryan), but some were clearly Indo-European but could not be ascribed to any known Iranian or Indo-Aryan language. This was a surprise because Indo-European languages are geographically divided into two main branches: eastern and western (see Renfrew 1987). Dubbed "Tocharian," this mysterious western Indo-European language was found in the desiccated ancient texts from the Tarim Basin of China. How could such a language be present so far to the east, so far away from its closest related languages, Celtic and Italic (Barber 1999:115–116)?

The second find is a series of frescoes depicting the life of the Buddha and his followers. Dating from the fourth to seventh centuries AD, these wall paintings show "knights with long swords" described as benefactors of the local Buddhist temples. According to Mallory and Mair (2000:173), the benefactors are depicted as Caucasians with blond or red hair and wearing long coats, and suspended from their chain belts is a long sword with a cross-like pommel. Could it be that contact between Europe and China not only occurred long before Marco Polo but also involved a migration of Europeans eastward into western China?

During the summer of 1988, Victor Mair, a professor of Asian and Middle Eastern Studies at the University of Pennsylvania, visited the museum in Ürümchi, the capital of Xinjiang Province in western China, to see a new gallery filled with mummies. These individuals were extremely lifelike and were dressed in brilliantly colored clothes woven from wool. Looking at the faces of these long-dead inhabitants of western China, Mair (1995b) was surprised to find that they looked like Europeans and not like modern Han Chinese. The mummies had been found at sites around the margins of the forbidding Tarim Basin.

Radiocarbon dating indicates that the mummies are several thousand years old. The earliest mummies date from 2000 to 1500 BC and were clothed only in plain-woven woolen blankets fastened in the front with a bone pin. Several individuals were buried with felt hats on their heads and a bundle of ephedra twigs on their chests (ephedra is a stimulant). Recovery of seeds and animal bones suggests that these people practiced a mixed economic strategy, combining agricultural production of western-derived wheat and barley with stockbreeding of western sheep, goats, and possibly camels and horses. Later Tarim mummies date from 1000 BC to AD 500. These individuals were found wearing fitted trousers decorated with red piping, coats, shirts, and jackets woven from sheep's wool in plaids and twills identified by Elizabeth Barber (1999:131–147) as nearly identical to those associated with the Celts of Europe.

HIGHLIGHT **12.3** *continued*

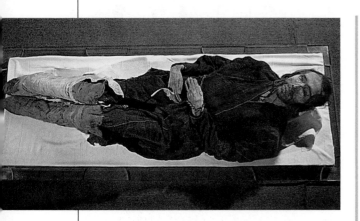

This 3,000-year-old male mummy was discovered at the Chärchän site in the Tarim Basin of western China. He had blond hair and was buried wearing brightly colored woolen clothing, all of which is well preserved. He was buried with three women, believed to be family members.

Do these European-looking mummies with Western-style clothing and diet represent migrants to China from the eastern European steppe? Following the lead of Russian archaeologist E. E. Kuzmina (1998), Irish archaeologists James Mallory and Victor Mair (2000) noted similarities in burial customs and metallurgy indicating that the early and late Tarim Basin mummies reflect separate migrations of Europeans from known archaeological cultures of the southern Russian steppe.

To test this hypothesis, Paolo Francalacci, of the University of Sassari, obtained tissue samples from 11 of the Tarim Basin mummies. One of the two samples tested in Italy yielded intact ancient DNA. Francalacci found the mtDNA of this mummy to belong to haplogroup H, the most common marker found among European populations. From this, Luigi Luca Cavalli-Sforza (2000) concluded that the DNA evidence supported the contention that the Tarim Basin mummies were Tocharian-speaking European immigrants from the Russian steppe.

Recent bioarchaeological studies by Brian Hemphill and James Mallory (2004) suggest that the situation is more complex (Schorr 2001). Hemphill and Mallory discovered that the Xianjiang mummies are not like the Russian steppe populations but rather reflect characteristics of Near Eastern peoples, 15 percent of whom also are in haplogroup H. Hemphill and Mallory found that the later Tarim mummies are closely related instead to earlier populations immediately to the west in south-central Asia. These populations belong to the Bronze Age, oasis-based, agricultural Oxus Civilization of Uzbekistan and Turkmenistan. According to Hemphill and Mallory, it is to the immediate west, among populations ancestral to the Persians, that the origins of the Tarim mummies can be traced.

So, who were the ancient mummies of western China? Archaeologists have not achieved consensus on the interpretation. Hemphill and Mallory's evidence casts doubt on the idea that they were Europeans. Nor are they Han Chinese. The Tarim mummies appear to be descendants of immigrants from the west rather than the northwest and may have had close ties with farmers of ancient Persia.

CRITICAL **THINKING** QUESTIONS

1. What is the archaeological significance of the Great Silk Road for interpreting peoples and cultures of the past?
2. What are the main interpretations of the origins of the Tarim mummies, and on what assumptions and hypotheses are they based?
3. What kinds of evidence can contribute to efforts to determine the origins and movements of prehistoric populations?
4. In the case of interpreting the Tarim Basin mummies, how do the cultural remains, historical linguistics, evidence about diet, DNA analysis, and findings from bioarchaeology interrelate?

transported to an unknown destination. The design of the ship, however, was found to be either Arab or Indian, and the vessel was constructed of materials from western Asia. Such early contact between China and the western Indian Ocean region was previously unknown; the ship and its cargo provided the earliest archaeological evidence of direct trade between the two areas. Political and social contacts must also have occurred, issues that will be investigated in the future.

The Archaeology of Warfare

Warfare is different from *intracultural* violence, such as assault or murder. **Warfare** is organized and sanctioned conflict between two cultures. It was widespread in the past and probably is as old as culture itself.

Warfare can occur on any scale, from two individuals of different cultures fighting each other to thousands of combatants in large battles. Evidence of warfare is present in the archaeological record in numerous forms, including (1) social and political organizations designed for military needs, (2) military facilities (e.g., bases and forts) and weapons (from ships to knives), (3) settlement patterns and defensive civilian facilities, (4) demographic patterns, and (5) actual remains from battles. The first three attest to the anticipation of, preparation for, or response to warfare. Demographic patterns may reflect only the results of warfare (e.g., higher mortality for military-age males), and actual conflict may be apparent only at battle sites (see Martin and Frayer 1997; Carman and Harding 1999).

Many of the archaeological manifestations of warfare are evident in the location of sites and in defensive architecture, such as medieval castles built on hilltops and equipped with high walls and moats. As the physical manifestations of potential or actual warfare become more numerous, the social and political organization necessary to undertake such conflict becomes more complex, ranging from basic leadership provided by a "war chief" to the presence of a formally conscripted and organized army and navy.

Evidence of actual warfare is present in damaged or destroyed facilities, such as burned towns with bodies. Evidence of warfare also can be found in the graves of soldiers killed in battle, such as the mass grave discovered at Towton, England (see Chapter 8), which contained many individuals with skeletal injuries consistent with battle. Many battlefield sites have been recorded, some still in good condition and containing the debris of battle, including spent or discarded weapons or projectiles, armor, supplies, and personal items. Other battle sites have changed over time, some so greatly that a great deal of environmental and geomorphological work is required to reconstruct the battle site itself (Highlight 12.4).

Archaeological investigations also can add to the record of known battle sites. For example, archaeological investigations have been conducted at the site of the battle of the Little Bighorn in 1876 (e.g., Scott and Fox 1987; Gray 1991; Fox 1993; Michno 1997). For more than 100 years, this battle between a U.S. force under the command of Lt. Col. George A. Custer and a combined Sioux and Cheyenne force has been romanticized as the gallant last stand of a doomed command. A new survey and the use of metal

HIGHLIGHT 12.4

Thermopylae, 480 BC

At one spot along the road from northern Greece to Athens, the mountains come very close to the sea. Travelers (and armies) moving south along the eastern coast of Greece must traverse a narrow pass if they want to get to Athens. At this narrow pass, called Thermopylae, a relatively small number of soldiers can defend against frontal assaults by a numerically superior enemy, and many battles have been fought there. The latest battle took place during World War II, when New Zealanders unsuccessfully tried to stop the Germans in 1941.

Probably the most famous battle at Thermopylae occured in 480 BC and was described by Herodotus and others many years later. Under King Xerxes, the Persians invaded Greece with a huge army, variously estimated at between 100,000 and 2 million men (the actual number most likely is closer to the lower end of the range). Xerxes conquered northern Greece and was moving south to attack Athens and other independent city-states. While the Greeks organized a defense, a small contingent of 300 Spartans occupied the pass just ahead of the Persians and fortified it. The Spartans were supported by several thousand troops from Thespia, Thebes, and Phokis, all under the command of the Spartan king, Leonidas. Because of the narrowness of the pass—perhaps only some 20 meters wide—the Persians were unable to bring their vastly superior numbers to bear, and the Spartans repeatedly repulsed their attacks.

At the same time, the Athenian Navy prevented the Persian Navy from landing troops behind the Spartan line.

At the end of the second day of fighting, a local herder sold Xerxes information about a route through the mountains that led to the rear of the Spartan position. That night, some 5,000 to 10,000 elite Persian troops took that route. In the morning, they attacked and overcame the Phokian rear guard and came upon the Greeks from behind. The Thebans surrendered. The Spartans and Thespians made a stand on a nearby hill, where they were all killed. Some of the Greek troops successfully retreated and later joined the main Greek army. Xerxes continued his advance on southern Greece and burned Athens. The Persian army was finally defeated by the combined Greek army at Plataea, and the Persian navy was defeated by the Greek fleet at Salamis. The Persians never again invaded Greece.

In the late 1880s and early 1900s, archaeological research was conducted to locate the battle site, the Spartan line, the route of the Persian flanking movement, the location where the Greek force protecting the back route fought the Persians, and the hill where the Spartans made their last stand. However, the "pass" at Thermopylae is now about three miles wide and does not match the description of Herodotus. Thus, considerable disagreement over the location of the battle ensues.

detectors led to a reinterpretation. Researchers plotted the location of bullets, shell casings, and other debris to reveal a detailed pattern of material. The material pattern suggests that Custer divided his command and encountered a vastly superior force. Evidence also indicated that many of Custer's men were killed trying to escape. Researchers also excavated the buried soldiers to assess their age, health, and actual cause of death (Scott et al. 1998).

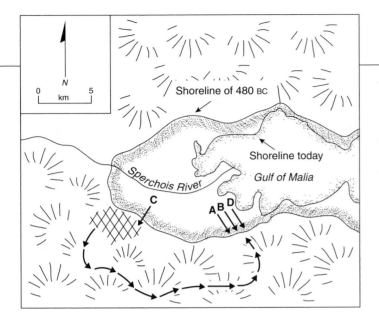

Shoreline of 480 BC

Shoreline today

Gulf of Malia

Sperchois River

C

A B D

0 5
km
N

This map of the pass at Thermopylae shows the shoreline of today and the 480 BC shoreline reconstructed from geomorphic data. The Greek defense line was probably at the narrowest portion of the pass (A), with the Greek camp (B) directly to the east and the Persian camp (C) to the west. The Persians crossed the mountains (dashed arrowed line) and trapped the Greeks on a hill (D), where they died to the last man.

Source: Adapted from Kraft et al. 1987, Figure 14.

Recently, geomorphic studies (Kraft et al. 1987) demonstrated that the geography of the pass has changed dramatically since 480 BC because of alluvial action. Deposition by several rivers has buried much of the ancient surface under alluvial fans and has pushed the shore back several miles. A reconstruction of the shoreline of 480 BC is consistent with Herodotus's description. Many of the features associated with the battle, including the Persian camp, the Greek defense lines, the main battlefield, and the Greek camp, apparently are buried under the alluvium. The top of the hill where the Greeks made their last stand and the battlefield where the Persians overcame the Phokians are still visible. Investigators using metal detectors discovered a large number of Persian-style metal arrowheads on the hill. The bodies of the Greek dead, said to have been buried there, have not been found and likely still lie beneath the alluvium. The battle of Thermopylae has been such a topic of interest that it has been the subject of several Hollywood films, including "The 300 Spartans" (1962) and "300" (2006).

CRITICAL **THINKING** QUESTIONS

1. How is evidence of warfare preserved in the archaeological record? What forms can that evidence take?
2. What are some of the challenges and benefits of reconstructing specific events from archaeological data?
3. What questions might future archaeologists ask when investigating the battle at Thermopylae? What methods might they use to learn more?

CONTENTSELECT

Search articles in the ContentSelect database using the key words *prehistoric migrations* and *human diasporas*. What are four examples of important prehistoric population movements in different parts of the world, and what were their effects? How can archaeologists reconstruct such broad-scale events?

New discoveries at the battlefield site of Custer's Last Stand on the Little Bighorn River have led to a reinterpretation of that event that more precisely fits the evidence. Ephemeral changes (events that pass quickly and leave little trace) are always a challenge for archaeologists to reconstruct and interpret. As new methods, technologies, and techniques become available, old well-worn sites can yield new findings and whole new ways of understanding culture conflict and culture change.

Chapter Summary

The study of change can be focused on culture history, cultural ecology, and political economy. Change occurs at various speeds and can be viewed both synchronically and diachronically. Archaeologists seek to document both short-term patterns of events and long-term changes.

Archaeologists use systems theory and evolutionary approaches to study change. Using systems theory, they examine how changes in one or more cultural subsystems alter the system as a whole. Using evolutionary approaches, they explore how changes in environment, culture, and technologies affected the evolution of cultures over time.

Invention and innovation are important mechanisms of change. Inventions and innovations may be spread by diffusion—by trade or other contact. Some technologies were independently invented in different regions.

Culture change also results from internal social or political movements intended to achieve some social or political goal.

The movement of people is another major mechanism of change. Migration is the movement of a population, such as an ethnic group, from one locality to another. A diaspora is the dispersal of segments of a population, often by force. Archaeologists can detect population movements by tracking various cultural and biological traits. Language is one of those traits. Changes in the structure, content, and distribution of languages over time can be used to model past population movements.

Detecting change involves the discovery and plotting of differences in traits across space and over time. Archaeologists begin by reconstructing events that took place at a specific time and comparing them to other events from different times to document evidence of change. In many sites, individual events and behaviors are difficult to detect. In most cases, archaeologists describe general patterns of remains in order to reconstruct general patterns of behavior.

All cultures have some contact with others. Among the outcomes of the constant interplay between groups are the diffusion of technology and ideas, immigration, emigration, and the exchange of mates. Direct contact between two cultures also can result in acculturation, assimilation, syncretism, pluralism, conflict, or some combination of these.

Trade is the movement of goods and services between cultures and is a primary mechanism of diffusion. Most trade focuses on obtaining materials not readily obtainable locally, from food to exotic materials such as precious metals or items of high-quality craftsmanship. Some trade was opportunistic, but most was planned. Trade took place over short and long distances, sometimes involving large-scale networks. Archaeologists study trade by identifying the source of traded materials, documenting trading facilities and means of transport, and then dating these components of the system. They then can reconstruct trading systems and formulate models of other aspects of past cultures, including social and political interaction.

Warfare is organized and sanctioned conflict between two cultures. Evidence of warfare is found in social and political organization, military facilities and weapons, settlement patterns and defensive civilian facilities, demographic patterns, and actual remains from battles. Fortifications, weapons, and the physical remains of persons killed in battle are the most common manifestations of war discovered in the archaeological record.

Key Concepts

Suggested Readings

If you want to learn more about the concepts and issues discussed in this chapter, consider looking at the following resources. (Some may be rather technical.)

Carman, John, and Anthony Harding (eds.). (1999). *Ancient Warfare: Archaeological Perspectives.* Stroud: Sutton.

Martin, Debra, and David W. Frayer (eds.). (1997). *Troubled Times: Violence and Warfare in the Past.* Sydney: Gordon and Breach.

Each of these books includes a series of articles that discuss how archaeologists study ancient warfare. Topics include weaponry, battlefield landscapes, bioarchaeology of battle dead, and the social and political implications of warfare.

Ericson, Jonathon E., and Timothy K. Earle (eds.). (1982). *Contexts for Prehistoric Exchange.* New York: Academic Press.

This book contains a series of articles that explain the various theoretical and methodological approaches to understanding the many aspects of regional exchange.

Leonard, Robert D. (2001). "Evolutionary Archaeology." In *Archaeological Theory Today,* Ian Hodder, ed., pp. 65–97. Cambridge: Polity Press.

This article clearly explains the subfield of evolutionary archaeology. It provides an outline to the approach, a discussion of its historical roots, and a detailed explanation of the basic principles of evolutionary theory as applied to archaeology.

Renfrew, Colin. (1987). *Archaeology & Language: The Puzzle of Indo-European Origins.* New York: Cambridge University Press.

Renfrew outlines the basic approach in the study of linguistic prehistory, the movement of languages and people through space and time. He uses the development and expansion of Indo-European as his primary example, but the principles apply to any study of ancient language movements.

chapter **13**

Cultural Resource Management

IN THE EARLY 1830s, beaver pelts were still highly desirable for the production of men's felt hats, which were the fashion rage among the upper classes in Europe and the eastern United States. However, the rivers and streams of eastern Canada and the United States, formerly home to millions of beavers, had become largely devoid of these furry relatives of the porcupine, and the area that trappers needed to cover to meet the high demand for pelts expanded dramatically. The American-run Columbia River Fishing and Trading Company saw an advantage to putting a fur-trading outpost along the Snake River in what is now southeastern Idaho to support fur trappers in that region and to develop a fishery to produce salmon for export. An additional advantage of this outpost was to gain an edge on the company's major competitor, British-owned Hudson's Bay Company.

ers and trappers, the fort served as an important way station along the Oregon Trail. During the summer of 1849 alone, an estimated 10,000 wagons passed through the fort on the way to California. However, Native American hostilities along the lower Snake River and the unpredictability of mercantile trade resulted in the official closing of Fort Hall in 1856. Over the next few years, the fort was used by various independent traders, and then was effectively destroyed by the flooding of the Snake River in 1862 and 1864.

Despite Fort Hall's historical importance, the actual location of its ruins remained in dispute. The term "Fort Hall" denoted various places along the river. Contradictory accounts of the location of the site in the historical record, and the changing river pattern after nearly a century and a half, added to the complexity of the issue. Along the Snake River on the Fort Hall Indian Reservation (north of Pocatello, Idaho), a historical marker had been erected in an area of earthen berms believed to represent the eroded adobe walls. But was this really Fort Hall? Although not absolutely certain about the locality, the National Park Service designated this Fort Hall "site" a National Historic Landmark because of its significance in U.S. history.

The need to determine the exact location of the fort became

In 1834, Nathaniel Wyeth of the Columbia River Fishing and Trading Company established a wooden stockade around the new trading post along the Snake River near the mouth of the Portneuf River above present-day American Falls, Idaho. Unfortunately, the outpost was plagued with employee incompetence, desertion, disease, and conflict with some of the local Native American groups. To add to these problems, men's fashions were shifting from beaver to silk, and the salmon exporting enterprise proved to be unprofitable. Wyeth soon recognized that his business was destined to fail, so he sold the troubled fort to Hudson's Bay Company in 1837.

In the hands of Hudson's Bay Company, Fort Hall proved to be a lucrative trading post for many years, despite the continuing decline in the numbers of beaver and a slowdown in the market for beaver pelts. The company reconstructed the exterior timber walls of the fort with adobe. In addition to supplying local trad-

critical when the Snake River started to encroach on the area. If the National Historic Landmark site was not the true location of Fort Hall, why spend perhaps millions of dollars to try to protect it? But if it *was* the actual location, time was of the essence.

Who is responsible for Fort Hall and its protection? Who will "manage" this cultural resource? The National Historic Preservation Act of 1966 requires federal agencies to recognize and document historic properties eligible for inclusion in the National Register of Historic Places. The law also requires federal agencies to restore and interpret important historic properties for public education purposes. Complicating the Fort Hall situation is the fact that several federal agencies might share responsibility for identifying and preserving the fort: the Bureau of Reclamation (because the site is along a river), the Army Corps of Engineers (for the same reason), and the Bureau of Indian Affairs (because the site is on an Indian reservation). Moreover, because the fort is a National Historic Landmark, it falls under the aegis of the National Park Service.

This multiple-agency interest resulted in great confusion about how to proceed. Several years passed while the federal government tried to decide who would pay for the archaeological investigation necessary to identify the exact location of the fort. Meanwhile, the Snake River rapidly encroached on the National Historic Landmark site. Another issue was the concerns of the Shoshone-Bannock Indians who occupy and manage the Fort Hall reservation. Their ancestors frequently camped outside the stockade of the fort, so

the history of their people is also represented at the site.

Fortunately, the state in which a resource is located has a say through the State Historic Preservation Office (SHPO; pronounced "ship-o"). After a series of meetings between the Idaho SHPO, the various federal agencies, and the Shoshone-Bannock tribes, some decisions were made. The Bureau of Reclamation would receive limited funding to pay for archaeological test excavations at Fort Hall. The Army Corps of Engineers would see what they could do about the encroaching river. The National Park Service would provide personnel to conduct site mapping and geophysical survey (proton magnetometry) work. Archaeological and Historical Services, a private archaeological firm operating out of Eastern Washington University with previous experience in excavating forts and Hudson's Bay Company sites, would do the test excavations for a fraction of their normal rate because of the importance of the opportunity.

The test excavations were completed in 1993, and the analysis of the exposed structures and recovered artifacts verified that the site really was Fort Hall. Key excavation units had exposed portions of the bastion and western wall that matched descriptions of the fort's size, configuration, and appearance in historic documents. The majority of the artifacts dated from the early to the mid-nineteenth century, which was consistent with the occupation of Fort Hall.

With the location of Fort Hall established, efforts are being made to protect and interpret the site. The immediate danger posed by the

Snake River was removed through temporary bank stabilization, and the multiagency and tribal groups continue to meet with the SHPO to work out plans for site interpretation and to control future river erosion. The process of cultural resource management succeeded in identifying and protecting an important archaeological resource that will provide information about the fur trade and tribal relations along the Snake River in the early nineteenth century.

For the location of Fort Hall and other sites mentioned in this chapter, see the map on page 355.

The Impact of Population Growth and Development on Archaeology

Undoubtedly the greatest threat to archaeological sites and related resources is the growth of human population worldwide. Whenever a new highway, housing development, bridge, or dam is built, archaeological sites are often endangered and frequently destroyed. Any time earth is moved in any significant way, the context of archaeological deposits may be permanently and irreparably damaged. Even activities as seemingly benign as cutting timber involve ancillary activities, such as the use of heavy equipment and the construction of landings to stack logs, that can compromise and damage many types of archaeological resources. Large-scale farming can scramble the context of shallow sites if not totally obliterate them. It is important to keep in mind, however, that many previously unknown archaeological sites have been uncovered by farming activities.

It is not just development that affects archaeological sites. Other human activities, many of them considered recreational, result in the unprecedented loss of the past. Off-road vehicles, especially four-wheel-drive sport-utility vehicles (SUVs) and motorcycles, can directly affect sites or lead to erosion that will expose and damage cultural deposits and features. In the United States, the drivers of these vehicles are unwittingly (in most cases) leveling countless archaeological sites. People are now able to go places that were nearly inaccessible 30 years ago, and many are making their own roads to get there! Most off-road recreationists are respectful of known archaeological sites, but a small percentage willfully vandalizes or loots these sites.

Looting or pothunting, for recreation or for profit, continues to increase in scope and incidence. In many poor, nonindustrial nations, the only way some people can survive is by looting archaeological sites. They sell pilfered artifacts to brokers, who move the objects on the world market. However, the destruction of archaeological sites is common in industrial nations as well, especially in the United States. Determined commercial looters in the American Southwest sometimes use heavy equipment such as backhoes to tear through buried pueblos and kivas in the hopes of finding unbroken painted pottery they can sell overseas for thousands of dollars. The Internet makes it much easier for today's

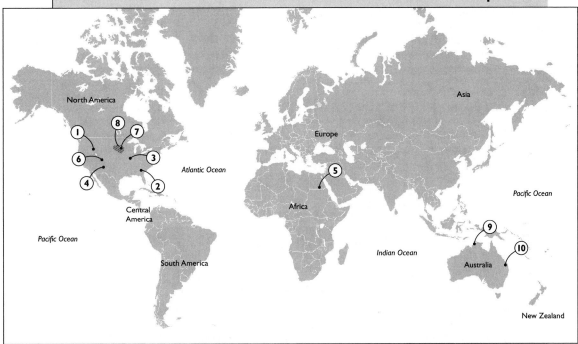

LOCATION MAP: **Sites Mentioned in Chapter 13**

1 ■ Fort Hall
  Snake River, Idaho

2 ■ Savannah River National Wildlife Refuge
  Savannah, Georgia

3 ■ Cahokia Mounds
  Cahokia, Illinois

4 ■ Pueblo Bonito
  New Mexico

5 ■ Abu Simbel
  Aswan, Egypt

6 ■ Mesa Verde
  Southwestern Colorado

7 ■ Little Rapids
  Minnesota

8 ■ Wahpeton Dakota culture
  North-central United States

9 ■ Kakadu National Park
  Northern Australia

10 ■ Peel Island
  Queensland, Australia

professional looters to bypass the brokers and sell their goods to a worldwide market. In addition, perhaps to a lesser degree, weekend "arrowhead collectors," many of whom have a genuine interest in prehistory, are also destroying the record of the past.

The Field of Cultural Resource Management

How do we save archaeological sites amid major development and the growth in popularity of outdoor recreation, off-road vehicles, and artifact collecting? How do we save the past for the future? Fortunately, there have been concerted efforts over the past few decades to record—and in some instances to preserve—archaeological sites for the benefit of future generations. It is recognized that with so much development around the world (particularly in North America), some means of identifying, documenting, and when possible protecting archaeological sites should be implemented. Within the federal government of the United States, the field of cultural resource management (CRM) has arisen as the result of legislation designed to recognize and document significant historical sites, unique historic architectural features, and archaeological sites. Laws also exist to safeguard archaeological sites on public and private lands in the United States and to prosecute people who damage protected resources. Furthermore, in both the United States and Canada, laws at the state (province) and federal levels exist to protect and repatriate human skeletal remains, as well as grave goods, to indigenous peoples (Native Hawaiians and Alaskan Inuit as well as American Indians). Similar statutes have been developed in Great Britain, Japan, and other parts of the world.

Antiquities Legislation in the United States

Awareness that archaeological sites, especially ruins on public lands in the American Southwest, were being robbed of their contents by antiquarians and commercial looters prompted Congress to enact the United States' first cultural resources statute in 1906. The **Antiquities Act of 1906** made it illegal to dig archaeological sites on public lands without a formal permit from the secretary of the interior, a permit that would be issued only to recognized professional archaeologists affiliated with educational institutions or museums. Nearly 30 years later, in 1935, Congress passed the Historic Sites Act, which empowered the National Park Service to develop programs to identify and document sites of historical significance, including archaeological sites.

In the early 1950s, there was renewed effort to build dams, reservoirs, and interstate highways, in part to accommodate the "baby boom" overtaking post–World War II United States. Then it suddenly became obvious that such activities were taking a toll on historical and archaeological sites that happened to be in the way of these projects. So the National Park Service, in conjunction with the Smithsonian Institution, launched the River Basin Surveys and the Interagency Archeological Salvage Program to salvage archaeological information from areas slated to be inundated by planned reservoir projects, many of them in the American Southeast and Northwest. To fund this effort, Congress passed the **Reservoir Salvage Act of 1960** to complete the work that had been started.

Antiquities legislation has provided a rationale for federal government oversight of public lands even when natural environmental changes, rather than public works projects, threaten archaeological sites. For example, the U.S. Fish and Wildlife Service, a branch of the Department of the Interior, commissioned an archaeological survey of sites in the coastal Southeast that were being threatened by rising sea levels (see Highlight 13.1).

HIGHLIGHT 13.1

Sea-Level Rise and U.S. Coastal Archaeology

At a depth of 1.5 meters, the anomaly became apparent: mixed with the solid mass of freshwater mussel shells (*Elliptio icterina*) were significant quantities of saltwater oyster shells (*Crassostera virginica*). Kneeling in the flooded base of the test pit, the archaeologist could clearly see the concentration in the pit profile, where wall seepage had washed the shells clean, exposing the hard, sharp-edged oyster shells against the soft lime of the mussel shells. Why were the oyster shells there? Were they carried in from miles downriver, where the river finally flowed into salt tidal water? Or—the more testable hypothesis—was the sea itself perhaps closer at the time the site was occupied?

The site was a low hummock adjacent to a canal in the Savannah River National Wildlife Refuge. Originally cypress swamp bordering the Savannah River, this land had been converted to rice cultivation in the early nineteenth century. Since the 1930s, the abandoned fields have been under the jurisdiction of the U.S. Fish and Wildlife Service for protection of migratory fowl and indigenous flora and fauna—including alligators like the ten-footer lassoed and hauled out of the excavation trench!

Below the surface debris of a twentieth-century liquor still (and a few nineteenth-century kaolin tobacco pipe fragments), the site was solidly prehistoric. It represented in successive layers each major archaeological phase of the region, from the end of the Mississippian (about AD 1600) back to the Refuge Phase of the Early Woodland (about 1000 BC). The principal occupation belonged to the earliest period: radiocarbon dates confirmed a span ranging from about 1000 to 500 BC.

Stratigraphically, the site was a 2.5-meter-thick shell midden based on a mud bed immediately above 1 meter of peat deposition. The peat overlay river sand of Pleistocene age. Stratification was not clearly discernible in the mud–clay mix of the midden, so excavation was conducted in arbitrary units—1 square meter across by 10 centimeters in depth, with a total of 24 levels.

The possibility of sea-level fluctuation inferred from the presence of saltwater oyster shells added a geological dimension to the study of the site. Cores were taken from across the surrounding swamp and analyzed for mineral and biotic content. Previous studies had established that Savannah River water differs from coastal/estuarine water in the mineral content of its sediments. Sediment typical of Savannah River water indicates a freshwater regime, whereas sediment from coastal water indicates saline conditions.

The cores were divided into 20-centimeter sections according to depth, and each section was appraised separately. Researchers discovered that freshwater conditions prevailed prior to site occupation. A

This Early Woodland shell midden at the Savannah River Refuge helped reveal the history of people's adaptations to a changing environment.

tuations in 500-year cycles for the past 6,000 years. Each successive sea-level rise was higher than its predecessor, resulting in an overall rise of about 5 meters.

The studies enabled archaeologists to reconstruct the history of occupation of the area. Originally, the site was a natural marsh levee that formed along a channel bank of the river. Early on, a shift in the river cut off the channel and it began filling in with fine sediment. People used the levee for seasonal resource gathering—deer (*Odocoileus virginianus*), hickory nuts, and acorns—and traveled downstream for saltwater fish and shellfish. Throughout much of the site occupation, dugout canoes allowed people ready access to the channel and surrounding areas. Cultural deposits of shell, animal bone, pottery, and other artifacts, along with sediments from occasional flooding, accumulated to a depth of 2.5 meters over a 15-meter area. After the Refuge Phase (about 1000 to 500 BC), usage of the site diminished and became intermittent as the channel over time became completely filled in with sediment (Lepionka et al. 1983).

Without an intimate understanding of the changing riverine and estuarine environments, the history of human occupation would not be known. In this case, it could be shown that people moved back and forth to the ocean to collect resources there as part of their overall subsistence and settlement patterns.

transition to estuarine conditions occurred during the early occupation period: a return to a full freshwater regime occurred during the later occupation. Diatoms (single-cell aqueous plants) are very species-specific in relation to water conditions such as salinity and temperature, and the distribution of diatom species in the cores was consistent with the mineral analysis.

These studies provided data for charting sea-level fluctuation over time along the South Carolina coast and also aided in the archaeological interpretation of the site. Radio carbon dating of soils below the water table and of occupation sites above the water table yielded dated maximums and minimums for sea level. These data revealed a pattern of 1- to 2-meter sea-level fluc-

CRITICAL **THINKING** QUESTIONS

1. In what ways might local environment influence the location of an archaeological site? How did the location of this site influence its occupation and use?
2. What physical process was involved in the formation of the Savannah River site?
3. How might a continuing rise in sea level affect the archaeology of the region? The sea-level rise endangering coastal sites is a national phenomenon. If public works projects such as a new dam on the Savannah River were planned, how would cultural resource management come into play?

The National Historic Preservation Act

The legislation that forever changed the face of American archaeology and historic preservation resulted from the urban renewal programs of the early 1960s. During the Kennedy administration, there was a push to "clean up" the decaying centers of American cities; in the process, buildings of historical significance, as well as architecturally unique buildings and entire historic communities, were destroyed with little or no documentation. Those interested in history were outraged, and soon the Johnson administration produced a report that outlined a national historic preservation program. In 1966 this program was enacted into law as the **National Historic Preservation Act (NHPA).** The NHPA has become the heart and soul of cultural resource management in the United States.

The NHPA established the **National Register of Historic Places,** an official listing of all historically significant resources (historic sites, buildings, structures, and archaeological sites) in the United States and its protectorates, including those identified on federal lands or during the course of federal activities. The National Park Service, which has been responsible for many cultural programs, including the administration of historic battlefields, administers the National Register. The law specifies that candidates for inclusion in the National Register must meet one of four established criteria. Most historical or archaeological sites are places that meet criterion d: they "have yielded, or may be likely to yield, information important in prehistory or history." Figure 13.1 provides the exact wording of the four criteria.

Archaeological sites determined to be eligible for nomination to the National Register would be appropriately documented and so recognized. How do sites gain such recognition? This is where Section 106 and Section 110 of the National Historic Preservation Act come into play.

SECTION 106 OF NHPA   According to **Section 106,** federal agencies are responsible for identifying and evaluating for National Register eligibility sites in all areas to be developed or impacted in a way that might destroy or "adversely effect" those sites. For

---

The quality of significance in American history, architecture, archaeology, engineering, and culture is present in districts, sites, buildings, structures, and objects that possess integrity of location, design, setting, materials, workmanship, feeling, and association.

(A) That are associated with events that have made a significant contribution to the broad patterns of our history; or

(B) That are associated with the lives of persons significant in our past; or

(C) That embody the distinctive characteristics of a type, period, or method of construction, or that represent the work of a master, or that possess high artistic values, or that represent a significant and distinguishable entity whose components may lack individual distinction; or

(D) That have yielded, or may be likely to yield, information important in history or prehistory.

figure 13.1

Criteria for Nomination to the National Register of Historic Places

Federal agencies, SHPOs, and, ultimately, the Keeper of the National Register use these criteria to determine the eligibility of historic properties for nomination to the National Register of Historic Places.

Source: 36 Code of Federal Regulations 60.4.

example, a federal agency planning an activity (known as an *undertaking*) that might damage any archaeological or historical site (such as the U.S. Forest Service planning to sell 640 acres of timber in a remote area of the Northwest) is responsible for identifying sites within the project area. A common tool used for identification is archaeological survey. If sites are found, it is necessary to determine their eligibility for nomination to the National Register. Test excavations may be needed to establish the presence of an intact subsurface deposit. Eligible properties are subject to **mitigation,** measures designed to lessen effects to such sites. Mitigation may include complete avoidance, simple recordation, or full recovery of data.

Only a small percentage of eligible sites are formally nominated and placed in the National Register. After eligibility has been determined, the lead agency should complete an extensive nomination form and submit it to the keeper of the National Register in Washington, D.C. Few agencies, however, appear to have the financial resources to complete the nomination process, even though Section 110 of the NHPA requires them to do so. Through Section 106, or the compliance process, thousands of archaeological sites are identified in many states, especially in the West, where federal holdings are vast (for example, nearly 85 percent of Nevada is public land).

SECTION 110 OF NHPA   According to **Section 110,** each federal agency is supposed to establish a formal historic preservation program to identify, evaluate, and nominate historic properties to the National Register, as well as protect those properties on an ongoing basis. Section 110 further obliges agencies to consider actions for which they are responsible. Suppose a proposed federally licensed dam will inundate shoreline sites and attract recreationists who will impact sites on adjacent lands. The pertinent agency—the Federal Energy Regulatory Commission—would be responsible for making certain that all affected sites were protected and monitored.

Section 110 also directs agencies to withhold funding if they are aware that the recipient of a federal grant, loan, assistance, or permit will use the federal aid to destroy a historic property. For example, a state planning to use federal funding to build a highway that would decimate a Pawnee village site would lose the federal money. Furthermore, according to Section 110, the heads of federal agencies are responsible for compliance with Section 106.

Interestingly, most federal agencies are at least familiar with project review under Section 106 but seldom know the details of Section 110. Many agencies have well-established and successful CRM programs and employ numerous historic preservation specialists; others struggle with the concept of Section 106 compliance nearly three and a half decades after the birth of the National Register, and rarely do they live up to their Section 110 responsibilities. Critics of CRM say that Section 106 actually is the "tail that wags the dog," because compliance (getting a "clearance") becomes more important than establishing a formal historic preservation program. *Compliance* has become the new watchword in CRM.

THE PRESERVATION PROCESS   How does one make sure that federal agencies faithfully comply with the NHPA and that the interests of each state are taken into consideration during federal undertakings? The NHPA establishes a system of checks and balances to ensure that the states and the federal agencies work together to identify and protect archaeological and historical sites (known collectively as *historic properties*). A **State Historic Preservation Of-**

fice (SHPO) in each of the 50 states assists federal agencies in their attempts to fulfill the provisions of NHPA. SHPOs consist of a state historic preservation officer, a deputy state historic preservation officer (usually the program administrator), and a staff. The staff may include a state archaeologist (in some states, this position may be a separate office in a completely different state agency). SHPOs employ experts in local archaeology, architectural history, and history who are well versed in historic preservation law. These experts assist in determinations of eligibility as well as interpretations of preservation statutes. Most SHPOs review federal undertakings to make certain that the state agrees with the federal agency's methods, findings, interpretations, and eligibility determinations.

If profound or irreconcilable disagreements arise between a SHPO and a federal agency, the **Advisory Council on Historic Preservation (ACHP)** can help adjudicate the contested issue. With headquarters in Washington, D.C., and a field office in Denver, Colorado, the ACHP consists of a 20-member council—several presidential appointees, the heads of various federal agencies, state and local governmental officials, Native American representatives, and representatives of the National Trust for Historic Preservation and the National Conference of State Historic Preservation Officers—and a staff of approximately 40 historic preservation specialists, or "caseworkers." The council meets only four times a year, so the majority of the work relating to oversight of Section 106 projects is carried out by the caseworkers. The federal agencies, the SHPOs, and the ACHP work together to move the Section 106 process along and help one another succeed in making sure both the spirit and the letter of the law are met (Figure 13.2).

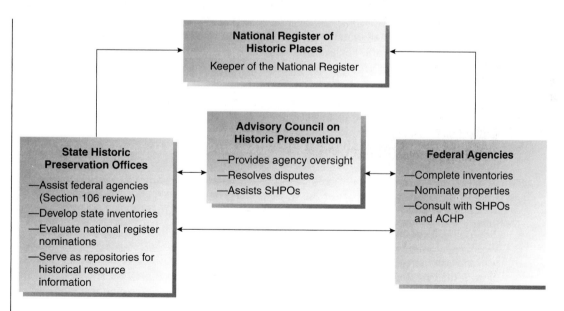

figure 13.2

Responsibilities and Interaction of the NHPA Partners

The National Historic Preservation Act established a system of checks and balances to protect eligible historic properties.

Compliance Archaeology

In an ideal world, every federal agency would have a historic preservation program that develops a complete inventory of all historic properties on lands under its jurisdiction. Except in some of the eastern states where federal land holdings are fairly small, few agencies in any state have complete inventories of their archaeological and historical sites. Many agencies, however, make a stalwart effort to meet this lofty goal, usually through project-driven Section 106 compliance activities.

INVENTORY   Archaeological survey is often conducted in advance of a federal undertaking. Unless an area was inventoried recently, every time an undertaking is proposed, a survey of the area is supposed to be executed. Agency archaeologists do such inventories or, if the project is large enough, contract the work out to a private archaeological consulting firm. In some agencies, cultural resource staffing is minimal, so most surveys for complex undertakings are contracted out. Usually the survey is limited to the *area of potential effect (APE)*—all of the land area that might be affected by a project, including areas that seem peripheral to the main activity. For example, the APE for a road project might include the proposed roadbed, gravel sources for construction, and areas where excavated soils are disposed.

When the survey is completed, each site is recorded and included in the agency's database. Archaeological sites usually are recorded on a standard form approved by the agencies' cultural resource staffs, the SHPOs, and the professional archaeological communities in each state. Figure 13.3 shows one page of a form used in California. The inclusion of site information in GIS databases allows for the development of predictive models with multiple overlays of data. For example, site location, elevation, degree of shade and sun exposure, and other factors can be considered together. Ideally, site information—along with a descriptive report of the exact locations, survey methodology, and findings—is sent to the SHPO in each state. In this way, the SHPO can serve as a central clearinghouse for all the historic resource information within a state. Agencies, archaeological consultants, and researchers can go to this clearinghouse to find archaeological data within their respective states. In large states, such as California, the SHPO provides funding for independent, regional "information centers" where archaeological data are maintained, updated, and managed; California has 12 such centers, including one run by the Yurok tribe in the northwestern part of the state.

The SHPO or consulting archaeological survey organization also gives a site a specific identifying number, usually based on the trinomial system established by the Smithsonian Institution. These trinomials (or "Smithsonian numbers") become the specific designation of a site. Trinomials include a state number or abbreviation, a county abbreviation, and an ordinal designation. Remember from Chapter 5 that the 103rd site recorded in Kern County, California, is CA-KER-103. Some states, such as Arizona, use alternative systems for designating sites.

EVALUATION   After a federal inventory is completed, the next task is to evaluate the recorded sites for eligibility for nomination to the National Register. As noted previously, most archaeological sites must meet National Register criterion D—they will be considered eligible for the National Register if they provide information that is important to

State of California -- The Resources Agency
DEPARTMENT OF PARKS AND RECREATION
ARCHAEOLOGICAL SITE RECORD

Primary #
Trinomial

Page of ***Resource Name or #:** ____________

***A1. Dimensions: a. Length:** ________ ( ) × **b. Width:** ________ ( )
Method of Measurement: ☐ Paced ☐ Taped ☐ Visual estimate ☐ Other: ____________
Method of Determination (Check any that apply.): ☐ Artifacts ☐ Features ☐ Soil ☐ Vegetation ☐ Topography ☐ Cut bank ☐ Animal burrow ☐ Excavation ☐ Property boundary ☐ Other (Explain):

Reliability of Determination: ☐ High ☐ Medium ☐ Low Explain:

Limitations (Check any that apply): ☐ Restricted access ☐ Paved/built over ☐ Site limits incompletely defined ☐ Disturbances ☐ Vegetation ☐ Other (Explain):

A2. Depth: ☐ None ☐ Unknown Method of Determination:
***A3. Human Remains:** ☐ Present ☐ Absent ☐ Possible ☐ Unknown (Explain):

***A4. Features** (Number, briefly describe, indicate size, list associated cultural constituents, and show location of each feature on sketch map.):

***A5. Cultural Constituents** (Describe and quantify artifacts, ecofacts, cultural residues, etc., not associated with features.):

***A6. Were Specimens Collected?** ☐ No ☐ Yes (If yes, attach Artifact Record or catalog and identify where specimens are curated.)
***A7. Site Condition:** ☐ Good ☐ Fair ☐ Poor:

***A8. Nearest Water** (Type, distance, and direction.):
***A9. Elevation:**
A10. Environmental Setting (Describe culturally relevant variables such as vegetation, fauna, soils, geology, landform, slope, aspect, exposure, etc.):

A11. Historical Information:

***A12. Age:** ☐ Prehistoric ☐ Protohistoric ☐ 1542-1769 ☐ 1769-1848 ☐ 1848-1880 ☐ 1880-1914 ☐ 1914-1945 ☐ Post 1945 ☐ Undetermined **Describe position in regional prehistoric chronology or factual historic dates if known:**

A13. Interpretations (Discuss data potential, function[s], ethnic affiliation, and other interpretations):

A14. Remarks:

A15. References (Documents, informants, maps, and other references):

A16. Photographs (List subjects, direction of view, and accession numbers or attach a Photograph Record.):

Original Media/Negatives Kept at:
***A17. Form Prepared by:** ____________ **Date:** ________
Affiliation and Address: ____________

DPR 523C (1/95) ***Required information**

figure 13.3

Page from a California Site Record Form

This is the first page of an archaeological site record form used by the archaeological inventory program of California. Most state archaeological site forms call for the exact site location and detailed descriptions of the site, the observed artifacts, and features. Federal and state agencies can use this information to keep track of sites.

our understanding of history or prehistory. In some cases, the scientific significance of an archaeological site is readily apparent because of the site's great size or complexity or the presence of monumental architecture, such as seen at Pueblo Bonito in New Mexico or the Cahokia Mounds site in Illinois (see the Location Map on page 355). What about sites with artifacts on the surface and some midden-like soil but no monumental architecture? A site that consists of a small surface scatter of lithic tool waste flakes is rarely eligible. What if there is a buried deposit that is deeply stratified and full of important data?

The only way to be certain of the eligibility of some archaeological sites is to conduct testing, or test excavations. Such excavations are designed to assess eligibility rather than to exhaustively investigate a site. Because agency staffs usually are small, most testing programs are awarded to private archaeological consulting firms by competitive bidding. Testing establishes site content and the depth and integrity of the archaeological deposit. If the deposit is intact, deep, and full of artifacts and features, it is certain to provide important information about prehistory, and the site would be considered eligible for nomination. Regional prehistories differ, however. A site that would be eligible in western Nevada might not be considered eligible in southern Maine.

NOMINATION   Once eligibility for nomination to the National Register is determined and agreed on by the SHPO, the appropriate federal agency is required to develop a strategy either to redesign the proposed project so it will not endanger eligible properties or, in consultation with the SHPO, to design a data recovery program that will "preserve" important information from the site. Because large-scale excavations for data recovery are extremely expensive (multi-million-dollar projects are not uncommon), most agencies and SHPOs try to convince the project proponents that redesigning the project to avoid and thus protect the site is the best way to proceed (for example, a site may be avoided by moving a road 200 feet to the west or placing a pipeline above ground, over the archaeological deposit). However, sometimes a project cannot be redesigned (it is hard to redesign a dam so that it will not inundate sites behind it), and mitigation in the form of data recovery is necessary. What "mitigation" means depends on where the project is and what local scholars and the SHPO consider to be "enough" site data to constitute appropriate data recovery.

What about nomination? Is it not the purpose of this process to nominate sites to the National Register? In the best of all possible worlds, this would be the case. But literally tens of thousands of federal actions each year require Section 106 review, and thousands of sites are determined eligible, yet few actually go through the process of being added to the Register. Most sites that are nominated to the Register are historical or architectural; few are archaeological—particularly prehistoric—in nature. Although the National Register is a federal entity, properties that are not on federal lands may be included. Many state-owned properties and archaeological sites on privately held lands have been included in the National Register.

In any case, nomination requires the completion of a form that contains detailed information about the site and its importance to regional history or prehistory. The effort to produce a nomination requires considerable time and resources because the research should be as complete as possible. Once completed, the form is submitted to the keeper of the National Register in Washington, D.C., at which time the Register staff determines the worthiness of the site for inclusion.

Both agency cultural resource staffs and SHPOs face ever-increasing numbers of federal projects and staggering workloads relating to basic Section 106 compliance. Therefore, it is impossible for either to produce as many nominations as they should. This fact is one of the sad ironies of federal preservation programs.

The Archaeological Resources Protection Act

As we have seen, the first step in protecting archaeological sites is to develop state inventories as a permanent record of these cultural resources. However, pothunters, vandals, and looters also know about many of these sites, and most of them are not particularly interested in preserving the archaeological record for future generations. Education by archaeologists and historic preservation professionals may keep otherwise law-abiding citizens from razing archaeological sites, but some individuals will never be persuaded to stop collecting from or digging into sites. Nor is it likely that commercial looters will be dissuaded. The greatest legal incentive designed to protect archaeological resources and sites on public lands from such abuses is the **Archaeological Resources Protection Act (ARPA).** Before the passage of ARPA in 1979, archaeological resources on public lands were protected under the Antiquities Act of 1906, but the language in that statute was so vague and the penalties so minimal that it barely discouraged anyone from illicit excavations on federal lands. In fact, between 1906 and 1979, only 18 Antiquities Act cases resulted in convictions by a federal court, resulting in a total of $4,000 in fines and two 90-day jail terms (Hutt et al. 1992).

During the 1970s, archaeologists convinced congressional leaders that something had to be done to protect sites from vandalism and collecting. ARPA made collecting or digging into an archaeological site on federal land a felony subject to prison terms of up to five years and a maximum penalty of $250,000. Amendments to the law in 1988 lowered the threshold of damages from $5,000 to $500, so now more agencies and U.S. prosecutors are willing to pursue criminal investigations and prosecution of offenders. ARPA prosecution and conviction rates have increased dramatically over the past decade.

The Native American Graves Protection and Repatriation Act

Although great tracts of public land exist in the United States, a large part of the nation is held by the states or is privately owned. Most states have some form of archaeological protection statute, frequently related to the discovery of aboriginal burials (so-called "burial laws"), that protects burials and their artifactual contents. Some states have emulated the NHPA, making it necessary to act on behalf of archaeological sites found on both state and private land undergoing development. For example, the California Environmental Quality Act, requires NHPA-type analysis and mitigation for "significant" archaeological sites in California prior to development.

Another federal statute that helps protect certain archaeological sites on public lands is the **Native American Graves Protection and Repatriation Act (NAGPRA).** Among other things, this statute, passed in 1990, makes it necessary for federal projects to cease and notify appropriate tribal representatives if aboriginal human remains are encountered as accidental discoveries during federal actions or archaeological investigations.

Repatriated Northern Cheyenne remains await burial at a 1993 ceremony in Busby, Montana.

Antiquities Legislation around the World

Nearly all nations have laws protecting antiquities and regulating the exportation of artifacts. As developed nations become increasingly prosperous, the desire for ancient objets d'art and artifacts for display increases dramatically. Unfortunately, this desire for ancient art fuels a booming international underground economy, especially in nations where poverty is rampant and people embrace any means of generating money in order to survive. The level of this problem is evident in the number of pre-Columbian artifacts of Maya origin auctioned during the last three decades by the auction house Sotheby's in the United States alone (Gilgan 2001) (Figure 13.4).

Worldwide, looting is not limited to digging up graves or archaeological deposits. From the Peruvian Andes to the jungles of Malaysia, temples, ruins, statuaries, rock art sites, and stelae are being chiseled, sawed, and broken to get at statues, paintings, figures, and inscriptions that represent the last several thousand years of human productivity. The recent war in Iraq led to the wholesale pillaging of the National Museum in Baghdad in 2003, where looters ransacked the facility and stole thousands of priceless artifacts related to the ancient Mesopotamian civilizations. Fortunately, most of the items were ultimately recovered. Despite the fact that in many countries looters face strict penalties, the lure of money (sometimes 50 to 100 times the average annual income of a typical citizen farmer in many countries, such as Niger) outweighs the potential consequences, including incarceration. Table 13.1 provides a list of some of the statutes that various countries have enacted in an effort to stem the tide of site destruction.

In 1970 the United Nations Educational, Scientific, and Cultural Organization (UNESCO) convened an international conference in Paris to address the problem of the illegal import, export, and transfer of artifacts and other cultural items. Participants

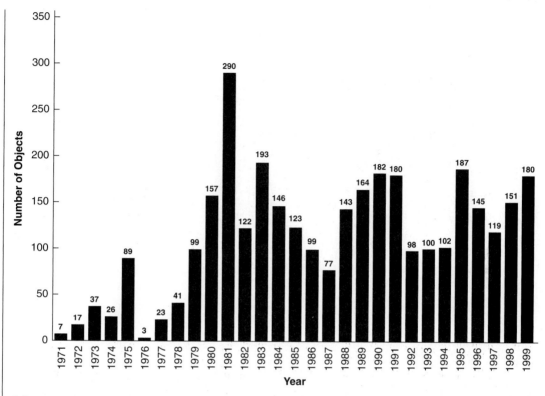

figure 13.4

Histogram of Auctioned Maya Artifacts

The number of Maya artifacts auctioned in the United States by Sotheby's increased greatly from 1971 to 1999. These numbers suggest that the vandalism of Maya sites and, by implication, vandalism in general continue to be major problems.

Source: Elizabeth Gilgan, 2001, "Looting and the Market for Maya Objects," in Neil Brodie, Jennifer Doole, and Colin Renfrew, eds., *Trade in Illicit Antiquities: The Destruction of the World's Heritage* (Cambridge, UK: The McDonald Institute for Archaeological Research), Figure 9.2. Used with permission.

drafted the **UNESCO Convention of 1970,** aimed at protecting not only archaeological materials but also significant or rare biological and paleontological resources (rare plants, animals, and fossils) considered to be part of a country's cultural heritage. However, more than 30 years later, several countries, including Great Britain, have yet to ratify the 26-article convention. Supplementing the UNESCO Convention of 1970 was the **Unidroit Convention of 1995** (issued by the International Institute for the Unification of Private Law), which outlawed stolen or illegally exported cultural objects, including items unlawfully excavated or unlawfully transported from legal excavations. Both conventions advocated the return of removed antiquities to their countries of origin. Several countries are abiding by these rules and have repatriated some artifacts. The United States, for example, recently returned some items to Peru.

table 13.1

Antiquities Protection Laws from around the World

STATUTE	COUNTRY	RESOURCES PROTECTED
Royal Proclamation (1666)	Sweden	Ancient monuments
Law for the Protection of Cultural Properties (1950)	Japan	Prehistoric/historic monuments and artifacts that are registered
Historic Monuments Act (1971)	Northern Ireland	Monuments and artifacts
Protection of Wrecks Act (1973)	United Kingdom	Shipwrecks
Ancient Monuments and Archaeological Areas Act (1979)	United Kingdom	Monuments and sites
Archaeological Resources Protection Act (1979)	United States	Archaeological sites, artifacts, and features
Norwegian Cultural Heritage Act (1979)	Norway	Ancient monuments, sites, and artifacts dating prior to AD 1573
Historic Heritage Law (1985)	Spain	Archaeological sites

The problem of archaeological site destruction for profit can be resolved by greatly reducing the demand for objects of antiquity by both private interests and museums. Many museums have adopted policies that prohibit the acquisition of illicit antiquities or any items whose provenience is unknown. Unfortunately, many museums in the United States do not fully comply with these rules, complicating efforts to stop looting (Brodie and Renfrew 2005).

Site Preservation and Restoration

Archaeologists are beginning to recognize that not every site can or should be excavated today and that measures must be taken to protect sites for future generations of scientists to examine. As you have read, some laws and conventions exist to reduce the antiquities market, thereby reducing site disturbance. Tourist dollars also reduce site disturbance. The pyramids at Giza, the Forum and Coliseum in Rome, Petra in Jordan, Aztec and Maya sites in Mexico and Central America, and the Acropolis in Greece are just a few examples of archaeological destinations that attract tens of thousands of visitors and their coveted vacation money to the host countries each year. The preservation and maintenance of these sites not only protects the cultural heritage of these countries but also provides an important economic boost as well.

Considerable resources and planning have gone into the preservation and restoration of certain archaeological sites, such as the removal and reconstruction of the Egyptian temple of Abu Simbel in the mid-1960s when construction of the Aswan Dam on Lake Nasser threatened to inundate this amazing Thirteenth Dynasty site (Highlight 13.2).

Preserving Abu Simbel

In the late 1950s, the government of Egypt decided to construct a large dam across the Nile River at Aswan in southern Egypt. The dam would provide hydroelectric power and flood control and would create a large lake, Lake Nasser, that would extend well into Sudan. The new lake would flood many thousands of acres, inundating many archaeological sites, including the two major temples at Abu Simbel dating from the time of Rameses II. These temples were one of the most recognized places in ancient Egypt and a major tourist attraction.

The two temples, located several hundred feet apart, were cut into the rock of cliffs overlooking the Nile and extended back into the cliff several hundred feet. Their construction was an engineering marvel in its day. The Great Temple was dedicated to Pharaoh Rameses II, the Small Temple to his wife, Queen Nofretari. There was widespread desire to save the temples from the rising waters, but time and money were limited.

Several ideas were proposed. One was to construct a small dam around the site so that it would remain dry even when the lake was full. Another was to move the temples in one piece to higher ground. Both proved unfeasible.

In 1962, after the Aswan Dam was completed and the waters of Lake Nasser were rising, it was proposed that each of the temples be cut into blocks that could be moved to higher ground immediately above their original positions and then reassembled. This idea was approved, and work began immediately. The project was cosponsored by UNESCO and paid for by donations from various countries and organizations.

Between 1964 and 1968, each of the temples was precisely mapped and cut into thousands of blocks with large rock saws. Each block was numbered and transported to a nearby storage yard. When all of

Workers at Abu Simbel rushed to complete the transfer of temple blocks to higher ground before rising waters behind the Aswan Dam drowned the site.

the blocks had been cut and moved, they were reassembled like pieces of a giant puzzle. They were repositioned with the aid of steel reinforcement bars and cement made to duplicate the color and texture of the rock. The workers had to place the reconstructed

HIGHLIGHT **13.2** *continued*

temples in exactly the same alignment as the originals because the ancient work crews had constructed them so that the Sun's rays would enter certain parts of the complex at certain times (Desroches-Nobelcourt and Gerster 1968). After the reconstruction was completed, the site once again became a tourist attraction and remains a symbol of the power and grandeur of ancient Egypt.

Increasingly, historical and archaeological sites are being seen as resources for economic development in the United States and elsewhere. Cultural tourism is a growing industry. Baby boomers, now reaching middle age, have more disposable income and higher education than previous generations, and many make museums, Civil War battlefields, historic town sites, and archaeological sites (e.g., Mesa Verde in Colorado, where great concentrations of prehistoric cliff dwellings are found in a spectacular setting) their holiday or vacation destination. The increase in the flow of tourists means more money for local communities, and many businesses in both urban and rural areas have made significant strides in attracting some of this new economic bounty. As a result, historical/archaeological resources are protected and maintained, and the communities benefit economically. Furthermore, sites that are professionally prepared and interpreted educate the public about the significance of such resources and why they need to be protected.

The Role of Public Education in Archaeological Preservation

As the archaeologist Charles McGimsey (1972:5) said, "there is no such thing as 'private archaeology.'" The greatest support system is the public. Interpreting history and prehistory in a way that everyone can enjoy increases people's appreciation and knowledge and justifies the funding of future programs that will accomplish these goals. Promoting archaeological education is an important role in professional archaeology. In the United States, both government agencies and educational institutions encourage and sponsor such efforts. For example, people can have hands-on experiences of field and laboratory work in the Passports in Time program developed by the U.S. Forest Service, and they can attend innovative, interactive educational exhibits, such as at the visitors' center at Cahokia Mounds State Historic Park in Illinois. Table 13.2 provides a list of some of the archaeological parks in the United States.

table 13.2

Selected Archaeological Parks in the United States

Alabama	Colorado	Iowa	Missouri
Moundville	Anasazi Heritage Center	Effigy Mounds	Graham Cave
Russell Cave	Hovenweep	Toolesboro Indian Mounds	Osage Village
Florence Indian Mound	Mesa Verde		**Montana**
		Kansas	Little Bighorn Battlefield
Arizona	**Florida**	Pawnee Village Site	
Besh-Ba-Gowah	Crystal River		**New Mexico**
Canyon de Chelly	Indian Temple Mound	**Kentucky**	Aztec Ruins
Casa Grande Ruins	Mission San Luis	Wickcliff Mounds	Chaco Canyon
Casa Malpais		Mammoth Cave	Gila Cliff Dwellings
Clover Ruin	**Georgia**		
Deer Valley Rock Art Center	Etowah Mounds	**Louisiana**	**North Carolina**
	Kolomoki Mounds	Marksville	Town Creek Indian Mound
Elden Pueblo		Poverty Point	
Homolovi Ruins	**Hawai'i**		**North Dakota**
Montezuma Castle National Monument	Kaloko-Honokohua	**Michigan**	Knife River Indian Village
	Pu'uhonua a Honaunau	Fort Michilimackinac	
Painted Rock Petroglyphs	Pu'ukohola Heiau	Sanilac Petroglyphs	**Ohio**
Pueblo Grande		St. Ignace Mission	Adena
Walnut Canyon	**Idaho**	Museum of Ojibwe Culture	Flint Ridge
	Nez Perce		Fort Ancient
		Minnesota	**Oklahoma**
Arkansas	**Illinois**	Grand Portage	Spiro Mounds
Parkin	Cahokia Mounds	Pipestone National Monument	
Toltec Mounds	Dickson Mounds		**Oregon**
			Fort Clatsop
California	**Indiana**	**Mississippi**	**South Carolina**
Indian Grinding Rocks State Park	Angel Mounds	Grand Village of the Natchez Indians	Oconee Station State Historic Site
	Mounds State Park		

States sponsor poster competitions as part of their activities and events for Archaeology Week. This poster features the archaeological excavation, reconstruction, and restoration of Edith Wharton's historic gardens at The Mount in Lenox, Massachusetts, a National Historic Landmark. The long-buried landscape design and gardens originally were built in 1901–1902. What did your state do for Archaeology Week most recently?

Many states have programs to inform people about the wonders of the past and the importance of preserving the past. Several programs are aimed at grade school children as well as adults. Most SHPOs and government agencies cooperate in sponsoring special lectures, museum and traveling exhibits intended to educate the public about the importance of archaeology and history, and "archaeology weeks" or "archaeology months" that are designed for adults as well as children and usually include public demonstrations of flintknapping, traditional basket construction, and other traditional activities. During these events, posters, flyers, and educational pamphlets are distributed to attract people to activities that explore curiosities of the past.

Avocational archaeological organizations also play a role in educating the public about archaeology. Most states have at least one such organization, and some have many. These organizations are sponsored or advised by professional archaeologists. Creditable archaeological societies have established codes of ethics that prohibit members from looting or vandalizing archaeological sites. Many of these associations assist professional archaeologists during extensive archaeological surveys. For example, the Archaeological Survey Association of Southern California conducted numerous field surveys and aided in many important excavations during the 1950s and 1960s. Many private organizations assist government agencies such as the Bureau of Land Management and the Forest Service in *archaeological site stewardship* as adjunct archaeologists. These workers monitor site conditions and report signs of site disturbance such as erosion, livestock trampling, and unauthorized digging.

The Internet is an important new source of educational information about archaeology and historic preservation worldwide. Many Web sites are sponsored by professional organizations. The Society for American Archaeology (SAA), for example, has entire sections devoted to public education, including listings of upcoming field and laboratory opportunities, workshops, presentations, and classes.

 # Cultural Resource Management among Traditional Peoples

In recent years, indigenous peoples across the globe have been asserting their rights to save, promote, and interpret their own cultural traditions and prehistories (see Watkins 2005). Native Americans, Native Hawaiians, Australian Aborigines, and the Maori of New Zealand are a few of the peoples who are taking a proactive role in developing their own cultural resource management programs. After years of being subjected to assimilation by Western cultures, many traditional groups are in danger of losing not only their traditional crafts and lifeways but their native languages as well. Interest in "saving" these cultures originated with European and American anthropologists during the late nineteenth and early twentieth centuries. Since then, many indigenous groups have gained political power and succeeded in obtaining funding and developing their own heritage preservation programs. The foci of these programs include native language classes, traditional interpretations of archaeological data, and repatriation efforts and the recovery of ethnological and archaeological collections from museums.

In North America, the Navajo, Zuni, Hopi, Nez Perce, Shoshone-Bannock, Confederated Salish-Kootnai, and Dakota are a few of the tribes that have active cultural resource programs. Some of these programs employ tribal anthropologists and archaeologists on a full-time basis to conduct surveys and site recordation on tribal lands. The Archaeology Department of the Navajo (Déné) cultural resource program is the largest Native American archaeological program in the Americas and is the only tribal organization that trains and employs native speakers as archaeologists. Too few archaeologists incorporate the views and research questions of the people whose past they study. An exception to this is the work of Janet Spector, as shown in Highlight 13.3.

Janet Spector and the Archaeology of the Dakota

As disciplines firmly rooted in the ebb and flow of Western culture, cultural anthropology and archaeology have been profoundly influenced by broader social movements, such as the civil rights and feminist movements of the twentieth century. Although the impact of feminist thought on anthropology can be traced back to the pioneering work of Margaret Mead in the 1920s, it was in the 1970s and 1980s, as men and women who participated in women's rights rallies came of age, that concerns with women's issues and gender systems really began to influence mainstream anthropological practice.

One of the classic articles to arise out of this early period of questioning and conceiving of feminist archaeology is "Archaeology and the Study of Gender," published in 1984 by Margaret Conkey and Janet Spector. Conkey and Spector (1984:22–23) suggested that one reason why an archaeology of gender had been slow in developing was that the effects of gender systems are most visible in the archaeological record at such a small scale—for example, in the internal organization of households. Traditional (processual) archaeology, with its emphasis on large-scale processes of development, simply was not looking where gender relations would be most evident.

Following this initial insight, feminist archaeologists began to think of their work as involving far more than what women did in the past; instead, they reworked the goals and priorities of archaeological practice to include a focus on daily life at the local level. At the same time, feminist archaeologists embraced multiple perspectives both in the present practice of archaeology and as part of the lived reality represented in the archaeological record. Thus, most feminist-inspired understandings of peoples of the past reflect the post-processual perspective in archaeology.

The best way to understand what this difference in perspective can mean to the practice of archaeology is to look at a case study by the pioneering author

Janet Spector. In her archaeological project at the village of Little Rapids, Minnesota, a Native American site occupied by members of the Wahpeton Dakota culture in the 1800s, Spector sought to implement many of the ideas she and Conkey had formulated in the abstract. She called her approach to understanding gender at the site the "task differentiation approach." The first step was to "examine the relationships between material and non-material aspects of gender in known or documented cases where we could learn about gender-specific tasks, behaviors, and beliefs and their material/spatial dimensions" (Spector 1991:390). In other words, she hoped that through comparative studies, "we could eventually isolate some material regularities or patterns about different types of task systems which then could be identified archaeologically" (Spector 1991:391).

Spector thought the task differentiation approach would help illuminate gender relations in the archaeological record and add representations of women to accounts of the Dakota past. As she began to work at Little Rapids, however, she discovered that the task approach actually "inhibited my ability to express what I'd learned through a variety of sources about Wahpeton men, women, and children who had lived at Little Rapids during a particularly disruptive period of their history when American colonial expansion was rapidly accelerating in Minnesota.... I abandoned my case study of task differentiation and began to experiment with a new way of presenting the archaeological and ethnohistoric knowledge I had acquired" (Spector 1991:393, 394).

Spector felt that the task orientation methodology still treated the Dakota as groups of people following rules and living out patterns without any individuality or spirit of their own. She felt she was in danger of "reinforcing Eurocentric stereotypes and images" of Native Americans as simple, unchanging, and undifferentiated and unmotivated as individuals (Spector

1991:393). How could she bring the past to life in a way that respects and humanizes the men, women, and children who lived it, while simultaneously preserving a place for "hard" (scientific) archaeological data?

As Spector pondered this problem, she proceeded with her project, striving to involve local descendants of the Wahpeton in the process. She found that her Native American collaborators had research questions, interpretations of the archaeological record, and final conclusions different from those her background in academic archaeology had taught her to ask and expect. In her book *What This Awl Means: Feminist Archaeology at a Wahpeton Dakota Village* (Spector 1993), she described how the involvement of members of another culture, like the inclusion of feminist perspectives, fundamentally altered archaeological questions and conclusions.

The awl mentioned in the book's title provided Spector with the inspiration for expressing her humanistic approach to archaeology. An awl is a piercing tool used by many cultures, particularly in the sewing of animal hides. Awls can be made of different materials, such as bone, antler, and even metal. At Little Rapids after European contact, many awls consisted of a metal tip set in an antler handle. Although most archaeological descriptions of awls emphasize the "working end" of the awl and its functional utility, Spector found ethnohistoric accounts describing the importance of the handles to their female owners, who sometimes painstakingly carved designs into them. Through the use of ethnohistoric sources, Spector (1991:395) discovered that the symbols carved on the handles recorded specific accomplishments, such as the completion of a hide robe.

After finding a decorated awl handle in the midden at Little Rapids, Spector (1993) wrote a fictional narrative imagining the moment of its deposition into the midden, and she used this story as the focal point for her book. The point of the story is to provide the reader with a moment of insight that is grounded in archaeological reality even though it is a product of

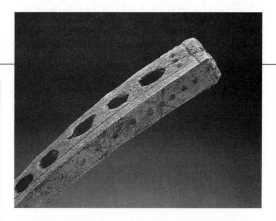

In her book about this awl, *What This Awl Means: Feminist Archaeology at a Wahpeton Dakota Village* (Spector 1993), Janet Spector brings to life the Dakota Indian men, women, and children who lived in Little Rapids, Minnesota, long ago.

Spector's imagination. The story also is infused with empathy for the real human being who once owned and used that handle. This approach illustrates the point Conkey and Spector made about changing the *scale* of the focus of archaeological research (in this case, centering a broader analysis of social change on a *single* artifact and its owner) and how changing the scale changes the questions that can be asked and answered about the past.

CRITICAL **THINKING** QUESTIONS

1. According to Janet Spector and other feminist archaeologists, why is the task differentiation approach to gender studies inadequate? What other approaches are possible?
2. How did Spector's work benefit from the use of ethnohistoric sources and her involvement of living descendants in archaeological excavation and interpretation?
3. How does feminist archaeology reflect the postprocessual approach in archaeology? What elements of the processual approach are included?

HIGHLIGHT 13.4

Heritage Management in Australia

The impact of European colonization on the indigenous peoples of Australia, known as Aborigines or Koori, has taken many forms. Over the centuries, they have been hunted and killed, forcibly relocated, fostered as children to families of European descent, and taught that their language and cultural ways were of no value (Chippindale 1993). In the latter part of the twentieth century, Aborigines made great strides toward regaining basic human rights as well as significant political power in their homeland. One area that has been a priority is gaining control of the cultural resources that represent their ancestral heritage.

In Australia a series of acts was passed in the 1960s and 1970s designed to protect archaeological resources and provide for heritage management, but these laws envisioned academically trained archaeologists as the experts who would be consulted and the caretakers who would manage and interpret sites (Flood 1989). These original laws have since been amended or reinterpreted to include stronger and more central roles for Australians of Aboriginal descent in heritage management. In response to these laws, as well as to archaeologists' growing sense of responsibility to involve the indigenous people, local Aboriginal communities were increasingly informed of archaeological projects and discoveries. In these early days of collaboration, however, the flow of information was very one-sided. Archaeologists and government officials usually told Aborigines what would be happening to archaeological resources, rather than asking for their opinions or their permission. Aborigines were

informed of developing ideas about their past, but they were not included in research design or stewardship of existing archaeological resources. In its own way, this situation represented a continuing "colonization" of the Aboriginal past by non-Aborigines: Australians of European descent were still the ultimate authorities in writing the history of the Aboriginal people, and Aboriginal accounts of the past and opinions on heritage management were marginalized.

In an effort to assert ownership over their ancestors' sites, the Tasmanian Aboriginal Land Council (TALC) demanded the return of archaeological materials that had been excavated by scholars from La Trobe University in Melbourne. The materials at issue in this highly publicized case did not include human skeletal remains but had been dated by archaeologists as being more than 30,000 years old. The archaeologists argued that the materials were so ancient that they should be considered "part of the universal history of humans and should be a source of history and pride to all Australians, Aboriginal and non-Aboriginal alike" (Allen 1995). The law, however, recognized them as the ancestral heritage of the indigenous people and ordered them returned to TALC's custody (Smith 1999). Some archaeologists saw this outcome as a blow to scientific progress, but others saw it as a long-overdue acknowledgment of the fact that indigenous peoples should have control over the remains of their past.

In other cases, Aborigines have been very interested in supporting archaeological research, especially when it helps undermine racist myths about their past.

Preservation efforts in other parts of the world by indigenous peoples include initiatives by the Australian Aborigines to record and protect heritage sites throughout Australia (Highlight 13.4). In 1996 the National Aboriginal History and Heritage Council (NAHHC) was formed to bring Aborigines together from different tribal and geographic affiliations for "the protection of Aboriginal Sites and Places considered to be 'at risk'" (NAHHC n.d.).

Kakadu National Park contains more than 1,000 sites, many as much as 30,000 years old. The park, a World Heritage site, is managed by the Australian Nature Conservation Agency and tribal elders working on behalf of the traditional owners, the Mirrar clan. Today the Mirrar are in a dispute with the Energy Resources of Australia company against a government-backed plan to mine uranium in this Aboriginal sacred land.

Until the early part of the twentieth century, Euro-Australians were taught that the land they had taken over had not been inhabited either very long or very intensely by Aborigines. The efforts of archaeologists, and especially the advent of radiometric dating methods, have extended the record of significant human occupation of the Australian continent to at least 40,000 years ago! Archaeologists from Australia National University were given permission by one Aboriginal group to use a small sample of human remains for dating and DNA analysis (Finkel 1998). In addition to being a source of pride for Aboriginal peoples, this type of research has produced strong evidence supporting legal arguments over landownership (Chippindale 1993).

An example of Aboriginal and archaeologist cooperation that moves beyond simple "keeping the locals informed of what the experts are up to" and into full-fledged collaboration comes from a project conducted on Peel Island in southeast Queensland. Anne Ross, the archaeologist in charge, spent several months working with the local indigenous community, explaining her research interests and how and why she wanted to excavate a specific site. Community members informed her that although they were interested in having research done on their land, they did not want the site that Ross had chosen excavated because it was not appropriate to answer the questions they had about their past (Ross and Coghill 2000). Together, Ross and the people of Quandamooka drew up a plan of archaeological research and heritage management that reflected the values and interests of the local community as its first priority. Later, having established a positive working relationship of mutual respect and cooperation, together the group decided to excavate at the site that had originally interested Ross (Ross and Coghill 2000). The archaeological research at Peel Island represents a potentially fruitful new direction for Aboriginal–archaeological collaboration.

CRITICAL **THINKING** QUESTIONS

1. How are cultural resource and antiquities management similar in Australia and the United States?
2. For the Aborigines, what are the main social and cultural issues surrounding heritage preservation?
3. What forms can cooperation between archaeologists and Aboriginal peoples take, and why is cooperation important to both groups?

Archaeology and Ethics

Recall from Chapter 5 that ethical precepts—moral principles that dictate appropriate behavior—apply in the field, laboratory, museum, and classroom. Professional archaeologists have an obligation to their colleagues, to the public, and to future generations to be diligent and respectful in their quest to understand the past. They have an obligation to adhere to a standard of ethics set by the archaeological community, especially today when so much archaeology is occurring (especially in the United States), often in the form of cultural resource management. But exactly what is the ethical code observed by archaeologists today?

Before the beginning of World War II, the number of practicing professional archaeologists was small enough that nearly everyone knew everyone else (McGimsey 1995). After the war, the field grew, and it soon became apparent that certain standards should be adopted. Not until 1961, however, did the Society for American Archaeology adopt four statements formalizing professional standards and a code of ethics for the organization. These statements, the core of the SAA's standards and ethics, consist of the following parts (after McGimsey 1995):

1. A definition of archaeology.
2. The proper methods of archaeology, which, if not followed, could lead to ejection from the organization.
3. Particular ethical issues, including making site information available to other scholars and reporting on findings in a timely manner. This part also prohibits buying and selling artifacts, excavating without permission, and willfully destroying archaeological sites.
4. Issues related to the training of professional archaeologists, suggestions about field experience beyond the bachelor's degree, and encouragement of prospective archaeologists to obtain a graduate degree.

The standards that define a professional archaeologist include a graduate degree in anthropology, evidence of supervised field and laboratory work, and evidence of carrying archaeological projects through to completion.

After the 1966 passage of the National Historic Preservation Act, the ensuing appearance of CRM created a new dichotomy in archaeology: no longer did archaeologists consist only of academics and a few government archaeologists; a whole new group of archaeologists from outside the university emerged. Peer review alone, which had kept people within the once-small archaeological community in check, would no longer work with the new CRM "outsiders." How could the concerned archaeological community keep tabs on the new generation of cultural resource managers and contract archaeologists? Ultimately, after much discussion among all concerned parties, a separate organization was established: the Society of Professional Archaeologists (SOPA).

The hope was that all members of the SAA who met the standards defining a professional archaeologist would apply for membership in SOPA, undergo a committee review, and then be accepted or rejected on the basis of that review process. A summary of the code of ethics adopted by the SAA and SOPA in 1995 is shown in Table 13.3. A grievance process also was established to investigate and sanction members found to be in violation of the code of ethics. In 1998 the Society of Professional Archaeologists became the **Register of Professional Archaeologists (RPA)**. Members of the Register are allowed to use the letters "RPA" after their names (following their graduate degree) to designate that they have met the stringent criteria set by the screening committee.

Ethical problems became more of a concern after the birth of CRM because the demand for archaeologists turned an academic tradition into a thriving business. When

table 13.3

Ethical Principles of Archaeology

PRINCIPLE	EXPLANATION
Stewardship	The archaeological record, sites, artifacts, and research records are irreplaceable and have to be protected, preserved, and used wisely.
Accountability	A reasonable effort must be made to consult with groups affected by archaeological work.
Commercialization	The buying and selling of artifacts must not be conducted.
Public education and outreach	Educating the public about archaeology and about the past is critical.
Intellectual property	The records and knowledge generated by archaeological investigations are not the property of the investigator and must be shared with others.
Public reporting and publication	Knowledge and information from archaeological investigations must be disseminated and shared as widely as possible.
Records and preservation	The collections, records, and reports of archaeological investigations must be preserved.
Training and resources	Archaeological work must be done by properly trained researchers with adequate resources to complete the work.

Source: Adapted from principles developed by the Society for American Archaeology. (See Lynott 1997.)

environmental firms and archaeological contract shops started charging to produce a product (e.g., a report identifying archaeological sites, determining site eligibility, or describing test excavation results), it was inevitable that some archaeologists would start cutting corners to turn a profit. There have been cases in which "archaeologists" with questionable scruples "missed" archaeological sites to appease a landowner or developer. It is hoped that the RPA and its grievance process can help eliminate once and for all unethical individuals who would call themselves professional archaeologists.

CONTENTSELECT

Search articles in the ContentSelect database using the key word *cultural resource management*. What are some examples of the kinds of sites commonly managed as cultural resources? What specific legal and humanistic issues pertaining to these sites do the articles address?

Chapter Summary

The growth of human population has led to the expansion of dwellings, dams, roadways, and shopping centers on lands inhabited by other people long ago. Recreational use of formerly remote areas with archaeological and historical resources has increased, leading to the unprecedented destruction of archaeological sites. To mitigate the disappearance of our fragile past, laws have been passed to protect archaeological sites from land-disturbing activities and artifact collectors. In the late 1960s, the United States enacted the National Historic Preservation Act in an attempt to make federal agencies responsible for identifying and protecting historical and archaeological resources on public land. This law created the National Register of Historic Places, a listing of historic sites, buildings, structures, and archaeological sites of significance to American history and prehistory. It also created State Historic Preservation Offices to represent each state in this federal process, and the Advisory Council on Historic Preservation to aid both the SHPOs and the federal agencies in some situations.

Steps also have been taken to protect artifacts and archaeological sites from illicit collectors. In the United States, Congress passed the Archaeological Resources Protection Act, making it a felony to destroy an archaeological site. Other nations have passed laws to reduce devastation of sites in their own countries as well as trafficking in antiquities, but further steps need to be taken. Because large and unusual archaeological sites seem to hold an interest for most people, these sites have commercial value as tourist attractions. Such sites serve to educate the public as well as to stimulate the economy of the surrounding community and provide revenue for site maintenance and further research.

In the United States, public education emphasizing the significance of history and prehistory aims to generate interest in these resources, instill a sense of respect for archaeological sites, and build a consensus favoring their protection. Federal programs (such as Passports in Time, which allows laypeople the opportunity to participate in archaeological research), avocational societies, and archaeological parks offer the public opportunities to learn about archaeology firsthand. State programs, such as "archaeology weeks," also assist in public education.

Traditional peoples around the globe are becoming more closely involved in the protection and interpretation of their past. Examples from the United States demonstrate the desire of native peoples to take a hand in preserving their cultures and interpreting the archaeological record. As indigenous peoples become more politically active, they are more frequently asserting their rights to be involved in archaeological research and have control over their cultural and human remains.

The explosion of archaeological work being conducted through cultural resource management projects raises questions about professional ethics. Professional archaeologists need a way to police themselves. Half a century ago, the archaeological community was small and could control behavior through peer pressure. Today, thousands of archaeologists are doing contract work, often under short deadlines, and opportunities for ethical breaches are increasing. The Society of American Archaeology code and the stringent entrance standards and grievance process of the Registry of Professional Archaeologists are intended to encourage ethical practice.

Key Concepts

Advisory Council on Historic Preservation (ACHP), 361
Antiquities Act of 1906, 356
Archaeological Resources Protection Act (ARPA), 365
mitigation, 360
National Historic Preservation Act (NHPA), 359

National Register of Historic Places, 359
Native American Graves Protection and Repatriation Act (NAGPRA), 365
Register of Professional Archaeologists (RPA), 378
Reservoir Salvage Act of 1960, 357

Section 106 of NHPA, 359
Section 110 of NHPA, 360
State Historic Preservation Office (SHPO), 360
UNESCO Convention of 1970, 367
Unidroit Convention of 1995, 367

Suggested Readings

If you want to learn more about the concepts and issues discussed in this chapter, consider looking at the following resources. (Some may be rather technical.)

Hunter, John, and Ian Ralston (eds.). (1997). *Archaeological Resource Management in the UK: An Introduction.* Phoenix Mill: Sutton.

This collection of papers written by British archaeologists provides insight into cultural resource management practices and issues outside of North America.

King, Thomas F. (1998). *Cultural Resource Law and Practice: An Introductory Guide.* Walnut Creek, CA: AltaMira Press.

King, Thomas F. (2001). *Federal Planning and Historic Places: The Section 106 Process.* Walnut Creek, CA: AltaMira Press.

Both of these works provide an excellent introduction and overview of the statutes that created and continue to govern the way cultural resource management is practiced in the United States. Written by a recognized expert in this field, these books are informative as well as entertaining.

Neumann, Thomas W., and Robert M. Sandford. (2001). *Cultural Resources Archaeology: An Introduction.* Walnut Creek, CA: AltaMira Press.

This book covers the nuts-and-bolts approach to understanding how cultural resource archaeology is practiced in the United States. A good primer for the introductory student.

Renfrew, Colin. (2000). *Loot, Legitimacy, and Ownership: The Ethical Crisis in Archaeology.* London: Gerald Duckworth.

Renfrew examines the perpetually vexing issue of looting, site destruction, and the selling of archaeological relics on the antiquities market.

Vitelli, Karen D. (1996). *Archaeological Ethics.* Walnut Creek, CA: AltaMira Press.

A collection of papers dealing with the issues of worldwide archaeological site looting, cultural resource management, professional behavior, and archaeologists' interaction with the public. A good examination of several ethical issues that face archaeologists today.

chapter **14**

Archaeology in the Real World

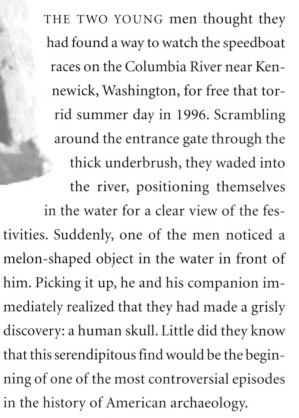

THE TWO YOUNG men thought they had found a way to watch the speedboat races on the Columbia River near Kennewick, Washington, for free that torrid summer day in 1996. Scrambling around the entrance gate through the thick underbrush, they waded into the river, positioning themselves in the water for a clear view of the festivities. Suddenly, one of the men noticed a melon-shaped object in the water in front of him. Picking it up, he and his companion immediately realized that they had made a grisly discovery: a human skull. Little did they know that this serendipitous find would be the beginning of one of the most controversial episodes in the history of American archaeology.

Once notified by the young men of this find, the coroner contacted the local archaeologist,

Dr. James Chatters. Was the find the result of a recent homicide or the remains of a prehistoric Native American that had eroded out of the riverbank? Chatters, a specialist in human osteology, initially thought that the skull likely belonged to a nineteenth-century white settler, given the long cranium and narrow face more typical of Caucasians than the rounder, wider-faced skulls of the indigenous populations of the Columbia Plateau. Supporting this early hypothesis was the fact that the remains were found in association with a historical archaeological site that was eroding into the river. Returning to the site, Chatters found additional skeletal material and ultimately recovered nearly 90 percent of the skeleton. The search team found numerous artifacts interspersed with the human bones dating to the late nineteenth and early twentieth centuries, lending yet further support to Chatters's initial impression.

But a more complete study was necessary, and Chatters undertook further analysis of the remains in his laboratory. The remains clearly were those of a robust adult male, then thought to be between 45 and 55 years of age. Most of the skull had been recovered, and every aspect of it—from the narrow, forward-projecting face to the configuration of the lower jaw—indicated Caucasoid rather than Native American. Even the femur, another indicator of racial affinity, was more Caucasoid than Asiatic in appearance. But Chatters noticed something peculiar in the ilium or blade of the pelvis: a partially healed wound with a hard, dark object still embedded in the bone. Was it a distorted bullet? Shrapnel from the Civil War? Or perhaps a stone

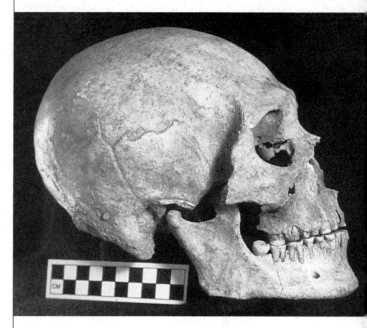

arrowpoint, a souvenir from an unfriendly encounter with the local Indian population more than 100 years ago?

Medical imaging equipment at a local hospital, including a CAT scan machine, clearly showed that the object was a stone projectile point, but the *type* of point it was made Chatters pause. The point was a Cascade projectile point—the most common style of dart point used on the Columbia Plateau between 5,000 and 9,000 years ago! What was an ancient projectile point doing in an early northwestern white settler?

Chatters knew that studies of the scant few remains of early human skeletons from the New World suggested that Paleoindians (the earliest occupants of the Americas) looked very different from later Native American peoples. In fact, they had features more commonly associated with Caucasoid populations (although they are clearly Asian

383

in origin). Could Kennewick Man be a Paleoindian? If so, this could be one of the most important North American scientific discoveries of the century. Chatters obtained permission to use radiocarbon dating to determine whether this new hypothesis could be supported. The results were staggering: Kennewick Man was 9,500 years old.

The place where the remains were found falls under the jurisdiction of the Army Corps of Engineers, a federal agency. According to the Native American Graves Protection and Repatriation Act (NAGPRA), it was the agency's responsibility to contact the local Native Americans for consultation. The interested tribes—the Yakama, the Umatilla, and the Colville—had been notified right after the discovery and updated on developments. After radiocarbon dating clarified that the remains were not those of a white settler, the Umatilla demanded that no further analysis be undertaken and that the remains be immediately repatriated for reburial—just days before Chatters was to take the remains to be examined by Dr. Doug Owsley, a renowned physical anthropologist at the Smithsonian Museum of Natural History. The Army Corps attorneys instructed the coroner to seize the remains from Chatters, who reluctantly surrendered the skeleton after only a two-hour warning that the remains were being repatriated. Much of the planned documentation and analysis was never completed, and Chatters feared that this significant discovery was going to be lost to science forever.

The scientific community, however, was not going to let the remains go without a fight. It was clear that the remains were Native American in a strictly literal sense, but did the Umatilla or any other tribe in the Northwest have the right to reclaim such ancient remains? Given the antiquity of the skeleton, it could be as closely related to indigenous peoples of South America as to any group now in North America. Furthermore, remains this rare can offer a unique glimpse into the prehistory of all humanity. The evidence should be studied by multiple scholars and the information made available to people worldwide. With this perspective, a group of eight prominent scientists, including both archaeologists and biological anthropologists, filed suit against the United States for the right to study the remains.

The suit alleged that the government had not adequately addressed the issue of the right of the Umatilla and several other tribes to claim the remains for reburial, because the tribes had not clearly proved direct affiliation with the remains (NAGPRA requires a "preponderance of evidence"). As a result of the lawsuit, the government conducted a four-year independent investigation of the remains. Physical anthropological, archaeological, and ethnological studies largely supported earlier conclusions that the remains were not affiliated with the tribes of the Northwest. Nevertheless, the United States argued that they did in fact demonstrate affiliation with those groups!

The Kennewick case has been in litigation since 1996, and only recently have there been significant developments. In August 2002, the district court ruled that the Kennewick remains were not Native American and set aside the decision made by the secretary of the interior that claimed otherwise. The government appealed the case to the U.S. Court of Appeals for the Ninth Circuit, where a unanimous opinion was rendered on February 4, 2004, to support the conclusion of the original district court allowing scientists the opportunity to study the remains. Although the Department of Justice has decided not to file an appeal, the concerned tribes still want to have some say in how the remains can be studied. The scientists have filed a motion to keep the tribes from further participation in the lawsuit, which was denied by the federal district court on August 17, 2004. The judge felt the tribes' role in the case had indeed ended with the original legal decision concluding that there was no link between the tribes and Kennewick Man. On September 9, 2004, the tribes fielded yet another motion, arguing that they have a right to intervene under several statutes other than NAGPRA, including ARPA and NHPA. This legal challenge was rejected by the courts, and Kennewick Man was turned over to the scientists for analysis. To prevent similar types of litigation, Congress is now considering an amendment to NAGPRA to clarify the law.

Studies of the Kennewick remains are now being conducted by physical anthropologist Douglas Owsley of the National Museum of Natural History, Smithsonian Institution. In 2005 and 2006, he and his team did a detailed examination of the remains and are subjecting samples of the bones to further radiometric dating assessments. Using advanced industrial CT technology, a new and more precise three-dimensional model of the Kennewick skull has been made (see page 211). Owsley's work suggests that the body of Kennewick Man was intentionally buried rather than buried naturally by fluvial processes. Further, it suggests he was in his late 30s rather than 45 to 50 years of age as originally proposed. The final report on the work is due for release in 2008.

For the location of Kennewick and other sites mentioned in this chapter, see the map on page 386.

Archaeology Today

Archaeology is no longer a simple matter of digging into archaeological sites and studying their contents. Over the past few decades, complex issues swirling around "ownership" of the past—and who has the right to study what—have emerged as some indigenous peoples around the world reject the interpretations of Western science in favor of traditional beliefs about cultural origins and past lifeways. Archaeologists are increasingly making it a point to include the viewpoints of traditional peoples in

LOCATION MAP: Sites Mentioned in Chapter 14

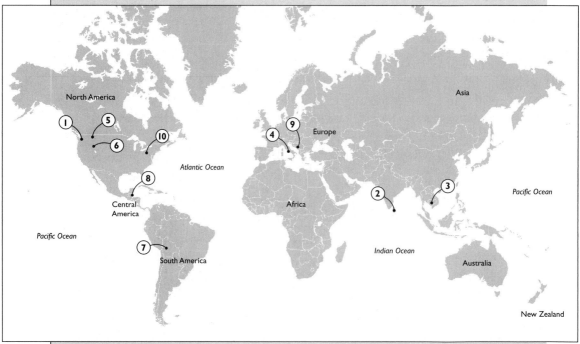

1 ■ Kennewick site
  Kennewick, Washington

2 ■ Sri Lanka

3 ■ Cambodia (Kampuchea)

4 ■ Ostia
  Italy

5 ■ Clark Fork River
  Montana

6 ■ Fort Hall
  Snake River, Idaho

7 ■ Llanos de Moxos
  Beni, Bolivia

8 ■ Pulltrouser Swamp
  Belize

9 ■ Bosnia

10 ■ United Airlines Flight No. 93 crash site
  Shanksville, Pennsylvania

archaeological interpretations, a change that can only enhance professional archaeologists' interpretations.

Not only are perceptions about interpreting the past being challenged, but the motivation for acquiring archaeological data is also changing. As discussed in Chapter 13, today a significant amount of the archaeological fieldwork undertaken in the United States is statute-related compliance archaeology rather than purely research-driven activity. Archaeology also is increasingly politically motivated. Some nations have used archaeology as a means of bolstering national pride and legitimizing claims to the right to remain within certain geographic areas or to acquire new territories.

Archaeology has practical applications that can help people with current problems of survival and adaptation. Knowledge about the overtaxing of the environment in the past, for instance, can help researchers design solutions for similar problems in the present. Archaeological methods have become popular in crime-scene investigations. Also, access to archaeology by the average citizen is becoming much easier with the advent of the Internet and interactive computer software, as well as the increase in cultural tourism and the popularity of archaeological sites as tourist destinations.

Archaeology and Politics

In addition to shedding light on the human past, archaeology has aided the reconstruction of cultural groups and ethnic origins and the dispersals of groups across geographic space. In some countries, archaeology has been a source of national pride—in Greece, Egypt, and Italy, for example, where the historical record and prehistoric remnants suggest the glory and splendor of ancient civilizations. The French are proud of their ancestors' resistance to Roman conquest, the Italians look proudly to their Roman forebears, the Irish rally around the notion of an ethnically pure Celtic origin, and the Israelis look to Iron Age archaeology to support their claims of statehood (Jones 1997). Many European archaeologists still work under the assumption that the material cultures they recover relate to specific ethnic groups. But can archaeology always truly identify ethnicity? As you read in Chapter 11, it is difficult to put a clear ethnic label on archaeological cultures. The difficulties in defining distinct ethnic groups in the archaeological record, however, have not stopped politicians from using archaeology as a tool to justify ignoble causes or promote distorted interpretations of the past to advance specific political viewpoints. For example, in Sri Lanka, both factions fighting a long civil war claim to be the original inhabitants of the island. Neither faction will allow any archaeological work for fear it may provide support for the other side.

Unfortunately, political agendas can and do cloud scientific objectivity, as in the case of the Nazis' use of the archaeological record to support their expansionist efforts during World War II. Long ignored before the rise of the Third Reich, German archaeology was reinvented by linguist and historian Gustav Kossinna, who claimed to be able to recognize "Germanic" artifact types throughout many parts of Europe. In his book, *German Prehistory: A Preeminently National Discipline* (1921), Kossinna cited spurious evidence of a

German "fatherland" that included most of Europe. The Nazis used this false prehistory as propaganda to support the reclamation of their ancient homeland through military expansion. New funding came to archaeology through the Third Reich and its wealthy supporters to find as much evidence as possible of the ancient Germanic presence while downplaying the significance of the influence of the Roman Empire. In 1941 a group of Nazi-supported archaeologists even claimed to have uncovered proof of a Neolithic presence of Germanic peoples in Greece (Arnold 1992)!

Benito Mussolini, Hitler's ally, used archaeology to inspire nationalistic pride among dispirited Italians. Mussolini glorified the Roman Empire (Kopff 2000). He poured money into archaeological excavation of sites of imperial Rome's golden era, such as the Roman seaport of Ostia (see the Location Map on page 386). Even the construction of the Foro Mussolini, a large sports arena built along the Tiber River in Rome during Mussolini's reign, was inspired by classical Roman architecture (Aicher 2000).

In the 1970s and 1980s, the Khmer Rouge in Cambodia, led by Pol Pot, used the ancient Khmer civilization as its inspiration, wanting to return Cambodia to its splendid past (see Highlight 4.5 in Chapter 4). To do that, the government set out to eliminate anything modern, including people with modern ideas. The Khmer Rouge forced people out of the cities and into the countryside. The result was mass starvation and the death of millions.

This prehistoric Puebloan kiva is a type of Native American house and ceremonial structure found in the southwestern United States. In what sense do archaeological finds such as this have more than one interpretation? How might an ancient Puebloan Indian, a contemporary Zuni elder, a processual archaeologist, and a postprocessual archaeologist interpret this feature?

Who Owns the Past?

The record of the past can be interpreted in any number of ways, such as by the archaeologists investigating it or by the descendants of the people who created it (Johnson 1999; Young 2006). Having alternative interpretations is not a problem; in fact, different views serve to strengthen research. For a long time, archaeologists tended to view their results as unassailable "truth," but in recent years, archaeology has become increasingly sensitive to the views and concerns of the descendants of the people being studied (such as Native Americans), and today more indigenous peoples are active participants in the research regarding their ancestors (see Highlight 14.1). This only broadens the scope of archaeological investigations, which is a good thing. However, in some cases indigenous groups claim the "truth" and oppose any investigations that might contradict their beliefs. Does any single group, archaeologists or descendants, have a monopoly on knowledge?

Some people argue that the past belongs to all people, that it is community property, and that the destruction of any part of the archaeological record without proper research is a crime against humanity. This view is the basis of much of the antiquities legislation around the world. Some governments, however, act to erase or alter evidence of the past that they do not like or that does not fit their agenda. For example, when the Spanish first conquered the Mexica and Inka, they dismantled their temples and used the stone for the construction of churches, substituting one system for another. More recently, when the Taliban, a fundamentalist Islamic government, controlled most of Afghanistan, they ordered the destruction of all images that were not Islamic. Ignoring international cries against the destruction of Afghanistan's irreplaceable archaeological treasures, the Taliban destroyed two huge statues of Buddha carved into a mountain.

In recent years, as Native Americans have gained more political power and greater public attention, there has been a call for greater consideration of their interpretations of the archaeological record. Many of these interpretations incorporate their traditional worldviews, intertwining religious beliefs, oral history, and creation stories. Indeed, the Native American viewpoint does provide alternative models for understanding the past, and this perspective has the potential to significantly enrich the body of archaeological knowledge once it is put in a scientifically testable framework.

Learning from the Past: Applying Archaeology to Contemporary Problems

Learning about past human successes and failures and about how people have adapted (or not) can inform us about how we might act in the future. Archaeological data can be used to address current problems. One example of a practical lesson from the past is

HIGHLIGHT 14.1

Indians and Archaeologists in the United States

The relationship between Native Americans and archaeologists has been as variable as the personalities, political climate, and specific circumstances involved. Some archaeologists have always worked very closely with Native Americans, treating the sites of their presumed ancestors with respect and involving tribal peoples directly in the excavation and the interpretation of certain features and artifacts. Other archaeologists have treated tribal concerns with indifference and have resisted or specifically avoided consulting local tribal representatives. Some Native Americans support the research efforts of prehistorians, but many others see archaeologists' attempts to study their past as disrespectful and even sacrilegious. Some objections to archaeological research have to do with traditional views of the appropriate treatment of the dead and their funerary materials. Some Native Americans strongly believe that handling the possessions of dead relatives, no matter how old, can result in illness, bad luck, and death among living people. Some refuse to enter museums that contain the skeletal remains of Native Americans. However, Native Americans' biggest complaint is that archaeologists attempt to reconstruct their people's past without consulting them about how to interpret the material culture and features. Many tribal people believe they are being misrepresented with an incomplete or false history.

With the enactment of the Native American Graves Protection and Repatriation Act and recent changes to the language in the regulations for the National Historic Preservation Act, government agencies are now required to consult more closely with Indian tribes. When archaeological projects based on Section 106 compliance are initiated, the federal government now routinely asks the appropriate tribes about their concerns over certain project areas and proposed archaeological research designs. In some cases, task groups are assembled that include State Historic Preservation Office staff, federal cultural resource personnel, and tribal representatives to work out the details of how archaeological projects should be organized and carried out.

A case in 1997 involved the Federal Energy Regulatory Commission hydropower plant relicensing project in Cabinet Gorge along the Clark Fork River in Montana and northern Idaho. A committee was formed consisting of representatives of several northwestern tribes (the Salish-Kootenai, the Kalispel, the Coeur d'Alene, and the Kootenai of Idaho), the SHPOs from Idaho and Montana, the U.S. Forest Service (which manages much of the land along the river), and the power company (Avista, formerly Washington Water and Power). Committee members worked together to balance traditional and scientific concerns about archaeological resources along the Clark Fork River. The result was a formal agreement to have the investigations conducted by an archaeological firm that had gained the trust and respect of local archaeologists and tribal peoples.

More and more tribes are beginning to establish cultural resource programs and tribal preservation offices, and these offices have begun to hire tribal archaeologists and anthropologists to represent the tribal perspective in interpreting native prehistory. Tribes and nations with full-time archaeologists include the Navajo, Zuni, Hopi, Potowatami, Choctaw, Shoshone-Bannock, and Ojibwe. Few of these archaeologists are Native American in ancestry. One of the few exceptions is Diana Yupe, a Shoshone woman with a university degree in anthropology and extensive experience as an archaeologist. She was the tribal anthropologist for the Shoshone-Bannock tribes at Fort Hall, Idaho (but is now with the U.S. Forest Service), and assisted her tribe with NHPA and NAGPRA consultation and with issues arising over cultural resource matters. "I have been living in two worlds: one of the Western

HIGHLIGHT **14.1** *continued*

scientist and the other of the traditional Indian people," says Yupe. "Some of my people think I have betrayed them because I do archaeology."

Yupe believes that she can provide a unique perspective for archaeology because she tries to understand archaeological sites—such as Wah'muza, located on the Fort Hall Reservation—as both a scientist and an Indian. Wah'muza is a habitation site occupied by the ancestors of the modern Shoshone for more than 4,000 years. Yupe worked there as a student at Idaho State University at Pocatello and used her traditional knowledge to help with interpretation of the site. "As an Indian archaeologist, I have to look within myself to understand my traditions and beliefs as an Indian, as an archaeologist, and as an Indian archaeologist," says Yupe. "Sometimes I don't like what I see or feel, but it is apparent that our ancestors are providing spiritual guidance to preserve our cultural ways for our tribal futures."

The importance of archaeologists and Native Americans working together is acknowledged today in American archaeology. Native American–sponsored symposia and workshops are becoming commonplace at the annual meetings of the Society for American Archaeology, and the relationship between Native Americans and archaeologists was a national conference topic at Dartmouth College in the spring of 2001. Joe Watkins, a Choctaw Indian who works for the Bureau of Indian Affairs as an anthropologist, was one of

Diana Yupe works at the excavation of a feature at a site in Idaho.

the conference organizers. Watkins stated, "Each of us American Indian archaeologists are trying to change not only the way archaeologists view American Indians, but the way American Indians view archaeologists."

CRITICAL **THINKING** QUESTIONS

1. What is the role of a tribal archaeologist? Why is this role important in American archaeology today?
2. What political and ideological factors are at work in relationships between archaeologists and indigenous peoples?

a call for reestablishing raised fields in northeastern Bolivia (the southwestern Amazon Basin) as in the ancient past. This area is alternately bone-dry savanna during the dry season and completely inundated during the winter floods. Raised fields provided an innovative means of farming long lost to prehistory (Coughlin 1995). Then Clark Erickson, an archaeologist from the University of Pennsylvania, recovered evidence of raised-field farming in the Llanos de Moxos region of Bolivia as old as 2,000 years.

Before the 1960s, specialists in the archaeology of the region could not imagine how an environment with such harsh seasonal extremes could have supported large populations in the past. Then in 1961, aerial photographs revealed the faint remnants of a complex series of raised fields. There was far more to the story of human occupation in this part of Amazonia than anyone had realized. Erickson's archaeological investigations,

HIGHLIGHT 14.2

The Ancient Maya and the Rain Forest

The Maya agricultural system was able to support a large population living in urban centers within a rain forest—without destroying the forest. How did the Maya do that? What lessons might we learn from them to help us use our forests without destroying them?

The Maya incorporated intensive and extensive horticultural techniques, creating a system of intensive agriculture (see Redfield and Rojas 1934; Kintz 1990; Wilk 1991; Fedick 1996), a system still used by the contemporary Maya. An understanding of Maya practices could lead to the development of techniques that could be utilized in contemporary rain forest settings, perhaps supporting large populations without the destruction of the forest.

Researchers originally thought that the Maya used swidden—a system in which land made suitable for cultivation by cutting and burning the vegetation was used on a repeated basis—as their primary agricultural technique. Swidden agriculture is fairly destructive but is sustainable with a relatively small population. Once archaeologists began to realize that what they thought were Maya ceremonial centers were actually Maya cities with large populations, they began to look for a more productive agricultural system and discovered the archaeological remains of nonswidden fields. In the hills, they found large numbers of small

stone-walled enclosures and small terraced gardens. In some swampy regions, they found raised fields; the best studied of these regions is Pulltrouser Swamp in southeastern Yucatán and northern Belize (Turner and Harrison 1983; Sharer 1994). To construct raised fields, the Maya dug ditches in the swamp and piled up the soil in a waffle-like pattern, raising the fields out of the water and creating canals between them. Soil dredged from the canals was added to the fields to maintain their fertility. The canals were colonized by turtles and fish, both of which the Maya ate.

Although our understanding of Maya agriculture is incomplete, some aspects of it are now clear. The Maya orchards blended into the forest. These trees were sources of food, lumber, and beauty. The Maya consructed small enclosed or terraced gardens where possible. In lowland areas not normally thought of as suitable for agriculture, they constructed raised fields. They also extensively utilized the swidden system. In addition, the Maya used a number of wild resources, such as deer and fruits, for food. These techniques composed a unified system that was highly productive and worked within the rain forest without destroying it.

Researchers hope that the Maya system can be understood and adapted for use by contemporary peoples around the world who farm in rain forests.

begun nearly two decades later, uncovered rectangular raised plots over a meter in height surrounded by canals. The features dated to between 100 BC and AD 1100 (Erickson 2000). Erickson wondered whether this means of adjusting to the local environment would work for present-day Bolivians trying to farm in the Llanos de Moxos. Experiments in replicating the raised fields demonstrated that the system worked well for growing manioc, maize, beans, and bananas. Though initially labor-intensive to build, the raised fields were easy to maintain once completed. They could be easily fertilized by scooping out the rotting vegetation from the bottoms of the adjacent canals and spreading it over the plot.

A swidden field in the forest

The ancient Maya used several techniques for farming in the rain forest, each of them suited to different conditions. Together, these methods provided a productive and sustainable agricultural system that supported the Maya for many centuries.

A small enclosed field

A small terraced field on a hillside

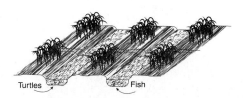

Turtles   Fish

Raised fields in swampy lowlands

Commonly used farming and ranching techniques result in destruction of the forest. If the Maya system could be adapted and adopted, rain forests could become very productive places capable of supporting large numbers of people in a sustained manner without sacrificing the forest.

CRITICAL **THINKING** QUESTIONS

1. How does this example show the practical aspects of learning about the past? In what countries might this knowledge be applied?
2. What other past knowledge or practices might be applied to other contemporary problems?

Some local farmers successfully adopted this farming strategy, and the idea of raised-field projects spread to neighboring communities. Because of this work, it may be possible for marginal farmers to succeed in the region for the first time in nearly 1,000 years. Similar studies on ancient farming practices in the Maya area of Mexico are providing useful alternatives for modern farmers in that region (Highlight 14.2).

In addition to providing possible solutions to contemporary problems related to agricultural practices, archaeology also furnishes clues about human impacts on the natural world that could serve as object lessons for the modern world. Archaeology has explained significant instances of human overexploitation of the environment that had negative repercussions in societies. An example from Highlight 9.1 in Chapter 9 is the overpopulation that led to the eventual deforestation and nearly complete environmental destruction of Easter Island. Another example is evidence suggesting that the destruction of forests surrounding certain ancient Maya sites in the lowlands of Guatemala probably was the result of excessive firewood cutting. The Maya used the wood to fuel fires needed for converting limestone dust into the plaster used in the maintenance of ceremonial center buildings (Woods and Titmus 1996).

The archaeological and paleontological records also reveal the role of humans in the disappearance of various animal species. A striking example is the rapid disappearance of some species of mammals after the appearance of humans on the Australian continent more than 40,000 years ago. Humans probably also were instrumental in the disappearance of American megafauna (giant animals such as mammoths and ground sloths), which became extinct shortly after human populations entered the New World. This information aids the conservation of plants and animals today. A goal of genome research, for example, is to preserve or re-create the genes from which medicinal plants and food crops originally arose.

Archaeology also is applied in forensic science. Because of their specialized knowledge and skills, archaeologists are the criminalists of the present as well as the past. They assist law enforcement agencies and international governments in excavating specific

Archaeological methods were used at the crash site of United Airlines Flight 93 in the Pennsylvania countryside following the terrorist takeover and subsequent crash of that flight. Forensic archaeologists also assisted at "ground zero" at the World Trade Center in New York City, destroyed by a terrorist attack on September 11, 2001.

types of crime scenes, especially homicides and body-disposal sites, and in recovering data from mass burials resulting from war and genocide as in Iraq, Argentina, Guatemala, and Afghanistan. For example, the coupling of archaeology and forensic science has been beneficial to exhume mass graves in Bosnia for war crimes investigations by the United Nations (see Brown 2006). In this effort, archaeologists discovered the criminals had murdered people, buried them, exhumed them, and reburied them in new mass graves. The evidence from soil and pollen enabled the archaeologists to reconstruct the events, and this evidence was used in the war crimes trials.

Archaeologists and human osteologists have teamed together as participants in international human rights missions across the globe, assisting foreign governments in their efforts to bring to justice perpetrators of mass homicide. Archaeologists are involved in ongoing attempts to recover the remains of American soldiers declared missing in action (MIAs) in Vietnam and Cambodia. Forensic anthropologists combine the skills of the archaeologist and the physical anthropologist at airplane crash sites and scenes of other catastrophic events, such as the terrorist attack and destruction of the World Trade Center in New York City on September 11, 2001. Highlight 14.3 describes an application of forensic archaeology to law enforcement.

Archaeology and Computer Technology

In the past three decades, the quality and availability of personal computers and software programs have revolutionized archaeology. Computer technology allows the processing of massive amounts of artifact data and provides increasingly accurate predictive models for archaeological site location using Geographic Information Systems (GIS) programs (McPherron and Dibble 2002). Computer-aided geophysical surveying techniques permit the nearly instantaneous mapping of subsurface anomalies. Sophisticated programs create rotating three-dimensional site maps, undertake complex statistical analyses of artifact data, and generate complicated predictive behavior models, such as modeling prehistoric population movements over time.

Significant advances in computer applications in field archaeology have been made in site mapping. The latest "total station" *laser transits* (distance-measuring devices using a fine laser beam) all have direct interface capabilities with computers. Each data point mapped with the laser (usually within a few centimeters of accuracy) can be instantly downloaded into three-dimensional graphics to show site boundaries, elevations, provenience of specific artifacts, and more. The laser transit allows for much more rapid mapping of sites, and provenience points generated by each transit shot can be manipulated to produce an accurate computer map. This site-mapping technology does in a few hours what would have taken days with standard low-tech equipment such as optical transits and drafting instruments. Computer technology also has contributed to locating sites accurately through the Global Positioning Systems (GPS): small handheld computers track satellite positions and provide nearly instant locational information. Archaeologists working in a remote area, such as parts of South America or Africa, can immediately place their sites on a map.

HIGHLIGHT 14.3

Murder in Idaho: Forensic Archaeology in Action

On a cool spring evening in 1995 in rural central Idaho, four young men ages 16 to 19 shoved their reluctant captive down a dirt path into the dark forest. Visiting from California, Jeffrey Towers was shocked when his supposed "friends" subdued him and bound his hands after inviting him to a summer cabin owned by the parents of one of the four men. Apparently (or at least in the minds of the four captors), Towers had committed some transgression that required that he "be taught a lesson." After mocking and humiliating the 19-year-old for more than an hour, the leader of the group pulled out a 9-mm pistol and put it to Towers's temple, threatening to kill him, then pulled the trigger. Jeffrey Towers was killed instantly in a "lesson" that had gone too far.

In an effort to erase any evidence of their deed, the four boys dug a shallow grave in the woods not far from where Towers was killed. They created a pyre of pine branches in the pit, dowsed the body with four gallons of kerosene, and spent the next four days incinerating the corpse. When the body was cremated to the group's satisfaction, the smoldering pile was covered over with about six inches of dirt and then with a "slash" pile (branches removed from trees during a logging operation; there had been logging in this area prior to the incident). Confident that the remains would never be discovered, they left the cabin and returned to their homes in Boise. Six months later, archaeologist Robert Yohe received a phone call from the Forensic Services Division of the Idaho Department of Law Enforcement. Here is his story.

As the state archaeologist for the state of Idaho and one of the few human osteologists in southern Idaho, I would occasionally get calls from law enforcement agencies and coroners to assist in the identification of skeletal material or badly decomposed bodies. This time I was asked if I could identify cremated human bone. I replied that I had worked with a number of

prehistoric human cremations and that I could probably be of assistance. It was then that I was told that a disgruntled youth complained to his probation officer that a local troublemaker and "wannabe gangsta" told him that he had killed a man and burned his body in the forest. He showed the youngster where he had hidden the body in the forest and bragged about his callous act. At the insistence of the parole officer, the youthful parolee took the police to the spot and showed them the pile of branches. Below the branches was an area of disturbed soil and burned earth. Wanting to make sure they were not digging up an old campfire, they asked me to join the recovery team to make the identifications on any human bone that was unearthed.

Accompanied by one of the head criminalists from Forensic Services, I arrived on the scene during November after one of the first major snows of the season. What had been dry during the spring was now under six inches of fresh snow, and more was on the way. I had managed to convince the various law enforcement agencies involved to allow me to excavate the crime scene using archaeological techniques that would maximize the amount of information we could recover from the location. First, I established a grid over the area as I would before any archaeological excavation (only here I used 5-foot squares instead of the 1-meter squares I would normally have used). I proceeded to defrost the frozen ground with large forced-air heaters and then excavated carefully with a trowel and other small hand tools. Before long, burned bone fragments began to emerge, many that were immediately identifiable as human. Then a piece of burned fabric. The partially burned remains of a Fila sports shoe. A belt buckle. Everything was mapped in place, and soils were wet-screened through a fine-mesh (one-eighth-inch) sieve. Then we found bullets, including the distorted copper jacket of a 9-mm slug (the temperatures of the fire exceeded the low melting point of lead, which had drained out through tears in the copper jacket). A disturbingly clear picture

HIGHLIGHT **14.3** *continued*

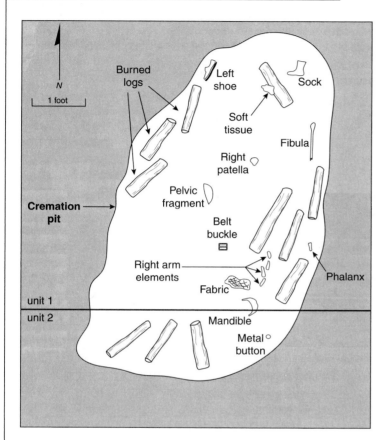

The killers of Jeff Towers tried to burn his body, but several items survived the cremation attempt. Looking at the map, can you discern any patterns in the remains that could provide clues to the orientation of the body, age of the cremation, age or sex of the individual, or other information?

of age; and robust characteristics of parts of the femur and mandible that suggested a male. Most of the teeth had exploded during the cremation process, and because Towers had not been to a dentist for seven years, dental records were of no use. Although I could not say with certainty that the remains were those of Towers, I was able to state that the remains were those of a young adult who was probably a male.

I took my data and conclusions and presented them in a preliminary hearing for the four men and a murder trial for one of the defendants. When faced with the evidence, three of the defendants plea-bargained to second degree murder or kidnapping and are spending between 5 and 25 years in prison. The fourth individual will spend at least 10 years in prison.

began to emerge as the positioning of the bones and the outlines of the cremation pit became evident.

Once back in the lab, I switched modes from field archaeologist to biological anthropologist. We had recovered more than 1,200 bone fragments during the fieldwork, and now the task at hand was to determine whether the remains were, in fact, those of Jeff Towers (who had since been reported missing). Only a surprisingly few bone fragments were unequivocally identifiable to specific parts of various bones, in part because most of the heat-distorted fragments were less than an inch in size! However, many clues became apparent: a fragment of the angle of the scapula with a partially fused epiphysis, a rib tip, and a fragmentary clavicle that suggested an age range of 17 to 20 years

CRITICAL **THINKING** QUESTIONS

1. How does the story of the murder in Idaho demonstrate the utility of contemporary practical applications of anthropological methods?
2. What information was derived from the archaeological excavation and bioanthropological analysis of the bones? How was that information used?

Until recently, catalogs of archaeological materials from particular sites were hand-written in immense logs that might fill dozens or even hundreds of pages. Analysis of artifacts required going back through the catalog to find the necessary information about the category of artifacts being analyzed. However, with computer cataloging, even the largest artifact inventory can be sorted in mere moments. Using a simple database program, with a few mouse clicks the archaeologist can, for example, create a list of all the obsidian projectile points from a particular stratum in five different excavation units. Statistical programs also enable archaeologists to process massive quantities of data and apply statistical tests more quickly and easily than in the past.

Archaeology, Mass Media, and Public Perception

Today, people have more access to misinformation about archaeology than at any other time in history. Mass media, especially the movies, tend to perpetuate old stereotypes about what archaeology is and what archaeologists do. Movies depict archaeologists as mercenaries, grave robbers, or romantic heroes, like the character Indiana Jones in the popular Steven Spielberg series. Films such as *The Mummy* (1999), *Laura Croft, Tomb Raider* (2001), and Disney's animated *Atlantis* (2001) all tend to equate archaeology with treasure hunting and even vandalism. Some professional archaeologists resent these misrepresentations of what archaeology really is all about.

Fortunately, people today also have more access to accurate information about archaeology, thanks to a wide variety of museum exhibits (and virtual tours), archaeological parks and exhibits, television documentaries, *Archaeology* and other magazines, and a vast array of archaeology-related Internet sites. For example, the Archaeology Channel (www.archaeologychannel.org) provides a large number of interesting videos on archaeology around the world, both for private and classroom viewing. In addition, the public is invited to experience fieldwork by participating in programs such as the U.S. Forest Service's Passport in Time and the Earth Watch "dig for a fee" programs run by professional archaeologists. The boom in cultural tourism is due in part to the fact that an increasingly well-informed public wants to see and experience archaeology and history. Archaeology is popular.

So What? The Significance of Archaeology

We hope that you have enjoyed this introductory journey into the amazing world of archaeology. Trying to address all the major questions about our past is a tall order. It is our hope that we were successful in convincing you that the effort is both fascinating and worthwhile. The work is often hard, the politics are frequently frustrating, and the results are sometimes long in coming, but we love our jobs! We anticipate that archaeologists in the future (perhaps some of you who read these very words) will face new challenges in their attempts to understand the past, and that these endeavors will be rewarded with a better, perhaps more complete, view of our long road to the present. We end with a recap of the various points in Chapter 1 describing the importance of archaeology.

1. Information that archaeology provides about human behavior in the past contributes to understanding current and future behavior.
2. Archaeology enlightens people about the value of all cultures, past and present. The documentation and preservation of cultural and biological diversity over time fosters understanding of how humans evolved and adapted.
3. Archaeology contributes to present-day debates about the roles of gender, religion, and power in past societies as well as in today's world.
4. Archaeology, and archaeological methods, are commonly used in the investigation of crime scenes and can contribute to the field of forensics.
5. Archaeology helps recover lost information about traditional knowledge, as well as the art, medicine, and philosophy of traditional cultures. Documented past traditional practices can be used to help the modern world.
6. Archaeologists study how people have interacted with their environments in the past, and they reconstruct past environments to understand how humans were influenced by their surroundings.
7. Archaeology is an important resource for cultural tourism, a major industry in many countries. Countries that are economically dependent on tourism focus on their cultural heritage and archaeological resources.
8. Archaeology sparks commercial interest and is widely used in films and television. In spite of the common misrepresentation of the discipline of archaeology by Hollywood, archaeology is a popular subject, and movies featuring archaeologists have made hundreds of millions of dollars.
9. Archaeology is just plain fun!

CONTENTSELECT

Search articles in the ContentSelect database using the key words *ecotourism* and *archaeological tourism*. How does tourism affect archaeological sites and the work of anthropologists? What problems and solutions do the articles address?

Chapter Summary

Archaeology today is not simply a matter of conducting field research and writing reports. In recent years, indigenous peoples have raised complex issues pertaining to "ownership" of the past. Some native peoples are rejecting the interpretations of Western science in favor of traditional beliefs about cultural origins and past lifeways. There is some movement toward incorporating traditional people's viewpoints in archaeology.

The motivations for acquiring archaeological data also are changing. A significant amount of archaeological fieldwork undertaken in the United States is compliance archaeology, not purely research-driven activity. Archaeology is also increasingly politically motivated. Some nations have used archaeology to bolster national pride and legitimize claims to the right to remain within certain geographic areas or to acquire new territories. Archaeology has practical applications that can help people with real-life problems. Archaeological methods are sometimes used in crime-scene investigations. The Internet and interactive computer software, television documentaries, cultural tourism, and archaeological sites that are tourist destinations provide ready access to accurate information about archaeology.

Suggested Readings

If you want to learn more about the concepts and issues discussed in this chapter, consider looking at the following resources. (Some may be rather technical.)

Chatters, James C. (2001). *Ancient Encounters: Kennewick Man and the First Americans.* New York: Simon & Schuster.

Chatters details the story of his collection, initial study, and documentation of this remarkable discovery, and then provides a discussion of what early skeletal materials can tell us about the earliest populations in the Americas.

Fine-Dare, Kathleen S. (2002). *Grave Injustice: The American Indian Movement and NAGPRA.* Lincoln: University of Nebraska Press.

A balanced discussion of the complex issue of the American Indian repatriation movement, as well as a history of the development of the Native American Graves Protection and Repatriation Act.

McPherron, Shannon P., and Harold L. Dibble. (2002). *Using Computers in Archaeology: A Practical Guide.* Boston: McGraw-Hill/Mayfield.

Explores recent developments in the application of computer technology to archaeological problems, specifically focusing on field applications of GIS for data collection, management, and interpretation.

Thomas, David Hurst. (2000). *Skull Wars: Kennewick Man, Archaeology, and the Battle for Native American Identity.* New York: Basic Books.

A famous American archaeologist looks at the Kennewick Man case, racism, and Native American–archaeologist relations in this interesting and thought-provoking work written for the general public.

Watkins, Joe. (2000). *Indigenous Archaeology: American Indian Values and Scientific Practice.* Walnut Creek, CA: AltaMira Press.

A well-researched treatment of American Indian–archaeologist conflict, repatriation, and indigenous archaeology by an archaeologist who is of Choctaw descent.

GLOSSARY

accelerator mass spectrometry (AMS) a technique of radiocarbon dating in which the ^{14}C atoms are directly counted.

acculturation an exchange of cultural features between two groups or societies in which parts of both cultures change but each group remains distinct.

Advisory Council on Historic Preservation (ACHP) an independent federal agency whose function is to mediate disputes between other agencies.

agricultural revolution a general description of the development of domestication and the shift from hunting and gathering to agriculture.

analogy an inference suggesting that if two things are similar in some ways, they probably will be similar in other ways.

antemortem changes in organic material that took place before death; generally used to refer to human remains.

anthropogenic human-caused changes in the environment; often used to refer to midden soils.

anthropology the study of humans, including their biology, culture, and language, both past and present.

antiquarians people interested in archaeology prior to the development of the formal discipline, primarily hobbyists.

Antiquities Act of 1906 The United States' first cultural resources statute, making it illegal to dig archaeological sites on public lands without a formal permit from the secretary of the interior.

appendicular skeleton the bones of the arms, hands, legs, and feet.

archaeoastronomy the study of ancient astronomical knowledge, practices, oral tradition, and cosmology.

archaeological culture an archaeological entity defined by a pattern of common traits, thought to possibly represent a past cultural group.

archaeological record the record of past human behavior, the material remains of past human activities distributed in patterns across the landscape and in varying degrees of condition.

Archaeological Resources Protection Act (ARPA) legislation designed to strengthen the Antiquities Act of 1906 with clearer language and greater penalties.

archaeology the study of the human past.

archaeomagnetism a dating technique in which the position of Earth's magnetic poles can be measured in certain materials, primarily clay, and compared to the known position of the poles over time; also known as *paleomagnetism.*

archaeometry the science of archaeological measurement, such as dating or other scientific techniques.

art a form of expression—symbolic, abstract, and representational. Art may be performance based, such as dance and theater, or representational, such as painting or sculpture.

artifact a portable object made, modified, or used by humans for a specific task. Artifacts are the basic "unit" of archaeological analysis.

assemblage all of the materials—artifacts and ecofacts—collected from a site and representing all of the evidence of the activities at a site.

assimilation the absorption of one group by another and disappearance of cultural differences.

attribute a descriptive aspect of an artifact or site, such as its size, content, material, or shape.

axial skeleton the skull, the vertebral column, the ribs and sternum (breastbone), the bones of the shoulder girdles (collar bones and shoulder blades), and the pelvic girdle.

band a small-scale society without formal leaders; the family is the primary sociopolitical and economic unit.

bioarchaeology the analysis of past people and their individual lives by studying and interpreting their mortal remains.

biostratigraphy a dating technique that uses the known ages of certain index fossils from one region to estimate the age of those same fossils in another region.

bioturbation any disturbance or movement of deposited materials by biological means.

block excavations a large excavation unit (2 to 10 meters square or larger) designed to expose a large area in a site.

botanical remains the remains of plants, from logs to pollen, found in archaeological sites.

Bronze Age one of the basic chronological periods in Old World archaeology, between about 5,500 and 3,000 years ago, a time when bronze was the most important metal.

carrying capacity a measure of the maximum number of individuals of a particular species that can be supported within a specific place for a specific time.

casual tools objects used as a tool once or twice for a specific purpose and discarded with no purposeful modification.

catchment analysis the study of where the materials found in a site were obtained, how much of an effort was necessary to procure those resources, and how that procurement affected settlement patterns.

chiefdom a society with a relatively large population, permanent settlements, some central authority, and a stratified social structure.

chronology a description and dated sequence of material.

chronometric dating a class of dating techniques that provide information on the actual age of a sample in years.

civilization a culture with a sociopolitical organization complex enough to be considered a state (*see* **state**); the highest stage of cultural development according to the original theory of unilinear cultural evolution.

classical archaeology the archaeology of "Classic" states, such as Greece and Rome, in the area of the Mediterranean Sea and surrounding regions.

classification the placement of materials into categories that can be used for identification and comparison.

cognitive archaeology the "study of past ways of thought as inferred from material remains" (Renfrew 1994:3).

component that portion of a site or site deposit representing occupation by an archaeologically specific culture over a specific time.

composite tool a tool made from more than one part, such as a knife with a stone blade and a wooden handle (*see* **simple tool**).

context the relationship between something and its surroundings in time and space.

core an artifact used as a source of material to manufacture flaked stone tools. Some cores were also used as tools, such as choppers or hammerstones.

cosmology the explanation of the origin of the universe and those things contained in it.

cremains burned human remains.

cremation the disposal of the dead by burning the body.

cross-dating the use of materials dated at one site to infer the age of similar materials at another site.

cultural chronology the description and sequences of cultures through space and time.

cultural conflict conflict of some sort between two groups, often due to competition for territory or for access to other resources.

cultural contact the constant interplay between groups, involving the diffusion of technology and ideas, immigration, emigration, exchange of mates, and the like.

cultural ecology the study of the cultural aspects of human interaction with the environment.

cultural materialism the theoretical framework based on the idea that human behavior is in response to practical problems.

cultural pluralism the maintenance of the distinctive aspects of multiple groups within a blended society, resulting in more than one cultural identity.

culture learned and shared behavior in humans passed from generation to generation.

culture history a description of past events and when and where they occurred.

curation the process of preparing archaeological materials for permanent storage, and the storage of that material.

data information resulting from the observation and recording of empirical and measurable phenomena.

datum the point from which measurements are taken for mapping.

dendrochronology a dating technique in which the tree rings of certain archaeological specimens are matched to a master ring plot to determine the age of the specimen.

diachronic data, hypotheses, or models that deal with a single time.

diaspora the breaking up of a population into smaller segments that then disperse into different areas without replacing the existing population; often caused by some force or circumstance, such as war or famine.

diet the long-term patterns and trends of foods that are and are not eaten, how and when foods are obtained and processed, their nutritional value, their overall role in the diet, and how those patterns change over time.

diffusion the movement of ideas or technologies from one culture to another without the movement of people.

direct historical approach the idea that the latest archaeological group in an area has continuity with the earliest ethnographic group in that same area.

DNA analysis the recovery of deoxyribonucleic acid (DNA) from archaeological specimens, replicated by polymerase chain reaction (PCR). The sequence of genes can be read to determine hereditary relationships between populations and even between individuals.

domestication a process by which organisms or landscapes are "controlled." In agriculture, domestication means that the genetic makeup of an organism is purposefully altered by humans to their advantage.

ecofact the unmodified remains of biological materials used by, or related to the activities of, people, such as discarded animal bone or charcoal from hearth fires or natural pollen in an archaeological site.

ecosystem an area where the abiotic and biotic components are tied together in a system.

ecotone the intersection of, and transition between, two ecozones, usually a more productive place than in either of the ecozones.

ecozone an area defined by biotic communities or geographic criteria (short for *environmental zone*).

electron-spin resonance a dating technique that uses microwave energy to measure residual energy trapped in archaeological materials, thus enabling an estimate of their age.

empirical objects and patterns that physically exist and can be observed, measured, and tested.

environment living (biotic) and nonliving (abiotic) systems interacting within a bounded geographic unit.

epiphyseal fusion the process of fusion of the ends of the long bones to the shaft of the bones, generally by the late teens or early twenties.

ethnoarchaeology the study of how living traditional people do things and how archaeologists might apply that information to the past.

ethnographic analogy the use of information about living cultures to help construct models of past cultures.

evolutionary archaeology a relatively new approach that studies the past from the perspective of Darwinian evolution, where the concepts of adaptation and selection are used in the analysis of cultural behaviors.

evolutionary ecology the application of the principles of biological selection to the understanding of how organisms adapt, used by archaeologists to study past cultural adaptation.

experimental archaeology the use of experiments with ancient materials and techniques to discover how and why things might have been done in the past.

faunal remains the remains of animals found in archaeological sites, including bone, flesh, hair, skin, hide, and chitin.

feature a nonportable thing constructed by humans for some task, such as a hearth, road, or dam.

fission–fusion pattern the seasonal and routine splitting (fission) of a group into several smaller groups and the recombination (fusion) of those groups later in time.

fission track dating a dating technique in which the damage (tracks) resulting from the decay of ^{238}U can be counted and used to estimate the age of the material.

flintknapping the process of making flaked stone tools.

food crisis theory a theory of the development of agriculture that suggests that the loss of many species at the end of the Pleistocene created a food crisis, forcing people to depend more heavily on remaining species and eventually leading to domestication and agriculture.

forager a classification of hunter-gatherers inferring small, very mobile groups.

FUN analysis a dating technique using the quantities of fluorine, uranium, and nitrogen to measure relative age in bone.

gender a culturally constructed category used to group people and defined by the role behavior that a person is expected to have in the culture, regardless of sex.

geoarchaeology the study of the relationship between geology and geological processes and archaeological interpretation.

geofact a naturally shaped stone that resembles an artifact.

geomorphology the study of landforms and how they change over time.

geophysical survey a group of noninvasive and nondestructive techniques to discover buried features within sites, such as walls, trenches, floors, pits, burials, and hearths.

ground-penetrating radar (GPR) a mapping method in which an active radar signal is beamed into the ground, reflecting off materials in the soil and returning a signal to the instrument to show subsurface features.

half-life the time it takes for one-half of the total amount of a given radioactive sample to decay.

Harris lines thin, bony, horizontal lines representing periods of arrested growth seen in the radiographs of long bones of individuals who experienced nutritional stress during their childhood or adolescence.

hilly flanks theory a theory of the development of agriculture that suggests that people began to exploit the native grasses, such as wheat and barley, that thrived along the hilly flanks of the Tigris-Euphrates River Valley, eventually domesticating them.

historical archaeology the archaeology of literate societies, primarily those of the recent past; often refers to the remains of European cultures outside of Europe.

horticulture low-intensity agriculture involving relatively small-scale fields, plots, and gardens; food raised primarily for personal consumption rather than for trade or a central authority.

human ecology the study of the relationships between humans and their environment.

hunter-gatherers groups that make their primary living from the exploitation of wild foods.

hydrology the study of water, particularly its geographic distribution and effect.

hypothesis a proposal to explain some relationship between two or more variables (data) that must be testable and refutable.

iconography the use of artistic images to represent information and aspects of belief systems.

independent invention the invention of the same ideas or technologies independently in different places or times.

index fossils specific species whose mere presence can be used to date strata because their age is known.

inhumation the intentional burial of a corpse; the disposal of the dead by burial.

innovation new ways of doing things by using already established methods, systems of organization, or technologies.

in situ a Latin term meaning "found in place," commonly applied to items discovered in place during an excavation.

intensive agriculture the large-scale production of domesticated plants, often using animal labor, equipment such as plows, and irrigation or other water-diversion techniques.

invention the creation of a new type of technology, often in response to a need to accomplish some task.

Iron Age one of the basic chronological periods in Old World archaeology, between about 3,000 and the present, a time when iron was the most important metal.

judgment samples a sample in which the choice of the sample unit is based on judgment.

laws universal generalizations about classes of facts.

Libby Curve of Knowns a series of radiocarbon dates on materials that matched their known ages and confirmed the accuracy of the radiocarbon dating method.

Libby half-life the original estimated half-life of radiocarbon, established at $5,568 \pm 30$ years.

locus a distinct place defined within a site, such as a cemetery, public square, or ceramic-manufacturing area.

manuport materials, such as an unusual stone from a distant source, clearly transported to a site by humans but showing no evidence of use or modification.

maritime archaeology the branch of archaeology that deals with any archaeological materials related to the marine environment (*also see* **nautical archaeology**).

Mesolithic the Middle Stone Age, the period that began once people started to domesticate plants and animals and after farming became the primary mode of making a living, from about 8,000 to 10,000 years ago.

metabolic pathways in reference to stable isotope analysis, the manner in which carbon dioxide is converted to energy by various types of plants. Two common metabolic pathways found in plants of economic importance to humans are the *Calvin cycle* and the *Hack-Slack pathway*.

midden site soil deposits containing broken and used-up artifacts plus decayed organic materials such as shell, plants, bones, grease, charcoal and ash from fires, and general household trash.

middle-range theory a combination of logic, analogy, and theory that link the materials within the archaeological record to human behavior.

migration the actual movement of a population of people, such as an ethnic group, from one locality to another.

mitigation in cultural resource management, the steps taken to lessen the adverse effects to archaeological and historic sites listed in, or eligible for nomination to, the National Register of Historic Places.

model a proposed construct of some entity, generally consisting of a series of interrelated hypotheses.

mortuary analysis the study of burial data to determine patterns of demography, status, and politics.

mummification the process of drying out a body so that it is preserved, sometimes occurring naturally and sometimes a purposeful procedure.

National Historic Preservation Act (NHPA) the act that requires federal agencies to recognize and document historic properties eligible for inclusion in the National Register of Historic Places, and to initiate the Section 106 and Section 110 processes.

National Register of Historic Places a federal list of properties and sites considered important to history and prehistory and afforded special preservation status.

Native American Graves Protection and Repatriation Act (NAGPRA) the federal law requiring that Native American skeletal remains be identified if possible and returned to their ancestors.

nautical archaeology the branch of maritime archaeology that deals specifically with ships, cargoes, maritime technology, and trade by sea.

Neolithic the New Stone Age, the time of preliterate, settled farmers in the Old World, from about 5,000 to 8,000 years ago.

nonstratified societies societies in which no one is significantly wealthier or more powerful or of higher status than anyone else.

oasis theory a theory of the development of agriculture that suggests that at the end of the Pleistocene, the environment changed, forcing people into close association with certain plants and animals, leading to domestication and agriculture.

obsidian hydration analysis a dating technique that measures the amount of water penetration into the surface of a break to estimate how long ago the piece was broken.

optimization model a model based on the premise that people will attempt to maximize their net efficiency and minimize their risk.

oral tradition an oral record of the beliefs, values, morals, and history of a group, transmitted from generation to generation through the narration of stories.

ossification the process by which cartilage takes on calcium phosphate, which hardens the cartilage to bone.

ossuary a location where the bones of individuals were interred together, having been removed from temporary graves where the bodies had been put to decompose.

osteobiography information about an individual's appearance, health, age at death, cause of death, and other characteristics derived from an analysis of the skeleton.

osteology the study of bones.

paleoclimate past climate, the long-term average of weather, including temperature and precipitation.

paleodemography the study of prehistoric populations, including their number, distribution, density, sex and age structure, mortality, and fertility.

paleoenvironment the study of the environment of the prehistoric past.

paleofeces preserved ancient human fecal matter.

Paleoindian the earliest occupants of the New World; occupation during the Pleistocene.

paleolinguistics the study of contemporary languages to reveal information about the structure and distribution of past languages and groups of speakers.

Paleolithic the Old Stone Age, commonly used to refer to the archaeology of Pleistocene hunters and gatherers, from the advent of humans about 10,000 to 4 million years ago.

palynology the study and analysis of pollen.

paradigm a philosophical framework within which a discipline operates.

pastoralism the herding, breeding, consumption, and use of managed or domesticated animals.

Pleistocene the geologic period lasting from about 1.9 million years to about 10,000 years ago, essentially the "Ice Ages."

polity an organized political entity of any size or scale.

postmortem changes in organic material that took place after death; generally used to refer to human remains.

postprocessual archaeology the theoretical paradigm in archaeology in which the past is believed to be subjective and thus unknowable.

potassium-argon (K/Ar) dating a radiometric dating technique in which radioactive potassium decays to argon at a known rate, good from about 100,000 to 4.6 billion years ago.

prehistoric archaeology the archaeology before written records from any time and any place.

prehistory the time before written records, comprising some 99 percent of the time humans have been on Earth.

preservation the state of decomposition of materials in archaeological sites. If things are well preserved, they are more likely to be recognized and recovered.

primary context the original location of an item before it is moved.

processual archaeology the theoretical paradigm in archaeology in which the past is believed to be objective and knowable.

protein residue analysis the chemical recovery and identification of plant or animal proteins surviving on tools, in paleofeces, or in soils.

radiocarbon dating a chronometric dating method in which the amount of radiocarbon (^{14}C) within an organic sample is measured and used to determine how long ago the specimen died.

radiocarbon years before present the unit of measurement reflected in a radiocarbon date. To equate to calendar years, the radiocarbon date has to be calibrated.

Register of Professional Archaeologists (RPA) a national organization of professional archaeologists designed to set standards and ethics of the profession and to lobby for archaeological causes.

remote sensing a group of techniques, from aerial photography to space-based laser imaging and mapping, that permit the detection of relatively large-scale phenomena unobserved or unnoticed by the human eye in a nondestructive manner from above the ground.

representational art primarily painting, inscription, and sculpture.

research design a plan for an archaeological investigation, stating the question(s) or problem(s) to be addressed, the theoretical approach, the biases of the investigators, the kinds of data sought to address the question, and the methods to be used to recover the data.

Reservoir Salvage Act of 1960 legislation requiring archaeological work in areas slated to be inundated by planned reservoir projects.

scientific method the method, employed in Western science, in which data are combined to form a hypothesis, which is tested against new data, rejected, or accepted, and either a new hypothesis is formed or the old one is retested.

screening the use of wire mesh to separate soils from objects in archaeological excavations so that artifacts and ecofacts can be recovered.

seasonal round the system of the timing and movement of groups across the landscape.

seasonal transhumance a seasonal round in which members of only one segment of the population, such as the herders, move with their animals seasonally while the rest of the population stays in one place.

secondary burial a burial exhumed from its original location and reburied elsewhere, such as in an ossuary.

secondary context the location of an item that has been moved out of its original (primary) location.

Section 106 of NHPA the section of the National Historic Preservation Act that created the National Register of Historic Places and directs federal agencies to identify and evaluate for NRHP eligibility sites in all areas to be developed or impacted in a way that might destroy or "adversely effect" those sites.

Section 110 of NHPA the section of the National Historic Preservation Act that obliges each federal agency to establish a formal historic preservation program to identify, evaluate, and nominate historic properties to the National Register, as well as protect those same properties, on an ongoing basis.

seriation a relative dating technique that plots specific changes in the frequencies of certain artifact styles over time to gauge their popularity at any point in the past, thus placing them in a sequence relative to each other.

settlement pattern the manner in which a particular group organized its settlements and occupied its geographic space.

simple tool a tool with only one part, such as a throwing stick (*see* **composite tool**).

site a geographic locality where there is some evidence of past human activity, such as artifacts or features.

skeletal age the age of a person calculated from measurements of the skeleton, such as the extent of epiphyseal fusion.

skeletal pathology evidence of disease or trauma that can be observed in the bones of the skeleton.

skeletal sex the sex of a person calculated from measurements of the skeleton, such as the size of the opening in the pelvic girdle.

skeletal stature the stature of a person calculated from measurements of the skeleton, such as the length of the long bones.

stable isotope analysis the measurement of stable isotopes in bone, primarily carbon and nitrogen, to analyze aspects of past behavior, such as diet.

standard excavation units regular excavation units (1 to 2 meters square) used in the excavation of a site.

state a society with a large population, complex social and political structures, central authority, complex record keeping, urban centers (cities), and monumental architecture.

State Historic Preservation Office (SHPO) the office in each state responsible for review and compliance in historic preservation law and the maintenance of the archaeological records in that state.

statistical sample a sample in which each sample unit has the same mathematical chance of being chosen as any other.

Stone Age one of the basic chronological periods in Old World archaeology, between about 2.6 million to 10,000 years ago, generally divided into the Paleolithic, Mesolithic, and Neolithic.

stratified society a society in which social roles and statuses are many and diverse, formally defined, inherited, and often institutionalized through the creation of castes or classes.

style a particular and distinctive form of an object or the way in which something is made.

surface collection a collection of materials lying on the surface of a site.

symbols material expressions of meanings and ideas, such as icons, writing, and art.

synchronic data, hypotheses, or models that deal with conditions at the same basic time period.

syncretism blended aspects of multiple cultures, such as the combination of animistic imagery and Christian iconography in early German art.

systems theory the idea that cultural systems operate in an equilibrium and that as conditions change, cultural subsystems will also change, reaching a new equilibrium.

taphonomy the study of what happens to biological materials after they enter the archaeological record.

temporal types artifacts of known age that can be used to date associated materials or activities.

test-level excavations small-scale excavations designed to determine the content, extent, and integrity of a site.

theory a systematic explanation for observations that relate to a particular aspect of the empirical world.

thermoluminescence (TL) dating a technique in which the energy trapped within the structure of certain minerals can be released, measured, and used to estimate the age of the specimen; commonly used to date pottery and burned clay features.

three-age system a chronology (Stone, Bronze, and Iron Age) developed for western Europe in the early nineteenth century.

trade the exchange of ideas or materials between individuals and groups.

transformation processes the various processes by which the archaeological record is transformed over time, such as decomposition and bioturbation.

trench a ditch from one to several meters wide and as long as necessary, dug for excavation.

trephining cutting a hole into the skull of an individual while the person is still alive.

tribe a society with a relatively large population, formal leaders, and some social segmentation based on criteria other than kinship.

typology the classification of materials into categories based on morphology.

UNESCO Convention of 1970 the international convention adopted by the United Nations Educational, Scientific, and Cultural Organization to address the problem of illegal import, export, and transfer of artifacts and other cultural items.

Unidroit Convention of 1995 the convention outlawing stolen or illegally exported cultural objects, including items unlawfully excavated or unlawfully transported from legal excavations.

unilinear cultural evolution the nineteenth-century theory that all cultures evolved upward through a specific series of stages, from savagery to barbarism to civilization.

uranium-thorium (U/Th) dating a chronometric dating method in which the ratio of uranium to thorium within a calcite sample is measured and used to estimate when the calcite formed, such as in cave deposits.

use-life the functional life of a tool, from its manufacture, to rejuvenation, to discard.

use-wear analysis examining the wear patterns—microscopic striations and polish—on the surface of tools to determine what the tools were used on.

warfare organized and sanctioned conflict between two groups.

Wilson bands small bands of thin enamel in teeth indicative of nutritional stress during tooth growth.

worldview a shared framework of assumptions held by a culture on how the world works.

zooarchaeology the study of archaeological faunal remains.

REFERENCES

Adams, Richard E. W.
   1991   *Prehistoric Mesoamerica.* Norman: University
           of Oklahoma Press.
Adams, Robert McC.
   1966   *The Evolution of Urban Society.* Chicago:
           Aldine.
   2001   Complexity in Archaic States. *Journal of
           Anthropological Archaeology* 20(3):345–360.
Adams, William Y., and Ernest W. Adams
   1991   *Archaeological Typology and Practical Reality.*
           Cambridge: Cambridge University Press.
Adovasio, J. M.
   1977   *Basketry Technology: A Guide to Identification
           and Analysis.* Chicago: Aldine.
Aicher, Peter
   2000   Mussolini's Forum and the Myth of Augustan
           Rome. *Classical Bulletin* 76(2).
Aikens, C. Melvin, and Takayasu Higuchi
   1982   *Prehistory of Japan.* New York: Academic Press.
Aldenderfer, Mark
   1998   Quantitative Methods in Archaeology: A
           Review of Recent Trends and Developments.
           Journal of Archaeological Research 6(2):91–120.
Aldenderfer, Mark, and Herbert D. G. Maschner, eds.
   1996   *Anthropology, Space, and Geographic Infor-
           mation Systems.* Oxford: Oxford University
           Press.
Allen, Jim
   1995   Letters: We Find That What's There Is Theirs—
           But What's Ours? *Weekend Australian,* Septem-
           ber 2–3.
Allen, Susan Heuck
   1999   *Finding the Walls of Troy: Frank Calvert and
           Heinrich Schliemann at Hisarlik.* Berkeley:
           University of California Press.
Alva, Walter
   1988   Discovering the New World's Richest Unlooted
           Tomb. *National Geographic* 174(4):510–549.
   1990   New Tomb of Royal Splendor. *National Geo-
           graphic* 177(6):2–15.
Alva, Walter, and Christopher B. Donnan
   1994   *Royal Tombs of Sipán.* 2nd edition. Los Angeles:
           Fowler Museum of Cultural History, University
           of California.

Ambrose, Stanley H., and John Krigbaum
   2003   Bone Chemistry and Bioarchaeology. *Journal
           of Anthropological Archaeology* 22(3):193–199.
Ammerman, Albert J.
   1992   Taking Stock of Quantitative Archaeology. *An-
           nual Review of Anthropology* 21:231–255.
Anschuetz, Kurt F., Richard H. Wilshusen, and Cherie L.
Scheick
   2001   An Archaeology of Landscapes: Perspectives
           and Directions. *Journal of Archaeological Re-
           search* 9(2):157–211.
Anthony, David W.
   1990   Migration in Archaeology: The Baby and
           the Bathwater. *American Anthropologist*
           92(4):895–914.
Arkush, Brooke S.
   1995   The Archaeology of CA-MNO-2122: A Study of
           Pre-Contact and Post-Contact Lifeways among
           the Mono Basin Paiute. *University of California
           Anthropological Records,* vol. 31, Berkeley.
Arnold, Bettina
   1992   The Past as Propaganada. *Archaeology*
           45(4):30–37.
Arnold, Jeanne E.
   2001   *The Origins of a Pacific Coast Chiefdom: The
           Chumash of the Channel Islands.* Salt Lake
           City: University of Utah Press.
   1992   Complex Hunter-Gatherer-Fishers of Pre-
           historic California: Chiefs, Specialists, and
           Maritime Adaptations of the Channel Islands.
           American Antiquity 57(1):60–84.
Arnold, Jeanne E., Roger H. Colton, and Scott Pleka
   1997   Contexts of Cultural Change in Insular Cali-
           fornia. *American Antiquity* 62(2):300–318.
Arnold, Philip J., III, and Brian S. Wilkens
   2001   On the VanPools' "Scientific" Postprocessual-
           ism. *American Antiquity* 66(2):361–366.
Ashmore, Wendy, and A. Bernard Knapp
   1999   *Archaeologies of Landscape: Contemporary Per-
           spectives.* Oxford: Blackwell.
Åström, Paul, and Sven A. Eriksson
   1980   *Fingerprints and Archaeology.* Studies in Medi-
           terranean Archaeology, vol 28. Göteborg: Paul
           Åströms Förlag.

Aufderheide, Authur C.
1989 Chemical Analysis of Skeletal Remains. In *Reconstruction of Life from the Skeleton*. Mehmet Y. Işcan and Kenneth A. R. Kennedy, eds. Pp. 237–260. New York: Alan R. Liss, Inc.

Aufderheide, Authur C., and Conrado Rodríguez-Martín
1998 *The Cambridge Encyclopedia of Human Paleopathology*. Cambridge: Cambridge University Press.

Aveni, Anthony F.
1981 Archaeostronomy. In *Advances in Archaeological Method and Theory*, vol. 4. Michael B. Schiffer, ed. Pp. 1–77. New York: Academic Press.
1993 *Ancient Astronomers*. Washington: Smithsonian Books.

Babbie, Earl
2001 *The Practice of Social Research*. 9th edition. Belmont, CA: Wadsworth/Thomson Learning.

Baillie, M. G.
1982 *Tree-Ring Dating and Archaeology*. Chicago: University of Chicago Press.

Baines, John, and Jaromir Malek
2000 *Cultural Atlas of Ancient Egypt*. Rev. edition. New York: Checkmark Books.

Banning, E. B.
2000 *The Archaeologist's Laboratory: The Analysis of Archaeological Data*. New York: Plenum Press.

Barber, Elizabeth Wayland
1999 *The Mummies of Ürümchi*. New York: Norton.

Barth, Fredrik
1956 Ecological Relationships of Ethnic Groups in Swat, Northern Pakistan. *American Anthropologist* 58(6):1079–1099.

Bartlett, John R.
1982 *Jericho*. Guildford, Surrey: Lutterworth Press.

Bar-Gal, G. Kahila, H. Khalaily, O. Mader, P. Ducos, and L. Kolska Horwitz
2002 Ancient DNA Evidence for the Transition from Wild to Domestic Status in Neolithic Goats: A Case Study from the Site of Abu Gosh, Israel. *Ancient Biomolecules* 4(1):9–17.

Bar-Yosef, Ofer, and Richard H. Meadow
1995 The Origins of Agriculture in the Near East. In *Last Hunters—First Farmers: New Perspectives on the Prehistoric Transition to Agriculture*. T. Douglas Price and Anne Birgitte Gebauer, eds. Pp. 39–94. Santa Fe: School of American Research Press.

Baraybar, José Pablo
1999 Diet and Death in a Fog Oasis Site in Central Coastal Peru: A Trace Element Study of Tomb 1 Malanche 22. *Journal of Archaeological Science* 26(5):471–482.

Baumhoff, M. A.
1981 The Carrying Capacity of Hunter-Gatherers. In *Affluent Foragers: Pacific Coasts East and West*. Shuzo Koyama and David Hurst Thomas, eds. Pp. 77–87. Senri Ethnological Studies No. 9. Osaka: National Museum of Ethnology.

Baxter, Jane Eva
2005 *The Archaeology of Childhood*. Walnut Creek, CA: AltaMira Press.

Bayman, James M.
2001 The Hohokam of Southwest North America. *Journal of World Prehistory* 15(3):257–311.

Beattie, Owen
1995 The Results of Multidisciplinary Research into Preserved Human Tissues from the Franklin Arctic Expedition of 1845. In *Proceedings of the I World Congress on Mummy Studies*, vol. 2. Pp. 579–586. Museo Arqueológico y Etnográfico de Tenerife.

Beck, Charlotte, and George T. Jones
1994 On-Site Artifact Analysis as an Alternative to Collection. *American Antiquity* 59(2):304–315.

Bell, James A.
1994a Interpretation and Testability in Theories about Prehistoric Thinking. In *The Ancient Mind: Elements of Cognitive Archaeology*. Colin Renfrew and Ezra B. W. Zubrow, eds. Pp. 15–21. Cambridge: Cambridge University Press.
1994b *Reconstructing Prehistory: Scientific Method in Archaeology*. Philadelphia: Temple University Press.

Bentley, R. Alexander, T. Douglas Price, and Elisabeth Stephan
2004 Determining the "Local" 87Sr/86Sr Range for Archaeological Skeletons: A Case Study from Neolithic Europe. *Journal of Archaeological Science* 31(4):365–375.

Bettinger, Robert L.
1987 Archaeological Approaches to Hunter-Gatherers. *Annual Review of Anthropology* 16:121–142.
1991 *Hunter-Gatherers: Archaeological and Evolutionary Theory*. New York: Plenum Press.

Bettinger, Robert L., and Martin A. Baumhoff
1982 The Numic Spread: Great Basin Cultures in Competition. *American Antiquity* 47(3):485–503.

Billman, Brian R., and Gary M. Feinman
1999 *Settlement Studies in the Americas: Fifty Years Since Virú*. Washington: Smithsonian Institution Press.

Binford, Lewis R.
1962 Archaeology as Anthropology. *American Antiquity* 28(2):217–225.

1964   A Consideration of Archaeological Research Design. *American Antiquity* 29(4):425–441.

1968   Post-Pleistocene Adaptations. In *New Perspectives in Archaeology.* Sally Binford and Lewis R. Binford, eds. Pp. 313–341. Chicago: Aldine.

1978   *Nunamiut Ethnoarchaeology.* New York: Academic Press.

1982   The Archaeology of Place. *Journal of Anthropological Archaeology* 1(1):5–31.

Blakely, Robert L.
1989   Bone Strontium in Pregnant and Lactating Females from Archaeological Samples. *American Journal of Physical Anthropology* 80(2):173–185.

Boas, Franz, and Helen Codere
1966   *Kwakiutl Ethnography.* Chicago: University of Chicago Press.

Bocek, Barbara
1986   Rodent Ecology and Burrowing Behavior: Predicted Effects on Archaeological Site Formation. *American Antiquity* 51(3):589–603.

Bocherens, Hervé, Caroline Polet, and Michel Toussaint
2007   Palaeodiet of Mesolithic and Neolithic Populations of Meuse Basin (Belgium): Evidence from Stable Isotopes. *Journal of Archaeological Science* 34(1):10–27.

Bocherens, Hervé, Marjan Mashkour, Dorothée G. Drucker, Issam Moussa, and Daniel Billiou
2006   Stable Isotope Evidence for Palaeodiets in Southern Turkmenistan During the Historical Period and Iron Age. *Journal of Archaeological Science* 33(2):253–264.

Bodley, John
1998   *Victims of Progress.* 4th edition. Mountain View, CA: Mayfield.

Bodner, Connie Cox, and Ralph M. Rowlett
1980   Separation of Bone, Charcoal, and Seeds by Chemical Flotation. *American Antiquity* 45(1):110–116.

Bond, George Clement, and Angela Gilliam, eds.
1994   *Social Construction of the Past: Representation of Power.* London: Routledge.

Boone, James L., and Eric Alden Smith
1998   Is It Evolution Yet? A Critique of Evolutionary Archaeology. *Current Anthropology* 39, Suppl. Pp. 141–173.

Bowdler, Sandra
1982   Prehistoric Archaeology in Tasmania. In *Advances in World Archaeology,* vol. 1. Fred Wendorf and Angela E. Close, eds. Pp. 1–49. New York: Academic Press.

Bowkett, Laurence, Stephen Hill, Diana Wardle, and K. A. Wardle
2001   *Classical Archaeology in the Field: Approaches.* London: Bristol Classical Press.

Bradford, Ernle D.
1982   *The Story of the "Mary Rose."* New York: Norton.

Braidwood, Robert
1960   The Agricultural Revolution. *Scientific American* 203:130–141.

Bresciani, J., W. Dansgaard, B. Fredskild, M. Ghisler, P. Grandjean, J. C. Hansen, J. P. Hart Hansen, N. Haarløv, B. Lorentzen, P. Nansen, A. M. Rørdam, and H. Tauber
1991   Living Conditions. In *The Greenland Mummies.* Jens Peder Hart Hansen, Jørgen Meldgaard, and Jørgen Nordqvist eds. Pp. 150–167. Washington: Smithsonian Institution Press.

Brew, J. O.
1979   Hopi Prehistory and History to 1850. In *Handbook of North American Indians,* vol. 9, *Southwest.* Alfonzo Ortiz, ed. Pp. 514–523. Washington: Smithsonian Institution.

Brewer, Douglas J.
1992   Zooarchaeology: Method, Theory, and Goals. In *Archaeological Method and Theory,* vol. 4. Michael B. Schiffer, ed. Pp. 195–244. Tucson: University of Arizona Press.

Brodie, Neil, and Colin Renfrew
2005   Looting and the World's Archaeological Heritage: The Inadequate Response. *Annual Review of Anthropology* 34:343–361.

Brodie, Neil, Jennifer Doole, and Colin Renfrew, eds.
2001   *Trade in Illicit Antiquities: The Destruction of the World's Archaeological Heritage.* Cambridge: McDonald Institute for Archaeological Research.

Broughton, Jack M.
1999   Resource Depression and Intensification during the Late Holocene, San Francisco Bay: Evidence from the Emeryville Shellmound Vertebrate Fauna. *University of California Anthropological Records,* vol. 32. Berkeley: University of California Press.

Brown, Ann Cynthia
1983   *Arthur Evans and the Palace of Minos.* Oxford: Ashmolean Museum.

Brown, A. G.
2006   The Use of Forensic Botany and Geology in War Crimes Investigations in NE Bosnia. *Forensic Science International* 163(3):204–210.

Brown, Michael D., Seyed H. Hosseini, Antonio Torroni, Hans-Jürgen Bandelt, Jon C. Allen, Theodore G. Schurr, Rosaria Scozzari, Fulvio Cruciani, and Douglas C. Wallace
1998   mtDNA Haplogroup X: An Ancient Link between Europe/Western Asia and North America? *American Journal of Human Genetics* 63:1852–1861.

Brück, Joanna, and Melissa Goodman
   1999   Introduction: Themes for a Critical Archae-
          ology of Prehistoric Settlement. In *Making
          Places in the Prehistoric World: Themes in
          Settlement Archaeology.* Joanna Brück and Me-
          lissa Goodman, eds. Pp. 1–19. London: UCL
          Press.
Brumfiel, Elizabeth J.
   2002   Origins of Social Inequality. In *Archae-
          ology: Original Readings in Method and Prac-
          tice.* Peter N. Peregrine, Carol R. Ember, and
          Melvin Ember, eds. Pp. 409–422. Upper Saddle
          River, NJ: Prentice Hall.
Burch, Ernest S., Jr., and Linda J. Ellanna, eds.
   1994   *Key Issues in Hunter-Gatherer Research.* Ox-
          ford: Berg Publishers.
Burton, James H., and T. Douglas Price
   2000   The Use and Abuse of Trace Elements for
          Paleodietary Research. In *Biogeochemical
          Approaches to Paleodietary Analysis.* Stanley
          H. Ambrose and M. Anne Katzenberg, eds.
          Pp. 159–171. New York: Kluwer Academic/
          Plenum.
Butler, Virginia L., and Roy A. Schroeder
   1996   Do Digestive Processes Leave Diagnostic
          Traces on Fish Bones? *Journal of Archaeo-
          logical Science* 25(10):957–971.
Butzer, Karl W.
   1976   *Early Hydraulic Civilization in Egypt: A Study
          in Cultural Ecology.* Chicago: University of
          Chicago Press.
   1982   *Archaeology as Human Ecology.* Cambridge:
          Cambridge University Press.
   2005   Environmental History in the Mediterranean
          World: Cross-Disciplinary Investigation of
          Cause-and-Effect for Degradation and Soil
          Erosion. *Journal of Archaeological Science*
          32(12):1773–1800.
Callen, Eric O.
   1967a Analysis of the Tehuacan Coprolites. In *The
          Prehistory of the Tehuacan Valley,* vol. 1. Doug-
          las S. Byers, ed. Pp. 261–289. Austin: University
          of Texas Press.
   1967b The First New World Cereal. *American Antiq-
          uity* 32(4):535–538.
Callen, Eric O., and T. W. M. Cameron
   1960   A Prehistoric Diet Revealed in Coprolites. *New
          Scientist* 8(190):35–40.
Campbell, Bernard G., and James D. Loy
   2002   *Humankind Emerging: The Concise Edition.*
          Boston: Allyn and Bacon.
Carman, John, and Anthony Harding, eds.
   1999   *Ancient Warfare: Archaeological Perspectives.*
          Stroud: Sutton.

Carneiro, Robert L.
   1970   A Theory of the Origin of the State. *Science*
          169:733–738.
Carver, Martin
   1998   *Sutton Hoo: Burial Ground for Kings?* Philadel-
          phia: University of Pennsylvania Press.
Casson, Lionel
   1994   *Travel in the Ancient World.* Baltimore: Johns
          Hopkins University Press.
Caton-Thompson, Gertrude
   1931   *The Zimbabwe Culture: Ruins and Reactions.*
          Oxford: Clarendon Press.
Cavalli-Sforza, Luigi L.
   2000   *Genes, Peoples, and Languages.* New York: Far-
          rar, Straus & Giroux.
Chakrabarti, Dilip K.
   1995   *The Archaeology of Ancient Indian Cities.* Delhi:
          Oxford University Press.
Chang, K. C., ed.
   1968   *Settlement Archaeology.* Palo Alto: National
          Press Books.
Chapman, John
   1997   Changing Gender Relations in the Later
          Prehistory of Eastern Hungary. In *Invisible
          People and Processes: Writing Gender and
          Childhood into European Archaeology.*
          Jenny Moore and Eleanor Scott, eds.
          Pp. 131–149. London: Leicester University
          Press.
Childe, V. Gordon
   1936   *Man Makes Himself.* London: Watts.
   1942   *What Happened in History.* Harmondsworth,
          Sussex: Pelican Books.
Ch'in Ping Ma Youg
   1996   *The Terracotta Army of Emperor Qin Shi
          Huang.* Pei-ching: Chung-kuo lü yu ch'u
          pan she.
Chippindale, Christopher
   1993   Editorial. *Antiquity* 67(256):469–476.
Chippindale, Christopher, and Paul S. C. Taçon
   1998   *The Archaeology of Rock-Art.* Cambridge: Cam-
          bridge University Press.
Claassen, Cheryl
   2002   Gender and Archaeology. In *Archaeology:
          Original Readings in Method and Practice.* Pe-
          ter N. Peregrine, Carol R. Ember, and Melvin
          Ember, eds. Pp. 210–224. Upper Saddle River,
          NJ: Prentice Hall.
Claassen, Cheryl, ed.
   1994   *Women in Archaeology.* Philadelphia: Univer-
          sity of Pennsylvania Press.
Clapp, Nicholas
   1998   *The Road to Ubar: Finding the Atlantis of the
          Sands.* Boston: Houghton Mifflin.

Clark, Anthony
1990 *Seeing beneath the Soil: Prospecting Methods in Archaeology.* London: Batsford.

Clark, Jeffery J.
2001 *Tracking Prehistoric Migrations: Pueblo Settlers among the Tonto Basin Hohokam.* Anthropological Papers of the University of Arizona No. 66. Tucson: University of Arizona.

Clarke, David L.
1968 *Analytical Archaeology.* London: Methuen.

Close, Angela E.
2000 Reconstructing Movement in Prehistory. *Journal of Archaeological Method and Theory* 7(1):49–77.

Clottes, Jean
2001 Paleolithic Europe. In *Handbook of Rock Art Research.* David S. Whitley, ed. Pp. 459–481. Walnut Creek, CA: AltaMira Press.

Cock, Guillermo
2002 Inca Rescue. *National Geographic* 201(5):78–91.

Codere, Helen
1950 *Fighting with Property: A Study of Kwakiutl Potlatching and Warfare, 1792–1930.* Monographs of the American Ethnological Society 18. Seattle: University of Washington Press.
1990 Kwakiutl: Traditional Culture. In *Handbook of North American Indians.* vol. 7, Northwest Coast, Wayne Suttles, ed. Pp. 359–377. Washington: Smithsonian Institution.

Coe, Michael D.
1999 *The Maya.* 6th edition. London: Thames and Hudson.

Cohen, Mark N.
1977 *The Food Crisis in Prehistory: Overpopulation and the Origins of Agriculture.* New Haven: Yale University Press.

Cohen, Mark N., and George J. Armelagos, eds.
1984 *Paleopathology at the Origins of Agriculture.* Orlando: Academic Press.

Cohen, Robin
1997 *Global Diasporas: An Introduction.* Seattle: University of Washington Press.

Coles, John
1973 *Archaeology by Experiment.* New York: Scribner.

Conkey, Margaret W., and Joan M. Gero
1997 Programme to Practice: Gender and Feminism in Archaeology. *Annual Review of Anthropology* 26:411–437.

Conkey, Margaret W., and Janet D. Spector
1984 Archaeology and the Study of Gender. In *Advances in Archaeological Method.* vol. 7. Michael J. Schiffer, ed. Pp. 1–38. New York: Academic Press.

Connolly, Peter
1990 *Pompeii.* Oxford: Oxford University Press.

Conyers, Lawrence B.
2004 *Ground-Penetrating Radar for Archaeology.* Walnut Creek, CA: AltaMira Press.

Cook, Delta Collins, and Kevin D. Hunt
1998 Sex Differences in Trace Elements: Status or Self–Selection? In *Sex and Gender in Paleopathological Perspective.* Anne L. Grauer and Patricia Stuart-MacAdam, eds. Pp. 64–78. Cambridge: Cambridge University Press.

Cosgrove, Richard
1999 Forty-Two Degrees South: The Archaeology of Late Pleistocene Tasmania. *Journal of World Prehistory* 13(4):357–402.

Costin, Cathy Lynne
1996 Exploring the Relationship between Gender and Craft in Complex Societies: Methodological and Theoretical Issues of Gender Attribution. In *Gender and Archaeology.* Rita P. Wright, ed. Pp. 111–140. Philadelphia: University of Pennsylvania Press.
2002 Cloth Production and Gender Relations in the Inka Empire. In *Archaeology: Original Readings in Method and Practice.* Peter N. Peregrine, Carol R. Ember, and Melvin Ember, eds. Pp. 261–279. Upper Saddle River, NJ: Prentice Hall.

Coughlin, Ellen K.
1995 Farming Lessons from Prehistory. *The Chronicle of Higher Education* 41(23):A10–A15.

Crabtree, Pam J.
1990 Zooarchaeology and Complex Societies: Some Uses of Faunal Analysis for the Study of Trade, Social Statues, and Ethnicity. In *Archaeological Method and Theory,* vol. 2, Michael B. Schiffer, ed. Pp. 155–205. Tucson: University of Arizona Press.

Cruz-Uribe, Katheryn, and Richard G. Klein
1986 Pascal Programs for Computing Taxonomic Abundance in Samples of Fossil Mammals. *Journal of Archaeological Science* 13(2):171–187.

Cullen, Bob
2003 Testimony from the Iceman. *Smithsonian* 33(11):42–50.

Cummings, Linda Scott
1996 Pollen Analysis of CA-SBR-1913, California. Appendix 6 in *Archaeological Investigations at Guapiabit: CA-SBR-1913,* by Mark Q. Sutton and Joan S. Schneider. *San Bernardino County Museum Association Quarterly* 43(4):74–76.

Dahlberg, Frances, ed.
  1981   *Woman the Gatherer.* New Haven: Yale University Press.
Darwin, Charles
  1859   *On the Origin of Species by Means of Natural Selection, or, The Preservation of Favoured Races in the Struggle for Life.* London: J. Murray.
Davis, Simon J. M.
  1987   *The Archaeology of Animals.* New Haven: Yale University Press.
Deagan, Kathleen
  1987   *Artifacts of the Spanish Colonies of Florida and the Caribbean, 1500–1800,* vol. 1: Ceramics, Glassware, and Beads. Washington: Smithsonian Institution Press.
Dean, Martin, Ben Ferrari, Ian Oxley, Mark Redknap, and Kit Watson, eds.
  1995   *Archaeology Underwater: The NAS Guide to Principles and Practice.* 2nd edition. London: Archetype Publications.
DeGusta, David, and Tim D. White
  1996   On the Use of Skeletal Collections for DNA Analysis. *Ancient Biomolecules* 1(1):89–92.
Delgado, James P.
  1998   *Encyclopedia of Underwater and Maritime Archaeology.* New Haven: Yale University Press.
DeSalle, Rob, John Gatesy, Ward Wheeler, and David Grimaldi
  1992   DNA Sequences from a Fossil Termite in Oligo-Miocene Amber and their Phylogenetic Implications. *Science* 257:1933–1936.
Desroches-Nobelcourt, Christiane, and Georg Gerster
  1968   *The World Saves Abu Simbel.* Vienna: Verlag A. F. Koska.
Dewar, Robert E.
  1984   Environmental Productivity, Population Regulation, and Carrying Capacity. *American Anthropologist* 86(3):601–614.
Diamond, Jared
  1992   *The Third Chimpanzee.* New York: HarperCollins.
  1995   Easter's End. *Discover* 16(8):62–69.
Días-Audreu, Margarita, and Timothy Champion
  1996   *Nationalism and Archaeology in Europe.* London: University College London Press.
Dincauze, Dena F.
  2000   *Environmental Archaeology: Principles and Practice.* Cambridge: Cambridge University Press.
Donnan, Christopher B.
  1976   *Moche Art and Iconography.* Los Angeles: University of California Latin American Center Publications.
  1988   Unraveling the Mystery of the Warrior-Priest. *National Geographic* 174(4):550–555.

  1990   Masterworks of Art Reveal a Remarkable Pre-Inca World. *National Geographic* 177(6):16–33.
Donnan, Christopher B.
  2001   Moche Burials Uncovered. *National Geographic* 199(3):58–73.
Donnan, Christopher B., and Luis Jaime Castillo
  1992   Finding the Tomb of a Moche Priestess. *Archaeology* 45(6):38–42.
Dowson, Thomas A., ed.
  2000   Why Queer Archaeology? An Introduction. *World Archaeology* 32(2):161–165.
Drennan, Robert D.
  1996   *Statistics for Archaeologists: A Commonsense Approach.* New York: Plenum Press.
Dudar, J. C., J. S. Waye, and S. R. Saunders
  2003   Determination of a Kinship System Using Ancient DNA, Mortuary Practice, and Historic Records in an Upper Canadian Pioneer Cemetery. *International Journal of Osteoarchaeology* 13(4):232–246.
Ehrenberg, Margaret
  1989   *Women in Prehistory.* Norman: University of Oklahoma Press.
El-Baz, Farouk, Bob Moores, and Claude E. Petrone
  1989   Remote Sensing at an Archaeological Site in Egypt. *American Scientist* 77(1):60–66.
Eliade, Mircea
  1973   *Australian Religions: An Introduction.* Ithaca: Cornell University Press.
El Mahdy, Christine
  1999   *Tutankhamen: The Life and Death of the Boy-King.* New York: St. Martin's Press.
Erickson, Clark L.
  2000   An Artificial Landscape-Scale Fishery in the Bolivian Amazon. *Nature* 408:190–193.
Ericson, Jonathon E.
  1982   Production for Obsidian Exchange in California. In *Contexts for Prehistoric Exchange.* Jonathon E. Ericson and Timothy K. Earle, eds. Pp. 129–148. New York: Academic Press.
Etienne, Robert
  1992   *Pompeii: The Day the City Died.* New York: Abrams.
Evershed, Richard P., and Noreen Tuross
  1996   Protenaceous Material from Potsherds and Associated Soils. *Journal of Archaeological Research* 23(3):429–436.
Ezzo, Joseph A., Clark M. Johnson, and T. Douglas Price
  1997   Analytical Perspectives on Prehistoric Migration: A Case Study from East-Central Arizona. *Journal of Archaeological Science* 24(5):447–466.
Fægri, Knut, Peter Emil Kaland, and Knut Krzywinski
  2000   *Textbook of Pollen Analysis.* 4th edition. Chichester: Wiley.

Fagan, Brian M.
 1999 *Floods, Famines and Emperors: El Niño and the Fate of Civilizations.* New York: Basic Books.

Farrell, Nancy
 1988 Analysis of Human Coprolites from CA-RIV-1179 and CA-RIV-2827. In *Archaeological Investigations at CA-RIV-1179, CA-RIV-2823, and CA-RIV-2827, La Quinta, Riverside County, California.* Mark Q. Sutton and Philip J. Wilke, eds. Pp. 129–142. Coyote Press Archives of California Prehistory No. 20. Salinas, CA: Coyote Press.

Farrer, K. T. H.
 1993 Lead and the Last Franklin Expedition. *Journal of Archaeological Research* 20(4):399–409.

Faulkner, Charles T.
 1991 Prehistoric Diet and Parasitic Infection in Tennessee: Evidence from the Analysis of Desiccated Human Paleofeces. *American Antiquity* 56(4):687–700.

Feder, Kenneth L.
 2006 *Frauds, Myths, and Mysteries: Science and Pseudoscience in Archaeology* (5th ed.). Boston: McGraw-Hill.

Fedick, Scott, ed.
 1996 *The View from Yalahau.* University of California, Riverside: UC Mexus.

Feinman, Gary M., and Joyce Marcus, eds.
 1998 *Archaic States.* Santa Fe: School of American Research.

Ferguson, Leland
 1992 *Uncommon Ground: Archaeology and Early African America, 1650–1800.* Washington: Smithsonian Institution Press.

Feulner, Mark A., and J. Barto Arnold III
 2005 Maritime Archaeology. In *Handbook of Archaeological Methods,* vol. 1. Herbert D. G. Maschner and Christopher Chippendale, eds. Pp. 270–305. Lanham, MD: AltaMira Press.

Finkel, Elizabeth
 1998 Aboriginal Groups Warm to Studies of Early Australians. *Science* 280(5368):1342.

Fiorato, Veronica, Anthea Boylston, and Christopher Knusel
 2000 *Blood Red Roses: The Archaeology of a Mass Grave from the Battle of Towton,* A.D. 1461. Oxford: Oxbow Books.

Fisher, John W., Jr.
 1995 Bone Surface Modifications in Zooarchaeology. *Journal of Archaeological Method and Theory* 2(1):7–68.

Fitton, J. Lesley
 1996 *The Discovery of the Greek Bronze Age.* Cambridge: Harvard University Press.

Flannery, Kent V.
 1967 Culture History vs. Cultural Process: A Debate in American Archaeology. *Scientific American* 217:119–122.
 1968 Archaeological Systems Theory and Early Mesoamerica. In *Anthropological Archaeology in the Americas.* Betty J. Meggers, ed. Pp. 67–87. Washington: Anthropological Society of Washington.
 1969 Origins and Ecological Effects of Domestication in Iran and the Near East. In *The Domestication and Exploitation of Plants and Animals.* Peter Ucko and George Dimbleby, eds. Pp. 73–100. London: Duckworth.
 1972 The Cultural Evolution of Civilizations. *Annual Review of Ecology and Systematics* 3:399–426.
 1976 Empirical Determination of Site Catchments in Oaxaca and Tehuacán. In *The Early Mesoamerican Village.* Kent V. Flannery, ed. Pp. 103–117. New York: Academic Press.
 2002 Prehistoric Social Evolution. In *Archaeology: Original Readings in Method and Practice.* Peter N. Peregrine, Carol R. Ember, and Melvin Ember, eds. Pp. 225–244. Upper Saddle River, NJ: Prentice Hall.

Flecker, Michael
 2001 A Ninth-Century A.D. Arab or Indian Shipwreck in Indonesia: First Evidence for Direct Trade with China. *World Archaeology* 32(3):335–354.

Flood, Josephine
 1989 Tread Softly for You Tread on My Bones: The Development of Cultural Resource Management in Australia. In *Archaeological Heritage Management in the Modern World.* H. Cleere, ed. Pp. 79–93. London: Unwin Hyman.

Foreman, Laura
 1999 *Cleopatra's Palace: In Search of a Legend.* Del Mar, CA: Discovery Books.

Fowler, Brenda
 2000 *Iceman: Uncovering the Life and Times of a Prehistoric Man Found in an Alpine Glacier.* New York: Random House.

Fox, Richard Allen, Jr.
 1993 *Archaeology, History, and Custer's Last Battle.* Norman: University of Oklahoma Press.

Frison, George C., R. L. Andrews, J. M. Adovasio, R. C. Carlisle, and Robert Edgar
 1986 A Late Paleoindian Animal Trapping Net from Northern Wyoming. *American Antiquity* 51(2):352–361.

Fritz, Gayle J.
1994   The Value of Archaeological Plant Remains for Paleodietary Reconstruction. In *Paleonutrition: The Diet and Health of Prehistoric Americans.* Kristin D. Sobolik, ed. Pp. 21–33. Occasional Paper No. 22. Carbondale: Southern Illinois University, Center for Archaeological Investigations.

Fry, Gary F.
1985   Analysis of Fecal Material. In *The Analysis of Prehistoric Diets.* Robert I. Gilbert, Jr., and James H. Mielke, eds. Pp. 127–154. Orlando: Academic Press.

Gallagher, Larry
2005   Stone Age Beer. *Discover* 26(11):54–59.

Galm, Jerry R.
1979   *The Uncas Site: A Late Prehistoric Manifestation in the Southern Plains.* Research Series No. 5. Norman: University of Oklahoma, Archaeological Research and Management Center.

Gargett, Robert H.
1989   Grave Shortcomings: The Evidence for Neanderthal Burial. *Current Anthropology* 30(2):157–190.

Garlake, Peter S.
1973   *Great Zimbabwe.* New York: Stein and Day.

Gee, Henry
1996   Box of Bones "Clinches" Identity of Piltdown Paleontology Hoaxer. *Nature* 381:262.

Genoves, S.
1967   Proportionality of the Long Bones and Their Relation to Stature among Mesoamericans. *American Journal of Physical Anthropology* 26:67–77.

Gero, Joan M., and Margaret W. Conkey, eds.
1991   *Engendering Archaeology: Women and Prehistory.* Oxford: Blackwell.

Gibbins, David, and Jonathan Adams, eds.
2001   Shipwrecks and Maritime Archaeology. *World Archaeology* 32(3):279–291.

Gilbert, M. T. P., A. J. Hansen, E. Willerslev, G. Turner-Walker, and M. Collins
2006   Insights into the Processes Behind the Contamination of Degraded Human Teeth and Bone Samples with Exogenous Sources of DNA. *International Journal of Osteoarchaeology* 16(2):156–164.

Gilgan, Elizabeth
2001   Looting and the Market for Mayan Objects: A Belizean Perspective. In *Trade in Illicit Antiquities: The Destruction of the World's Archaeological Heritage.* Neil Brodie, Jennifer Doole, and Colin Renfrew, eds. Pp. 73–87. Cambridge: McDonald Institute for Archaeological Research.

Gillings, Mark, David Mattingly, and Jan van Dalen, eds.
1999   *Geographic Information Systems and Landscape Archaeology.* Oxford: Oxbow Books.

Gillings, Mark, and David Wheatley
2005   Geographic Information Systems. In *Handbook of Archaeological Methods,* vol. 1. Herbert D. G. Maschner and Christopher Chippendale, eds. Pp. 373–422. Lanham, MD: AltaMira Press.

Gilreath, Amy J., and William R. Hildebrandt
1997   *Prehistoric Use of the Coso Volcanic Field.* Contributions of the University of California Archaeological Research Facility No. 56. Berkeley: University of California.

Glassow, Michael A.
1978   The Concept of Carrying Capacity in the Study of Culture Process. In *Advances in Archaeological Method and Theory,* vol. 1. Michael B. Schiffer, ed. Pp. 31–48. New York: Academic Press.

Gobalet, Kenneth W.
1989   Remains of Tiny Fish from a Late Prehistoric Pomo Site near Clear Lake, California. *Journal of California and Great Basin Anthropology* 11(2):231–239.

Goddio, Franck, André Bernard, Etienne Bernand, Ibrahim Darwish, Zsolt Kiss, and Jean Yoyotte, eds.
1998   *Alexandria: The Submerged Royal Quarters.* London: Periplus.

Golley, Frank B.
1993   *A History of the Ecosystems Concept in Ecology.* New Haven: Yale University Press.

Gordon, Elizabeth A.
1993   Screen Size and Differential Faunal Recovery: A Hawaiian Example. *Journal of Field Archaeology* 20(4):453–460.

Gosden, Christopher
1999   *Anthropology and Archaeology: A Changing Relationship.* London: Routledge.

Gosden, Christopher, ed.
2001   Making Sense: Archaeology and Aesthetics. *World Archaeology* 33(2):163–167.

Goudie, Andrew
1994   *The Human Impact on the Natural Environment.* 4th edition. Cambridge: Massachusetts Institute of Technology Press.

Gould, Richard A.
2000   *Archaeology and the Social History of Ships.* Cambridge: Cambridge University Press.

Grant, Michael
1976   *Cities of Vesuvius: Pompeii and Herculaneum.* New York: Penguin Books.

Graslund, Bo
1987   *The Birth of Prehistoric Chronology: Dating Methods and Dating Systems in Nineteenth-Century Scandinavian Archaeology.* Cambridge: Cambridge University Press.

Gray, John S.
    1991   *Custer's Last Campaign: Mitch Boyer and the Little Bighorn Reconstructed.* Lincoln: University of Nebraska Press.
Grayson, Donald K.
    1983   *The Establishment of Human Antiquity.* New York: Academic Press.
    1984   *Quantitative Zooarchaeology.* New York: Academic Press.
    2001   The Archaeological Record of Human Impacts on Animal Populations. *Journal of World Prehistory* 15(1):1–68.
Green, Jeremy
    2004   *Maritime Archaeology: A Technical Handbook.* (2nd ed.) Amsterdam: Academic Press.
Greig, James
    1984   Garderobes, Sewers, Cesspits and Latrines. *Current Archaeology* 85:49–52.
Grinde, Donald A., and Bruce E. Johansen
    1995   *Ecocide of Native America: Environmental Destruction of Indian Lands and Peoples.* Santa Fe: Clear Light.
Guillet, David
    1987   Terracing and Irrigation in the Peruvian Highlands. *Current Anthropology* 28(4):409–430.
Gvozdover, Marianna D.
    1989   The Typology of Female Figurines of the Kostenki Paleolithic Culture. *Soviet Anthropology and Archaeology* 27(4):32–94.
Hamilton, Donny L.
    1991   A Decade of Excavations at Port Royal, Jamaica. In *Underwater Archaeology Proceedings from the Society for Historical Archaeology Conference.* John D. Broadwater, ed. Pp. 90–94. Tucson: Society for Historical Archaeology.
Hansen, Joyce, and Gary McGowan
    1998   *Breaking Ground, Breaking Silence: The Story of New York's African Burial Ground.* New York: Holt.
Hansen, Jens Peder Hart, Jørgen Meldgaard, and Jørgen Nordqvist, eds.
    1991   *The Greenland Mummies.* Washington: Smithsonian Institution Press.
Hardesty, Donald L.
    1975   The Niche Concept: Suggestions for Its Use in Studies of Human Ecology. *Human Ecology* 3(2):71–85.
Harding, D. W.
    1974   *The Iron Age in Lowland Britain.* London: Routledge and Kegan Paul.
Hardy, Bruce L., Rudolf A. Raff, and Venu Raman
    1997   Recovery of Mammalian DNA from Middle Paleolithic Stone Tools. *Journal of Archaeological Science* 24:601–611.

Harner, Michael
    1977   The Ecological Basis for Aztec Sacrifice. *American Ethnologist* 4(1):117–135.
Harrington, Spencer P. M.
    1993   Bones and Bureaucrats: New York's Great Cemetery Imbroglio. *Archaeology* 46(2):28–38.
Harris, David, and Gordon Hillman, eds.
    1989   *Foraging and Farming: The Evolution of Plant Exploitation.* Cambridge: Cambridge University Press.
Harris, Marvin
    1979   *Cultural Materialism: The Struggle for a Science of Culture.* New York: Random House.
Hastorf, Christine A., and Virginia S. Popper, eds.
    1988   *Current Paleoethnobotany.* Chicago: University of Chicago Press.
Haury, Emil W.
    1976   *The Hohokam: Desert Farmers and Craftsmen.* Tucson: University of Arizona Press.
Hawass, Zahi
    2000   *Valley of the Golden Mummies.* New York: Abrams.
Hawkins, D.
    1990   The Black Death and New London Cemeteries of 1348. *Antiquity* 64:637–642.
Headland, Thomas, and Lawrence A. Reid
    1989   Hunter-Gatherers and Their Neighbors from Prehistory to the Present. *Current Anthropology* 30(1):43–66.
Heath, Barbara J.
    1999   *The Archaeology of Slave Life at Thomas Jefferson's Poplar Forest.* Charlottesville: University Press of Virginia.
Hedges, Robert E. M.
    2003   On Bone Collagen-Apatite-Carbonate Isotopic Relationships. *International Journal of Osteoarchaeology* 13(1–2):66–79.
Heggie, D. C.
    1982   *Archaeoastronomy in the Old World.* Cambridge: Cambridge University Press.
Hegmon, Michelle
    1992   Archaeological Research on Style. *Annual Review of Anthropology* 21:517–536.
    2003   Setting Theoretical Egos Aside: Issues and Theory in North American Archaeology. *American Antiquity* 68(2):213–243.
Heimmer, Don H., and Steven L. De Vore
    2000   Near-Surface, High Resolution Geophysical Methods for Cultural Resource Management and Archaeological Investigations. In *Science and Technology in Historic Preservation.* Ray A. Williamson and Paul R. Nickens, eds. Pp. 53–73. New York: Kluwer Academic/Plenum.

Heizer, Robert F., and Martin A. Baumhoff
  1962   *Prehistoric Rock Art of Eastern California and Nevada.* Berkeley: University of California Press.

Hemphill, Brian E.
  1999   Wear and Tear: Osteoarthritis as an Indicator of Mobility among Great Basin Hunter-Gatherers. In *Prehistoric Lifeways in the Great Basin Wetlands: Bioarchaeological Reconstruction and Interpretation.* Brian E. Hemphill and Clark Spencer Larsen, eds. Pp. 241–289. Salt Lake City: University of Utah Press.

Hemphill, Brian E., and James P. Mallory
  2004   Horse-Mounted Invaders from the Russo-Kazakh Steppe or Agricultural Colonists from Western Central Asia? A Craniometric Investigation of the Bronze Age Settlement of Xinjiang. *American Journal of Physical Anthropology* 124(3):199–222.

Henry, Donald O.
  1995   *Prehistoric Cultural Ecology and Evolution: Insights from Southern Jordan.* New York: Plenum Press.

Heron, Carl, and Richard P. Evershed
  1993   The Analysis of Organic Residues and the Study of Pottery Use. In *Archaeological Method and Theory,* vol. 5. Michael B. Schiffer, ed. Pp. 247–286. Tucson: University of Arizona Press.

Heron, Carl, Richard P. Evershed, and L. J. Goad
  1991   Effects of Migration of Soil Lipids on Organic Residues Associated with Buried Potsherds. *Journal of Archaeological Science* 18:641–659.

Herz, Norman, and Ervan G. Garrison
  1998   *Geological Methods for Archaeology.* Oxford: Oxford University Press.

Hester, Thomas R., Harry J. Shafer, and Kenneth L. Feder, eds.
  1997   *Field Methods in Archaeology.* 7th edition. Mountain View, CA: Mayfield.

Heyerdahl, Thor
  1972   *The Ra Expeditions.* Harmondsworth: Penguin.

Hill, Erica
  1998   Gender-Informed Archaeology: The Priority of Definition, the Use of Analogy, and the Multivariate Approach. *Journal of Archaeological Method and Theory* 5(1):99–128.

Hill, James N., and Joel Gunn, eds.
  1977   *The Individual in Prehistory: Studies of Variability in Style in Prehistoric Technologies.* New York: Academic Press.

Hillman, Gordon C.
  1986   Plant Foods in Ancient Diet: The Archaeological Role of Palaeofaeces in General and Lindow Man's Gut Contents in Particular. In *Lindow Man: The Body in the Bog.* I. M. Stead, J. B. Bourke, and Don Brothwell, eds. Pp. 99–115. Ithaca: Cornell University Press.

Hillson, Simon W.
  1986   *Teeth.* Cambridge: Cambridge Manuals in Archaeology.
  1996   *Dental Anthropology.* Cambridge: Cambridge University Press.

Hodder, Ian
  1982   *Symbols in Action: Ethnoarchaeological Studies of Material Culture.* Cambridge: Cambridge University Press.
  1991   *Reading the Past: Current Approaches to Interpretation in Archaeology.* 2nd edition. Cambridge: Cambridge University Press.
  1999   *The Archaeological Process: An Introduction.* Oxford: Blackwell.

Holden, Timothy G.
  1986   Preliminary Report on the Detailed Analyses of the Macroscopic Remains from the Gut of Lindow Man. In *Lindow Man: The Body in the Bog.* I. M. Stead, J. B. Bourke, and Don Brothwell, eds. Pp. 116–125. Ithaca: Cornell University Press.
  1994   Dietary Evidence from the Intestinal Contents of Ancient Humans with Particular Reference to Desiccated Remains from Northern Chile. In *Tropical Archaeobotany: Applications and New Developments.* Jon G. Hather, ed. Pp. 65–85. London: Routledge.

Holland, Mitchell M., Deborah L. Fisher, Lloyd G. Mitchell, William C. Rodriquez, James J. Canik, Carl R. Merril, and Victor W. Weedn
  1993   Mitrochondrial DNA Sequence Analysis of Human Skeletal Remains: Identification of Remains from the Vietnam War. *Journal of Forensic Sciences* 38(3):542–553.

Honch, Noah V., T. F. G. Higham, J. Chapman, B. Gaydarska, and Robert E. M. Hedges
  2006   A Palaeodietary Investigation of Carbon ($^{13}C/^{12}C$) and Nitrogen ($^{15}N/^{14}N$) in Human and Faunal Bones from the Copper Age Cemeteries of Varna I and Durankulak, Bulgaria. *Journal of Archaeological Science* 33(11):1493–1504.

Hong, S., J. P. Candelone, C. Patterson, and C. F. Boutron
  1996   History of Ancient Copper Smelting Pollution during Roman and Mediaeval Times Recorded in the Greenland Ice. *Science* 272:246–249.

Hood, Sinclair
  1971   *The Minoans: Crete in the Bronze Age.* London: Thames and Hudson.

Hoppe, Kathryn A., Paul L. Koch, and T. T. Furutani
　2003　Assessing the Preservation of Biogenic Strontium in Fossil Bones and Tooth Enamel. *International Journal of Osteoarchaeology* 13(1–2):20–28.

Hu, Yaowu, Stanley H. Ambrose, and Changsui Wang
　2006　Stable Isotopic Analysis of Human Bones from the Jiahu Site, Henan, China: Implications for the Transition to Agriculture. *Journal of Archaeological Science* 33(9):1319–1330.

Hudson, Jean
　1990　*Advancing Methods in Zooarchaeology: An Ethnoarchaeological Study among the Aka Pygmies.* Ph.D. dissertation, University of California, Santa Barbara.

Hudson, Jean, ed.
　1993　*From Bones to Behavior: Ethnoarchaeological and Experimental Contributions to the Interpretation of Faunal Remains.* Occasional Paper No. 21. Carbondale: Southern Illinois University, Center for Archaeological Investigations.

Hunt, Robert C.
　1988　Size and Structure of Authority in Canal Irrigation Systems. *Journal of Anthropological Research* 44(4):335–355.

Hunt, Terry L.
　2007　Rethinking Easter Island's Ecological Catastrophe. *Journal of Archaeological Science* 34(3):485–502.

Huss-Ashmore, Rebecca, Alan H. Goodman, and George J. Armelagos
　1982　Nutritional Inference from Paleopathology. In *Advances in Archaeological Method and Theory,* vol. 5. Michael B. Schiffer, ed. Pp. 395–474. New York: Academic Press.

Hutson, Scott R.
　2001　Synergy through Disunity: Science as Social Practice: Comments on VanPool and VanPool. *American Antiquity* 66(2):349–360.

Hutt, Sherry, Elwood W. Jones, and Martin E. McAllister
　1992　*Archaeological Resource Protection.* Washington: Preservation Press.

Ikawa-Smith, Fumiko
　2001　*The Upper Paleolithic along the Pacific Margin of Northeast Asia.* Paper presented at the Annual Meetings of the Society for American Archaeology, New Orleans.

Ingold, Tim
　1987　*The Appropriation of Nature: Essays on Human Ecology and Social Relations.* Iowa City: University of Iowa Press.

Jackson, Donald Dale
　1992　How Lord Elgin First Won—and Lost—His Marbles. *Smithsonian* 23(9):135–146.

Jefferson, Thomas
　1787　*Notes on the State of Virginia.* London: J. Stockdale.

Jochim, Michael A.
　1983　Optimization Models in Context. In *Archaeological Hammers and Theories.* James A. Moore and Authur S. Keene, eds. Pp. 157–172. New York: Academic Press.
　1998　*A Hunter-Gatherer Landscape: Southwest Germany in the Late Paleolithic and Mesolithic.* New York: Plenum Press.

Johnson, Mathew
　1999　*Archaeological Theory: An Introduction.* Oxford: Blackwell.

Jones, Andrew K. G.
　1986　Fish Bone Survival in the Digestive System of the Pig, Dog, and Man: Some Experiments. In *Fish and Archaeology: Studies in Osteometry, Taphonomy, Seasonality and Fishing Methods.* D. C. Brinkhuizen and A. T. Claseneds, eds. Pp. 53–61. British Archaeological Reports. International Series No. 294. Oxford: British Archaeological Reports.

Jones, Kevin T., and David B. Madsen
　1989　Calculating the Cost of Resource Transportation: A Great Basin Example. *Current Anthropology* 30(4):529–534.

Jones, Rhys
　1978　Why Did the Tasmanians Stop Eating Fish? In *Explorations in Ethnoarchaeology.* Richard Gould, ed. Pp. 11–48. Albuquerque: University of New Mexico Press.
　1995　Tasmanian Archaeology: Establishing the Sequences. *Annual Review of Anthropology* 24:423–446.

Jones, Siâm
　1997　*The Archaeology of Ethnicity: Constructing Identities in the Past and Present.* London: Routledge.

Kaestle, Frederika A., and David Glenn Smith
　2001　Ancient Mitochondrial DNA Evidence for Prehistoric Population Movement: The Numic Expansion. *American Journal of Physical Anthropology* 115(1):1–12.

Kamp, Kathryn A.
　2001　Where Have All the Children Gone? The Archaeology of Childhood. *Journal of Archaeological Methods and Theory* 8(1):1–34.

Kamp, Kathryn A., Nichole Timmerman, Greg Lind, Jules Graybill, and Ian Natowsky
　1999　Discovering Childhood: Using Fingerprints to Find Children in the Archaeological Record. *American Antiquity* 64(2):309–315.

Kaplan, Abraham
　1964　*The Conduct of Inquiry.* San Francisco: Chandler.

Katzenberg, M. Anne, and Roman G. Harrison
 1997 What's in a Bone? Recent Advances in Archaeological Bone Chemistry. *Journal of Archaeological Research* 5(3):265–293.
Keenleyside, A., X. Song, D. R. Chettle, and C. E. Weber
 1996 The Lead Content of Human Bones from the
 1845 Franklin Expedition. *Journal of Archaeological Science* 23(3):461–465.
Kelly, Robert L.
 1995 *The Foraging Spectrum: Diversity in Hunter-
 Gatherer Lifeways.* Washington: Smithsonian
 Institution.
Kenoyer, Jonathon M.
 1998 *Ancient Cities of the Indus Civilization.* Karachi:
 Oxford University Press.
Kent, Susan
 1992 Anemia through the Ages: Changing Perspec-
 tives and Their Implications. In *Diet Demography, and Disease: Changing Perspectives on
 Anemia.* Patricia Stuart-Macadam and Susan
 Kent, eds. Pp. 1–30. New York: Aldine De
 Gruyter.
Kenworthy, Mary Anne, Eleanor M. King, Mary Elizabeth
 Ruwell, and Trudy Van Houten
 1985 *Preserving Field Records: Archival Techniques
 for Archaeologists and Anthropologists.* Philadel-
 phia: University Museum of Archaeology and
 Anthropology.
Kenyon, Kathleen M.
 1957 *Digging Up Jericho.* London: Ernest Benn.
 1979 *Archaeology in the Holy Land.* 4th edition.
 London: Ernest Benn.
Kidder, Alfred V.
 1924 *An Introduction to the Study of Southwestern
 Archaeology, with a Preliminary Account of
 the Excavations at Pecos.* New Haven, CT: Yale
 University Press, Papers of the Southwestern
 Expedition, Phillips Academy, No. 1.
Kintz, Ellen
 1990 *Life under the Tropical Canopy: Tradition and
 Change among the Yucatec Maya.* New York:
 Holt, Rinehart and Winston.
Kirch, Patrick V.
 1977 Valley Agricultural Systems in Prehistoric
 Hawai'i: An Archaeological Consideration.
 Asian Perspectives 20:246–280.
 1984 *Evolution of Polynesian Chiefdoms.* New York:
 Cambridge University Press.
 1994 *The Wet and The Dry: Irrigation and Agri-
 cultural Intensification in Polynesia.* Chicago:
 University of Chicago Press.
 1997 The Cultural Landscape of Kipapa and
 Nakaohu ahupua'a: A Preliminary Report on
 an Intensive Archaeological Survey. In *Na Mea*

*Kahiko o Kahikinui: Studies in the Archaeology
 of Kahikinui, Maui, Hawaiian Islands.* Patrick
 V. Kirch, ed. Pp. 12–27. Berkeley, CA: Archaeological Research Facility, Oceanic Archaeological Laboratory, Special Publication No. 1.
Kirch, Patrick V., and Marshall Sahlins
 1992 *Anahulu: The Anthropology of History in the
 Kingdom of Hawai'i,* 2 vols. Chicago: University of Chicago Press.
Kirner, Donna, R. Burky, K. Selsor, D. George, R. E. Taylor,
 and J. R. Southon
 1997 Dating the Spirit Cave Mummy: The Value
 of Reexamination. *Nevada Historical Society
 Quarterly* 40(1):54–56.
Klippel, W. E.
 2001 Sugar Monoculture, Bovid Skeletal Part Frequencies, and Stable Carbon Isotopes: Interpreting Enslaved African Diet at Brimstone
 Hill, St Kitts, West Indies. *Journal of Archaeological Science* 28(11):1191–1198.
Koerper, Henry C.
 1999 *A Numismatic Example of Stylistic Seriation:
 The Satyr-and-Nymph Motif of Thasos.* Paper
 presented at the Annual Meeting of the Society
 for American Archaeology, Chicago.
Kohl, Philip L.
 1998 Nationalism and Archaeology: On the Construction of Nations and the Reconstructions
 of the Remote Past. *Annual Review of Anthropology* 27:223–246.
Kolman, Connie J., and Noreen Tuross
 2000 Ancient DNA Analysis of Human Populations.
 American Journal of Physical Anthropology
 111(1):5–23.
Kopff, E. Christian
 2000 Italian Fascism and the Roman Empire. *Classical Bulletin* 76(2).
Kormondy, Edward J., and Daniel E. Brown
 1998 *Fundamentals of Human Ecology.* Upper Saddle
 River, NJ: Prentice Hall.
Kossinna, Gustaf
 1921 *German Prehistory: A Preeminently National Discipline* [*Die deutsche Vorgeschichte: eine hervorragend
 nationale Wissenschaft*]. Mannus-Biblioteck 9.
Kowal, Walter, Owen B. Beattie, Halfdan Baadsgaard, and
 Peter M. Krahn
 1991 Source Identification of Lead Found in Tissues
 of Sailors from the Franklin Arctic Expedition
 of 1845. *Journal of Archaeological Research*
 18(2):193–203.
Kraft, John C., George Rapp, Jr., George J. Szemler,
 Christos Tziavos, and Edward W. Kase
 1987 The Pass at Thermopylae, Greece. *Journal of
 Field Archaeology* 14(2):181–198.

Kramer, Carol, ed.

1979   *Ethnoarchaeology: Implications of Ethnography for Archaeology.* New York: Columbia University Press.

Krech, Shepard

1999   *The Ecological Indian: Myth and History.* New York: Norton.

Krupp, E. C.

1983   *Echos of the Ancient Skies: The Astronomy of Lost Civilizations.* New York: Harper & Row.

1984   *Archaeoastronomy and the Roots of Science.* Boulder: Westview Press.

Kunzig Robert

2000   Life Boats. *Discover* 21(4):42–49.

Kuzmina, E. E.

1998   Cultural Connections of the Tarim Basin People and Pastoralists of the Asian Steppes in the Bronze Age. In *The Bronze Age and Early Iron Age Peoples of Eastern Central Asia.* Victor H. Mair, ed. Pp. 63–93. University of Pennsylvania Museum Publication, vol. 1. Philadelphia: University Museum of Archaeology and Anthropology.

Kuznar, Lawrence A.

1997   *Reclaiming a Scientific Anthropology.* Walnut Creek, CA: AltaMira Press.

Kvamme, Kenneth L.

1989   Geographic Information Systems in Regional Archaeological Research and Data Management. In *Archaeological Method and Theory,* vol. 1. Michael B. Schiffer, ed. Pp. 139–203. Tucson: University of Arizona Press.

2005   Terrestrial Remote Sensing in Archaeology. In *Handbook of Archaeological Methods,* vol. 1. Herbert D. G. Maschner and Christopher Chippendale, eds. Pp. 423–477. Lanham, MD: AltaMira Press.

Lambert, Joseph B.

2005   Archaeological Chemistry. In *Handbook of Archaeological Methods,* vol. 1. Herbert D. G. Maschner and Christopher Chippendale, eds. Pp. 478–500. Lanham, MD: AltaMira Press.

Lambert, Patricia M.

1993   Health in Prehistoric Populations of the Santa Barbara Channel Islands. *American Antiquity* 58(3):509–522.

La Riche, William

1996   *Alexandria: The Sunken City.* London: Weidenfeld & Nicolson.

Larsen, Clark Spenser

1987   Bioarchaeological Interpretations of Subsistence Economy and Behavior from Human Skeletal Remains. In *Advances in Archaeological Method and Theory,* vol. 10. Michael B. Schiffer, ed. Pp. 339–445. New York: Academic Press.

1997   *Bioarchaeology: Interpreting Behavior from the Human Skeleton.* Cambridge Studies in Biological Anthropology 21. Cambridge: Cambridge University Press.

2000   *Skeletons in Our Closet: Revealing Our Past through Bioarchaeology.* Princeton: Princeton University Press.

Lawton, Harry W.

1987   Riverside's First Chinatown and the Boom of the Eighties. In *Wong Ho Luen: An American Chinatown.* Great Basin Foundation, eds. Pp. 1–52. San Diego, CA: Great Basin Foundation.

Leakey, Mary D., and R. L. Hay

1979   Pliocene Footprints in the Laetoli Beds at Laetoli, Northern Tanzania. *Nature* 278:317–323.

Lee, Richard B., and Irven DeVore, eds.

1968   *Man the Hunter.* Chicago: Aldine.

1976   *Kalahari Hunter-Gatherers: Studies of the !Kung San and Their Neighbors.* Cambridge: Harvard University Press.

Lee-Thorpe, Julia A., Judith C. Sealy, and Nikolaas J. van der Merwe

1989   Stable Carbon Isotope Ratio Differences between Bone Collagen and Bone Apatite, and Their Relationship to Diet. *Journal of Archaeological Science* 16:585–599.

Leonard, Robert D.

2001   Evolutionary Archaeology. In *Archaeological Theory Today.* Ian Hodder, ed. Pp. 65–97. Cambridge: Polity Press.

Leone, Mark P.

1984   Interpreting Ideology in Historical Archaeology: Using the Rules of Perspective in the William Paca Garden in Annapolis, Maryland. In *Ideology, Power, and Prehistory.* Daniel Miller and Christopher Tilley, eds. Pp. 25–35. Cambridge: Cambridge University Press.

Levy, Thomas E., James D. Anderson, Mark Waggoner, Neil Smith, Adolfo Muniz, and Russell B. Adams

2001   Interface: Archaeology and Technology: Digital Archaeology 2001: GIS-Based Excavation Recording in Jordan. *The SAA Archaeological Record* 1(3):23–29.

Lewis, Henry T.

1973   *Patterns of Indian Burning in California: Ecology and Ethnohistory.* Ballena Press Anthropological Papers No. 1. Ramona, CA: Ballena Press.

1982   Fire Technology and Resource Management in Aboriginal North America and Australia. In *Resource Managers: North American and Australian Hunter-Gatherers.* Nancy M. Williams and Eugene S. Hunn, eds. Pp. 45–67. Boulder, CO: Westview Press.

Lewis, Martin
1992 *Green Delusions.* Raleigh: Duke University Press.

Likovsky, Jakub, Markéta Urbanova, Martin Hájek, Viktor Černý, and Petřech
2006 Two Cases of Leprosy from Žatec (Bohemia), Dated to the Turn of the 12th Century and Confirmed by DNA Analysis for *Mycobacterium leprae. Journal of Archaeological Science* 33(9):1276–1283.

Lillie, Malcolm C., and Kenneth Jacobs
2006 Stable Isotope Analysis of 14 Individuals from the Mesolithic Cemetery of Vasilyevka II, Dnieper Rapids Region, Ukraine. *Journal of Archaeological Science* 33(6):880–886.

Limp, W. Fredrick
2000 Geographic Information Systems in Historic Preservation. In *Science and Technology in Historic Preservation.* Ray A. Williamson and Paul R. Nickens, eds. Pp. 231–247. New York: Kluwer Academic/Plenum.

Little, Barbara J.
1994 Consider the Hermaphroditic Mind: Comment on "The Interplay of Evidential Constraints and Political Interests: Recent Archaeological Research on Gender." *American Antiquity* 59(3):539–544.

Little, John D. C., and Elizabeth A. Little
1997 Analysing Prehistoric Diets by Linear Programming. *Journal of Archaeological Science* 24(8):741–747.

Lobell, Jarrett A.
2003 Warriors of Clay. *Archaeology* 56(2):36–39.

Loewe, Michael, and Edward L. Shaughnessy
1999 *The Cambridge History of Ancient China.* Cambridge: Cambridge University Press.

Longacre, William A., and James M. Skibo, eds.
1994 *Kalinga Ethnoarchaeology: Expanding Archaeological Method and Theory.* Washington: Smithsonian Institution Press.

Lowell, Percival
1906 *Mars and Its Canals.* New York: Macmillan.

Lubbock, Sir John
1865 *Pre-historic Times: As Illustrated by Ancient Remains and the Manners and Customs of Modern Savages.* London: Williams and Norgate.

Lyell, Charles
1830 *Principles of Geology* (Volume I). London: John Murray.

Lyman, R. Lee
1982 Archaeofaunas and Subsistence Studies. In *Advances in Archaeological Method and Theory,* vol. 5. Michael B. Schiffer, ed. Pp. 331–393. New York: Academic Press.
1987 Archaeofaunas and Butchery Studies: An Archaeological Perspective. In *Advances in Archaeological Method and Theory,* vol. 10. Michael B. Schiffer, ed. Pp. 249–337. New York: Academic Press.
1994 *Vertebrate Taphonomy.* Cambridge: Cambridge University Press.

Lyman, R. Lee, and Michael J. O'Brien
1998 The Goals of Evolutionary Archaeology: History and Explanation. *Current Anthropology* 39(5):615–652.
2001 The Direct Historical Approach, Analogical Reasoning, and Theory in Americanist Archaeology. *Journal of Archaeological Method and Theory* 8(4):303–342.

Lynott, Mark J.
1997 Ethical Principles and Archaeological Practice: Development of an Ethics Policy. *American Antiquity* 62(4):589–599.

MacNeish, Richard
1992 *The Origins of Agriculture and Settled Life.* Norman: University of Oklahoma Press.

Madsen, David B.
1986 *Leap and Grab: Energetic Efficiency Tests of Cricket Use.* Paper presented at the Great Basin Anthropological Conference, Las Vegas.

Madsen, David B., and James E. Kirkman
1988 Hunting Hoppers. *American Antiquity* 53(3):593–604.

Madsen, David B., and Dave N. Schmitt
1998 Mass Collecting and the Diet Breadth Model: A Great Basin Example. *Journal of Archaeological Science* 25(5):445–455.

Magnier, Mark
2000 Japan Amazed as Archaeologist's Magic Exposed as Sleight of Hand. *Los Angeles Times,* November 9: A-1, A-24.

Mair, Victor H.
1995a Mummies of the Tarim Basin. *Archaeology* 48(2):28–35.
1995b Prehistoric Caucasoid Corpses of the Tarim Basin. *Journal of Indo-European Studies* 23 (3–4):281–307.

Maiuri, Amedeo
1958 Pompeii. *Scientific American* 198(4):68–78.

Mallory, James P., and Victor H. Mair
2000 *The Tarim Mummies.* New York: Thames and Hudson.

Marlar, Richard A., Banks L. Leonard, Brian R. Billman, Patricia M. Lambert, and Jennifer E. Marlar
2000 Biochemical Evidence of Cannibalism at a Prehistoric Puebloan Site in Southwestern Colorado. *Nature* 407:74–78.

Marsden, Peter
  2003   *Sealed by Time: The Loss and Recovery of the Mary Rose.* Portsmouth: Mary Rose Trust.

Marshall, Fiona, and Tom Pilgram
  1993   NISP vs. MNI in Quantification of Body-Part Representation. *American Antiquity* 58(2): 261–269.

Martin, Debra L., and George J. Armelagos
  1986   Histological Analysis of Bone Remodeling in Prehistoric Sudanese Nubian Specimens (350 BC–AD 1100). In *Science in Egyptology.* R. A. David, ed. Pp. 389–397. Manchester: Manchester University Press.

Martin, Debra, and David W. Frayer, eds.
  1997   *Troubled Times: Violence and Warfare in the Past.* Sydney: Gordon and Breach.

Maschner, Herbert D. G., ed.
  1996   *Darwinian Archaeologies.* New York: Plenum Press.

Masters, P. M., and N. C. Flemming, eds.
  1983   *Quaternary Coastlines and Marine Archaeology: Towards the Prehistory of Land Bridges and Continental Shelves.* London: Academic Press.

Matson, P. A., W. J. Parton, A. G. Power, and M. J. Swift
  1997   Agricultural Intensification and Ecosystem Properties. *Science* 227:504–509.

Mays, Simon
  1998   *The Archaeology of Human Bones.* London: Routledge.

Mays, Simon, and Marina Faerman
  2001   Sex Identification in Some Putative Infanticide Victims from Roman Britain Using Ancient DNA. *Journal of Archaeological Science* 28(5):555–559.

McCall, Grant
  1994   *Rapanui: Tradition and Survival on Easter Island.* 2nd edition. Honolulu: University of Hawaii Press.

McDougall, Dennis P.
  1990   The Bottles of the Hoff Store Site. In *The Hoff Store Site and Gold Rush Merchandise from San Francisco, California.* Allen G. Pastron and Eugene M. Hattori, eds. Pp. 58–74. Society for Historical Archaeology Special Publication Series No. 7. Pleasant Hill, CA: Society for Historical Archaeology.

McGimsey, Charles R., III
  1972   *Public Archaeology.* Orlando: Academic Press.
  1995   Standards, Ethics, and Archaeology: A Brief History. In *Ethics in American Archaeology: Challenges for the 1990s.* Mark J. Lynott and Alison Wylie, eds. Pp. 11–13. Washington: Society for American Archaeology.

McGovern, Patrick E., and Robert G. Mondavi
  2007   *Ancient Wine: The Search for the Origins of Viniculture.* Princeton, NJ: Princeton University Press.

McGuire, Randall H.
  1992   *A Marxist Archaeology.* San Diego: Academic Press.
  1993   Archaeology and Marxism. In *Archaeological Method and Theory,* vol. 5. Michael B. Schiffer, ed. Pp. 101–157. Tucson: University of Arizona Press.

McGuire, Randall H., and Robert Paynter, eds.
  1991   *The Archaeology of Inequality.* Oxford: Blackwell.

McIntosh, Roderick J.
  1998   Riddle of the Great Zimbabwe. *Archaeology* 51(4):44–49.

McKee, Alexander
  1974   *King Henry VIII's "Mary Rose."* New York: Stein and Day.

McPherron, Shannon P., and Harold L. Dibble
  2002   *Using Computers in Archaeology: A Practical Guide.* New York: McGraw-Hill/Mayfield.

Meindl, Richard S., and Katherine F. Russell
  1998   Recent Advances in Method and Theory in Paleodemography. *Annual Review of Anthropology* 27:375–399.

Meltzer, David J.
  1995   Clocking the First Americans. *Annual Review of Anthropology* 24:21–45.

Menon, Shanti
  1998   Indus Valley, Inc. *Discover* 19(12):67–71.

Meyer, William B.
  1996   *Human Impact on the Earth.* Cambridge: Cambridge University Press.

Michno, Gregory F.
  1997   *Lakota Noon: The Indian Narrative of Custer's Defeat.* Missoula, MT: Mountain Press.

Miller, Naomi F.
  2002   The Analysis of Archaeological Plant Remains. In *Archaeology: Original Readings in Method and Practice.* Peter N. Peregrine, Carol R. Ember, and Melvin Ember, eds. Pp. 81–91. Upper Saddle River, NJ: Prentice Hall.

Mithen, Steven
  1994   From Domain Specific to Generalized Intelligence: A Cognitive Interpretation of the Middle/Upper Palaeolithic Transition. In *The Ancient Mind: Elements of Cognitive Archaeology.* Colin Renfrew and Ezra B. W. Zubrow, eds. Pp. 29–39. Cambridge: Cambridge University Press.
  2001   Archaeological Theory and Theories of Cognitive Evolution. In *Archaeological Theory Today.* Ian Hodder, ed. Pp. 98–121. Cambridge: Polity Press.

Moore, John H., Margot P. Liberty, and A. Terry Straus
  2001   Cheyenne. In *Handbook of North American Indians,* vol. 13 (pt. 2), *Plains.* Raymond J. De-Mallie, ed. Pp. 863–885. Washington: Smithsonian Institution.

Morehead, Caroline
  1996   *Lost and Found: The 9,000 Treasures of Troy: Heinrich Schliemann and the Gold That Got Away.* New York: Penguin.

Morgan, Lewis Henry
  1877   *Ancient Society or, Researches in the Line of Human Progress from Savagery through Barbarism to Civilization.* Chicago: C. H. Kerr.

Morris, Ian
  2000   *Archaeology as Cultural History.* Oxford: Blackwell.

Muckelroy, Keith
  1978   *Maritime Archaeology.* Cambridge: Cambridge University Press.

Mulligan, Connie J.
  2006   Anthropological Applications of Ancient DNA: Problems and Prospects. *American Antiquity* 71(2):365–380.

Munsey, Cecil
  1970   *The Illustrated Guide to Collecting Bottles.* New York: Hawthorn Books.

Nash, Stephen E.
  2002   Archaeological Tree-Ring Dating at the Millennium. *Journal of Archaeological Research* 10(3):243–275.

Neff, Hector
  2000   On Evolutionary Ecology and Evolutionary Archaeology: Some Common Ground? *Current Anthropology* 41(3):427–429.

Nelson, Mark R.
  2002   The Mummy's Curse: Historical Cohort Study. *British Medical Journal* 325:21–28.

Nelson, Sarah Milledge
  2004   *Gender in Archaeology: Analyzing Power and Prestige.* 2nd edition. Walnut Creek, CA: AltaMira Press.

Nelson, Sarah Milledge ed.
  2006   *Handbook of Gender in Archaeology.* Lanham, MD: AltaMira Press.

Newman, Margaret E., Robert M. Yohe II, Howard Ceri, and Mark Q. Sutton
  1993   Immunological Protein Residue Analysis of Non-Lithic Archaeological Materials. *Journal of Archaeological Science* 20(1):93–100.

Newman, Margaret E., Robert M. Yohe II, B. Cooyman, and Howard Ceri
  1997   "Blood" from Stones? Probably: A Response to Fiedel. *Journal of Archaeological Science* 24(11):1023–1027.

Nichols, Johanna
  1997   Modeling Ancient Population Structures and Movement in Linguistics. *Annual Review of Anthropology* 26:359–384.

Normile, Dennis
  2001   Japanese Fraud Highlights Media-Driven Research Ethic. *Science* 291:34–35.

Oates, Joan
  1993   Trade and Power in the Fifth and Fourth Millennia BC: New Evidence from Northern Mesopotamia. *World Archaeology* 24(3):403–422.

O'Brien, Michael J., ed.
  1996   *Evolutionary Archaeology: Theory and Application.* Salt Lake City: University of Utah Press.

O'Brien, Michael J., and R. Lee Lyman
  2000   *Applying Evolutionary Archaeology: A Systematic Approach.* New York: Kluwer Academic/Plenum.

O'Connell, James F.
  1995   Ethnoarchaeology Needs a General Theory of Behavior. *Journal of Archaeological Research* 3(3):205–255.

Odum, Eugene P.
  1953   *Fundamentals of Ecology.* Philadelphia: Saunders.

Orser, Charles E., and Brian M. Fagan
  1995   *Historical Archaeology.* New York: HarperCollins.

Ortiz de Montellano, Bernard R.
  1978   Aztec Cannibalism: An Ecological Necessity? *Science* 200(4342):611–617.

Orton, Clive
  2000   *Sampling in Archaeology.* Cambridge: Cambridge University Press.

Orton, Clive, Paul Tyers, and Alan Vince
  1993   *Pottery in Archaeology.* Cambridge: Cambridge University Press.

Osborne, Richard H.
  1998   The Experimental Replication of a Stone Mortar. *Lithic Technology* 23(3):116–123.

Otto, John Solomon
  1984   *Cannon's Point Plantation, 1794–1860: Living Conditions and Status Patterns in the Old South.* Orlando: Academic Press.

Parkes, P. A.
  1986   *Current Scientific Techniques in Archaeology.* New York: St. Martin's Press.

Parr, Robert E.
  1989   *Archaeological Investigation of the Huntoon Pronghorn Trap Complex, Mineral County, Nevada.* Masters thesis, University of California, Riverside.

Patterson, Thomas C.
  1999   The Political Economy of Archaeology in the United States. *Annual Review of Anthropology* 28:115–174.

Pawson, Michael, and David Buisseret
  2000   *Port Royal, Jamaica.* Kingston: University of West Indies Press.

Paynter, Robert
  1989   The Archaeology of Equality and Inequality. *Annual Review of Anthropology* 18:369–399.
  2000   Historical Archaeology and the Post-Columbian World of North America. *Journal of Archaeological Research* 8(3):169–217.

Paynter, Robert, and Randall H. McGuire
  1991   The Archaeology of Inequality: Material Culture, Domination, and Resistance. In *The Archaeology of Inequality,* Randall H. McGuire and Robert Paynter, eds. Pp. 1–27. Oxford: Blackwell.

Pearsall, Deborah M.
  1989   *Paleoethnobotany: A Handbook of Procedures.* San Diego: Academic Press.

Peebles, Christopher S., and Glenn A. Black
  1987   Moundville from 1000 to 1500 AD as Seen from 1840 to 1985 AD. In *Chiefdoms in the Americas.* Robert D. Drennan and Carlos A. Uribe, eds. Pp. 21–41. Lanham, MD: University Press of America.

Peebles, Christopher S., and Susan M. Kus
  1977   Some Archaeological Correlates of Ranked Societies. *American Antiquity* 42(3):421–448.

Pendleton, Lorann S., and David Hurst Thomas
  1983   The Fort Sage Drift Fence, Washoe County, Nevada. *Anthropological Papers of the American Museum of Natural History* 58(2):1–38.

Petsche, Jerome E.
  1974   *The Steamboat "Bertrand": History, Excavation, and Architecture.* Publications in Archeology 11. Washington: National Park Service.

Phillipson, David W.
  1977   *The Later Prehistory of Eastern and Southern Africa.* New York: Africana.
  1985   *African Archaeology.* Cambridge: Cambridge University Press.

Piggott, Stuart
  1950   *Ancient India.* Harmondsworth: Penguin.

Pikirayi, Innocent
  2001   *The Zimbabwe Culture: Origins and Decline in Southern Zambezian States.* Walnut Creek, CA: AltaMira Press.

Pimentel, David, M. Herdendorf, S. Eisenfeld, L. Olander, M. Carroquino, C. Corson, J. McDade, Y. Chung, W. Cannon, J. Roberts, L. Bluman, and J. Gregg
  1994   Achieving a Secure Energy Future: Environmental and Economic Issues. *Ecological Economics* 9(3):201–219.

Piperno, Doloris R., and Deborah M. Pearsall
  1993   The Nature and Status of Phytolith Analysis. In *Current Research in Phytolith Analysis: Applications in Archaeology and Paleoecology.* Deborah M. Pearsall and Dolores R. Piperno, eds. Pp. 9–18. MASCA Research Papers in Science and Archaeology, vol. 10. Philadelphia: University Museum of Archaeology and Anthropology.

Poirier, David A., and Kenneth L. Feder, eds.
  2001   *Dangerous Places: Health, Safety, and Archaeology.* Westport, CT: Bergin & Garvey.

Pollard, A. Mark, and Carl Heron
  1996   *Archaeological Chemistry.* Cambridge: The Royal Society of Chemistry.

Powell, Eric A.
  2002   Shooting Up the Old West. *Archaeology* 55(3):16.

Powell, Jerry A., and Charles L. Hogue
  1979   *California Insects.* Berkeley: University of California Press.

Preucel, Robert W.
  1995   The Postprocessual Condition. *Journal of Archaeological Research* 3(2):147–175.

Price, David H.
  1994   Wittfogel's Neglected Hydraulic/Hydroagricultural Distinction. *Journal of Anthropological Research* 50(2):187–204.

Price, Mary F.
  1999   All in the Family: The Impact of Gender and Family Constructs on the Study of Prehistoric Settlement. In *Making Places in the Prehistoric World: Themes in Settlement Archaeology.* Joanna Brück and Melissa Goodman, eds. Pp. 30–51. London: UCL Press.

Price, T. Douglas, and James A. Brown, eds.
  1985   *Prehistoric Hunter-Gatherers: The Emergence of Cultural Complexity.* Orlando: Academic Press.

Price, T. Douglas, and Anne Birgitte Gebauer, eds.
  1995a   *Last Hunters—First Farmers: New Perspectives on the Prehistoric Transition to Agriculture.* Santa Fe: School of American Research Press.

Price, T. Douglas, and Anne Birgitte Gebauer
  1995b   New Perspectives on the Transition to Agriculture. In *Last Hunters—First Farmers: New Perspectives on the Prehistoric Transition to Agriculture.* T. Douglas Price and Anne Birgitte Gebauer, eds. Pp. 3–19. Santa Fe: School of American Research Press.

Price, T. Douglas, Linda Manzanilla, and William D. Middleton
  2000   Immigration and the Ancient City of Teotihuacan in Mexico: A Study Using Strontium Isotope Ratios in Human Bone and Teeth. *Journal of Archaeological Science* 27(10): 903–913.

Pringle, Heather
  2001a   The Incorruptibles. *Discover* 22(6):66–71.

2001b Secrets of the Alpaca Mummies. *Discover* 22(4):58–65.

Pyatt, F. B., G. Gilmore, J. P. Grattan, C. O. Hunt, and S. McLaren
2000 An Imperial Legacy? An Exploration of the Environmental Impact of Ancient Metal Mining and Smelting in Southern Jordan. *Journal of Archaeological Science* 27(9):771–778.

Rainbird, Paul
2002 A Message for Our Future? The Rapa Nui (Easter Island) Ecodisaster and Pacific Island Environments. *World Archaeology* 33(3):436–451.

Rapp, George, Jr., and Christopher L. Hill
1998 *Geoarchaeology: Earth-Science Approach to Archaeological Interpretation.* New Haven: Yale University Press.

Rathje, William L.
1999 An Archaeology of Space Garbage. *Discovering Archaeology* 1(5):108–111.

Rathje, William L., W. W. Hughes, D. C. Wilson, M. K. Tani, G. H. Archer, R. G. Hunt, and T. W. Jones
1992 The Archaeology of Contemporary Landfills. *American Antiquity* 57(3):437–447.

Rathje, William L., and Cullen Murphy
2001 *Rubbish! The Archaeology of Garbage.* Tucson: University of Arizona Press.

Redding, Richard W.
2002 The Study of Human Subsistence Behavior Using Faunal Evidence from Archaeological Sites. In *Archaeology: Original Readings in Method and Practice.* Peter N. Peregrine, Carol R. Ember, and Melvin Ember, eds. Pp. 92–110. Upper Saddle River, NJ: Prentice Hall.

Redfield, Robert, and Alfonso Villa Rojas
1934 *Chan Kom, a Maya Village.* Washington: Carnegie Institute of Washington.

Redman, Charles L.
1999 *Human Impact on Ancient Environments.* Tucson: University of Arizona Press.

Rega, Elizabeth
1997 Age, Gender and Biological Reality in the Early Bronze Age Cemetery at Mokrin. In *Invisible People and Processes: Writing Gender and Childhood into European Archaeology.* Jenny Moore and Eleanor Scott, eds. Pp. 229–247. London: Leicester University Press.

Reid, J. Jefferson, and Stephanie M. Whittlesey
1997 *The Archaeology of Ancient Arizona.* Tucson: University of Arizona Press.

Reinhard, Karl J.
1998a Mummy Studies and Archaeoparasitology. In *Mummies, Disease, and Ancient Cultures.* 2nd edition. Aidan Cockburn, Eve Cockburn, and Theodore A. Reyman, eds. Pp. 377–380. Cambridge: Cambridge University Press.
1998b Mummy Studies and Paleonutrition. In *Mummies, Disease, and Ancient Cultures.* 2nd edition. Aidan Cockburn, Eve Cockburn, and Theodore A. Reyman, eds. Pp. 372–377. Cambridge: Cambridge University Press.

Reinhard, Karl J., and Vaughn M. Bryant, Jr.
1992 Coprolite Analysis: A Biological Perspective on Archaeology. In *Archaeological Method and Theory,* vol. 4. Michael B. Schiffer, ed. Pp. 245–288. Tucson: University of Arizona Press.
1995 Investigating Mummified Intestinal Contents: Reconstructing Diet and Parasitic Disease. In *Proceedings of the I World Congress on Mummy Studies,* vol. 1. pp. 403–408. Tenerife: Museo Arqueológico Y Etnográfico de Tenerife.

Reitz, Elizabeth J., and Elizabeth S. Wing
1999 *Zooarchaeology.* Cambridge: Cambridge Manuals in Archaeology.

Renfrew, Colin
1987 *Archaeology and Language: The Puzzle of Indo-European Origins.* New York: Cambridge University Press.
1994 Towards a Cognitive Archaeology. In T*he Ancient Mind: Elements of Cognitive Archaeology.* Colin Renfrew and Ezra B. W. Zubrow, eds. Pp. 3–12. Cambridge: Cambridge University Press.
2000 *Loot, Legitimacy and Ownership: The Ethical Crisis in Archaeology.* London: Duckworth.

Renfrew, Colin, and Paul Bahn
1996 *Archaeology.* 2nd edition. London: Thames and Hudson.
2004 *Archaeology.* 4th edition. London: Thames and Hudson.

Rice, Prudence M.
1987 *Pottery Analysis: A Sourcebook.* Chicago: University of Chicago Press.

Richards, Martin P., Kate Smalley, Bryan C. Sykes, and Robert E. M. Hedges
1993 Archaeology and Genetics: Analyzing DNA from Skeletal Remains. *World Archaeology* 25(1):18–28.

Richerson, Peter J., and Robert Boyd
1992 Cultural Inheritance and Evolutionary Ecology. In *Evolutionary Ecology and Human Behavior.* Eric Alden Smith and Bruce Winterhalder, eds. Pp. 61–92. New York: Aldine.

Richerson, Peter J., Robert Boyd, and Robert L. Bettinger
2001 Was Agriculture Impossible during the Pleistocene but Mandatory during the Holocene? A Climate Change Hypothesis. *American Antiquity* 66(3):387–411.

Rindos, David
    1984   *The Origins of Agriculture: An Evolutionary Perspective.* Orlando: Academic Press.
Robb, John E.
    1998   The Archaeology of Symbols. *Annual Review of Anthropology* 27:329–346.
Robins, Don, Keith Sales, Duro Oduwole, Tim Holden, and Gordon Hillman
    1986   Postscript: Last Minute Results from ESR Spectroscopy Concerning the Cooking of Lindow Man's Last Meal. In *Lindow Man: The Body in the Bog.* I. M. Stead, J. B. Bourke, and Don Brothwell, eds. Pp. 140–142. Ithaca: Cornell University Press.
Romey, Kristin M.
    2001   "God's Hands" Did the Devil's Work. *Archaeology* 54(1):16.
Roper, Donna C.
    1979   The Method and Theory of Site Catchment Analysis: A Review. In *Advances in Archaeological Method and Theory,* vol. 2. Michael B. Schiffer, ed. Pp. 119–140. New York: Academic Press.
Rose, Jerome C., Keith W. Condon, and Alan H. Goodman
    1985   Diet and Dentition: Developmental Disturbances. In *The Analysis of Prehistoric Diets.* Robert I. Gilbert, Jr., and James H. Mielke, eds. Pp. 281–306. New York: Academic Press.
Rose, Mark
    1997   Origins of Syphilis. *Archaeology* 50(1):24–25.
Roskams, Steve
    2001   *Excavation.* Cambridge: Cambridge Manuals in Archaeology.
Ross, Anne, and Shane Coghill
    2000   Conducting a Community-Based Archaeological Project: An Archaeologist's and Koenpul Man's Perspective. *Australian Aboriginal Studies,* Spring/Fall: 76.
Rouse, Irving
    1986   *Mitigations in Prehistory: Inferring Population Movement from Cultural Remains.* New Haven: Yale University Press.
Rovner, Irwin
    1983   Plant Opal Phytolith Analysis: Major Advances in Archaeobotanical Research. In *Advances in Archaeological Method and Theory,* vol. 6. Michael B. Schiffer, ed. Pp. 225–266. New York: Academic Press.
Rowley-Conwy, Peter, ed.
    2002   Ancient Ecodisasters. *World Archaeology* 33(3):361–528.
Royce, Anya P.
    1982   *Ethnic Identity: Strategies of Diversity.* Bloomington: Indiana University Press.

Ruddiman, William F.
    2003   The Anthropogenic Greenhouse Era Began Thousands of Years Ago. *Climatic Change* 61(3):261–293.
Ruff, Christopher B., Brigitte M. Holt, Vladimir Sládek, Margit Berner, William A. Murphy, Jr., Dieter zur Nedden, Horst Seidler, and Wolfgang Recheis
    2006   Body Size, Body Proportions, and Mobility in the Tyrolean "Iceman." *Journal of Human Evolution* 51(1):91–101.
Ruspoli, Mario
    1987   *The Cave of Lascaux: The Final Photographs.* New York: Abrams.
Rylander, Kate Aasen
    1994   Corn Preparation among the Basketmaker Anasazi: A Scanning Electron Microscope Study of *Zea Mays* Remains from Coprolites. In *Paleonutrition: The Diet and Health of Prehistoric Americans.* Kristin D. Sobolik, ed. Pp. 115–133. Occasional Paper No. 22. Carbondale: Southern Illinois University, Center for Archaeological Investigations.
Safont, S., A. Malgosa, M. E. Subirà, and J. Gibert
    1998   Can Trace Elements in Fossils Provide Information About Palaeodiet? *International Journal of Osteoarchaeology* 8(1):23–37.
Sakellarakes, Giannes
    1997   *Minoan Crete in a New Light,* 2 vols. London: Eleni Nakou Foundation.
Samuels, Stephan R., ed.
    1991   *Ozette Archaeological Project Research Reports,* vol. 1. *House Structure and Floor Midden.* Department of Anthropology Reports of Investigations 63. Pullman: Washington State University.
Schiffer, Michael B.
    1987   *Formation Processes of the Archaeological Record.* Albuquerque: University of New Mexico Press.
    1995   *Behavioral Archaeology: First Principles.* Salt Lake City: University of Utah Press.
Schliemann, Heinrich
    1968   *Troy and Its Remains: A Narrative of Researches*
    [1875] *and Discoveries Made on the Site of Ilium and in the Trojan Plain.* Philip Smith, ed. New York: Dover.
Schmidt, Robert A., and Barbara L. Voss, eds.
    2000   *Archaeologies of Sexuality.* New York: Routledge.
Schneider, Joan S.
    2002   Analyses of "Ground Stone" Milling and Processing Implements, Decorative and Ritual Objects, Cutting and Abrading Tools. In *Archaeological Laboratory Methods: An Introduction.* 3rd edition. Mark Q. Sutton and Brooke

S. Arkush, eds. Pp. 68–104. Dubuque: Kendall/Hunt.

Schulting, Rick J., and Michael P. Richards
2001 Dating Women and Becoming Farmers: New Paleodietary and AMS Dating Evidence from the Breton Mesolithic Cemeteries of Téviec and Hoëdic. *Journal of Anthropological Archaeology* 20(3):314–344.

Schutkowski, Holger, Bernd Herrmann, Felicitas Wiedemann, Hervé Bocherens, and Gisela Grupe
1999 Diet, Status and Decomposition at Weingarten: Trace Element and Isotope Analyses on Early Mediaeval Skeletal Material. *Journal of Archaeological Science* 26(6):675–685.

Scott, Douglas D., and Richard A. Fox
1987 *Archaeological Insights into the Custer Battle: An Assessment of the 1984 Field Season.* Norman: University of Oklahoma Press.

Scott, Douglas D., P. Willey, and Melissa A. Connor
1998 *They Died with Custer: Soldiers' Bones of the Little Bighorn.* Norman: University of Oklahoma Press.

Scott, Elizabeth M., ed.
1994 *Those of Little Note: Gender, Race, and Class in Historical Archaeology.* Tuscon: University of Arizona Press.

Semenov, S. A.
1964 *Prehistoric Technology.* London: Cory, Adams & McKay.

Sever, Thomas L.
2000 Remote Sensing Methods. In *Science and Technology in Historic Preservation.* Ray A. Williamson and Paul R. Nickens, eds. Pp. 21–51. New York: Kluwer Academic/Plenum.

Service, Elman R.
1962 *Primitive Social Organization: An Evolutionary Perspective.* New York: Random House.

Shaffer, Brian S.
1992 Quarter-Inch-Screening: Understanding Biases in Recovery of Vertebrate Faunal Remains. *American Antiquity* 57(1):129–136.

Shaffer, Brian S., and Julia L. J. Sanchez
1994 Comparison of ⅛" and ¼" Mesh Recovery of Controlled Samples of Small-to-Medium-Sized Mammals. *American Antiquity* 59(3):525–530.

Shanks, Michael, and Christopher Tilley
1987 *Re-Constructing Archaeology: Theory and Practice.* Cambridge: Cambridge University Press.

Shanks, Orin C., Marcel Kornfeld, and Dee Dee Hawk
1999 Protein Analysis of Bugas-Holding Tools: New Trends in Immunological Studies. *Journal of Archaeological Science* 26(9):1183–1191.

Shanks, Orin C., Larry Hodges, Lucas Tilley, Marcel Kornfeld, Mary Lou Larson, and Walt Ream
2005 DNA from Ancient Stone Tools and Bones Excavated at Bugas-Holding, Wyoming. *Journal of Archaeological Science* 32(1):27–38.

Sharer, Robert
1994 *The Ancient Maya.* 5th edition. Stanford: Stanford University Press.

Shaw, Ian, ed.
2000 *The Oxford History of Ancient Egypt.* Oxford: Oxford University Press.

Sheets, Payson D.
1992 *The Ceren Site: A Prehistoric Village Buried by Volcanic Ash in Central America.* Fort Worth: Harcourt Brace Jovanovich College.

Sheler, Jeffery
1999 *Is the Bible True?* San Francisco: Harper.

Shennan, Stephen
2002 *Genes, Memes and Human History: Darwinian Archaeology and Cultural Evolution.* London: Thames & Hudson.

Sigurdsson, Haraldur, Steven Carey, Winton Cornell, and Tullio Pescatore
1985 The Eruption of Vesuvius in A.D. 79. *National Geographic Research* 1(3):332–387.

Silverberg, Robert
1968 *Mound Builders of Ancient America: The Archaeology of a Myth.* Greenwich, CT: New York Graphic Society.

Simms, Steven R.
1984 *Aboriginal Great Basin Foraging Strategies: An Evolutionary Analysis.* Ph.D. dissertation, University of Utah.

Singleton, Theresa A.
1995 The Archaeology of Slavery in the United States. *Annual Review of Anthropology* 24:119–140.

Slayman, Andrew L.
1997 The *New* Pompeii. *Archaeology* 50(6):27–36.

Smith, Eric Alden
1983 Anthropological Applications of Optimal Foraging Theory: A Critical Review. *Current Anthropology* 24(5):625–651.

Smith, Laurajane
1999 The Last Archaeologist? Material Culture and Contested Identities. *Australian Aboriginal Studies* 1999(2):25.

Sobolik, Kristin D.
1990 A Nutritional Analysis of Diet as Revealed in Prehistoric Human Coprolites. *The Texas Journal of Science* 42(1):23–36.

Sobolik, Kristin D., and Deborah J. Gerick
1992 Prehistoric Medicinal Plant Usage: A Case Study from Coprolites. *Journal of Ethnobiology* 12(2):203–211.

Sobolik, Kristin D., Kristen J. Gremillion, Patricia L. Whitten, and Patty Jo Watson
1996 Technical Note: Sex Determination of Prehistoric Human Paleofeces. *American Journal of Physical Anthropology* 101(2):283–290.

Soffer, O., J. M. Adovasio, and D. C. Hyland
2000 The "Venus" Figurines: Textiles, Basketry, Gender, and Status in the Upper Paleolithic. *Current Anthropology* 41(4):511–537.

Solecki, Ralph S.
1971 *Shanidar: The First Flower People.* New York: Knopf.

Spaulding, Albert
1953 Statistical Techniques for the Discovery of Artifact Types. *American Antiquity* 18:305–313.

Spector, Janet D.
1991 What This Awl Means: Toward a Feminist Archaeology. In *Engendering Archaeology: Women and Prehistory.* Joan M. Gero and Margaret W. Conkey, eds. Pp. 388–406. Cambridge: Blackwell.
1993 *What This Awl Means: Feminist Archaeology at a Wahpeton Dakota Village.* St. Paul: Minnesota Historical Society Press.

Spencer, Charles S.
1997 Evolutionary Approaches in Archaeology. *Journal of Archaeological Research* 5(3):209–264.

Spencer-Wood, Suzanne M.
2006 Feminist Theory and Gender Research in Historical Archaeology. In *Handbook of Gender in Archaeology.* Sarah Milledge Nelson, ed. Pp. 59–104. Lanham, MD: AltaMira Press.

Stannard, David E.
1992 *American Holocaust: Columbus and the Conquest of the New World.* Oxford: Oxford University Press.

Stark, Miriam T., ed.
1998 *The Archaeology of Social Boundaries.* Washington: Smithsonian Institution Press.

Steward, Julian H.
1938 Basin-Plateau Aboriginal Sociopolitical Groups. *Bureau of American Ethnology Bulletin* 120.
1955 *Theory of Culture Change.* Urbana: University of Illinois Press.

Stewart, Francis L., and Peter W. Stahl
1977 Cautionary Note on Edible Meat Poundage Figures. *American Antiquity* 42(2):267–270.

Stirland, A. J.
2000 *Raising the Dead: The Skeleton Crew of Henry VIII's Great Ship, the* Mary Rose. Chichester: John Wiley & Sons.

Stokes, Marvin A., and Terah L. Smiley
1996 *An Introduction to Tree-Ring Dating.* Tucson: University of Arizona Press.

Stuart-Macadam, Patricia L.
1989 Nutritional Deficiency Diseases: A Survey of Scurvy, Rickets, and Iron-Deficiency Anemia. In *Reconstruction of Life from the Skeleton.* Mehmet Yaşar İşcan and Kenneth A. R. Kennedy, eds. Pp. 201–222. New York: Liss.
1998 Iron Deficiency Anemia: Exploring the Difference. In *Sex and Gender in Paleopathological Perspective.* Anne L. Grauer and Patricia Stuart-MacAdam, eds. Pp. 45–63. Cambridge: Cambridge University Press.

Sutton, Mark Q.
1993 Midden and Coprolite Derived Subsistence Evidence: An Analysis of Data from the La Quinta Site, Salton Basin, California. *Journal of Ethnobiology* 13(1):1–15.
1995 Archaeological Aspects of Insect Use. *Journal of Archaeological Method and Theory* 2(3):253–298.
1998 Cluster Analysis of Paleofecal Data Sets: A Test of Late Prehistoric Settlement and Subsistence Patterns in the Northern Coachella Valley, California. *American Antiquity* 63(1):86–107.

Sutton, Mark Q., and E. N. Anderson
2004 *Introduction to Cultural Ecology.* Walnut Creek, CA: AltaMira Press.

Sutton, Mark Q., and Brooke S. Arkush
2006 *Archaeological Laboratory Methods: An Introduction.* 4th edition. Dubuque: Kendall/Hunt.

Sutton, Mark Q., Minnie Malik, and Andrew Ogram
1996 Experiments on the Determination of Gender from Coprolites by DNA Analysis. *Journal of Archaeological Science* 23(2):263–267.

Sutton, Mark Q., and Karl J. Reinhard
1995 Cluster Analysis of the Coprolites from Antelope House: Implications for Anasazi Diet and Cuisine. *Journal of Archaeological Science* 22(6):741–750.

Sutton, Mark Q., and Joan S. Schneider
1996 Archaeological Investigations at Guapiabit: CA-SBR-1913. *San Bernardino County Museum Association Quarterly* 43(4).

Sutton, Mark Q., and Philip J. Wilke, eds.
1988 *Archaeological Investigations at CA-RIV-1179, CA-RIV-2823, and CA-RIV-2827, La Quinta, Riverside County, California.* Coyote Press Archives of California Prehistory No. 20. Salinas, CA: Coyote Press.

Switzer, Ronald R.
1974 *The Bertrand Bottles: A Study of 19th Century Glass and Ceramic Containers.* Publications in Archaeology 12. Washington: National Park Service.

Tattersall, Ian, Eric Delson, and John Van Couvering, eds.
1988 *Encyclopedia of Human Evolution and Prehistory.* New York: Garland.

Taylor, R. E.
  1987 *Radiocarbon Dating: An Archaeological Perspective.* Orlando: Academic Press.
Taylor, R. E., and Martin Aitken, eds.
  1997 *Chronometric Dating in Archaeology.* New York: Plenum Press.
Taylor, Walter W.
  1948 *A Study of Archaeology.* Menasha, WI: American Anthropological Association.
Testart, Alain
  1982 The Significance of Food Storage among Hunter-Gatherers: Residence Patterns, Population Densities, and Social Inequalities. *Current Anthropology* 23(5):523–537.
  1988 Some Major Problems in the Social Anthropology of Hunter-Gatherers. *Current Anthropology* 29(1):1–31.
Thomas, Brian W.
  1998 Power and Community: The Archaeology of Slavery at the Hermitage Plantation. *American Antiquity* 63(4):531–551.
Thomas, Cyrus
  1894 Report on the Mound Explorations of the Bureau of Ethnology. In *Twelfth Annual Report of Bureau of Ethnology, 1890–1891.* Washington: Bureau of Ethnology.
Thomas, David Hurst
  1969 Great Basin Hunting Patterns: A Quantitative Method for Treating Faunal Remains. *American Antiquity* 34(4):392–401.
  1986 Contemporary Hunter-Gatherer Archaeology in America. In *American Archaeology: Past and Future.* David J. Meltzer, Don D. Fowler, and Jeremy A. Sabloff, eds. Pp. 237–276. Washington: Smithsonian Institution Press.
Thomas, Julian
  2001 Archaeologies of Place and Landscape. In *Archaeological Theory Today.* Ian Hodder, ed. Pp. 165–186. Cambridge: Polity Press.
Thomsen, Christian
  1848 *Guide to Northern Archaeology.* London: J. Bain.
Torroni, Antonio
  2000 Mitochrondrial DNA and the Origin of Native Americans. In *America Past, America Present: Genes and Languages in the Americas and Beyond.* Colin Renfrew, ed. Pp. 77–87. Cambridge: McDonald Institute for Archaeological Research.
Traill, David A.
  1995 *Schliemann and Troy: Treasure and Deceit.* New York: St. Martin's Press.
Trigg, Heather B., Richard I. Ford, John G. Moore, and Louise D. Jessop
  1994 Coprolite Evidence for Prehistoric Foodstuffs, Condiments, and Medicines. In *Eating on the Wild Side: The Pharmacologic, Ecological, and Social Implications of Using Noncultigens.* Nina L. Etkin, ed. Pp. 210–223. Tucson: University of Arizona Press.
Trigger, Bruce G.
  1993 Marxism in Contemporary Western Archaeology. In *Archaeological Method and Theory,* vol. 5. Michael B. Schiffer, ed. Pp. 159–200. Tucson: University of Arizona Press.
Trotter, M., and Gleser, G. C.
  1952 Estimation of Stature from Long Bones of American Whites and Negroes. *American Journal of Physical Anthropology* 9:311–324.
  1977 Corrigenda to "Estimation of Stature from Long Bones of American Whites and Negroes." *American Journal of Physical Anthropology* 47:355–356.
Tschauner, Hartmut
  1996 Middle-Range Theory, Behavioral Archaeology, and Postempiricist Philosophy of Science in Archaeology. *Journal of Archaeological Method and Theory* 3(1):1–30.
Turner, B. L., and Peter D. Harrison
  1983 *Pulltrouser Swamp: Ancient Maya Habitat, Agriculture, and Settlement in Northern Belize.* Austin: University of Texas Press.
Turner, B. L., J. L. Edwards, E. A. Quinn, J. D. Kingston, and D. P. Van Gerven
  2006 Age–Related Variation in Isotopic Indicators of Diet at Medieval Kulubnarti, Sudanese Nubia. *International Journal of Osteoarchaeology* 17(1):1–25.
Turner, Christy G., and Jacqueline A. Turner
  1999 *Man Corn: Cannibalism and Violence in the Prehistoric American Southwest.* Salt Lake City: University of Utah Press.
Tylor, Edward B.
  1871 *Primitive Culture.* New York: Henry Holt.
Van Buren, Mary
  2001 The Archaeology of El Niño Events and Other "Natural" Disasters. *Journal of Archaeological Method and Theory* 8(2):129–149.
van der Merwe, Nikolaas J., Robert H. Tykot, Norman Hammond, and Kim Oakberg
  2000 Diet and Animal Husbandry of the Preclassic Maya at Cuello, Belize: Isotopic and Zooarchaeological Evidence. In *Biogeochemical Approaches to Paleodietary Analysis,* Stanley H. Ambrose and M. Anne Katzenberg, eds. Pp. 23–38. New York: Kluwer Academic/ Plenum.
VanPool, Christine S., and Todd L. VanPool
  1999 The Scientific Nature of Postprocessualism. *American Antiquity* 64(1):33–53.

VanPool, Todd L., and Christine S. VanPool
2001 Postprocessualism and the Nature of Science: A Response to Comments by Hutson and Arnold and Wilkens. *American Antiquity* 66(2):367–375.

Van Riper, A. Bowdoin
1993 *Men among the Mammoths: Victorian Science and the Discovery of Human Prehistory.* Chicago: University of Chicago Press.

Van Tilburg, Jo Anne
1994 *Easter Island: Archaeology, Ecology, and Culture.* Washington: Smithsonian Institution Press.

Vita-Finzi, C., and E. S. Higgs
1970 Prehistoric Economy in the Mount Carmel Area of Palestine: Site Catchment Analysis. *Proceedings of the Prehistoric Society* 36:1–37.

Vitousek, Peter M., Harold A. Mooney, Jane Lubchenco, and Jerry M. Melillo
1997 Human Domination of Earth's Ecosystem. *Science* 277:494–499.

Vogel, Joe
1997 *Encyclopedia of Precolonial Africa.* Walnut Creek, CA: AltaMira Press.

von Däniken, Erich
1970 *Chariots of the Gods.* New York: Putnam.

Wall, Diana diZerega
1994 *The Archaeology of Gender: Separating the Spheres in Urban America.* New York: Plenum Press.

Ward-Perkins, John, and Amanda Claridge
1978 *Pompeii, A.D. 79.* New York: Knopf.

Waselkov, Gregory A.
1987 Shellfish Gathering and Shell Midden Archaeology. In *Advances in Archaeological Method and Theory,* vol. 10. Michael B. Schiffer, ed. Pp. 93–210. New York: Academic Press.

Watkins, Joe
2005 Through Wary Eyes: Indigenous Perspectives on Archaeology. *Annual Review of Anthropology* 34:429–449.

Watters, Meg
2001 Another Tool for the Kit. *The SAA Archaeological Record* 1(2):17–20.

Wenli, Zhang
1996 *The Qin Terracotta Army: Treasures of Lintong.* London: Scala Books.

Wescott, Konnie L., and R. Joe Brandon, eds.
2000 *Practical Applications of GIS for Archaeologists: A Predictive Modeling Toolkit.* London: Taylor & Francis.

Wheeler, Sir Mortimer
1947 Harappa 1946: The Defences and Cemetery R 37. *Ancient India* 3:58–130.
1955 *Archaeology from the Earth.* Oxford: Clarendon Press.

1968 *The Indus Civilization.* 3rd edition. Cambridge: Cambridge University Press.

White, J. Peter, and James F. O'Connell
1982 *A Prehistory of Australia, New Guinea and Sahul.* Sydney: Academic Press.

White, Richard
1997 Indian People and the Natural World: Asking the Right Questions. In *Rethinking American Indian History.* Donald L. Fixico, ed. Pp. 87–100. Albuquerque: University of New Mexico Press.

White, Theodore E.
1953 A Method of Calculating the Dietary Percentage of Various Food Animals Utilized by Aboriginal Peoples. *American Antiquity* 18(4):396–398.

White, Tim D.
1992 *Prehistoric Cannibalism at Mancos 5MUMR-2346.* Princeton: Princeton University Press.

Whitley, David S., ed.
2001 *Handbook of Rock Art Research.* Walnut Creek, CA: AltaMira Press.

Whitney, Eleanor Noss, and Sharon Rady Rolfes
1996 *Understanding Nutrition.* 7th edition. Minneapolis/St. Paul: West.

Wilk, Richard R.
1991 *Household Ecology: Economic Change and Domestic Life among the Kekchi Maya of Belize.* Tucson: University of Arizona Press.

Wilk, Richard R., and William L. Rathje
1982 Household Archaeology. *American Behavioral Scientist* 25(6):617–639.

Wilke, Philip J.
1978 *Late Prehistoric Human Ecology at Lake Cahuilla, Coachella Valley, California.* Contributions of the University of California Archaeological Research Facility No. 38. Berkeley: University of California.
1988 Bow Staves Harvested from Juniper Trees by Indians of Nevada. *Journal of California and Great Basin Anthropology* 10(1):3–31.

Wilkie, Laurie A., and Katherine Howlett Hayes
2006 Engendered and Feminist Archaeologies of the Recent and Documented Pasts. *Journal of Archaeological Research* 14(3):243–264.

Wilkinson, T. J.
2000 Regional Approaches to Mesopotamian Archaeology: The Contribution of Archaeological Surveys. *Journal of Archaeological Research* 8(3):219–267.

Willet, Frank
1993 *African Art.* London: Thames and Hudson.

Willey, Gordon R.
1953 Prehistoric Settlement Patterns in the Virú Valley, Perú. *Bureau of American Ethnology Bulletin* 155.

Willey, Gordon R., and Philip Phillips
1958　*Method and Theory in American Archaeology.* Chicago: University of Chicago Press.

Willey, Gordon R., and Jeremy A. Sabloff
1993　*A History of American Archaeology.* 3rd edition. New York: Freeman.

Willey, P., and T. E. Emerson
1993　The Osteology and Archaeology of the Crow Creek Massacre. *Plains Anthropologist* 38: 227–269.

Williamson, Ray A., ed.
1981　*Archaeostronomy in the Americas.* Ballena Press Anthropological Papers No. 22. Los Altos, CA: Ballena Press.

Winkelman, Michael
1998　Aztec Human Sacrifice: Cross-Cultural Assessments of the Ecological Hypothesis. *Ethnology* 37(3):285–298.

Winterhalder, Bruce
1981　Optimal Foraging Strategies and Hunter-Gatherer Research in Anthropology: Theory and Models. In *Hunter-Gatherer Foraging Strategies: Ethnographic and Archaeological Analyses.* Bruce Winterhalder and Eric Alden Smith, eds. Pp. 13–35. Chicago: University of Chicago Press.

Wittfogel, Karl
1957　*Oriental Despotism.* New Haven: Yale University Press.

Woods, James C., and Gene L. Titmus
1996　Stone on Stone: Perspectives on Maya Civilization from Lithic Studies. In *Eighth Palenque Round Table, 1993.* Martha Macri and Jan McHargue, eds. Pp. 479–489. The Palenque Round Table Series, vol. 10. San Francisco: Pre-Columbian Art Research Institute.

Wright, Rita P., ed.
1996　*Gender and Archaeology.* Philadelphia: University of Pennsylvania Press.

Wylie, Alison
1992　The Interplay of Evidential Constraints and Political Interests: Recent Archaeological Research on Gender. *American Antiquity* 57(1):15–35.

Yerkes, R. W., and P. N. Kardulias
1993　Recent Developments in the Analysis of Lithic Artifacts. *Journal of Archaeological Research* 1(2):89–120.

Yohe, Robert M., II
1992　*A Reevaluation of Western Great Basin Cultural Chronology and Evidence for the Timing of the Introduction of the Bow and Arrow to Eastern California Based on New Excavations at the Rose Spring Site (CA-INY-327).* Ph.D. dissertation, University of California, Riverside.

2002　Analysis of Flaked Stone Artifacts. In *Archaeological Laboratory Methods: An Introduction.* 3rd edition. Mark Q. Sutton and Brooke S. Arkush, eds. Pp. 37–67. Dubuque: Kendall/Hunt.

Yohe, Robert M., II, and Linda Scott Cummings
2001　*Dental Calculus and Dietary Variability: A Comparison of Prehistoric and Historic Samples.* Paper presented at the Annual Meetings of the Society for American Archaeology, New Orleans.

Yohe, Robert M., II, and Max G. Pavesic
2002　*Dietary Implications of the Isotopic Analysis of the Human Skeletons from the Braden Site, Western Idaho.* Paper presented at the October 2002 Great Basin Anthropological Conference, Elko.

Yohe, Robert M., II, Margaret E. Newman, and Joan S. Schneider
1991　Immunological Identification of Small-Mammal Proteins on Aboriginal Milling Equipment. *American Antiquity* 56(4):659–666.

Young, James O.
2006　Cultures and the Ownership of Archaeological Finds. In *The Ethics of Archaeology: Philosophical Perspectives on Archaeological Practice.* Chris Scarre and Geoffrey Scarre, eds. Pp. 15–31. Cambridge: Cambridge University Press.

Zanker, Paul
1998　*Pompeii: Public and Private Life.* Cambridge: Harvard University Press.

Zhang, Juzhong, Garman Harbottle, Changsui Wang, and Zhaochen Kong
1999　Oldest Playable Musical Instruments Found at Jiahu, Early Neolithic Site in China. *Nature* 401:366–368.

Zimmerman, Larry J.
2003　*Presenting the Past.* Walnut Creek, CA: AltaMira Press.

INDEX

432

PHOTO CREDITS